매일 3단계로 푸는 영어독해

고1

전국연합 학력평가 기출

시간은 없고 과목은 많은 통합 수능! 절대평가인 영어부터 끝내는 것이 최적의 전략입니다.

수능 기본 단어부터 필수 구문과 유형별 독해 Tip까지, <매3영 고1>로 단 2주에 완벽 정리하세요!

- 수능 영어에 대한 근거 있는 자신감을 키워주는 책
- 수능+내신 필수 단어/구문을 끝내주는 책
- 친절한 해설로 독학 영어의 길잡이가 되어주는 책

고등 영어 마스터, <매3영>이라면 가능합니다!

체계적인 **3단계** 학습으로
내신·학력평가 동시대비

구성과 특징

STEP 1

모든 영어 공부의 시작은 단어!

수능 필수 단어 & 어구 익히기

❶ 수능 필수 단어 LIST

문제 풀이에 앞서 지문 속 필수 어휘를
완벽하게 정리할 수 있습니다.

❸ 단어 SELF-TEST

암기한 단어를 확인해 보고, 놓친 단어는
그 자리에서 바로 정리할 수 있습니다.

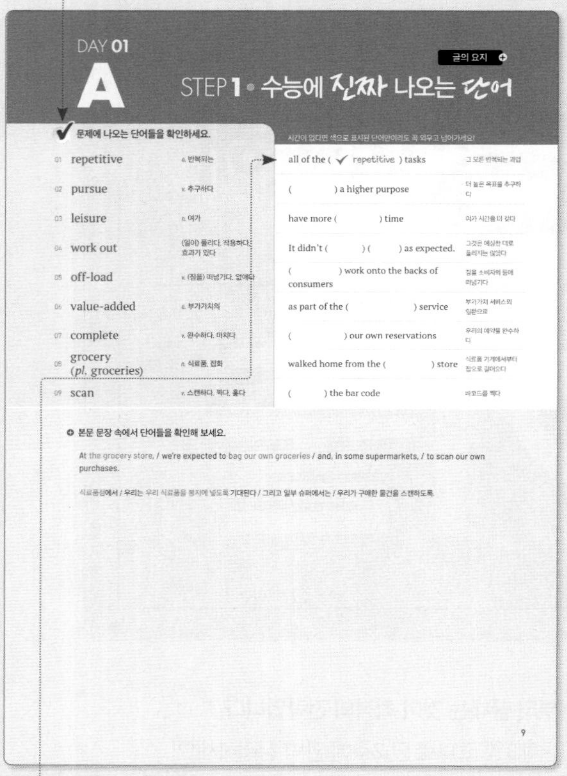

DAY 01

A

STEP 1 • 수능에 진짜 나오는 단어

글의 요지

✔ 문제에 나오는 단어들을 확인하세요.

시간이 없다면 색으로 표시된 단어만이라도 꼭 외우고 넘어가세요!

01	repetitive	a. 반복되는	all of the (✔ repetitive) tasks	그 모든 반복되는 과업
02	pursue	v. 추구하다	( ) a higher purpose	더 높은 목표를 추구하다
03	leisure	n. 여가	have more ( ) time	여가 시간을 더 갖다
04	work out	(일이) 풀리다, 작용하다; 효과가 있다	It didn't ( ) ( ) as expected.	그것은 예상한 대로 풀리지는 않았다
05	off-load	v. (짐을) 떠넘기다, 없애다	( ) work onto the backs of consumers	짐을 소비자의 등에 떠넘기다
06	value-added	a. 부가가치의	as part of the ( ) service	부가가치 서비스의 일환으로
07	complete	v. 완수하다, 마치다	( ) our own reservations	우리의 예약을 완수하다
08	grocery (*pl.* groceries)	n. 식료품, 잡화	walked home from the ( ) store	식료품 가게에서부터 집으로 걸어오다
09	scan	v. 스캔하다, 찍다, 훑다	( ) the bar code	바코드를 찍다

⊕ 본문 문장 속에서 단어들을 확인해 보세요.

At the grocery store, / we're expected to bag our own groceries / and, in some supermarkets, / to scan our own purchases.

식료품점에서 / 우리는 우리 식료품을 봉지에 넣도록 기대된다 / 그리고 일부 슈퍼에서는 / 우리가 구매한 물건을 스캔하도록

9

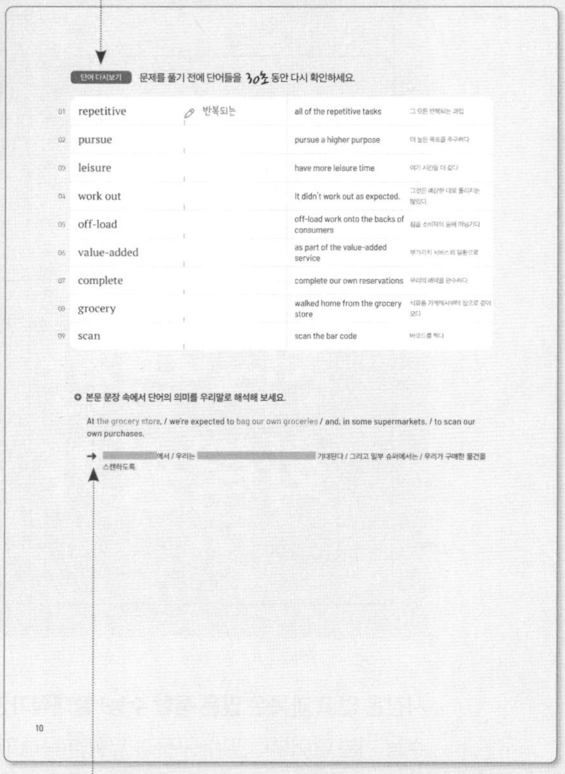

단어 다시보기 문제를 풀기 전에 단어들을 30초 동안 다시 확인하세요.

01	repetitive	반복되는	all of the repetitive tasks	그 모든 반복되는 과업
02	pursue		pursue a higher purpose	더 높은 목표를 추구하다
03	leisure		have more leisure time	여가 시간을 더 갖다
04	work out		It didn't work out as expected.	그것은 예상한 대로 풀리지는 않았다
05	off-load		off-load work onto the backs of consumers	짐을 소비자의 등에 떠넘기다
06	value-added		as part of the value-added service	부가가치 서비스의 일환으로
07	complete		complete our own reservations	우리의 예약을 완수하다
08	grocery		walked home from the grocery store	식료품 가게에서부터 집으로 걸어오다
09	scan		scan the bar code	바코드를 찍다

⊕ 본문 문장 속에서 단어의 의미를 우리말로 해석해 보세요.

At the grocery store, / we're expected to bag our own groceries / and, in some supermarkets, / to scan our own purchases.

→ ________에서 / 우리는 ________ 기대된다 / 그리고 일부 슈퍼에서는 / 우리가 구매한 물건을 스캔하도록

10

❷ 예문 확인 & 빈칸 채우기

지문에 실제로 쓰인 표현에서 단어의 용법을
확인하며 쉽게 암기할 수 있습니다.

❹ 문장 속 단어 CHECK

외운 단어를 문장 속에서 직접 해석해 보며
단어의 응용력을 기를 수 있습니다.

STEP 2

좋은 기출 문제도 풀어야 내 것!

문제 풀이 실전 훈련

❶ 시간 & 난이도 확인

유형 및 난이도에 따른 문제 풀이 제한 시간을 확인하고, 실전처럼 시간 안배를 연습할 수 있습니다.

❸ 종합 성적표 REVIEW

3일마다 종합 성적표를 작성해 보면서 나의 문제 풀이 습관을 돌아볼 수 있습니다.

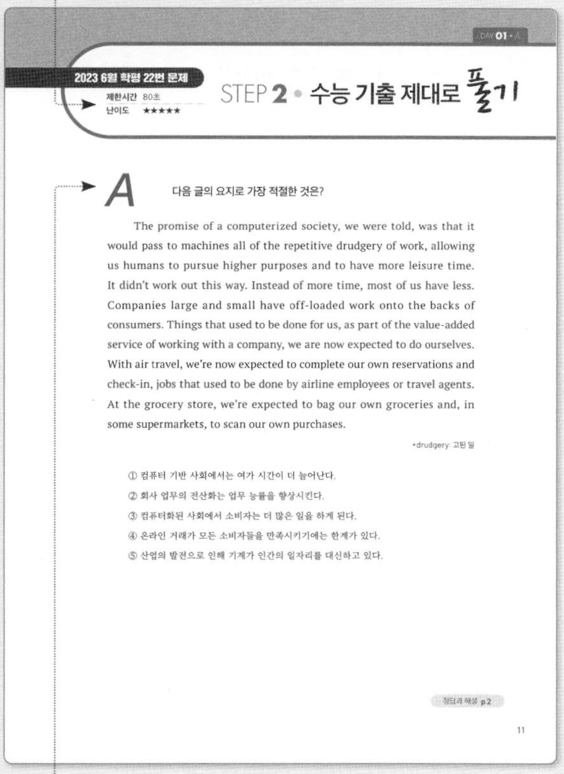

DAY 01 • A

2023 6월 학평 22번 문제
제한시간 80초
난이도 ★★★★★

STEP 2 • 수능 기출 제대로 풀기

A 다음 글의 요지로 가장 적절한 것은?

The promise of a computerized society, we were told, was that it would pass to machines all of the repetitive drudgery of work, allowing us humans to pursue higher purposes and to have more leisure time. It didn't work out this way. Instead of more time, most of us have less. Companies large and small have off-loaded work onto the backs of consumers. Things that used to be done for us, as part of the value-added service of working with a company, we are now expected to do ourselves. With air travel, we're now expected to complete our own reservations and check-in, jobs that used to be done by airline employees or travel agents. At the grocery store, we're expected to bag our own groceries and, in some supermarkets, to scan our own purchases.

*drudgery: 고된 일

① 컴퓨터 기반 사회에서는 여가 시간이 더 늘어난다.
② 회사 업무의 전산화는 업무 능률을 향상시킨다.
③ 컴퓨터화된 사회에서 소비자는 더 많은 일을 하게 된다.
④ 온라인 거래가 모든 소비자들을 만족시키기에는 한계가 있다.
⑤ 산업의 발전으로 인해 기계가 인간의 일자리를 대신하고 있다.

정답과 해설 p.2

11

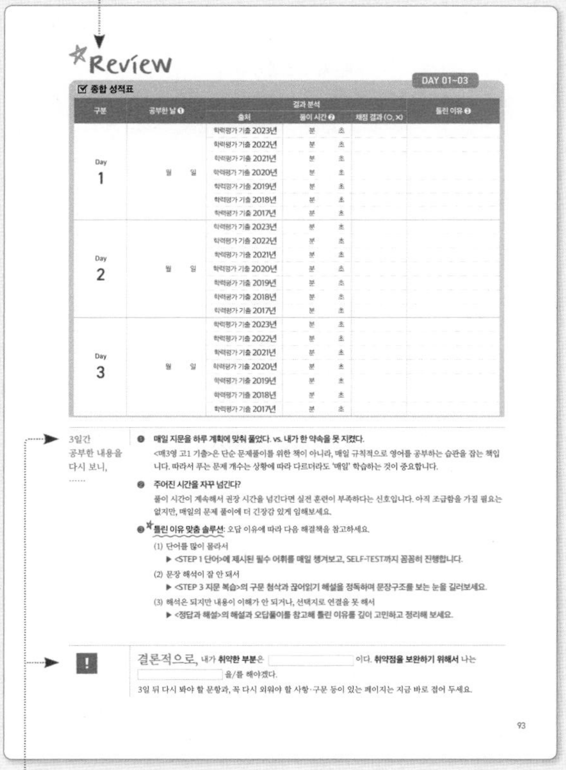

Review

☑ 종합 성적표 DAY 01~03

구분	공부한 날 ❶	결과 분석 출처	풀이 시간 ❷	채점 결과 (O, X)	틀린 이유 ❸
Day 1	월 일	학력평가 기출 2023년	분 초		
		학력평가 기출 2022년	분 초		
		학력평가 기출 2021년	분 초		
		학력평가 기출 2020년	분 초		
		학력평가 기출 2019년	분 초		
		학력평가 기출 2018년	분 초		
		학력평가 기출 2017년	분 초		
Day 2	월 일	학력평가 기출 2023년	분 초		
		학력평가 기출 2022년	분 초		
		학력평가 기출 2021년	분 초		
		학력평가 기출 2020년	분 초		
		학력평가 기출 2019년	분 초		
		학력평가 기출 2018년	분 초		
		학력평가 기출 2017년	분 초		
Day 3	월 일	학력평가 기출 2023년	분 초		
		학력평가 기출 2022년	분 초		
		학력평가 기출 2021년	분 초		
		학력평가 기출 2020년	분 초		
		학력평가 기출 2019년	분 초		
		학력평가 기출 2018년	분 초		
		학력평가 기출 2017년	분 초		

3일간 공부한 내용을 다시 보니, ……

❶ **매일 지문을 하루 계획에 맞춰 풀었다. vs. 내가 한 약속을 못 지켰다.**
<매3영 고1 기출>은 단순 문제풀이를 위한 책이 아니라, 매일 규칙적으로 영어를 공부하는 습관을 잡는 책입니다. 따라서 푸는 문제 개수는 상황에 따라 다르더라도 '매일' 학습하는 것이 중요합니다.

❷ **주어진 시간을 자꾸 넘긴다?**
풀이 시간이 계속해서 권장 시간을 넘긴다면 실전 훈련이 부족하다는 신호입니다. 아직 조급함을 가질 필요는 없지만, 매일의 문제 풀이에 더 긴장감 있게 임해보세요.

❸ **틀린 이유 맞춤 솔루션**: 오답 이유에 따라 다음 해결책을 참고하세요.
(1) 단어를 많이 몰라서
▶ <STEP 1 단어>에 제시된 필수 어휘를 매일 챙겨보고, SELF-TEST까지 꼼꼼히 진행합니다.
(2) 문장 해석이 잘 안 돼서
▶ <STEP 3 지문 복습>의 구문 첨삭과 끊어읽기 해설을 정독하며 문장구조를 보는 눈을 길러보세요.
(3) 해석은 되지만 내용이 이해가 안 되거나, 선택지로 연결을 못 해서
▶ <정답과 해설>의 해설과 오답풀이를 참고해 틀린 이유를 깊이 고민하고 정리해 보세요.

! 결론적으로, 내가 **취약한 부분**은 ______ 이다. **취약점을 보완하기 위해서** 나는 ______ 을/를 해야겠다.
3일 뒤 다시 봐야 할 문항과, 꼭 다시 외워야 할 사항·구문 등이 있는 페이지는 지금 바로 접어 두세요.

93

❷ 매일 실전 훈련 연습

매일 유형별 문제풀이로 실전 감각을 기를 수 있습니다.

❹ 맞춤 솔루션 찾기

나의 문제 풀이 상황에 따라 맞춤 솔루션을 찾고, 앞으로의 학습 방향을 설계할 수 있습니다.

체계적인 **3단계** 학습으로
내신·학력평가 동시대비

구성과 특징

STEP 3

작은 단어, 구문도 놓치지 않는다!

첨삭 해설로 지문 복습하기

❶ 전 문장 직독직해

끊어읽기로 모든 문장을 직독직해 해보고 정확한 해석 능력을 기를 수 있습니다.

❸ 지문 속 단어 복습

STEP 1에서 외웠던 단어가 지문 속에 어떻게 활용되었는지 최종 확인하고, 암기 여부를 재점검할 수 있습니다.

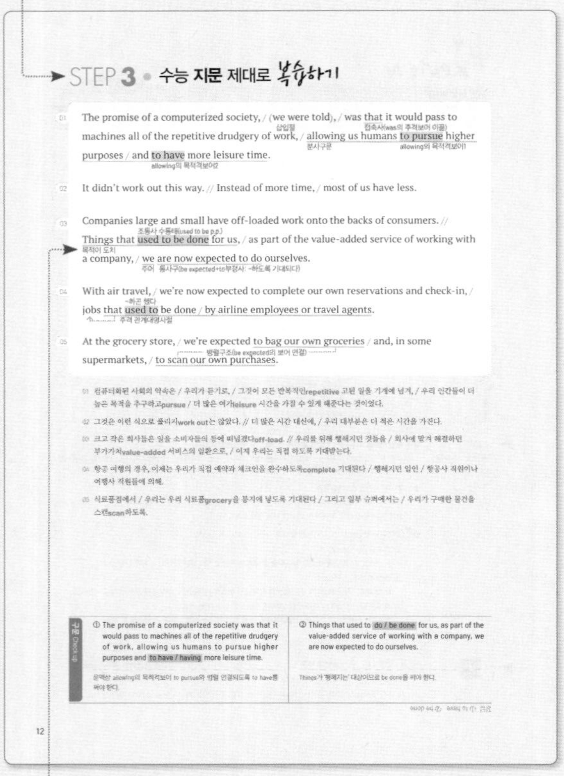
STEP 3 • 수능 지문 제대로 복습하기

01 The promise of a computerized society, / (we were told), / was that it would pass to machines all of the repetitive drudgery of work, / allowing us humans to pursue higher purposes / and to have more leisure time.

02 It didn't work out this way. // Instead of more time, / most of us have less.

03 Companies large and small have off-loaded work onto the backs of consumers. // Things that used to be done for us, / as part of the value-added service of working with a company, / we are now expected to do ourselves.

04 With air travel, / we're now expected to complete our own reservations and check-in, / jobs that used to be done / by airline employees or travel agents.

05 At the grocery store, / we're expected to bag our own groceries / and, in some supermarkets, / to scan our own purchases.

① The promise of a computerized society was that it would pass to machines all of the repetitive drudgery of work, allowing us humans to pursue higher purposes and to have / having more leisure time.

② Things that used to do / be done for us, as part of the value-added service of working with a company, we are now expected to do ourselves.

12

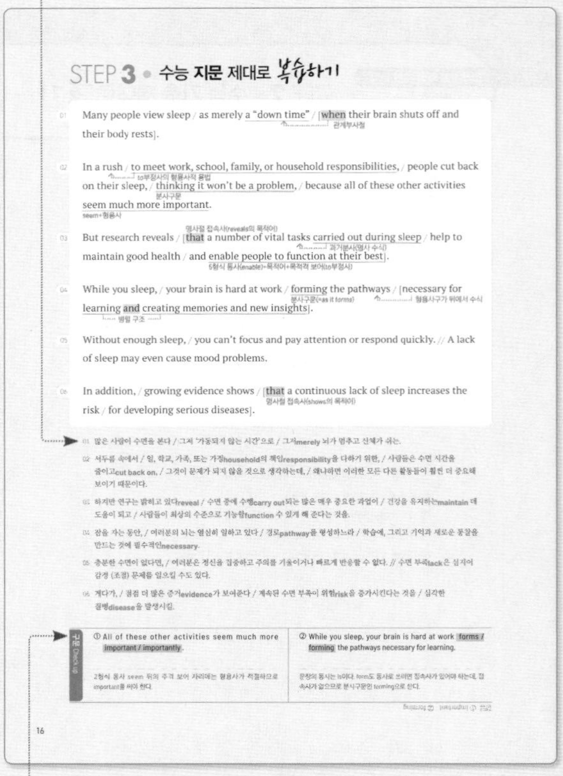
STEP 3 • 수능 지문 제대로 복습하기

01 Many people view sleep / as merely a "down time" / [when their brain shuts off and their body rests].

02 In a rush / to meet work, school, family, or household responsibilities, / people cut back on their sleep, / thinking it won't be a problem, / because all of these other activities seem much more important.

03 But research reveals / [that a number of vital tasks carried out during sleep / help to maintain good health / and enable people to function at their best].

04 While you sleep, / your brain is hard at work / forming the pathways / [necessary for learning and creating memories and new insights].

05 Without enough sleep, / you can't focus and pay attention or respond quickly. // A lack of sleep may even cause mood problems.

06 In addition, / growing evidence shows / [that a continuous lack of sleep increases the risk / for developing serious diseases].

① All of these other activities seem much more important / importantly.

② While you sleep, your brain is hard at work forms / forming the pathways necessary for learning.

16

❷ 구문 첨삭 해설

실제 수능에 자주 나오는 구문을 꼼꼼히 학습하고, 다음 문제 풀이에 적용할 수 있습니다.

❹ 구문 CHECK-UP

첨삭 해설로 학습한 구문 포인트를 어법 변형 문제로 한 번 더 정리할 수 있습니다.

"Extra" STEP

기본기를 독해력으로 끌어올린다!

정답 및 해설

❶ 해석

직독직해로 읽은 의미를
매끄러운 말로 확인할 수 있습니다.

❸ 상세 오답 풀이

선택지 함정과 오답의 근거를
자세히 설명해주는 오답 풀이를 통해
나의 약점을 보완할 수 있습니다.

❷ 해설

근거 중심의 자세한 해설로
정답 도출의 과정을 확인할 수 있습니다.

❹ 구문플러스 & 유형플러스

필수 구문/어법 사항, 유형별 주의 사항을
추가로 확인하며 실전력을 기를 수 있습니다.

Contents

14일 만에 완성하는 내신과 학력평가 등급up 프로그램

좋은 기출 문제와 기본기가 튼튼해지는 영어 공부법의 만남

최신 7개년 고1 전국연합 학력평가 기출문제
⊕ 독해 유형별 훈련 시스템 ⊕ 모든 지문 문장별 첨삭 해설

공부한 날	단원		페이지	학습일
Day 8	내용 불일치	Day 8A 2023년 학평 Day 8B 2022년 학평 Day 8C 2021년 학평 Day 8D 2020년 학평 Day 8E 2019년 학평 Day 8F 2018년 학평 Day 8G 2016년 학평	p.209	____월 ____일
Day 9	어휘의 이해	Day 9A 2023년 학평 Day 9B 2022년 학평 Day 9C 2021년 학평 Day 9D 2020년 학평 Day 9E 2019년 학평 Day 9F 2018년 학평 Day 9G 2017년 학평	p.237	____월 ____일
Day 10	어법의 이해	Day 10A 2023년 학평 Day 10B 2022년 학평 Day 10C 2021년 학평 Day 10D 2020년 학평 Day 10E 2019년 학평 Day 10F 2018년 학평 Day 10G 2017년 학평	p.267	____월 ____일
Day 11	글의 순서 배열	Day 11A 2023년 학평 Day 11B 2022년 학평 Day 11C 2021년 학평 Day 11D 2020년 학평 Day 11E 2019년 학평 Day 11F 2018년 학평 Day 11G 2017년 학평	p.295	____월 ____일
Day 12	주어진 문장 넣기	Day 12A 2023년 학평 Day 12B 2022년 학평 Day 12C 2021년 학평 Day 12D 2020년 학평 Day 12E 2019년 학평 Day 12F 2018년 학평 Day 12G 2017년 학평	p.323	____월 ____일
Day 13	요약문 완성	Day 13A 2023년 학평 Day 13B 2022년 학평 Day 13C 2021년 학평 Day 13D 2020년 학평 Day 13E 2019년 학평 Day 13F 2018년 학평 Day 13G 2017년 학평	p.353	____월 ____일
Day 14	장문의 이해	Day 14A 2023년 학평 Day 14B 2022년 학평 Day 14C 2021년 학평 Day 14D 2020년 학평 Day 14E 2019년 학평 Day 14F 2018년 학평 Day 14G 2017년 학평	p.381	____월 ____일

<매3영>이 제시하는 3단계로

유형 3일 훈련

DAY 01~03

공부한 날			출처	페이지
DAY 1	월	일	학력평가 기출 2023년 학력평가 기출 2022년 학력평가 기출 2021년 학력평가 기출 2020년 학력평가 기출 2019년 학력평가 기출 2018년 학력평가 기출 2017년	9
DAY 2	월	일	학력평가 기출 2023년 학력평가 기출 2022년 학력평가 기출 2021년 학력평가 기출 2020년 학력평가 기출 2019년 학력평가 기출 2018년 학력평가 기출 2017년	37
DAY 3	월	일	학력평가 기출 2023년 학력평가 기출 2022년 학력평가 기출 2021년 학력평가 기출 2020년 학력평가 기출 2019년 학력평가 기출 2018년 학력평가 기출 2017년	65

DAY 01

A

글의 요지 ⊕

STEP 1 • 수능에 진짜 나오는 단어

✔ 문제에 나오는 단어들을 확인하세요.

시간이 없다면 색으로 표시된 단어만이라도 꼭 외우고 넘어가세요!

01	repetitive	*a.* 반복되는	all of the (✔ repetitive) tasks	그 모든 반복되는 과업
02	pursue	*v.* 추구하다	( ) a higher purpose	더 높은 목표를 추구하다
03	leisure	*n.* 여가	have more ( ) time	여가 시간을 더 갖다
04	work out	(일이) 풀리다, 작용하다, 효과가 있다	It didn't ( ) ( ) as expected.	그것은 예상한 대로 풀리지는 않았다.
05	off-load	*v.* (짐을) 떠넘기다, 없애다	( ) work onto the backs of consumers	짐을 소비자의 등에 떠넘기다
06	value-added	*a.* 부가가치의	as part of the ( ) service	부가가치 서비스의 일환으로
07	complete	*v.* 완수하다, 마치다	( ) our own reservations	우리의 예약을 완수하다
08	grocery (*pl.* groceries)	*n.* 식료품, 잡화	walked home from the ( ) store	식료품 가게에서부터 집으로 걸어오다
09	scan	*v.* 스캔하다, 찍다, 훑다	( ) the bar code	바코드를 찍다

⊕ 본문 문장 속에서 단어들을 확인해 보세요.

At the grocery store, / we're expected to bag our own groceries / and, in some supermarkets, / to scan our own purchases.

식료품점에서 / 우리는 우리 식료품을 봉지에 넣도록 기대된다 / 그리고 일부 슈퍼에서는 / 우리가 구매한 물건을 스캔하도록.

단어 다시보기 문제를 풀기 전에 단어들을 30초 동안 다시 확인하세요.

01	repetitive	반복되는	all of the repetitive tasks	그 모든 반복되는 과업
02	pursue		pursue a higher purpose	더 높은 목표를 추구하다
03	leisure		have more leisure time	여가 시간을 더 갖다
04	work out		It didn't work out as expected.	그것은 예상한 대로 풀리지는 않았다.
05	off-load		off-load work onto the backs of consumers	짐을 소비자의 등에 떠넘기다
06	value-added		as part of the value-added service	부가가치 서비스의 일환으로
07	complete		complete our own reservations	우리의 예약을 완수하다
08	grocery		walked home from the grocery store	식료품 가게에서부터 집으로 걸어오다
09	scan		scan the bar code	바코드를 찍다

⊕ 본문 문장 속에서 단어의 의미를 우리말로 해석해 보세요.

At the grocery store, / we're expected to bag our own groceries / and, in some supermarkets, / to scan our own purchases.

→ ______에서 / 우리는 ______ 기대된다 / 그리고 일부 슈퍼에서는 / 우리가 구매한 물건을 스캔하도록.

2023 6월 학평 22번 문제

제한시간 80초

난이도 ★★★★★

STEP 2 • 수능 기출 제대로 풀기

A 다음 글의 요지로 가장 적절한 것은?

The promise of a computerized society, we were told, was that it would pass to machines all of the repetitive drudgery of work, allowing us humans to pursue higher purposes and to have more leisure time. It didn't work out this way. Instead of more time, most of us have less. Companies large and small have off-loaded work onto the backs of consumers. Things that used to be done for us, as part of the value-added service of working with a company, we are now expected to do ourselves. With air travel, we're now expected to complete our own reservations and check-in, jobs that used to be done by airline employees or travel agents. At the grocery store, we're expected to bag our own groceries and, in some supermarkets, to scan our own purchases.

*drudgery: 고된 일

① 컴퓨터 기반 사회에서는 여가 시간이 더 늘어난다.

② 회사 업무의 전산화는 업무 능률을 향상시킨다.

③ 컴퓨터화된 사회에서 소비자는 더 많은 일을 하게 된다.

④ 온라인 거래가 모든 소비자들을 만족시키기에는 한계가 있다.

⑤ 산업의 발전으로 인해 기계가 인간의 일자리를 대신하고 있다.

정답과 해설 p.2

STEP 3 • 수능 지문 제대로 복습하기

01 The promise of a computerized society, / (we were told), / was that it would pass to machines all of the repetitive drudgery of work, / allowing us humans to pursue higher purposes / and to have more leisure time.

삽입절 / 접속사(was의 주격보어 이끎) / 분사구문 / allowing의 목적격보어1 / allowing의 목적격보어2

02 It didn't work out this way. // Instead of more time, / most of us have less.

03 Companies large and small have off-loaded work onto the backs of consumers. // Things that used to be done for us, / as part of the value-added service of working with a company, / we are now expected to do ourselves.

조동사 수동태(used to be p.p.) / 목적어 도치 / 주어 / 동사구(be expected+to부정사: ~하도록 기대되다)

04 With air travel, / we're now expected to complete our own reservations and check-in, / jobs that used to be done / by airline employees or travel agents.

~하곤 했다 / 주격 관계대명사절

05 At the grocery store, / we're expected to bag our own groceries / and, in some supermarkets, / to scan our own purchases.

병렬구조(be expected의 보어 연결)

01 컴퓨터화된 사회의 약속은 / 우리가 듣기로, / 그것이 모든 반복적인**repetitive** 고된 일을 기계에 넘겨, / 우리 인간들이 더 높은 목적을 추구하고**pursue** / 더 많은 여가**leisure** 시간을 가질 수 있게 해준다는 것이었다.

02 그것은 이런 식으로 풀리지**work out**는 않았다. // 더 많은 시간 대신에, / 우리 대부분은 더 적은 시간을 가진다.

03 크고 작은 회사들은 일을 소비자들의 등에 떠넘겼다**off-load**. // 우리를 위해 행해지던 것들을 / 회사에 맡겨 해결하던 부가가치**value-added** 서비스의 일환으로, / 이제 우리는 직접 하도록 기대받는다.

04 항공 여행의 경우, 이제는 우리가 직접 예약과 체크인을 완수하도록**complete** 기대된다 / 행해지던 일인 / 항공사 직원이나 여행사 직원들에 의해.

05 식료품점에서 / 우리는 우리 식료품**grocery**을 봉지에 넣도록 기대된다 / 그리고 일부 슈퍼에서는 / 우리가 구매한 물건을 스캔**scan**하도록.

구문 Check up

① The promise of a computerized society was that it would pass to machines all of the repetitive drudgery of work, allowing us humans to pursue higher purposes and to have / having more leisure time.

문맥상 allowing의 목적격보어 to pursue와 병렬 연결되도록 to have를 써야 한다.

② Things that used to do / be done for us, as part of the value-added service of working with a company, we are now expected to do ourselves.

Things가 '행해지는' 대상이므로 be done을 써야 한다.

정답 ① to have ② be done

B

STEP 1 • 수능에 진짜 나오는 단어

글의 요지 +

✔ 문제에 나오는 단어들을 확인하세요.

시간이 없다면 색으로 표시된 단어만이라도 꼭 외우고 넘어가세요!

01	merely	ad. 그저, 단지	view sleep as (✔ merely) a "down time"	수면을 그저 '가동되지 않는 시간'으로 보다
02	household	n. 가정, 가족	the average ( )	평균적인 가정
03	responsibility	n. 책임	meet family ( )ies	가족의 책임을 다하다
04	cut back on	~을 줄이다	( ) ( ) ( ) their sleep	그들의 수면 시간을 줄이다
05	reveal	v. 밝히다	( ) the fact	사실을 밝히다
06	carry out	~을 수행하다	( ) ( ) many tasks	많은 과업을 수행하다
07	maintain	v. 유지하다	( ) good health	건강을 유지하다
08	function	v. 기능하다	( ) at their best	최상의 수준으로 기능하다
09	pathway	n. 경로	form the ( )s	경로를 형성하다
10	necessary	a. 필수적인	( ) for learning	학습에 필수적인
11	lack	n. 부족	a ( ) of sleep	수면 부족
12	evidence	n. 증거	growing ( )	점점 더 많은 증거
13	risk	n. 위험	increase the ( )	위험을 증가시키다
14	disease	n. 질병	develop serious ( )s	심각한 질병을 발생시키다

⊕ 본문 문장 속에서 단어들을 확인해 보세요.

In addition, / growing evidence shows / that a continuous lack of sleep increases the risk / for developing serious diseases.

게다가, / 점점 더 많은 증거가 보여준다 / 계속된 수면 부족이 위험을 증가시킨다는 것을 / 심각한 질병을 발생시킬.

단어 다시보기 문제를 풀기 전에 단어들을 30초 동안 다시 확인하세요.

01	merely	그저, 단지	view sleep as merely a "down time"	수면을 그저 '가동되지 않는 시간'으로 보다
02	household		the average household	평균적인 가정
03	responsibility		meet family responsibilities	가족의 책임을 다하다
04	cut back on		cut back on their sleep	그들의 수면 시간을 줄이다
05	reveal		reveal the fact	사실을 밝히다
06	carry out		carry out many tasks	많은 과업을 수행하다
07	maintain		maintain good health	건강을 유지하다
08	function		function at their best	최상의 수준으로 기능하다
09	pathway		form the pathways	경로를 형성하다
10	necessary		necessary for learning	학습에 필수적인
11	lack		a lack of sleep	수면 부족
12	evidence		growing evidence	점점 더 많은 증거
13	risk		increase the risk	위험을 증가시키다
14	disease		develop serious diseases	심각한 질병을 발생시키다

⊕ 본문 문장 속에서 단어의 의미를 우리말로 해석해 보세요.

In addition, / growing evidence shows / that a continuous lack of sleep increases the risk / for developing serious diseases.

→ 게다가, / 점점 더 많은 ______가 보여준다 / 계속된 수면 ______이 ______을 증가시킨다는 것을 / 심각한 ______을 발생시킬.

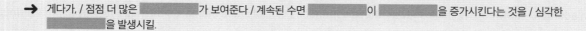

2022 3월 학평 22번 문제

제한시간 50초

난이도 ★☆☆☆☆

STEP 2 • 수능 기출 제대로 풀기

B 다음 글의 요지로 가장 적절한 것은?

Many people view sleep as merely a "down time" when their brain shuts off and their body rests. In a rush to meet work, school, family, or household responsibilities, people cut back on their sleep, thinking it won't be a problem, because all of these other activities seem much more important. But research reveals that a number of vital tasks carried out during sleep help to maintain good health and enable people to function at their best. While you sleep, your brain is hard at work forming the pathways necessary for learning and creating memories and new insights. Without enough sleep, you can't focus and pay attention or respond quickly. A lack of sleep may even cause mood problems. In addition, growing evidence shows that a continuous lack of sleep increases the risk for developing serious diseases.

*vital: 매우 중요한

① 수면은 건강 유지와 최상의 기능 발휘에 도움이 된다.

② 업무량이 증가하면 필요한 수면 시간도 증가한다.

③ 균형 잡힌 식단을 유지하면 뇌 기능이 향상된다.

④ 불면증은 주위 사람들에게 부정적인 영향을 미친다.

⑤ 꿈의 내용은 깨어 있는 시간 동안의 경험을 반영한다.

정답과 해설 p.2

STEP 3 • 수능 지문 제대로 복습하기

01 Many people view sleep / as merely a "down time" / [when their brain shuts off and their body rests].
관계부사절

02 In a rush / to meet work, school, family, or household responsibilities, / people cut back on their sleep, / thinking it won't be a problem, / because all of these other activities seem much more important.
to부정사의 형용사적 용법
분사구문
seem+형용사

03 But research reveals / [that a number of vital tasks carried out during sleep / help to maintain good health / and enable people to function at their best].
명사절 접속사(reveals의 목적어)
과거분사(명사 수식)
5형식 동사(enable)+목적어+목적격 보어(to부정사)

04 While you sleep, / your brain is hard at work / forming the pathways / [necessary for learning and creating memories and new insights].
분사구문(=as it forms)
형용사구가 뒤에서 수식
병렬 구조

05 Without enough sleep, / you can't focus and pay attention or respond quickly. // A lack of sleep may even cause mood problems.

06 In addition, / growing evidence shows / [that a continuous lack of sleep increases the risk / for developing serious diseases].
명사절 접속사(shows의 목적어)

01 많은 사람이 수면을 본다 / 그저 '가동되지 않는 시간'으로 / 그저**merely** 뇌가 멈추고 신체가 쉬는.

02 서두름 속에서 / 일, 학교, 가족, 또는 가정**household**의 책임**responsibility**을 다하기 위한, / 사람들은 수면 시간을 줄이고**cut back on**, / 그것이 문제가 되지 않을 것으로 생각하는데, / 왜냐하면 이러한 모든 다른 활동들이 훨씬 더 중요해 보이기 때문이다.

03 하지만 연구는 밝히고 있다**reveal** / 수면 중에 수행**carry out**되는 많은 매우 중요한 과업이 / 건강을 유지하는**maintain** 데 도움이 되고 / 사람들이 최상의 수준으로 기능할**function** 수 있게 해 준다는 것을.

04 잠을 자는 동안, / 여러분의 뇌는 열심히 일하고 있다 / 경로**pathway**를 형성하느라 / 학습에, 그리고 기억과 새로운 통찰을 만드는 것에 필수적인**necessary**.

05 충분한 수면이 없다면, / 여러분은 정신을 집중하고 주의를 기울이거나 빠르게 반응할 수 없다. // 수면 부족**lack**은 심지어 감정 (조절) 문제를 일으킬 수도 있다.

06 게다가, / 점점 더 많은 증거**evidence**가 보여준다 / 계속된 수면 부족이 위험**risk**을 증가시킨다는 것을 / 심각한 질병**disease**을 발생시킬.

구문 Check up

① All of these other activities seem much more important / importantly.	② While you sleep, your brain is hard at work forms / forming the pathways necessary for learning.
2형식 동사 seem 뒤의 주격 보어 자리에는 형용사가 적절하므로 important를 써야 한다.	문장의 동사는 is이다. form도 동사로 쓰려면 접속사가 있어야 하는데, 접속사가 없으므로 분사구문인 forming으로 쓴다.

정답 ① important ② forming

C

글의 요지 ➕

STEP 1 • 수능에 진짜 나오는 단어

✔ 문제에 나오는 단어들을 확인하세요.

시간이 없다면 색으로 표시된 단어만이라도 꼭 외우고 넘어가세요!

01	independently	ad. 독자적으로	think (✔ independently)	독자적으로 생각하다
02	trustworthy	a. 신뢰할 수 있는	a ( ) group of people	신뢰할 수 있는 집단
03	extremely	ad. 매우	( ) difficult	매우 어려운
04	ultimately	ad. 궁극적으로	( ) better for you	당신에게 궁극적으로 더 좋은
05	faith	n. 믿음	have ( )	믿음을 갖다
06	probably	ad. 아마도	You're ( ) blind.	당신은 아마도 보지 못한다.
07	blind	a. 보지 못하는, 눈먼	be ( ) to their way of thinking	그들이 생각하는 방식을 보지 못하다
08	evidence	n. 증거	All the ( ) is against you.	모든 증거가 당신에게 불리하다.
09	incredibly	ad. 믿을 수 없을 정도로	( ) open-minded	믿을 수 없을 정도로 마음을 연
10	repeatedly	ad. 반복적으로	( ) encounter something	무언가를 반복적으로 겪다
11	encounter	v. 겪다, 맞닥뜨리다	( ) lots of pain	많은 고통을 겪다
12	bet	v. 확신하다	( ) that they were right	그들이 옳았다고 확신하다

➕ 본문 문장 속에서 단어들을 확인해 보세요.

If you can't understand their view, / you're probably just blind / to their way of thinking.

만약 여러분이 그들의 생각을 이해할 수 없다면, / 여러분은 아마도 단지 보지 못하는 것이다 / 그들이 생각하는 방식을.

단어 다시보기 문제를 풀기 전에 단어들을 30초 동안 다시 확인하세요.

01	independently	독자적으로	think independently	독자적으로 생각하다
02	trustworthy		a trustworthy group of people	신뢰할 수 있는 집단
03	extremely		extremely difficult	매우 어려운
04	ultimately		ultimately better for you	당신에게 궁극적으로 더 좋은
05	faith		have faith	믿음을 갖다
06	probably		You're probably blind.	당신은 아마도 보지 못한다.
07	blind		be blind to their way of thinking	그들이 생각하는 방식을 보지 못하다
08	evidence		All the evidence is against you.	모든 증거가 당신에게 불리하다.
09	incredibly		incredibly open-minded	믿을 수 없을 정도로 마음을 연
10	repeatedly		repeatedly encounter something	무언가를 반복적으로 겪다
11	encounter		encounter lots of pain	많은 고통을 겪다
12	bet		bet that they were right	그들이 옳았다고 확신하다

⊕ 본문 문장 속에서 단어의 의미를 우리말로 해석해 보세요.

If you can't understand their view, / you're probably just blind / to their way of thinking.

➜ 만약 여러분이 그들의 생각을 이해할 수 없다면, / 여러분은 ____________________ 것이다 / 그들이 생각하는 방식을.

2021 9월 학평 22번 문제

제한시간 80초

난이도 ★★★★☆

STEP 2 • 수능 기출 제대로 풀기

C

다음 글의 요지로 가장 적절한 것은?

It's important that you think independently and fight for what you believe in, but there comes a time when it's wiser to stop fighting for your view and move on to accepting what a trustworthy group of people think is best. This can be extremely difficult. But it's smarter, and ultimately better for you to be open-minded and have faith that the conclusions of a trustworthy group of people are better than whatever you think. If you can't understand their view, you're probably just blind to their way of thinking. If you continue doing what you think is best when all the evidence and trustworthy people are against you, you're being dangerously confident. The truth is that while most people can become incredibly open-minded, some can't, even after they have repeatedly encountered lots of pain from betting that they were right when they were not.

① 대부분의 사람들은 진리에 도달하지 못하고 고통을 받는다.

② 맹목적으로 다른 사람의 의견을 받아들이는 것은 위험하다.

③ 남을 설득하기 위해서는 타당한 증거로 주장을 뒷받침해야 한다.

④ 믿을 만한 사람이 누구인지 판단하려면 열린 마음을 가져야 한다.

⑤ 자신의 의견이 최선이 아닐 수 있다는 것을 인정하는 것이 필요하다.

정답과 해설 p.2

STEP 3 • 수능 지문 제대로 복습하기

01 It's important / [that you think independently / and fight for what you believe in], / but there comes a time / when it's wiser / [to stop fighting for your view / and move on to accepting / what a trustworthy group of people think is best].

가주어 / 진주어(that절) / 관계대명사 what절(전치사의 목적어) / 도치(동사+주어) / 관계부사 / 가주어 / 진주어(to부정사) / 관계대명사 what절 (accepting의 목적어) / 삽입구문

02 This can be extremely difficult. // But / it's smarter, and ultimately better / [for you to be open-minded and have faith / that the conclusions of a trustworthy group of people are better / than whatever you think].

가주어 / 의미상 주어 / 진주어(to부정사) / 동격의 that절(=faith) / 복합관계대명사(=anything that: ~한 무엇이든)

03 If you can't understand their view, / you're probably just blind / to their way of thinking.

04 If you continue doing / what you think is best / when all the evidence and trustworthy people are against you, / you're being dangerously confident.

삽입구문 / 관계대명사 what절(doing의 목적어) / 현재진행형

05 The truth is / that while most people can become incredibly open-minded, / some can't, / even after they have repeatedly encountered lots of pain / from betting that they were right when they were not.

명사절 접속사(보어) / (become incredibly open-minded) / right 생략 / 명사절 접속사(betting의 목적어) / 대동사

01 중요하다 / 당신이 독자적으로**independently** 생각하고 / 자신이 믿는 것을 위해 싸우는 것이, / 하지만 때가 온다 / 더 현명한 (때가) / 자신의 생각을 위해 싸우는 것을 중단하고 / 받아들이는 쪽으로 나아 가는 것이 (더 현명한) / 신뢰할 수 있는**trustworthy** 집단이 생각하기에 가장 좋은 것을.

02 이것은 매우**extremely** 어려울 수 있다. // 하지만 / 더 영리하고 궁극적으로**ultimately** 더 좋다 / 여러분이 마음을 열고 믿음**faith**을 갖는 것이 / 신뢰할 수 있는 집단의 결론이 낫다는 (믿음) / 여러분이 생각하는 그 무엇보다.

03 만약 여러분이 그들의 생각을 이해할 수 없다면, / 여러분은 아마도**probably** 단지 보지 못하는**blind** 것이다 / 그들이 생각하는 방식을.

04 당신이 하기를 계속한다면, / 당신이 생각하기에 최선인 것을 / 모든 증거**evidence**와 신뢰할 수 있는 사람들이 당신에게 반대할 때, / 당신은 위험할 정도로 자신감에 차 있는 것이다.

05 사실은 / 대부분의 사람들은 믿을 수 없을 정도로**incredibly** 마음을 열 수 있는 반면에, / 어떤 사람들은 그럴 수 없다는 것이다 / 많은 고통을 반복적으로**repeatedly** 겪은**encounter** 후에도 / 자신이 옳지 않았을 때 옳았다고 확신하는**bet** 것으로부터.

구문 Check up

① It's important that you think independently and fight for which / what you believe in.

전치사 for의 목적어 자리에 명사가 와야 하고, 뒤에 불완전한 문장이 오므로, 선행사(명사)를 포함하는 관계대명사 what을 쓴다.

② They have repeatedly encountered lots of pain from betting that they were right when they were / did not.

내용상 앞의 were right를 부정문으로 바꾸어 써야 하므로 이와 일치되도록 be동사 were를 쓴다.

정답 ① what ② were

D

주제 추론

STEP 1 • 수능에 진짜 나오는 단어

✔ 문제에 나오는 단어들을 확인하세요.

시간이 없다면 색으로 표시된 단어만이라도 꼭 외우고 넘어가세요!

01	engage in	~에 참여하다	(✔ engage) (in) play activities	놀이 활동에 참여하다
02	behavior	n. 행동	practice ( )s	행동을 연습하다
03	survival	n. 생존	for future ( )	미래 생존을 위해
04	development	n. 발달	important functions during ( )	발달하는 동안 주요한 기능들
05	infancy	n. 유아기	the earliest beginnings in ( )	유아기의 가장 초기
06	try out	시도하다	allow children to ( ) ( )	아이들에게 시도하게 해주다
07	acquire	v. 습득하다, 얻다	( ) values	가치를 습득하다
08	trait	n. 특성	personality ( )s	성격적인 특성들
09	compete	v. 경쟁하다	( ) with others	다른 이들과 경쟁하다
10	cooperate	v. 협력하다	( ) with others	다른 이들과 협력하다
11	contrast	n. 차이, 대조	( )s between human and animal play	인간과 동물 놀이의 차이
12	stage	n. 단계	various developmental ( )s	다양한 발달상의 단계들

⊕ 본문 문장 속에서 단어들을 확인해 보세요.

In animals, / play has long been seen / as a way of learning and practicing skills and behaviors / that are necessary for future survival.

동물에게 있어 / 놀이는 오랫동안 여겨져 왔다 / 기술과 행동을 학습하고 연마하는 방식으로 / 미래 생존에 필요한.

단어 다시보기 문제를 풀기 전에 단어들을 30초 동안 다시 확인하세요.

01	engage in	~에 참여하다	engage in play activities	놀이 활동에 참여하다
02	behavior		practice behaviors	행동을 연습하다
03	survival		for future survival	미래 생존을 위해
04	development		important functions during development	발달하는 동안 주요한 기능들
05	infancy		the earliest beginnings in infancy	유아기의 가장 초기
06	try out		allow children to try out	아이들에게 시도하게 해주다
07	acquire		acquire values	가치를 습득하다
08	trait		personality traits	성격적인 특성들
09	compete		compete with others	다른 이들과 경쟁하다
10	cooperate		cooperate with others	다른 이들과 협력하다
11	contrast		contrasts between human and animal play	인간과 동물 놀이의 차이
12	stage		various developmental stages	다양한 발달상의 단계들

⊕ 본문 문장 속에서 단어의 의미를 우리말로 해석해 보세요.

In animals, / play has long been seen / as a way of learning and practicing skills and behaviors / that are necessary for future survival.

➜ 동물에게 있어 / 놀이는 오랫동안 여겨져 왔다 / 기술과 ________을 학습하고 연마하는 방식으로 / ________에 필요한.

2020 9월 학평 23번 문제

제한시간 70초

난이도 ★★★☆☆

STEP 2 • 수능 기출 제대로 풀기

D

다음 글의 주제로 가장 적절한 것은?

Animals as well as humans engage in play activities. In animals, play has long been seen as a way of learning and practicing skills and behaviors that are necessary for future survival. In children, too, play has important functions during development. From its earliest beginnings in infancy, play is a way in which children learn about the world and their place in it. Children's play serves as a training ground for developing physical abilities — skills like walking, running, and jumping that are necessary for everyday living. Play also allows children to try out and learn social behaviors and to acquire values and personality traits that will be important in adulthood. For example, they learn how to compete and cooperate with others, how to lead and follow, how to make decisions, and so on.

① necessity of trying out creative ideas

② roles of play in children's development

③ contrasts between human and animal play

④ effects of children's physical abilities on play

⑤ children's needs at various developmental stages

정답과 해설 p.3

STEP 3 • 수능 지문 제대로 복습하기

01 Animals as well as humans / engage in play activities.
A as well as B: B뿐만 아니라 A도 / 수 일치(A)

02 In animals, / play has long been seen / as a way of learning and practicing skills and behaviors / that are necessary for future survival. // In children, too, / play has important functions / during development.
현재완료 수동태 / 선행사 / 관계대명사절

03 From its earliest beginnings in infancy, / play is a way / in which children learn / about the world and their place in it.
전치사+관계대명사절 / (=play)

04 Children's play serves as a training ground / for developing physical abilities / — skills like walking, running, and jumping / that are necessary for everyday living.
전치사구 / 주격 관계대명사절

05 Play also allows children [to try out and learn social behaviors] / and [to acquire values and personality traits / that will be important in adulthood].
5형식 동사 / 목적어 / 목적격 보어(to부정사) 병렬구조 / 선행사 / 주격 관계대명사절

06 For example, / they learn [how to compete and cooperate with others, / how to lead and follow, / how to make decisions, and so on].
learn의 목적어(how+to부정사)

01 인간뿐만 아니라 동물도 / 놀이 활동에 참여한다**engage in**.

02 동물에게 있어 / 놀이는 오랫동안 여겨져 왔다 / 기술과 행동**behavior**을 학습하고 연마하는 방식으로 / 미래 생존**future survival**에 필요한. // 아이들에게 있어서도 / 놀이는 중요한 기능을 한다 / 발달하는 동안**during development**.

03 유아기**infancy**의 가장 초기부터, / 놀이는 방식이다 / 아이들이 배우는 / 세상과 그 안에서의 그들의 위치에 대해.

04 아이들의 놀이는 훈련의 토대로서 역할을 한다 / 신체능력을 발달시키기 위한 / 걷기, 달리기, 그리고 점프하기와 같은 기술을 / 매일의 삶에 필요한.

05 놀이는 또한 아이들이 사회적 행동을 시도하고**try out** 배우게 한다 / 그리고 가치와 성격적 특성**personality trait**을 습득하게**acquire** 한다 / 성인기에 중요할.

06 예를 들어, / 그들은 다른 사람들과 경쟁하고 협력하는**compete and cooperate with others** 방식을 배운다 / 그리고 이끌고 따르는 방식, / 결정하는 방식 등을.

구문 Check up

① In animals, play has long [seen / been seen] as a way of learning and practicing skills and behaviors.

놀이가 '아는' 것이 아니라 '여겨지는' 것이므로 현재완료의 수동태인 been seen을 쓴다.

② Play also allows children [try / to try] out and learn social behaviors and to acquire values.

동사 allow는 5형식 동사로 목적격 보어로 to부정사가 오므로 to try를 쓴다.

정답 ① been seen ② to try

E

주제 추론 +

STEP 1 • 수능에 진짜 나오는 단어

✓ 문제에 나오는 단어들을 확인하세요.

시간이 없다면 색으로 표시된 단어만이라도 꼭 외우고 넘어가세요!

01	communicate	v. 전달하다	(✓ communicate) information	정보를 전달하다
02	sheer	a. 단순한, 순전한	( ) delight	순전한 기쁨
03	knowledge	n. 지식	true ( )	진정한 지식
04	rely on	~에 의존하다	We should ( ) ( ) our own judgement.	우리는 우리 자신의 판단에 의존해야 한다.
05	polish	v. 다듬다, (광을 내어) 닦다, 손질하다	( ) the shoes	신발을 닦다
06	write out	자세히 쓰다	( ) ( ) your feelings	당신의 감정을 자세히 쓰다
07	critically	ad. 비판적으로	look back ( ) at the result	결과를 비판적으로 되돌아보다
08	embarrassing	a. 당황스러운	( ) ideas	당황스러운 생각들

⊕ 본문 문장 속에서 단어들을 확인해 보세요.

Therefore you don't learn the details of your thinking / until speaking or writing it out in detail / and looking back critically at the result.

그러므로 여러분은 여러분 사고의 세부 내용을 알지 못한다 / 그것을 상세하게 이야기하거나 쓸 때까지 / 그리고 그 결과를 비판적으로 되돌아볼 때까지.

단어 다시보기 문제를 풀기 전에 단어들을 30초 동안 다시 확인하세요.

01	communicate	전달하다	communicate information	정보를 전달하다
02	sheer		sheer delight	순전한 기쁨
03	knowledge		true knowledge	진정한 지식
04	rely on		We should rely on our own judgement.	우리는 우리 자신의 판단에 의존해야 한다.
05	polish		polish the shoes	신발을 닦다
06	write out		write out your feelings	당신의 감정을 자세히 쓰다
07	critically		look back critically at the result	결과를 비판적으로 되돌아보다
08	embarrassing		embarrassing ideas	당황스러운 생각들

⊕ **본문 문장 속에서 단어의 의미를 우리말로 해석해 보세요.**

Therefore you don't learn the details of your thinking / until speaking or writing it out in detail / and looking back critically at the result.

→ 그러므로 여러분은 여러분 사고의 세부 내용을 알지 못한다 / ______ 이야기하거나 ______ 때까지 / 그리고 ______ ______ 때까지.

2019 11월 학평 23번 문제

제한시간 80초

난이도 ★★★★★

STEP 2 • 수능 기출 제대로 풀기

E

다음 글의 주제로 가장 적절한 것은?

You can say that information sits in one brain until it is communicated to another, unchanged in the conversation. That's true of *sheer* information, like your phone number or the place you left your keys. But it's not true of knowledge. Knowledge relies on judgements, which you discover and polish in conversation with other people or with yourself. Therefore you don't learn the details of your thinking until speaking or writing it out in detail and looking back critically at the result. "Is what I just said foolish, or is what I just wrote a deep truth?" In the speaking or writing, you uncover your bad ideas, often embarrassing ones, and good ideas too, sometimes fame-making ones. Thinking requires its expression.

① critical roles of speaking or writing in refining thoughts

② persuasive ways to communicate what you think to people

③ important tips to select the right information for your writing

④ positive effects of logical thinking on reading comprehension

⑤ enormous gaps between spoken language and written language

정답과 해설 p.3

STEP 3 • 수능 지문 제대로 복습하기

01 You can say / that information sits in one brain / until it is communicated to another, / unchanged in the conversation.
명사절 접속사 (that) / 분사구문 (unchanged)

02 That's true of *sheer* information, / like your phone number / or the place you left your keys.
전치사(~처럼) (like) / where 생략 / 관계부사절 (you left your keys)

03 But it's not true of knowledge. // Knowledge relies on judgements, / which you discover and polish / in conversation with other people or with yourself.
계속적 용법(judgements 설명) (which)

04 Therefore you don't learn the details of your thinking / until speaking or writing it out in detail / and looking back critically at the result.
분사구문(=until you speak or write ~ and look back ~)

05 "Is what I just said foolish, / or is what I just wrote a deep truth?"

06 In the speaking or writing, / you uncover your bad ideas, / often embarrassing ones, / and good ideas too, / sometimes fame-making ones. // Thinking requires its expression.
부정대명사(=ideas) (ones)

01 여러분은 말할 수 있다 / 정보가 한 뇌에 머물러 있다고 / 그것이 다른 뇌로 전달될**communicate** 때까지 / 그리고 대화 속에서 변하지 않는다고.

02 이는 '단순**sheer**' 정보에 대해서는 사실이다 / 여러분의 전화번호나 / 여러분이 열쇠를 놓아둔 장소처럼.

03 하지만 이것은 지식에 대해서는 사실이 아니다. // 지식**knowledge**은 판단에 의존하는데**rely on**, / 여러분은 그 판단을 발견하고 다듬는다**polish** / 다른 사람들 혹은 자신과의 대화 속에서.

04 그러므로 여러분은 여러분 사고의 세부 내용을 알지 못한다 / 그것을 상세하게 이야기하거나 쓸**write out** 때까지 / 그리고 그 결과를 비판적으로**critically** 되돌아볼 때까지.

05 "내가 방금 이야기한 것이 바보 같은가, / 혹은 내가 방금 쓴 것이 깊은 진실인가?"

06 말하거나 쓸 때, / 여러분은 형편없는 생각들을 발견하게 된다 / 흔히 당황스러운**embarrassing** 것들 / 또한 좋은 생각들도 / 때로는 유명하게 만들어 주는 것들. // 사고는 그것의 표현이 필요하다.

구문 Check up

① That's true of *sheer* information, like / alike your phone number or the place you left your keys.

뒤에 A or B 형태의 명사구가 나오므로 전치사 like를 써야 한다. alike는 보어 역할만 할 수 있는 형용사이다.

② Therefore you don't learn the details of your thinking until speaking or writing it out in detail and look / looking back critically at the result.

speaking or writing과 and로 병렬 연결될 현재분사 자리이므로 looking이 적절하다.

정답 ① like ② looking

F

글의 요지

STEP 1 • 수능에 진짜 나오는 단어

✔ 문제에 나오는 단어들을 확인하세요.

시간이 없다면 색으로 표시된 단어만이라도 꼭 외우고 넘어가세요!

01	praise	v. 칭찬하다 n. 칭찬	(✓ praise) your child	아이를 칭찬하다
02	intelligence	n. 지능	a child's ( )	어린아이의 지능
03	talent	n. 재능	praise one's ( )	재능을 칭찬하다
04	boost	v. 북돋우다, 높이다	( ) one's self-esteem	자존감을 높이다
05	motivate	v. 동기를 부여하다	( ) a child	어린아이에게 동기를 부여하다
06	backfire	v. 역효과를 일으키다 n. 역효과, 역풍	This sort of praise ( )s.	이런 종류의 칭찬은 역효과를 일으킨다.
07	colleague	n. 동료	her ( )s	그녀의 동료들
08	demonstrate	v. 보여주다, 증명하다	( ) the effect	효과를 보여주다
09	experimental	a. 실험적인	( ) studies	실험적 연구
10	cautious	a. 조심스러운	become more ( )	더 조심하게 되다
11	challenge	n. 도전	avoid ( )s	도전을 피하다
12	appraisal	n. 평가	the high ( )	높은 평가
13	helpless	a. 무기력한	feel ( )	무기력하게 느끼다

⊕ 본문 문장 속에서 단어들을 확인해 보세요.

It might seem / that praising your child's intelligence or talent / would boost his self-esteem and motivate him.

보일지도 모른다 / 당신의 아이의 지능 또는 재능을 칭찬하는 것은 / 그의 자존감을 높이고 그에게 동기를 부여하는 것처럼.

단어 다시보기 문제를 풀기 전에 단어들을 30초 동안 다시 확인하세요.

01	praise	칭찬하다, 칭찬	praise your child	아이를 칭찬하다
02	intelligence		a child's intelligence	어린아이의 지능
03	talent		praise one's talent	재능을 칭찬하다
04	boost		boost one's self-esteem	자존감을 높이다
05	motivate		motivate a child	어린아이에게 동기를 부여하다
06	backfire		This sort of praise backfires.	이런 종류의 칭찬은 역효과를 일으킨다.
07	colleague		her colleagues	그녀의 동료들
08	demonstrate		demonstrate the effect	효과를 보여주다
09	experimental		experimental studies	실험적 연구
10	cautious		become more cautious	더 조심하게 되다
11	challenge		avoid challenges	도전을 피하다
12	appraisal		the high appraisal	높은 평가
13	helpless		feel helpless	무기력하게 느끼다

⊕ 본문 문장 속에서 단어의 의미를 우리말로 해석해 보세요.

It might seem / that praising your child's intelligence or talent / would boost his self-esteem and motivate him.

→ 보일지도 모른다 / ________ 또는 ________을 칭찬하는 것은 / 그의 자존감을 ________ 그에게 ________ 것처럼.

2018 9월 학평 21번 문제

제한시간 70초

난이도 ★★★☆☆

STEP 2 • 수능 기출 제대로 풀기

F

다음 글의 요지로 가장 적절한 것은?

It might seem that praising your child's intelligence or talent would boost his self-esteem and motivate him. But it turns out that this sort of praise backfires. Carol Dweck and her colleagues have demonstrated the effect in a series of experimental studies: "When we praise kids for their ability, kids become more cautious. They avoid challenges." It's as if they are afraid to do anything that might make them fail and lose your high appraisal. Kids might also get the message that intelligence or talent is something that people either have or don't have. This leaves kids feeling helpless when they make mistakes. What's the point of trying to improve if your mistakes indicate that you lack intelligence?

① 놀이 시간의 부족은 아이의 인지 발달을 지연시킨다.

② 구체적인 칭찬은 아이의 자존감 발달에 도움이 된다.

③ 아이의 능력에 맞는 도전 과제를 제시할 필요가 있다.

④ 자신의 잘못을 인정하는 태도는 꾸준한 대화를 통해 길러진다.

⑤ 아이의 지능과 재능에 대한 칭찬은 아이에게 부정적 영향을 끼친다.

정답과 해설 p.4

STEP 3 • 수능 지문 제대로 복습하기

01 It might seem / [that praising your child's intelligence or talent / would boost his self-esteem and motivate him].
(It: 가주어 / that ~ talent: 진주어(that절) / praising ~ talent: that절의 주어(동명사))

02 But it turns out / that this sort of praise backfires. // Carol Dweck and her colleagues have demonstrated the effect / in a series of experimental studies:
(it: 가주어 / that ~: 진주어(that절) / have demonstrated: 현재완료)

03 "When we praise kids for their ability, / kids become more cautious. // They avoid challenges."
(more cautious: 형용사의 비교급)

04 It's as if they are afraid to do anything / that might make them fail and lose your high appraisal.
(as if: 마치 ~인 것처럼 / that: 주격 관계대명사 / make them fail and lose ~: 사역동사+목적어+목적격보어(원형부정사))

05 Kids might also get the message / [that intelligence or talent is something / that people either have or don't have]. // This leaves kids feeling helpless / when they make mistakes.
(that ~ have: 동격의 that절(=the message) / that: 목적격 관계대명사 / either A or B: A 또는 B 둘 중 하나 / leaves kids feeling helpless: leave+목적어+목적격 보어(현재분사구))

06 What's the point of trying to improve / if your mistakes indicate / that you lack intelligence?
(trying to improve: ~하려고 노력하다(≠try+-ing: 시험삼아 해보다) / that: 명사절 접속사)

01 보일지도 모른다 / 당신 아이의 지능intelligence과 재능talent을 칭찬하는praise 것이 / 그의 자존감을 높이고boost 그에게 동기를 부여하는motivate 것처럼.

02 그러나 밝혀진다 / 이런 종류의 칭찬은 역효과를 일으키는backfire 것으로. // Carol Dweck과 그녀의 동료colleague들은 그 효과를 보여주었다demonstrate / 일련의 실험적experimental 연구들에서.

03 "우리가 그들의 능력에 대해 아이들을 칭찬할 때, / 아이들은 더 조심하게cautious 된다. // 그들은 도전challenge을 피한다."

04 그것은 마치 그들이 그 어떤 것도 하길 두려워하는 것과 같다 / 자신들을 실패하게 만들고 당신의 높은 평가appraisal를 잃게 할지도 모를 (그 어떤 것).

05 아이들은 또한 메시지를 받을지도 모른다 / 지능이나 재능이 어떤 것이라는 / 사람들이 가지거나 가지지 못하는 (어떤 것). // 이것은 아이들이 무기력하게helpless 느끼도록 만든다 / 그들이 실수했을 때.

06 향상하도록 노력하는 것이 무슨 소용이겠는가 / 만약 당신의 실수가 나타낸다면 / 당신이 지능이 부족하다는 것을?

구문 Check up

① It might seem that [praise / praising] your child's intelligence or talent would boost his self-esteem and motivate him.

명사절 that절의 주어 역할을 해야 하기 때문에 동사인 praise가 아닌 동명사 praising이 와야 한다.

② This leaves kids [feeling / felt] helpless when they make mistakes.

목적어인 kids와 목적격 보어 feel의 관계가 능동이므로 현재분사 feeling이 적절하다.

정답 ① praising ② feeling

G

주제 추론

STEP 1 • 수능에 진짜 나오는 단어

✔ 문제에 나오는 단어들을 확인하세요.

시간이 없다면 색으로 표시된 단어만이라도 꼭 외우고 넘어가세요!

01	gadget	n. 기기, 장치	a new (✔ gadget)	새로운 기기
02	random	a. 무작위의	( ) junk	무작위의 잡동사니
03	turn into	~으로 변하다, 되다	( ) ( ) a hobby	취미가 되다
04	pleasure	n. 기쁨	( ) in creating things	물건들을 만드는 기쁨
05	satisfaction	n. 만족	the same kind of ( )	같은 종류의 만족감
06	rush	n. 흥분, 열기	a similar ( )	유사한 흥분
07	temporary	a. 일시의, 임시의	a ( ) solution	임시 해결책
08	recommendation	n. 추천, 권고	the ( ) of a doctor	의사의 권고
09	craft	n. 공예기술	learn more about ( )	공예기술에 대해 더 배우다
10	online	ad. 온라인상으로	learn more ( )	온라인상으로 더 배우다
11	end up ~ing	결국 ~하다	( ) ( ) spend( ) money	결국 돈을 쓰다
12	stuff	n. 물건	a collection of ( )	수집 물건
13	decrease	v. 감소하다, 떨어지다	( ) in value	가치가 떨어지다

⊕ 본문 문장 속에서 단어들을 확인해 보세요.

Shopping for new gadgets, clothes, or just random junk / can turn into a hobby / in itself.

새로운 기기, 옷, 혹은 단지 무작위 잡동사니들을 사는 것은 / 취미가 될 수 있다 / 그 자체로.

단어 다시보기 문제를 풀기 전에 단어들을 30초 동안 다시 확인하세요.

01	gadget	기기, 장치	a new gadget	새로운 기기
02	random		random junk	무작위의 잡동사니
03	turn into		turn into a hobby	취미가 되다
04	pleasure		pleasure in creating things	물건들을 만드는 기쁨
05	satisfaction		the same kind of satisfaction	같은 종류의 만족감
06	rush		a similar rush	유사한 흥분
07	temporary		a temporary solution	임시 해결책
08	recommendation		the recommendation of a doctor	의사의 권고
09	craft		learn more about craft	공예기술에 대해 더 배우다
10	online		learn more online	온라인상으로 더 배우다
11	end up ~ing		end up spending money	결국 돈을 쓰다
12	stuff		a collection of stuff	수집 물건
13	decrease		decrease in value	가치가 떨어지다

⊕ **본문 문장 속에서 단어의 의미를 우리말로 해석해 보세요.**

Shopping for new gadgets, clothes, or just random junk / can turn into a hobby / in itself.

→ 새로운 ______, 옷, 혹은 단지 ______ 잡동사니들을 사는 것은 / ______ 수 있다 / 그 자체로.

2017 9월 학평 22번 문제

제한시간 70초
난이도 ★★★☆☆

STEP 2 • 수능 기출 제대로 풀기

G

다음 글의 주제로 가장 적절한 것은?

Shopping for new gadgets, clothes, or just random junk can turn into a hobby in itself. If you'd rather save your money, try finding pleasure in creating things rather than buying things. We get the same kind of satisfaction from making things that we do from buying things. If you draw something you're proud of or write something you enjoy, you've now got a new thing in your life that makes you happy. Buying a new gadget might give you a similar rush, but it's also probably more temporary. Of course, our recommendation can cost money, too. However, when you can't spend money, you can always learn more about your craft online or practice with what you already have. Even if you end up spending money making things yourself, you're at least building a skill rather than a collection of stuff that's quickly decreasing in value.

① misconceptions about gadget collecting as a hobby
② why creating things is better than shopping
③ negative effects of expensive hobbies
④ ways to purchase clothing wisely
⑤ shopping for clothes as a hobby

정답과 해설 p.4

STEP 3 • 수능 지문 제대로 복습하기

01 Shopping for new gadgets, clothes, or just random junk / can turn into a hobby / in itself.
주어(동명사) / 동사구

02 If you'd rather save your money, / try finding pleasure in creating things / rather than buying things.
try+-ing: ~해보다 / ~하기보다는

03 We get the same kind of satisfaction from making things / that we do from buying things. // If you draw something you're proud of / or write something you enjoy, / you've now got a new thing in your life / that makes you happy.
목적격 관계대명사 / 대동사 do(=get ~ satisfaction) / 목적격 관계대명사 생략 / 목적격 관계대명사 생략 / 주격 관계대명사절

04 Buying a new gadget / might give you a similar rush, / but it's also probably more temporary. // Of course, our recommendation can cost money, too.
주어(동명사) / give+간접목적어+직접목적어

05 However, / when you can't spend money, / you can always learn more about your craft online / or practice with what you already have.
관계대명사 what절(전치사의 목적어)

06 Even if you end up spending money / making things yourself, / you're at least building a skill / rather than a collection of stuff / that's quickly decreasing in value.
end up -ing: 결국 ~하게 되다 / 부사절 접속사(양보): ~에도 불구하고 / spend+돈+-ing: ~하는 데 돈을 쓰다 / 주격 관계대명사절

01 새로운 기기**gadget**, 옷, 혹은 단지 무작위**random** 잡동사니들을 사는 것은 / 취미가 될 수 있다**turn into a hobby** / 그 자체로.

02 여러분이 다소 돈을 절약하고 싶다면, / 무언가를 만드는 데서 즐거움**pleasure**을 찾아 보아라 / 물건을 사기보다는.

03 우리는 무언가를 만드는 것으로부터 똑같은 만족감**satisfaction**을 얻는다 / 우리가 물건을 사는 것으로부터 얻는 (것과 똑같은 만족감을). // 만약에 여러분이 자랑스러워하는 무언가를 그리거나 / 즐기는 무언가를 글로 쓴다면, / 이제 여러분은 새로운 것을 삶에서 얻은 것이다 / 여러분을 행복하게 만들어 주는.

04 새로운 기기를 사는 것이 / 여러분에게 비슷한 흥분감**a similar rush**을 줄 수 있지만 / 그것은 아마도 더 일시적일**temporary** 것이다. // 물론, 우리가 추천하는 것**recommendation**도 돈이 들 수 있다.

05 그러나 / 여러분이 돈을 쓸 수 없다면, / 여러분은 언제나 온라인에서**online** 공예기술**craft**에 관해서 더 배우거나 / 여러분이 이미 가지고 있는 것을 연습할 수 있다.

06 비록 여러분이 결국 돈을 쓰게**end up spending** 될지라도 / 직접 무언가를 만드는 데, / 여러분은 적어도 기술을 키워 나가고 있는 것이다 / 물건**stuff**을 수집하기보다는 / 가치가 급격히 떨어지게 될**decrease in value**.

구문 Check up

① If you'd rather save your money, try finding pleasure in creating things rather than buy / buying things.

rather than은 문법적으로 대등한 형태를 연결한다. 따라서 동명사 creating과 형태를 맞추어 buying을 써야 한다.

② Even if you end up to spend / spending money making things yourself, you're at least building a skill.

end up 동사구 다음에는 동명사가 와야 하므로 spending이 적절하다. 그리고 <spend+금액> 다음에도 동명사가 오는 것에 유의한다.

정답 ① buying ② spending

A STEP 1 • 수능에 진짜 나오는 단어

✔ 문제에 나오는 단어들을 확인하세요.

시간이 없다면 색으로 표시된 단어만이라도 꼭 외우고 넘어가세요!

01	intended	a. 의도된	the (✔ intended) path	의도된 길
02	reward	v. 보상하다 n. 보상	be well ()ed for your efforts	노력에 대해 잘 보상받다
03	slippery	a. 미끄러운	a () road	미끄러운 길
04	superhuman	a. 초인적인	a () effort	초인적인 노력
05	effectively	ad. 사실상, 효과적으로	He is, (), leading the team.	그가 사실상 팀을 이끌고 있다.
06	stuck	a. 갇힌, 막힌, 꼼짝 못하는	I feel like I'm ().	나는 갇힌 기분이다.
07	secure	a. 안정적인	a () income	안정적인 수입
08	well-paying	a. 보수가 좋은	a () job	보수가 좋은 직업

✛ 본문 문장 속에서 단어들을 확인해 보세요.

If you are good at something / and are well rewarded for doing it, / you may want to keep doing it / even if you stop enjoying it.

여러분이 어떤 일을 잘하고 / 그것을 하는 것에 대한 보상을 잘 받는다면, / 여러분은 계속 그것을 하고 싶을 수도 있다 / 여러분이 그것을 즐기지 않게 되더라도.

단어 다시보기 문제를 풀기 전에 단어들을 30초 동안 다시 확인하세요.

01	intended	의도된	the intended path	의도된 길
02	reward		be well rewarded for your efforts	노력에 대해 잘 보상받다
03	slippery		a slippery road	미끄러운 길
04	superhuman		a superhuman effort	초인적인 노력
05	effectively		He is, effectively, leading the team.	그가 사실상 팀을 이끌고 있다.
06	stuck		I feel like I'm stuck.	나는 갇힌 기분이다.
07	secure		a secure income	안정적인 수입
08	well-paying		a well-paying job	보수가 좋은 직업

⊕ 본문 문장 속에서 단어의 의미를 우리말로 해석해 보세요.

If you are good at something / and are well rewarded for doing it, / you may want to keep doing it / even if you stop enjoying it.

➜ 여러분이 어떤 일을 잘하고 / ______________________면, / 여러분은 계속 그것을 하고 싶을 수도 있다 / 여러분이 그것을 즐기지 않게 되더라도.

2023 3월 학평 24번 문제

제한시간 70초

난이도 ★★★☆☆

STEP 2 • 수능 기출 제대로 풀기

A

다음 글의 제목으로 가장 적절한 것은?

Success can lead you off your intended path and into a comfortable rut. If you are good at something and are well rewarded for doing it, you may want to keep doing it even if you stop enjoying it. The danger is that one day you look around and realize you're so deep in this comfortable rut that you can no longer see the sun or breathe fresh air; the sides of the rut have become so slippery that it would take a superhuman effort to climb out; and, effectively, you're stuck. And it's a situation that many working people worry they're in now. The poor employment market has left them feeling locked in what may be a secure, or even well-paying — but ultimately unsatisfying — job.

*rut: 틀에 박힌 생활

① Don't Compete with Yourself

② A Trap of a Successful Career

③ Create More Jobs for Young People

④ What Difficult Jobs Have in Common

⑤ A Road Map for an Influential Employer

정답과 해설 p.5

STEP 3 • 수능 지문 제대로 복습하기

01 Success can lead you off your intended path / and into a comfortable rut.

02 If you are good at something / and are well rewarded for doing it, / you may want to keep doing it / even if you stop enjoying it.

(If: 접속사(만약 ~한다면) / keep doing: keep+동명사(계속 ~하다) / even if: 접속사(~하더라도) / stop enjoying: stop+동명사(~하기를 멈추다))

03 The danger is / that one day you look around and realize / [you're so deep in this comfortable rut / that you can no longer see the sun or breathe fresh air]; / [the sides of the rut have become so slippery / that it would take a superhuman effort to climb out; / and, effectively, you're stuck].

(that: 접속사(is의 보어 연결) / [you're so deep ... fresh air]: realize의 목적절1 / so ~ that …: 너무 ~해서 …하다 / [the sides of ... stuck]: realize의 목적절2 / so ~ that …: 너무 ~해서 …하다 / it: 가주어 / to climb out: 진주어)

04 And it's a situation / that many working people worry / they're in now.

(a situation: 선행사 / that many working people worry: 목적격 관계대명사절 / 접속사 that 생략 / 목적어 생략)

05 The poor employment market / has left them feeling locked in / what may be a secure, or even well-paying — but ultimately unsatisfying — job.

(has left them feeling locked in: leave+목적어+현재분사: ~이 …하게 두다 / what may be ... job: 명사절(in의 목적어))

01 성공은 여러분이 의도된**intended** 길에서 벗어나게 이끌 수 있다 / 그리고 틀에 박힌 편안한 생활로 (들어가게).

02 여러분이 어떤 일을 잘하고 / 그것을 하는 것에 대한 보상을 잘 받는다**be well rewarded**면, / 여러분은 계속 그것을 하고 싶을 수도 있다 / 여러분이 그것을 즐기지 않게 되더라도.

03 위험한 점은 ~이다 / 어느 날 여러분이 주위를 둘러보며 알게 된다는 것 / 여러분이 이 틀에 박힌 편안한 생활에 너무나 깊이 빠져서 / 여러분이 더 이상은 태양을 보거나 신선한 공기를 마시지 못한다는 것을 / 그 틀에 박힌 생활의 양쪽 면이 너무나 미끄러워져서**slippery** / 기어올라 나오려면 초인적인**superhuman** 노력이 필요할 것이고 / 사실상**effectively** 여러분이 꼼짝할 수 없다**stuck**는 것을.

04 그리고 그것은 상황이다 / 많은 근로자가 걱정하는 / 현재 자신이 처해 있다고.

05 열악한 고용 시장이 / 그들을 갇혀 있다고 느끼게 하였다 / 안정적**secure**이거나 심지어 보수가 좋을**well-paying** 수도 있지만, 궁극적으로는 만족스럽지 못한 일에.

구문 Check up

① If you are good at something and are well rewarded for doing it, you may want to keep doing it even if you stop to enjoy / enjoying it.

문맥상 즐기는 것을 '관두더라도' 일을 계속하게 된다는 의미이다. 따라서 「stop+동명사(~하는 것을 멈추다)」의 enjoying을 쓴다.

② The sides of the rut have become so slippery that / which it would take a superhuman effort to climb out.

「so ~ that …(너무 ~해서 …하다)」 구문이므로 접속사 that이 적합하다.

정답 ① enjoying ② that

DAY 02

B

제목 추론

STEP 1 • 수능에 진짜 나오는 단어

✔ 문제에 나오는 단어들을 확인하세요.

시간이 없다면 색으로 표시된 단어만이라도 꼭 외우고 넘어가세요!

01	accurately	ad. 정확하게	speak (✔ accurately)	정확히 말하다
02	recognize	v. 인식하다, 알아보다	( ) one's old friend	옛 벗을 알아보다
03	label	v. ~에 라벨(이름 등)을 붙이다	( ) each item	각 품목에 라벨을 붙이다
04	emotion	n. 감정	recognize and label ( )s	감정을 인식하고 그것에 이름을 붙이다
05	refer to A as B	A를 B라 부르다	be ( )red ( ) ( ) the "snowball effect"	'스노우볼 효과'라고 불리다
06	psychologist	n. 심리학자	in the words of a ( )	한 심리학자의 말에 의하면
07	vocabulary	n. 어휘	have a rich ( )	풍부한 어휘를 갖다
08	absolutely	ad. 절대적으로	( ) impossible	절대적으로 불가능한
09	transformative	a. (사람을) 변화시키는	It is ( ).	그것은 (사람을) 변화시킬 수 있는 힘이 있다.
10	distinguish	v. 구별하다	( ) between good and evil	선악을 구별하다
11	a range of	광범위한, 다양한	( ) ( ) ( ) emotions	광범위한 감정들
12	ordinary	a. 평범한	( ) existence	평범한 존재
13	regulation	n. 조절	great emotion ( )	탁월한 감정 조절

⊕ 본문 문장 속에서 단어들을 확인해 보세요.

Our ability to accurately recognize and label emotions / is often referred to as *emotional granularity*.

감정을 정확하게 인식하고 그것에 이름을 붙일 수 있는 우리의 능력은 / 흔히 '감정 입자도'라고 불린다.

단어 다시보기 문제를 풀기 전에 단어들을 30초 동안 다시 확인하세요.

01	accurately	정확하게	speak accurately	정확히 말하다
02	recognize		recognize one's old friend	옛 벗을 알아보다
03	label		label each item	각 품목에 라벨을 붙이다
04	emotion		recognize and label emotions	감정을 인식하고 그것에 이름을 붙이다
05	refer to A as B		be referred to as the "snowball effect"	'스노우볼 효과'라고 불리다
06	psychologist		in the words of a psychologist	한 심리학자의 말에 의하면
07	vocabulary		have a rich vocabulary	풍부한 어휘를 갖다
08	absolutely		absolutely impossible	절대적으로 불가능한
09	transformative		It is transformative.	그것은 (사람을) 변화시킬 수 있는 힘이 있다.
10	distinguish		distinguish between good and evil	선악을 구별하다
11	a range of		a range of emotions	광범위한 감정들
12	ordinary		ordinary existence	평범한 존재
13	regulation		great emotion regulation	탁월한 감정 조절

⊕ 본문 문장 속에서 단어의 의미를 우리말로 해석해 보세요.

Our ability to accurately recognize and label emotions / is often referred to as *emotional granularity*.

→ ____________ 수 있는 우리의 능력은 / 흔히 '감정 입자도' ____________.

2022 3월 학평 24번 문제

제한시간 70초

난이도 ★★★☆☆

STEP 2 • 수능 기출 제대로 풀기

B

다음 글의 제목으로 가장 적절한 것은?

Our ability to accurately recognize and label emotions is often referred to as *emotional granularity*. In the words of Harvard psychologist Susan David, "Learning to label emotions with a more nuanced vocabulary can be absolutely transformative." David explains that if we don't have a rich emotional vocabulary, it is difficult to communicate our needs and to get the support that we need from others. But those who are able to distinguish between a range of various emotions "do much, much better at managing the ups and downs of ordinary existence than those who see everything in black and white." In fact, research shows that the process of labeling emotional experience is related to greater emotion regulation and psychosocial well-being.

*nuanced: 미묘한 차이가 있는

① True Friendship Endures Emotional Arguments

② Detailed Labeling of Emotions Is Beneficial

③ Labeling Emotions: Easier Said Than Done

④ Categorize and Label Tasks for Efficiency

⑤ Be Brave and Communicate Your Needs

정답과 해설 p.5

STEP 3 ● 수능 지문 제대로 복습하기

01 Our ability to accurately recognize and label emotions / is often referred to as *emotional granularity.*

to부정사의 형용사적 용법

02 In the words of Harvard psychologist Susan David, / "Learning to label emotions with a more nuanced vocabulary / can be absolutely transformative."

주어(동명사)

03 David explains / that if we don't have a rich emotional vocabulary, / it is difficult / [to communicate our needs] / and [to get the support that we need from others].

명사절 접속사(explains의 목적어) / 가주어 / 진주어(병렬 구조) / 목적격 관계대명사절

04 But / those who are able to distinguish between a range of various emotions / "do much, much better / at managing the ups and downs of ordinary existence / than those who see everything in black and white."

주격 관계대명사절 / 주격 관계대명사절

05 In fact, / research shows / that the process of labeling emotional experience / is related to greater emotion regulation and psychosocial well-being.

명사절 접속사(shows의 목적절 연결)

01 감정**emotion**을 정확하게**accurately** 인식하고**recognize** 그것에 이름을 붙일**label** 수 있는 우리의 능력은 / 흔히 '감정 입자도'라고 불린다**be referred to as**.

02 Harvard 대학의 심리학자**psychologist**인 Susan David의 말에 의하면, / "더 미묘한 차이가 있는 어휘**vocabulary**로 감정에 이름을 붙이는 법을 배우는 것은 / 절대적으로**absolutely** (사람을) 변화시킬 수 있다**transformative**."

03 David는 설명한다 / 우리가 풍부한 감정 어휘를 갖고 있지 않으면, / 어렵다고 / 우리의 욕구를 전달하는 것이 / 그리고 우리가 필요로 하는 지지를 다른 사람들로부터 얻는 것이.

04 그러나 / 광범위한**a range of** 다양한 감정을 구별할**distinguish** 수 있는 사람들은 / "훨씬 훨씬 더 잘한다 / 평범한**ordinary** 존재로 사는 중에 겪는 좋은 일들과 궂은 일들을 관리하는 것을 / 모든 것을 흑백 논리로 보는 사람들보다."

05 사실, / 연구 결과가 보여 준다 / 감정 경험에 이름을 붙이는 과정은 / 더 탁월한 감정 조절**regulation** 및 심리 사회적 행복과 관련되어 있다는 것을.

구문 Check up

① Learn / Learning to label emotions with a more nuanced vocabulary can be absolutely transformative.

이 문장의 동사는 can be로, 주어가 필요하기 때문에 동명사 형태인 Learning으로 써야 한다.

② If we don't have a rich emotional vocabulary, it is difficult to communicate our needs and to get the support that / what we need from others.

앞에 선행사(the support)가 존재하고 뒤에 불완전한 절(we need)이 이어지므로 목적격 관계대명사 that이 적절하다.

정답 ① Learning ② that

C

제목 추론

STEP 1 • 수능에 진짜 나오는 단어

✔ 문제에 나오는 단어들을 확인하세요.

시간이 없다면 색으로 표시된 단어만이라도 꼭 외우고 넘어가세요!

01	rarely	ad. 거의 ~않는	(✔ rarely) consider it	그것을 거의 고려하지 않는다
02	critical	a. 중요한	a ( ) role	중요한 역할
03	vertical	a. 수직의	( ) transportation	수직 운송 수단
04	billion	n. 10억	more than 7 ( ) journeys	70억회 이상의 이동
05	efficient	a. 효율적인	( ) vertical transportation	효율적인 수직 운송 수단
06	expand	v. 확장시키다	( ) our ability	우리의 능력을 확장하다
07	skyscraper	n. 마천루, 고층 건물	taller ( )s	더 높은 고층 건물들
08	institute	n. (교육) 기관, 협회	( ) of Technology	공과대학
09	advance	n. 발전 v. 나아가다	( )s in elevators	엘리베이터의 발전
10	construction	n. 건설, 건축	under ( )	건설 중인

⊕ 본문 문장 속에서 단어들을 확인해 보세요.

When people think about the development of cities, / rarely do they consider / the critical role of vertical transportation.

사람들은 도시 발전에 대해 생각할 때, / 거의 고려하지 않는다 / 수직 운송 수단의 중요한 역할을.

단어 다시보기 문제를 풀기 전에 단어들을 30초 동안 다시 확인하세요.

01	rarely	거의 ~않는	rarely consider it	그것을 거의 고려하지 않는다
02	critical		a critical role	중요한 역할
03	vertical		vertical transportation	수직 운송 수단
04	billion		more than 7 billion journeys	70억회 이상의 이동
05	efficient		efficient vertical transportation	효율적인 수직 운송 수단
06	expand		expand our ability	우리의 능력을 확장하다
07	skyscraper		taller skyscrapers	더 높은 고층 건물들
08	institute		Institute of Technology	공과대학
09	advance		advances in elevators	엘리베이터의 발전
10	construction		under construction	건설 중인

⊕ 본문 문장 속에서 단어의 의미를 우리말로 해석해 보세요.

When people think about the development of cities, / rarely do they consider / the critical role of vertical transportation.

→ 사람들은 도시 발전에 대해 생각할 때, / ________ 고려하지 ________ / ________ 운송 수단의 ________ 역할을.

2021 6월 학평 24번 문제

제한시간 70초

난이도 ★★★☆☆

STEP 2 • 수능 기출 제대로 풀기

C

다음 글의 제목으로 가장 적절한 것은?

When people think about the development of cities, rarely do they consider the critical role of vertical transportation. In fact, each day, more than 7 billion elevator journeys are taken in tall buildings all over the world. Efficient vertical transportation can expand our ability to build taller and taller skyscrapers. Antony Wood, a Professor of Architecture at the Illinois Institute of Technology, explains that advances in elevators over the past 20 years are probably the greatest advances we have seen in tall buildings. For example, elevators in the Jeddah Tower in Jeddah, Saudi Arabia, under construction, will reach a height record of 660m.

① Elevators Bring Buildings Closer to the Sky

② The Higher You Climb, the Better the View

③ How to Construct an Elevator Cheap and Fast

④ The Function of the Ancient and the Modern City

⑤ The Evolution of Architecture: Solutions for Overpopulation

정답과 해설 p.5

STEP 3 • 수능 지문 제대로 복습하기

01 When people think about the development of cities, / rarely do they consider / the critical role of vertical transportation.
부정어구 도치(rarely+조동사+주어+동사원형)

02 In fact, / each day, / more than 7 billion elevator journeys are taken / in tall buildings all over the world.
수동태

03 Efficient vertical transportation can expand our ability / to build taller and taller skyscrapers.
to부정사의 형용사적 용법

04 Antony Wood, a Professor of Architecture at the Illinois Institute of Technology, explains / that advances in elevators over the past 20 years / are probably the greatest advances / we have seen in tall buildings.
명사절 접속사(explains의 목적어)
목적격 관계대명사 생략

05 For example, / elevators in the Jeddah Tower in Jeddah, Saudi Arabia, under construction, / will reach a height record of 660m.
주격 관계대명사+be동사(which are) 생략

01 사람들은 도시 발전에 대해 생각할 때, / 거의 고려하지 않는다**rarely do they consider** / 수직 운송 수단**vertical transportation**의 중요한**critical** 역할을.

02 실제로 / 매일 / 70억**7 billion** 회 이상의 엘리베이터 이동이 이루어진다 / 전 세계 높은 빌딩에서.

03 효율적인**efficient** 수직 운송 수단은 우리의 능력을 확장시킬**expand** 수 있다 / 점점 더 높은 고층 건물**skyscraper**을 만들 수 있는.

04 일리노이 공과대학**Institute of Technology**의 건축학과 교수인 Antony Wood는 설명한다 / 지난 20년 간의 엘리베이터의 발전**advance**은 / 아마도 가장 큰 발전이라고 / 우리가 높은 건물에서 봐 왔던.

05 예를 들어, / 사우디 아라비아 Jeddah의 Jeddah Tower에 있는 엘리베이터는 / 건설 중인**under construction** / 660미터라는 기록적인 높이에 이를 것이다.

구문 Check up

① When people think about the development of cities, rarely [they consider / do they consider] the critical role of vertical transportation.

부정어구 rarely가 문장 앞에 나오므로 주어, 동사가 도치된 구문으로 써야 한다. 따라서 do they consider가 적절하다.

② Antony Wood explains [that / which] advances in elevators over the past 20 years are probably the greatest advances we have seen in tall buildings.

동사 explain의 목적어 자리이다. 뒤에 완전한 절이 나오고 있으므로 목적어 역할의 명사절을 이끄는 접속사 that을 쓴다.

정답 ① do they consider ② that

D

제목 추론 ⊕

STEP 1 • 수능에 진짜 나오는 단어

✔ 문제에 나오는 단어들을 확인하세요.

시간이 없다면 색으로 표시된 단어만이라도 꼭 외우고 넘어가세요!

01	cause	v. ~하게 만들다, 원인이 되다	(✔ cause) you to smile	여러분을 미소 짓게 만들다
02	chemical	n. 화학물질	feel-good ( )s	기분 좋아지는 화학물질
03	force	v. 억지로 ~하게 하다	( ) your face to smile	억지로 얼굴이 미소 짓게 하다
04	muscular	a. 근육의	facial ( ) pattern	안면 근육의 형태
05	link	v. 연결하다	be ( )ed to all the happy networks	모든 행복 연결망과 연결되다
06	calm	v. 안정시키다	( ) you down	여러분을 안정시키다
07	chemistry	n. 화학작용	change your brain ( )	뇌의 화학작용을 바꾸다
08	release	v. 배출시키다	( ) the feel-good chemicals	기분 좋은 화학 물질을 배출시키다
09	genuine	a. 진정한	a ( ) and forced smile	진정한 미소와 억지 미소
10	perform	v. 수행하다	( ) stressful tasks	스트레스가 상당한 과업을 수행하다
11	intensity	n. 강도	the ( ) of the stress	스트레스의 강도
12	lower	v. 낮추다	( ) heart rate levels	심장 박동 수치를 낮추다
13	recover	v. 회복하다	( ) from the stress	스트레스에서 회복하다

⊕ 본문 문장 속에서 단어들을 확인해 보세요.

Every event that causes you to smile / makes you feel happy / and produces feel-good chemicals / in your brain.

여러분을 미소 짓게 만드는 온갖 사건들은 / 여러분이 행복감을 느끼게 하고, / 기분 좋아지는 화학물질을 생산한다 / 여러분의 뇌에서.

단어 다시보기 문제를 풀기 전에 단어들을 30초 동안 다시 확인하세요.

01	cause	~하게 만들다, 원인이 되다	cause you to smile	여러분을 미소 짓게 만들다
02	chemical		feel-good chemicals	기분 좋아지는 화학물질
03	force		force your face to smile	억지로 얼굴이 미소 짓게 하다
04	muscular		facial muscular pattern	안면 근육의 형태
05	link		be linked to all the happy networks	모든 행복 연결망과 연결되다
06	calm		calm you down	여러분을 안정시키다
07	chemistry		change your brain chemistry	뇌의 화학작용을 바꾸다
08	release		release the feel-good chemicals	기분 좋은 화학물질을 배출시키다
09	genuine		a genuine and forced smile	진정한 미소와 억지 미소
10	perform		perform stressful tasks	스트레스가 상당한 과업을 수행하다
11	intensity		the intensity of the stress	스트레스의 강도
12	lower		lower heart rate levels	심장 박동 수치를 낮추다
13	recover		recover from the stress	스트레스에서 회복하다

⊕ 본문 문장 속에서 단어의 의미를 우리말로 해석해 보세요.

Every event that causes you to smile / makes you feel happy / and produces feel-good chemicals / in your brain.

→ ______ 온갖 사건들은 / 여러분이 행복감을 느끼게 하고, / ______을 생산한다 / 여러분의 뇌에서.

2020 6월 학평 24번 문제

제한시간 70초

난이도 ★★★☆☆

STEP 2 • 수능 기출 제대로 풀기

D

다음 글의 제목으로 가장 적절한 것은?

Every event that causes you to smile makes you feel happy and produces feel-good chemicals in your brain. Force your face to smile even when you are stressed or feel unhappy. The facial muscular pattern produced by the smile is linked to all the "happy networks" in your brain and will in turn naturally calm you down and change your brain chemistry by releasing the same feel-good chemicals. Researchers studied the effects of a genuine and forced smile on individuals during a stressful event. The researchers had participants perform stressful tasks while not smiling, smiling, or holding chopsticks crossways in their mouths (to force the face to form a smile). The results of the study showed that smiling, forced or genuine, during stressful events reduced the intensity of the stress response in the body and lowered heart rate levels after recovering from the stress.

① Causes and Effects of Stressful Events

② Personal Signs and Patterns of Stress

③ How Body and Brain React to Stress

④ Stress: Necessary Evil for Happiness

⑤ Do Faked Smiles Also Help Reduce Stress?

정답과 해설 p.6

STEP 3 ● 수능 지문 제대로 복습하기

01 Every event that causes you to smile / makes you feel happy / and produces feel-good chemicals / in your brain.

주어(every+명사) / 주격 관계대명사절 / 단수동사(병렬구조)

02 Force your face to smile / even when you are stressed or feel unhappy.

~할 때조차(양보)

03 The facial muscular pattern produced by the smile / is linked to all the "happy networks" in your brain / and will in turn naturally calm you down / and change your brain chemistry / by releasing the same feel-good chemicals.

주어 / 과거분사 / 그 결과

04 Researchers studied / the effects of a genuine and forced smile on individuals / during a stressful event.

05 The researchers had participants perform stressful tasks / while not smiling, smiling, / or holding chopsticks crossways in their mouths (to force the face to form a smile).

사역동사+목적어+목적격 보어(원형부정사) / 병렬구조 (접속사가 남아있는 분사구문)

06 The results of the study showed / [that smiling, (forced or genuine), / during stressful events / reduced the intensity of the stress response in the body / and lowered heart rate levels / after recovering from the stress].

명사절 접속사 / 삽입구 / 주어(동명사) / 동사

01 여러분을 미소 짓게 만드는cause 온갖 사건들은 / 여러분이 행복감을 느끼게 하고, / 기분을 좋게 만들어주는 화학물질chemical을 생산한다 / 여러분의 뇌에서.

02 얼굴에 미소를 지어보자force / 심지어 스트레스를 받거나 불행하다고 느낄 때조차.

03 미소에 의해 만들어지는 안면 근육의 형태the facial muscular pattern는 / 뇌의 모든 "행복 연결망"과 연결되어 있고be linked to / 따라서 자연스럽게 여러분을 안정시키고calm down / 뇌의 화학작용chemistry을 변화시킬 것이다 / 기분을 좋게 만들어주는 동일한 화학물질들을 배출함release으로써.

04 연구자들은 연구하였다 / 진정한 미소와 억지 미소a genuine and forced smile가 개개인들에게 미치는 영향을 / 스트레스가 상당한 상황에서.

05 연구자들은 참가자들이 스트레스를 수반한 과업을 수행하도록perform stressful tasks 했다 / 미소 짓지 않거나, 미소 짓거나, / 또는 (억지 미소를 짓게 하기 위해) 입에 젓가락을 옆으로 물고서.

06 연구의 결과는 보여주었다 / 미소가 억지이든 진정한 것이든, / 스트레스가 상당한 상황에서 / 인체의 스트레스 반응의 강도intensity를 줄였고, / 심장 박동 수치도 낮추었다lower heart rate levels는 것을 / 스트레스로부터 회복한recover 후에.

구문 Check up

① Every event that causes you to smile **make / makes** you feel happy and produces feel-good chemicals in your brain.

동사 make의 주어는 Every event로, 단수이기 때문에 makes로 쓴다.

② The facial muscular pattern **producing / produced** by the smile is linked to all the "happy networks" in your brain.

주어(The facial ~ pattern)는 '미소에 의해 만들어지는' 것이므로, 수동의 의미를 표현하는 과거분사로 수식한다. 따라서 produced가 정답이다.

정답 ① makes ② produced

DAY 02

E

제목 추론 ⊕

STEP 1 • 수능에 진짜 나오는 단어

✔ 문제에 나오는 단어들을 확인하세요.

시간이 없다면 색으로 표시된 단어만이라도 꼭 외우고 넘어가세요!

01	neighborhood	*n.* 동네	a newcomer to a (✔ neighborhood)	동네에 새로 온 사람
02	neighbor	*n.* 이웃, 주변 사람	a new ( )	새 이웃
03	favor	*n.* 호의, 친절	ask for a ( )	도움을 요청하다
04	cite	*v.* 인용하다	( ) a law	법률을 인용하다
05	maxim	*n.* 격언, 금언	cite an old ( )	옛 격언을 인용하다
06	immediate	*a.* 즉각적인	the ( ) invitation	즉각적인 초대
07	interaction	*n.* 상호작용	social ( )	사회적인 상호작용
08	encounter	*n.* 만남 *v.* 마주치다	at first ( )	첫 만남에
09	latter	*n.* 후자	the ( ) ↔ the former	후자 ↔ 전자
10	familiarity	*n.* 친밀감	increase the ( )	친밀감을 증진시키다
11	overcome	*v.* 극복하다	( ) fear	두려움을 극복하다
12	hesitancy	*n.* 머뭇거림, 망설임	overcome natural ( )	당연한 머뭇거림을 극복하다
13	mutual	*a.* 상호간의	overcome ( ) fear	상호간의 두려움을 극복하다

⊕ 본문 문장 속에서 단어들을 확인해 보세요.

In that manner, / both parties could overcome / their natural hesitancy and mutual fear of the stranger.

그러한 방식으로, / 양쪽은 극복할 수 있을 것이다 / 낯선 사람에 대한 당연한 머뭇거림과 상호간의 두려움을.

단어 다시보기 문제를 풀기 전에 단어들을 30초 동안 다시 확인하세요.

01	neighborhood	동네	a newcomer to a neighborhood	동네에 새로 온 사람
02	neighbor		a new neighbor	새 이웃
03	favor		ask for a favor	도움을 요청하다
04	cite		cite a law	법률을 인용하다
05	maxim		cite an old maxim	옛 격언을 인용하다
06	immediate		the immediate invitation	즉각적인 초대
07	interaction		social interaction	사회적인 상호작용
08	encounter		at first encounter	첫 만남에
09	latter		the latter ↔ the former	후자 ↔ 전자
10	familiarity		increase the familiarity	친밀감을 증진시키다
11	overcome		overcome fear	두려움을 극복하다
12	hesitancy		overcome natural hesitancy	당연한 머뭇거림을 극복하다
13	mutual		overcome mutual fear	상호간의 두려움을 극복하다

⊕ 본문 문장 속에서 단어의 의미를 우리말로 해석해 보세요.

In that manner, / both parties could overcome / their natural hesitancy and mutual fear of the stranger.

→ 그러한 방식으로, / 양쪽은 ________ 수 있을 것이다 / 낯선 사람에 대한 당연한 ______과 ______ 두려움을.

2019 9월 학평 24번 문제

제한시간 70초

난이도 ★★★☆☆

STEP 2 • 수능 기출 제대로 풀기

E

다음 글의 제목으로 가장 적절한 것은?

Benjamin Franklin once suggested that a newcomer to a neighborhood ask a new neighbor to do him or her a favor, citing an old maxim: He that has once done you a kindness will be more ready to do you another than he whom you yourself have obliged. In Franklin's opinion, asking someone for something was the most useful and immediate invitation to social interaction. Such asking on the part of the newcomer provided the neighbor with an opportunity to show himself or herself as a good person, at first encounter. It also meant that the latter could now ask the former for a favor, in return, increasing the familiarity and trust. In that manner, both parties could overcome their natural hesitancy and mutual fear of the stranger.

*oblige: ~에게 친절을 베풀다

① How to Present Your Strengths to Others
② A Relationship Opener: Asking for a Favor
③ Why Do We Hesitate to Help Strangers?
④ What You Ask for Shows Who You Are
⑤ Polite Ways of Inviting Our Neighbors

정답과 해설 p.6

STEP 3 • 수능 지문 제대로 복습하기

01 Benjamin Franklin once suggested / that a newcomer to a neighborhood / ask a new neighbor to do him or her a favor, / citing an old maxim: / He that has once done you a kindness / will be more ready to do you another / than he whom you yourself have obliged.

(should 생략 / 명사절 접속사 / 5형식 동사 / 목적어 / 목적격 보어 / 분사구문(부대상황: ~하면서) / 주격 관계대명사절 / kindness / 목적격 관계대명사절)

02 In Franklin's opinion, / asking someone for something / was the most useful and immediate invitation / to social interaction.

(주어(동명사) / 동사(단수))

03 Such asking on the part of the newcomer / provided the neighbor / with an opportunity to show himself or herself as a good person, / at first encounter.

(provide A with B: A에게 B를 제공하다 / to부정사의 형용사적 용법)

04 It also meant / that the latter could now ask the former for a favor, / in return, / increasing the familiarity and trust.

(분사구문)

05 In that manner, / both parties could overcome / their natural hesitancy and mutual fear of the stranger.

01 Benjamin Franklin은 예전에 제안했다 / 동네에 새로 온 사람**a newcomer to a neighborhood**은 / 새 이웃**a new neighbor**에게 도움**favor**을 요청해야 한다고 / 옛 격언을 인용하며**cite an old maxim** / '너에게 친절을 행한 적이 있는 사람은 / 너에게 또 다른 친절을 행할 준비가 더 되어 있을 것이다 / 네가 친절을 베풀었던 사람보다도'라는 (격언을).

02 Franklin의 의견으로는, / 누군가에게 무언가를 요구하는 것은 / 가장 유용하고 즉각적인 초대**immediate invitation**이다 / 사회적 상호작용**social interaction**으로의.

03 새로 온 사람 쪽에서의 그러한 요청은 / 이웃에게 제공했던 것이다 / 자신을 좋은 사람으로 보여줄 수 있는 기회를 / 첫 만남에**at first encounter**.

04 또한 그것은 의미했다 / 이제 후자(이웃)**the latter**가 전자(새로 온 사람)에게 부탁할 수 있으며, / 그 보답으로, / 그러면서 친밀함과 신뢰를 증진시킨다**increase the familiarity**는 것을.

05 그러한 방식으로, / 양쪽은 극복할**overcome** 수 있을 것이다 / 낯선 사람에 대한 당연한 머뭇거림과 상호 두려움**natural hesitancy and mutual fear**을.

구문 Check up

① Benjamin Franklin once suggested that a newcomer to a neighborhood asked / ask a new neighbor to do him or her a favor.

제안의 동사 suggested 뒤로 연결되는 목적절(that ~)이 당위(~해야 한다)의 의미로 해석되면 목적절의 동사는 <(should)+동사원형>으로 써야 한다. 따라서 ask가 정답이다.

② It also meant that the latter could now ask the former for a favor, in return, increase / increasing the familiarity and trust.

that절의 동사는 could ask로, 만약 increase를 이와 병렬연결되는 동사로 쓰고 싶다면 접속사가 있어야 하지만 접속사가 없기 때문에 분사구문으로 쓴다. 따라서 increasing이 정답이다.

정답 ① ask ② increasing

DAY 02

F

제목 추론

STEP 1 • 수능에 진짜 나오는 단어

✔ 문제에 나오는 단어들을 확인하세요.

시간이 없다면 색으로 표시된 단어만이라도 꼭 외우고 넘어가세요!

01	mammal	n. 포유류	(✔ Mammal)s tend to be less colorful.	포유류는 색이 덜 화려한 경향이 있다.
02	purpose	n. 목적	serve a ( )	목적을 수행하다
03	role	n. 역할	the colors' ( )	색의 역할
04	obvious	a. 명확한	always ( )	항상 명확한
05	gain	v. 얻다	( ) benefits from having stripes	줄무늬를 지님으로써 이득을 얻다
06	puzzle	v. 곤혹스럽게 하다	( ) scientists	과학자들을 곤혹스럽게 하다
07	solve	v. 풀다, 해결하다	( ) this mystery	이 수수께끼를 풀다
08	biologist	n. 생물학자	wildlife ( )	야생 생물학자
09	decade	n. 10년	more than a ( )	10년 이상
10	rule out	배제하다	( ) ( ) the theory	이론을 배제하다
11	confuse	v. 혼란스럽게 하다	( ) predators	포식자들을 혼란스럽게 하다
12	comparison	n. 비교, 대비	for ( )	(~와) 대비하여
13	avoid	v. 피하다	( ) landing	앉는 것을 피하다

⊕ 본문 문장 속에서 단어들을 확인해 보세요.

The question / of what zebras can gain from having stripes / has puzzled scientists / for more than a century.

이 질문은 / 얼룩말이 줄무늬를 지님으로써 얻을 수 있는 것이 무엇인지에 대한 / 과학자들을 곤혹스럽게 했다 / 1세기가 넘도록.

단어 다시보기 문제를 풀기 전에 단어들을 30초 동안 다시 확인하세요.

01	mammal	포유류	Mammals tend to be less colorful.	포유류는 색이 덜 화려한 경향이 있다.
02	purpose		serve a purpose	목적을 수행하다
03	role		the colors' role	색의 역할
04	obvious		always obvious	항상 명확한
05	gain		gain benefits from having stripes	줄무늬를 지님으로써 이득을 얻다
06	puzzle		puzzle scientists	과학자들을 곤혹스럽게 하다
07	solve		solve this mystery	이 수수께끼를 풀다
08	biologist		wildlife biologist	야생 생물학자
09	decade		more than a decade	10년 이상
10	rule out		rule out the theory	이론을 배제하다
11	confuse		confuse predators	포식자들을 혼란스럽게 하다
12	comparison		for comparison	(~와) 대비하여
13	avoid		avoid landing	앉는 것을 피하다

⊕ 본문 문장 속에서 단어의 의미를 우리말로 해석해 보세요.

The question / of what zebras can gain from having stripes / has puzzled scientists / for more than a century.

➔ 이 질문은 / 얼룩말이 ______ 수 있는 것이 무엇인지에 대한 / ______ / 1세기가 넘도록.

2018 6월 학평 23번 문제

제한시간 70초

난이도 ★★★☆☆

STEP 2 • 수능 기출 제대로 풀기

F

다음 글의 제목으로 가장 적절한 것은?

Mammals tend to be less colorful than other animal groups, but zebras are strikingly dressed in black-and-white. What purpose do such high contrast patterns serve? The colors' roles aren't always obvious. The question of what zebras can gain from having stripes has puzzled scientists for more than a century. To try to solve this mystery, wildlife biologist Tim Caro spent more than a decade studying zebras in Tanzania. He ruled out theory after theory — stripes don't keep them cool, stripes don't confuse predators — before finding an answer. In 2013, he set up fly traps covered in zebra skin and, for comparison, others covered in antelope skin. He saw that flies seemed to avoid landing on the stripes. After more research, he concluded that stripes can literally save zebras from disease-carrying insects.

*antelope: 영양(羚羊)

① Zebras' Stripes: Nature's Defense Against Flies

② Which Mammal Has the Most Colorful Skin?

③ What Animals Are Predators of Zebras?

④ Patterns: Not for Hiding, But for Showing Off

⑤ Each Zebra Is Born with Its Own Unique Stripes

정답과 해설 p.7

STEP 3 ● 수능 지문 제대로 복습하기

01 Mammals tend to be less colorful / than other animal groups, / but zebras are strikingly dressed in black-and-white.
(tend to: ~하는 경향이 있다)

02 What purpose do such high contrast patterns serve? // The colors' roles aren't always obvious. // The question / of what zebras can gain from having stripes / has puzzled scientists / for more than a century.
(목적어 생략 / what(의문사+불완전한 문장) / has puzzled: 현재완료(계속))

03 To try to solve this mystery, / wildlife biologist Tim Caro spent more than a decade / studying zebras in Tanzania.
(To try to solve this mystery: 부사적 용법(목적) / spend+시간/돈+-ing)

04 He ruled out theory after theory / — stripes don't keep them cool, / stripes don't confuse predators — / before finding an answer.
(접속사가 남아있는 분사구문(=before he found an answer))

05 In 2013, / he set up fly traps / covered in zebra skin / and, for comparison, / others covered in antelope skin.
(covered: 과거분사 / others: (=other traps) / covered: 과거분사)

06 He saw / that flies seemed to avoid landing on the stripes. // After more research, / he concluded / that stripes can literally save zebras / from disease-carrying insects.
(that: 명사절 접속사 / landing: 동명사(avoid의 목적어) / that: 명사절 접속사 / disease-carrying: 복합형용사(명사+분사))

01 포유류mammal는 색이 덜 화려한 경향이 있지만 / 다른 동물군에 비해 / 얼룩말은 두드러지게 흑백의 모습을 하고 있다.

02 이런 높은 대비의 무늬가 무슨 목적purpose을 수행할까? // 색의 역할role이 항상 명확한obvious 것은 아니다. // 이 질문은 / 줄무늬를 지님으로써 얼룩말이 얻을gain 수 있는 것이 무엇인지에 대한 / 과학자들을 곤혹스럽게 했다puzzle / 1세기가 넘도록.

03 이 신비를 풀기solve 위해, / 야생 생물학자biologist Tim Caro는 10년decade 이상을 보냈다 / 탄자니아에서 얼룩말을 연구하면서.

04 그는 이론을 하나씩 하나씩 배제해rule out 나갔다 / — 줄무늬는 얼룩말들을 시원하게 유지시켜 주지도 않았고, / 줄무늬는 포식자들을 혼란스럽게 하지confuse도 않았다 — / 답을 찾기 전에.

05 2013년에 / 그는 파리 덫을 설치했다 / 얼룩말의 가죽으로 덮인 / 그리고 이와 대비comparison하여 / 영양의 가죽으로 덮인 다른 덫들도 (준비했다).

06 그는 알게 되었다 / 파리가 줄무늬 위에 앉는 것을 피하는avoid 것처럼 보인다는 것을. // 더 많은 연구 후에, / 그는 결론을 내렸다 / 줄무늬가 얼룩말을 말 그대로 구할 수 있다고 / 질병을 옮기는 곤충으로부터.

구문 Check up

① The question of how / what zebras can gain from having stripes has puzzled scientists for more than a century.

전치사 of의 목적어 자리에 명사가 와야 하고, 뒤에 불완전한 문장이 오므로 명사절을 이끌 수 있는 의문사 what을 쓴다.

② He saw that flies seemed to avoid landing / to land on the stripes.

avoid는 동명사만 목적어로 취하는 동사이므로 landing이 적절하다.

정답 ① what ② landing

DAY 02

G

제목 추론

STEP 1 • 수능에 진짜 나오는 단어

✔ 문제에 나오는 단어들을 확인하세요.

시간이 없다면 색으로 표시된 단어만이라도 꼭 외우고 넘어가세요!

01	overprotective	a. 과잉보호하는	(✔ overprotective) parents	과잉보호하는 부모
02	spare	v. (불쾌한 경험을) 경험하지 않게 하다, 아끼다	( ) kids from bullying	아이들이 괴롭힘을 경험하지 않게 하다
03	consequence	n. 결과	all natural ( )s	모든 자연스런 결과들
04	lack	v. 결핍되다, 부족하다	( ) a clear understanding	명확한 이해가 부족하다
05	bounce back	회복하다, 되살아나다	( ) ( ) from failure	실패로부터 회복되다
06	prevent A from -ing	A가 ~하지 못하게 하다	( ) them ( ) making poor choices	그들이 잘못된 선택을 하지 못하게 하다
07	conclude	v. 결론을 내리다, 결정하다	( ) not to go	가지 않기로 결정하다
08	opportunity	n. 기회	an ( ) to learn	배울 기회
09	experience	v. 경험하다	( ) pain	고통을 경험하다
10	prepare	v. 준비하다, 준비시키다	( ) for a party	파티를 준비하다
11	adulthood	n. 성인, 성인기	prepare children for ( )	성인기를 아이들에게 준비시키다
12	potential	a. 잠재적인, 잠재력이 있는	the ( ) consequences	잠재적인 결과
13	choice	n. 선택	the potential consequences of their ( )s	선택이 가져오는 잠재적인 결과

⊕ 본문 문장 속에서 단어들을 확인해 보세요.

Overprotective **parents** / spare kids from all natural consequences.

과잉보호하는 **부모들은** / 아이들이 모든 자연적 결과를 경험하지 못하게 막는다.

단어 다시보기 문제를 풀기 전에 단어들을 30초 동안 다시 확인하세요.

01	overprotective	과잉보호하는	overprotective parents	과잉보호하는 부모
02	spare		spare kids from bullying	아이들이 괴롭힘을 경험하지 않게 하다
03	consequence		all natural consequences	모든 자연스런 결과들
04	lack		lack a clear understanding	명확한 이해가 부족하다
05	bounce back		bounce back from failure	실패로부터 회복되다
06	prevent A from -ing		prevent them from making poor choices	그들이 잘못된 선택을 하지 못하게 하다
07	conclude		conclude not to go	가지 않기로 결정하다
08	opportunity		an opportunity to learn	배울 기회
09	experience		experience pain	고통을 경험하다
10	prepare		prepare for a party	파티를 준비하다
11	adulthood		prepare children for adulthood	성인기를 아이들에게 준비시키다
12	potential		the potential consequences	잠재적인 결과
13	choice		the potential consequences of their choices	선택이 가져오는 잠재적인 결과

⊕ **본문 문장 속에서 단어의 의미를 우리말로 해석해 보세요.**

Overprotective parents / spare kids from all natural consequences.

➜ ______ 부모들은 / ______.

2017 9월 학평 23번 문제

제한시간 60초

난이도 ★★☆☆☆

STEP 2 • 수능 기출 제대로 풀기

G

다음 글의 제목으로 가장 적절한 것은?

Overprotective parents spare kids from all natural consequences. Unfortunately, their kids often lack a clear understanding of the reasons behind their parents' rules. They never learn how to bounce back from failure or how to recover from mistakes because their parents prevented them from making poor choices. Rather than learning, "I should wear a jacket because it's cold outside," a child may conclude, "I have to wear a jacket because my mom makes me." Without an opportunity to experience real-world consequences, kids don't always understand why their parents make certain rules. Natural consequences prepare children for adulthood by helping them think about the potential consequences of their choices.

① Dark Sides of the Virtual World

② Let Natural Consequences Teach Kids

③ The More Choices, the More Mistakes

④ Listen to Kids to Improve Relationships

⑤ The Benefits of Overprotective Parenting

정답과 해설 p.7

STEP 3 ● 수능 지문 제대로 복습하기

01 Overprotective parents / spare kids from all natural consequences.
spare A from~: A가 ~하지 못하게 하다

02 Unfortunately, / their kids often lack a clear understanding of the reasons / behind their parents' rules.
명사를 수식하는 전치사구

03 They never learn / how to bounce back from failure / or how to recover from mistakes / because their parents prevented them from making poor choices.
learn의 목적어(의문사+to부정사)
(=the kids)

04 Rather than learning, / "I should wear a jacket because it's cold outside," / a child may conclude, / "I have to wear a jacket because my mom makes me."
사역동사 원형부정사구 wear a jacket 생략

05 Without an opportunity to experience real-world consequences, / kids don't always understand / why their parents make certain rules.
to부정사의 형용사적 용법(명사 수식)
don't understand의 목적어(의문사절)

06 Natural consequences prepare children for adulthood / by helping them think / about the potential consequences of their choices.
전치사+ -ing
help+A+(to)동사원형: A가 ~하는 것을 돕다

01 과잉보호하는 부모들**overprotective parents**은 / 아이들이 모든 자연적 결과**all natural consequences**를 경험하지 못하게 막는다**spare**.

02 불행히도, / 그들의 자녀는 종종 이유를 명확하게 이해하지 못한다**lack** / 부모가 정한 규칙 이면에 있는.

03 아이들은 결코 배우지 못한다 / 실패로부터 다시 일어나거나**bounce back** / 실수로부터 회복하는 법을 / 부모들이 아이들이 잘못된 선택을 하지 않도록 막았기**prevent** 때문에.

04 배우기보다는 / "밖에 날씨가 춥기 때문에 외투를 입어야지"라고, / 아이는 결론을 낼지도**conclude** 모른다 / "엄마가 시키니까 외투를 입어야지"라고.

05 실제 세상이 주는 결과를 경험할 기회**an opportunity to experience**가 없으면, / 아이들은 항상 이해하는 것은 아니다 / 그들의 부모가 왜 특정한 규칙들을 만드는지를.

06 자연적 결과는 아이들이 성인기를 대비할**prepare children for adulthood** 수 있도록 해준다 / 그들이 생각하게 도움으로써 / 자신들의 선택**choice**이 가져오는 잠재적인**potential** 결과에 대해.

구문 Check up

① The kids never learn how to bounce back from failure or how to recover from mistakes because their parents prevented them / themselves from making poor choices.

prevented의 주어는 their parents인데 목적어는 문맥상 the kids이다. 따라서 인칭대명사 them을 쓴다. 재귀대명사는 주어와 목적어가 동일할 때 쓴다.

② Natural consequences prepare children for adulthood by help / helping them think about the potential consequences of their choices.

전치사 by의 목적어가 필요하기 때문에 동명사 helping을 쓴다.

정답 ① them ② helping

A STEP 1 • 수능에 진짜 나오는 단어

필자의 주장 ⊕

✔ 문제에 나오는 단어들을 확인하세요.

시간이 없다면 색으로 표시된 단어만이라도 꼭 외우고 넘어가세요!

01	overhear	v. 우연히 듣다, 엿듣다	(✔ overhear) their conversation	그들의 대화를 우연히 듣다
02	priority	n. 우선순위	a high ( )	높은 우선순위
03	take the high road	올바른 길로 가다	( ) ( ) ( ) ( )	올바른 길로 가다
04	tempting	a. 유혹적인	look ( )	유혹적으로 보이다
05	act on	~에 따라 행동하다	( ) ( ) your values	가치관에 따라 행동하다
06	uphold	v. 유지하다	( ) those values	그러한 가치들을 유지하다
07	respect	v. 존중하다	( ) others	타인들을 존중하다
08	compassion	n. 연민	show ( )	연민을 보이다
09	concern	n. 걱정	our ( ) about the environment	환경에 관한 우리의 걱정
10	suffer	v. 괴로워하다, 고통받다	( ) from pain	통증으로 괴로워하다
11	self-discipline	n. 자제력	show our own ( )	우리 자신의 자제력을 보여주다

⊕ 본문 문장 속에서 단어들을 확인해 보세요.

We can show them our compassion and concern / when others are suffering, / and our own self-discipline, courage and honesty / as we make difficult decisions.

우리는 그들에게 우리의 연민과 걱정을 보여줄 수 있다 / 타인이 괴로워하고 있을 때 / 그리고 우리 자신의 자제력과 용기와 정직을 / 우리가 어려운 결정을 할 때.

단어 다시보기 문제를 풀기 전에 단어들을 30초 동안 다시 확인하세요.

01	overhear	우연히 듣다, 엿듣다	overhear their conversation	그들의 대화를 우연히 듣다
02	priority		a high priority	높은 우선순위
03	take the high road		take the high road	올바른 길로 가다
04	tempting		look tempting	유혹적으로 보이다
05	act on		act on your values	가치관에 따라 행동하다
06	uphold		uphold those values	그러한 가치들을 유지하다
07	respect		respect others	타인들을 존중하다
08	compassion		show compassion	연민을 보이다
09	concern		our concern about the environment	환경에 관한 우리의 걱정
10	suffer		suffer from pain	통증으로 괴로워하다
11	self-discipline		show our own self-discipline	우리 자신의 자제력을 보여주다

⊕ 본문 문장 속에서 단어의 의미를 우리말로 해석해 보세요.

We can show them our compassion and concern / when others are suffering, / and our own self-discipline, courage and honesty / as we make difficult decisions.

➔ 우리는 그들에게 ______을 보여줄 수 있다 / 타인이 ______ 때 / 그리고 ______과 용기와 정직을 / 우리가 어려운 결정을 할 때.

2023 9월 학평 20번 문제

제한시간 50초
난이도 ★☆☆☆☆

STEP 2 • 수능 기출 제대로 풀기

A

다음 글에서 필자가 주장하는 바로 가장 적절한 것은?

We are always teaching our children something by our words and our actions. They learn from seeing. They learn from hearing and from *overhearing*. Children share the values of their parents about the most important things in life. Our priorities and principles and our examples of good behavior can teach our children to take the high road when other roads look tempting. Remember that children do not learn the values that make up strong character simply by being *told* about them. They learn by seeing the people around them *act* on and *uphold* those values in their daily lives. Therefore show your child good examples of life by your action. In our daily lives, we can show our children that we respect others. We can show them our compassion and concern when others are suffering, and our own self-discipline, courage and honesty as we make difficult decisions.

① 자녀를 타인과 비교하는 말을 삼가야 한다.

② 자녀에게 행동으로 삶의 모범을 보여야 한다.

③ 칭찬을 통해 자녀의 바람직한 행동을 강화해야 한다.

④ 훈육을 하기 전에 자녀 스스로 생각할 시간을 주어야 한다.

⑤ 자녀가 새로운 것에 도전할 때 인내심을 가지고 지켜봐야 한다.

정답과 해설 p.8

STEP 3 • 수능 지문 제대로 복습하기

01 We are always teaching our children something / by our words and our actions. // They learn from seeing. // They learn from hearing and from *overhearing*.

4형식 teach+간접목적어+직접목적어: ~에게 …을 가르치다 / 전치사+동명사 / 병렬 연결

02 Children share the values of their parents / about the most important things in life. // Our priorities and principles and our examples of good behavior / can teach our children to take the high road / when other roads look tempting.

5형식 teach+목적어+to부정사: ~이 …하도록 가르치다

03 Remember / that children do not learn the values / that make up strong character / simply by being *told* about them. // They learn / by seeing the people around them *act* on and *uphold* those values / in their daily lives.

명령문(~하라) / 접속사(~것) / 주격 관계대명사 / 동명사의 수동태(being+p.p.) / 지각동사 / 목적어 / 목적격보어

04 Therefore / show your child good examples of life / by your action. // In our daily lives, / we can show our children / [that we respect others].

명령문(~하라) / 명사절(can show의 직접목적어)

05 We can show them our compassion and concern / when others are suffering, / and (can show them) our own self-discipline, courage and honesty / as we make difficult decisions.

동사 / 간접목적어 / 직접목적어1 / 직접목적어2 / 접속사(~할 때)

01 우리는 항상 우리 자녀에게 무언가를 가르치고 있다 / 우리의 말과 행동으로. // 그들은 보는 것으로부터 배운다. // 그들은 듣고 또 '우연히 듣는**overhear** 것'으로부터 배운다.

02 아이들은 그들 부모의 가치관을 공유한다 / 인생에서 가장 중요한 것에 관한. // 우리의 우선순위**priority**와 원칙, 그리고 훌륭한 행동에 대한 본보기는 / 우리 자녀가 올바른 길로 가도록**take the high road** 가르칠 수 있다 / 다른 길이 유혹적**tempting**으로 보일 때.

03 기억하라 / 아이들은 가치를 배우지 않는다는 것을 / 확고한 인격을 구성하는 (가치) / 단순히 그것에 대해 '들음'으로써. // 그들은 배운다 / 주변 사람들이 그러한 가치에 따라 '행동'하고 '유지'하는**act on and uphold** 것을 봄으로써 / 그들의 일상생활에서.

04 그러므로 / 여러분의 자녀에게 삶의 모범을 보이라 / 여러분의 행동으로. // 우리 일상생활에서 / 우리는 자녀에게 보여줄 수 있다 / 우리가 타인을 존중하는**respect** 것을.

05 우리는 그들에게 우리의 연민**compassion**과 걱정**concern**을 보여줄 수 있다 / 타인이 괴로워하고**suffer** 있을 때 / 그리고 우리 자신의 자제력**self-discipline**과 용기와 정직을 (보여줄 수 있다) / 우리가 어려운 결정을 할 때.

구문 Check up

① Remember that children do not learn the values that make up strong character simply by telling / being told about them.

문맥상 아이들이 이야기를 '듣는' 것이므로 동명사의 수동태인 being told가 알맞다.

② Our examples of good behavior can teach our children take / to take the high road when other roads look tempting.

teach의 목적격보어로는 to부정사가 적절하므로 to take를 써야 한다.

정답 ① being told ② to take

B

글의 목적

STEP 1 • 수능에 진짜 나오는 단어

✔ 문제에 나오는 단어들을 확인하세요.

시간이 없다면 색으로 표시된 단어만이라도 꼭 외우고 넘어가세요!

01	guardian	n. 보호자	Dear (✔ guardian)s	보호자들께
02	hold	v. (모임 등을) 열다	( ) a class party	학급 파티를 열다
03	sweet	n. 사탕류(~s)	bring in ( )s	사탕류를 가져오다
04	crisp	n. 파삭파삭한 감자칩(~s)	have ( )s for a snack	간식으로 감자칩을 먹다
05	request	v. 요청하다	( ) that children do not bring in food	아이들이 음식을 가져오지 않기를 요청하다
06	seal	v. 밀봉하다	a ( )ed packet	밀봉된 꾸러미
07	ingredient	n. 성분	list the ( )s	성분을 목록으로 작성하다
08	contain	v. 포함하다, 함유하다	( ) nuts	견과류를 포함하다
09	severe	a. 심각한	a ( ) illness	심각한 병
10	allergy	n. 알레르기, 알러지	nut ( )ies	견과류 알레르기
11	continue	v. 지속하다	( )d support	지속적인 지원
12	cooperation	n. 협조, 협동	support and ( )	지원과 협조

⊕ 본문 문장 속에서 단어들을 확인해 보세요.

All food should arrive in a sealed packet / with the ingredients clearly listed.

모든 음식은 밀봉된 꾸러미로 와야 합니다 / 성분이 명확하게 목록으로 작성된 채로.

단어 다시보기 문제를 풀기 전에 단어들을 30초 동안 다시 확인하세요.

01	guardian	보호자	Dear guardians	보호자들께
02	hold		hold a class party	학급 파티를 열다
03	sweet		bring in sweets	사탕류를 가져오다
04	crisp		have crisps for a snack	간식으로 감자칩을 먹다
05	request		request that children do not bring in food	아이들이 음식을 가져오지 않기를 요청하다
06	seal		a sealed packet	밀봉된 꾸러미
07	ingredient		list the ingredients	성분을 목록으로 작성하다
08	contain		contain nuts	견과류를 포함하다
09	severe		a severe illness	심각한 병
10	allergy		nut allergies	견과류 알레르기
11	continue		continued support	지속적인 지원
12	cooperation		support and cooperation	지원과 협조

⊕ **본문 문장 속에서 단어의 의미를 우리말로 해석해 보세요.**

All food should arrive in a sealed packet / with the ingredients clearly listed.

→ 모든 음식은 ______ 꾸러미로 와야 합니다 / ______이 명확하게 목록으로 작성된 채로.

2022 9월 학평 18번 문제

제한시간 50초

난이도 ★☆☆☆☆

STEP 2 • 수능 기출 제대로 풀기

B

다음 글의 목적으로 가장 적절한 것은?

Dear Parents/Guardians,

Class parties will be held on the afternoon of Friday, December 16th, 2022. Children may bring in sweets, crisps, biscuits, cakes, and drinks. We are requesting that children do not bring in home-cooked or prepared food. All food should arrive in a sealed packet with the ingredients clearly listed. Fruit and vegetables are welcomed if they are pre-packed in a sealed packet from the shop. Please DO NOT send any food into school containing nuts as we have many children with severe nut allergies. Please check the ingredients of all food your children bring carefully. Thank you for your continued support and cooperation.

Yours sincerely,
Lisa Brown, Headteacher

① 학급 파티 일정 변경을 공지하려고

② 학교 식당의 새로운 메뉴를 소개하려고

③ 학생의 특정 음식 알레르기 여부를 조사하려고

④ 학부모의 적극적인 학급 파티 참여를 독려하려고

⑤ 학급 파티에 가져올 음식에 대한 유의 사항을 안내하려고

정답과 해설 p.8

STEP 3 • 수능 지문 제대로 복습하기

01 Dear Parents/Guardians, // Class parties will be held / on the afternoon of Friday, December 16th, 2022.

02 Children may bring in sweets, crisps, biscuits, cakes, and drinks. // We are requesting / that children do not bring in home-cooked or prepared food.
명사절 접속사(are requesting의 목적어)

03 All food should arrive in a sealed packet / with the ingredients clearly listed.
과거분사 / with+명사+과거분사(~가 ~된 채로)

04 Fruit and vegetables are welcomed / if they are pre-packed / in a sealed packet from the shop.

05 Please DO NOT send any food into school / containing nuts / as we have many children / with severe nut allergies.
접속사(~이니까) / 현재분사(명사 수식)

06 Please check the ingredients of all food / your children bring / carefully. // Thank you for your continued support and cooperation. // Yours sincerely, Lisa Brown, Headteacher
목적격 관계대명사 that 생략 / 관계대명사절

01 부모님들/보호자**guardian**들께, // 학급 파티가 열릴**be held** 것입니다 / 2022년 12월 16일 금요일 오후에.

02 아이들은 사탕류**sweets**, 감자칩**crisps**, 비스킷, 케이크, 그리고 음료를 가지고 올 수 있습니다. // 우리는 요청합니다**request** / 아이들이 집에서 만들거나 준비한 음식을 가져오지 않기를.

03 모든 음식은 밀봉된**sealed** 꾸러미로 와야 합니다 / 성분**ingredient**이 명확하게 목록으로 작성된 채로.

04 과일과 채소는 환영합니다 / 사전 포장된 것이라면 / 가게에서 밀봉된 꾸러미로.

05 그 어떤 음식도 학교에 보내지 마십시오 / 견과류가 포함**contain**된 (음식) / 아이들이 많이 있으니 / 심각한**severe** 견과류 알레르기**allergy**를 가진.

06 모든 음식의 성분을 확인해 주십시오 / 아이들이 가져오는 / 주의 깊게. // 여러분의 지속적인**continued** 지원과 협조**cooperation**에 감사드립니다. // 교장 Lisa Brown 드림

구문 Check up

① All food should arrive in a sealed packet with the ingredients clearly [listing / listed].

<with+명사+분사>의 형태에서 명사 the ingredients와 동사 list의 관계가 수동이므로 과거분사 listed를 쓴다.

② Please DO NOT send any food into school [contain / containing] nuts as we have many children with severe nut allergies.

문장(명령문)의 동사는 DO NOT send이다. send와 contain을 병렬연결할 접속사가 없고, 내용상 contain nuts가 food를 수식해야 하므로 현재분사 containing으로 쓴다.

정답 ① listed ② containing

C

글의 목적 +

STEP 1 • 수능에 진짜 나오는 단어

✔ 문제에 나오는 단어들을 확인하세요.

시간이 없다면 색으로 표시된 단어만이라도 꼭 외우고 넘어가세요!

01	literature	n. 문학	a (✔ literature) group	문학 모임
02	raise	v. 모금하다, 올리다	( ) enough money	충분한 돈을 모금하다
03	remodel	v. 리모델링하다, 개조하다	( ) the library building	도서관 건물을 리모델링하다
04	local	a. 지역의	our ( ) builder	우리 지역의 건축업자
05	volunteer	v. 자원하다	( ) to help	돕기로 자원하다
06	assistance	n. 도움	He needs ( ).	그는 도움이 필요하다.
07	hammer	n. 망치	a ( ) or a paint brush	망치나 페인트 붓
08	donate	v. 기부하다	( ) your time	당신의 시간을 기부하다
09	information	n. 정보	for more ( )	더 많은 정보를 원하면

⊕ 본문 문장 속에서 단어들을 확인해 보세요.

By grabbing a hammer or a paint brush / and donating your time, / you can help with the construction.

망치나 페인트 붓을 쥐고 / 시간을 기부함으로써, / 여러분은 공사를 도울 수 있습니다.

단어 다시보기 문제를 풀기 전에 단어들을 30초 동안 다시 확인하세요.

01	literature	문학	a literature group	문학 모임
02	raise		raise enough money	충분한 돈을 모금하다
03	remodel		remodel the library building	도서관 건물을 리모델링하다
04	local		our local builder	우리 지역의 건축업자
05	volunteer		volunteer to help	돕기로 자원하다
06	assistance		He needs assistance.	그는 도움이 필요하다.
07	hammer		a hammer or a paint brush	망치나 페인트 붓
08	donate		donate your time	당신의 시간을 기부하다
09	information		for more information	더 많은 정보를 원하면

⊕ 본문 문장 속에서 단어의 의미를 우리말로 해석해 보세요.

By grabbing a hammer or a paint brush and / donating your time, / you can help with the construction.

→ ______나 페인트 붓을 쥐고 / 시간을 ______으로써, / 여러분은 공사를 도울 수 있습니다.

2021 3월 학평 18번 문제

제한시간 50초
난이도 ★☆☆☆☆

STEP 2 • 수능 기출 제대로 풀기

C

다음 글의 목적으로 가장 적절한 것은?

Dear members of Eastwood Library,

Thanks to the Friends of Literature group, we've successfully raised enough money to remodel the library building. John Baker, our local builder, has volunteered to help us with the remodelling but he needs assistance. By grabbing a hammer or a paint brush and donating your time, you can help with the construction. Join Mr. Baker in his volunteering team and become a part of making Eastwood Library a better place! Please call 541-567-1234 for more information.

Sincerely,
Mark Anderson

① 도서관 임시 휴관의 이유를 설명하려고
② 도서관 자원봉사자 교육 일정을 안내하려고
③ 도서관 보수를 위한 모금 행사를 제안하려고
④ 도서관 공사에 참여할 자원봉사자를 모집하려고
⑤ 도서관에서 개최하는 글쓰기 대회를 홍보하려고

정답과 해설 p.8

STEP 3 ● 수능 지문 제대로 복습하기

01 Dear members of Eastwood Library, // Thanks to the Friends of Literature group, / we've successfully raised enough money / to remodel the library building.

전치사(~덕분에)

enough+명사+to부정사: ~하기에 충분한 (명사)

02 John Baker, our local builder, / has volunteered / to help us with the remodelling / but he needs assistance.

help A with B: B에 대해서 A를 돕다

03 By grabbing a hammer or a paint brush / and donating your time, / you can help with the construction.

병렬연결(전치사by의 목적어)

04 Join Mr. Baker in his volunteering team / and become a part / of making Eastwood Library a better place!

병렬연결(명령문)

make(5형식)+목적어+목적격 보어: ~를 …로 만들다

05 Please call 541-567-1234 for more information. // Sincerely, Mark Anderson

01 Eastwood 도서관 회원들께, // '문학**literature**의 친구들' 모임 덕분에, / 우리는 충분한 돈을 성공적으로 모금하였습니다**raise enough money** / 도서관 건물을 리모델링하기**remodel** 위한.

02 우리 지역의 건축업자**local builder**인 John Baker 씨가 / 자원했습니다**volunteer** / 우리의 리모델링을 돕기로, / 하지만 그는 도움**assistance**이 필요합니다.

03 망치**hammer**나 페인트 붓을 쥐고 / 시간을 기부함**donate**으로써, / 여러분은 공사를 도울 수 있습니다.

04 Baker 씨의 자원봉사 팀에 동참하십시오 / 그리고 참여하십시오 / Eastwood 도서관을 더 좋은 곳으로 만드는 데!

05 더 많은 정보**information**를 원하시면 541-567-1234로 전화해 주십시오. // Mark Anderson 드림

구문 Check up

① Thanks to the Friends of Literature group, we've successfully raised enough money [to remodel / remodelling] the library building.

<enough+명사+to부정사> 구조를 써서 '~하기에 충분한 …'이라는 의미를 나타내고 있으므로 to remodel을 쓴다.

② By grabbing a hammer or a paint brush and [donate / donating] your time, you can help with the construction.

전치사 by 뒤의 동명사 grabbing과 병렬 연결되는 구조이므로 동명사 donating을 쓴다.

정답 ① to remodel ② donating

D

필자의 주장 +

STEP 1 • 수능에 진짜 나오는 단어

✔ 문제에 나오는 단어들을 확인하세요.

시간이 없다면 색으로 표시된 단어만이라도 꼭 외우고 넘어가세요!

01	keep	v. (계속) ~하게 하다	(✔ keep) good ideas floating	좋은 생각이 떠돌게 하다
02	float	v. 떠돌다	good ideas ( )ing around in your head	머릿속에 떠도는 좋은 생각
03	ensure	v. 보장하다	( ) that it won't happen	일어나지 않을 것이라고 보장하다
04	tip	n. 조언	take a ( )	조언을 얻다
05	come to life	생명력을 얻다	the only good ideas that ( ) ( ) ( )	생명력을 얻는 유일한 좋은 생각
06	aim	v. 목표로 하다	( ) to hit one hundred dreams	꿈이 100개가 되는 것을 목표로 하다
07	reminder	n. 상기시키는 것[사람]	a ( ) to get going on	시작되게 상기시키는 것
08	motivator	n. 동기 부여 요소	a powerful ( )	강력한 동기 부여 요소
09	burden	n. 부담	the ( ) of remembering all of them	그 모든 것을 기억하는 부담
10	action	n. 실행	put them into ( )	그것들을 실행하다

+ 본문 문장 속에서 단어들을 확인해 보세요.

Take a tip from writers, / who know / that the only good ideas that come to life / are the ones that get written down.

작가들로부터 조언을 얻어라 / 그들은 안다 / 생명력을 얻는 유일한 좋은 생각은 / 적어둔 것이라는 점을.

단어 다시보기 문제를 풀기 전에 단어들을 30초 동안 다시 확인하세요.

01	keep	(계속) ~하게 하다	keep good ideas floating	좋은 생각이 떠돌게 하다
02	float		good ideas floating around in your head	머릿속에 떠도는 좋은 생각
03	ensure		ensure that it won't happen	일어나지 않을 것이라고 보장하다
04	tip		take a tip	조언을 얻다
05	come to life		the only good ideas that come to life	생명력을 얻는 유일한 좋은 생각
06	aim		aim to hit one hundred dreams	꿈이 100개가 되는 것을 목표로 하다
07	reminder		a reminder to get going on	시작되게 상기시키는 것
08	motivator		a powerful motivator	강력한 동기 부여 요소
09	burden		the burden of remembering all of them	그 모든 것을 기억하는 부담
10	action		put them into action	그것들을 실행하다

⊕ 본문 문장 속에서 단어의 의미를 우리말로 해석해 보세요.

Take a tip from writers, / who know / that the only good ideas that come to life / are the ones that get written down.

→ 작가들로부터 ______ / 그들은 안다 / ______ 유일한 좋은 생각은 / 적어둔 것이라는 점을.

2020 3월 학평 20번 문제

제한시간 60초

난이도 ★★☆☆☆

STEP 2 • 수능 기출 제대로 풀기

D

다음 글에서 필자가 주장하는 바로 가장 적절한 것은?

Keeping good ideas floating around in your head is a great way to ensure that they won't happen. Take a tip from writers, who know that the only good ideas that come to life are the ones that get written down. Take out a piece of paper and record everything you'd love to do someday — aim to hit one hundred dreams. You'll have a reminder and motivator to get going on those things that are calling you, and you also won't have the burden of remembering all of them. When you put your dreams into words you begin putting them into action.

① 친구의 꿈을 응원하라.

② 하고 싶은 일을 적으라.

③ 신중히 생각한 후 행동하라.

④ 효과적인 기억법을 개발하라.

⑤ 실현 가능한 목표에 집중하라.

정답과 해설 p.9

STEP 3 • 수능 지문 제대로 복습하기

동명사 주어

01 Keeping good ideas floating around in your head / is a great way / to ensure that they won't happen.

keep+목적어+목적격 보어(현재분사) / 동사(단수) / 형용사적 용법

02 Take a tip from writers, / who know / that the only good ideas that come to life / are the ones that get written down.

=and they / 명사절 접속사 / 관계대명사절 / 관계대명사절

목적격 관계대명사 that 생략

03 Take out a piece of paper / and record everything you'd love to do someday / — aim to hit one hundred dreams.

관계대명사절

04 You'll have a reminder and motivator / to get going on those things that are calling you, / and you also won't have / the burden of remembering all of them.

주격 관계대명사절

05 When you put your dreams into words / you begin putting them into action.

begin의 목적어(동명사)

01 좋은 생각을 머릿속에 떠돌게 하는**keep good ideas floating** 것은 / 확실한 방법이다 / 그것이 이루어지지 않게 보장하는**ensure**.

02 작가들로부터 조언을 얻어라**take a tip** / 그들은 안다 / 생명력을 얻는**come to life** 유일한 좋은 생각은 / 적어둔 것(생각)이라는 점을.

03 종이 한 장을 꺼내 / 언젠가 하고 싶은 모든 것을 기록하는데, / 꿈이 100개가 되는 것을 목표로 해라**aim to hit one hundred dreams**.

04 상기시키는 것**reminder** 과 동기 부여 요소**motivator**를 갖게 될 것이고 / 여러분을 부르고 있는 그것들을 시작하도록 / 또한 갖지 않을 것이다 / 그 모든 것을 기억하는 부담**burden**을.

05 꿈을 글로 적을 때 / 여러분은 그것을 실행하기**put them into action** 시작하는 것이다.

구문 Check up

① Keeping good ideas floating around in your head is a great way ensures / to ensure that they won't happen.

문장의 동사는 is이고, 이에 동사 ensure를 병렬 연결해줄 접속사가 앞에 없다. 따라서 way를 수식할 수 있는 형태인 형용사적 용법의 to부정사 to ensure를 쓴다.

② When you put your dreams into words you begin put / putting them into action.

동사 begin의 목적어 자리에는 동명사나 to부정사 형태만 쓸 수 있으므로 putting이 정답이다.

정답 ① to ensure ② putting

E

필자의 주장 +

STEP 1 • 수능에 진짜 나오는 단어

✔ 문제에 나오는 단어들을 확인하세요.

시간이 없다면 색으로 표시된 단어만이라도 꼭 외우고 넘어가세요!

01	tough	a. 어려운, 힘든	It can be (✔ tough).	어려울 수 있다.
02	settle down to	~에 집중하기 시작하다	( ) ( ) ( ) study	공부에 집중하기 시작하다
03	distraction	n. 집중을 방해하는 것	many ( )s	집중을 방해하는 많은 것들
04	combine	v. 병행하다, 결합하다	( ) homework with other activities	숙제와 다른 활동을 병행하다
05	instant	a. 즉각적인	( ) messaging	즉각적인 메시지 주고받기
06	profile	n. 신상 명세	update a ( ) on a social-networking site	SNS에 신상 명세를 올리다
07	multi-task	v. 한꺼번에 여러 일을 처리하다	You can ( ).	당신은 여러 일을 할 수 있다.
08	at once	한번에	multi-task ( ) ( )	한번에 여러 일을 하다
09	concentrate	v. 집중하다	( ) on study	공부에 집중하다
10	catch up on	따라잡다, (앞서 못했던 일을) 하다	( ) ( ) ( ) work	일을 따라잡다(만회하다)
11	pastime	n. 취미, 소일거리	just a ( )	단지 소일거리

⊕ 본문 문장 속에서 단어들을 확인해 보세요.

It can be tough / to settle down to study / when there are so many distractions.

힘들 수 있다 / 공부에 집중하기 시작하는 것은 / 집중을 방해하는 것들이 너무 많이 있을 때.

단어 다시보기 문제를 풀기 전에 단어들을 30초 동안 다시 확인하세요.

01	tough	어려운, 힘든	It can be tough.	어려울 수 있다.
02	settle down to		settle down to study	공부에 집중하기 시작하다
03	distraction		many distractions	집중을 방해하는 많은 것들
04	combine		combine homework with other activities	숙제와 다른 활동을 병행하다
05	instant		instant messaging	즉각적인 메시지 주고받기
06	profile		update a profile on a social-networking site	SNS에 신상 명세를 올리다
07	multi-task		You can multi-task.	당신은 여러 일을 할 수 있다.
08	at once		multi-task at once	한번에 여러 일을 하다
09	concentrate		concentrate on study	공부에 집중하다
10	catch up on		catch up on work	일을 따라잡다(만회하다)
11	pastime		just a pastime	단지 소일거리

⊕ 본문 문장 속에서 단어의 의미를 우리말로 해석해 보세요.

It can be tough / to settle down to study / when there are so many distractions.

➔ ____ 수 있다 / 공부 ____ 것은 / ____ 이 너무 많이 있을 때.

2019 3월 학평 21번 문제

제한시간 70초

난이도 ★★★☆☆

STEP 2 • 수능 기출 제대로 풀기

E

다음 글에서 필자가 주장하는 바로 가장 적절한 것은?

It can be tough to settle down to study when there are so many distractions. Most young people like to combine a bit of homework with quite a lot of instant messaging, chatting on the phone, updating profiles on social-networking sites, and checking emails. While it may be true that you can multi-task and can focus on all these things at once, try to be honest with yourself. It is most likely that you will be able to work best if you concentrate on your studies but allow yourself regular breaks — every 30 minutes or so — to catch up on those other pastimes.

① 공부할 때는 공부에만 집중하라.

② 평소 주변 사람들과 자주 연락하라.

③ 피로감을 느끼지 않게 충분한 휴식을 취하라.

④ 자투리 시간을 이용하여 숙제를 하라.

⑤ 학습에 유익한 취미 활동을 하라.

정답과 해설 p.9

STEP 3 • 수능 지문 제대로 복습하기

01 It can be tough / to settle down to study / when there are so many distractions.
가주어(it) 진주어(to부정사)

02 Most young people like to combine a bit of homework / with quite a lot of instant messaging, / chatting on the phone, / updating profiles on social-networking sites, / and checking emails.
4개의 (동)명사구 병렬연결

03 While it may be true/ that you can multi-task / and can focus on all these things at once, / try to be honest with yourself.
가주어(it) 진주어(that절) 명령문

04 It is most likely that you will be able to work best / if you concentrate on your studies / but allow yourself regular breaks / — every 30 minutes or so — / to catch up on those other pastimes.
시간과 조건의 부사절에서는 현재가 미래를 대신함 가주어 진주어(that절) allow(4형식)+간접 목적어+직접 목적어 부사적 용법(목적)

01 힘들**tough** 수 있다 / 공부에 전념하는**settle down to study** 것은 / 집중을 방해하는 것**distraction**들이 너무 많이 있을 때.

02 많은 젊은이들이 숙제를 찔끔하는 것을 병행하고**combine** 싶어 한다 / 즉각적인**instant** 메시지 주고받기, / 전화로 잡담하기, / SNS에 신상 정보**profile** 업데이트하기, / 그리고 이메일 확인하기를 잔뜩 하는 것과.

03 사실일지도 모르지만 / 여러분이 동시에**at once** 여러 가지 일을 처리할**multi-task** 수 있고 / 이러한 모든 일들에 집중할 수 있다는 것이, / 자신에게 솔직해지려고 노력해라.

04 여러분은 아마도 가장 잘 공부할 수 있을 것이다 / 여러분이 공부에 집중하되**concentrate on study** / 자기 자신에게 규칙적인 휴식을 허락한다면 / 30분 정도마다 / 그런 다른 소일거리를 하기**catch up on those other pastimes** 위해.

구문 Check up

① It can be tough settle / to settle down to study when there are so many distractions.

가주어 it의 진주어로 to부정사가 자연스럽기 때문에 to settle을 쓴다.

② It is most likely that you will be able to work best if you will concentrate / concentrate on your studies.

조건을 나타내는 if절에서는 현재가 미래를 대신한다. 따라서 현재시제인 concentrate가 적절하다.

정답 ① to settle ② concentrate

글의 목적

STEP 1 • 수능에 진짜 나오는 단어

문제에 나오는 단어들을 확인하세요.

시간이 없다면 색으로 표시된 단어만이라도 꼭 외우고 넘어가세요!

01	inquiry	n. 문의	a reply to your (✓ inquiry)	당신의 문의에 대한 회신
02	shipment	n. 배송	( ) status	배송 상황
03	purchase	v. 구매하다	( ) at our store	우리 가게에서 구매하다
04	delivery	n. 배송	( ) of your desk	당신의 책상 배송
05	warehouse	n. 도매점, 창고	a ( ) store	창고형 할인점
06	manufacturer	n. 제조업체	the furniture ( )	가구 제조업체
07	replacement	n. 대체품	an exact ( )	똑같은 대체품
08	expect	v. 기대하다	( ) the delivery	그 배송을 기대하다
09	immediately	ad. 바로, 즉시	telephone ( )	바로 전화하다
10	convenient	a. 편리한	( ) delivery time	편리한 배송 시간
11	regret	v. 후회하다, 유감으로 생각하다	( ) the inconvenience	불편에 대해 유감으로 생각하다
12	delay	n. 지연	shipment ( )	배송 지연
13	cause	v. 일으키다, 야기하다	( ) the inconvenience	불편을 일으키다

본문 문장 속에서 단어들을 확인해 보세요.

We regret the inconvenience / this delay has caused you.

우리는 불편에 대해 유감으로 생각합니다 / 이 지연이 당신에게 일으킨.

단어 다시보기 문제를 풀기 전에 단어들을 30초 동안 다시 확인하세요.

01	inquiry	문의	a reply to your inquiry	당신의 문의에 대한 회신
02	shipment		shipment status	배송 상황
03	purchase		purchase at our store	우리 가게에서 구매하다
04	delivery		delivery of your desk	당신의 책상 배송
05	warehouse		a warehouse store	창고형 할인점
06	manufacturer		the furniture manufacturer	가구 제조업체
07	replacement		an exact replacement	똑같은 대체품
08	expect		expect the delivery	그 배송을 기대하다
09	immediately		telephone immediately	바로 전화하다
10	convenient		convenient delivery time	편리한 배송 시간
11	regret		regret the inconvenience	불편에 대해 유감으로 생각하다
12	delay		shipment delay	배송 지연
13	cause		cause the inconvenience	불편을 일으키다

⊕ **본문 문장 속에서 단어의 의미를 우리말로 해석해 보세요.**

We regret the inconvenience / this delay has caused you.

➔ 우리는 ______ / 이 지연이 당신에게 ______.

2018 9월 학평 18번 문제

제한시간 60초

난이도 ★★☆☆☆

STEP 2 • 수능 기출 제대로 풀기

F 다음 글의 목적으로 가장 적절한 것은?

Dear Mr. Stevens,

This is a reply to your inquiry about the shipment status of the desk you purchased at our store on September 26. Unfortunately, the delivery of your desk will take longer than expected due to the damage that occurred during the shipment from the furniture manufacturer to our warehouse. We have ordered an exact replacement from the manufacturer, and we expect that delivery will take place within two weeks. As soon as the desk arrives, we will telephone you immediately and arrange a convenient delivery time. We regret the inconvenience this delay has caused you.

Sincerely,

Justin Upton

① 영업시간 변경을 공지하려고

② 고객 서비스 만족도를 조사하려고

③ 상품의 배송 지연에 대해 설명하려고

④ 구매한 상품의 환불 절차를 안내하려고

⑤ 배송된 상품의 파손에 대해 항의하려고

정답과 해설 p.10

STEP 3 • 수능 지문 제대로 복습하기

01 Dear Mr. Stevens, // This is a reply to your inquiry / about the shipment status of the desk / you purchased at our store / on September 26.
목적격 관계대명사 that(which)생략

02 Unfortunately, / the delivery of your desk / will take longer than expected / due to the damage / that occurred during the shipment / from the furniture manufacturer to our warehouse.
전치사(~때문에) 명사 주격 관계대명사

03 We have ordered an exact replacement from the manufacturer, / and we expect / that delivery will take place / within two weeks.
현재완료

04 As soon as the desk arrives, / we will telephone you immediately / and arrange a convenient delivery time.
~하자마자(시간) 시간의 부사절에서는 현재시제가 미래를 대신함

05 We regret the inconvenience / this delay has caused you. // Sincerely, Justin Upton
목적격 관계대명사 생략 cause(4형식)+간접 목적어+직접 목적어(~에게 ~을 안겨주다)

01 Stevens 씨께, // 이것은 문의**inquiry**에 대한 회신입니다 / 책상의 배송**shipment** 상황에 대한 / 당신이 우리 가게에서 구매한**purchase** / 9월 26일에.

02 불행히도, / 당신의 책상 배송**delivery**이 / 예상된 것보다 더 오래 걸릴 것입니다 / 파손 때문에 / 배송되는 동안 발생한 / 가구 제조업체**manufacturer**에서 우리 창고**warehouse**로.

03 우리는 제조업체로부터 똑같은 대체품**replacement**을 주문했고, / 예상합니다**expect** / 그 배송이 이뤄질 것으로 / 2주 안에.

04 그 책상이 도착하자마자 / 우리는 당신에게 바로**immediately** 전화해서 / 편리한**convenient** 배송 시간을 정할 것입니다.

05 우리는 불편에 대해 유감으로 생각합니다**regret** / 이 지연**delay**이 당신에게 일으킨**cause**. // 진심을 담아, Justin Upton 드림

구문 Check up

① Unfortunately, the delivery of your desk will take longer than expected [due to / because] the damage that occurred during the shipment from the furniture manufacturer to our warehouse.

뒤에 관계대명사절의 수식을 받는 명사구가 나오므로 전치사 due to가 적절하다.

② As soon as the desk [arrives / will arrive], we will telephone you immediately and arrange a convenient delivery time.

시간과 조건의 부사절에서는 현재시제가 미래시제를 대신하므로 현재 동사인 arrives가 적절하다.

정답 ① due to ② arrives

G

필자의 주장 ⊕

STEP 1 • 수능에 진짜 나오는 단어

✔ 문제에 나오는 단어들을 확인하세요.

시간이 없다면 색으로 표시된 단어만이라도 꼭 외우고 넘어가세요!

01	judge	v. 판단하다	(✔ judge) him guilty	그를 유죄로 판단하다
02	action	n. 행동	put more value in ( )	행동에 더 많은 가치를 두다
03	volume	n. 음량(볼륨), 소리	speak ( )s louder	더 큰 소리로 말하다
04	exhibit	v. 보여주다, 전시하다	( ) new products	새로운 제품을 보여주다
05	reserve	v. 유보하다, 연기하다	( ) judgement	판단을 유보하다
06	define	v. 규정하다, 정의하다	( )d by their behavior	그들의 행동으로 정의되는
07	bossy	a. 거만한	the ( ) one	거들먹거리는 사람
08	mean	a. 심술궂은, 비열한	( ) things	비열한 일들
09	desirable	a. 바람직한	( ) behavior	바람직한 행동
10	assumption	n. 추측, 추정	make an ( )	추정하다
11	eliminate	v. 지우다, 없애다	( ) mosquitoes	모기를 없애다
12	observation	n. 관찰	a brief ( )	단시간의 관찰

⊕ 본문 문장 속에서 단어들을 확인해 보세요.

However, / when someone exhibits some difficult behavior, / you might want to reserve judgement / for later.

하지만, / 누군가가 난해한 행동을 보일 때, / 여러분은 판단을 유보하기를 원할 수도 있다 / 나중으로.

단어 다시보기 문제를 풀기 전에 단어들을 30초 동안 다시 확인하세요.

01	judge	판단하다	judge him guilty	그를 유죄로 판단하다
02	action		put more value in action	행동에 더 많은 가치를 두다
03	volume		speak volumes louder	더 큰 소리로 말하다
04	exhibit		exhibit new products	새로운 제품을 보여주다
05	reserve		reserve judgement	판단을 유보하다
06	define		defined by their behavior	그들의 행동으로 정의되는
07	bossy		the bossy one	거들먹거리는 사람
08	mean		mean things	비열한 일들
09	desirable		desirable behavior	바람직한 행동
10	assumption		make an assumption	추정하다
11	eliminate		eliminate mosquitoes	모기를 없애다
12	observation		a brief observation	단시간의 관찰

⊕ 본문 문장 속에서 단어의 의미를 우리말로 해석해 보세요.

However, / when someone exhibits some difficult behavior, / you might want to reserve judgement / for later.

→ 하지만, / 누군가가 난해한 행동을 ________ 때, / 여러분은 ________________를 원할 수도 있다 / 나중으로.

2017 9월 학평 20번 문제

제한시간 60초

난이도 ★★☆☆☆

STEP 2 • 수능 기출 제대로 풀기

G

다음 글에서 필자가 주장하는 바로 가장 적절한 것은?

It is easy to judge people based on their actions. We are often taught to put more value in actions than words, and for good reason. The actions of others often speak volumes louder than their words. However, when someone exhibits some difficult behavior, you might want to reserve judgement for later. People are not always defined by their behavior. It is common to think, "He is so bossy," or "She is so mean," after observing less-than-desirable behavior in someone. But you should never make such assumptions right away. You should give someone a second chance before you label them and shut them out forever. You may find a great co-worker or best friend in someone, so don't eliminate a person from your life based on a brief observation.

① 단시간의 관찰로 타인을 성급하게 판단하지 마라.

② 자신의 적성을 찾기 위해 다양한 경험을 쌓아라.

③ 바람직하지 않은 습관을 고치기 위해 노력하라.

④ 원만한 인간관계를 위해 칭찬을 아끼지 마라.

⑤ 말보다는 행동으로 삶의 모범을 보여라.

정답과 해설 p.10

STEP 3 • 수능 지문 제대로 복습하기

01 It is easy to judge people / based on their actions. // We are often taught / to put more value in actions than words, / and for good reason.
가주어(it) 진주어(to부정사) <teach+목적어+to부정사>의 수동태

02 The actions of others often speak volumes louder / than their words.
-er than: 비교급

03 However, / when someone exhibits some difficult behavior, / you might want to reserve judgement / for later.
부사절 접속사

04 People are not always defined by their behavior. // It is common to think, / "He is so bossy," / or "She is so mean," / after observing less-than-desirable behavior in someone.
부분 부정: 항상 ~하는 것은 아니다 가주어 진주어 <접속사+-ing>의 분사구문

05 But you should never make such assumptions right away. // You should give someone a second chance / before you label them / and shut them out forever.
give+간접목적어+직접목적어

06 You may find a great co-worker or best friend in someone, / so don't eliminate a person from your life / based on a brief observation.

01 사람들을 판단하는**judge** 것은 쉽다 / 행동을 기반으로. // 우리는 종종 배운다 / 말보다 행동**action**에 더 많은 가치를 두도록, / 그리고 그럴 만한 충분한 이유가 있다.

02 다른 사람의 행동은 종종 더 큰 소리**volume**로 말한다 / 그들의 말보다.

03 하지만, / 누군가가 난해한 행동을 보일 때**exhibit**, / 여러분은 판단을 유보하기**reserve judgement**를 원할 수도 있다 / 나중으로.

04 사람들은 항상 그들의 행동으로 정의되는**define** 것은 아니다. // 보통 생각한다 / "그는 너무 거들먹거려**bossy**," / 또는 "그녀는 너무 심술궂어**mean**,"라고 / 누군가의 별로 바람직하지**desirable** 않은 행동을 관찰한 후에.

05 그러나 여러분은 그러한 추측**assumption**을 즉시 내려서는 안 된다. // 여러분은 다시 한 번 기회를 줘야 한다 / 그들을 낙인 찍기 전에 / 그리고 영원히 차단해 버리기 전에.

06 여러분은 누군가가 훌륭한 동료 또는 절친한 친구라는 것을 알게 될 수도 있다, / 그러므로 사람을 여러분의 삶에서 제거하지**eliminate** 말라 / 단시간의 관찰**a brief observation**을 근거로.

구문 Check up

① It is easy judge / to judge people based on their actions.

가주어 it에 대한 진주어로는 to부정사가 적절하므로 to judge를 쓴다.

② We often teach / are often taught to put more value in actions than words, and for good reason.

teach는 '가르치다'라는 의미이고 문맥상 '우리가 ~하도록 배운다'라는 뜻이 적절하기 때문에 수동태 are taught를 쓴다.

정답 ① to judge ② are often taught

Review

DAY 01~03

☑ 종합 성적표

구분	공부한 날 ❶	결과 분석			틀린 이유 ❸
		출처	풀이 시간 ❷	채점 결과 (O, X)	
Day 1	월 일	학력평가 기출 2023년	분 초		
		학력평가 기출 2022년	분 초		
		학력평가 기출 2021년	분 초		
		학력평가 기출 2020년	분 초		
		학력평가 기출 2019년	분 초		
		학력평가 기출 2018년	분 초		
		학력평가 기출 2017년	분 초		
Day 2	월 일	학력평가 기출 2023년	분 초		
		학력평가 기출 2022년	분 초		
		학력평가 기출 2021년	분 초		
		학력평가 기출 2020년	분 초		
		학력평가 기출 2019년	분 초		
		학력평가 기출 2018년	분 초		
		학력평가 기출 2017년	분 초		
Day 3	월 일	학력평가 기출 2023년	분 초		
		학력평가 기출 2022년	분 초		
		학력평가 기출 2021년	분 초		
		학력평가 기출 2020년	분 초		
		학력평가 기출 2019년	분 초		
		학력평가 기출 2018년	분 초		
		학력평가 기출 2017년	분 초		

3일간 공부한 내용을 다시 보니, ……

❶ **매일 지문을 하루 계획에 맞춰 풀었다. vs. 내가 한 약속을 못 지켰다.**

<매3영 고1 기출>은 단순 문제풀이를 위한 책이 아니라, 매일 규칙적으로 영어를 공부하는 습관을 잡는 책입니다. 따라서 푸는 문제 개수는 상황에 따라 다르더라도 '매일' 학습하는 것이 중요합니다.

❷ **주어진 시간을 자꾸 넘긴다?**

풀이 시간이 계속해서 권장 시간을 넘긴다면 실전 훈련이 부족하다는 신호입니다. 아직 조급함을 가질 필요는 없지만, 매일의 문제 풀이에 더 긴장감 있게 임해보세요.

❸ **틀린 이유 맞춤 솔루션**: 오답 이유에 따라 다음 해결책을 참고하세요.

(1) 단어를 많이 몰라서

▶ <STEP 1 단어>에 제시된 필수 어휘를 매일 챙겨보고, SELF-TEST까지 꼼꼼히 진행합니다.

(2) 문장 해석이 잘 안 돼서

▶ <STEP 3 지문 복습>의 구문 첨삭과 끊어읽기 해설을 정독하며 문장구조를 보는 눈을 길러보세요.

(3) 해석은 되지만 내용이 이해가 안 되거나, 선택지로 연결을 못 해서

▶ <정답과 해설>의 해설과 오답풀이를 참고해 틀린 이유를 깊이 고민하고 정리해 보세요.

!

결론적으로, 내가 **취약한 부분**은 ____________ 이다. **취약점을 보완하기 위해서** 나는 ____________ 을/를 해야겠다.

3일 뒤 다시 봐야 할 문항과, 꼭 다시 외워야 할 사항·구문 등이 있는 페이지는 지금 바로 접어 두세요.

<매3영>이 제시하는 3단계로

유형 3일 훈련

DAY 04~06

공부한 날			출처	페이지
DAY 4	월	일	학력평가 기출 2023년 학력평가 기출 2022년 학력평가 기출 2021년 학력평가 기출 2020년 학력평가 기출 2019년 학력평가 기출 2018년 학력평가 기출 2016년	95
DAY 5	월	일	학력평가 기출 2023년 학력평가 기출 2022년 학력평가 기출 2021년 학력평가 기출 2020년 학력평가 기출 2019년 학력평가 기출 2018년 학력평가 기출 2017년	123
DAY 6	월	일	학력평가 기출 2023년 학력평가 기출 2022년 학력평가 기출 2021년 학력평가 기출 2020년 학력평가 기출 2019년 학력평가 기출 2018년 학력평가 기출 2017년	151

DAY 04

A

도표의 이해

STEP 1 • 수능에 진짜 나오는 단어

문제에 나오는 단어들을 확인하세요.

01	share	n. 점유율
02	land	n. 토지, 땅
03	region	n. 지역
04	decline	v. 감소하다
05	among	prep. ~ 중에서
06	gap	n. 격차, 차이
07	in terms of	~ 면에서

시간이 없다면 색으로 표시된 단어만이라도 꼭 외우고 넘어가세요!

Africa's (✓ share) of forest area	아프리카의 산림 면적의 점유율
the share of forest area in total (　　　) area	총 토지 면적에서 산림 면적의 점유율
by (　　　)	지역별로
The share (　　　)d from 1990 to 2019.	점유율은 1990년부터 2019년까지 감소했다.
the largest (　　　) the five regions	다섯 개 지역 중에서 가장 큰
the smallest (　　　) between 1990 and 2019	1990년과 2019년 사이의 가장 작은 격차
(　　) (　　　) (　　) the share of forest area	산림 면적의 점유율 면에서

⊕ 본문 문장 속에서 단어들을 확인해 보세요.

The above graph shows / the share of forest area in total land area by region / in 1990 and 2019.

위 도표는 보여준다 / 지역별 총 토지 면적에서 산림 면적의 점유율을 / 1990년과 2019년의.

단어 다시보기 문제를 풀기 전에 단어들을 30초 동안 다시 확인하세요.

01	share	점유율	Africa's share of forest area	아프리카의 산림 면적의 점유율
02	land		the share of forest area in total land area	총 토지 면적에서 산림 면적의 점유율
03	region		by region	지역별로
04	decline		The share declined from 1990 to 2019.	점유율은 1990년부터 2019년까지 감소했다.
05	among		the largest among the five regions	다섯 개 지역 중에서 가장 큰
06	gap		the smallest gap between 1990 and 2019	1990년과 2019년 사이의 가장 작은 격차
07	in terms of		in terms of the share of forest area	산림 면적의 점유율 면에서

⊕ 본문 문장 속에서 단어의 의미를 우리말로 해석해 보세요.

The above graph shows / the share of forest area in total land area by region / in 1990 and 2019.

→ 위 도표는 보여준다 / ____________________ / 1990년과 2019년의.

2023 6월 학평 25번 문제

제한시간 60초

난이도 ★★☆☆☆

STEP 2 • 수능 기출 제대로 풀기

A

다음 도표의 내용과 일치하지 않는 것은?

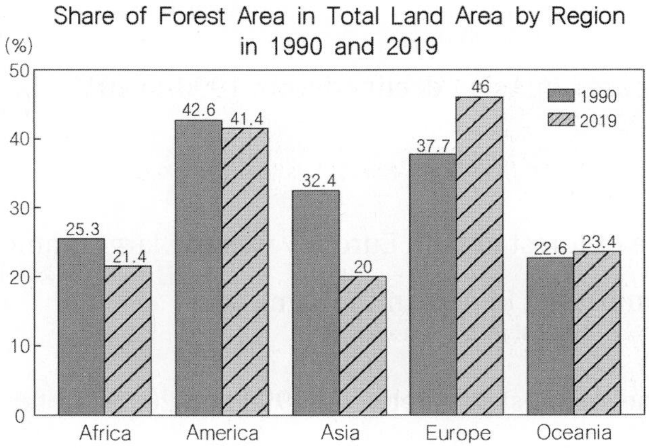

The above graph shows the share of forest area in total land area by region in 1990 and 2019. ① Africa's share of forest area in total land area was over 20% in both 1990 and 2019. ② The share of forest area in America was 42.6% in 1990, which was larger than that in 2019. ③ The share of forest area in Asia declined from 1990 to 2019 by more than 10 percentage points. ④ In 2019, the share of forest area in Europe was the largest among the five regions, more than three times that in Asia in the same year. ⑤ Oceania showed the smallest gap between 1990 and 2019 in terms of the share of forest area in total land area.

정답과 해설 p.11

STEP 3 • 수능 지문 제대로 복습하기

01 The above graph shows / the share of forest area in total land area by region / in 1990 and 2019.
목적어

02 Africa's share of forest area in total land area / was over 20% in both 1990 and 2019.
주어(단수) 동사

03 The share of forest area in America / was 42.6% in 1990, / which was larger than that in 2019.
선행사 계속적 용법

04 The share of forest area in Asia / declined from 1990 to 2019 / by more than 10 percentage points.
~만큼

05 In 2019, / the share of forest area in Europe / was the largest among the five regions, / more than three times that in Asia in the same year.
최상급+among: ~ 중에서 가장 …한
~ 이상, 넘게 (=the share of forest area)

06 Oceania showed the smallest gap between 1990 and 2019 / in terms of the share of forest area in total land area.
~ 면에서, ~에 있어

01 위 도표는 보여준다 / 지역별 총 토지 면적에서 산림 면적의 점유율을**the share of forest area in total land area by region** / 1990년과 2019년의.

02 아프리카의 전체 토지 면적에서 산림 면적의 점유율이 / 1990년과 2019년 둘 다 20%를 넘었다.

03 아메리카의 산림 면적 점유율은 / 1990년에 42.6%였고, / 이는 2019년의 그것보다 더 컸다.

04 아시아의 산림 면적 점유율은 / 1990년부터 2019년까지 감소했다**decline** / 10퍼센트포인트 넘게.

05 2019년 / 유럽의 산림 면적 점유율은 / 다섯 개 지역 중에서**among** 가장 컸고, / 같은 해 아시아에서의 비율의 세 배(→두 배)가 넘었다.

06 오세아니아는 1990년과 2019년 사이에 가장 작은 차이**gap**를 보였다 / 총 토지 면적에서의 산림 면적의 점유율 면에서**in terms of.**

구문 Check up

① The share of forest area in America was 42.6% in 1990, that / which was larger than that in 2019.

that은 계속적 용법으로 쓸 수 없으므로, 콤마 뒤의 관계대명사로 which가 적절하다.

② In 2019, the share of forest area in Europe was the largest among the five regions, more than three times those / that in Asia in the same year.

the share of forest area를 받는 단수 지시대명사가 필요하므로 that이 적절하다.

정답 ① which ② that

B

도표의 이해 +

STEP 1 • 수능에 진짜 나오는 단어

✔ 문제에 나오는 단어들을 확인하세요.

시간이 없다면 색으로 표시된 단어만이라도 꼭 외우고 넘어가세요!

01	above	a. 위의	the (✔ above) graph	위의 도표
02	percentage	n. 비율	the ( ) of people	사람들의 비율
03	material	n. 자료	online learning ( )s	온라인 학습 자료
04	least	a. 가장 적은 ad. 가장 적게(덜)	the ( ) important	가장 덜 중요한
05	be likely to	~할 것 같다, ~할 가능성이 있다	( ) ( ) ( ) use online courses	온라인 강의를 이용할 가능성이 있다
06	gap	n. 차이	the ( ) between those	그것들 사이의 차이
07	one in five	다섯 중 하나	more than ( ) ( ) ( ) people	다섯 명 중 한 명 이상의 사람

⊕ 본문 문장 속에서 단어들을 확인해 보세요.

Those aged 65 and older / were the least likely to use online courses / among the six age groups.

65세 이상인 사람들이 / 온라인 강의를 이용할 가능성이 가장 낮았다 / 여섯 개의 연령 집단 가운데서.

단어 다시보기 문제를 풀기 전에 단어들을 30초 동안 다시 확인하세요.

01	above	위의	the above graph	위의 도표
02	percentage		the percentage of people	사람들의 비율
03	material		online learning materials	온라인 학습 자료
04	least		the least important	가장 덜 중요한
05	be likely to		be likely to use online courses	온라인 강의를 이용할 가능성이 있다
06	gap		the gap between those	그것들 사이의 차이
07	one in five		more than one in five people	다섯 명 중 한 명 이상의 사람

⊕ 본문 문장 속에서 단어의 의미를 우리말로 해석해 보세요.

Those aged 65 and older / were the least likely to use online courses / among the six age groups.

→ 65세 이상인 사람들이 / 온라인 강의를 이용할 __________ / 여섯 개의 연령 집단 가운데서.

2022 3월 학평 25번 문제

제한시간 70초
난이도 ★★★☆☆

STEP 2 • 수능 기출 제대로 풀기

B

다음 도표의 내용과 일치하지 않는 것은?

Percentage of UK People
Who Used Online Course and Online Learning Material
(in 2020, by age group)

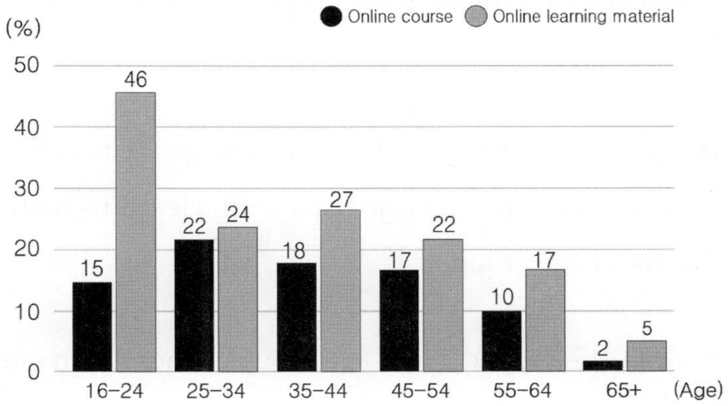

The above graph shows the percentage of people in the UK who used online courses and online learning materials, by age group in 2020. ① In each age group, the percentage of people who used online learning materials was higher than that of people who used online courses. ② The 25-34 age group had the highest percentage of people who used online courses in all the age groups. ③ Those aged 65 and older were the least likely to use online courses among the six age groups. ④ Among the six age groups, the gap between the percentage of people who used online courses and that of people who used online learning materials was the greatest in the 16-24 age group. ⑤ In each of the 35-44, 45-54, and 55-64 age groups, more than one in five people used online learning materials.

정답과 해설 p.11

STEP 3 • 수능 지문 제대로 복습하기

01 The above graph shows the percentage of people in the UK / who used online courses and online learning materials, / by age group / in 2020.
주격 관계대명사절

02 In each age group, / the percentage of people who used online learning materials / was higher than that of people who used online courses.
주격 관계대명사절 (=the percentage) 주격 관계대명사절

03 The 25-34 age group had the highest percentage / of people who used online courses / in all the age groups.
주격 관계대명사절

04 Those aged 65 and older / were the least likely to use online courses / among the six age groups.
과거분사

05 Among the six age groups, / the gap / [between the percentage of people who used online courses / and that of people who used online learning materials] / was the greatest / in the 16-24 age group.
주어 주격 관계대명사절 주격 관계대명사절 동사(단수)

06 In each of the 35-44, 45-54, and 55-64 age groups, / more than one in five people / used online learning materials.

01 위above 도표는 영국 사람들의 비율percentage을 보여준다 / 온라인 강의와 온라인 학습 자료material를 이용한 (영국 사람들) / 연령 집단별로 / 2020년도에.

02 각 연령 집단에서, / 온라인 학습 자료를 이용한 사람들의 비율이 / 온라인 강의를 이용한 사람들의 비율보다 더 높았다.

03 25세에서 34세 연령 집단이 비율이 가장 높았다 / 온라인 강의를 이용한 사람들의 (비율) / 모든 연령 집단 중.

04 65세 이상인 사람들이 / 온라인 강의를 이용할 가능성이 가장 낮았다be the least likely to / 여섯 개의 연령 집단 가운데서.

05 여섯 개의 연령 집단 가운데서, / 차이gap는 / 온라인 강의를 이용한 사람들의 비율과 / 온라인 학습 자료를 이용한 사람들의 비율 간의 / 가장 컸다 / 16세에서 24세 연령 집단에서.

06 35세에서 44세, 45세에서 54세, 55세에서 64세(→삭제)의 각 연령 집단에서, / 다섯 명 중 한 명one in five 이상의 사람들이 / 온라인 학습 자료를 이용했다.

구문 Check up

① The percentage of people who used online learning materials was higher than that / those of people who used online courses.

the percentage를 대신하는 대명사이므로 단수 표현인 that이 적절하다.

② The gap between the percentage of people who used online courses and that of people who used online learning materials was / were the greatest in the 16-24 age group.

이 문장의 주어는 The gap이므로 단수로 수 일치하여 was를 쓴다.

정답 ① that ② was

C

도표의 이해

STEP 1 • 수능에 진짜 나오는 단어

✔ 문제에 나오는 단어들을 확인하세요.

시간이 없다면 색으로 표시된 단어만이라도 꼭 외우고 넘어가세요!

01	source	n. 출처	information (✔ source)s	정보의 출처
02	survey	n. 설문 조사 v. 조사하다	based on a ( )	설문 조사에 기반하여
03	customer	n. 고객, 소비자	users or ( )s	사용자들이나 고객들
04	hold	v. 가지다, 지니다	( ) trust	믿음을 갖다
05	distrust	n. 불신 v. 불신하다	hold ( )	불신을 갖다
06	gap	n. 차이	the smallest ( )	가장 작은 차이
07	one-fifth	n. 5분의 1	fewer than ( )	5분의 1보다 적은
08	A be outweighed by B	B가 A를 능가하다	The benefits ( ) ( ) ( ) the risks.	위험이 이득을 능가한다.
09	three times	세 배	more than ( ) ( )	세 배 이상의

⊕ 본문 문장 속에서 단어들을 확인해 보세요.

Fewer than one-fifth of adults say / they trust information from television advertising, / outweighed by the share / who distrust such information.

미국 성인의 5분의 1보다 적은 수치가 말했는데 / 그들이 텔레비전 광고로부터의 정보를 신뢰한다고, / 이것을 그 점유율이 능가했다 / 그러한 정보를 불신하는.

단어 다시보기 문제를 풀기 전에 단어들을 30초 동안 다시 확인하세요.

01	source	출처	information sources	정보의 출처
02	survey		based on a survey	설문 조사에 기반하여
03	customer		users or customers	사용자들이나 고객들
04	hold		hold trust	믿음을 갖다
05	distrust		hold distrust	불신을 갖다
06	gap		the smallest gap	가장 작은 차이
07	one-fifth		fewer than one-fifth	5분의 1보다 적은
08	A be outweighed by B		The benefits are outweighed by the risks.	위험이 이득을 능가한다.
09	three times		more than three times	세 배 이상의

⊕ 본문 문장 속에서 단어의 의미를 우리말로 해석해 보세요.

Fewer than one-fifth of adults say / they trust information from television advertising, / outweighed by the share / who distrust such information.

→ 미국 성인의 ________ 수치가 말했는데 / 그들이 텔레비전 광고로부터의 정보를 신뢰한다고, / ________ ________ / 그러한 정보를 ________.

2021 9월 학평 25번 문제

제한시간 60초

난이도 ★★☆☆☆

STEP 2 • 수능 기출 제대로 풀기

C

다음 도표의 내용과 일치하지 않는 것은?

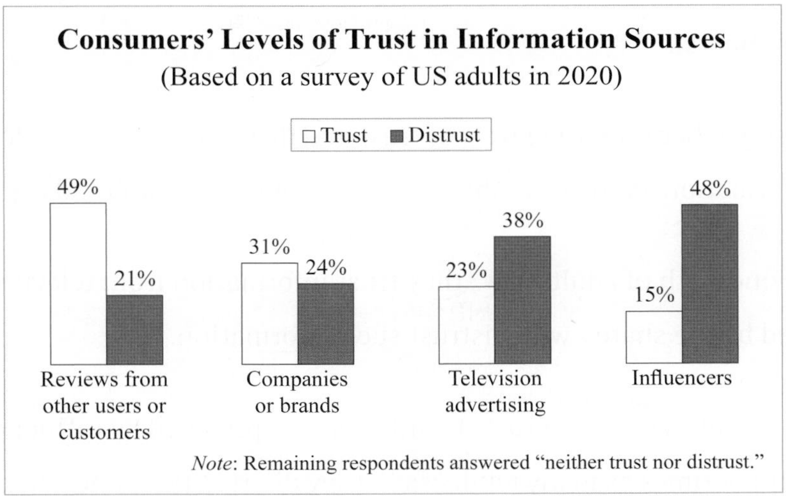

The graph above shows the consumers' levels of trust in four different types of information sources, based on a survey of US adults in 2020. ① About half of US adults say they trust the information they receive from reviews from other users or customers. ② This is more than double those who say they hold distrust for reviews from other users or customers. ③ The smallest gap between the levels of trust and distrust among the four different types of information sources is shown in the companies or brands' graph. ④ Fewer than one-fifth of adults say they trust information from television advertising, outweighed by the share who distrust such information. ⑤ Only 15% of adults say they trust the information provided by influencers, while more than three times as many adults say they distrust the same source of information.

정답과 해설 p.11

STEP 3 • 수능 지문 제대로 복습하기

01 The graph above shows the consumers' levels of trust / in four different types of information sources, / based on a survey of US adults in 2020.

02 About half of US adults say / they trust the information / they receive from reviews from other users or customers.
(주어(half of+복수명사) / 동사(adults에 수 일치) / 목적격 관계대명사 생략)

03 This is more than double / those [who say they hold distrust / for reviews from other users or customers].
(주격 관계대명사절 / 명사절 접속사 that 생략)

04 The smallest gap between the levels of trust and distrust / among the four different types of information sources / is shown / in the companies or brands' graph.
(주어 / 동사(수동태))

05 Fewer than one-fifth of adults say / they trust information from television advertising, outweighed by the share / who distrust such information.
(which is 생략 / 명사절 접속사 that 생략 / 주격 관계대명사절)

06 Only 15% of adults say / they trust the information provided by influencers, / while more than three times as many adults say / they distrust the same source of information.
(명사절 접속사 that 생략 / 과거분사구 / ~인 반면에 / (as 15%) / 배수표현(배수사+as+원급+as))

01 위 그래프는 소비자의 신뢰 정도를 보여준다 / 네 가지 다른 종류의 정보 출처**source**들에 대한 / 2020년 미국 성인들을 대상으로 한 설문 조사에 기반하여**based on a survey**.

02 미국 성인의 절반 정도가 말했다 / 정보를 믿는다고 / 다른 사용자들이나 고객**customer**들로부터의 상품평에서 얻은.

03 이것은 두 배 이상이다 / 불신을 갖는다고**hold distrust** 말한 사람들의 / 다른 사용자들이나 고객들로부터의 상품평에 대해.

04 신뢰와 불신 정도 사이의 가장 작은 차이**gap**는 / 네 가지 다른 종류의 정보 출처들 중에서 / 보인다 / 회사나 상표의 그래프에서.

05 미국 성인의 5분의 1보다 적은(→많은) 수치**fewer than one-fifth**가 말했는데 / 그들이 텔레비전 광고로부터의 정보를 신뢰한다고, / 이것을 그 점유율이 능가했다**be outweighed by** / 그러한 정보를 불신하는.

06 미국 성인의 15%만 말했다 / 인플루언서에게 제공받은 정보를 신뢰한다고, / 반면에 세 배 이상의**more than three times** 미국 성인들이 말했다 / 바로 그 정보 출처를 불신한다고.

구문 Check up

① About half of US adults [say / says] they trust the information they receive from reviews from other users or customers.

주어에 부분을 나타내는 명사(half)가 쓰였으므로, of 뒤에 오는 전체 명사에 수 일치한다. 즉 US adults가 복수이므로, 복수형 say가 적절하다.

② The smallest gap between the levels of trust and distrust among the four different types of information sources [shows / is shown] in the companies or brands' graph.

주어인 '가장 작은 차이(The smallest gap)'가 그래프에서 보여지는 것이므로 수동태인 is shown을 쓴다.

정답 ① say ② is shown

D

도표의 이해 +

STEP 1 • 수능에 진짜 나오는 단어

✔ 문제에 나오는 단어들을 확인하세요.

시간이 없다면 색으로 표시된 단어만이라도 꼭 외우고 넘어가세요!

01	device	n. 기기, 장치	the most important (✓ device)	가장 중요한 기기
02	access	n. 접속 v. 접속하다	Internet ( )	인터넷 접속
03	consider	v. 고려하다	British people ( )	영국민이 고려하다
04	a third	1/3(3분의 1)	( ) ( ) of internet users	인터넷 사용자의 1/3
05	overtake	v. 압도하다	( ) the laptop	노트북을 압도하다
06	in contrast	대조적으로	( ) ( ) = on the contrary	대조적으로

⊕ 본문 문장 속에서 단어들을 확인해 보세요.

More than a third of UK Internet users / considered smartphones to be their most important device / for accessing the Internet / in 2016.

3분의 1이 넘는 영국 인터넷 사용자들은 / 스마트폰을 그들의 가장 중요한 장치로 생각했다 / 인터넷 접속을 위한 / 2016년에.

단어 다시보기 문제를 풀기 전에 단어들을 30초 동안 다시 확인하세요.

01	device	기기, 장치	the most important device	가장 중요한 기기
02	access		Internet access	인터넷 접속
03	consider		British people consider	영국민이 고려하다
04	a third		a third of Internet users	인터넷 사용자의 1/3
05	overtake		overtake the laptop	노트북을 압도하다
06	in contrast		in contrast = on the contrary	대조적으로

⊕ **본문 문장 속에서 단어의 의미를 우리말로 해석해 보세요.**

More than a third of UK Internet users / considered smartphones to be their most important device / for accessing the Internet / in 2016.

→ 3분의 1이 넘는 영국 인터넷 사용자들은 / 스마트폰을 ________________로 ________ / ________을 위한 / 2016년에.

2020 6월 학평 25번 문제

제한시간 70초

난이도 ★★★☆☆

STEP 2 • 수능 기출 제대로 풀기

D

다음 도표의 내용과 일치하지 않는 것은?

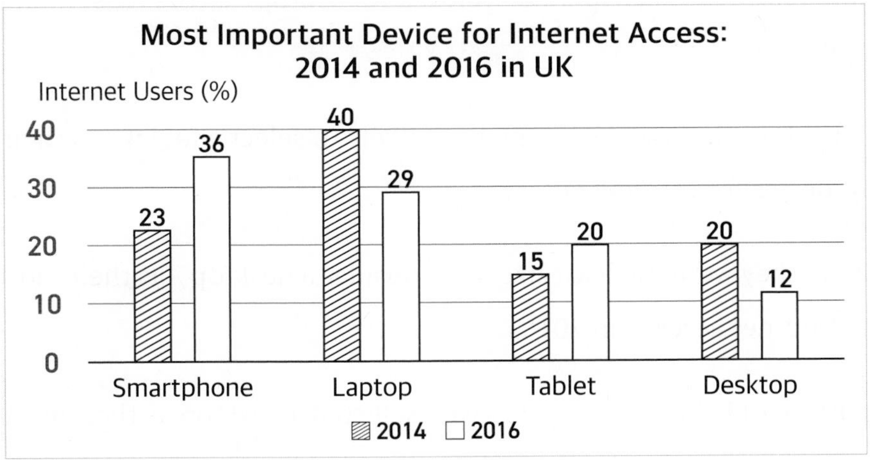

The above graph shows what devices British people considered the most important when connecting to the Internet in 2014 and 2016. ① More than a third of UK Internet users considered smartphones to be their most important device for accessing the Internet in 2016. ② In the same year, the smartphone overtook the laptop as the most important device for Internet access. ③ In 2014, UK Internet users were the least likely to select a tablet as their most important device for Internet access. ④ In contrast, they were the least likely to consider a desktop as their most important device for Internet access in 2016. ⑤ The proportion of UK Internet users who selected a desktop as their most important device for Internet access increased by half from 2014 to 2016.

*proportion: 비율

정답과 해설 p.12

STEP 3 • 수능 지문 제대로 복습하기

01 The above graph shows / [what devices British people considered the most important / when connecting to the Internet / in 2014 and 2016].
(what: 의문형용사(어떤)+명사+주어+동사 / when connecting to the Internet: <접속사+-ing>의 분사구문)

02 More than a third of UK Internet users / considered smartphones to be their most important device / for accessing the Internet / in 2016.
(a third of UK Internet users: 주어(부분+of+전체) / considered: 5형식 동사 / smartphones: 목적어 / to be their most important device: 목적격 보어 / for accessing: 전치사+ -ing)

03 In the same year, / the smartphone overtook the laptop / as the most important device for Internet access.
(as: 전치사(~로서))

04 In 2014, / UK Internet users were the least likely to select a tablet / as their most important device for Internet access.

05 In contrast, / they were the least likely to consider a desktop / as their most important device for Internet access / in 2016.

06 The proportion of UK Internet users / who selected a desktop as their most important device for Internet access / increased by half from 2014 to 2016.
(The proportion of UK Internet users: 주어 / who selected ... access: 주격 관계대명사절 / increased: 동사 / by: ~만큼)

01 위 도표는 보여 준다 / 영국인들이 어떤 장치**device**들을 가장 중요하다고 생각했는지**consider**를 / 인터넷 접속을 할 때 / 2014년과 2016년에.

02 3분의 1이 넘는**more than a third** 영국 인터넷 사용자들은 / 스마트폰을 가장 중요한 장치로 생각했다 / 인터넷 접속**access the Internet**을 위한 / 2016년에.

03 같은 해에, / 스마트폰이 노트북을 추월하였다**overtake the laptop** / 인터넷 접속을 위해 가장 중요한 장치로서.

04 2014년에, / 영국 인터넷 사용자들은 태블릿을 가장 적게 선택하는 경향이 있었다 / 인터넷 접속을 위한 가장 중요한 장치로.

05 대조적으로**in contrast**, / 그들은 데스크톱을 가장 적게 선택하는 경향이 있었다 / 인터넷 접속을 위한 가장 중요한 장치로 / 2016년에는.

06 영국 인터넷 사용자들의 비율은 / 인터넷 접속을 위한 가장 중요한 장치로 데스크톱을 선택한 / 2016년도에 2014년도 비율의 절반만큼 증가하였다(→ 감소하였다).

구문 Check up

① The above graph shows what devices British people considered the most important when connects / connecting to the Internet in 2014 and 2016.

부사절의 주어가 없을 때는 <접속사+-ing/-ed>의 분사구문으로 쓸 수 있기 때문에 connecting이 정답이다.

② More than a third of UK Internet users considered smartphones to be their most important device for access / accessing the Internet in 2016.

the Internet을 목적어로 취하면서 동시에 전치사 for의 목적어 역할을 하는 동명사가 와야 하므로 accessing이 적절하다.

정답 ① connecting ② accessing

DAY 04

E

도표의 이해

STEP 1 • 수능에 진짜 나오는 단어

✔ 문제에 나오는 단어들을 확인하세요.

시간이 없다면 색으로 표시된 단어만이라도 꼭 외우고 넘어가세요!

01	invention	n. 발명	health science (✔ invention)	건강 과학 발명
02	interest	n. 흥미	invention ( )s	발명 흥미
03	web-based	a. 웹 기반의	( ) invention	웹 기반의 발명품
04	environmental	a. 환경의	( ) invention	환경 관련 발명
05	survey	n. 조사	a ( ) on invention interests	발명 흥미에 대한 조사
06	category	n. 범주	the five invention ( )ies	다섯 개의 발명 범주
07	male	a. 남성의 n. 남성	a ( ) respondent	남성 응답자
08	respondent	n. 응답자	the percentage of male ( )s	남성 응답자의 비율
09	female	a. 여성의 n. 여성	a ( ) respondent	여성 응답자
10	gap	n. 차이	the ( ) between males and females	남성과 여성의 차이
11	gender	n. 성별	each ( ) group	각 성별 집단

⊕ 본문 문장 속에서 단어들을 확인해 보세요.

Among the five invention categories, / the highest percentage of male respondents / showed interest / in inventing consumer products.

다섯 개의 발명 범주 중에서 / 가장 높은 비율의 남성 응답자가 / 흥미를 나타냈다 / 소비재를 발명하는 것에 대해.

단어 다시보기 문제를 풀기 전에 단어들을 30초 동안 다시 확인하세요.

01	invention	발명	health science invention	건강 과학 발명
02	interest		invention interests	발명 흥미
03	web-based		web-based invention	웹 기반의 발명품
04	environmental		environmental invention	환경 관련 발명
05	survey		a survey on invention interests	발명 흥미에 대한 조사
06	category		the five invention categories	다섯 개의 발명 범주
07	male		a male respondent	남성 응답자
08	respondent		the percentage of male respondents	남성 응답자의 비율
09	female		a female respondent	여성 응답자
10	gap		the gap between males and females	남성과 여성의 차이
11	gender		each gender group	각 성별 집단

⊕ **본문 문장 속에서 단어의 의미를 우리말로 해석해 보세요.**

Among the five invention categories, / the highest percentage of male respondents / showed interest / in inventing consumer products.

→ 다섯 개의 __________ 중에서 / 가장 높은 비율의 __________가 / __________를 나타냈다 / 소비재를 발명하는 것에 대해.

2019 9월 학평 25번 문제

제한시간 60초
난이도 ★★☆☆☆

STEP 2 • 수능 기출 제대로 풀기

E

다음 도표의 내용과 일치하지 않는 것은?

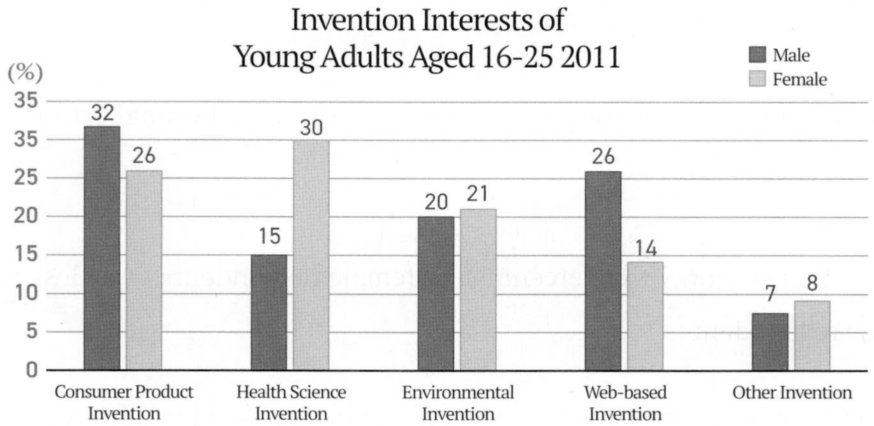

The graph above shows the results of a survey on invention interests in young adults aged 16 to 25 in 2011. ① Among the five invention categories, the highest percentage of male respondents showed interest in inventing consumer products. ② For health science invention, the percentage of female respondents was twice as high as that of male respondents. ③ The percentage point gap between males and females was the smallest in environmental invention. ④ For web-based invention, the percentage of female respondents was less than half that of male respondents. ⑤ In the category of other invention, the percentage of respondents from each gender group was less than 10 percent.

정답과 해설 p.12

STEP 3 • 수능 지문 제대로 복습하기

01 The graph above shows / the results of a survey on invention interests / in young adults aged 16 to 25 / in 2011.
과거분사

02 Among the five invention categories, / the highest percentage of male respondents / showed interest / in inventing consumer products.
~ 중에서(범위 표현) the+최상급(가장 ~한)

03 For health science invention, / the percentage of female respondents / was twice as high as that of male respondents.
(=the percentage)
배수 표현+as+원급+as…: …의 몇 배만큼 ~한

04 The percentage point gap between males and females / was the smallest / in environmental invention.
주어 동사(단수)

05 For web-based invention, / the percentage of female respondents / was less than half that of male respondents.
~보다 덜한
(=the percentage)

06 In the category of other invention, / the percentage of respondents from each gender group / was less than 10 percent.

01 위 그래프는 보여 준다 / 발명 흥미 분야에 관한 조사**a survey on invention interests**의 결과를 / 16세부터 25세까지의 청년들의 / 2011년에 실시한.

02 다섯 개 범주의 발명 분야**the five invention categories** 중에서 / 가장 높은 비율의 남성 응답자**male respondent**가 / 흥미를 나타냈다 / 소비재를 발명하는 것에 대해.

03 건강 과학 발명 분야에서, / 여성 응답자**female respondent**의 비율은 / 남성 응답자의 비율의 2배만큼 높았다.

04 남성과 여성 간 비율의 차이**gap**가 / 가장 작았다 / 환경**environmental** 관련 발명 분야에서.

05 웹 기반**web-based** 발명 분야에서, / 여성 응답자의 비율은 / 남성 응답자의 비율의 절반보다 적었다(→ 많았다).

06 기타 발명 분야의 범주에서 / 각 성별**gender** 집단의 응답자 비율은 / 10퍼센트보다 적었다.

구문 Check up

① For health science invention, the percentage of female respondents was twice as high / higher as that of male respondents.

배수표현은 원급과 비교급을 둘 다 활용할 수 있지만, as ~ as가 오면 때는 형용사나 부사의 원급을 쓴다. 따라서 high가 적절하다.

② For web-based invention, the percentage of female respondents was less than half those / that of male respondents.

단수명사인 the percentage끼리 비교하는 것이므로 단수대명사 that을 쓴다.

정답 ① high ② that

STEP 1 • 수능에 진짜 나오는 단어

✔ 문제에 나오는 단어들을 확인하세요.

시간이 없다면 색으로 표시된 단어만이라도 꼭 외우고 넘어가세요!

01	count	n. 계산, 집계	the medal (✔ count)	메달 집계
02	bronze	a. 청동의, 구릿빛의	( ) medals	동메달
03	graph	n. 그래프, 도표	the above ( )	위의 그래프
04	show	v. 보여주다	( ) the number	수를 보여주다
05	win	v. 이기다, (상을) 획득하다	( ) a medal	메달을 획득하다
06	based on	~에 기반하여, ~을 바탕으로	( ) ( ) the evidence	증거를 바탕으로
07	committee	n. 위원회	the International Olympic ( )	국제올림픽위원회
08	when it comes to	~의 경우, ~에 관해서	( ) ( ) ( ) ( ) gold medals	금메달의 경우
09	twice	ad. 두 배로	less than ( )	두 배보다 적은

⊕ 본문 문장 속에서 단어들을 확인해 보세요.

Of the 5 countries, / the United States won the most medals in total, / about 120.

5개 국가들 중, / 미국이 합계상 가장 많은 메달을 획득하였다 / 약 120개로.

단어 다시보기 문제를 풀기 전에 단어들을 30초 동안 다시 확인하세요.

01	count	계산, 집계	the medal count	메달 집계
02	bronze		bronze medals	동메달
03	graph		the above graph	위의 그래프
04	show		show the number	수를 보여주다
05	win		win a medal	메달을 획득하다
06	based on		based on the evidence	증거를 바탕으로
07	committee		the International Olympic Committee	국제올림픽위원회
08	when it comes to		when it comes to gold medals	금메달의 경우
09	twice		less than twice	두 배보다 적은

⊕ **본문 문장 속에서 단어의 의미를 우리말로 해석해 보세요.**

Of the 5 countries, / the United States won the most medals in total, / about 120.

➔ 5개 국가들 중, / 미국이 합계상 ________________ / 약 120개로.

2018 6월 학평 24번 문제

제한시간 70초

난이도 ★★★☆☆

STEP 2 • 수능 기출 제대로 풀기

F

다음 도표의 내용과 일치하지 않는 것은?

2016 Summer Olympic Games Medal Count

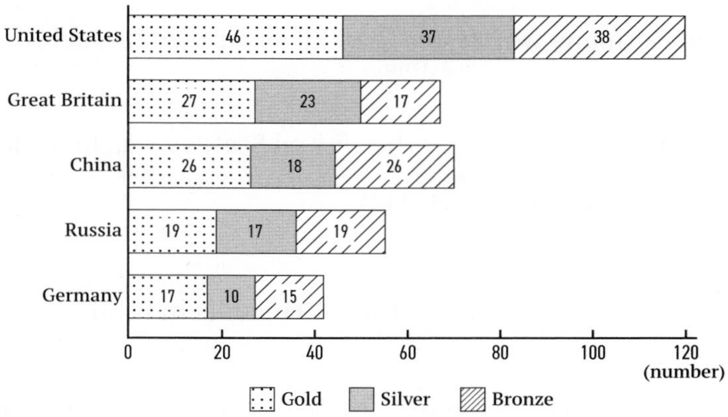

The above graph shows the number of medals won by the top 5 countries during the 2016 Summer Olympic Games, based on the medal count of the International Olympic Committee (IOC). ① Of the 5 countries, the United States won the most medals in total, about 120. ② When it comes to gold medals, Great Britain won more than China did. ③ China, Russia, and Germany won fewer than 20 silver medals each. ④ The number of bronze medals won by the United States was less than twice the number of bronze medals won by Germany. ⑤ Each of the top 5 countries won more than 40 medals in total.

정답과 해설 p.13

STEP 3 • 수능 지문 제대로 복습하기

01 The above graph shows the number of medals / won by the top 5 countries / during the 2016 Summer Olympic Games, / based on the medal count of the International Olympic Committee (IOC).
(the number of+복수명사(~의 수) / 과거분사)

02 Of the 5 countries, / the United States won the most medals in total, / about 120.
(~ 중에서 / 최상급(가장 ~한) / 약, 대략)

03 When it comes to gold medals, / Great Britain won more than China did.
(~에 관하여, ~의 경우 / 대동사(=won))

04 China, Russia, and Germany won fewer than 20 silver medals each.
(비교급+than / 각각(부사))

05 The number of bronze medals won by the United States / was less than twice the number of bronze medals won by Germany.
(주어(the number of+복수명사: 단수 취급) / 과거분사 / 동사 / 과거분사)

06 Each of the top 5 countries / won more than 40 medals in total.

01 위 그래프**graph**는 메달의 수를 보여주고 있다**show** / 상위 5개 국가들이 획득한**win** / 2016년 하계 올림픽 동안 / 국제올림픽위원회**committee**의 메달 집계**count**를 바탕으로**based on**.

02 5개 국가들 중, / 미국이 가장 많은 총 메달을 획득하였다 / 약 120개로.

03 금메달의 경우**when it comes to**, / 영국이 중국보다 더 많이 획득하였다.

04 중국, 러시아, 독일은 각각 20개 미만의 은메달을 획득하였다.

05 미국이 획득한 동메달**bronze medal** 수는 / 독일이 획득한 동메달 수의 두 배**twice**보다 적었다(→ 많았다).

06 상위 5개 국가는 각각 / 총 40개 이상의 메달을 획득하였다.

구문 Check up

① When it comes to gold medals, Great Britain won more than China was / did.

앞에 나온 일반동사(won)를 대신해야 하므로 did가 적절하다.

② China, Russia, and Germany won few / fewer than 20 silver medals each.

비교 대상을 나타내는 전치사 than이 쓰였으므로 비교급인 fewer가 적절하다.

정답 ① did ② fewer

G

도표의 이해 +

STEP 1 • 수능에 진짜 나오는 단어

✔ 문제에 나오는 단어들을 확인하세요.

시간이 없다면 색으로 표시된 단어만이라도 꼭 외우고 넘어가세요!

01	amenity	n. 편의 서비스	the top four hotel (✔ amenities)	상위 네 개의 호텔 편의 서비스
02	accessibility	n. 접근성	( ) to mass transportation	대중교통에의 접근성
03	mass	a. 대중의, 대중적인	the ( ) media	대중 매체
04	transportation	n. 운송, 교통	mass ( )	대중 교통
05	leisure	n. 여가	( ) travelers	여가 여행자들
06	deciding	a. 결정적인	the ( ) game	결정적인 경기
07	factor	n. 요인	the deciding ( )	결정적인 요인
08	popular	a. 인기 있는	a ( ) singer	인기 가수
09	rank	v. (순위를) 차지하다	( ) second in the world	전세계에서 2위를 차지하다

⊕ 본문 문장 속에서 단어들을 확인해 보세요.

The graph above shows the top four hotel amenities / leisure and business travelers selected as the deciding factor / when choosing a hotel.

위 그래프는 상위 네 개의 호텔 편의 서비스를 보여준다 / 여가 여행자들과 출장 여행자들이 결정적 요인으로 고른 / 호텔 선택 시.

단어 다시보기 문제를 풀기 전에 단어들을 30초 동안 다시 확인하세요.

01	amenity	편의 서비스	the top four hotel amenities	상위 네 개의 호텔 편의 서비스
02	accessibility		accessibility to mass transportation	대중교통에의 접근성
03	mass		the mass media	대중 매체
04	transportation		mass transportation	대중 교통
05	leisure		leisure travelers	여가 여행자들
06	deciding		the deciding game	결정적인 경기
07	factor		the deciding factor	결정적인 요인
08	popular		a popular singer	인기 가수
09	rank		rank second in the world	전세계에서 2위를 차지하다

⊕ 본문 문장 속에서 단어의 의미를 우리말로 해석해 보세요.

The graph above shows the top four hotel amenities / leisure and business travelers selected as the deciding factor / when choosing a hotel.

➔ 위 그래프는 __________ 를 보여준다 / 여가 여행자들과 출장 여행자들이 __________ 으로 고른 / 호텔 선택 시.

2016 9월 학평 24번 문제

제한시간 50초

난이도 ★☆☆☆☆

STEP 2 • 수능 기출 제대로 풀기

G

다음 도표의 내용과 일치하지 않는 것은?

Top Hotel Amenities

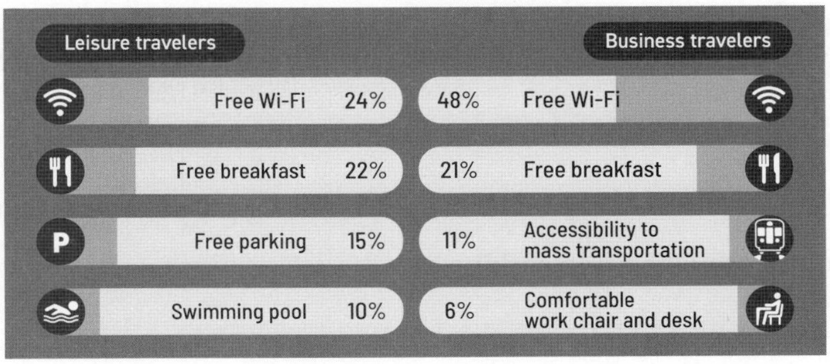

The graph above shows the top four hotel amenities leisure and business travelers selected as the deciding factor when choosing a hotel. ① For both types of traveler, free Wi-Fi is the most popular choice. ② Free breakfast ranks second for both types of traveler, with 22 percent of leisure travelers and 21 percent of business travelers selecting it. ③ Accessibility to mass transportation is not as popular as free breakfast for business travelers. ④ Fifteen percent of leisure travelers chose a swimming pool as their top amenity while ten percent selected free parking. ⑤ Having a comfortable work chair and desk is the least popular choice on the list of the top four amenities for business stays.

정답과 해설 p.13

STEP 3 • 수능 지문 제대로 복습하기

01 The graph above shows the top four hotel amenities / (that 생략) leisure and business travelers selected as the deciding factor / when choosing a hotel.
목적격 관계대명사절
분사구문: 접속사가 있어 의미가 더 명확해짐

02 For both types of traveler, / free Wi-Fi is the most popular choice.
최상급: the most+형용사/부사

03 Free breakfast ranks second / for both types of traveler, / with 22 percent of leisure travelers and 21 percent of business travelers selecting it.
with+A+현재분사(A가 ~하면서, 한 채로)

04 Accessibility to mass transportation / is not as popular as free breakfast / for business travelers.
not as ~ as…: …만큼 ~하지 않은

05 Fifteen percent of leisure travelers chose a swimming pool as their top amenity / while ten percent selected free parking.
부사절 접속사: ~인 반면에

06 Having a comfortable work chair and desk / is the least popular choice / on the list of the top four amenities for business stays.
주어(동명사) 동사(단수) the least+형용사/부사(가장 덜 ~한)

01 위 그래프는 상위 네 개의 호텔 편의 서비스**amenity**를 보여준다 / 여가 여행자들**leisure traveler**과 출장 여행자들이 결정적 요인**deciding factor**으로 고른 / 호텔을 선택할 때.

02 두 유형의 여행자 모두에게 / 무료 Wi-Fi가 가장 인기 있는 선택**popular choice**이었다.

03 무료 조식은 2위에 올랐다**rank second** / 두 유형의 여행자 모두에서 / 여가 여행자들 중 22퍼센트와 출장 여행자들 중 21퍼센트가 그것을 선택해서.

04 대중교통에의 접근성**accessibility to mass transportation**은 / 무료 조식만큼 인기 있지 않다 / 출장 여행자들에게.

05 여가 여행자의 15퍼센트(→10퍼센트)가 수영장을 그들의 중요한 편의 서비스로 선택했고 / 반면 10퍼센트(→15퍼센트)가 무료 주차를 선택했다.

06 편안한 업무용 의자와 책상을 가지는 것이 / 가장 덜 인기 있는 선택이었다 / 출장 체류를 위한 상위 네 개의 편의 서비스 목록 중.

구문 Check up

① The graph above shows the top four hotel amenities leisure and business travelers selected as the deciding factor when choose / choosing a hotel.

내용상 '호텔을 선택할 때'라는 의미가 되어야 하는데, when 이후 주어가 없으므로 <접속사+분사> 형태의 분사구문으로 쓴다. 따라서 choosing이 정답이다.

② Free breakfast ranks second for both types of traveler, with 22 percent of leisure travelers and 21 percent of business travelers select / selecting it.

분사구문 중 <with+명사+-ing/-ed>의 형태에서 명사가 and로 연결되어 길어진 것으로, 분사 형태인 selecting을 쓴다.

정답 ① choosing ② selecting

DAY 05

A

빈칸 추론 I

STEP 1 • 수능에 진짜 나오는 단어

✔ 문제에 나오는 단어들을 확인하세요.

시간이 없다면 색으로 표시된 단어만이라도 꼭 외우고 넘어가세요!

01	individual	n. 개인, 사람	(✔ Individual)s who perform at a high level in their field	자기 분야에서 높은 수준으로 수행하는 개인들
02	profession	n. 직업	the legal ( )	법률 쪽 직업
03	instant	a. 즉각적인	( ) happiness	즉각적인 행복
04	credibility	n. 신뢰(성)	high ( )	높은 신뢰성
05	have nothing to do with	~와 전혀 관련이 없다	( ) ( ) ( ) ( ) ( ) your effort	너의 노력과는 전혀 관련이 없다
06	world-famous	a. 세계적으로 유명한	a ( ) basketball player	세계적으로 유명한 농구 선수
07	knowledge	n. 지식	his ( ) of the products	제품에 대한 그의 지식
08	expertise	n. 전문 지식, 전문성	his ( ) on engines	엔진에 대한 그의 전문 지식
09	admire	v. 존경하다	( ) his talent	그의 재능을 존경하다

⊕ 본문 문장 속에서 단어들을 확인해 보세요.

Individuals who perform at a high level in their profession / often have instant credibility with others.

자기 직업에서 높은 수준으로 수행하는 사람들은 / 흔히 다른 사람들에게 즉각적인 신뢰를 얻는다.

단어 다시보기 문제를 풀기 전에 단어들을 30초 동안 다시 확인하세요.

01	individual	개인, 사람	Individuals who perform at a high level in their field	자기 분야에서 높은 수준으로 수행하는 개인들
02	profession		the legal profession	법률 쪽 직업
03	instant		instant happiness	즉각적인 행복
04	credibility		high credibility	높은 신뢰성
05	have nothing to do with		have nothing to do with your effort	너의 노력과는 전혀 관련이 없다
06	world-famous		a world-famous basketball player	세계적으로 유명한 농구 선수
07	knowledge		his knowledge of the products	제품에 대한 그의 지식
08	expertise		his expertise on engines	엔진에 대한 그의 전문 지식
09	admire		admire his talent	그의 재능을 존경하다

⊕ 본문 문장 속에서 단어의 의미를 우리말로 해석해 보세요.

Individuals who perform at a high level in their profession / often have instant credibility with others.

→ 자기 ________에서 높은 수준으로 수행하는 ________은 / 흔히 다른 사람들에게 ________________.

2023 6월 학평 31번 문제

제한시간 80초

난이도 ★★★★★

STEP 2 • 수능 기출 제대로 풀기

A

다음 빈칸에 들어갈 말로 가장 적절한 것은?

Individuals who perform at a high level in their profession often have instant credibility with others. People admire them, they want to be like them, and they feel connected to them. When they speak, others listen — even if the area of their skill has nothing to do with the advice they give. Think about a world-famous basketball player. He has made more money from endorsements than he ever did playing basketball. Is it because of his knowledge of the products he endorses? No. It's because of what he can do with a basketball. The same can be said of an Olympic medalist swimmer. People listen to him because of what he can do in the pool. And when an actor tells us we should drive a certain car, we don't listen because of his expertise on engines. We listen because we admire his talent. ______________ connects. If you possess a high level of ability in an area, others may desire to connect with you because of it.

*endorsement: (유명인의 텔레비전 등에서의 상품) 보증 선전

① Patience

② Sacrifice

③ Honesty

④ Excellence

⑤ Creativity

정답과 해설 p.14

STEP 3 • 수능 지문 제대로 복습하기

01 Individuals who perform at a high level in their profession / often have instant credibility with others.
주어(복수) 주격 관계대명사절 동사

02 People admire them, / they want to be like them, / and they feel connected to them. // When they speak, / others listen / — even if the area of their skill has nothing to do with the advice they give.
비록 ~이지만 목적격 관계대명사절

03 Think about a world-famous basketball player. // He has made more money from endorsements / than he ever did playing basketball. // Is it because of his knowledge of the products he endorses? // No. // It's because of what he can do with a basketball.
명령문(~하라) 비교급+than: ~보다 더 …한 대동사(= made money) 목적격 관계대명사절

04 The same can be said of an Olympic medalist swimmer. // People listen to him / because of what he can do in the pool.
전치사(~ 때문에) 명사절

05 And when an actor tells us we should drive a certain car, / we don't listen because of his expertise on engines. // We listen because we admire his talent.
접속사(~ 때문에)

06 Excellence connects. // If you possess a high level of ability in an area, / others may desire to connect with you because of it.
desire+to부정사: ~하기를 원하다

01 자기 직업**profession**에서 높은 수준으로 수행하는 사람**individual**들은 / 흔히 다른 사람들에게 즉각적인 신뢰**instant credibility**를 얻는다.

02 사람들은 그들을 존경하고, / 그들처럼 되고 싶어 하고, / 그들과 연결되어 있다고 느낀다. // 그들이 말할 때, / 다른 사람들은 경청한다 / 비록 그들의 기술 분야가 그들이 주는 조언과 전혀 관련이 없을지라도**have nothing to do with**.

03 세계적으로 유명한**world-famous** 농구 선수를 생각해 보라. // 그는 광고로부터 더 많은 돈을 벌었다 / 그가 농구를 하면서 그간 벌었던 것보다. // 그것이 그가 광고하는 제품에 대한 지식**knowledge** 때문일까? // 아니다. // 그것은 그가 농구로 할 수 있는 것 때문이다.

04 올림픽 메달리스트 수영 선수에 관해서도 똑같은 것을 말할 수 있다. // 사람들은 그의 말을 경청한다 / 그가 수영장에서 할 수 있는 것 때문에.

05 그리고 어떤 배우가 우리에게 특정 자동차를 운전해야 한다고 말할 때, / 우리는 엔진에 대한 그의 전문 지식**expertise** 때문에 경청하는 것은 아니다. // 우리는 그의 재능을 존경하기**admire** 때문에 경청한다.

06 탁월함이 연결된다. // 만약 당신이 어떤 분야에서 높은 수준의 능력을 갖고 있다면, / 다른 사람들은 그것 때문에 당신과 연결되기를 원할 수도 있다.

구문 Check up

① Individuals who perform at a high level in their profession often has / have instant credibility with others.

주어 Individuals가 복수명사이므로 동사 have가 적절하다.

② People listen to him because / because of what he can do in the pool.

'what ~ the pool'이 명사절이므로, 전치사 because of가 적절하다.

정답 ① have ② because of

B

빈칸 추론 I

STEP 1 • 수능에 진짜 나오는 단어

✔ 문제에 나오는 단어들을 확인하세요.

시간이 없다면 색으로 표시된 단어만이라도 꼭 외우고 넘어가세요!

01	warehouse	n. 창고, 저장소	the large (✔ warehouse)s	거대한 창고들
02	shelf	n. 선반	grab products off ( )es	선반에서 상품을 집어내다
03	instruction	n. 지시 사항	give ( )s	지시하다
04	minimise	v. 최소화하다	( ) error	실수를 최소화하다
05	maximise	v. 최대화하다	( ) profit	이익을 최대화하다
06	productivity	n. 생산성	maximise ( )	생산성을 최대화하다
07	condition	n. 조건, 상황	work in such ( )s	그러한 조건에서 일하다
08	flesh	n. 살, 육체	made of ( )	살로 만들어진
09	adapt	v. 적응하다	ask us to ( )	적응하라고 요구하다
10	take over	인수하다, 넘겨받다	( ) ( ) the thought process	사고 과정을 가져가다
11	treat A as B	A를 B로 취급하다	( ) workers ( ) a source	작업자들을 자원으로 취급하다
12	inexpensive	a. 값싼, 저렴한	an ( ) source	값싼 자원
13	opposable thumbs	마주 보는 엄지 손가락(엄지가 다른 네 손가락과 맞닿아 물건을 쥘 수 있음)	have a pair of ( ) ( )	한 쌍의 마주 보는 엄지 손가락이 있다

⊕ 본문 문장 속에서 단어들을 확인해 보세요.

Working in such conditions / reduces people / to machines made of flesh.

그러한 조건에서 일하는 것은 / 사람을 격하시킨다 / 살로 만들어진 기계로.

단어 다시보기 문제를 풀기 전에 단어들을 30초 동안 다시 확인하세요.

01	warehouse	창고, 저장소	the large warehouses	거대한 창고들
02	shelf		grab products off shelves	선반에서 상품을 집어내다
03	instruction		give instructions	지시하다
04	minimise		minimise error	실수를 최소화하다
05	maximise		maximise profit	이익을 최대화하다
06	productivity		maximise productivity	생산성을 최대화하다
07	condition		work in such conditions	그러한 조건에서 일하다
08	flesh		made of flesh	살로 만들어진
09	adapt		ask us to adapt	적응하라고 요구하다
10	take over		take over the thought process	사고 과정을 가져가다
11	treat A as B		treat workers as a source	작업자들을 자원으로 취급하다
12	inexpensive		an inexpensive source	값싼 자원
13	opposable thumbs		have a pair of opposable thumbs	한 쌍의 마주 보는 엄지손가락이 있다

⊕ **본문 문장 속에서 단어의 의미를 우리말로 해석해 보세요.**

Working in such conditions / reduces people / to machines made of flesh.

→ 그러한 ______에서 일하는 것은 / 사람을 격하시킨다 / ______로 만들어진 기계로.

2022 9월 학평 31번 문제

제한시간 80초

난이도 ★★★★★

STEP 2 • 수능 기출 제대로 풀기

B 다음 빈칸에 들어갈 말로 가장 적절한 것은?

We worry that the robots are taking our jobs, but just as common a problem is that the robots are taking our ______________. In the large warehouses so common behind the scenes of today's economy, human 'pickers' hurry around grabbing products off shelves and moving them to where they can be packed and dispatched. In their ears are headpieces: the voice of Jennifer', a piece of software, tells them where to go and what to do, controlling the smallest details of their movements. Jennifer breaks down instructions into tiny chunks, to minimise error and maximise productivity — for example, rather than picking eighteen copies of a book off a shelf, the human worker would be politely instructed to pick five. Then another five. Then yet another five. Then another three. Working in such conditions reduces people to machines made of flesh. Rather than asking us to think or adapt, the Jennifer unit takes over the thought process and treats workers as an inexpensive source of some visual processing and a pair of opposable thumbs.

*dispatch: 발송하다 **chunk: 덩어리

① reliability

② judgment

③ endurance

④ sociability

⑤ cooperation

정답과 해설 p.14

STEP 3 • 수능 지문 제대로 복습하기

01 We worry that the robots are taking our jobs, / but just as common a problem is / as this 생략
명사절 접속사(worry의 목적어)　　　　　　　　　　　　　　　　　　　　　　　<as+형용사+관사+명사> 어순
that the robots are taking our judgment.

02 In the large warehouses / so common behind the scenes of today's economy, / human
　　　　　　　　　　　　　형용사구(명사 수식)
'pickers' hurry around / grabbing products off shelves /and moving them / to where
　　　　　　　　　　　　병렬구조(분사구문: ~하면서)　　　　　선행사 생략(the place)
they can be packed and dispatched.

03 In their ears are headpieces: / the voice of Jennifer', a piece of software, / tells them
장소 부사구　　　　　도치(동사+주어)
where to go and what to do, / controlling the smallest details of their movements.
　　　　　　　　　　　　　분사구문: ~하면서

04 Jennifer breaks down instructions into tiny chunks, / to minimise error and maximise
　　　　　　　　　　　　　　　　　　　　　　　　　　　　to부정사의 부사적 용법
productivity / — for example, rather than picking eighteen copies of a book off a shelf,
/ the human worker would be politely instructed / to pick five. // Then another five. //
　　　　　　　　　　5형식 문장의 수동태: be p.p.+목적격 보어(to부정사)
Then yet another five. // Then another three.

05 Working in such conditions / reduces people / to machines made of flesh.
동명사 주어(단수 취급)　　　　동사　　　　　　　　　　　과거분사구(명사 수식)

06 Rather than asking us to think or adapt, / the Jennifer unit takes over the thought
　　　　　　5형식 동사(ask)+목적어+목적격 보어(to부정사)
process / and treats workers as an inexpensive source / of some visual processing and a
　　　　　　　　　　　　　　　　　　　　　　　　전치사구
pair of opposable thumbs.

01 우리는 로봇이 우리의 직업을 빼앗고 있다고 걱정한다, / 하지만 그만큼 흔한 문제는 / 로봇이 우리의 판단력을 빼앗고 있다는 것이다.

02 거대한 창고warehouse에서 / 오늘날의 경제 배후에서 아주 흔한 (창고), / 인간 '집게들'은 서두른다 / 선반shelf에서 상품을 집어내느라 / 그리고 그것들을 이동시키느라 / 그것들이 포장되고 발송될 수 있는 곳으로.

03 그들의 귀에는 헤드폰이 있다, / 한 소프트웨어 프로그램인 'Jennifer'의 목소리가 / 그들에게 어디로 갈지와 무엇을 할지를 말한다 / 그들 움직임의 가장 작은 세부 사항들을 조종하면서.

04 Jennifer는 지시 사항instruction을 아주 작은 덩어리로 쪼갠다/ 실수를 줄이고minimise 생산성을 최대화하기maximise productivity 위해 / — 예를 들어, 선반에서 책 18권을 집어내기보다는, / 인간 작업자는 정중하게 지시받을 것이다 / 5권을 집어내라고. // 그러고 나서 또 다른 5권을. // 그러고 나서 다시 또 다른 5권을. // 그러고 나서 또 다른 3권을.

05 그러한 조건condition에서 일하는 것은 / 사람을 격하시킨다 / 살flesh로 만들어진 기계로.

06 우리에게 생각하거나 적응하라고adapt 요구하기보다는, / Jennifer라는 장치는 사고 과정을 가져가고take over / 작업자들을 값싼 자원으로 취급한다treat workers as an inexpensive source / 약간의 시각적인 처리 과정과 한 쌍의 마주 보는 엄지손가락opposable thumbs을 가진.

구문 Check up	① Human 'pickers' hurry around grab / grabbing products off shelves.	② Rather than asking us think / to think or adapt, the Jennifer unit takes over the thought process.
	문장의 동사는 hurry이고, 이와 grab를 병렬연결해 줄 접속사가 없으므로 분사구문인 grabbing으로 쓴다.	5형식 동사 ask는 목적격 보어로 to부정사를 취하므로 to think를 쓴다.

정답 ① grabbing ② to think

C

빈칸 추론 I

STEP 1 • 수능에 진짜 나오는 단어

문제에 나오는 단어들을 확인하세요.

시간이 없다면 색으로 표시된 단어만이라도 꼭 외우고 넘어가세요!

01	aspect	n. 측면	the most important (aspect)s	가장 중요한 측면들
02	make sure	반드시 ~하도록 하다	( ) ( ) that an animal's needs are met	동물의 욕구가 반드시 충족되게 하다
03	need	n. 욕구, 요구	an animal's ( )s	동물의 욕구
04	consistently	ad. 일관되게	meet the needs ( )	일관되게 욕구를 충족시키다
05	predictably	ad. 예측 가능하게	( ) happen	예측 가능하게 발생하다
06	control	n. 통제 v. 통제하다	a sense of ( )	통제감
07	distress	n. 괴로움	experience ( )	괴로움을 겪다
08	ensure	v. 보장하다	( ) that it is predictable	그것이 예측 가능함을 보장하다
09	available	a. 이용 가능한	Water is ( ).	물이 이용 가능하다.
10	discomfort	n. 불편	to the point of ( )	불편할 정도로
11	companion	n. 친구, 동료	human ( )s	인간 친구들
12	display	v. 보여주다	( ) support	지지를 보여주다
13	withhold	v. 주지 않다, 보류하다	( ) love	사랑을 주지 않다

⊕ 본문 문장 속에서 단어들을 확인해 보세요.

One of the most important aspects of providing good care / is making sure / that an animal's needs are being met / consistently and predictably.

좋은 보살핌을 제공하는 것의 가장 중요한 측면 중 한 가지는 / 반드시 되도록 하는 것이다 / 동물의 욕구가 충족되도록 / 일관되게 그리고 예측 가능하게.

단어 다시보기 문제를 풀기 전에 단어들을 30초 동안 다시 확인하세요.

01	aspect	측면	the most important aspects	가장 중요한 측면들
02	make sure		make sure that an animal's needs are met	동물의 욕구가 반드시 충족되도록 하다
03	need		an animal's needs	동물의 욕구
04	consistently		meet the needs consistently	일관되게 욕구를 충족시키다
05	predictably		predictably happen	예측 가능하게 발생하다
06	control		a sense of control	통제감
07	distress		experience distress	괴로움을 겪다
08	ensure		ensure that it is predictable	그것이 예측 가능함을 보장하다
09	available		Water is available.	물이 이용 가능하다.
10	discomfort		to the point of discomfort	불편할 정도로
11	companion		human companions	인간 친구들
12	display		display support	지지를 보여주다
13	withhold		withhold love	사랑을 주지 않다

⊕ 본문 문장 속에서 단어의 의미를 우리말로 해석해 보세요.

One of the most important aspects of providing good care / is making sure / that an animal's needs are being met / consistently and predictably.

➔ 좋은 보살핌을 제공하는 것의 가장 중요한 ______ 중 한 가지는 / ______ 이다 / 동물의 ______ 가 충족되도록 / ______ 그리고 ______.

2021 3월 학평 31번 문제

제한시간 80초

난이도 ★★★★★

STEP 2 • 수능 기출 제대로 풀기

C

다음 빈칸에 들어갈 말로 가장 적절한 것은?

One of the most important aspects of providing good care is making sure that an animal's needs are being met consistently and predictably. Like humans, animals need a sense of control. So an animal who may get enough food but doesn't know when the food will appear and can see no consistent schedule may experience distress. We can provide a sense of control by ensuring that our animal's environment is ___________: there is always water available and always in the same place. There is always food when we get up in the morning and after our evening walk. There will always be a time and place to eliminate, without having to hold things in to the point of discomfort. Human companions can display consistent emotional support, rather than providing love one moment and withholding love the next. When animals know what to expect, they can feel more confident and calm.

*eliminate: 배설하다

① silent

② natural

③ isolated

④ dynamic

⑤ predictable

정답과 해설 p.14

STEP 3 • 수능 지문 제대로 복습하기

01 One of the most important aspects of providing good care / is making sure / that an animal's needs are being met / consistently and predictably. // Like humans, / animals need a sense of control.

주어(단수 취급) / 수 일치 / 명사절 접속사 / 현재진행 수동태

02 So / an animal / [who may get enough food / but doesn't know when the food will appear / and can see no consistent schedule] / may experience distress.

주격 관계대명사 / 병렬구조

03 We can provide a sense of control / by ensuring / that our animal's environment is predictable: / there is always water available / and always in the same place.

by+동명사: ~함으로써 / 명사절 접속사(ensuring의 목적어) / 콜론: 부연 설명

04 There is always food / when we get up in the morning / and after our evening walk. // There will always be a time and place / to eliminate, / without having to hold things in / to the point of discomfort.

병렬구조 / 시간 부사절 / 시간 전치사구 / to부정사의 형용사적 용법 / without+동명사: ~하지 않고

05 Human companions can display consistent emotional support, / rather than providing love one moment and withholding love the next.

병렬구조 (동명사)

06 When animals know / what to expect, / they can feel more confident and calm.

의문사+to부정사(무엇을 ~할지) / 감각동사+주격보어(형용사)

01 좋은 보살핌을 제공하는 것의 가장 중요한 측면**aspect** 중 한 가지는 / 반드시 되도록 하는**make sure** 것이다 / 동물의 욕구**need**가 충족되도록 / 일관되게**consistently** 그리고 예측 가능하게**predictably**. // 사람과 마찬가지로, / 동물은 통제감**sense of control**이 필요하다.

02 그러므로 / 동물은 / 충분한 음식을 제공받고 있는 / 하지만 음식이 언제 나타날지 모르는 / 그리고 일관된 일정을 알 수 없는 (동물은) / 괴로움을 겪을지도**experience distress** 모른다.

03 우리는 통제되고 있다는 느낌을 줄 수 있다 / 보장함**ensure**으로써 / 우리 동물의 환경이 예측 가능하도록. // 즉, 물이 늘 있고**available**, / 늘 같은 곳에 있다.

04 늘 음식이 있다 / 우리가 아침에 일어날 때 / 그리고 저녁 산책 후에. // 시간과 장소가 늘 있을 것이다 / (변을) 배설할 수 있는 / 참아야 할 필요 없이 / 불편할**discomfort** 정도로.

05 사람 친구**companion**는 일관된 정서적 지지를 보여주면**display** 된다 / 한순간에는 애정을 주다가 그 다음에는 애정을 주지 않기**withhold**보다는.

06 동물이 알고 있을 때 / 기대할 수 있는 것이 무엇인지, / 동물은 자신감과 차분함을 더 많이 느낄 수 있다.

구문 Check up

① We can provide a sense of control by ensuring that / what our animal's environment is predictable.

뒤따르는 절이 완전하므로 명사절 접속사 that이 적절하다.

② When animals know what to expect, they can feel more confident and calm / confidently and calmly.

동사 feel은 보어인 형용사와 함께 쓰여 '~함을 느끼다'라는 의미가 된다. 따라서 confident and calm이 적절하다.

정답 ① that ② confident and calm

DAY 05

D

빈칸 추론 I

STEP 1 • 수능에 진짜 나오는 단어

✔ 문제에 나오는 단어들을 확인하세요.

시간이 없다면 색으로 표시된 단어만이라도 꼭 외우고 넘어가세요!

01	critically	ad. 비판적으로	think (✓ critically)	비판적으로 생각하다
02	observation	n. 관찰	( )s are recorded.	관찰이 기록된다.
03	make sense	합리적이다, 이치에 맞다	Conclusions ( ) ( ).	결론이 합리적이다.
04	source	n. 출처	the ( )s of information	정보의 출처
05	reliable	a. 믿을 만한	the ( ) sources	믿을 만한 출처
06	conduct	v. 수행하다	( ) the experiment	실험을 수행하다
07	unbiased	a. 한쪽으로 치우치지 않은, 편견 없는	The scientist is ( ).	과학자는 편견이 없다.
08	profit	v. 이득을 보다	The drug company ( )s.	제약 회사가 이득을 본다.
09	involve	v. 관련시키다	a special interest is ( )d	특별한 이익이 관련되다
10	benefit	v. ~에 이익이 되다, 이익을 주다	( ) the drug company	제약 회사에 이익이 되다
11	assess	v. 평가하다	( ) results	결과를 평가하다
12	untrustworthy	a. 신뢰할 수 없는	Its product is ( ).	그 제품은 신뢰할 수 없다.
13	decisive	a. 결단력 있는	They are ( ).	그들은 결단력 있다.

⊕ 본문 문장 속에서 단어들을 확인해 보세요.

You should also ask / if the scientist or group conducting the experiment / was unbiased.

당신은 역시 물어야 한다 / 실험을 수행한 그 과학자나 그룹이 / 한쪽으로 치우치지 않았는지.

단어 다시보기 문제를 풀기 전에 단어들을 30초 동안 다시 확인하세요.

01	critically	비판적으로	think critically	비판적으로 생각하다
02	observation		Observations are recorded.	관찰이 기록된다.
03	make sense		Conclusions make sense.	결론이 합리적이다.
04	source		the sources of information	정보의 출처
05	reliable		the reliable sources	믿을 만한 출처
06	conduct		conduct the experiment	실험을 수행하다
07	unbiased		The scientist is unbiased.	과학자는 편견이 없다.
08	profit		The drug company profits.	제약 회사가 이득을 본다.
09	involve		a special interest is involved	특별한 이익이 관련되다
10	benefit		benefit the drug company	제약 회사에 이익이 되다
11	assess		assess results	결과를 평가하다
12	untrustworthy		Its product is untrustworthy.	그 제품은 신뢰할 수 없다.
13	decisive		They are decisive.	그들은 결단력 있다.

⊕ 본문 문장 속에서 단어의 의미를 우리말로 해석해 보세요.

You should also ask / if the scientist or group conducting the experiment / was unbiased.

➔ 당신은 역시 물어야 한다 / 실험을 ________ 그 과학자나 그룹이 / ________________.

2020 6월 학평 31번 문제

제한시간 80초

난이도 ★★★★★

STEP 2 • 수능 기출 제대로 풀기

D

다음 빈칸에 들어갈 말로 가장 적절한 것은?

When reading another scientist's findings, think critically about the experiment. Ask yourself: Were observations recorded during or after the experiment? Do the conclusions make sense? Can the results be repeated? Are the sources of information reliable? You should also ask if the scientist or group conducting the experiment was unbiased. Being unbiased means that you have no special interest in the outcome of the experiment. For example, if a drug company pays for an experiment to test how well one of its new products works, there is a special interest involved: The drug company profits if the experiment shows that its product is effective. Therefore, the experimenters aren't ____________. They might ensure the conclusion is positive and benefits the drug company. When assessing results, think about any biases that may be present!

① inventive

② objective

③ untrustworthy

④ unreliable

⑤ decisive

정답과 해설 p.15

STEP 3 • 수능 지문 제대로 복습하기

01 When reading another scientist's findings, / think critically about the experiment.
접속사가 있는 분사구문(=When you read ~)

02 Ask yourself: / Were observations recorded / during or after the experiment? // Do the conclusions make sense?

03 Can the results be repeated? // Are the sources of information reliable? // You should also ask / if the scientist or group conducting the experiment / was unbiased.
명사절 접속사(~인지 아닌지) / 현재분사(명사 수식)

04 Being unbiased means / that you have no special interest / in the outcome of the experiment.
동명사 주어 / 명사절 접속사(means의 목적어)

05 For example, / if a drug company pays for an experiment / to test how well one of its new products works, / there is a special interest involved: / The drug company profits / if the experiment shows that its product is effective.
부사절 접속사(만약) / 의문사절(to test의 목적어) / 과거분사 / 부사절 접속사(만약) / 명사절 접속사

06 Therefore, / the experimenters aren't objective. // They might ensure / the conclusion is positive / and benefits the drug company. // When assessing results, / think about any biases that may be present!
명사절 접속사 that 생략 / 병렬구조(동사 연결) / 접속사가 있는 분사구문(=When you assess ~) / 주격 관계대명사절

01 다른 과학자의 실험 결과물을 읽을 때, / 그 실험에 대해 비판적으로 생각하라**think critically**.

02 당신 자신에게 물어라. / 관찰들이**observation** 기록되었나 / 실험 도중에 혹은 후에? // 결론이 합리적인가**make sense**?

03 그 결과들은 반복될 수 있는가? // 정보의 출처**the sources of information**는 신뢰할 만한가**reliable**? // 당신은 역시 물어야 한다 / 실험을 수행한**conduct the experiment** 그 과학자나 그룹이 / 한쪽으로 치우치지 않았는지.

04 한쪽으로 치우치지 않음**being unbiased**은 의미한다 / 당신이 특별한 이익을 얻지 않는다는 것을 / 실험의 결과로.

05 예를 들면, / 만약 한 제약 회사가 실험에 대한 비용을 지불한다면 / 그 회사의 새로운 제품 중 하나가 얼마나 잘 작용하는지 시험해보기 위해, / 특별한 이익이 관련된**a special interest involved** 것이다. / 그 제약 회사는 이익을 본다**profit** / 만약 실험이 그 제품이 효과 있음을 보여준다면.

06 따라서, / 그 실험자들은 객관적이지 않다. // 그들은 보장할지도 모른다 / 결론이 우호적이고 / 제약 회사에 이익을 주도록**benefit**. // 결과들을 평가할**assess results** 때, / 있을 수 있는 어떤 치우침에 대해 생각하라!

구문 Check up

① You should also ask if / that the scientist or group conducting the experiment was unbiased.	② The drug company profits if the experiment shows that it / its product is effective.
동사 ask 다음에 '~인지 아닌지'의 의미인 명사절이 올 때 접속사는 if(=whether)를 쓴다.	that절에서 주어는 product이고 product는 the drug company의 제품이기 때문에 소유격으로 its를 쓴다.

정답 ① if ② its

DAY 05

E

빈칸 추론 I ⊕

STEP 1 • 수능에 진짜 나오는 단어

✔ 문제에 나오는 단어들을 확인하세요.

시간이 없다면 색으로 표시된 단어만이라도 꼭 외우고 넘어가세요!

01	creativity	n. 창의력	(✔ Creativity) is a skill.	창의력은 능력이다.
02	uniquely	ad. 특별히, 고유하게	consider it ( ) human	그것을 특별히 인간적이라고 간주하다
03	creative	a. 창의적인	a ( ) being	창의적인 존재
04	nest	n. 둥지	make a ( )	둥지를 만들다
05	species	n. 종	other ( ) on Earth	지구상의 다른 종
06	display	v. 보여주다	( ) creativity	창의력을 보여주다
07	amazing	a. 놀라운	( ) things	놀라운 일들
08	acquire	v. 습득하다	( ) the ability	능력을 습득하다
09	artificial	a. 인공적인	the ( ) intelligence	인공지능
10	boom	n. 급속한 발전	the artificial intelligence ( )	인공지능의 급속한 발전
11	recognize	v. 인식하다	( ) faces	얼굴을 인식하다
12	translate	v. 번역하다	( ) languages	언어를 번역하다
13	all of a sudden	갑자기	( ) ( ) ( ) ( ) = suddenly	갑자기
14	possibility	n. 가능성	face the ( )	가능성에 직면하다

⊕ 본문 문장 속에서 단어들을 확인해 보세요.

Creativity is a skill / we usually consider uniquely human.

창의력은 능력이다 / 우리가 일반적으로 특별히 인간적이라고 간주하는.

단어 다시보기 문제를 풀기 전에 단어들을 30초 동안 다시 확인하세요.

01	creativity	창의력	Creativity is a skill.	창의력은 능력이다.
02	uniquely		consider it uniquely human	그것을 특별히 인간적이라고 간주하다
03	creative		a creative being	창의적인 존재
04	nest		make a nest	둥지를 만들다
05	species		other species on Earth	지구상의 다른 종
06	display		display creativity	창의력을 보여주다
07	amazing		amazing things	놀라운 일들
08	acquire		acquire the ability	능력을 습득하다
09	artificial		the artificial intelligence	인공지능
10	boom		the artificial intelligence boom	인공지능의 급속한 발전
11	recognize		recognize faces	얼굴을 인식하다
12	translate		translate languages	언어를 번역하다
13	all of a sudden		all of a sudden = suddenly	갑자기
14	possibility		face the possibility	가능성에 직면하다

⊕ 본문 문장 속에서 단어의 의미를 우리말로 해석해 보세요.

Creativity is a skill / we usually consider uniquely human.

→ ________은 능력이다 / 우리가 일반적으로 ________ 인간적이라고 간주하는.

2019 6월 학평 31번 문제

제한시간 80초

난이도 ★★★★★

STEP 2 • 수능 기출 제대로 풀기

E

다음 빈칸에 들어갈 말로 가장 적절한 것은?

Creativity is a skill we usually consider uniquely human. For all of human history, we have been the most creative beings on Earth. Birds can make their nests, ants can make their hills, but no other species on Earth comes close to the level of creativity we humans display. However, just in the last decade we have acquired the ability to do amazing things with computers, like developing robots. With the artificial intelligence boom of the 2010s, computers can now recognize faces, translate languages, take calls for you, write poems, and beat players at the world's most complicated board game, to name a few things. All of a sudden, we must face the possibility that our ability to be creative is not ______________.

① unrivaled

② learned

③ universal

④ ignored

⑤ challenged

정답과 해설 p.15

STEP 3 • 수능 지문 제대로 복습하기

01 Creativity is a skill / we usually consider uniquely human.
(목적격 관계대명사 that 생략)

02 For all of human history, / we have been the most creative beings on Earth.
(For all of human history: 기간 부사구 / have been: 현재완료)

03 Birds can make their nests, / ants can make their hills, / but no other species on Earth / comes close to the level of creativity / we humans display.
(목적격 관계대명사 that 생략)

04 However, just in the last decade / we have acquired the ability / to do amazing things with computers, / like developing robots.
(to do amazing things with computers: to부정사의 형용사적 용법)

05 With the artificial intelligence boom of the 2010s, / computers can now recognize faces, / translate languages, / take calls for you, / write poems, / and beat players at the world's most complicated board game, / to name a few things.
(can: 조동사 / recognize: 동사원형1 / translate: 동사원형2 / take: 동사원형3 / write: 동사원형4 / beat: 동사원형5 / to name a few things: 몇 가지를 말하자면)

06 All of a sudden, / we must face the possibility / that our ability to be creative is not unrivaled.
(that our ability to be creative is not unrivaled: 동격의 that절(=the possibility))

01 창의력creativity은 능력이다 / 우리가 일반적으로 특별히uniquely 인간적이라고 간주하는.

02 인류 역사를 통틀어, / 우리는 지구상에서 가장 창의적인 존재creative being였다.

03 새는 둥지를 틀 수 있고make a nest, / 개미는 개미탑을 쌓을 수 있지만, / 지구상의 그 어떤 다른 종species도 / 창의력 수준에 가까이 도달하지 못한다 / 우리 인간이 보여주는display.

04 하지만, 불과 지난 10년 만에 / 우리는 능력을 습득하였다acquire the ability / 컴퓨터로 놀라운amazing 것을 할 수 있는 (능력) / 로봇 개발처럼.

05 2010년대의 인공 지능의 급속한 발전the artificial intelligence boom으로, / 컴퓨터는 이제 얼굴을 인식하고recognize faces, / 언어를 번역하고translate languages, / 여러분을 대신해 전화를 받고, / 시를 쓸 수 있으며 / 세계에서 가장 복잡한 보드게임에서 선수들을 이길 수 있다 / 몇 가지를 언급하자면.

06 갑작스럽게all of a sudden, / 우리는 가능성에 직면해야face the possibility 할 것이다 / 우리의 창의력이 경쟁할 상대가 없지 않게 되는.

구문 Check up

① We have acquired the ability [done / to do] amazing things with computers, like developing robots.	② We must face the possibility [that / which] our ability to be creative is not unrivaled.
앞의 명사 ability를 수식하고 능동의 의미가 문맥상 적절하므로 to부정사 to do를 쓴다.	뒤의 문장이 완전한 문장이고 앞의 possibility를 추가 설명해 주는 것이기 때문에 동격의 절을 이끄는 that을 쓴다.

정답 ① to do ② that

STEP 1 • 수능에 *진짜* 나오는 *단어*

✔ 문제에 나오는 단어들을 확인하세요.

시간이 없다면 색으로 표시된 단어만이라도 꼭 외우고 넘어가세요!

01	outcome	n. 결과	an (✔ outcome) of motivation	동기부여의 결과
02	behavior	n. 행동	preparatory ()s	준비 행동
03	considerable	a. 상당한	() effort	상당한 노력
04	vehicle	n. 차, 탈 것	research ()s	차들을 검색하다
05	dealership	n. (자동차) 대리점	visit ()s	대리점들을 방문하다
06	weight	n. 무게, 몸무게	lose ()	몸무게를 줄이다
07	portion	n. 1인분	smaller ()s	더 적은 1인분의 양
08	motivate	v. 동기를 부여하다	be ()d to exercise	운동하고자 하는 동기가 있다
09	drive	v. 몰아붙이다, 이끌어내다	() the final behaviors	최종 행동을 이끌다
10	goal	n. 목표	bring a ()	목표를 가져오다
11	willingness	n. 의지	create ()	의지를 만들다
12	expend	v. 쓰다, 지출하다	() time and energy	시간과 에너지를 쓰다
13	extra	a. 여분의, 추가적인	() money	추가적인 돈

⊕ 본문 문장 속에서 단어들을 확인해 보세요.

One outcome of motivation is behavior / that takes considerable effort.

동기 부여의 한 가지 결과는 행동이다 / 상당한 노력을 필요로 하는.

단어 다시보기 문제를 풀기 전에 단어들을 30초 동안 다시 확인하세요.

01	outcome	결과	an outcome of motivation	동기부여의 결과
02	behavior		preparatory behaviors	준비 행동
03	considerable		considerable effort	상당한 노력
04	vehicle		research vehicles	차들을 검색하다
05	dealership		visit dealerships	대리점들을 방문하다
06	weight		lose weight	몸무게를 줄이다
07	portion		smaller portions	더 적은 1인분의 양
08	motivate		be motivated to exercise	운동하고자 하는 동기가 있다
09	drive		drive the final behaviors	최종 행동을 이끌다
10	goal		bring a goal	목표를 가져오다
11	willingness		create willingness	의지를 만들다
12	expend		expend time and energy	시간과 에너지를 쓰다
13	extra		extra money	추가적인 돈

⊕ 본문 문장 속에서 단어의 의미를 우리말로 해석해 보세요.

One outcome of motivation is behavior / that takes considerable effort.

→ 동기 부여의 한 가지 ____는 ____이다 / ____을 필요로 하는.

2018 6월 학평 31번 문제

제한시간 70초

난이도 ★★★☆☆

STEP 2 • 수능 기출 제대로 풀기

F

다음 빈칸에 들어갈 말로 가장 적절한 것은?

One outcome of motivation is behavior that takes considerable ____________. For example, if you are motivated to buy a good car, you will research vehicles online, look at ads, visit dealerships, and so on. Likewise, if you are motivated to lose weight, you will buy low-fat foods, eat smaller portions, and exercise. Motivation not only drives the final behaviors that bring a goal closer but also creates willingness to expend time and energy on preparatory behaviors. Thus, someone motivated to buy a new smartphone may earn extra money for it, drive through a storm to reach the store, and then wait in line to buy it.

*preparatory: 준비의

① risk

② effort

③ memory

④ fortune

⑤ experience

정답과 해설 p.16

STEP 3 • 수능 지문 제대로 복습하기

01 One outcome of motivation is behavior / that takes considerable effort.
take effort: 노력을 필요로 하다
주격 관계대명사절

02 For example, / if you are motivated to buy a good car, / you will research vehicles online, / look at ads, / visit dealerships, and so on.
be motivated+to부정사: ~하도록 동기 부여받다

03 Likewise, / if you are motivated to lose weight, / you will buy low-fat foods, / eat smaller portions, / and exercise.
조건의 부사절에서는 현재시제가 미래를 나타냄
동사 buy, eat, exercise 병렬구조

04 Motivation not only drives the final behaviors / that bring a goal closer / but also creates willingness / to expend time and energy on preparatory behaviors.
not only A but also B: A뿐만 아니라 B도
주격 관계대명사절
형용사적 용법

05 Thus, / someone motivated to buy a new smartphone / may earn extra money for it, / drive through a storm to reach the store, / and then wait in line to buy it.
과거분사
부사적 용법(목적)
부사적 용법(목적)

01 동기 부여의 한 가지 결과**outcome**는 행동이다 / 상당한**considerable** 노력을 필요로 하는.

02 예를 들면, / 만약 좋은 차를 사고자 하는 동기가 있다면, / 당신은 온라인으로 차**vehicle**들을 검색하고, / 광고를 자세히 보며, / 자동차 대리점**dealership**들을 방문하는 것 등을 할 것이다.

03 마찬가지로, / 몸무게**weight**를 줄이고자 하는 동기가 있다면**be motivated**, / 당신은 저지방 식품을 사고, / 더 적은 1인분의 양**portion**을 먹으며, / 운동을 할 것이다.

04 동기 부여는 최종 행동을 이끌**drive** 뿐만 아니라, / 목표**goal**를 더 가까이 가져오는 / 의지**willingness**를 만들기도 한다 / 준비 행동**behavior**에 시간과 에너지를 쓸**expend**.

05 따라서 / 새 스마트폰을 사고자 하는 동기가 있는 사람은 / 그것을 위해 추가적인**extra** 돈을 벌고, / 가게에 가기 위해 폭풍 속을 운전하며, / 그것을 사려고 줄을 서서 기다릴지도 모른다.

구문 Check up

① Likewise, if you are motivated to lose weight, you will buy low-fat foods, eat smaller portions, and exercise / exercising.

조동사 will 뒤에 세 개의 동사(buy, eat, exercise)가 병렬연결된 구조이므로 exercise를 써야 한다.

② Motivation not only drives the final behaviors that / what bring a goal closer but also creates willingness to expend time and energy on preparatory behaviors.

앞에 선행사(the final behaviors)가 존재하므로 관계대명사 that이 적절하다.

정답 ① exercise ② that

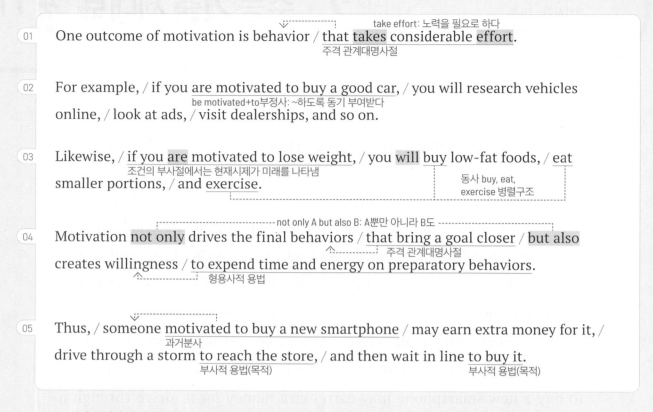

G

STEP 1 • 수능에 진짜 나오는 단어

✔ 문제에 나오는 단어들을 확인하세요.

시간이 없다면 색으로 표시된 단어만이라도 꼭 외우고 넘어가세요!

01	routinely	ad. 주기적으로	be (✔ routinely) checked	주기적으로 점검받다
02	stop by	~에 들르다	( ) ( ) at the office	사무실에 들르다
03	particular	a. 특정한	be trained on a ( ) skill	특정한 기술에 대해 훈련을 받다
04	cater	v. (음식을) 제공하다, ~의 요구를 맞추다	( ) meals for the family	그 가족에게 식사를 제공하다
05	gesture	n. 몸짓, 표시	a ( ) of support	도움의 표시
06	fiercely	ad. 맹렬하게, 열렬히, 치열하게	( ) compete	치열하게 경쟁하다
07	loyal	a. 충성스러운	fiercely ( )	열렬히 충성스러운
08	go the extra mile	한층 더 노력하다	They don't mind ( )ing ( ) ( ) ( ) for their boss.	그들은 자기 상사를 위해 한층 더 노력하기를 사리지 않는다.
09	voluntarily	ad. 자진해서	go ( )	자진해서 가다
10	suggest	v. 제안하다	( ) creative ideas	창의적인 아이디어를 제안하다

⊕ 본문 문장 속에서 단어들을 확인해 보세요.

They have employees / who absolutely do not mind going the extra mile for their boss.

이들은 부하 직원을 두고 있다 / 자기 상사를 위해 한층 더 노력하기를 전혀 사리지 않는.

단어 다시보기 문제를 풀기 전에 단어들을 30초 동안 다시 확인하세요.

01	routinely	주기적으로	be routinely checked	주기적으로 점검받다
02	stop by		stop by at the office	사무실에 들르다
03	particular		be trained on a particular skill	특정한 기술에 대해 훈련을 받다
04	cater		cater meals for the family	그 가족에게 식사를 제공하다
05	gesture		a gesture of support	도움의 표시
06	fiercely		fiercely compete	치열하게 경쟁하다
07	loyal		fiercely loyal	열렬히 충성스러운
08	go the extra mile		They don't mind going the extra mile for their boss.	그들은 자기 상사를 위해 한층 더 노력하기를 사리지 않는다.
09	voluntarily		go voluntarily	자진해서 가다
10	suggest		suggest creative ideas	창의적인 아이디어를 제안하다

⊕ 본문 문장 속에서 단어의 의미를 우리말로 해석해 보세요.

They have employees / who absolutely do not mind going the extra mile for their boss.

→ 이들은 부하 직원을 두고 있다 / 자기 상사를 위해 ____________를 전혀 사리지 않는.

2017 11월 학평 31번 문제

제한시간 80초

난이도 ★★★★☆

STEP 2 • 수능 기출 제대로 풀기

G 다음 빈칸에 들어갈 말로 가장 적절한 것은?

Imagine for a moment that your boss remembers all of your children's names and ages, routinely stops by your desk and asks about them, and then listens as you talk about them. Imagine that same boss tells you about a skill you need to develop and opens up an opportunity for you to be trained on that particular skill. Imagine there is a death in the family, and the boss has your company cater meals for your family after the funeral as a gesture of support. All of these are real scenarios, and guess what? All the bosses who engaged in these acts of care and concern have fiercely loyal employees. They have employees who absolutely do not mind going the extra mile for their boss. They enjoy going to work and voluntarily suggest creative ideas that save the company money and increase sales. These bosses influence the behavior of their team not by telling them what to do differently, but by ______________.

① caring

② warning

③ training

④ pretending

⑤ evaluating

정답과 해설 p.16

STEP 3 • 수능 지문 제대로 복습하기

01 Imagine for a moment / that your boss remembers all of your children's names and ages, / routinely stops by your desk and asks about them, / and then listens as you talk about them.

명령문(~하라) 접속사(~것) 동사1 동사2 동사3 접속사(~할 때)

02 Imagine that same boss tells you / about a skill you need to develop / and opens up an opportunity / for you to be trained on that particular skill.

지시대명사(그) 동사1 목적격 관계대명사절 동사2 목적어 수식(형용사적 용법)

03 Imagine there is a death in the family, / and the boss has your company cater meals for your family / after the funeral / as a gesture of support.

접속사 that 생략 사역동사 목적어 원형부정사 전치사(~로서)

04 All of these are real scenarios, / and guess what? // All the bosses who engaged in these acts of care and concern / have fiercely loyal employees.

주어(복수) 주격 관계대명사절 동사

05 They have employees / who absolutely do not mind going the extra mile for their boss. // They enjoy going to work / and voluntarily suggest creative ideas / that save the company money and increase sales.

주격 관계대명사절 주격 관계대명사절 save A B: A에게 B를 아껴주다

06 These bosses influence the behavior of their team / not by telling them what to do differently, / but by caring.

not A but B: A가 아니라 B인

01 잠시 상상해 보라 / 여러분의 상사가 여러분 자녀의 이름과 나이를 모두 기억해주고, / 주기적으로**routinely** 여러분 자리에 들러서**stop by** 그들에 관해 물어봐주고, / 그런 뒤 여러분이 그들에 관해 이야기할 때 들어준다고.

02 바로 그 상사가 여러분에게 이야기해준다고 상상해 보라 / 여러분이 개발해야 할 능력에 관해 / 그리고 기회를 열어준다고 / 그 특정**particular** 능력을 여러분이 교육받을.

03 가족상이 있다고 상상해 보라 / 그리고 여러분의 상사가 회사에서 여러분의 가족들에게 식사를 제공하게**cater** 해준다고 / 장례식 후에 / 도와주려는 표시**gesture**로.

04 이 모든 것들은 실제 시나리오인데, / 어떻게 생각하는가? // 이런 배려와 관심의 행동을 했던 모든 상사는 / 열렬히 충성스러운**fiercely loyal** 부하 직원을 두고 있다.

05 이들은 부하 직원을 두고 있다 / 자기 상사를 위해 한층 더 노력하기**go the extra mile**를 전혀 사리지 않는. // 그들은 출근하는 것을 즐기며, / 창의적인 아이디어를 자진해서 제안한다**voluntarily suggest** / 회사 돈을 아끼고 매출을 증대시킬.

06 이런 상사들은 자기 팀원들의 행동에 영향을 끼친다 / 그들에게 무엇을 달리 할지 말해줘서가 아니라 / 배려를 통해서.

구문 Check up

① Imagine that same boss tells you about a skill you need to develop and open / opens up an opportunity for you to be trained on that particular skill.

that same boss에 연결되는 동사가 'tells ~ and opens up ~'으로 병렬 연결되는 구조이므로 opens가 정답이다.

② All the bosses who engaged in these acts of care and concern has / have fiercely loyal employees.

All the bosses가 복수명사 주어이므로 have가 적절하다.

정답 ① opens ② have

빈칸 추론 II ➕

STEP 1 • 수능에 *진짜* 나오는 *단어*

✔️ **문제에 나오는 단어들을 확인하세요.**

시간이 없다면 색으로 표시된 단어만이라도 꼭 외우고 넘어가세요!

01	race	*n.* 경주, 인종 *v.* (심장이) 뛰다	take part in a (✔️ race)	경주에 참가하다
02	countryside	*n.* 시골	through the ()	시골을 통과하여
03	discover	*v.* 발견하다	() a fact	사실을 발견하다
04	evolutionary	*a.* 진화의	an () principle	진화의 원칙
05	evolve	*v.* 진화하다, 발전하다	() to run faster	더 빨리 달리게 진화하다
06	generation	*n.* 세대	make a new () of rabbits	새로운 토끼 세대를 만들다
07	pass on	전해주다, 물려주다	() () news	소식을 전해주다
08	gene	*n.* 유전자	have the same ()s	똑같은 유전자를 갖다
09	species	*n.* (생물) 종	save a rare ()	희귀종을 보호하다

➕ **본문 문장 속에서 단어들을 확인해 보세요.**

In Lewis Carroll's *Through the Looking-Glass*, / the Red Queen takes Alice on a race through the countryside.

Lewis Carroll의 <Through the Looking-Glass>에서 / 붉은 여왕은 Alice를 시골을 통과하는 경주에 데리고 간다.

단어 다시보기 문제를 풀기 전에 단어들을 30초 동안 다시 확인하세요.

01	race	경주, 인종 (심장이) 뛰다	take part in a race	경주에 참가하다
02	countryside		through the countryside	시골을 통과하여
03	discover		discover a fact	사실을 발견하다
04	evolutionary		an evolutionary principle	진화의 원칙
05	evolve		evolve to run faster	더 빨리 달리게 진화하다
06	generation		make a new generation of rabbits	새로운 토끼 세대를 만들다
07	pass on		pass on news	소식을 전해주다
08	gene		have the same genes	똑같은 유전자를 갖다
09	species		save a rare species	희귀종을 보호하다

⊕ 본문 문장 속에서 단어의 의미를 우리말로 해석해 보세요.

In Lewis Carroll's *Through the Looking-Glass*, / the Red Queen takes Alice on a race through the countryside.

→ Lewis Carroll의 <Through the Looking-Glass>에서 / 붉은 여왕은 Alice를 ________________ 에 데리고 간다.

2023 3월 학평 33번 문제

제한시간 80초

난이도 ★★★★★

STEP 2 • 수능 기출 제대로 풀기

A 다음 빈칸에 들어갈 말로 가장 적절한 것은?

In Lewis Carroll's *Through the Looking-Glass*, the Red Queen takes Alice on a race through the countryside. They run and they run, but then Alice discovers that they're still under the same tree that they started from. The Red Queen explains to Alice: "*here*, you see, it takes all the running you can do, to keep in the same place." Biologists sometimes use this Red Queen Effect to explain an evolutionary principle. If foxes evolve to run faster so they can catch more rabbits, then only the fastest rabbits will live long enough to make a new generation of bunnies that run even faster — in which case, of course, only the fastest foxes will catch enough rabbits to thrive and pass on their genes. Even though they might run, the two species ______________________.

*thrive: 번성하다

① just stay in place

② end up walking slowly

③ never run into each other

④ won't be able to adapt to changes

⑤ cannot run faster than their parents

정답과 해설 p.17

STEP 3 • 수능 지문 제대로 복습하기

01 In Lewis Carroll's *Through the Looking-Glass*, / the Red Queen takes Alice on a race through the countryside.

02 They run and they run, / but then Alice discovers / that they're still under the same tree / that they started from.
접속사(~것) 선행사(the same+명) 목적격 관계대명사(the same과 짝꿍)

03 The Red Queen explains to Alice: / "*here*, you see, / it takes all the running you can do, / to keep in the same place."
explains의 목적어(직접 인용문) 부사적 용법(목적)

04 Biologists sometimes use this Red Queen Effect / to explain an evolutionary principle.
부사적 용법(목적)

05 If foxes evolve to run faster / so (that) they can catch more rabbits, / then only the fastest rabbits will live long enough / to make a new generation of bunnies / that run even faster / — in which case, of course, / only the fastest foxes will catch enough rabbits / to thrive and pass on their genes.
접속사(~하기 위해) 주격 관계대명사절 형/부+enough+to부정사: ~할 만큼 충분히 …한/하게 enough+명+to부정사: ~할 만큼 충분한 …

06 Even though they might run, / the two species just stay in place.
접속사(~하더라도)

01 Lewis Carroll의 <Through the Looking-Glass>에서 / 붉은 여왕은 Alice를 시골**countryside**을 통과하는 경주**race**에 데리고 간다.

02 그들은 달리고 또 달리지만, / 그러다가 Alice는 발견한다**discover** / 그들이 나무 아래에 여전히 있음을 / 자신들이 출발했던.

03 붉은 여왕은 Alice에게 설명한다 / "'여기서는' 보다시피 / 네가 할 수 있는 모든 뜀박질을 해야 한단다 / 같은 장소에 머물러 있으려면."이라고.

04 생물학자들은 때때로 이 '붉은 여왕 효과'를 이용한다 / 진화**evolutionary** 원리를 설명하기 위해.

05 만약 여우가 더 빨리 달리게 진화한다**evolve**면 / 그들이 더 많은 토끼를 잡기 위해 / 그러면 오직 가장 빠른 토끼만이 충분히 오래 살아 / 새로운 세대**generation**의 토끼를 낳을 텐데, / 훨씬 더 빨리 달리는 / 이 경우 당연하게도 / 가장 빠른 여우만이 충분한 토끼를 잡을 것이다 / 번성하여 자기 유전자를 물려줄**pass on their genes** 만큼.

06 그 두 종**species**이 달린다 해도, / 그것들은 제자리에 머무를 뿐이다.

구문 Check up

① They run and they run, but then Alice discovers that / what they're still under the same tree that they started from.

they're still under the same tree가 완전한 문장이므로 접속사 that이 적절하다. what 뒤에는 불완전한 문장이 나온다.

② *Here*, you see, it takes all the running you can do, keeps / to keep in the same place."

주절인 'it takes ~ do'와 콤마로 분리된 부사구 자리이므로, to keep(~하기 위해)을 쓴다.

정답 ① that ② to keep

DAY 06

B

빈칸 추론 II

STEP 1 • 수능에 진짜 나오는 단어

✔ 문제에 나오는 단어들을 확인하세요.

시간이 없다면 색으로 표시된 단어만이라도 꼭 외우고 넘어가세요!

01	intellectually	ad. 지적으로, 지성에 관해서는	(✔ intellectually) active	지적으로 활발한
02	superior	a. 우월한	( ) to its competitors	경쟁자들보다 우월한
03	modify	v. 변형하다	( ) the form	형태를 변형하다
04	gene	n. 유전자	modify the ( )	유전자를 변형하다
05	receptor	n. 수용체	the hormone ( )	호르몬 수용체
06	chemical	n. 화학 물질	a brain ( )	뇌의 화학 물질
07	genetically	ad. 유전적으로	( ) modified food	유전자 조작 식품
08	inferior	a. 열등한	intellectually ( )	지적으로 열등한
09	standard	a. 표준의	a ( ) cage	표준 우리
10	interaction	n. 상호작용	lots of social ( )	많은 사회적 상호작용
11	handicap	v. 불리한 입장에 두다	be genetically ( )ped	유전적으로 불리한
12	perform	v. 수행하다	They ( )ed well.	그들은 잘 수행했다.
13	triumph	n. 승리	a real ( )	진정한 승리
14	nurture	n. 양육, (천성과 대비되는) 후천성, 환경	the nature-( ) issue	유전과 (양육) 환경의 논쟁

⊕ 본문 문장 속에서 단어들을 확인해 보세요.

One group was made intellectually superior / by modifying the gene for the glutamate receptor.

한 집단은 지적으로 우월하게 만들어졌다 / 글루타민산염 수용체에 대한 유전자를 변형함으로써.

단어 다시보기 문제를 풀기 전에 단어들을 30초 동안 다시 확인하세요.

01	intellectually	지적으로, 지성에 관해서는	intellectually active	지적으로 활발한
02	superior		superior to its competitors	경쟁자들보다 우월한
03	modify		modify the form	형태를 변형하다
04	gene		modify the gene	유전자를 변형하다
05	receptor		the hormone receptor	호르몬 수용체
06	chemical		a brain chemical	뇌의 화학 물질
07	genetically		genetically modified food	유전자 조작 식품
08	inferior		intellectually inferior	지적으로 열등한
09	standard		a standard cage	표준 우리
10	interaction		lots of social interaction	많은 사회적 상호작용
11	handicap		be genetically handicapped	유전적으로 불리한
12	perform		They performed well.	그들은 잘 수행했다.
13	triumph		a real triumph	진정한 승리
14	nurture		the nature-nurture issue	유전과 (양육) 환경의 논쟁

⊕ **본문 문장 속에서 단어의 의미를 우리말로 해석해 보세요.**

One group was made intellectually superior / by modifying the gene for the glutamate receptor.

→ 한 집단은 ________ 만들어졌다 / 글루타민산염 ________에 대한 ________를 ________으로써.

2022 6월 학평 33번 문제

제한시간 80초

난이도 ★★★★★

STEP 2 • 수능 기출 제대로 풀기

B

다음 빈칸에 들어갈 말로 가장 적절한 것은?

In a study at Princeton University in 1992, research scientists looked at two different groups of mice. One group was made intellectually superior by modifying the gene for the glutamate receptor. Glutamate is a brain chemical that is necessary in learning. The other group was genetically manipulated to be intellectually inferior, also done by modifying the gene for the glutamate receptor. The smart mice were then raised in standard cages, while the inferior mice were raised in large cages with toys and exercise wheels and with lots of social interaction. At the end of the study, although the intellectually inferior mice were genetically handicapped, they were able to perform just as well as their genetic superiors. This was a real triumph for nurture over nature. Genes are turned on or off ________________________.

*glutamate: 글루타민산염
**manipulate: 조작하다

① by themselves for survival

② free from social interaction

③ based on what is around you

④ depending on genetic superiority

⑤ so as to keep ourselves entertained

정답과 해설 p.17

STEP 3 • 수능 지문 제대로 복습하기

01 In a study at Princeton University in 1992, / research scientists looked at two different groups of mice.

02 One group was made intellectually superior / by modifying the gene for the glutamate receptor. // Glutamate is a brain chemical / that is necessary in learning.
5형식 동사의 수동태: be p.p. + 목적격 보어(형용사구)
주격 관계대명사절

03 The other group was genetically manipulated / to be intellectually inferior, / also done by modifying the gene / for the glutamate receptor.
선행사
which was 생략

04 The smart mice were then raised in standard cages, / while the inferior mice were raised in large cages / with toys and exercise wheels and with lots of social interaction.
접속사: ~하는 반면에

05 At the end of the study, / although the intellectually inferior mice / were genetically handicapped, / they were able to perform just as well / as their genetic superiors.
원급 비교(as+형용사/부사+as+명사): …만큼 ~하게

06 This was a real triumph for nurture / over nature. // Genes are turned on or off / based on what is around you.
구동사의 수동태(be p.p.+부사/전치사)
관계대명사 what절(전치사 on의 목적어)

01 1992년 프린스턴 대학의 한 연구에서, / 연구 과학자들은 두 개의 다른 쥐 집단을 관찰했다.

02 한 집단은 지적으로 우월하게**intellectually superior** 만들어졌다 / 글루타민산염 수용체**receptor**에 대한 유전자**gene**를 변형**modify**함으로써. // 글루타민산염은 뇌 화학 물질**chemical**이다 / 학습에 필수적인.

03 다른 집단도 유전적으로**genetically** 조작되었는데 / 지적으로 열등하도록**inferior**, / 이것도 역시 유전자를 변형함으로써 이루어졌다 / 글루타민산염 수용체에 대한 (유전자).

04 그 후 똑똑한 쥐들은 표준**standard** 우리에서 길러졌고, / 반면에 열등한 쥐들은 큰 우리에서 길러졌다 / 장난감과 운동용 쳇바퀴가 있고 사회적 상호작용**interaction**이 많은.

05 연구가 끝날 무렵, / 비록 지적으로 열등한 쥐들이 / 유전적으로 불리했지만**be handicapped**, / 그들은 잘 수행할**perform** 수 있었다 / 그들보다 유전적으로 우월한 쥐들만큼.

06 이것은 양육(후천적 환경)**nurture**의 진정한 승리**triumph**였다 / 천성(선천적 성질)에 대한. // 유전자는 켜지거나 꺼진다 / 여러분 주변에 있는 것에 따라.

구문 Check up

① One group made / was made intellectually superior by modifying the gene for the glutamate receptor.

'~하게 만들어졌다'라는 수동의 의미이므로 was made를 쓴다.

② Genes are turned on or off based on that / what is around you.

전치사 on의 목적어가 없고, 뒤에 불완전한 절이 오므로, 선행사(명사)를 포함하는 관계대명사 what을 쓴다.

정답 ① was made ② what

C

STEP 1 • 수능에 진짜 나오는 단어

✔ 문제에 나오는 단어들을 확인하세요.

시간이 없다면 색으로 표시된 단어만이라도 꼭 외우고 넘어가세요!

01	evolutionary	a. 진화의	(✔ evolutionary) biologists	진화 생물학자들
02	trade	v. 거래하다	need to ( )	거래해야 하다
03	establish	v. 확립하다, 정하다	( ) trust	신뢰를 확립하다
04	handy	a. 편리한	Language is very ( ).	언어는 매우 편리하다.
05	conduct	v. 수행하다	( ) business with someone	누군가와 거래를 수행하다
06	bowl	n. 그릇	wooden ( )s	나무로 만든 그릇
07	bunch	n. 다발	six ( )es of bananas	여섯 다발의 바나나
08	nearly	ad. 거의	( ) impossible	거의 불가능한
09	confuse	v. 혼란스럽게 하다	( )ing noises	혼란스러운 소음
10	carry out	실행하다	( ) it ( )	그것을 실행하다
11	according to	~에 따라서	( ) ( ) terms	조항에 따라서
12	term	n. 조항 (보통 복수형태로 씀)	agree on ( )s	조항에 합의하다
13	bond	n. 결속	a ( ) of trust	신뢰라는 결속
14	specific	a. 구체적인	Language allows us to be ( ).	언어는 우리를 구체적이도록 해 준다.

⊕ 본문 문장 속에서 단어들을 확인해 보세요.

Language is very handy / when you are trying to conduct business with someone.

언어는 매우 편리하다 / 당신이 누군가와 거래를 수행하려고 할 때.

단어 다시보기 문제를 풀기 전에 단어들을 30초 동안 다시 확인하세요.

01	evolutionary	진화의	evolutionary biologists	진화 생물학자들
02	trade		need to trade	거래해야 하다
03	establish		establish trust	신뢰를 확립하다
04	handy		Language is very handy.	언어는 매우 편리하다.
05	conduct		conduct business with someone	누군가와 거래를 수행하다
06	bowl		wooden bowls	나무로 만든 그릇
07	bunch		six bunches of bananas	여섯 다발의 바나나
08	nearly		nearly impossible	거의 불가능한
09	confuse		confusing noises	혼란스러운 소음
10	carry out		carry it out	그것을 실행하다
11	according to		according to terms	조항에 따라서
12	term		agree on terms	조항에 합의하다
13	bond		a bond of trust	신뢰라는 결속
14	specific		Language allows us to be specific.	언어는 우리를 구체적이도록 해 준다.

⊕ 본문 문장 속에서 단어의 의미를 우리말로 해석해 보세요.

Language is very handy / when you are trying to conduct business with someone.

→ 언어는 매우 ________ / 당신이 누군가와 거래를 ________ 할 때.

2021 9월 학평 32번 문제

제한시간 70초

난이도 ★★★☆☆

STEP 2 • 수능 기출 제대로 풀기

C

다음 빈칸에 들어갈 말로 가장 적절한 것은?

Many evolutionary biologists argue that humans ______________________________. We needed to trade, and we needed to establish trust in order to trade. Language is very handy when you are trying to conduct business with someone. Two early humans could not only agree to trade three wooden bowls for six bunches of bananas but establish rules as well. What wood was used for the bowls? Where did you get the bananas? That business deal would have been nearly impossible using only gestures and confusing noises, and carrying it out according to terms agreed upon creates a bond of trust. Language allows us to be specific, and this is where conversation plays a key role.

① used body language to communicate

② instinctively knew who to depend on

③ often changed rules for their own needs

④ lived independently for their own survival

⑤ developed language for economic reasons

정답과 해설 p.17

STEP 3 • 수능 지문 제대로 복습하기

01 Many evolutionary biologists argue / that humans developed language / for economic reasons.
(that: 명사절 접속사)

02 We needed to trade, / and we needed to establish trust / in order to trade. // Language is very handy / when you are trying to conduct business with someone.
(in order to trade: to부정사 부사적 용법(~하기 위해))

03 Two early humans / could not only agree / to trade three wooden bowls for six bunches of bananas / but establish rules as well.
(not only A but B as well: A뿐만 아니라 B도(as well: 또한))

04 What wood was used for the bowls? // Where did you get the bananas?

05 That business deal would have been nearly impossible / [using only gestures and confusing noises], / and [carrying it out / according to terms agreed upon] / creates a bond of trust.
(would have been: 가정법 과거완료 주절 / using only gestures and confusing noises: 분사구문 / carrying it out: 동명사 주어(단수 취급) / agreed upon: 과거분사 / creates: 동사)

06 Language allows us to be specific, / and this is where conversation plays a key role.
(allows us to be specific: 5형식 동사(allow)+목적어+목적격 보어(to부정사) / is where: 장소 선행사(the place) 생략)

01 많은 진화 생물학자**evolutionary biologist**들은 주장한다 / 인간이 언어를 발달시켰다고 / 경제적인 이유로.

02 우리는 거래해야**trade** 했고, / 우리는 신뢰를 확립해야**establish trust** 했다 / 거래하기 위해서는. // 언어는 매우 편리하다**very handy** / 당신이 누군가와 거래를 수행하려고**conduct business** 할 때.

03 초창기의 두 인간은 / 동의할 수 있었을 뿐만 아니라 / 세 개의 나무로 만든 그릇**bowl**을 여섯 다발**bunch**의 바나나와 거래하기로 / 규칙을 정할 수도 있었다.

04 무슨 나무가 그 그릇들을 만드는 데 사용되었나? // 당신은 어디서 그 바나나를 얻었나?

05 그 상업 거래는 거의 불가능했을**nearly impossible** 것이다 / 단지 제스처와 혼란스런 소음**confusing noise**만을 사용해서는, / 그리고 그것을 실행하는**carry out** 것이 / 합의된 조항에 따라서**according to terms** / 신뢰라는 결속**bond**을 만든다.

06 언어는 우리가 구체적이도록**specific** 해 주고 / 이것이 대화가 중요한 역할을 하는 지점이다.

구문 Check up

① Two early humans could not only agree to trade three wooden bowls for six bunches of bananas but establish / establishing rules as well.

not only A but B as well 구문으로, 조동사 could에 이어지는 동사구를 병렬 연결하는 구조이므로 동사원형 establish를 쓴다.

② Carry / Carrying it out according to terms agreed upon creates a bond of trust.

문장의 동사는 creates이고 주어가 필요하기 때문에 동명사 형태인 Carrying으로 써야 한다.

정답 ① establish ② Carrying

D

빈칸 추론 II

STEP 1 • 수능에 진짜 나오는 단어

문제에 나오는 단어들을 확인하세요.

시간이 없다면 색으로 표시된 단어만이라도 꼭 외우고 넘어가세요!

01	infant	n. 유아	newborns and (infant)s	신생아와 유아
02	comfort	v. 편하게 하다	Infants are ( )ed.	유아가 편안해한다.
03	rock	v. 흔들다	be comforted by ( )ing	흔들림에 의해 편안해지다
04	convincing	a. 설득력 있는	( ) data	설득력 있는 자료
05	demonstrate	v. 입증하다, 설명하다	( ) a relationship	관계를 입증하다
06	significant	a. 상당한, 중요한	a ( ) relationship	상당한 관계
07	pregnancy	n. 임신	during ( )	임신 기간 동안
08	response	n. 반응	a newborn's ( ) to rocking	신생아의 흔들림에 대한 반응
09	associate	v. 연관시키다	( ) rocking with being fed	흔들림과 수유를 연관시키다
10	gentle	a. 부드러운	( ) rocking	부드러운 흔들림
11	repetitive	a. 반복적인	( ) movement	반복적인 움직임
12	associative	a. 연관되기 쉬운	( ) learning	연관 학습
13	fondness	n. 선호, 좋아함	acquire a ( )	좋아하게 되다
14	consistent	a. 지속적인	( ) feeding	지속적인 수유

⊕ 본문 문장 속에서 단어들을 확인해 보세요.

Parents understand / that rocking quiets a newborn, / and they very often provide gentle, repetitive movement / during feeding.

부모는 알고 있다 / 흔들어 주는 것이 신생아를 달래 준다는 것을 / 그리고 그들은 부드럽고, 반복적인 움직임을 매우 자주 제공한다 / 젖을 주는 동안.

단어 다시보기 문제를 풀기 전에 단어들을 30초 동안 다시 확인하세요.

01	infant	유아	newborns and infants	신생아와 유아
02	comfort		Infants are comforted.	유아가 편안해한다.
03	rock		be comforted by rocking	흔들림에 의해 편안해지다
04	convincing		convincing data	설득력 있는 자료
05	demonstrate		demonstrate a relationship	관계를 입증하다
06	significant		a significant relationship	상당한 관계
07	pregnancy		during pregnancy	임신 기간 동안
08	response		a newborn's response to rocking	신생아의 흔들림에 대한 반응
09	associate		associate rocking with being fed	흔들림과 수유를 연관시키다
10	gentle		gentle rocking	부드러운 흔들림
11	repetitive		repetitive movement	반복적인 움직임
12	associative		associative learning	연관 학습
13	fondness		acquire a fondness	좋아하게 되다
14	consistent		consistent feeding	지속적인 수유

⊕ 본문 문장 속에서 단어의 의미를 우리말로 해석해 보세요.

Parents understand / that rocking quiets a newborn, / and they very often provide gentle, repetitive movement / during feeding.

→ 부모는 알고 있다 / ________이 신생아를 달래 준다는 것을 / 그리고 그들은 ________________을 매우 자주 제공한다 / 젖을 주는 동안.

2020 9월 학평 34번 문제

제한시간 80초

난이도 ★★★★★

STEP 2 • 수능 기출 제대로 풀기

D

다음 빈칸에 들어갈 말로 가장 적절한 것은?

We're often told that newborns and infants are comforted by rocking because this motion is similar to what they experienced in the womb, and that they must take comfort in this familiar feeling. This may be true; however, to date there are no convincing data that demonstrate a significant relationship between the amount of time a mother moves during pregnancy and her newborn's response to rocking. Just as likely is the idea that newborns come to associate gentle rocking with being fed. Parents understand that rocking quiets a newborn, and they very often provide gentle, repetitive movement during feeding. Since the appearance of food is a primary reinforcer, newborns may ______________ because they have been conditioned through a process of associative learning.

*womb: 자궁
**reinforcer: 강화물

① acquire a fondness for motion

② want consistent feeding

③ dislike severe rocking

④ remember the tastes of food

⑤ form a bond with their mothers

정답과 해설 p.18

STEP 3 ● 수능 지문 제대로 복습하기

01 We're often told / that newborns and infants are comforted by rocking / because this motion is similar / to what they experienced in the womb, / and that they must take comfort in this familiar feeling.

병렬구조(직접목적어를 이끄는 that절) / 관계대명사 what절(전치사 to의 목적어) / ~임에 틀림없다

02 This may be true; / however, to date / there are no convincing data / that demonstrate a significant relationship / [between the amount of time a mother moves during pregnancy / and her newborn's response to rocking].

현재까지 / 주격 관계대명사 / 전치사구(between A and B) / 관계부사절(when 생략)

03 Just as likely is the idea / that newborns come to associate gentle rocking with being fed.

보어(형용사구) / 도치(동사+주어) / 동격절(=the idea) / 동명사의 수동태 (being p.p.)

04 Parents understand / that rocking quiets a newborn, / and they very often provide gentle, repetitive movement / during feeding.

명사절 접속사

05 Since the appearance of food is a primary reinforcer, / newborns may acquire a fondness for motion / because they have been conditioned / through a process of associative learning.

접속사(때문에) / 현재완료 수동태

01 우리는 자주 듣는다 / 신생아와 유아**newborns and infants**가 흔들림에 의해 편안해하는데**be comforted by rocking** / 이것은 이런 움직임이 유사하기 때문이라고 / 자궁 안에서 그들이 경험했던 것과, / 그리고 그들이 이런 친숙한 느낌에서 편안해지는 것이 틀림없다고.

02 이것은 사실일 수 있다. / 하지만, 현재까지 / 설득력 있는**convincing** 데이터는 없다 / 상당한**significant** 관계가 있음을 입증하는**demonstrate** / 임신**pregnancy** 기간 동안 엄마가 움직이는 시간의 양과 / 흔들림에 대한 신생아의 반응**response** 사이에.

03 생각도 그만큼 가능할 법하다 / 신생아가 부드러운**gentle** 흔들림을 젖을 먹는 것과 연관시키게**associate** 된다는 (생각).

04 부모는 알고 있다 / 흔들어 주는 것이 신생아를 달래 준다는 것을 / 그리고 그들은 부드럽고, 반복적인**repetitive** 움직임을 매우 자주 제공한다 / 젖을 주는 동안.

05 음식의 등장은 일차 강화물이기 때문에, / 신생아는 아마도 움직임을 좋아하게 되고**acquire a fondness**, / 그 이유는 그들이 조건화되어 왔기 때문이다 / 연관 학습**associative learning**의 과정을 통해.

구문 Check up

① We're often told that / what newborns and infants are comforted by rocking because this motion is similar to what they experienced in the womb.

4형식 동사 tell의 수동태 문장이다. 뒤따르는 절이 완전하므로 tell의 직접목적어 역할을 하는 명사절이 되도록 명사절 접속사 that을 쓴다.

② Since / Because of the appearance of food is a primary reinforcer, newborns may acquire a fondness for motion because they have been conditioned.

뒤에 문장이 나오므로 접속사 Since를 쓴다. because of 뒤에는 명사구가 나온다.

정답 ① that ② Since

E

빈칸 추론 II

STEP 1 • 수능에 진짜 나오는 단어

문제에 나오는 단어들을 확인하세요.

시간이 없다면 색으로 표시된 단어만이라도 꼭 외우고 넘어가세요!

01	vision	n. 비전, 미래상	the old (vision)	기존의 비전
02	unpredictable	a. 예측할 수 없는	in ( ) ways	예측할 수 없는 방식으로
03	optimistic	a. 낙관적인, 긍정적인	( ) ↔ pessimistic	낙관적인 ↔ 비관적인
04	forecast	n. 예측 v. 예측하다	an optimistic ( )	낙관적인 예측
05	blow away	날려버리다	( ) ( ) his forecast	그의 예측을 날려버리다
06	competition	n. 경쟁	aggressive ( )	공격적인 경쟁
07	foresee	v. 예견하다	( ) the recession	경기 침체를 예견하다
08	skyrocket	v. 급등하다	Sales can ( ).	판매가 급등할 수 있다.
09	stick to	~을 고수하다	( ) ( ) the old vision	기존의 비전을 고수하다
10	modify	v. 수정하다	( ) the vision	비전을 수정하다
11	abandon	v. 버리다	( ) the vision	비전을 버리다
12	defend	v. 옹호하다, 방어하다	( ) the wrong decisions	잘못된 결정을 옹호하다
13	conform to	~에 따르다, 맞추다	( ) ( ) the new reality	새로운 현실에 맞추다

⊕ 본문 문장 속에서 단어들을 확인해 보세요.

There is nothing wrong / in modifying your vision / or even abandoning it, / as necessary.

잘못된 것이 아니다 / 당신의 비전을 수정하거나 / 심지어 그것을 버리는 것은 / 필요할 때.

단어 다시보기 문제를 풀기 전에 단어들을 30초 동안 다시 확인하세요.

01	vision	비전, 미래상	the old vision	기존의 비전
02	unpredictable		in unpredictable ways	예측할 수 없는 방식으로
03	optimistic		optimistic ↔ pessimistic	낙관적인 ↔ 비관적인
04	forecast		an optimistic forecast	낙관적인 예측
05	blow away		blow away his forecast	그의 예측을 날려버리다
06	competition		aggressive competition	공격적인 경쟁
07	foresee		foresee the recession	경기 침체를 예견하다
08	skyrocket		Sales can skyrocket.	판매가 급등할 수 있다.
09	stick to		stick to the old vision	기존의 비전을 고수하다
10	modify		modify the vision	비전을 수정하다
11	abandon		abandon the vision	비전을 버리다
12	defend		defend the wrong decisions	잘못된 결정을 옹호하다
13	conform to		conform to the new reality	새로운 현실에 맞추다

⊕ 본문 문장 속에서 단어의 의미를 우리말로 해석해 보세요.

There is nothing wrong / in modifying your vision / or even abandoning it, / as necessary.

➔ 잘못된 것이 아니다 / ____________________ / 심지어 그것을 __________은 / 필요할 때.

2019 9월 학평 34번 문제

제한시간 70초

난이도 ★★★☆☆

STEP 2 • 수능 기출 제대로 풀기

E

다음 빈칸에 들어갈 말로 가장 적절한 것은?

Vision is like shooting at a moving target. Plenty of things can go wrong in the future and plenty more can change in unpredictable ways. When such things happen, you should be prepared to __________________________________. For example, a businessman's optimistic forecast can be blown away by a cruel recession or by aggressive competition in ways he could not have foreseen. Or in another scenario, his sales can skyrocket and his numbers can get even better. In any event, he will be foolish to stick to his old vision in the face of new data. There is nothing wrong in modifying your vision or even abandoning it, as necessary.

*recession: 경기 침체

① explain your vision logically to others

② defend the wrong decisions you've made

③ build a community to share your experience

④ make your vision conform to the new reality

⑤ consult experts to predict the future economy

정답과 해설 p.18

STEP 3 • 수능 지문 제대로 복습하기

01 Vision is like shooting at a moving target. // Plenty of things can go wrong / in the future / and plenty more can change / in unpredictable ways.
(like: 전치사(~처럼), shooting at a moving target: 동명사구)

02 When such things happen, / you should be prepared / to make your vision conform to the new reality.
(make+목적어+목적격 보어(동사원형))

03 For example, / a businessman's optimistic forecast can be blown away / by a cruel recession or by aggressive competition / in ways he could not have foreseen.
(could not have p.p.: ~할 수 없었을 것이다 / 목적격 관계대명사절)

04 Or in another scenario, / his sales can skyrocket / and his numbers can get even better.
(even: 비교급 강조)

05 In any event, / he will be foolish / to stick to his old vision / in the face of new data.
(to stick: 부사적 용법(이유, 판단의 근거))

06 There is nothing wrong / in modifying your vision / or even abandoning it, / as necessary.
(병렬연결(전치사 in의 목적어))

01 비전vision은 움직이는 목표물을 쏘아 맞히는 것과 같다. // 많은 것들이 잘못될 수 있고 / 미래에 / 더 많은 것들이 변할 수 있다 / 예측할 수 없는 방식들로in unpredictable ways.

02 그러한 일들이 일어날 때, / 당신은 준비되어야 한다 / 당신의 비전을 새로운 현실에 맞출conform to 수 있도록.

03 예를 들어, / 한 사업가의 낙관적인 예측optimistic forecast은 날아갈blow away 수 있다 / 잔혹한 경기 침체나 공격적인 경쟁aggressive competition에 의해 / 그가 예견할foresee 수 없었을 방식으로.

04 혹은 또 다른 시나리오에서는 / 그의 판매가 급등하거나skyrocket / 그의 수익이 훨씬 더 나아질 수 있다.

05 어떤 상황에서도, / 그에게 어리석은 일이 될 것이다 / 그의 기존의 비전을 고수하는stick to his old vision 것은 / 새로운 데이터에 직면했을 때.

06 잘못된 것이 아니다 / 당신의 비전을 수정하거나modify / 심지어 그것을 버리는abandon 것은 / 필요할 때.

구문 Check up

① You should be prepared to make your vision conform / to conform to the new reality.

5형식 동사 make는 목적격 보어로 동사원형이 오기 때문에 conform을 써야 한다.

② There is nothing wrong in modifying your vision or even abandoning / to abandon it.

modifying에 이어 전치사 in의 목적어 역할을 하는 동명사 abandoning이 와야 한다.

정답 ① conform ② abandoning

STEP 1 • 수능에 *진짜* 나오는 *단어*

✔ 문제에 나오는 단어들을 확인하세요.

시간이 없다면 색으로 표시된 단어만이라도 꼭 외우고 넘어가세요!

01	physicist	n. 물리학자	a nuclear (✔ physicist)	핵물리학자
02	marble	n. 구슬	the falling ()	떨어지는 구슬
03	vacuum	n. 진공, 진공상태	in a ()	진공 상태에서
04	surround	v. 둘러싸다	The building is ()ed by air.	건물은 공기로 둘러싸여 있다
05	friction	n. 마찰	the () on the marble	구슬에 가해지는 마찰
06	substantially	ad. 상당히, 많이	increase ()	꽤 증가하다
07	simplify	v. 단순화하다	() the problem	문제를 단순화하다
08	affect	v. 영향을 미치다	() the answer	그 답에 영향을 주다
09	assumption	n. 가정	make ()s	가정을 하다
10	complex	a. 복잡한	the () world	복잡한 세상
11	produce	v. 생산하다	() goods	상품을 생산하다

⊕ 본문 문장 속에서 단어들을 확인해 보세요.

Assuming the marble falls in a vacuum / **simplifies** the problem / **without** substantially affecting the answer.

구슬이 진공상태에서 떨어진다고 가정하는 것은 / 그 문제를 단순화한다 / 그 답에 크게 영향을 주지 않고.

단어 다시보기 문제를 풀기 전에 단어들을 30초 동안 다시 확인하세요.

01	physicist	물리학자	a nuclear physicist	핵물리학자
02	marble		the falling marble	떨어지는 구슬
03	vacuum		in a vacuum	진공 상태에서
04	surround		The building is surrounded by air.	건물은 공기로 둘러싸여 있다
05	friction		the friction on the marble	구슬에 가해지는 마찰
06	substantially		increase substantially	꽤 증가하다
07	simplify		simplify the problem	문제를 단순화하다
08	affect		affect the answer	그 답에 영향을 주다
09	assumption		make assumptions	가정을 하다
10	complex		the complex world	복잡한 세상
11	produce		produce goods	상품을 생산하다

⊕ **본문 문장 속에서 단어의 의미를 우리말로 해석해 보세요.**

Assuming the marble falls in a vacuum / simplifies the problem / without substantially affecting the answer.

→ ______고 가정하는 것은 / 그 문제를 ______ / ______ 않고.

2018 9월 학평 34번 문제

제한시간 80초

난이도 ★★★★★

STEP 2 • 수능 기출 제대로 풀기

F

다음 빈칸에 들어갈 말로 가장 적절한 것은?

If you ask a physicist how long it would take a marble to fall from the top of a ten-story building, he will likely answer the question by assuming that the marble falls in a vacuum. In reality, the building is surrounded by air, which applies friction to the falling marble and slows it down. Yet the physicist will point out that the friction on the marble is so small that its effect is negligible. Assuming the marble falls in a vacuum simplifies the problem without substantially affecting the answer. Economists make assumptions for the same reason: Assumptions can simplify the complex world and make it easier to understand. To study the effects of international trade, for example, we might assume that the world consists of only two countries and that each country produces only two goods. By doing so, we can ______________________. Thus, we are in a better position to understand international trade in the complex world.

*negligible: 무시할 수 있는

① prevent violations of consumer rights

② understand the value of cultural diversity

③ guarantee the safety of experimenters in labs

④ focus our thinking on the essence of the problem

⑤ realize the differences between physics and economics

정답과 해설 p.19

STEP 3 • 수능 지문 제대로 복습하기

01 If you ask a physicist / [how long it would take a marble to fall / from the top of a ten-story building], / he will likely answer the question / by assuming that the marble falls in a vacuum.
(의문사절(ask의 직접목적어) / likely: 부사(아마도) / that: 명사절 접속사)

02 In reality, / the building is surrounded by air, / which applies friction to the falling marble / and slows it down.
(air: 선행사 / which: 주격 관계대명사(계속적 용법))

03 Yet the physicist will point out / that the friction on the marble is so small / that its effect is negligible. // Assuming the marble falls in a vacuum / simplifies the problem / without substantially affecting the answer.
(that: 명사절 접속사 / so 형용사 that: 너무 ~해서 …하다 / Assuming the marble falls in a vacuum: 주어(동명사, 단수 취급) / simplifies: 수 일치)

04 Economists make assumptions / for the same reason: / Assumptions can simplify the complex world / and make it easier to understand.
(make it easier to understand: 5형식 동사+목적어+목적격 보어(형용사구))

05 To study the effects of international trade, / for example, / we might assume / that the world consists of only two countries / and that each country produces only two goods. // By doing so, / we can focus our thinking / on the essence of the problem. // Thus, / we are in a better position / to understand international trade in the complex world.
(To study the effects of international trade: 부사적 용법(목적) / that … that: 병렬구조(명사절 접속사 that) / By doing so: by+-ing: ~함으로써 / to understand …: 형용사적 용법)

01 만약 당신이 물리학자**physicist**에게 묻는다면, / 구슬**marble**이 떨어지는 데 시간이 얼마나 걸리는지 / 10층 건물 꼭대기에서, / 그는 그 질문에 아마 답할 것이다 / 진공상태**vacuum**에서 구슬이 떨어지는 것을 가정하고.

02 실제로 / 건물은 공기로 둘러싸여**be surrounded** 있는데, / 그것이 떨어지는 구슬에 마찰**friction**을 가하며 / 그것의 속도를 떨어뜨린다.

03 그러나 그 물리학자는 지적할 것이다 / 구슬에 가해지는 마찰이 너무 작아서 / 그것의 효과는 무시할 수 있다는 점을. // 구슬이 진공상태에서 떨어진다고 가정하는 것은 / 그 문제를 단순화한다**simplify** / 그 답에 크게**substantially** 영향을 주지**affect** 않고.

04 경제학자들도 가정**assumption**을 한다 / 같은 이유로. / 가정은 복잡한**complex** 세상을 단순화하고 / 이해하기 더 쉽게 만들 수 있다.

05 국제무역의 효과를 연구하기 위해 / 예를 들어, / 우리는 가정할 수 있다 / 세상이 단 두 국가로만 구성되었고, / 각각의 국가들이 두 상품만을 생산한다**produce**고. // 그렇게 함으로써, / 우리는 우리의 사고를 집중할 수 있다 / 문제의 본질에. // 따라서 / 우리는 더 나은 위치에 있게 된다 / 복잡한 세상에서의 국제무역을 이해할.

구문 Check up

① In reality, the building is surrounded by air, that / which applies friction to the falling marble and slows it down.

관계대명사 that은 계속적 용법으로 쓸 수 없으므로 which가 적절하다.

② Assuming the marble falls in a vacuum simplify / simplifies the problem without substantially affecting the answer.

동명사(Assuming)는 단수 취급하므로 수 일치하여 simplifies를 쓴다.

정답 ① which ② simplifies

G

빈칸 추론 II

STEP 1 • 수능에 진짜 나오는 단어

문제에 나오는 단어들을 확인하세요.

시간이 없다면 색으로 표시된 단어만이라도 꼭 외우고 넘어가세요!

01	executive	n. 경영진	a chief (executive)	최고 경영자
02	complaint	n. 불평	plenty of ( )s	많은 불평
03	regarding	prep. ~에 대해	( ) feedback	피드백에 대해
04	handler	n. 취급하는 사람	baggage ( )s	수하물 담당자
05	reduce	v. 줄이다	( ) the average wait time	평균 대기 시간을 줄이다
06	result in	결과적으로 ~되다	( ) ( ) satisfaction	결과적으로 만족하다
07	occupy	v. 차지하다, 사용되다	( ) one corner	한쪽 구석을 차지하다
08	exaggerate	v. 부풀리다, 과장하다	( ) about the time	시간에 대해 과장하다
09	bothersome	a. 성가신	a ( ) side effect	성가신 부작용

⊕ 본문 문장 속에서 단어들을 확인해 보세요.

Houston Airport executives faced plenty of complaints / regarding baggage claim time, / so they increased the number of baggage handlers.

Houston 공항의 경영자들은 많은 불평에 직면했다 / 수하물을 찾는 데 걸리는 시간에 대한 / 그래서 그들은 수하물 담당자들의 수를 늘렸다.

단어 다시보기 문제를 풀기 전에 단어들을 30초 동안 다시 확인하세요.

01	executive	경영진	a chief executive	최고 경영자
02	complaint		plenty of complaints	많은 불평
03	regarding		regarding feedback	피드백에 대해
04	handler		baggage handlers	수하물 담당자
05	reduce		reduce the average wait time	평균 대기 시간을 줄이다
06	result in		result in satisfaction	결과적으로 만족하다
07	occupy		occupy one corner	한쪽 구석을 차지하다
08	exaggerate		exaggerate about the time	시간에 대해 과장하다
09	bothersome		a bothersome side effect	성가신 부작용

⊕ 본문 문장 속에서 단어의 의미를 우리말로 해석해 보세요.

Houston Airport executives faced plenty of complaints / regarding baggage claim time, / so they increased the number of baggage handlers.

→ Houston 공항의 ______은 많은 ______에 직면했다 / 수하물을 찾는 데 걸리는 시간______ / 그래서 그들은 ______의 수를 늘렸다.

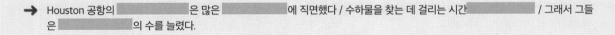

2017 9월 학평 33번 문제

제한시간 70초

난이도 ★★★☆☆

STEP 2 • 수능 기출 제대로 풀기

G

다음 빈칸에 들어갈 말로 가장 적절한 것은?

Houston Airport executives faced plenty of complaints regarding baggage claim time, so they increased the number of baggage handlers. Although it reduced the average wait time to eight minutes, complaints didn't stop. It took about a minute to get from the arrival gate to baggage claim, so the passengers spent seven more minutes waiting for their bags. The solution was to move the arrival gates away from the baggage claim so it took passengers about seven minutes to walk there. It resulted in complaints reducing to almost zero. Research shows occupied time feels shorter than unoccupied time. People usually exaggerate about the time they waited, and what they find most bothersome is time spent unoccupied. Thus, occupying the passengers' time by ______________________ gave them the idea they didn't have to wait as long.

*baggage claim (area): 수하물 찾는 곳

① having them wait in line

② making them walk longer

③ producing more advertisements

④ bothering them with complaints

⑤ hiring more staff to handle bags

정답과 해설 p.19

STEP 3 • 수능 지문 제대로 복습하기

01 Houston Airport executives faced plenty of complaints / regarding baggage claim time, / so they increased the number of baggage handlers. // Although it reduced the average wait time to eight minutes, / complaints didn't stop.

(regarding: 전치사: ~에 관해 / the number of~: ~의 숫자 / Although: 양보의 접속사: ~에도 불구하고)

02 It took about a minute / to get from the arrival gate to baggage claim, / so the passengers spent seven more minutes waiting for their bags.

(It took about a minute / to get: it takes+시간+to부정사: ~하는 데 (시간)이 걸리다 / spent seven more minutes waiting: spend+시간+-ing: (시간)을 ~하는 데 쓰다)

03 The solution was to move the arrival gates away from the baggage claim / so (that) it took passengers about seven minutes / to walk there.

(to move: to부정사의 명사적 용법(보어) / so (that): 접속사(결과, 목적))

04 It resulted in / complaints reducing to almost zero. // Research shows / occupied time feels shorter than unoccupied time.

(resulted in: 결과적으로 ~되다 / complaints: 동명사의 의미상 주어 / reducing: 동명사(전치사 in의 목적어) / 접속사 that 생략 / occupied: 과거분사)

05 People usually exaggerate about the time / they waited, / and what they find most bothersome / is time spent unoccupied.

(when 생략 / what they find most bothersome: 주어(관계대명사 what절) / is: 동사(단수) / spent: 과거분사(명사 수식))

06 Thus, occupying the passengers' time / by making them walk longer / gave them the idea / they didn't have to wait as long.

(occupying: 주어(동명사) / gave them the idea: 수여동사+간접목적어+직접목적어 / 동격의 that 생략 / they didn't have to wait as long: the idea의 의미를 보충)

01 Houston 공항의 임원들**executive**은 많은 불평**complaint**에 직면했다 / 수하물 찾는 데 걸리는 시간에 대한**regarding** / 그래서 그들은 수하물 담당자들**baggage handler**의 수를 늘렸다. // 비록 이것이 기다리는 평균 시간을 8분으로 줄였지만**reduce** / 불평은 멈추지 않았다.

02 약 1분의 시간이 걸렸다 / 도착 게이트에서 수하물을 찾는 곳까지 도달하는 데 / 그래서 탑승객들은 그들의 가방을 기다리며 7분을 더 보냈다.

03 그 해결책은 도착 게이트를 수하물 찾는 곳으로부터 더 멀리 이동시키는 것이었고 / 그 결과 탑승객들에게 약 7분의 시간이 걸렸다 / 걸어가는 데.

04 이는 결과를 가져왔다**result in** / 불평이 거의 0으로 줄어드는. // 연구는 보여준다 / 사용되는 시간**occupied time**이 사용되지 않은 시간보다 더 짧게 느껴진다는 것을.

05 사람들은 보통 시간에 대해 과장한다**exaggerate** / 그들이 기다렸던 / 그리고 그들이 가장 성가신**bothersome** 것으로 여기는 것은 / 사용되지 않은 채로 보내진 시간이다.

06 그래서 탑승객들의 시간을 차지하는 것은 / 그들을 더 오래 걷게 함으로써 / 그들에게 생각을 갖게 했다 / 그렇게 오래 기다릴 필요가 없다는.

구문 Check up

① It / That took about a minute to get from the arrival gate to baggage claim, so the passengers spent seven more minutes waiting for their bags.

<it takes+시간+to부정사> 구문이므로 It을 쓴다. 이 It은 원칙적으로 다른 대명사로 대체될 수 없다.

② People usually exaggerate about the time they waited, and what they find most bothersome is / are time spent unoccupied.

주어가 what they find most bothersome으로 관계대명사 what절이기 때문에 단수 취급한다. 따라서 is를 쓴다.

정답 ① It ② is

Review

DAY 04~06

종합 성적표

구분	공부한 날 ❶	결과 분석			틀린 이유 ❸
		출처	풀이 시간 ❷	채점 결과 (O, X)	
Day 4	월 일	학력평가 기출 2023년	분 초		
		학력평가 기출 2022년	분 초		
		학력평가 기출 2021년	분 초		
		학력평가 기출 2020년	분 초		
		학력평가 기출 2019년	분 초		
		학력평가 기출 2018년	분 초		
		학력평가 기출 2016년	분 초		
Day 5	월 일	학력평가 기출 2023년	분 초		
		학력평가 기출 2022년	분 초		
		학력평가 기출 2021년	분 초		
		학력평가 기출 2020년	분 초		
		학력평가 기출 2019년	분 초		
		학력평가 기출 2018년	분 초		
		학력평가 기출 2017년	분 초		
Day 6	월 일	학력평가 기출 2023년	분 초		
		학력평가 기출 2022년	분 초		
		학력평가 기출 2021년	분 초		
		학력평가 기출 2020년	분 초		
		학력평가 기출 2019년	분 초		
		학력평가 기출 2018년	분 초		
		학력평가 기출 2017년	분 초		

3일간 공부한 내용을 다시 보니, ……

❶ **매일 지문을 하루 계획에 맞춰 풀었다. vs. 내가 한 약속을 못 지켰다.**

<매3영 고1 기출>은 단순 문제풀이를 위한 책이 아니라, 매일 규칙적으로 영어를 공부하는 습관을 잡는 책입니다. 따라서 푸는 문제 개수는 상황에 따라 다르더라도 '매일' 학습하는 것이 중요합니다.

❷ **주어진 시간을 자꾸 넘긴다?**

풀이 시간이 계속해서 권장 시간을 넘긴다면 실전 훈련이 부족하다는 신호입니다. 아직 조급함을 가질 필요는 없지만, 매일의 문제 풀이에 더 긴장감 있게 임해보세요.

❸ **틀린 이유 맞춤 솔루션**: 오답 이유에 따라 다음 해결책을 참고하세요.

(1) 단어를 많이 몰라서

▶ <STEP 1 단어>에 제시된 필수 어휘를 매일 챙겨보고, SELF-TEST까지 꼼꼼히 진행합니다.

(2) 문장 해석이 잘 안 돼서

▶ <STEP 3 지문 복습>의 구문 첨삭과 끊어읽기 해설을 정독하며 문장구조를 보는 눈을 길러보세요.

(3) 해석은 되지만 내용이 이해가 안 되거나, 선택지로 연결을 못 해서

▶ <정답과 해설>의 해설과 오답풀이를 참고해 틀린 이유를 깊이 고민하고 정리해 보세요.

!

결론적으로, 내가 **취약한 부분**은 ______ 이다. **취약점을 보완하기 위해서** 나는 ______ 을/를 해야겠다.

3일 뒤 다시 봐야 할 문항과, 꼭 다시 외워야 할 사항·구문 등이 있는 페이지는 지금 바로 접어 두세요.

<매3영>이 제시하는 3단계로

유형3일 훈련

DAY 07~09

공부한 날			출처	페이지
DAY 7	월	일	학력평가 기출 2023년 학력평가 기출 2022년 학력평가 기출 2021년 학력평가 기출 2020년 학력평가 기출 2019년 학력평가 기출 2018년 학력평가 기출 2017년	181
DAY 8	월	일	학력평가 기출 2023년 학력평가 기출 2022년 학력평가 기출 2021년 학력평가 기출 2020년 학력평가 기출 2019년 학력평가 기출 2018년 학력평가 기출 2016년	209
DAY 9	월	일	학력평가 기출 2023년 학력평가 기출 2022년 학력평가 기출 2021년 학력평가 기출 2020년 학력평가 기출 2019년 학력평가 기출 2018년 학력평가 기출 2017년	237

DAY 07

A

함축적 의미 추론 ⊕

STEP 1 • 수능에 진짜 나오는 단어

✔ 문제에 나오는 단어들을 확인하세요.

시간이 없다면 색으로 표시된 단어만이라도 꼭 외우고 넘어가세요!

01	purchase	*n.* 구매 *v.* 구매하다, 사다	make a big (✔ purchase)	대량 구매하다
02	influence	*n.* 영향(력)	understand the ( )	영향력을 이해하다
03	likelihood	*n.* 가능성	the ( ) of purchase	구매 가능성
04	return	*v.* 반품하다	( ) the product	제품을 반품하다
05	encourage	*v.* 권장하다	( ) others to purchase the product	다른 사람들에게 제품을 사라고 권장하다
06	satisfied	*a.* 만족한	( ) customers	만족한 고객들
07	ambassador	*n.* 대사, 사절	a brand ( )	브랜드 (홍보) 대사
08	advertisement	*n.* 광고	TV ( )s	TV 광고
09	continually	*ad.* 지속적으로	( ) monitor your customer's satisfaction	고객의 만족을 지속적으로 관찰하다
10	word-of-mouth	*a.* 입소문의, 구전의	negative ( ) advertising	부정적인 입소문 광고

⊕ 본문 문장 속에서 단어들을 확인해 보세요.

By continually monitoring your customer's satisfaction after the sale, / you have the ability to avoid negative word-of-mouth advertising.

판매 후 고객의 만족을 지속적으로 관찰하여, / 당신은 부정적인 입소문 광고를 피할 수 있는 능력을 얻는다.

단어 다시보기 문제를 풀기 전에 단어들을 30초 동안 다시 확인하세요.

01	purchase	구매, 구매하다, 사다	make a big purchase	대량 구매하다
02	influence		understand the influence	영향력을 이해하다
03	likelihood		the likelihood of purchase	구매 가능성
04	return		return the product	제품을 반품하다
05	encourage		encourage others to purchase the product	다른 사람들에게 제품을 사라고 권장하다
06	satisfied		satisfied customers	만족한 고객들
07	ambassador		a brand ambassador	브랜드 (홍보) 대사
08	advertisement		TV advertisements	TV 광고
09	continually		continually monitor your customer's satisfaction	고객의 만족을 지속적으로 관찰하다
10	word-of-mouth		negative word-of-mouth advertising	부정적인 입소문 광고

⊕ 본문 문장 속에서 단어의 의미를 우리말로 해석해 보세요.

By continually monitoring your customer's satisfaction after the sale, / you have the ability to avoid negative word-of-mouth advertising.

→ 판매 후 고객의 만족을 __________ 관찰하여, / 당신은 __________를 피할 수 있는 능력을 얻는다.

2023 6월 학평 21번 문제

제한시간 80초

난이도 ★★★★☆

STEP 2 • 수능 기출 제대로 풀기

A

밑줄 친 become unpaid ambassadors가 다음 글에서 의미하는 바로 가장 적절한 것은?

Why do you care how a customer reacts to a purchase? Good question. By understanding post-purchase behavior, you can understand the influence and the likelihood of whether a buyer will repurchase the product (and whether she will keep it or return it). You'll also determine whether the buyer will encourage others to purchase the product from you. Satisfied customers can become unpaid ambassadors for your business, so customer satisfaction should be on the top of your to-do list. People tend to believe the opinions of people they know. People trust friends over advertisements any day. They know that advertisements are paid to tell the "good side" and that they're used to persuade them to purchase products and services. By continually monitoring your customer's satisfaction after the sale, you have the ability to avoid negative word-of-mouth advertising.

① recommend products to others for no gain

② offer manufacturers feedback on products

③ become people who don't trust others' words

④ get rewards for advertising products overseas

⑤ buy products without worrying about the price

정답과 해설 p.20

STEP 3 • 수능 지문 제대로 복습하기

01 Why do you care how a customer reacts to a purchase? // Good question.
간접의문문(care의 목적절)

02 By understanding post-purchase behavior, / you can understand the influence and the likelihood / of whether a buyer will repurchase the product / (and whether she will keep it or return it). // You'll also determine / whether the buyer will encourage others to purchase the product from you.
~함으로써(수단) / ~인지 아닌지 / 동사구 / 목적어 / the likelihood 수식 / 목적절(~인지 아닌지) / encourage+목적어+to부정사: ~이 …하도록 권장하다

03 Satisfied customers can become unpaid ambassadors for your business, / so customer satisfaction should be on the top of your to-do list.

04 People tend to believe the opinions of people they know. // People trust friends over advertisements any day.
목적격 관계대명사절(whom 생략)

05 They know / that advertisements are paid to tell the "good side" / and that they're used to persuade them to purchase products and services.
목적절1 / 목적절2(be used to+동사원형: ~하려고 이용되다)

06 By continually monitoring your customer's satisfaction after the sale, / you have the ability to avoid negative word-of-mouth advertising.
형용사적 용법

01 왜 당신은 고객이 구매**purchase**에 어떻게 반응하는지 신경 쓰는가? // 좋은 질문이다.

02 구매 후 행동을 이해함으로써, / 당신은 그 영향력**influence**과 가능성**likelihood**을 이해할 수 있다 / 구매자가 제품을 재구매할지의 / (그리고 그 사람이 제품을 가질지 또는 반품할지**return**). // 당신은 또한 알아낼 것이다 / 구매자가 다른 사람들에게 당신에게서 제품을 구매하도록 권장할지**encourage** 아닐지도.

03 만족한**satisfied** 고객은 당신의 사업을 위한 무급 대사**ambassador**가 될 수 있으므로, / 고객 만족은 할 일 목록의 최상단에 있어야 한다.

04 사람들은 자기가 아는 사람들의 의견을 믿는 경향이 있다. // 사람들은 언제든 광고**advertisement**보다 친구를 더 신뢰한다.

05 그들은 알고 있다 / 광고는 '좋은 면'을 말하려고 돈을 받는다는 것 / 그리고 그것들은 제품과 서비스를 구매하도록 그들을 설득하는 데 이용된다는 것을.

06 판매 후 고객의 만족을 지속적으로**continually** 관찰하여, / 당신은 부정적인 입소문**word-of-mouth** 광고를 피할 수 있는 능력을 얻는다.

구문 Check up

① By understanding post-purchase behavior, you can understand the influence and the likelihood of that / whether a buyer will repurchase the product.

문맥상 '~인지 아닌지'라는 의미를 나타내면서 전치사 of의 목적절을 이끄는 접속사 자리이므로 whether가 적절하다. 접속사 that은 전치사 뒤에 나올 수 없다.

② They know that advertisements are paid to tell the "good side" and what / that they're used to persuade them to purchase products and services.

and 앞뒤로 know의 목적절이 병렬 연결된 'that ~ and that ~' 구조이다. 따라서 that이 적절하다. 뒤에 <be used to+동사원형>이 포함된 완전한 문장이 연결되었다.

정답 ① whether ② that

DAY 07

B

STEP 1 • 수능에 진짜 나오는 단어

함축적 의미 추론 +

✔ 문제에 나오는 단어들을 확인하세요.

시간이 없다면 색으로 표시된 단어만이라도 꼭 외우고 넘어가세요!

01	psychology	n. 심리학	child (✓ psychology)	아동 심리학
02	professor	n. 교수	a psychology ( )	한 심리학 교수
03	management	n. 관리	stress ( )	스트레스 관리
04	principle	n. 원칙	the basic ( )s	기본 원리
05	absolute	a. 절대적인	the ( ) weight	절대적 무게
06	matter	v. 중요하다	It doesn't ( ).	그것은 중요하지 않다.
07	depend on	~에 달려 있다	It ( )s ( ) your mind.	그것은 네 마음에 달려 있다.
08	severe	a. 심각한	( ) losses	심각한 손실
09	pain	n. 고통	severe ( )	심각한 고통
10	nod one's head	고개를 끄덕이다	The class ( )ded ( ) ( )s.	반 학생들은 고개를 끄덕였다.
11	agreement	n. 동의	in ( )	동의하며
12	continue	v. 계속하다	She ( )d.	그녀는 (말을) 계속했다.
13	sign	n. 신호	a strong ( )	강력한 신호

⊕ 본문 문장 속에서 단어들을 확인해 보세요.

The absolute weight of this glass doesn't matter.

이 잔의 절대적 무게는 중요하지 않습니다.

단어 다시보기 문제를 풀기 전에 단어들을 30초 동안 다시 확인하세요.

01	psychology	심리학	child psychology	아동 심리학
02	professor		a psychology professor	한 심리학 교수
03	management		stress management	스트레스 관리
04	principle		the basic principles	기본 원리
05	absolute		the absolute weight	절대적 무게
06	matter		It doesn't matter.	그것은 중요하지 않다.
07	depend on		It depends on your mind.	그것은 네 마음에 달려 있다.
08	severe		severe losses	심각한 손실
09	pain		severe pain	심각한 고통
10	nod one's head		The class nodded their heads.	반 학생들은 고개를 끄덕였다.
11	agreement		in agreement	동의하며
12	continue		She continued.	그녀는 (말을) 계속했다.
13	sign		a strong sign	강력한 신호

⊕ 본문 문장 속에서 단어의 의미를 우리말로 해석해 보세요.

The absolute weight of this glass doesn't matter.

→ 이 잔의 ________ 무게는 ________ 않습니다.

2022 6월 학평 21번 문제

제한시간 60초

난이도 ★★☆☆☆

STEP 2 • 수능 기출 제대로 풀기

B

밑줄 친 put the glass down이 다음 글에서 의미하는 바로 가장 적절한 것은?

A psychology professor raised a glass of water while teaching stress management principles to her students, and asked them, "How heavy is this glass of water I'm holding?" Students shouted out various answers. The professor replied, "The absolute weight of this glass doesn't matter. It depends on how long I hold it. If I hold it for a minute, it's quite light. But, if I hold it for a day straight, it will cause severe pain in my arm, forcing me to drop the glass to the floor. In each case, the weight of the glass is the same, but the longer I hold it, the heavier it feels to me." As the class nodded their heads in agreement, she continued, "Your stresses in life are like this glass of water. If you still feel the weight of yesterday's stress, it's a strong sign that it's time to put the glass down."

① pour more water into the glass

② set a plan not to make mistakes

③ let go of the stress in your mind

④ think about the cause of your stress

⑤ learn to accept the opinions of others

정답과 해설 p.20

STEP 3 • 수능 지문 제대로 복습하기

01 A psychology professor raised a glass of water / while teaching stress management principles to her students, / and asked them, / "How heavy is this glass of water / I'm holding?"

(raised: 동사1 / asked: 동사2 / while teaching ~: 접속사가 남아있는 분사구문(=while she taught ~) / this glass of water / I'm: 목적격 관계대명사 생략)

02 Students shouted out various answers. // The professor replied, / "The absolute weight of this glass doesn't matter. // It depends on how long I hold it.

(how long I hold it: 의문사절(전치사 on의 목적어))

03 If I hold it for a minute, / it's quite light. // But, if I hold it for a day straight, / it will cause severe pain in my arm, / forcing me to drop the glass to the floor.

(forcing me to drop the glass to the floor: 분사구문: 5형식 동사+목적어+목적격 보어(to부정사))

04 In each case, / the weight of the glass is the same, / but the longer I hold it, / the heavier it feels to me."

(the 비교급 ~, the 비교급 …: ~하면 할수록 더 …하다)

05 As the class nodded their heads in agreement, / she continued, / "Your stresses in life are like this glass of water.

(like: 전치사(~처럼))

06 If you still feel the weight of yesterday's stress, / it's a strong sign / that it's time to put the glass down."

(that it's time to put the glass down: a strong sign을 자세히 설명해주는 동격의 that절)

01 한 심리학 교수psychology professor가 물이 든 유리잔을 들어 올렸다 / 학생들에게 스트레스 관리management 원칙principle을 가르치던 중에, / 그리고 물었다, / "이 물 잔은 얼마나 무거울까요 / 제가 들고 있는?"

02 학생들은 다양한 대답을 외쳤다. // 그 교수가 답했다, / "이 잔의 절대적absolute 무게는 중요하지matter 않습니다. // 이는 제가 이 잔을 얼마나 오래 들고 있느냐에 달려 있죠depend on.

03 만약 제가 이것을 1분 동안 들고 있다면, / 꽤 가볍죠. // 하지만, 만약 제가 이것을 하루 종일 들고 있다면, / 이것은 제 팔에 심각한 고통severe pain을 야기하고, / 잔을 바닥에 떨어뜨리게 할 것입니다.

04 각 사례에서, / 잔의 무게는 같은데, / 하지만 제가 오래 들고 있을수록 / 그것은 저에게 더 무겁게 느껴지죠."

05 학생들은 동의하며 고개를 끄덕였고nod their heads in agreement, / 교수는 말을 계속했다continue, / "여러분이 인생에서 느끼는 스트레스들도 이 물잔과 같습니다.

06 만약 아직도 어제 받은 스트레스의 무게를 느낀다면, / 그것은 강력한 신호sign입니다 / 잔을 내려놓아야 할 때라는."

구문 Check up

① But, if I hold it for a day straight, it will cause severe pain in my arm, forcing me drop / to drop the glass to the floor.

동사 force의 목적격 보어 자리이므로 to부정사인 to drop이 적절하다.

② If you still feel the weight of yesterday's stress, it's a strong sign that / which it's time to put the glass down.

뒤따르는 절이 완전하고, 내용상 앞의 a strong sign을 자세히 설명하므로 동격의 절을 이끄는 that을 쓴다.

정답 ① to drop ② that

C

함축적 의미 추론

STEP 1 • 수능에 진짜 나오는 단어

문제에 나오는 단어들을 확인하세요.

시간이 없다면 색으로 표시된 단어만이라도 꼭 외우고 넘어가세요!

01	tendency	n. 경향	have a (✓ tendency)	경향이 있다
02	interpret	v. 해석하다	( ) events	사건을 해석하다
03	selectively	ad. 선택적으로	interpret events ( )	사건을 선택적으로 해석하다
04	stack	v. 쌓다	( ) evidence	증거를 쌓다
05	viewpoint	n. 관점	support a ( )	관점을 뒷받침하다
06	perception	n. 지각, 인식	selective ( )	선택적인 지각
07	stand out	두드러지다	seem to ( ) ( )	두드러져 보이다
08	may well	~할 수도 있다, 아마 ~일 것이다	( ) ( ) be wrong	틀릴 수도 있다
09	current	a. 현재의	( ) demands	현재의 요구들
10	nail	n. 못	look like a ( )	못처럼 보이다
11	quote	n. 인용문	The ( ) highlights the phenomenon.	인용문은 그 현상을 강조한다.
12	phenomenon	n. 현상	the ( ) of selective perception	선택적 지각 현상
13	as though	마치 ~인 것처럼	( ) ( ) it is full of nails	마치 못이 가득한 것처럼

⊕ 본문 문장 속에서 단어들을 확인해 보세요.

Selective perception / is based on / what seems to us to stand out.

선택적인 지각은 / 기반을 둔다 / 우리에게 두드러져 보이는 것에.

단어 다시보기 문제를 풀기 전에 단어들을 30초 동안 다시 확인하세요.

01	tendency	경향	have a tendency	경향이 있다
02	interpret		interpret events	사건을 해석하다
03	selectively		interpret events selectively	사건을 선택적으로 해석하다
04	stack		stack evidence	증거를 쌓다
05	viewpoint		support a viewpoint	관점을 뒷받침하다
06	perception		selective perception	선택적인 지각
07	stand out		seem to stand out	두드러져 보이다
08	may well		may well be wrong	틀릴 수도 있다
09	current		current demands	현재의 요구들
10	nail		look like a nail	못처럼 보이다
11	quote		The quote highlights the phenomenon.	인용문은 그 현상을 강조한다.
12	phenomenon		the phenomenon of selective perception	선택적 지각 현상
13	as though		as though it is full of nails	마치 못이 가득한 것처럼

⊕ 본문 문장 속에서 단어의 의미를 우리말로 해석해 보세요.

Selective perception / is based on / what seems to us to stand out.

→ ______은 / 기반을 둔다 / 우리에게 ______ 보이는 것에.

2021 6월 학평 21번 문제

제한시간 80초

난이도 ★★★★★

STEP 2 • 수능 기출 제대로 풀기

C

밑줄 친 want to use a hammer가 다음 글에서 의미하는 바로 가장 적절한 것은?

We have a tendency to interpret events selectively. If we want things to be "this way" or "that way" we can most certainly select, stack, or arrange evidence in a way that supports such a viewpoint. Selective perception is based on what seems to us to stand out. However, what seems to us to be standing out may very well be related to our goals, interests, expectations, past experiences, or current demands of the situation — "with a hammer in hand, everything looks like a nail." This quote highlights the phenomenon of selective perception. If we want to use a hammer, then the world around us may begin to look as though it is full of nails!

① are unwilling to stand out

② make our effort meaningless

③ intend to do something in a certain way

④ hope others have a viewpoint similar to ours

⑤ have a way of thinking that is accepted by others

정답과 해설 p.20

STEP 3 • 수능 지문 제대로 복습하기

01 We have a tendency / to interpret events selectively.
to부정사의 형용사적 용법

02 If we want things to be "this way" or "that way" / we can most certainly select, stack, or arrange evidence / in a way that supports such a viewpoint.
5형식 동사(want)+목적어+목적격 보어(to부정사)
주격 관계대명사절

03 Selective perception / is based on / what seems to us to stand out.
seem+to부정사: ~하는 것으로 보이다
관계대명사 what절(전치사 on의 목적어)

04 However, / what seems to us to be standing out / may very well be related / to our goals, interests, expectations, past experiences, or current demands of the situation / — "with a hammer in hand, / everything looks like a nail."
may well+동사원형: ~할 수도 있다, 아마 ~일 것이다
관계대명사 what절(주어)
대시(—): 인용구 연결
주어(단수 취급)

05 This quote highlights the phenomenon of selective perception. // If we want to use a hammer, / then the world around us may begin to look / as though it is full of nails!
마치 ~인 것처럼(=as if)

01 우리는 경향**tendency**이 있다 / 사건을 선택적으로 해석하는**interpret events selectively**.

02 만약 우리가 일이 "이렇게" 또는 "그렇게" 되기를 원한다면, / 우리는 아주 틀림없이 증거를 선택하거나 쌓거나**stack** 배열할 수 있다 / 그러한 관점**viewpoint**을 뒷받침하는 방식으로.

03 선택적인 지각**selective perception**은 / 기반을 둔다 / 우리에게 두드러져**stand out** 보이는 것에.

04 그러나 / 우리에게 두드러져 보이고 있는 것은 / 매우 관련 있을지도 모른다**may very well be related to** / 우리의 목표, 관심사, 기대, 과거의 경험 또는 상황에 대한 현재의**current** 요구와 / — 즉, "망치를 손에 들고 있으면, / 모든 것은 못**nail**처럼 보인다."

05 이 인용문**quote**은 선택적 지각 현상**phenomenon**을 강조한다. // 만약 우리가 망치를 사용하기를 원하면, / 우리 주변의 세상은 보이기 시작할지도 모른다 / 마치 못으로 가득한 것처럼**as though it is full of nails**!

구문 Check up

① If we want things [be / to be] "this way" or "that way" we can most certainly select, stack, or arrange evidence in a way that supports such a viewpoint.

동사 want는 5형식 동사로 쓰일 때 목적격 보어로 to부정사를 쓴다. 따라서 to be가 적절하다.

② Selective perception is based on [that / what] seems to us to stand out.

전치사 on의 목적어가 없고, 뒤에 불완전한 문장이 오므로 선행사(명사)를 포함하는 관계대명사 what이 적절하다.

정답 ① to be ② what

D

무관한 문장 찾기

STEP 1 • 수능에 진짜 나오는 단어

문제에 나오는 단어들을 확인하세요.

시간이 없다면 색으로 표시된 단어만이라도 꼭 외우고 넘어가세요!

01	pay attention to	~에 주의를 기울이다	(✓ pay)(attention)(to) some people	몇몇 사람에게 주의를 기울이다
02	reflect	v. 나타내다, 반영하다	( ) a hard fact	명백한 사실을 나타내다
03	limit	n. 한계 v. 제한하다	( )s on the number of people	사람의 수에 대한 한계
04	stable	a. 안정적인	( ) social relationships	안정적인 사회 관계
05	background	n. 배경	different ( )s	다른 배경
06	colorful	a. 다채로운	Your life becomes ( ).	삶이 다채로워진다.
07	be capable of	~를 할 수 있다	( )( )( ) forming	형성할 수 있다
08	form	v. 형성하다	( ) meaningful relationships	의미 있는 관계를 형성하다
09	maximum	n. 최대	a ( ) of a hundred people	최대 100명
10	assume	v. 가정하다	( ) that we can't be real friends	우리가 진정한 친구가 될 수 없다고 가정하다

본문 문장 속에서 단어들을 확인해 보세요.

It just reflects a hard fact: / there are limits on the number of people / we can possibly pay attention to / or develop a relationship with.

그것은 단지 명백한 사실을 반영할 뿐인데, / 사람의 수에 한계가 있다는 것이다 / 우리가 아마 주의를 기울이거나 / 관계를 발전시킬 수 있는.

단어 다시보기 문제를 풀기 전에 단어들을 30초 동안 다시 확인하세요.

01	pay attention to	~에 주의를 기울이다	pay attention to some people	몇몇 사람에게 주의를 기울이다
02	reflect		reflect a hard fact	명백한 사실을 나타내다
03	limit		limits on the number of people	사람의 수에 대한 한계
04	stable		stable social relationships	안정적인 사회 관계
05	background		different backgrounds	다른 배경
06	colorful		Your life becomes colorful.	삶이 다채로워진다.
07	be capable of		be capable of forming	형성할 수 있다
08	form		form meaningful relationships	의미 있는 관계를 형성하다
09	maximum		a maximum of a hundred people	최대 100명
10	assume		assume that we can't be real friends	우리가 진정한 친구가 될 수 없다고 가정하다

⊕ 본문 문장 속에서 단어의 의미를 우리말로 해석해 보세요.

It just reflects a hard fact: / there are limits on the number of people / we can possibly pay attention to / or develop a relationship with.

➔ 그것은 단지 명백한 사실을 ______ 뿐인데, / 사람의 수에 ______가 있다는 것이다 / 우리가 아마 ______ / 관계를 발전시킬 수 있는.

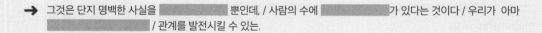

2020 3월 학평 39번 문제

제한시간 70초

난이도 ★★★☆☆

STEP 2 • 수능 기출 제대로 풀기

D

다음 글에서 전체 흐름과 관계 없는 문장은?

Paying attention to some people and not others doesn't mean you're being dismissive or arrogant. ① It just reflects a hard fact: there are limits on the number of people we can possibly pay attention to or develop a relationship with. ② Some scientists even believe that the number of people with whom we can continue stable social relationships might be limited naturally by our brains. ③ The more people you know of different backgrounds, the more colorful your life becomes. ④ Professor Robin Dunbar has explained that our minds are only really capable of forming meaningful relationships with a maximum of about a hundred and fifty people. ⑤ Whether that's true or not, it's safe to assume that we can't be real friends with everyone.

*dismissive: 무시하는
**arrogant: 거만한

정답과 해설 p.21

STEP 3 • 수능 지문 제대로 복습하기

01 Paying attention to some people and not others / doesn't mean / you're being dismissive or arrogant.
주어(동명사) 동사(단수) 접속사 that 생략

02 It just reflects a hard fact: / there are limits on the number of people / we can possibly pay attention to or develop a relationship with.
콜론: 부연 설명 관계대명사 who(m) 생략

03 Some scientists even believe / that the number of people with whom we can continue stable social relationships / might be limited naturally / by our brains.
명사절 접속사 전치사+관계대명사절

04 The more people you know of different backgrounds, / the more colorful your life becomes.
the 비교급 ~, the 비교급 …: ~하면 할수록 더 …하다

05 Professor Robin Dunbar has explained / that our minds are only really capable of forming meaningful relationships / with a maximum of about a hundred and fifty people.
명사절 접속사

06 Whether that's true or not, / it's safe to assume / that we can't be real friends with everyone.
부사절 접속사: ~이든 아니든 가주어 진주어(to부정사) 명사절 접속사

01 일부 사람들에게 주의를 기울이고**pay attention to** 다른 사람들에게 그렇게 하지 않는 것이 / 의미하지는 않는다 / 여러분이 남을 무시하고 있다거나 거만하게 굴고 있다는 것을.

02 그것은 단지 명백한 사실을 나타낼**reflect a hard fact** 뿐인데, / 사람의 수에 한계**limits on the number of people**가 있다는 것이다 / 우리가 가능한대로(최대한) 주의를 기울이거나 관계를 발전시킬 수 있는.

03 일부 과학자는 심지어 믿는다 / 우리가 안정된 사회적 관계**stable social relationships**를 지속할 수 있는 사람의 수가 / 자연스럽게 제한되는 것일지도 모른다고 / 우리의 뇌에 의해.

04 (여러분이 다른 배경**background**의 사람들을 더 많이 알수록, / 여러분의 삶은 더 다채로워진다**colorful.**)

05 Robin Dunbar 교수는 설명했다 / 우리의 마음은 실제로 의미 있는 관계를 형성할 수 있을**be capable of forming** 뿐이라고 / 최대**maximum** 약 150명의 사람과.

06 그것이 사실이든 아니든, / 가정하는**assume** 것이 안전하다 / 우리가 모든 사람과 진정한 친구가 될 수 있는 것은 아니라고.

구문 Check up

① The number of people whom / with whom we can continue stable social relationships might be limited naturally by our brains.

뒤따르는 절(we ~ relationships)에 이미 목적어가 있으므로 목적격 관계대명사를 단독으로 쓸 수 없다. 의미상 '사람들과 관계를 맺는다'는 뜻이 되도록 <전치사+목적격 관계대명사>인 with whom을 쓴다.

② If / Whether that's true or not, it's safe to assume that we can't be real friends with everyone.

or not과 함께 부사절 '~이든 아니든'을 이끌 수 있는 접속사는 Whether이다. if(~인지 아닌지)는 명사절로만 쓰인다.

정답 ① with whom ② Whether

DAY 07

E

함축적 의미 추론 +

STEP 1 • 수능에 진짜 나오는 단어

✔ 문제에 나오는 단어들을 확인하세요.

시간이 없다면 색으로 표시된 단어만이라도 꼭 외우고 넘어가세요!

01	doubtful	a. 의심스러운	(✔ doubtful) advantages	의심스러운 이점
02	balance	v. 균형을 이루다	( ) cost versus demand	비용과 수요의 균형을 맞추다
03	decision-making	n. 의사 결정	a ( ) process	의사 결정 과정
04	available	a. 사용 가능한	free information ( )	사용 가능한 무료 정보
05	issue	n. 문제, 사안	information on the ( )	문제에 대한 정보
06	search for	~을 찾다	( ) ( ) answers	답을 찾다
07	keep in mind	명심하다	a point to ( ) ( ) ( )	명심할 점
08	seemingly	ad. 겉보기에, 외견상으로	the ( ) impossible	겉보기에 불가능한 것
09	accomplish	v. 성취하다, 이루다	( ) the seemingly impossible	겉보기에 불가능한 것을 이루다
10	analysis	n. 분석	the simple ( )	단순한 분석
11	access	v. 접근하다	( ) free information	무료 정보에 접근하다
12	due to	~ 때문에	( ) ( ) too much information	너무 많은 정보 때문에

⊕ 본문 문장 속에서 단어들을 확인해 보세요.

To be successful in anything today, / we have to keep in mind / that in the land of the blind, / a one-eyed person can accomplish the seemingly impossible.

오늘날 어떤 일에 있어서 성공하기 위해서는, / 우리는 명심해야 한다 / 눈먼 사람들의 세계에서는 / 한 눈으로 보는 사람이 겉보기에 불가능한 일을 이룰 수 있다는 것을.

단어 다시보기 문제를 풀기 전에 단어들을 30초 동안 다시 확인하세요.

01	doubtful	의심스러운	doubtful advantages	의심스러운 이점
02	balance		balance cost versus demand	비용과 수요의 균형을 맞추다
03	decision-making		a decision-making process	의사 결정 과정
04	available		free information available	사용 가능한 무료 정보
05	issue		information on the issue	문제에 대한 정보
06	search for		search for answers	답을 찾다
07	keep in mind		a point to keep in mind	명심할 점
08	seemingly		the seemingly impossible	겉보기에 불가능한 것
09	accomplish		accomplish the seemingly impossible	겉보기에 불가능한 것을 이루다
10	analysis		the simple analysis	단순한 분석
11	access		access free information	무료 정보에 접근하다
12	due to		due to too much information	너무 많은 정보 때문에

⊕ 본문 문장 속에서 단어의 의미를 우리말로 해석해 보세요.

To be successful in anything today, / we have to keep in mind / that in the land of the blind, / a one-eyed person can accomplish the seemingly impossible.

➔ 오늘날 어떤 일에 있어서 성공하기 위해서는, / 우리는 ________ 한다 / 눈먼 사람들의 세계에서는 / 한 눈으로 보는 사람이 ________ 수 있다는 것을.

2019 3월 학평 30번 문제

제한시간 80초

난이도 ★★★★☆

STEP 2 • 수능 기출 제대로 풀기

E

밑줄 친 information blinded가 다음 글에서 의미하는 바로 가장 적절한 것은?

Technology has doubtful advantages. We must balance too much information versus using only the right information and keeping the decision-making process simple. The Internet has made so much free information available on any issue that we think we have to consider all of it in order to make a decision. So we keep searching for answers on the Internet. This makes us information blinded, like deer in headlights, when trying to make personal, business, or other decisions. To be successful in anything today, we have to keep in mind that in the land of the blind, a one-eyed person can accomplish the seemingly impossible. The one-eyed person understands the power of keeping any analysis simple and will be the decision maker when he uses his one eye of intuition.

* intuition: 직관

① unwilling to accept others' ideas

② unable to access free information

③ unable to make decisions due to too much information

④ indifferent to the lack of available information

⑤ willing to take risks in decision-making

정답과 해설 p.21

STEP 3 • 수능 지문 제대로 복습하기

01 Technology has doubtful advantages. // We must balance too much information / versus using only the right information and keeping the decision-making process simple.

balance A versus B: A와 B 사이에서 균형을 잡다
keep+목적어+목적격 보어(형용사)

02 The Internet has made so much free information / available on any issue / that we think we have to consider all of it / in order to make a decision.

so ~ that: 너무 ~해서 …하다
5형식 동사+목적어+목적격 보어(형용사구)
부사적 용법(목적)

03 So we keep searching for answers / on the Internet. // This makes us information blinded, / like deer in headlights, / when trying to make personal, business, or other decisions.

keep+-ing(계속해서 ~하다)
5형식 동사+목적어+목적격 보어(형용사구)
<접속사+-ing>의 분사구문

04 To be successful in anything today, / we have to keep in mind / [that in the land of the blind, / a one-eyed person can accomplish the seemingly impossible].

keep in mind의 목적어(명사절)
the+형용사: 복수명사(~한 것들)

05 The one-eyed person understands the power / of keeping any analysis simple / and will be the decision maker / when he uses his one eye of intuition.

전치사구

01 기술은 의문의 여지가 있는 이점**doubtful advantage**을 지니고 있다. // 우리는 너무 많은 정보와 ~ (사이에서) 균형을 이루어야**balance** 한다 / 올바른 정보만 사용하고 의사 결정 과정**decision-making process**을 간소하게 하는 것 사이에서.

02 인터넷은 너무 많은 무료 정보를 만들었다 / 어떤 문제**issue**에 대해서도 이용 가능하도록**available** / 그래서 우리는 그 모든 정보를 고려해야 한다고 생각한다 / 어떤 결정을 하기 위해서.

03 그래서 우리는 계속 답을 검색한다**keep searching for answers** / 인터넷에서. // 이것이 우리를 정보에 눈멀게 만든다 / 전조등 불빛에 노출된 사슴처럼, / 우리가 개인적, 사업적, 혹은 다른 결정을 하려고 애쓸 때.

04 오늘날 어떤 일에 있어서 성공하기 위해서는, / 우리는 명심해야 한다**keep in mind** / 눈먼 사람들의 세계에서는 / 한 눈으로 보는 사람이 겉보기에 불가능한 일을 이룰 수**accomplish the seemingly impossible** 있다는 것을.

05 한 눈으로 보는 사람은 힘을 이해한다 / 어떤 분석**analysis**이든 단순하게 하는 것의 / 그리고 의사 결정자가 될 것이다 / 직관이라는 한 눈을 사용할 때.

구문 Check up

① The Internet has made so much free information available on any issue that / which we think we have to consider all of it in order to make a decision.

<so ~ that …> 구문으로, '너무 ~해서 …하다'라는 의미이다. 여기서 정답인 that은 결과의 부사절 접속사이다.

② The one-eyed person understands the power of keeping any analysis simple / simply.

keep의 목적격 보어로는 형용사가 올 수 있고 부사는 올 수 없다. 따라서 simple이 적절하다.

정답 ① that ② simple

F

무관한 문장 찾기 ⊕

STEP 1 • 수능에 진짜 나오는 단어

✔ 문제에 나오는 단어들을 확인하세요.

시간이 없다면 색으로 표시된 단어만이라도 꼭 외우고 넘어가세요!

01	ultimate	a. 궁극적인	the (✓ ultimate) commons	궁극적인 공유 자원
02	boundless	a. 한없는, 끝없는	( ) watercourses	끝없는 강
03	protect	v. 보호하다	( ) water	물을 보호하다
04	rule	n. 규칙	( )s change.	규칙은 변한다.
05	redefine	v. 재정의하다	( ) wise use	현명한 사용을 재정의하다
06	nation	n. 국가	the first ( )	첫 번째 국가
07	constitution	n. 헌법, 구조	in its ( )	헌법에
08	proclaim	v. 주장하다	They ( ) that rivers and forests have their own rights.	그들은 강과 숲이 자기만의 권리를 갖는다고 주장한다.
09	property	n. 재산, 자산	simple ( )	단순한 재산
10	flourish	v. 번영하다, 번창하다	the right to ( )	번영할 권리
11	file	v. (문서를) 보관하다, (소송을) 제기하다	( ) suit	소송을 제기하다
12	on behalf of	대신하여	( ) ( ) ( ) others	다른 사람들을 대신하여
13	acknowledge	v. 인정하다	( ) nature's rights	자연의 권리를 인정하다

⊕ 본문 문장 속에서 단어들을 확인해 보세요.

Once, / watercourses seemed boundless / and the idea of protecting water was considered silly.

한때, / 강들은 끝없는 것처럼 보였고 / 물을 보호한다는 발상은 어리석게 여겨졌다.

단어 다시보기 문제를 풀기 전에 단어들을 30초 동안 다시 확인하세요.

01	ultimate	궁극적인	the ultimate commons	궁극적인 공유 자원
02	boundless		boundless watercourses	끝없는 강
03	protect		protect water	물을 보호하다
04	rule		Rules change.	규칙은 변한다.
05	redefine		redefine wise use	현명한 사용을 재정의하다
06	nation		the first nation	첫 번째 국가
07	constitution		in its constitution	헌법에
08	proclaim		They proclaim that rivers and forests have their own rights.	그들은 강과 숲이 자기만의 권리를 갖는다고 주장한다.
09	property		simple property	단순한 재산
10	flourish		the right to flourish	번영할 권리
11	file		file suit	소송을 제기하다
12	on behalf of		on behalf of others	다른 사람들을 대신하여
13	acknowledge		acknowledge nature's rights	자연의 권리를 인정하다

⊕ 본문 문장 속에서 단어의 의미를 우리말로 해석해 보세요.

Once, / watercourses seemed boundless / and the idea of protecting water was considered silly.

→ 한때, / 강들은 ________ 것처럼 보였고 / ________는 발상은 어리석게 여겨졌다.

2018 9월 학평 35번 문제

제한시간 80초

난이도 ★★★★★

STEP 2 • 수능 기출 제대로 풀기

F

다음 글에서 전체 흐름과 관계 없는 문장은?

Water is the ultimate commons. Once, watercourses seemed boundless and the idea of protecting water was considered silly. But rules change. Time and again, communities have studied water systems and redefined wise use. ① Now Ecuador has become the first nation on Earth to put the rights of nature in its constitution. ② This move has proclaimed that rivers and forests are not simply property but maintain their own right to flourish. ③ Developing a water-based transportation system will modernize Ecuador's transportation infrastructure. ④ According to the constitution, a citizen might file suit on behalf of an injured watershed, recognizing that its health is crucial to the common good. ⑤ More countries are acknowledging nature's rights and are expected to follow Ecuador's lead.

*commons: 공유 자원
**watershed: (강) 유역

정답과 해설 p.22

STEP 3 ● 수능 지문 제대로 복습하기

01 Water is the ultimate commons. // Once, / watercourses seemed boundless / and the idea of protecting water was considered silly.

seem+형용사

5형식 수동태: 수동태(be+p.p.)+목적격 보어(형용사)

02 But rules change. // Time and again, / communities have studied water systems / and (have 생략) redefined wise use. // Now Ecuador has become the first nation on Earth / to put the rights of nature in its constitution.

동사1 / 동사2 / 현재완료 / 형용사적 용법(the first nation 수식)

03 This move has proclaimed / that rivers and forests are not simply property / but maintain their own right to flourish.

명사절 접속사 / not A but B: A가 아니라 B / 형용사적 용법

04 Developing a water-based transportation system / will modernize Ecuador's transportation infrastructure.

주어(동명사)

05 According to the constitution, / a citizen might file suit / on behalf of an injured watershed, / recognizing that its health is crucial to the common good.

과거분사(watershed 수식) / 분사구문(=as he recognizes ~)

06 More countries are acknowledging nature's rights / and are expected to follow Ecuador's lead.

5형식 수동태: 수동태(be+p.p.)+목적격 보어(to부정사)

01 물은 궁극적인**ultimate** 공유 자원이다. // 한때, / 강들은 끝없는**boundless** 것처럼 보였고 / 물을 보호한다**protect**는 발상은 어리석게 여겨졌다.

02 그러나 규칙**rule**은 변한다. // 반복적으로 / 사회는 수계(水系)를 연구해 왔고 / 현명한 사용을 재정의해**redefine** 왔다. // 현재 에콰도르는 지구상 첫 번째 국가**nation**가 되었다 / 헌법**constitution**에 자연의 권리를 포함시킨.

03 이러한 움직임은 주장한다**proclaim** / 강과 숲이 단순히 재산**property**이 아니라 / 그들 스스로가 번영할**flourish** 권리를 가진다고.

04 (수로 기반 교통체제를 발달시키는 것은 / 에콰도르의 교통 기반 시설을 현대화시킬 것이다.)

05 이 헌법에 따라, / 시민은 소송을 제기할**file suit** 수도 있다 / 훼손된 (강) 유역을 대표해서**on behalf of** / 강의 건강은 공공의 선에 필수적임을 인식하며.

06 더 많은 국가들이 자연의 권리를 인정하고**acknowledge** 있으며 / 에콰도르의 주도를 따를 것으로 기대된다.

구문 Check up

① Once, watercourses seemed [boundless / boundlessly] and the idea of protecting water was considered silly.

2형식 동사 seem의 보어로는 형용사가 적절하므로 boundless를 써야 한다.

② According to the constitution, a citizen might file suit on behalf of an [injuring / injured] watershed, recognizing that its health is crucial to the common good.

수식을 받는 명사(watershed)와의 관계가 수동이므로 과거분사 injured가 적절하다.

정답 ① boundless ② injured

G

무관한 문장 찾기

STEP 1 • 수능에 진짜 나오는 단어

문제에 나오는 단어들을 확인하세요.

시간이 없다면 색으로 표시된 단어만이라도 꼭 외우고 넘어가세요!

01	knowledgeable	*a.* 해박한, 유식한	(✓ knowledgeable) about history	역사에 해박한
02	sort	*n.* 종류, 부류	all (　　　)s of fancy careers	온갖 종류의 멋진 직업
03	brilliant	*a.* 훌륭한, 멋진	a (　　　) scientist	훌륭한 과학자
04	vocation	*n.* 직업	brilliant (　　　)s	훌륭한 직업들
05	exploration	*n.* 탐구, 탐험	the (　　　) of the Amazon	아마존의 탐험
06	humanity	*n.* 인류	things for (　　　)	인류를 위한 일들
07	sociologist	*n.* 사회학자	Korean (　　　)s	한국의 사회학자들
08	economist	*n.* 경제학자	(　　　)s around the world	전세계의 경제학자
09	historian	*n.* 역사학자	a career as a (　　　)	역사학자로서의 경력
10	rare	*a.* 드문	a (　　　) job	드문 직업
11	interrelationship	*n.* 상관관계	(　　　)s with the present	현재와의 상관관계

⊕ 본문 문장 속에서 단어들을 확인해 보세요.

Studying history can make you / more knowledgeable or interesting to talk to / or can lead to all sorts of brilliant vocations, explorations, and careers.

역사를 공부하는 것은 여러분을 만들어 줄 수 있다 / 함께 말하기에 더 유식하거나 재미있게 / 또는 모든 종류의 멋진 직업, 탐구, 그리고 경력으로 이어질 수 있다.

단어 다시보기 문제를 풀기 전에 단어들을 30초 동안 다시 확인하세요.

01	knowledgeable	해박한, 유식한	knowledgeable about history	역사에 해박한
02	sort		all sorts of fancy careers	온갖 종류의 멋진 직업
03	brilliant		a brilliant scientist	훌륭한 과학자
04	vocation		brilliant vocations	훌륭한 직업들
05	exploration		the exploration of the Amazon	아마존의 탐험
06	humanity		things for humanity	인류를 위한 일들
07	sociologist		Korean sociologists	한국의 사회학자들
08	economist		economists around the world	전세계의 경제학자
09	historian		a career as a historian	역사학자로서의 경력
10	rare		a rare job	드문 직업
11	interrelationship		interrelationships with the present	현재와의 상관관계

⊕ 본문 문장 속에서 단어의 의미를 우리말로 해석해 보세요.

Studying history can make you / more knowledgeable or interesting to talk to / or can lead to all sorts of brilliant vocations, explorations, and careers.

→ 역사를 공부하는 것은 여러분을 만들어 줄 수 있다 / 함께 말하기에 더 ______ 재미있게 / 또는 ______ 으로 이어질 수 있다.

2017 9월 학평 39번 문제

제한시간 70초

난이도 ★★★☆☆

STEP 2 • 수능 기출 제대로 풀기

G

다음 글에서 전체 흐름과 관계 없는 문장은?

Studying history can make you more knowledgeable or interesting to talk to or can lead to all sorts of brilliant vocations, explorations, and careers. ① But even more importantly, studying history helps us ask and answer humanity's Big Questions. ② If you want to know why something is happening in the present, you might ask a sociologist or an economist. ③ But if you want to know deep background, you ask historians. ④ A career as a historian is a rare job, which is probably why you have never met one. ⑤ That's because they are the people who know and understand the past and can explain its complex interrelationships with the present.

정답과 해설 p.22

STEP 3 • 수능 지문 제대로 복습하기

01 Studying history can make you / more knowledgeable or interesting to talk to / or can lead to all sorts of brilliant vocations, explorations, and careers.

(Studying history: 동명사 주어 / make: 5형식 동사 / you: 목적어 / more knowledgeable or interesting: 목적격 보어 / to talk to: 부사적 용법(형용사 수식))

02 But even more importantly, / studying history helps us ask and answer / humanity's Big Questions.

(studying history: 주어(동명사) / helps us ask and answer: help+목적어(A)+(to)동사원형: A가 ~하는 것을 돕다)

03 If you want to know / why something is happening in the present, / you might ask a sociologist or an economist.

(why something is happening in the present: to know의 목적어(의문사절))

04 But if you want to know deep background, / you ask historians.

(if: 조건절의 접속사)

05 A career as a historian is a rare job, / which is probably why you have never met one.

(which: 계속적 용법(=and it) / 선행사 the reason 생략 / why you have never met one: 관계부사절)

06 That's because they are the people / who know and understand the past / and can explain its complex interrelationships with the present.

(That's because: ~이기 때문이다(뒤에 원인) / who: 주격 관계대명사절)

01 역사를 공부하는 것은 여러분을 만들어 줄 수 있다 / 함께 말하기에 더 유식하거나**knowledgeable** 재미있게 / 또는 모든 종류의**all sorts of** 멋진 직업**brilliant vocations**, 탐구**exploration**, 그리고 경력으로 이어질 수 있다.

02 하지만 훨씬 더 중요한 것은 / 역사를 공부하는 것이 우리가 묻고 답하는 데 도움을 준다는 점이다 / 인류**humanity**의 '중대 문제'를.

03 만약 여러분이 알기를 원한다면 / 현재 무언가가 왜 발생하고 있는지, / 여러분은 사회학자**sociologist**나 경제학자**economist**에게 물어볼지도 모른다.

04 그러나 만약 여러분이 (그에 대한) 깊은 배경지식을 알고 싶다면, / 여러분은 역사가**historian**에게 질문한다.

05 (역사가와 같은 직업은 드문 직업**rare job**이고, / 이것이 아마 여러분이 역사가를 만나 본 적이 없는 이유인 것이다.)

06 그것은 그들이 사람이기 때문이다 / 과거를 알고 이해하며 / 현재와의 복잡한 상관관계**complex interrelationship**를 설명할 수 있는 (사람).

구문 Check up

① Studying history can make you more knowledgeable / knowledgeably or can lead to all sorts of brilliant vocations, explorations, and careers.

5형식 문장의 목적격보어 자리이므로 형용사 knowledgeable이 적절하다.

② But even more importantly, studying history helps us ask and answer / answers humanity's Big Questions.

문맥상 helps가 아니라 원형부정사인 ask와 병렬연결되는 부분이다. 따라서 answer가 정답이다.

정답 ① knowledgeable ② answer

DAY 08

A

내용 불일치 ⊕

STEP 1 • 수능에 진짜 나오는 단어

✔ 문제에 나오는 단어들을 확인하세요.

시간이 없다면 색으로 표시된 단어만이라도 꼭 외우고 넘어가세요!

01	grow up	자라다, 성장하다	(✓ grow) (up) in New York	뉴욕에서 자라다
02	financial	a. 금융의	a deep interest in ( ) issues	금융 문제에 대한 깊은 관심
03	graduate from	~을 졸업하다	( ) ( ) high school	고등학교를 졸업하다
04	major in	~을 전공하다	( ) ( ) economics	경제학을 전공하다
05	dissatisfied	a. 불만족한	be ( ) with his economic education	그가 받은 경제학 교육에 불만족하다
06	handle	v. (문제나 상황을) 다루다	( ) real problems	현실적인 문제를 다루다
07	degree	n. 학위	earn a doctor's ( )	박사 학위를 취득하다
08	doctoral	a. 박사의	a ( ) paper	박사 논문
09	contribution	n. 기여, 이바지	an important ( ) to economics	경제학에 대한 중요한 기여
10	award	v. 상을 주다	be ( )ed the Nobel Prize	노벨상을 받다

⊕ 본문 문장 속에서 단어들을 확인해 보세요.

After graduating from high school, / Becker went to Princeton University, / where he majored in economics.

고등학교를 졸업한 후, / Becker는 Princeton University로 진학했고, / 거기서 그는 경제학을 전공했다.

단어 다시보기 문제를 풀기 전에 단어들을 30초 동안 다시 확인하세요.

01	grow up	자라다, 성장하다	grow up in New York	뉴욕에서 자라다
02	financial		a deep interest in financial issues	금융 문제에 대한 깊은 관심
03	graduate from		graduate from high school	고등학교를 졸업하다
04	major in		major in economics	경제학을 전공하다
05	dissatisfied		be dissatisfied with his economic education	그가 받은 경제학 교육에 불만족하다
06	handle		handle real problems	현실적인 문제를 다루다
07	degree		earn a doctor's degree	박사 학위를 취득하다
08	doctoral		a doctoral paper	박사 논문
09	contribution		an important contribution to economics	경제학에 대한 중요한 기여
10	award		be awarded the Nobel Prize	노벨상을 받다

⊕ 본문 문장 속에서 단어의 의미를 우리말로 해석해 보세요.

After graduating from high school, / Becker went to Princeton University, / where he majored in economics.

➜ ________________ 후, / Becker는 Princeton University로 진학했고, / 거기서 그는 ________________.

2023 6월 학평 26번 문제

제한시간 60초

난이도 ★★☆☆☆

STEP 2 • 수능 기출 제대로 풀기

A

Gary Becker에 관한 다음 글의 내용과 일치하지 않는 것은?

Gary Becker was born in Pottsville, Pennsylvania in 1930 and grew up in Brooklyn, New York City. His father, who was not well educated, had a deep interest in financial and political issues. After graduating from high school, Becker went to Princeton University, where he majored in economics. He was dissatisfied with his economic education at Princeton University because "it didn't seem to be handling real problems." He earned a doctor's degree in economics from the University of Chicago in 1955. His doctoral paper on the economics of discrimination was mentioned by the Nobel Prize Committee as an important contribution to economics. Since 1985, Becker had written a regular economics column in *Business Week*, explaining economic analysis and ideas to the general public. In 1992, he was awarded the Nobel Prize in economic science.

*discrimination: 차별

① New York City의 Brooklyn에서 자랐다.

② 아버지는 금융과 정치 문제에 깊은 관심이 있었다.

③ Princeton University에서의 경제학 교육에 만족했다.

④ 1955년에 경제학 박사 학위를 취득했다.

⑤ *Business Week*에 경제학 칼럼을 기고했다.

정답과 해설 p.24

STEP 3 • 수능 지문 제대로 복습하기

01 Gary Becker was born in Pottsville, Pennsylvania in 1930 / and grew up in Brooklyn, New York City.

02 His father, / who was not well educated, / had a deep interest in financial and political issues.
(His father: 주어 / who was not well educated: 삽입절(주어 보충) / had: 동사)

03 After graduating from high school, / Becker went to Princeton University, / where he majored in economics. // He was dissatisfied with his economic education at Princeton University / because "it didn't seem to be handling real problems."
(After graduating from high school: 분사구문(= After he graduated from high school) / Princeton University: 선행사(장소) / where he majored in economics: 계속적 용법 / seem to be handling real problems: seem+to부정사: ~하는 것 같다)

04 He earned a doctor's degree in economics from the University of Chicago in 1955. // His doctoral paper on the economics of discrimination / was mentioned by the Nobel Prize Committee / as an important contribution to economics.
(His doctoral paper on the economics of discrimination: 주어 / was mentioned: 동사(수동태) / as: ~로서)

05 Since 1985, / Becker had written a regular economics column in *Business Week*, / explaining economic analysis and ideas to the general public.
(had written: 과거완료 / explaining economic analysis and ideas to the general public: 분사구문)

06 In 1992, / he was awarded the Nobel Prize in economic science.
(was awarded: 4형식 수동태 / the Nobel Prize in economic science: 직접목적어)

01 Gary Becker는 1930년 Pennsylvania 주 Pottsville에서 태어났고 / New York City의 Brooklyn에서 자랐다**grow up**.

02 그의 아버지는 / 교육을 제대로 받지 못한 / 금융**financial**과 정치 문제에 깊은 관심이 있었다.

03 고등학교를 졸업한**graduate from** 후, / Becker는 Princeton University로 진학했고, / 거기서 그는 경제학을 전공했다**major in**. // 그는 Princeton University에서 그가 받은 경제학 교육에 불만족했다**dissatisfied** / '그것이 현실적인 문제를 다루고**handle** 있는 것처럼 보이지 않았기' 때문에.

04 그는 1955년에 University of Chicago에서 경제학 박사 학위**degree**를 취득했다. // 차별의 경제학에 대한 그의 박사**doctoral** 논문은 노벨상 위원회에 의해 언급되었다 / 경제학에 대한 중요한 기여**contribution**로.

05 1985년부터, / Becker는 〈Business Week〉에 경제학 칼럼을 정기적으로 기고했다 / 경제학적 분석과 아이디어를 일반 대중에게 설명하는.

06 1992년에, / 그는 노벨 경제학상을 수상했다**award**.

구문 Check up

① His father, who was not well educated, having / had a deep interest in financial and political issues.

주어 His father 뒤로 동사가 필요하므로 had가 적절하다.

② In 1992, he awarded / was awarded the Nobel Prize in economic science.

주어 he가 '상을 받는' 대상이므로 was awarded가 적절하다. 동사 뒤의 the Nobel Prize는 목적어이다.

정답 ① had ② was awarded

B

내용 불일치 +

STEP 1 • 수능에 진짜 나오는 단어

✔ 문제에 나오는 단어들을 확인하세요.

시간이 없다면 색으로 표시된 단어만이라도 꼭 외우고 넘어가세요!

01	composer	n. 작곡가	He is a (✔ composer).	그는 작곡가이다.
02	classical music	클래식 음악	study ( ) ( )	클래식 음악을 공부하다
03	as a youth	젊었을 때	He studied music ( ) ( ) ( ).	그는 젊었을 때 음악을 공부했다.
04	teenager	n. 10대	I'm a ( ).	나는 10대이다.
05	amateur	a. 아마추어의	an ( ) contest	아마추어 대회
06	successful	a. 성공적인	a ( ) film music composer	성공적인 영화 음악 작곡가
07	collaborate	v. 협업하다	( ) with him	그와 협업하다
08	flutist	n. 플루트 연주자	collaborate with a ( )	플루트 연주자와 협업하다
09	publish	v. 발매하다, 출간하다	( ) *Suite for Flute*	*Suite for Flute*를 발매하다
10	well-known for	~로 잘 알려진	He is ( ) ( ) *Suite for Flute*.	그는 *Suite for Flute*로 잘 알려져 있다.

⊕ 본문 문장 속에서 단어들을 확인해 보세요.

In 1975, / he collaborated with flutist Rampal / and published *Suite for Flute and Jazz Piano Trio*, / which he became most well-known for.

1975년에, / 그는 플루트 연주자 Rampal과 협업했고, / <Suite for Flute and Jazz Piano Trio>를 발매했으며, / 그것으로 가장 잘 알려지게 되었다.

단어 다시보기 문제를 풀기 전에 단어들을 30초 동안 다시 확인하세요.

01	composer	작곡가	He is a composer.	그는 작곡가이다.
02	classical music		study classical music	클래식 음악을 공부하다
03	as a youth		He studied music as a youth.	그는 젊었을 때 음악을 공부했다.
04	teenager		I'm a teenager.	나는 10대이다.
05	amateur		an amateur contest	아마추어 대회
06	successful		a successful film music composer	성공적인 영화 음악 작곡가
07	collaborate		collaborate with him	그와 협업하다
08	flutist		collaborate with a flutist	플루트 연주자와 협업하다
09	publish		publish *Suite for Flute*	*Suite for Flute*를 발매하다
10	well-known for		He is well-known for *Suite for Flute.*	그는 *Suite for Flute*로 잘 알려져 있다.

⊕ 본문 문장 속에서 단어의 의미를 우리말로 해석해 보세요.

In 1975, / he collaborated with flutist Rampal / and published *Suite for Flute and Jazz Piano Trio,* / which he became most well-known for.

→ 1975년에, / 그는 ________ Rampal과 ________, / <Suite for Flute and Jazz Piano Trio>를 ________, / 그것으로 가장 ________ 되었다.

2022 6월 학평 26번 문제

제한시간 50초

난이도 ★☆☆☆☆

STEP 2 • 수능 기출 제대로 풀기

B

Claude Bolling에 관한 다음 글의 내용과 일치하지 않는 것은?

Pianist, composer, and big band leader, Claude Bolling, was born on April 10, 1930, in Cannes, France, but spent most of his life in Paris. He began studying classical music as a youth. He was introduced to the world of jazz by a schoolmate. Later, Bolling became interested in the music of Fats Waller, one of the most excellent jazz musicians. Bolling became famous as a teenager by winning the Best Piano Player prize at an amateur contest in France. He was also a successful film music composer, writing the music for more than one hundred films. In 1975, he collaborated with flutist Rampal and published *Suite for Flute and Jazz Piano Trio*, which he became most well-known for. He died in 2020, leaving two sons, David and Alexandre.

① 1930년에 프랑스에서 태어났다.

② 학교 친구를 통해 재즈를 소개받았다.

③ 20대에 Best Piano Player 상을 받았다.

④ 성공적인 영화 음악 작곡가였다.

⑤ 1975년에 플루트 연주자와 협업했다.

정답과 해설 p.24

STEP 3 • 수능 지문 제대로 복습하기

01 Pianist, composer, and big band leader, Claude Bolling, / was born on April 10, 1930, in Cannes, France, / but spent most of his life in Paris.
주어 동격(지위 설명) / 주어 / 동사1 / 동사2

02 He began studying classical music / as a youth. // He was introduced to the world of jazz / by a schoolmate.
수동태 / by+행위자

03 Later, / Bolling became interested in the music of Fats Waller, / one of the most excellent jazz musicians.
동격

04 Bolling became famous as a teenager / by winning the Best Piano Player prize / at an amateur contest in France.
by+동명사: ~함으로써

05 He was also a successful film music composer, / writing the music for more than one hundred films.
분사구문

06 In 1975, / he collaborated with flutist Rampal / and published *Suite for Flute and Jazz Piano Trio*, / which he became most well-known for.
선행사 / 계속적 용법의 관계대명사(목적격)

07 He died in 2020, / leaving two sons, David and Alexandre.
분사구문 / 동격

01 피아니스트, 작곡가**composer**, 그리고 빅 밴드 리더인 Claude Bolling은 / 1930년 4월 10일 프랑스 칸에서 태어났지만, / 그의 삶의 대부분을 파리에서 보냈다.

02 그는 클래식 음악**classical music**을 공부하기 시작했다 / 젊었을 때**as a youth**. // 그는 재즈의 세계를 소개받았다 / 학교 친구에게.

03 후에, / Bolling은 Fats Waller의 음악에 관심을 가졌다 / 최고의 재즈 음악가들 중 한 명인.

04 그는 10대**teenager** 때 유명해졌다 / Best Piano Player 상을 수상하며 / 프랑스의 아마추어**amateur** 대회에서.

05 그는 또한 성공적인**successful** 영화 음악 작곡가였고, / 100편이 넘는 영화의 음악을 작곡했다.

06 1975년에, / 그는 플루트 연주자**flutist** Rampal과 협업했고**collaborate**, / 〈Suite for Flute and Jazz Piano Trio〉를 발매했으며**publish**, / 그것으로 가장 잘 알려지게**well-known for** 되었다.

07 그는 2020년 사망했다 / 두 아들 David와 Alexandre를 남기고.

구문 Check up

① He was introducing / introduced to the world of jazz by a schoolmate.

그가 재즈의 세계에 '소개받은' 것이므로 수동태 과거분사 introduced로 쓴다.

② He was also a successful film music composer, wrote / writing the music for more than one hundred films.

문장의 동사는 was이다. write도 동사로 쓰려면 was와 병렬연결시켜 줄 접속사가 있어야 하는데, 접속사가 없으므로 분사구문인 writing으로 쓴다.

정답 ① introduced ② writing

C

내용 불일치 +

STEP 1 • 수능에 진짜 나오는 단어

✔ 문제에 나오는 단어들을 확인하세요.

시간이 없다면 색으로 표시된 단어만이라도 꼭 외우고 넘어가세요!

01	on account of	~ 때문에	(✔ on) (account) (of) their appearance	그것들의 겉모양 때문에
02	appearance	n. 겉모양	the unique rock-like ( )	독특한 바위 같은 겉모양
03	native	a. 태어난 곳의, 원산지인	be ( ) to the deserts	사막이 원산지이다
04	nursery	n. 종묘원, 묘목(시)장	be sold in ( )ies	종묘원에서 팔리다
05	compacted	a. 빡빡한	( ) soil	빡빡한 토양
06	extreme	a. 극도의, 극한의	( ) conditions	극한의 조건
07	temperature	n. 온도	hot ( )s	높은 온도
08	rarely	ad. 거의 ~않다	( ) get more than an inch	거의 1인치 이상이 되지 않는다
09	resemble	v. 닮다	( ) the foot	발을 닮다
10	grayish	a. 회색 빛을 띠는	( ) brown	회갈색 빛을 띠는
11	stem	n. 줄기	have no true ( )	실제 줄기가 없다
12	underground	a. 땅속에 묻혀 있는	Much of the plant is ( ).	식물의 대부분이 땅속에 묻혀 있다.
13	conserve	v. 보존하다	( ) moisture	수분을 보존하다

⊕ 본문 문장 속에서 단어들을 확인해 보세요.

Lithops are plants / that are often called 'living stones' / on account of their unique rock-like appearance.

Lithops는 식물이다 / 종종 '살아있는 돌'로 불리는 / 독특한 바위 같은 겉모양 때문에.

단어 다시보기 문제를 풀기 전에 단어들을 30초 동안 다시 확인하세요.

01	on account of	~ 때문에	on account of their appearance	그것들의 겉모양 때문에
02	appearance		the unique rock-like appearance	독특한 바위 같은 겉모양
03	native		be native to the deserts	사막이 원산지이다
04	nursery		be sold in nurseries	종묘원에서 팔리다
05	compacted		compacted soil	빡빡한 토양
06	extreme		extreme conditions	극한의 조건
07	temperature		hot temperatures	높은 온도
08	rarely		rarely get more than an inch	거의 1인치 이상이 되지 않는다
09	resemble		resemble the foot	발을 닮다
10	grayish		grayish brown	회갈색 빛을 띠는
11	stem		have no true stem	실제 줄기가 없다
12	underground		Much of the plant is underground.	식물의 대부분이 땅속에 묻혀 있다.
13	conserve		conserve moisture	수분을 보존하다

⊕ 본문 문장 속에서 단어의 의미를 우리말로 해석해 보세요.

Lithops are plants / that are often called 'living stones' / on account of their unique rock-like appearance.

→ Lithops는 식물이다 / 종종 '살아있는 돌'로 불리는 / 독특한 바위 같은 __________.

2021 6월 학평 26번 문제

제한시간 70초

난이도 ★★★☆☆

STEP 2 • 수능 기출 제대로 풀기

C

Lithops에 관한 다음 글의 내용과 일치하지 않는 것은?

Lithops are plants that are often called 'living stones' on account of their unique rock-like appearance. They are native to the deserts of South Africa but commonly sold in garden centers and nurseries. Lithops grow well in compacted, sandy soil with little water and extreme hot temperatures. Lithops are small plants, rarely getting more than an inch above the soil surface and usually with only two leaves. The thick leaves resemble the cleft in an animal's foot or just a pair of grayish brown stones gathered together. The plants have no true stem and much of the plant is underground. Their appearance has the effect of conserving moisture.

*cleft: 갈라진 틈

① 살아있는 돌로 불리는 식물이다.

② 원산지는 남아프리카 사막 지역이다.

③ 토양의 표면 위로 대개 1인치 이상 자란다.

④ 줄기가 없으며 땅속에 대부분 묻혀 있다.

⑤ 겉모양은 수분 보존 효과를 갖고 있다.

정답과 해설 p.24

STEP 3 • 수능 지문 제대로 복습하기

01 Lithops are plants / [that are often called 'living stones' / on account of their unique rock-like appearance].
주격 관계대명사절

02 They are native to the deserts of South Africa / but commonly sold / in garden centers and nurseries.
주격 보어 병렬 구조(are에 연결)

03 Lithops grow well / in compacted, sandy soil with little water / and extreme hot temperatures.
명사구 병렬 구조(in에 연결)

04 Lithops are small plants, / rarely getting more than an inch above the soil surface / and usually with only two leaves.
분사구문(주어 보충)
전치사구(주어 보충)

05 The thick leaves resemble / the cleft in an animal's foot / or just a pair of grayish brown stones / gathered together.
목적어1
목적어2
과거분사

06 The plants have no true stem / and much of the plant is underground. // Their appearance has the effect of conserving moisture.
주어(much of+단수명사)
동사

01 Lithops는 식물이다 / 종종 '살아있는 돌'로 불리는 / 독특한 바위 같은 겉모양**appearance** 때문에**on account of**.

02 그것들은 원산지가 남아프리카 사막이지만**native to the deserts**, / 흔히 팔린다 / 식물원과 종묘원**nursery**에서.

03 Lithops는 잘 자란다 / 수분이 거의 없는 빽빽한**compacted** 모래 토양과 / 극단적인 높은 온도**extreme hot temperatures**에서.

04 Lithops는 작은 식물로, / 토양의 표면 위로 거의 1인치 이상이 되지 않고**rarely get more than an inch** / 보통 단 두 개의 잎을 가지고 있다.

05 두꺼운 잎은 닮았다**resemble** / 동물 발의 갈라진 틈을 / 또는 한 쌍의 회갈색 빛을 띠는**grayish brown** 돌을 / 함께 모여있는 (돌).

06 이 식물은 실제 줄기**stem**는 없고 / 식물의 대부분이 땅속에 묻혀 있다**underground**. // 겉모양은 수분을 보존하는**conserve** 효과를 가지고 있다.

구문 Check up

① They are native to the deserts of South Africa but commonly sell / sold in garden centers and nurseries.

주어 They(=Lithops)가 '파는' 것이 아니라 '팔리는' 것이므로 수동태를 쓴다. 따라서 sold가 적절하다.

② Lithops are small plants, rarely get / getting more than an inch above the soil surface.

문장의 동사는 are이다. get을 동사로 쓰려면 접속사가 있어야 하는데, 접속사가 없으므로 분사구문인 getting으로 쓴다.

정답 ① sold ② getting

D

내용 불일치

STEP 1 • 수능에 진짜 나오는 단어

✔ 문제에 나오는 단어들을 확인하세요.

시간이 없다면 색으로 표시된 단어만이라도 꼭 외우고 넘어가세요!

01	graduate from	~를 졸업하다	(✔ graduate) (from) college	대학을 졸업하다
02	in addition to	~ 외에도	( ) ( ) ( ) writing novels	소설을 쓰는 것 외에도
03	editor	*n.* 편집자	work as a journal ( )	저널 편집자로 일하다
04	encourage	*v.* 고무시키다	( ) many writers	많은 작가를 고무시키다
05	fiction	*n.* 소설	a ( ) writer	소설 작가
06	critic	*n.* 비평가	receive good reviews from ( )s	비평가들에게서 좋은 평을 받다
07	ultimately	*ad.* 결국에는	( ) = finally	결국에는
08	claim	*v.* 주장하다	( ) her pride	자부심을 주장하다
09	racial	*a.* 인종의	her ( ) background	그녀의 인종 배경
10	identity	*n.* 정체성	her racial ( )	그녀의 인종적 정체성

⊕ 본문 문장 속에서 단어들을 확인해 보세요.

In it, / she tells the story of a black girl / who could pass for white / but ultimately claims her racial identity and pride.

그 작품에서, / 그녀는 한 흑인 소녀의 이야기를 했다 / 백인으로 여겨질 수 있었던 / 하지만 결국에는 자신의 인종적 정체성과 자부심을 주장하는.

단어 다시보기 문제를 풀기 전에 단어들을 30초 동안 다시 확인하세요.

01	graduate from	~를 졸업하다	graduate from college	대학을 졸업하다
02	in addition to		in addition to writing novels	소설을 쓰는 것 외에도
03	editor		work as a journal editor	저널 편집자로 일하다
04	encourage		encourage many writers	많은 작가를 고무시키다
05	fiction		a fiction writer	소설 작가
06	critic		receive good reviews from critics	비평가들에게서 좋은 평을 받다
07	ultimately		ultimately = finally	결국에는
08	claim		claim her pride	자부심을 주장하다
09	racial		her racial background	그녀의 인종 배경
10	identity		her racial identity	그녀의 인종적 정체성

⊕ **본문 문장 속에서 단어의 의미를 우리말로 해석해 보세요.**

In it, / she tells the story of a black girl / who could pass for white / but ultimately claims her racial identity and pride.

➜ 그 작품에서, / 그녀는 한 흑인 소녀의 이야기를 했다 / 백인으로 여겨질 수 있었던 / 하지만 ____________________.

2020 9월 학평 26번 문제

제한시간 60초
난이도 ★★☆☆☆

STEP 2 • 수능 기출 제대로 풀기

D

Jessie Redmon Fauset에 관한 다음 글의 내용과 일치하지 않는 것은?

Jessie Redmon Fauset was born in Snow Hill, New Jersey, in 1884. She was the first black woman to graduate from Cornell University. In addition to writing novels, poetry, short stories, and essays, Fauset taught French in public schools in Washington, D.C. and worked as a journal editor. While working as an editor, she encouraged many well-known writers of the Harlem Renaissance. Though she is more famous for being an editor than for being a fiction writer, many critics consider her novel *Plum Bun* Fauset's strongest work. In it, she tells the story of a black girl who could pass for white but ultimately claims her racial identity and pride. Fauset died of heart disease April 30, 1961, in Philadelphia.

*pass for: ~으로 여겨지다

① Cornell University를 졸업한 최초의 흑인 여성이었다.
② Washington, D.C.의 공립학교에서 프랑스어를 가르쳤다.
③ 편집자보다는 소설가로서 더 유명하다.
④ 흑인 소녀의 이야기를 다룬 소설을 썼다.
⑤ Philadelphia에서 심장병으로 사망했다.

정답과 해설 p.25

STEP 3 • 수능 지문 제대로 복습하기

01 Jessie Redmon Fauset was born / in Snow Hill, New Jersey, in 1884. // She was the first black woman / to graduate from Cornell University.
to부정사의 형용사적 용법

02 In addition to writing novels, poetry, short stories, and essays, / Fauset taught French in public schools in Washington, D.C. / and worked as a journal editor.
~ 외에도(to가 전치사) 동명사구 동사1 동사2 전치사(~로서)

03 While working as an editor, / she encouraged many well-known writers of the Harlem Renaissance.
<접속사+-ing>의 분사구문: 접속사가 있어 의미가 더 명확해짐

04 Though she is more famous for being an editor / than for being a fiction writer, / many critics consider her novel *Plum Bun* Fauset's strongest work.
접속사(뒤에 문장) 비교급+than: ~보다 더 …한 5형식 동사 목적어 목적격 보어

05 In it, / she tells the story of a black girl / who could pass for white / but ultimately claims her racial identity and pride.
동사1 주격 관계대명사절 동사2

06 Fauset died of heart disease / April 30, 1961, in Philadelphia.

01 Jessie Redmon Fauset은 태어났다 / 1884년 New Jersey의 Snow Hill에서. // 그녀는 최초의 흑인 여성이었다 / Cornell University를 졸업한**graduate from**.

02 소설, 시, 단편 소설, 수필을 쓰는 것 외에도**in addition to** / Fauset은 Washington, D.C.의 공립학교에서 프랑스어를 가르쳤고, / 저널 편집자**editor**로서 일했다.

03 편집자로 일하는 동안, / 그녀는 Harlem Renaissance(흑인 예술 문화 부흥 운동)의 많은 유명한 작가들을 고무시켰다**encourage**.

04 비록 그녀는 편집자로서 더 유명하지만 / 소설가**fiction writer**로서보다, / 많은 비평가**critic**들은 그녀의 소설 〈Plum Bun〉을 Fauset의 가장 뛰어난 작품으로 간주한다.

05 그 작품에서, / 그녀는 한 흑인 소녀의 이야기를 한다 / 백인으로 여겨질 수 있었지만 / 결국에는**ultimately** 자신의 인종적 정체성**racial identity**과 자부심을 주장하는**claim**.

06 Fauset은 심장병으로 사망했다 / 1961년 4월 30일에 Philadelphia에서.

구문 Check up

① In addition to writing novels, poetry, short stories, and essays, Fauset taught French in public schools in Washington, D.C. and [working / worked] as a journal editor.

문맥상 과거시제 동사 taught에 병렬 연결되는 동사 자리이므로 worked를 쓴다.

② [Despite / Though] she is more famous for being an editor than for being a fiction writer, many critics consider her novel *Plum Bun* Fauset's strongest work.

'she is more famous ~'가 <주어+동사>를 갖춘 문장이므로 접속사 Though를 쓴다.

정답 ① worked ② Though

E

내용 불일치 +

STEP 1 • 수능에 진짜 나오는 단어

✔ 문제에 나오는 단어들을 확인하세요.

시간이 없다면 색으로 표시된 단어만이라도 꼭 외우고 넘어가세요!

01	well-to-do	a. 잘 사는, 부유한	a (✔ well-to-do) family	부유한 가정
02	childhood	n. 어린 시절	travel in her ( )	어린 시절에 여행을 하다
03	approve	v. 찬성하다	( ) the plan	그 계획을 찬성하다
04	desire	n. 갈망, 욕망	a strong ( )	강한 갈망
05	bravely	ad. 용감하게	live ( )	용감하게 살아가다
06	take the steps	걸음을 떼다, 밟아나가다	bravely ( ) ( ) ( )	용감하게 밟아나가다
07	admire	v. 감탄하다, 칭찬하다, 존경하다	( ) the work of Edgar Degas	Edgar Degas의 작품에 감탄하다
08	inspiration	n. 영감	a great ( )	큰 영감
09	sight	n. 시력	lose ( )	시력을 잃다
10	later	a. 만년의, 늦은	during the ( ) years of her life	그녀의 노년에는
11	at the age of	~ 나이에, ~일 때	( ) ( ) ( ) ( ) seventy	70세 나이에

+ 본문 문장 속에서 단어들을 확인해 보세요.

She admired the work of Edgar Degas / and was able to meet him in Paris, / which was a great inspiration.

그녀는 Edgar Degas의 작품에 감탄했고 / 파리에서 그를 만날 수 있었는데, / 그것은 큰 영감이 되었다.

단어 다시보기 문제를 풀기 전에 단어들을 30초 동안 다시 확인하세요.

01	well-to-do	잘 사는, 부유한	a well-to-do family	부유한 가정
02	childhood		travel in her childhood	어린 시절에 여행을 하다
03	approve		approve the plan	그 계획을 찬성하다
04	desire		a strong desire	강한 갈망
05	bravely		live bravely	용감하게 살아가다
06	take the steps		bravely take the steps	용감하게 밟아나가다
07	admire		admire the work of Edgar Degas	Edgar Degas의 작품에 감탄하다
08	inspiration		a great inspiration	큰 영감
09	sight		lose sight	시력을 잃다
10	later		during the later years of her life	그녀의 노년에는
11	at the age of		at the age of seventy	70세 나이에

⊕ 본문 문장 속에서 단어의 의미를 우리말로 해석해 보세요.

She admired the work of Edgar Degas / and was able to meet him in Paris, / which was a great inspiration.

→ 그녀는 Edgar Degas의 작품에 ______ / 파리에서 그를 만날 수 있었는데, / 그것은 큰 ______이 되었다.

2019 9월 학평 26번 문제

제한시간 60초

난이도 ★★☆☆☆

STEP 2 • 수능 기출 제대로 풀기

E

Mary Cassatt에 관한 다음 글의 내용과 일치하지 않는 것은?

Mary Cassatt was born in Pennsylvania, the fourth of five children born in her well-to-do family. Mary Cassatt and her family traveled throughout Europe in her childhood. Her family did not approve when she decided to become an artist, but her desire was so strong, she bravely took the steps to make art her career. She studied first in Philadelphia and then went to Paris to study painting. She admired the work of Edgar Degas and was able to meet him in Paris, which was a great inspiration. Though she never had children of her own, she loved children and painted portraits of the children of her friends and family. Cassatt lost her sight at the age of seventy, and, sadly, was not able to paint during the later years of her life.

① 유년 시절에 유럽 전역을 여행했다.

② 화가가 되는 것을 가족이 찬성하지 않았다.

③ Edgar Degas를 파리에서 만났다.

④ 자기 자녀의 초상화를 그렸다.

⑤ 70세에 시력을 잃었다.

정답과 해설 p.25

STEP 3 ● 수능 지문 제대로 복습하기

01 Mary Cassatt was born in Pennsylvania, / the fourth of five children born in her well-to-do family.
과거분사(명사 수식)

02 Mary Cassatt and her family traveled throughout Europe / in her childhood.

03 Her family did not approve / when she decided to become an artist, / but her desire was so strong, / she bravely took the steps / to make art her career.
so 형용사 (that) ~: 너무 …해서 ~하다 (that이 생략되고 콤마로 대체)
형용사적 용법

04 She studied first in Philadelphia / and then went to Paris / to study painting.
부사적 용법(목적)

05 She admired the work of Edgar Degas / and was able to meet him in Paris, / which was a great inspiration.
선행사
관계대명사의 계속적 용법(=and it)

06 Though she never had children of her own, / she loved children / and painted portraits of the children of her friends and family.
양보의 부사절: 비록 ~이지만

07 Cassatt lost her sight at the age of seventy, / and, sadly, was not able to paint / during the later years of her life.
전치사(~동안)
기간 명사구

01 Mary Cassatt은 Pennsylvania에서 태어났다 / 부유한**well-to-do** 가정에서 태어난 다섯 아이들 중 넷째로.

02 Mary Cassatt과 그녀의 가족은 유럽 전역을 여행했다 / 유년 시절에**in her childhood.**

03 그녀의 가족은 찬성하지**approve** 않았다 / 그녀가 화가가 되려고 결심했을 때, / 그러나 그녀의 열망**desire**은 매우 강해서 / 과정을 용감하게 밟아나갔다**bravely take the steps** / 미술을 그녀의 진로 분야로 삼기 위한.

04 그녀는 먼저 필라델피아에서 공부했고 / 그리고 나서 파리로 갔다 / 그림을 공부하기 위해.

05 그녀는 Edgar Degas의 작품에 감탄했고**admire the work** / 파리에서 그를 만날 수 있었는데, / 그것은 큰 영감**a great inspiration**이 되었다.

06 비록 그녀는 자기 자녀는 없었지만, / 아이들을 사랑했고 / 그녀의 친구들과 가족의 자녀의 초상화를 그렸다.

07 Cassatt은 70세에**at the age of seventy** 시력을 잃었고**lose sight,** / 슬프게도 그림을 그릴 수 없었다 / 노년**the later years**에는.

구문 Check up

① She admired the work of Edgar Degas and was able to meet him in Paris, which / that was a great inspiration.

앞에 콤마(,)가 있으면 관계대명사의 계속적 용법으로 관계대명사 that은 쓰지 않는다. 따라서 which가 정답이다.

② Though / Despite she never had children of her own, she loved children and painted portraits.

뒤에 문장이 나오므로 접속사 Though를 써야 한다. Despite는 의미는 같지만 전치사이다.

정답 ① which ② Though

F

내용 불일치 +

STEP 1 • 수능에 진짜 나오는 단어

✔ 문제에 나오는 단어들을 확인하세요.

시간이 없다면 색으로 표시된 단어만이라도 꼭 외우고 넘어가세요!

01	develop	v. 발달시키다, 개발하다	(✔ develop) his passion	그의 열정을 키우다
02	passion	n. 열정	the ( ) for photography	사진에 대한 열정
03	teens	n. 십대 시절	in his ( )	그의 십대 시절에
04	capture	v. 포획하다, 촬영하다	( ) scenes	장면을 촬영하다
05	combat	n. 전투, 전쟁	a ( ) photographer	종군 사진 기자
06	staff	n. 직원	become a ( )	직원이 되다
07	daily	a. 매일의, 일간의	a ( ) evening newspaper	매일 나오는 석간 신문
08	earn	v. 벌다, 가져다 주다	( ) him the prize	그에게 상을 가져다 주다
09	prize	n. 상	The Pulitzer ( )	퓰리처상
10	shoot	v. 쏘다, 촬영하다	( ) covers	표지를 촬영하다
11	magazine	n. 잡지	covers of ( )s	잡지 표지
12	portrait	n. 초상화, 인물 사진	a ( ) of a lady	여인의 초상화
13	political	a. 정치적인	( ) leaders	정치 지도자들

⊕ 본문 문장 속에서 단어들을 확인해 보세요.

After graduating, / he joined the United States Marine Corps, / where he captured scenes from the Korean War / as a combat photographer.

졸업 후, / 그는 미국 해병대에 입대했고, / 그곳에서 그는 한국 전쟁에서의 장면을 촬영했다 / 종군 사진 기자로.

단어 다시보기 문제를 풀기 전에 단어들을 30초 동안 다시 확인하세요.

01	develop	발달시키다, 개발하다	develop his passion	그의 열정을 키우다
02	passion		the passion for photography	사진에 대한 열정
03	teens		in his teens	그의 십대 시절에
04	capture		capture scenes	장면을 촬영하다
05	combat		a combat photographer	종군 사진 기자
06	staff		become a staff	직원이 되다
07	daily		a daily evening newspaper	매일 나오는 석간 신문
08	earn		earn him the prize	그에게 상을 가져다 주다
09	prize		The Pulitzer Prize	퓰리처상
10	shoot		shoot covers	표지를 촬영하다
11	magazine		covers of magazines	잡지 표지
12	portrait		a portrait of a lady	여인의 초상화
13	political		political leaders	정치 지도자들

⊕ 본문 문장 속에서 단어의 의미를 우리말로 해석해 보세요.

After graduating, / he joined the United States Marine Corps, / where he captured scenes from the Korean War / as a combat photographer.

➔ 졸업 후, / 그는 미국 해병대에 입대했고, / 그곳에서 그는 한국 전쟁에서의 ______________ / ______________로.

2018 9월 학평 25번 문제

제한시간 60초

난이도 ★★☆☆☆

STEP 2 • 수능 기출 제대로 풀기

F

Eddie Adams에 관한 다음 글의 내용과 일치하지 않는 것은?

Eddie Adams was born in New Kensington, Pennsylvania. He developed his passion for photography in his teens, when he became a staff photographer for his high school paper. After graduating, he joined the United States Marine Corps, where he captured scenes from the Korean War as a combat photographer. In 1958, he became staff at the *Philadelphia Evening Bulletin*, a daily evening newspaper published in Philadelphia. In 1962, he joined the Associated Press (AP), and after 10 years, he left the AP to work as a freelancer for *Time* magazine. The Saigon Execution photo that he took in Vietnam earned him the Pulitzer Prize for Spot News Photography in 1969. He shot more than 350 covers of magazines with portraits of political leaders such as Deng Xiaoping, Richard Nixon, and George Bush.

① 10대 시절에 사진에 대한 열정을 키웠다.

② 종군 사진 기자로 한국전쟁의 장면을 촬영했다.

③ 1962년부터 *Time* 잡지사에서 일했다.

④ 베트남에서 촬영한 사진으로 퓰리처상을 받았다.

⑤ 정치 지도자들의 잡지 표지용 사진을 촬영했다.

정답과 해설 p.26

STEP 3 • 수능 지문 제대로 복습하기

01 Eddie Adams was born / in New Kensington, Pennsylvania. // He developed his passion for photography / in his teens, / when he became a staff photographer / for his high school paper.

be born: 태어나다 / 선행사(시간) / 계속적 용법(그리고 이때)

02 After graduating, / he joined the United States Marine Corps, / where he captured scenes from the Korean War / as a combat photographer.

선행사(장소) / =and there

03 In 1958, / he became staff at the *Philadelphia Evening Bulletin*, / a daily evening newspaper / published in Philadelphia.

동격 / 과거분사

04 In 1962, / he joined the Associated Press (AP), / and after 10 years, / he left the AP / to work as a freelancer for *Time* magazine.

부사적 용법(목적)

05 The Saigon Execution photo / that he took in Vietnam / earned him the Pulitzer Prize for Spot News Photography / in 1969. // He shot more than 350 covers of magazines / with portraits of political leaders / such as Deng Xiaoping, Richard Nixon, and George Bush.

목적격 관계대명사절 / 4형식 동사 / 간접목적어 / 직접목적어 / ~와 같은

01 Eddie Adams는 태어났다 / 펜실베니아 주 New Kensington에서. // 그는 사진에 대한 열정**passion**을 키웠다**develop** / 십대 시절**teens**에, / 이때 그는 사진 기자가 되었다 / 자신의 고등학교 신문의.

02 졸업 후, / 그는 미국 해병대에 입대했고, / 그곳에서 한국 전쟁 장면을 촬영했다**capture** / 종군 사진 기자**combat photographer**로.

03 1958년, / 그는 〈Philadelphia Evening Bulletin〉의 직원**staff**이 되었다 / 석간 신문**daily evening newspaper**인 / 필라델피아에서 발간된.

04 1962년에 / 그는 연합통신사(AP)에 입사했고, / 10년 뒤, / 그는 연합통신사를 떠났다 / 〈Time〉 잡지사에서 프리랜서로 일하기 위해.

05 〈Saigon Execution〉 사진은 / 그가 베트남에서 촬영한 (사진) / 그에게 특종기사 보도 사진 부문의 퓰리처상**prize**을 가져다 주었다**earn** / 1969년에. // 그는 350개가 넘는 잡지**magazine** 표지를 촬영했다**shoot** / 정치**political** 지도자들의 사진**portrait**으로 / Deng Xiaoping, Richard Nixon, George Bush와 같은.

구문 Check up

① In 1958, he became staff at the *Philadelphia Evening Bulletin*, a daily evening newspaper published / publishing in Philadelphia.

수식을 받는 명사(newspaper)와의 관계가 수동이므로 과거분사 published가 적절하다.

② The Saigon Execution photo what / that he took in Vietnam earned him the Pulitzer Prize for Spot News Photography in 1969.

앞에 선행사(photo)가 존재하므로 목적격 관계대명사 that이 적절하다.

정답 ① published ② that

G

내용 불일치 +

STEP 1 • 수능에 진짜 나오는 단어

✔ 문제에 나오는 단어들을 확인하세요.

시간이 없다면 색으로 표시된 단어만이라도 꼭 외우고 넘어가세요!

01	wealthy	*a.* 부유한	a (✔ wealthy) family	한 부유한 가정
02	educate	*v.* 교육하다	( )d in the US	미국에서 교육 받은
03	tutor	*n.* 가정 교사	private ( )s	개인 가정 교사들
04	architecture	*n.* 건축	a great love of ( )	건축에 매우 큰 애정
05	devote	*v.* 쏟다, 바치다	( ) much of her time	많은 시간을 쏟다
06	assist	*v.* 돕다	( ) children	아이들을 돕다
07	orphan	*n.* 고아	assist ( )s	고아들을 돕다
08	raise	*v.* 모으다	( ) money	돈을 모으다
09	fund	*n.* 기금	raise ( )s	기금을 모으다
10	support	*v.* 부양하다	( ) two children	두 아이를 부양하다

⊕ 본문 문장 속에서 단어들을 확인해 보세요.

During World War I, / she devoted much of her time / to assisting orphans from France and Belgium / and helped raise funds / to support them.

1차 세계대전 동안 / 그녀는 많은 시간을 쏟았다 / 프랑스와 벨기에의 고아들을 돕는 것에 / 그리고 기금을 모으는 것을 도왔다 / 그들을 부양하기 위해.

단어 다시보기 문제를 풀기 전에 단어들을 30초 동안 다시 확인하세요.

01	wealthy	부유한	a wealthy family	한 부유한 가정
02	educate		educated in the US	미국에서 교육 받은
03	tutor		private tutors	개인 가정 교사들
04	architecture		a great love of architecture	건축에 매우 큰 애정
05	devote		devote much of her time	많은 시간을 쏟다
06	assist		assist children	아이들을 돕다
07	orphan		assist orphans	고아들을 돕다
08	raise		raise money	돈을 모으다
09	fund		raise funds	기금을 모으다
10	support		support two children	두 아이를 부양하다

본문 문장 속에서 단어의 의미를 우리말로 해석해 보세요.

During World War I, / she devoted much of her time / to assisting orphans from France and Belgium / and helped raise funds / to support them.

→ 1차 세계대전 동안 / 그녀는 많은 시간을 ______ / 프랑스와 벨기에의 ______에 / 그리고 ______을 도왔다 / 그들을 ______ 위해.

2016 9월 학평 25번 문제

제한시간 60초

난이도 ★★☆☆☆

STEP 2 • 수능 기출 제대로 풀기

G

Edith Wharton에 관한 다음 글의 내용과 일치하지 않는 것은?

Edith Wharton was born into a wealthy family in 1862 in New York City. Educated by private tutors at home, she enjoyed reading and writing early on. After her first novel, *The Valley of Decision*, was published in 1902, she wrote many novels and some gained her a wide audience. Wharton also had a great love of architecture, and she designed and built her first real home. During World War I, she devoted much of her time to assisting orphans from France and Belgium and helped raise funds to support them. After the war, she settled in Provence, France, and she finished writing *The Age of Innocence* there. This novel won Wharton the 1921 Pulitzer Prize, making her the first woman to win the award.

① 1902년에 첫 소설이 출판되었다.
② 건축에 관심이 있어 자신의 집을 설계했다.
③ 프랑스와 벨기에의 고아를 도왔다.
④ 전쟁 중 *The Age of Innocence*를 완성했다.
⑤ 여성 최초로 Pulitzer상을 받았다.

정답과 해설 p.26

STEP 3 • 수능 지문 제대로 복습하기

01 Edith Wharton was born into a wealthy family / in 1862 in New York City. //
Educated by private tutors at home, / she enjoyed reading and writing early on.
분사구문(=As she was educated ~)

02 After her first novel, *The Valley of Decision*, was published in 1902, / she wrote many novels / and some gained her a wide audience.
동격
gain+간접목적어+직접목적어: ~에게 …를 얻게 하다

03 Wharton also had a great love of architecture, / and she designed and built her first real home.
~에 대단한 애정을 갖다

04 During World War I, / she devoted much of her time / to assisting orphans from France and Belgium / and helped raise funds / to support them.
devote A to B: A를 B에 바치다
목적어(원형부정사) 부사적 용법(목적)

05 After the war, / she settled in Provence, France, / and she finished writing *The Age of Innocence* there.
finish+동명사(목적어)

06 This novel won Wharton the 1921 Pulitzer Prize, / [making her the first woman to win the award].
4형식 동사 간접목적어 직접목적어 분사구문(=and it made~) 형용사적 용법

01 Edith Wharton은 한 부유한 가정**a wealthy family**에서 태어났다 / 1862년에 뉴욕 시에서. // 가정에서 개인 교사들**private tutor**에 의해 교육을 받아서**be educated** / 그녀는 일찍이 독서와 글쓰기를 즐겼다.

02 그녀의 첫 번째 소설인 〈The Valley of Decision〉이 1902년에 출판된 후, / 그녀는 많은 소설을 집필했고 / 몇몇 작품은 그녀에게 폭넓은 독자층을 가져다 주었다.

03 Wharton은 또한 건축**architecture**에 매우 큰 애정이 있었고 / 그녀는 자신의 첫 번째 실제 집을 설계하여 건축했다.

04 1차 세계대전 동안 / 그녀는 많은 시간을 쏟았다**devote** / 프랑스와 벨기에의 고아들을 돕는 데**assist orphans** / 그리고 기금을 모으는**raise funds** 것을 도왔다 / 그들을 부양하기**support** 위해.

05 전쟁 후 / 그녀는 프랑스의 Provence에 정착했으며 / 거기에서 〈The Age of Innocence〉의 집필을 끝마쳤다.

06 이 소설은 Wharton이 1921년 Pulitzer상을 받을 수 있게 했으며 / 그녀를 이 상을 받은 최초의 여성으로 만들어 주었다.

구문 Check up

① Educating / Educated by private tutors at home, she enjoyed reading and writing early on.

의미상 주어 she가 '교육을 하는 것'이 아니라 '교육을 받는 것'이기 때문에 -ed의 과거분사구문으로 써야 한다. 따라서 Educated가 정답이다.

② During World War I, she devoted much of her time to assist / assisting orphans from France and Belgium and helped raise funds to support them.

<devote A to B>는 'A를 B에 바치다'라는 의미로, 여기서 to는 전치사이기 때문에 목적어로 동명사 assisting이 온다.

정답 ① Educated ② assisting

어휘의 이해 +

A STEP 1 • 수능에 진짜 나오는 단어

✔ 문제에 나오는 단어들을 확인하세요.

시간이 없다면 색으로 표시된 단어만이라도 꼭 외우고 넘어가세요!

01	philosophical	a. 철학적인	the major (✔ philosophical) shift	주요한 철학적 변화
02	industrial	a. 산업의	( ) societies	산업 사회
03	competitive	a. 경쟁력 있는, 경쟁적인	a ( ) price	경쟁력 있는 가격
04	geographically	ad. 지리적으로	( ) remote areas	지리적으로 먼 지역
05	spread out	퍼뜨리다, 펼치다	papers ( ) ( ) on the desk	책상 위에 펼쳐둔 서류들
06	quality	a. 양질의, 고급의	produce a ( ) product	양질의 제품을 만들다
07	reasonable	a. 적당한, 합리적인	at a ( ) price	적당한 가격에
08	essential	a. 매우 중요한, 필수적인, 핵심적인	an ( ) part	필수적인 부분
09	deliver	v. 내놓다, 산출하다	( ) products that customers actually wanted	소비자들이 실제 원했던 제품을 내놓다
10	modernization	n. 현대화	the ( ) of society	사회의 현대화
11	revolution	n. 혁명	a marketing ( )	마케팅 혁명
12	demand	n. 수요, 요구 v. 요구하다	create the ( )	수요를 창출하다

⊕ 본문 문장 속에서 단어들을 확인해 보세요.

In fact, / it was equally essential / to deliver products / that customers actually wanted.

사실, / 마찬가지로 매우 중요했다 / 제품을 내놓는 것이 / 고객이 실제로 원하는.

단어 다시보기 문제를 풀기 전에 단어들을 30초 동안 다시 확인하세요.

01	philosophical	철학적인	the major philosophical shift	주요한 철학적 변화
02	industrial		industrial societies	산업 사회
03	competitive		a competitive price	경쟁력 있는 가격
04	geographically		geographically remote areas	지리적으로 먼 지역
05	spread out		papers spread out on the desk	책상 위에 펼쳐둔 서류들
06	quality		produce a quality product	양질의 제품을 만들다
07	reasonable		at a reasonable price	적당한 가격에
08	essential		an essential part	필수적인 부분
09	deliver		deliver products that customers actually wanted	소비자들이 실제 원했던 제품을 내놓다
10	modernization		the modernization of society	사회의 현대화
11	revolution		a marketing revolution	마케팅 혁명
12	demand		create the demand	수요를 창출하다

⊕ 본문 문장 속에서 단어의 의미를 우리말로 해석해 보세요.

In fact, / it was equally essential / to deliver products / that customers actually wanted.

→ 사실, / 마찬가지로 매우 ______ / ______ 것이 / 고객이 실제로 원하는.

2023 3월 학평 30번 문제

제한시간 80초

난이도 ★★★★★

STEP 2 • 수능 기출 제대로 풀기

A

다음 글의 밑줄 친 부분 중, 문맥상 낱말의 쓰임이 적절하지 않은 것은?

The major philosophical shift in the idea of selling came when industrial societies became more affluent, more competitive, and more geographically spread out during the 1940s and 1950s. This forced business to develop ① closer relations with buyers and clients, which in turn made business realize that it was not enough to produce a quality product at a reasonable price. In fact, it was equally ② essential to deliver products that customers actually wanted. Henry Ford produced his best-selling T-model Ford in one color only (black) in 1908, but in modern societies this was no longer ③ possible. The modernization of society led to a marketing revolution that ④ strengthened the view that production would create its own demand. Customers, and the desire to ⑤ meet their diverse and often complex needs, became the focus of business.

*affluent: 부유한

정답과 해설 p.27

STEP 3 • 수능 지문 제대로 복습하기

01 The major philosophical shift in the idea of selling / came / when industrial societies became more affluent, more competitive, and more geographically spread out / during the 1940s and 1950s.
주어 / 수식 / 동사

02 This forced business / to develop closer relations with buyers and clients, / which in turn made business realize / that it was not enough / to produce a quality product at a reasonable price.
force+목적어+to부정사: ~이 어쩔 수 없이 ~하게 하다 / 계속적 용법(앞 문장 보충) / 사역동사 / 원형부정사 / 가주어 / 진주어

03 In fact, / it was equally essential / to deliver products / that customers actually wanted.
가주어 / 진주어 / 목적격 관계대명사절

04 Henry Ford produced his best-selling T-model Ford / in one color only (black) / in 1908, / but in modern societies / this was no longer possible.
지시대명사(=but 앞 내용)

05 The modernization of society led to a marketing revolution / that strengthened the view / that production would create its own demand.
주격 관계대명사절 / 동격(=the view)

06 Customers, / and the desire to meet their diverse and often complex needs, / became the focus of business.
주어1 / 주어2 / 형용사적 용법 / 동사

01 판매 개념에 주요한 철학적**philosophical** 변화가 / 일어났다 / 산업**industrial** 사회가 더 부유해지고, 더 경쟁적이게**competitive** 되고, 더 지리적으로 퍼지면서**geographically spread out** / 1940년대와 1950년대 동안.

02 이것은 기업이 어쩔 수 없이 하게 했고 / 구매자 및 고객과 더 긴밀한 관계를 발전시키게 / 이것은 결과적으로 기업이 깨닫게 했다 / 충분하지 않다는 것을 / 적당한**reasonable** 가격에 양질의**quality** 제품을 생산하는 것으로는.

03 사실, / 마찬가지로 매우 중요했다**essential** / 제품을 내놓는**deliver** 것이 / 고객이 실제로 원하는.

04 Henry Ford는 가장 많이 팔린 T-모델 Ford를 생산했지만 / 딱 한 색상(검은색)으로만 / 1908년에 / 현대 사회에서는 / 이것이 더 이상 가능하지 않았다.

05 사회의 현대화**modernization**는 마케팅 혁명**revolution**으로 이어졌다 / 견해를 강화하는(→ 파괴하는) / 생산이 그 자체의 수요**demand**를 창출할 것이라는.

06 고객 / 그리고 그들의 다양하고 흔히 복잡한 욕구를 충족하고자 하는 욕망이 / 기업의 초점이 되었다.

구문 Check up

① That / It was not enough to produce a quality product at a reasonable price.

가주어 자리이므로 It이 적절하다.

② The modernization of society led to a marketing revolution that destroyed the view which / that production would create its own demand.

뒤에 완전한 문장이 나오는 것으로 보아 접속사 that이 적절하다. 이 that 절은 the view와 동격을 이루는 명사절이다.

정답 ① It ② that

B

어휘의 이해 +

STEP 1 • 수능에 진짜 나오는 단어

문제에 나오는 단어들을 확인하세요.

시간이 없다면 색으로 표시된 단어만이라도 꼭 외우고 넘어가세요!

01	herb	n. 허브, 식용(약용) 식물	Certain (✓ herb)s improve health.	어떤 허브들은 건강을 향상시킨다.
02	organ	n. (몸의) 장기, 기관	the work of certain ( )s	특정 장기의 기능
03	cure	v. 고치다, 치료하다	( ) specific diseases	특정 질병들을 고치다
04	statement	n. 진술, 말	unscientific ( )s	비과학적인 진술
05	groundless	a. 근거 없는	( ) statements	근거 없는 진술
06	circulation	n. 순환	your blood ( )	당신의 혈액 순환
07	aggressive	a. 적극적인, 공격적인	an ( ) attempt	적극적인 시도
08	eliminate	v. 제거하다	( ) the herbs	허브를 제거하다
09	temporary	a. 일시적인	a ( ) feeling of a high	일시적으로 좋은 기분
10	condition	n. 상태	your health ( )	당신의 건강 상태
11	intelligence	n. 지성, 지능	have the ( )	지성을 갖다
12	regain	v. 되찾다	( ) health	건강을 되찾다
13	otherwise	ad. 그렇지 않으면	( ) = if not	그렇지 않으면

+ 본문 문장 속에서 단어들을 확인해 보세요.

Sometimes herbs appear to work, / since they tend to increase your blood circulation / in an aggressive attempt by your body / to eliminate them from your system.

때때로 허브는 효과가 있는 것처럼 보이는데, / 이는 그것들이 혈액 순환을 증가시키는 경향이 있기 때문이다 / 당신 몸의 적극적인 시도 속에서 / 당신의 신체로부터 그것들을 제거하려는.

단어 다시보기 문제를 풀기 전에 단어들을 30초 동안 다시 확인하세요.

01	herb	허브, 식용 식물	Certain herbs improve health.	어떤 허브들은 건강을 향상시킨다.
02	organ		the work of certain organs	특정 장기의 기능
03	cure		cure specific diseases	특정한 질병을 고치다
04	statement		unscientific statements	비과학적인 진술
05	groundless		groundless statements	근거 없는 진술
06	circulation		your blood circulation	당신의 혈액 순환
07	aggressive		an aggressive attempt	적극적인 시도
08	eliminate		eliminate the herbs	허브를 제거하다
09	temporary		a temporary feeling of a high	일시적으로 좋은 기분
10	condition		your health condition	당신의 건강 상태
11	intelligence		have the intelligence	지성을 갖다
12	regain		regain health	건강을 되찾다
13	otherwise		otherwise = if not	그렇지 않으면

⊕ 본문 문장 속에서 단어의 의미를 우리말로 해석해 보세요.

Sometimes herbs appear to work, / since they tend to increase your blood circulation / in an aggressive attempt by your body / to eliminate them from your system.

→ 때때로 ________는 효과가 있는 것처럼 보이는데, / 이는 그것들이 혈액 ________을 증가시키는 경향이 있기 때문이다 / 당신 몸의 ________ 시도 속에서 / 당신의 신체로부터 그것들을 ________.

2022 9월 학평 30번 문제

제한시간 80초

난이도 ★★★★☆

STEP 2 • 수능 기출 제대로 풀기

B

다음 글의 밑줄 친 부분 중, 문맥상 낱말의 쓰임이 적절하지 않은 것은?

It is widely believed that certain herbs somehow magically improve the work of certain organs, and "cure" specific diseases as a result. Such statements are unscientific and groundless. Sometimes herbs appear to work, since they tend to ① increase your blood circulation in an aggressive attempt by your body to eliminate them from your system. That can create a ② temporary feeling of a high, which makes it seem as if your health condition has improved. Also, herbs can have a placebo effect, just like any other method, thus helping you feel better. Whatever the case, it is your body that has the intelligence to ③ regain health, and not the herbs. How can herbs have the intelligence needed to direct your body into getting healthier? That is impossible. Try to imagine how herbs might come into your body and intelligently ④ fix your problems. If you try to do that, you will see how impossible it seems. Otherwise, it would mean that herbs are ⑤ less intelligent than the human body, which is truly hard to believe.

*placebo effect: 위약 효과

정답과 해설 p.27

01 It is widely believed / [that certain herbs somehow magically improve the work of
가주어 진주어(that절)
certain organs, / and "cure" specific diseases as a result]. // Such statements are

unscientific and groundless.

02 Sometimes herbs appear to work, / since they tend to increase your blood circulation /

in an aggressive attempt by your body / to eliminate them from your system.
 to부정사의 형용사적 용법 마치 ~인 것처럼
03 That can create a temporary feeling of a high, / which [makes it seem / as if your health
 5형식 동사+목적어+목적격 보어(동사원형)
condition has improved]. // Also, herbs can have a placebo effect, / just like any other
 분사구문: 5형식 동사+목적어+목적격 보어(동사원형)
method, / thus helping you feel better.

 is 생략
04 Whatever the case, / it is your body / that has the intelligence to regain health, / and
무엇이든지(=No matter what) ┆------ it that 강조구문 ------┆ to부정사의 형용사적 용법
not the herbs. // How can herbs have the intelligence / needed to direct your body into
 과거분사구(명사 수식)
getting healthier? // That is impossible.

05 Try to imagine / [how herbs might come into your body / and intelligently fix your
명령문 의문사절(to imagine의 목적어)
problems]. // If you try to do that, / you will see / how impossible it seems.
 의문사절(see의 목적어)
06 Otherwise, // it would mean / that herbs are less intelligent than the human body, /
 명사절 접속사(would mean의 목적어)
which is truly hard to believe.
계속적 용법의 관계대명사

01 널리 알려져 있다 / 어떤 허브herb들은 다소 마법처럼 특정 장기organ의 기능을 향상시키고, / 그 결과 특정한 질병을
'고친다cure'고. // 그러한 진술statement은 비과학적이고 근거가 없다groundless.

02 때때로 허브는 효과가 있는 것처럼 보이는데, / 이는 그것들이 혈액 순환circulation을 증가시키는 경향이 있기 때문이다 /
당신 몸의 적극적인aggressive 시도 속에서 / 당신의 신체로부터 그것들을 제거eliminate하려는.

03 그것은 일시적temporary으로 좋은 기분을 만들어 줄 수 있는데, / 이는 보이게 만든다 / 마치 당신의 건강
상태condition가 향상된 것처럼. // 또한 허브는 위약 효과를 가지고 있는데, / 다른 아무 방법과 마찬가지로, / 그래서
당신이 더 나아졌다고 느끼도록 도와준다.

04 어떠한 경우든, / 바로 당신의 몸이다 / 건강을 되찾게regain 하는 지성intelligence을 가진 것은 / 허브가 아니라.
// 허브가 어떻게 지성을 가질 수 있겠는가 / 당신의 몸을 더 건강해지는 방향으로 인도하는 데 요구되는? // 그것은
불가능하다.

05 상상해 보라 / 어떻게 허브가 당신의 몸 안으로 들어가 / 영리하게 당신의 문제를 해결할 수 있는지. // 만약 당신이 그렇게
해 본다면, / 당신은 알게 될 것이다 / 그것이 얼마나 불가능하게 보이는지를.

06 그렇지 않다면otherwise, / 그것은 의미하게 되는데 / 허브가 인간의 몸보다 덜(→더) 지적이라는 것을, / 이는 정말로
믿기 어렵다.

구문 Check up	① That can create a temporary feeling of a high, which makes it seem / to seem as if your health condition has improved.	② Also, herbs can have a placebo effect, just like any other method, thus help / helping you feel better.
	5형식 사역동사 make의 목적격 보어는 동사원형으로 쓰므로 seem이 적절하다.	문장의 동사는 have로, 이와 help를 병렬연결해 줄 접속사가 없으므로 분사구문인 helping으로 써야 한다.

정답 ① seem ② helping

C

어휘의 이해 +

STEP 1 • 수능에 진짜 나오는 단어

✔ 문제에 나오는 단어들을 확인하세요.

시간이 없다면 색으로 표시된 단어만이라도 꼭 외우고 넘어가세요!

01	fundamental	a. 기본적인	something (✔ fundamental)	기본적인 어떤 것
02	chances are (that)	아마 …일 것이다	( ) ( ) you are reading it.	아마 너는 그것을 읽고 있을 것이다.
03	moreover	ad. 또한, 게다가	( ) = furthermore	게다가
04	probably	ad. 아마도	( ) never	아마 전혀 아닌
05	worth	a. ~할 만한 가치가 있는	Using artificial light was ( ) it.	인공조명을 이용하는 것은 그럴 만한 가치가 있었다.
06	notice	v. 의식하다	( ) the cost	비용을 의식하다
07	light up	밝히다, (불을) 켜다	( ) ( ) the world	세상을 밝히다
08	enter	v. 들어오다, 들어가다	Natural light ( )s the building.	자연광이 건물에 들어온다.

⊕ 본문 문장 속에서 단어들을 확인해 보세요.

Moreover, / you probably never thought / about whether using artificial light for reading was worth it.

또한, / 여러분은 아마 한번도 생각하지 않았을 것이다 / 독서를 위해 인공조명을 이용하는 것이 그럴 만한 가치가 있는지에 대해.

단어 다시보기 문제를 풀기 전에 단어들을 30초 동안 다시 확인하세요.

01	fundamental	기본적인	something fundamental	기본적인 어떤 것
02	chances are (that)		Chances are you are reading it.	아마 너는 그것을 읽고 있을 것이다.
03	moreover		moreover = furthermore	게다가
04	probably		probably never	아마 전혀 아닌
05	worth		Using artificial light was worth it.	인공조명을 이용하는 것은 그럴 만한 가치가 있었다.
06	notice		notice the cost	비용을 의식하다
07	light up		light up the world	세상을 밝히다
08	enter		Natural light enters the building.	자연광이 건물에 들어온다.

⊕ 본문 문장 속에서 단어의 의미를 우리말로 해석해 보세요.

Moreover, / you probably never thought / about whether using artificial light for reading was worth it.

→ ________, / 여러분은 ________________ 것이다 / 독서를 위해 인공조명을 이용하는 것이 그럴 만한 ____________지에 대해.

2021 3월 학평 30번 문제

제한시간 80초

난이도 ★★★★☆

STEP 2 • 수능 기출 제대로 풀기

C

다음 글의 밑줄 친 부분 중, 문맥상 낱말의 쓰임이 적절하지 않은 것은?

When the price of something fundamental drops greatly, the whole world can change. Consider light. Chances are you are reading this sentence under some kind of artificial light. Moreover, you probably never thought about whether using artificial light for reading was worth it. Light is so ① cheap that you use it without thinking. But in the early 1800s, it would have cost you four hundred times what you are paying now for the same amount of light. At that price, you would ② notice the cost and would think twice before using artificial light to read a book. The ③ increase in the price of light lit up the world. Not only did it turn night into day, but it allowed us to live and work in big buildings that ④ natural light could not enter. Nearly nothing we have today would be ⑤ possible if the cost of artificial light had not dropped to almost nothing.

*artificial: 인공의

정답과 해설 p.27

STEP 3 • 수능 지문 제대로 복습하기

01 When the price of something fundamental drops greatly, / the whole world can change. // Consider light.
-thing으로 끝나는 명사는 형용사가 뒤에서 수식
명령문

02 Chances are / you are reading this sentence / under some kind of artificial light. // Moreover, / you probably never thought / about whether using artificial light for reading was worth it.
명사절 접속사 that 생략
~인지 아닌지 whether절의 동명사 주어(단수 취급)

03 Light is so cheap / that you use it without thinking.
so ~ that …: 너무 ~해서 …하다

04 But / in the early 1800s, / it would have cost you / four hundred times / what you are paying now / for the same amount of light.
4형식 동사(cost)+간접 목적어+직접 목적어
가정법 과거완료
관계대명사 what절

05 At that price, / you would notice the cost / and would think twice / [before using artificial light / to read a book]. // The increase in the price of light / lit up the world.
병렬구조(가정법 과거)
전치사+동명사

06 Not only did it turn night into day, / but it [allowed us to live and work in big buildings / that natural light could not enter].
not only A but (also) B: A뿐만 아니라 B도
도치(not only+조동사+주어+동사원형)
5형식 동사(allow)+목적어+목적격 보어(to부정사)
목적격 관계대명사절

07 Nearly nothing we have today would be possible / if the cost of artificial light had not dropped / to almost nothing.
목적격 관계대명사 that 생략
혼합가정법(가정법 과거 주절+과거완료 종속절)

01 기본적인**fundamental** 어떤 것의 가격이 크게 하락할 때, / 온 세상이 바뀔 수 있다. // 조명을 생각해 보자.

02 아마**chances are (that)** / 여러분은 이 문장을 읽고 있을 것이다 / 어떤 유형의 인공조명 아래에서. // 또한**moreover**, / 여러분은 아마**probably** 한번도 생각하지 않았을 것이다 / 독서를 위해 인공조명을 이용하는 것이 그럴 만한 가치가 있는지**be worth it**에 대해.

03 조명 값이 너무 싸서 / 여러분은 생각 없이 그것을 이용한다.

04 하지만 / 1800년대 초반에는, / 당신에게 비용이 들었을 것이다 / 400배만큼 / 오늘날 지불하고 있는 것의 / 같은 양의 조명에 대해.

05 그 가격이면, / 여러분은 비용을 의식할**notice** 것이고 / 다시 한번 생각할 것이다 / 인공조명을 이용하기 전에 / 책을 읽기 위해. // 조명 가격의 증가(→ 하락)는 / 세상을 밝혔다**light up the world**.

06 그것은 밤을 낮으로 바꾸었을 뿐 아니라, / 큰 건물에서 우리가 살고 일할 수 있게 해 주었다 / 자연광이 들어올**enter** 수 없는.

07 우리가 오늘날 누리는 것들은 거의 불가능할 것이다 / 만약 인공조명의 비용이 하락하지 않았더라면 / 거의 공짜 수준으로.

구문 Check up

① Light is so cheap **which / that** you use it without thinking.

이 문장은 '너무 ~해서 …하다'라는 뜻의 <so ~ that …> 구문으로 접속사 that을 써야 한다.

② It allowed us **live / to live** and work in big buildings that natural light could not enter.

동사 allow가 5형식으로 쓰일 때는 <allow+목적어+목적격 보어(to부정사)>의 형태로 쓴다. 따라서 to live가 정답이다.

정답 ① that ② to live

DAY 09

D

어휘의 이해 +

STEP 1 • 수능에 진짜 나오는 단어

✔ 문제에 나오는 단어들을 확인하세요.

시간이 없다면 색으로 표시된 단어만이라도 꼭 외우고 넘어가세요!

01	make up	차지하다, 구성하다	(✔ make) (up) just two percent	단지 2퍼센트를 차지하다
02	newborn	n. 신생아	a ( ) in the bed	침대에 있는 신생아
03	no less than	자그마치 (~인)	( ) ( ) ( ) 65 percent	자그마치 65퍼센트인
04	partly	ad. 부분적으로	( ) agree	부분적으로 동의하다
05	exhaust	v. 피곤하게 하다	( ) them	그들을 피곤하게 하다
06	reserve	n. 비축, 저장고	an energy ( )	에너지 저장고
07	quarter	n. 4분의 1	a ( ) of the total	전체의 4분의 1
08	matter	n. 물질	per unit of ( )	물질의 단위당
09	marvelously	ad. 대단히, 훌륭하게	( ) efficient	대단히 효율적인
10	require	v. 필요로 하다, 요구하다	( ) four hundred calories of energy	400칼로리의 에너지를 필요로 하다

⊕ 본문 문장 속에서 단어들을 확인해 보세요.

The brain makes up / just two percent of our body weight / but uses 20 percent of our energy.

뇌는 차지한다 / 몸무게의 2퍼센트만을 / 하지만 우리의 에너지의 20퍼센트를 사용한다.

단어 다시보기 문제를 풀기 전에 단어들을 30초 동안 다시 확인하세요.

01	make up	차지하다, 구성하다	make up just two percent	단지 2퍼센트를 차지하다
02	newborn		a newborn in the bed	침대에 있는 신생아
03	no less than		no less than 65 percent	자그마치 65퍼센트인
04	partly		partly agree	부분적으로 동의하다
05	exhaust		exhaust them	그들을 피곤하게 하다
06	reserve		an energy reserve	에너지 저장고
07	quarter		a quarter of the total	전체의 4분의 1
08	matter		per unit of matter	물질의 단위당
09	marvelously		marvelously efficient	대단히 효율적인
10	require		require four hundred calories of energy	400칼로리의 에너지를 필요로 하다

⊕ **본문 문장 속에서 단어의 의미를 우리말로 해석해 보세요.**

The brain makes up / just two percent of our body weight / but uses 20 percent of our energy.

➔ 뇌는 ____________ / 몸무게의 2퍼센트만을 / 하지만 우리의 에너지의 20퍼센트를 사용한다.

2020 6월 학평 30번 문제

제한시간 70초

난이도 ★★★☆☆

STEP 2 • 수능 기출 제대로 풀기

D

(A), (B), (C)의 각 네모 안에서 문맥에 맞는 낱말로 가장 적절한 것은?

The brain makes up just two percent of our body weight but uses 20 percent of our energy. In newborns, it's no less than 65 percent. That's partly why babies sleep all the time — their growing brains (A) [warn / exhaust] them — and have a lot of body fat, to use as an energy reserve when needed. Our muscles use even more of our energy, about a quarter of the total, but we have a lot of muscle. Actually, per unit of matter, the brain uses by far (B) [more / less] energy than our other organs. That means that the brain is the most expensive of our organs. But it is also marvelously (C) [creative / efficient]. Our brains require only about four hundred calories of energy a day — about the same as we get from a blueberry muffin. Try running your laptop for twenty-four hours on a muffin and see how far you get.

	(A)		(B)		(C)
①	warn	……	less	……	efficient
②	warn	……	more	……	efficient
③	exhaust	……	more	……	efficient
④	exhaust	……	more	……	creative
⑤	exhaust	……	less	……	creative

정답과 해설 p.28

STEP 3 • 수능 지문 제대로 복습하기

01 The brain makes up / just two percent of our body weight / but uses 20 percent of our energy. // In newborns, / it's no less than 65 percent.
자그마치 ~만큼 많은

02 That's partly why babies sleep all the time / — (their growing brains exhaust them) — / and have a lot of body fat, / to use as an energy reserve / when needed.
병렬연결 / ( ): 삽입절(앞 내용 보충) / 부사적 용법(목적)

03 Our muscles use even more of our energy, / about a quarter of the total, / but we have a lot of muscle.
비교급 강조 / 부사(약, 대략)

04 Actually, / per unit of matter, / the brain uses by far more energy / than our other organs. // That means / that the brain is the most expensive / of our organs.
비교급 강조 / 명사절 접속사 / 최상급

05 But it is also marvelously efficient. // Our brains require / only about four hundred calories of energy a day / — about the same as we get from a blueberry muffin.
~과 똑같이

06 Try running your laptop / for twenty-four hours on a muffin / and see how far you get.
try+-ing: 시험삼아 ~하다 / 의문사절

01 뇌는 차지한다**make up** / 몸무게의 2퍼센트만을 / 하지만 우리의 에너지의 20퍼센트를 사용한다. // 갓 태어난 아기**newborn**의 경우, / 그 비율은 자그마치**no less than** 65퍼센트에 달한다.

02 그것은 아기들이 항상 잠을 자는 부분적인**partly** 이유이다 / — 아기들의 성장하는 뇌가 그들을 소진시킨다**exhaust** — / 그리고 (아기들이) 많은 체지방을 보유하는 이유이다 / (그것을) 에너지 저장고**energy reserve**로 사용하기 위해 / 필요할 때.

03 근육은 훨씬 더 많은 에너지를 사용한다 / 전체의 약 4분의 1 정도**a quarter of the total**로 / 하지만, 우리가 많은 근육을 가지고 있기도 하다.

04 실제로, / 물질 단위당**per unit of matter**, / 뇌는 훨씬 더 많은 에너지를 사용한다 / 다른 기관보다. // 그것은 의미한다 / 뇌가 단연 가장 에너지 소모가 많다는 것을 / 우리 장기 중.

05 하지만 그것은 또한 놀랍도록 효율적이다**marvelously efficient**. // 뇌는 필요로 한다**require** / 하루에 약 400칼로리의 에너지만을 / 블루베리 머핀에서 얻는 것과 거의 같은.

06 노트북을 작동시켜 보라 / 머핀으로 24시간 동안 / 그리고 얼마나 가는지를 보라.

구문 Check up

① That's partly why babies sleep all the time and have a lot of body fat, use / to use as an energy reserve when needed.

콤마 앞이 완전한 절인데 접속사가 따로 있지 않아 동사를 추가할 수 없으므로, to use를 써야 한다. 이는 목적을 나타낸다.

② Actually, per unit of matter, the brain uses by far more energy as / than our other organs.

앞에 비교급인 more가 나오므로 than을 써야 한다.

정답 ① to use ② than

E

어휘의 이해 +

STEP 1 • 수능에 진짜 나오는 단어

✔ 문제에 나오는 단어들을 확인하세요.

시간이 없다면 색으로 표시된 단어만이라도 꼭 외우고 넘어가세요!

01	assignment	n. 숙제, 과제	a school (✔ assignment)	학교 과제
02	emphasis	n. 강조	the ( ) on work	일에 대한 강조
03	productivity	n. 생산성	individual ( )	개별적인 생산성
04	collective	a. 집단적인	( ) memory	집단 기억
05	independence	n. 독립성	have more ( )	더 많은 독립성을 갖다
06	factor	n. 요인	a necessary ( )	필수 요인
07	requirement	n. 필요, 필수 요건	a ( ) for everyone	모든 이에게 있어서의 필수 요건
08	consequently	ad. 그 결과, 따라서	( ) = as a result	그 결과
09	arrange	v. 마련하다, 처리하다	( ) group work	모둠 활동을 마련하다
10	acquire	v. 습득하다, 얻다	( ) teamwork skills	팀워크 기술을 습득하다
11	insist	v. 주장하다, 요구하다	( ) on a refund	환불을 요구하다
12	evidence	n. 증거	provide ( )	증거를 요구하다
13	interdependence	n. 상호 의존성	independence and ( )	독립성과 상호 의존성
14	ensure	v. 보장하다	( ) success	성공을 보장하다

⊕ 본문 문장 속에서 단어들을 확인해 보세요.

This emphasis on individual productivity / reflected an opinion / that independence is a necessary factor for success.

이러한 개별 생산성의 강조는 / 의견을 반영했던 것이다 / 독립성이 성공의 필수 요인이라는.

단어 다시보기 문제를 풀기 전에 단어들을 30초 동안 다시 확인하세요.

01	assignment	숙제, 과제	a school assignment	학교 과제
02	emphasis		the emphasis on work	일에 대한 강조
03	productivity		individual productivity	개별적인 생산성
04	collective		collective memory	집단 기억
05	independence		have more independence	더 많은 독립성을 갖다
06	factor		a necessary factor	필수 요인
07	requirement		a requirement for everyone	모든 이에게 있어서의 필수 요건
08	consequently		consequently = as a result	그 결과
09	arrange		arrange group work	모둠 활동을 마련하다
10	acquire		acquire teamwork skills	팀워크 기술을 습득하다
11	insist		insist on a refund	환불을 요구하다
12	evidence		provide evidence	증거를 요구하다
13	interdependence		independence and interdependence	독립성과 상호 의존성
14	ensure		ensure success	성공을 보장하다

⊕ 본문 문장 속에서 단어의 의미를 우리말로 해석해 보세요.

This emphasis on individual productivity / reflected an opinion / that independence is a necessary factor for success.

→ 이러한 개별 ______의 ______는 / 의견을 반영했던 것이다 / ______이 성공의 필수 ______이라는.

2019 6월 학평 30번 문제

제한시간 80초

난이도 ★★★★★

STEP 2 • 수능 기출 제대로 풀기

E

(A), (B), (C)의 각 네모 안에서 문맥에 맞는 낱말로 가장 적절한 것은?

School assignments have typically required that students work alone. This emphasis on (A) [collective / individual] productivity reflected an opinion that independence is a necessary factor for success. Having the ability to take care of oneself without depending on others was considered a requirement for everyone. Consequently, teachers in the past (B) [more / less] often arranged group work or encouraged students to acquire teamwork skills. However, since the new millennium, businesses have experienced more global competition that requires improved productivity. This situation has led employers to insist that newcomers to the labor market provide evidence of traditional independence but also interdependence shown through teamwork skills. The challenge for educators is to ensure individual competence in basic skills while (C) [adding / decreasing] learning opportunities that can enable students to also perform well in teams.

*competence: 능력

	(A)		(B)		(C)
①	individual	……	less	……	adding
②	collective	……	less	……	decreasing
③	individual	……	less	……	decreasing
④	collective	……	more	……	decreasing
⑤	individual	……	more	……	adding

정답과 해설 p.28

STEP 3 • 수능 지문 제대로 복습하기

01 School assignments have typically required / that students work alone. // This emphasis on individual productivity / reflected an opinion / that independence is a necessary factor for success.

should 생략 / required의 목적어(명사절) / an opinion을 설명해주는 동격절

02 [Having the ability to take care of oneself / without depending on others] / was considered a requirement for everyone.

주어(동명사) / 형용사적 용법 / 수동태: ~로 간주되다 / 주격보어(능동태의 목적격보어가 주격보어로 변경됨)

03 Consequently, / teachers in the past / less often arranged group work / or encouraged students / to acquire teamwork skills.

동사1 / 동사2: encourage+목적어+목적격 보어(to부정사)

04 However, since the new millennium, / businesses have experienced more global competition / that requires improved productivity.

기간 부사구 / 현재완료 / 주격 관계대명사절

05 This situation has led employers to insist / [that newcomers to the labor market provide evidence of traditional independence / but also interdependence shown through teamwork skills].

should 생략 / to insist의 목적어(명사절) / 과거분사(명사 수식)

06 The challenge for educators / is to ensure individual competence in basic skills / while adding learning opportunities / that can enable students to also perform well in teams.

<접속사+-ing> 분사구문 / 주격 관계대명사절

01 학교 과제school assignment는 전형적으로 요구해 왔다 / 학생들이 혼자 하도록. // 이러한 개별 생산성productivity의 강조emphasis는 / 의견을 반영했던 것이다 / 독립성independence이 성공의 필수 요인factor이라는.

02 자신을 관리하는 능력을 가지는 것이 / 타인에게 의존하지 않고 / 모든 사람에게 요구되는 것requirement으로 간주되었다.

03 따라서consequently, / 과거의 교사들은 / 덜 자주 모둠 활동을 마련하거나arrange group work / (덜 자주) 학생들에게 권장했다 / 팀워크 기술을 배우는acquire teamwork skills 것을.

04 그러나 뉴 밀레니엄 시대 이후 / 기업들은 더 많은 국제적 경쟁을 경험하고 있다 / 향상된 생산성을 요구하는.

05 이러한 상황은 고용주들로 하여금 요구하도록insist 만들었다 / 노동 시장의 초입자들이 / 전통적인 독립성을 입증해야provide evidence 한다고 / 그런데 팀워크 기술을 통해 보여지는 상호 의존성interdependence 또한.

06 교육자의 도전 과제는 / 기본적인 기술에서의 개별 능력을 보장하는ensure 것이다 / 학습 기회를 늘려주는 동시에 / 학생들이 팀에서도 잘 수행할 수 있도록 하는.

구문 Check up

① Having the ability to take care of oneself without depending on others considered / was considered a requirement for everyone.

동사 consider는 능동으로 쓸 때 목적어 다음에 목적격 보어가 오는 5형식 동사로, 여기서는 의미상 '간주되다'가 적절하고 뒤에 목적격 보어만 나와 있기 때문에 수동태인 was considered로 쓴다.

② Newcomers to the labor market provide evidence of traditional independence but also interdependence showing / shown through teamwork skills.

의미상 '팀워크 기술을 통해 보여진'이라는 수동의 뜻이 어울리기 때문에 과거분사 shown으로 쓴다.

정답 ① was considered ② shown

F

어휘의 이해 +

STEP 1 • 수능에 진짜 나오는 단어

✔ 문제에 나오는 단어들을 확인하세요.

시간이 없다면 색으로 표시된 단어만이라도 꼭 외우고 넘어가세요!

01	innately	ad. 선천적으로	be (✔ innately) inclined	선천적으로 경향이 있다
02	cause	n. 원인, 이유	( )s of events	사건의 원인
03	form	v. 형성하다, 구성하다	( ) explanations	설명을 구성하다
04	persuasive	a. 설득력 있는	a ( ) medium	설득력 있는 수단
05	provide	v. 제공하다	( ) examples	사례를 제공하다
06	instance	n. 사건, 경우	new ( )s	새로운 경우
07	generalization	n. 일반화	form ( )s	일반화하다
08	attribution	n. (원인의) 귀착, 귀속	these causal ( )s	이러한 인과관계의 귀착
09	complex	a. 복잡한	a ( ) chain of events	복잡한 일련의 사건들
10	contribute to	~에 기여하다, ~의 원인이 되다	( ) ( ) the result	결과의 원인이 되다
11	occur	v. 발생하다, 일어나다	events ( )	사건이 발생하다
12	causal	a. 인과 관계의, 원인이 되는	a ( ) act	원인이 되는 행동
13	assign	v. 선정하다, 부여하다	( ) one cause	하나의 원인을 선정하다

+ 본문 문장 속에서 단어들을 확인해 보세요.

Rather, / there is a complex chain of events / that all contribute to the result; / if any one of the events would not have occurred, / the result would be different.

오히려 / 복잡한 일련의 사건들이 있다 / 모두 그 결과의 원인이 되는. / 만일 사건들 중에 어느 하나라도 발생하지 않았었다면, / 결과는 다를 것이다.

단어 다시보기 문제를 풀기 전에 단어들을 30초 동안 다시 확인하세요.

01	innately	선천적으로	be innately inclined	선천적으로 경향이 있다
02	cause		causes of events	사건의 원인
03	form		form explanations	설명을 구성하다
04	persuasive		a persuasive medium	설득력 있는 수단
05	provide		provide examples	사례를 제공하다
06	instance		new instances	새로운 경우
07	generalization		form generalizations	일반화하다
08	attribution		these causal attributions	이러한 인과관계의 귀착
09	complex		a complex chain of events	복잡한 일련의 사건들
10	contribute to		contribute to the result	결과의 원인이 되다
11	occur		events occur	사건이 발생하다
12	causal		a causal act	원인이 되는 행동
13	assign		assign one cause	하나의 원인을 선정하다

⊕ 본문 문장 속에서 단어의 의미를 우리말로 해석해 보세요.

Rather, / there is a complex chain of events / that all contribute to the result; / if any one of the events would not have occurred, / the result would be different.

→ 오히려 / ________이 있다 / 모두 그 결과________. / 만일 사건들 중에 어느 하나라도 ________ 않았었다면, / 결과는 다를 것이다.

2018 9월 학평 29번 문제

제한시간 80초

난이도 ★★★★★

STEP 2 • 수능 기출 제대로 풀기

F

다음 글의 밑줄 친 부분 중, 문맥상 낱말의 쓰임이 적절하지 않은 것은?

People are innately inclined to look for causes of events, to form explanations and stories. That is one reason storytelling is such a ① persuasive medium. Stories resonate with our experiences and provide examples of new instances. From our experiences and the stories of others we tend to form ② generalizations about the way people behave and things work. We attribute causes to events, and as long as these cause-and-effect ③ pairings make sense, we use them for understanding future events. Yet these causal attributions are often mistaken. Sometimes they implicate the ④ wrong causes, and for some things that happen, there is no single cause. Rather, there is a complex chain of events that all contribute to the result; if any one of the events would not have occurred, the result would be ⑤ similar. But even when there is no single causal act, that doesn't stop people from assigning one.

*resonate: 떠올리게 하다
**implicate: 연관시키다

정답과 해설 p.29

STEP 3 • 수능 지문 제대로 복습하기

01 People are innately inclined / to look for causes of events, / to form explanations and stories. // That is one reason storytelling is such a persuasive medium.

be inclined to: ~하는 경향이 있다 / 동격 / 관계부사 why 생략 / such+관사+형용사+명사: 그토록 ~한 …

02 Stories resonate with our experiences / and provide examples of new instances. // From our experiences and the stories of others / we tend to form generalizations / about the way people behave and things work.

관계부사 how 생략(the way와 how는 함께 쓰지 않음)

03 We attribute causes to events, / and as long as these cause-and-effect pairings make sense, / we use them for understanding future events.

attribute A to B: A를 B의 탓으로 돌리다 / 조건 접속사(~하는 한)

04 Yet / these causal attributions are often mistaken. // Sometimes / they implicate the wrong causes, / and for some things that happen, / there is no single cause.

수동태(be+p.p.) / 주격 관계대명사절

05 Rather, / there is a complex chain of events / that all contribute to the result; / if any one of the events would not have occurred, / the result would be similar.

선행사(복수) / 수 일치 / 주격 관계대명사절 / 혼합가정법(과거의 원인이 달랐더라면 현재의 결과도 달랐을 것이라는 의미)

06 But even when there is no single causal act, / that doesn't stop people from assigning one.

대명사 주어 / stop A from+-ing: A가 ~하는 것을 막다 / =a single casual act

01 사람들은 선천적으로**innately** 경향이 있다 / 사건의 원인**cause**을 찾는 / 즉, 설명과 이야기를 구성하려는**form**. // 그것이 한 가지 이유이다 / 스토리텔링이 그토록 설득력 있는**persuasive** 수단인.

02 이야기는 우리의 경험을 떠올리게 하고 / 새로운 경우**instance**의 사례를 제공한다**provide**. // 우리의 경험과 다른 이들의 이야기로부터 / 우리는 일반화**generalization**하는 경향이 있다 / 방식에 관해 / 사람들이 행동하고 상황이 작동하는.

03 우리는 사건에 원인을 귀착시키고 / 이러한 원인과 결과 쌍이 이치에 맞는 한, / 그것을 미래의 사건을 이해하는 데 사용한다.

04 하지만 / 이러한 인과관계의 귀착**attribution**은 종종 잘못되기도 한다. // 때때로 / 그것은 잘못된 원인을 연관시키기도 하고, / 발생하는 어떤 일에 있어서 / 원인이 하나만 있지 않기도 하다.

05 오히려 / 복잡한**complex** 일련의 사건들이 있다 / 모두 그 결과의 원인이 되는**contribute to**. / 만일 사건들 중에 어느 하나라도 발생하지**occur** 않았었다면, / 결과는 유사할(→다를) 것이다.

06 하지만 원인이 되는**causal** 행동이 단 하나가 아닐 때조차도, / 사람들이 하나(원인 행동 하나)를 선정하는**assign** 것을 막지는 못한다.

구문 Check up

① From our experiences and the stories of others we tend to form generalizations about the way / the way how people behave and things work.

선행사 the way와 관계부사 how는 함께 쓸 수 없으므로 how 없이 the way만 쓴다.

② Sometimes they implicate the wrong causes, and for some things what / that happen, there is no single cause.

앞에 선행사(some things)가 존재하고 뒤에 불완전한 문장이 이어지므로 주격 관계대명사 that이 적절하다.

정답 ① the way ② that

G

어휘의 이해 +

STEP 1 • 수능에 진짜 나오는 단어

✔ 문제에 나오는 단어들을 확인하세요.

시간이 없다면 색으로 표시된 단어만이라도 꼭 외우고 넘어가세요!

01	within	prep. ~안에, 내부에	(✔ within) a few years	몇 년 안에
02	society	n. 사회	early ( )ies	초창기 사회
03	religion	n. 종교	found in ( )	종교에서 발견된
04	inadequate	a. 충분하지 않은	( ) explanations	불충분한 설명
05	reason	n. 이성	based on ( )	이성에 근거하여
06	consistency	n. 일관성	lack ( )	일관성이 부족하다
07	shift	n. 변화 v. 바꾸다	a ( ) in history	역사에서의 변화
08	mark	v. 표시하다, 나타내다	( ) the birth of philosophy	철학의 탄생을 나타내다
09	inquire	v. 조사하다	( ) into the nature	본질을 조사하다
10	likewise	ad. 마찬가지로	( ) unhappy	마찬가지로 불행한
11	rationally	ad. 이성적으로	( ) ↔ irrationally	이성적으로 ↔ 비이성적으로
12	satisfactory	a. 만족스러운	a ( ) explanation	만족스러운 설명

⊕ 본문 문장 속에서 단어들을 확인해 보세요.

Some people, however, / found the traditional religious explanations inadequate, / and they began to search for answers / based on reason.

그러나 몇몇 사람들은 / 그 전통적인 종교적 설명이 충분하지 않다는 것을 알게 되었고, / 답을 찾기 시작하였다 / 이성에 근거하여.

단어 다시보기 문제를 풀기 전에 단어들을 30초 동안 다시 확인하세요.

01	within	~안에, 내부에	within a few years	몇 년 안에
02	society		early societies	초창기 사회
03	religion		found in religion	종교에서 발견된
04	inadequate		inadequate explanations	불충분한 설명
05	reason		based on reason	이성에 근거하여
06	consistency		lack consistency	일관성이 부족하다
07	shift		a shift in history	역사에서의 변화
08	mark		mark the birth of philosophy	철학의 탄생을 나타내다
09	inquire		inquire into the nature	본질을 조사하다
10	likewise		likewise unhappy	마찬가지로 불행한
11	rationally		rationally ↔ irrationally	이성적으로 ↔ 비이성적으로
12	satisfactory		a satisfactory explanation	만족스러운 설명

⊕ 본문 문장 속에서 단어의 의미를 우리말로 해석해 보세요.

Some people, however, / found the traditional religious explanations inadequate, / and they began to search for answers / based on reason.

→ 그러나 몇몇 사람들은 / 그 전통적인 종교적 설명이 ________ 것을 알게 되었고, / 답을 찾기 시작하였다 / 이성에 근거하여.

2017 9월 학평 29번 문제

제한시간 80초

난이도 ★★★★☆

STEP 2 • 수능 기출 제대로 풀기

G

(A), (B), (C)의 각 네모 안에서 문맥에 맞는 낱말로 가장 적절한 것은?

From the beginning of human history, people have asked questions about the world and their place within it. For early societies, the answers to the most basic questions were found in (A) [religion / science]. Some people, however, found the traditional religious explanations inadequate, and they began to search for answers based on reason. This (B) [consistency / shift] marked the birth of philosophy, and the first of the great thinkers that we know of was Thales of Miletus. He used reason to inquire into the nature of the universe, and encouraged others to do likewise. He passed on to his followers not only his answers but also the process of thinking (C) [rationally / irrationally], together with an idea of what kind of explanations could be considered satisfactory.

	(A)		(B)		(C)
①	religion	……	consistency	……	rationally
②	religion	……	shift	……	irrationally
③	religion	……	shift	……	rationally
④	science	……	shift	……	irrationally
⑤	science	……	consistency	……	rationally

정답과 해설 p.29

STEP 3 • 수능 지문 제대로 복습하기

01 From the beginning of human history, / people have asked questions / about the world and their place within it.
기간 부사구 / 현재완료 / 대명사(=the world)

02 For early societies, / the answers to the most basic questions / were found in religion.
주어 / 동사(복수+수동태)

03 Some people, however, / found the traditional religious explanations inadequate, / and they began to search for answers / based on reason.
5형식 동사 / 목적어 / 목적격 보어

04 This shift marked the birth of philosophy, / and the first of the great thinkers / that we know of / was Thales of Miletus.
주어 / 목적격 관계대명사절 / 수 일치(단수)

05 He used reason / to inquire into the nature of the universe, / and encouraged others to do likewise.
to부정사의 부사적 용법(목적: ~하기 위해서) / encourage+목적어+목적격 보어(to부정사)

06 He passed on to his followers / not only his answers but also the process of thinking rationally, / together with an idea of [what kind of explanations could be considered satisfactory].
not only A but also B: A뿐만 아니라 B도 / 의문사절(전치사 of의 목적어) / 5형식 수동태 / 주격보어(능동태의 목적격보어가 주격보어로 변경됨)

01 인류 역사의 시작부터, / 사람들은 질문해 왔다 / 세상과 그 세상 속에 있는**within** 그들의 장소에 관하여.

02 초기 사회**early societies**에 있어, / 가장 기초적 의문에 대한 대답은 / 종교**religion**에서 발견되었다.

03 그러나 몇몇 사람들은 / 그 전통적인 종교적 설명이 충분하지 않다는**inadequate** 것을 알게 되었고, / 답을 찾기 시작하였다 / 이성에 근거하여**based on reason**.

04 이러한 변화**shift**는 철학의 탄생을 보여주었고**marked the birth of philosophy**, / 위대한 사상가들 중 첫 번째 사람은 / 우리가 아는 (사상가들) / Miletus의 Thales였다.

05 그는 이성을 사용하였다 / 우주의 본질을 탐구하기**inquire** 위해, / 그리고 다른 사람들도 이와 같이**likewise** 하도록 권장하였다.

06 그는 자신의 추종자들에게 전했다 / 자신의 대답뿐만 아니라 이성적으로**rationally** 생각하는 과정도 / 어떤 종류의 설명이 만족스러운 것으로 여겨질**be considered satisfactory** 수 있는가에 대한 생각과 함께.

구문 Check up

① For early societies, the answers to the most basic questions found / were found in religion.

대답들이 '발견되었다'는 수동의 의미이기 때문에 수동태인 were found를 써야 한다.

② He passed on to his followers not only his answers but also the process, together with an idea of what kind of explanations could consider / be considered satisfactory.

어떤 설명들이 만족스럽게 '여겨진다'는 뜻이므로 수동태인 be considered로 쓴다. 앞에 조동사 could가 있어 원형인 be를 쓴다.

정답 ① were found ② be considered

★Review

DAY 07~09

☑ 종합 성적표

구분	공부한 날 ❶	결과 분석			틀린 이유 ❸
		출처	풀이 시간 ❷	채점 결과 (O, X)	
Day 7	월 일	학력평가 기출 2023년	분 초		
		학력평가 기출 2022년	분 초		
		학력평가 기출 2021년	분 초		
		학력평가 기출 2020년	분 초		
		학력평가 기출 2019년	분 초		
		학력평가 기출 2018년	분 초		
		학력평가 기출 2017년	분 초		
Day 8	월 일	학력평가 기출 2023년	분 초		
		학력평가 기출 2022년	분 초		
		학력평가 기출 2021년	분 초		
		학력평가 기출 2020년	분 초		
		학력평가 기출 2019년	분 초		
		학력평가 기출 2018년	분 초		
		학력평가 기출 2016년	분 초		
Day 9	월 일	학력평가 기출 2023년	분 초		
		학력평가 기출 2022년	분 초		
		학력평가 기출 2021년	분 초		
		학력평가 기출 2020년	분 초		
		학력평가 기출 2019년	분 초		
		학력평가 기출 2018년	분 초		
		학력평가 기출 2017년	분 초		

3일간 공부한 내용을 다시 보니, ……

❶ **매일 지문을 하루 계획에 맞춰 풀었다. vs. 내가 한 약속을 못 지켰다.**

<매3영 고1 기출>은 단순 문제풀이를 위한 책이 아니라, 매일 규칙적으로 영어를 공부하는 습관을 잡는 책입니다. 따라서 푸는 문제 개수는 상황에 따라 다르더라도 '매일' 학습하는 것이 중요합니다.

❷ **주어진 시간을 자꾸 넘긴다?**

풀이 시간이 계속해서 권장 시간을 넘긴다면 실전 훈련이 부족하다는 신호입니다. 아직 조급함을 가질 필요는 없지만, 매일의 문제 풀이에 더 긴장감 있게 임해보세요.

❸ **틀린 이유 맞춤 솔루션**: 오답 이유에 따라 다음 해결책을 참고하세요.

(1) 단어를 많이 몰라서

▶ **<STEP 1 단어>에 제시된 필수 어휘를 매일 챙겨보고, SELF-TEST까지 꼼꼼히 진행합니다.**

(2) 문장 해석이 잘 안 돼서

▶ **<STEP 3 지문 복습>의 구문 첨삭과 끊어읽기 해설을 정독하며 문장구조를 보는 눈을 길러보세요.**

(3) 해석은 되지만 내용이 이해가 안 되거나, 선택지로 연결을 못 해서

▶ **<정답과 해설>의 해설과 오답풀이를 참고해 틀린 이유를 깊이 고민하고 정리해 보세요.**

!

결론적으로, 내가 **취약한 부분**은 ______ 이다. **취약점을 보완하기 위해서** 나는 ______ 을/를 해야겠다.

3일 뒤 다시 봐야 할 문항과, 꼭 다시 외워야 할 사항·구문 등이 있는 페이지는 지금 바로 접어 두세요.

<매3영>이 제시하는 3단계로

유형 3일 훈련

DAY

10~12

공부한 날			출처	페이지
DAY 10	월	일	학력평가 기출 2023년 학력평가 기출 2022년 학력평가 기출 2021년 학력평가 기출 2020년 학력평가 기출 2019년 학력평가 기출 2018년 학력평가 기출 2017년	267
DAY 11	월	일	학력평가 기출 2023년 학력평가 기출 2022년 학력평가 기출 2021년 학력평가 기출 2020년 학력평가 기출 2019년 학력평가 기출 2018년 학력평가 기출 2017년	295
DAY 12	월	일	학력평가 기출 2023년 학력평가 기출 2022년 학력평가 기출 2021년 학력평가 기출 2020년 학력평가 기출 2019년 학력평가 기출 2018년 학력평가 기출 2017년	323

DAY 10

A

어법의 이해 +

STEP 1 • 수능에 진짜 나오는 단어

✔ 문제에 나오는 단어들을 확인하세요.

시간이 없다면 색으로 표시된 단어만이라도 꼭 외우고 넘어가세요!

01	exist	v. 존재하다	Do ghosts (✔ exist)?	귀신이 존재할까?
02	specialized	a. 전문적인	( ) skills	전문적인 기술들
03	degree	n. 학위	a ( ) in sport management	스포츠 경영 분야의 학위
04	expertise	n. 전문 지식	without any ( )	어떤 전문 지식도 없는
05	executive	n. 임원	a skilled ( )	노련한 임원
06	respective	a. 각자의, 저마다의	in their ( ) fields	각자 자기 분야에서
07	criticism	n. 비난	face ( )	비난에 직면하다
08	accountant	n. 회계사	a qualified ( )	자격이 있는 회계사

⊕ 본문 문장 속에서 단어들을 확인해 보세요.

Executives in sport management / have decades of knowledge and experience / in their respective fields.

스포츠 경영 임원진들은 / 수십 년의 지식과 경험을 가지고 있다 / 각자 자기 분야에서.

단어 다시보기 문제를 풀기 전에 단어들을 30초 동안 다시 확인하세요.

01	exist	존재하다	Do ghosts exist?	귀신이 존재할까?
02	specialized		specialized skills	전문적인 기술들
03	degree		a degree in sport management	스포츠 경영 분야의 학위
04	expertise		without any expertise	어떤 전문 지식도 없는
05	executive		a skilled executive	노련한 임원
06	respective		in their respective fields	각자 자기 분야에서
07	criticism		face criticism	비난에 직면하다
08	accountant		a qualified accountant	자격이 있는 회계사

⊕ 본문 문장 속에서 단어의 의미를 우리말로 해석해 보세요.

Executives in sport management / have decades of knowledge and experience / in their respective fields.

→ 스포츠 경영 ______은 / 수십 년의 지식과 경험을 가지고 있다 / ______ 자기 분야에서.

2023 9월 학평 29번 문제

제한시간 80초

난이도 ★★★★★

STEP 2 • 수능 기출 제대로 풀기

A

다음 글의 밑줄 친 부분 중, 어법상 틀린 것은?

There is a reason the title "Monday Morning Quarterback" exists. Just read the comments on social media from fans discussing the weekend's games, and you quickly see how many people believe they could play, coach, and manage sport teams more ① successfully than those on the field. This goes for the boardroom as well. Students and professionals with years of training and specialized degrees in sport business may also find themselves ② being given advice on how to do their jobs from friends, family, or even total strangers without any expertise. Executives in sport management ③ have decades of knowledge and experience in their respective fields. However, many of them face criticism from fans and community members telling ④ themselves how to run their business. Very few people tell their doctor how to perform surgery or their accountant how to prepare their taxes, but many people provide feedback on ⑤ how sport organizations should be managed.

*boardroom: 이사회실

정답과 해설 p.30

STEP 3 • 수능 지문 제대로 복습하기

01 There is a reason (관계부사 why) the title “Monday Morning Quarterback” exists.

02 Just read the comments on social media / from fans discussing the weekend’s games, / and you quickly see / how many people believe / they could play, coach, and manage sport teams more successfully / than those on the field. // This goes for the boardroom as well.

(명령문+and: ~하라, 그러면 … / 현재분사구 / 동사구 / 비교급 부사 / ~인 사람들 / ~도, 또한)

03 Students and professionals with years of training and specialized degrees in sport business / may also find themselves being given advice / on how to do their jobs / from friends, family, or even total strangers without any expertise.

(주어 / 전치사구 / find+목적어+목적격보어: ~가 …하다는 것을 알다 / how to-V: 어떻게 ~할지)

04 Executives in sport management / have decades of knowledge and experience / in their respective fields. // However, / many of them face criticism from fans and community members / telling them how to run their business.

(주어(복수) / 수 일치 / 현재분사구 / =executives)

05 Very few people / tell their doctor how to perform surgery / or their accountant how to prepare their taxes, / but many people provide feedback / on how sport organizations should be managed.

(거의 없는 / 4형식 동사 / 간접목적어1 / 직접목적어1 / 간접목적어2 / 직접목적어2 / 의문사절(on의 목적어))

01 이유가 있다 / ‘Monday Morning Quarterback’이라는 이름이 존재하는**exist**.

02 그저 소셜 미디어의 댓글을 읽어 보라 / 주말 경기에 대해 토론하는 팬들의 / 그러면 여러분은 금방 알 수 있다 / 얼마나 많은 사람들이 믿는지 / 자신이 더 성공적으로 경기를 뛰고, 감독하고, 스포츠팀을 관리할 수 있다고 / 경기장에 있는 사람들보다. // 이것은 이사회실에서도 마찬가지이다.

03 스포츠 사업에서 수년간의 훈련을 받고 전문적인 학위**specialized degree**를 가진 학생들과 전문가들도 / 또한 충고를 듣고 있는 자신을 발견할지도 모른다 / 어떻게 그들의 일을 해야 할지에 관해 / 전문 지식**expertise**이 전혀 없는 가족, 혹은 완전한 타인으로부터.

04 스포츠 경영 임원진들**executive**은 / 수십 년의 지식과 경험을 가지고 있다 / 각자**respective** 자기 분야에서. // 하지만, / 그들 중 많은 사람들이 팬들과 지역 사회 구성원들의 비난에 직면한다**face criticism** / 그들에게 사업 운영 방식을 알려주는.

05 ~한 사람은 거의 없다 / 의사에게 수술하는 방법을 알려주거나 / 회계사**accountant**에게 세금을 준비하는 방법을 알려주는 / 하지만 많은 사람들이 피드백을 제공한다 / 스포츠 조직이 어떻게 관리되어야 하는지에 대한.

구문 Check up

① Just read the comments on social media from fans [discussing / discussed] the weekend’s games.

맥락상 fans가 ‘논의하는’ 주체이므로 능동을 나타내는 현재분사인 discussing이 알맞다.

② But many people provide feedback on how sport organizations should [manage / be managed].

how절의 주어 sport organizations는 ‘관리되는’ 대상이다. 따라서 be managed가 적절하다.

정답 ① discussing ② be managed

B

어법의 이해 ⊕

STEP 1 • 수능에 진짜 나오는 단어

✔ 문제에 나오는 단어들을 확인하세요.

시간이 없다면 색으로 표시된 단어만이라도 꼭 외우고 넘어가세요!

01	shrink	v. 줄다	(✔ shrink) in mass	부피가 줄다
02	peak	v. 정점에 도달하다	( ) in size	크기가 정점에 도달하다
03	predator	n. 포식자	dangerous ( )s	위험한 포식자들
04	have one's wits about	~에 대해 빈틈이 없다	( ) their ( ) ( ) dangerous predators	위험한 포식자들에 대해 빈틈이 없다
05	domesticate	v. 길들이다	( ) animals	동물들을 길들이다
06	immediate	a. 즉각적인	avoid ( ) death	즉각적인 죽음을 피하다
07	obtain	v. 얻다	( ) food	음식을 얻다
08	outsource	v. (작업을 외부에) 위탁하다, 아웃소싱하다	( ) the tasks to the wider society	과업을 더 넓은 사회로 위탁하다
09	ancestor	n. 조상	smaller than ( )s	조상보다 더 작은
10	characteristic	n. 특징	a ( ) of animals	동물들의 특징
11	domestic	a. 가축의, 가정의, 국내의	( ) animals	가축
12	dumb	a. 어리석은	( )er than our ancestors	우리 조상들보다 더 어리석은
13	not necessarily	반드시 ~인 것은 아닌	brain size is ( ) ( ) a critical factor	뇌 크기가 반드시 결정적인 요소는 아니다
14	indicator	n. 지표	an ( ) of human intelligence	인간 지능의 지표
15	wire	v. 연결하다, 구성하다, 설정하다	Our brains are ( )d to avoid pain.	우리의 뇌는 고통을 피하도록 설정돼 있다.

⊕ 본문 문장 속에서 단어들을 확인해 보세요.

It is a characteristic of domestic animals / that they are generally smaller than their wild cousins.

가축 동물들의 한 특징이다 / 그들이 일반적으로 그들의 야생 사촌들보다 더 작은 것이.

단어 다시보기 문제를 풀기 전에 단어들을 30초 동안 다시 확인하세요.

01	shrink	줄다	shrink in mass	부피가 줄다
02	peak		peak in size	크기가 정점에 도달하다
03	predator		dangerous predators	위험한 포식자들
04	have one's wits about		have their wits about dangerous predators	위험한 포식자들에 대해 빈틈이 없다
05	domesticate		domesticate animals	동물들을 길들이다
06	immediate		avoid immediate death	즉각적인 죽음을 피하다
07	obtain		obtain food	음식을 얻다
08	outsource		outsource the tasks to the wider society	과업을 더 넓은 사회로 위탁하다
09	ancestor		smaller than ancestors	조상보다 더 작은
10	characteristic		a characteristic of animals	동물들의 특징
11	domestic		domestic animals	가축
12	dumb		dumber than our ancestors	우리 조상들보다 더 어리석은
13	not necessarily		brain size is not necessarily a critical factor	뇌 크기가 반드시 결정적인 요소는 아니다
14	indicator		an indicator of human intelligence	인간 지능의 지표
15	wire		Our brains are wired to avoid pain.	우리의 뇌는 고통을 피하도록 설정돼 있다.

⊕ **본문 문장 속에서 단어의 의미를 우리말로 해석해 보세요.**

It is a characteristic of domestic animals / that they are generally smaller than their wild cousins.

→ ________ 동물들의 한 ________이다 / 그들이 일반적으로 그들의 야생 사촌들보다 더 작은 것이.

2022 9월 학평 29번 문제

제한시간 70초

난이도 ★★★☆☆

STEP 2 • 수능 기출 제대로 풀기

B

다음 글의 밑줄 친 부분 중, 어법상 틀린 것은?

The human brain, it turns out, has shrunk in mass by about 10 percent since it ① peaked in size 15,000—30,000 years ago. One possible reason is that many thousands of years ago humans lived in a world of dangerous predators ② where they had to have their wits about them at all times to avoid being killed. Today, we have effectively domesticated ourselves and many of the tasks of survival — from avoiding immediate death to building shelters to obtaining food — ③ has been outsourced to the wider society. We are smaller than our ancestors too, and it is a characteristic of domestic animals ④ that they are generally smaller than their wild cousins. None of this may mean we are dumber — brain size is not necessarily an indicator of human intelligence — but it may mean that our brains today are wired up differently, and perhaps more efficiently, than ⑤ those of our ancestors.

정답과 해설 p.30

STEP 3 • 수능 지문 제대로 복습하기

01 The human brain, / it turns out, / has shrunk in mass by about 10 percent / since it peaked in size 15,000—30,000 years ago.
주어 / 삽입절 / 동사(현재완료) / 대략, 약 / ~만큼 / 기간 부사구(~ 이래로)

02 One possible reason is / that many thousands of years ago / humans lived in a world of dangerous predators / [where they had to have their wits about them at all times / to avoid being killed].
명사절 접속사(보어) / 관계부사절 / to부정사의 부사적 용법(~하기 위해)

03 Today, / we have effectively domesticated ourselves / and many of the tasks of survival / — from avoiding immediate death / to building shelters / to obtaining food — / have been outsourced to the wider society.
주어(many of+복수명사) / from A to B to C: A에서 B, C까지 / 동사(복수+현재완료 수동태)

04 We are smaller than our ancestors too, / and it is a characteristic of domestic animals / that they are generally smaller than their wild cousins.
가주어 / 진주어(that절)

05 None of this may mean / we are dumber / — (brain size is not necessarily an indicator of human intelligence) — / but it may mean / that our brains today are wired up / differently, and perhaps more efficiently, / than those of our ancestors.
명사절 접속사 that 생략 / ( ): that절 부연 설명 / 명사절 접속사 / (=brains)

01 인간의 뇌는 / 밝혀졌다 / 부피가 약 10퍼센트만큼 줄어든**shrink** 것으로 / 15,000년에서 30,000년 전에 크기가 정점에 도달한**peak** 이후.

02 한 가지 가능한 이유는 / 수천 년 전에 / 인간은 위험한 포식자**predator**들의 세계에서 살았다는 것이다 / 항상 포식자들에 대해 빈틈이 없어야 했던**have their wits about them** / 죽임을 당하는 것을 피하기 위해.

03 오늘날, / 우리는 우리 자신을 효율적으로 길들여**domesticate** 왔고 / 생존의 많은 과업이/ 즉각적인**immediate** 죽음을 피하는 것부터 / 은신처를 짓는 일까지 / 그리고 음식을 얻는**obtain** 일까지 / 더 넓은 사회로 위탁**outsource**되어 왔다.

04 또한 우리는 우리의 조상**ancestor**들보다 더 작다 / 그리고 가축**domestic** 동물들의 한 특징**characteristic**이다 / 그들이 일반적으로 그들의 야생 사촌들보다 더 작은 것이.

05 이것의 어떤 것도 의미하지는 않는다 / 우리가 더 어리석다**dumb**는 것을 / 뇌 크기가 반드시 인간 지능의 지표는 아니다**not necessarily an indicator** / 하지만 그것은 의미할지도 모른다 / 오늘날 우리의 뇌가 구성되어 있다**be wired**는 것을 / 다르게, 그리고 아마도 더 효율적으로 / 우리 조상들의 그것들보다.

구문 Check up

① The human brain, it turns out, has / have shrunk in mass by about 10 percent since it peaked in size 15,000—30,000 years ago.

주어가 The human brain이므로 단수로 수 일치한다. 따라서 has가 정답이다.

② Humans lived in a world of dangerous predators where they had to have their wits about them at all times to avoid to be / being killed.

avoid의 목적어 자리에는 동명사를 쓰므로 being이 적절하다. 참고로 <being p.p.>는 동명사의 수동태이다.

정답 ① has ② being

C

어법의 이해 +

STEP 1 • 수능에 진짜 나오는 단어

✔ 문제에 나오는 단어들을 확인하세요.

시간이 없다면 색으로 표시된 단어만이라도 꼭 외우고 넘어가세요!

01	hold	v. 주장하다	a theory (✔ hold)s that	한 이론이 ~라고 주장하다
02	goods	n. 물품, 상품	sell ( )	물품을 팔다
03	dismiss	v. 해고하다, 떨쳐버리다	( ) workers	직원들을 해고하다
04	unemployment	n. 실업	( ) is impossible.	실업은 불가능하다.
05	picture	v. 상상하다	( ) the level of spending	지출의 정도를 상상하다
06	apply	v. 적용되다	Say's Law ( )ies.	세이의 법칙이 적용된다.
07	earning	n. 수입, 소득(주로 복수형)	use all their ( )s	모든 수입을 사용하다
08	save	v. 저축하다	( ) some of it	그것의 일부를 저축하다
09	leakage	n. 누수, 누출, 샘	Savings are a ( ) of spending.	저축은 지출의 누수이다.

⊕ 본문 문장 속에서 단어들을 확인해 보세요.

Say's Law applies / because people use all their earnings / to buy things.

세이의 법칙은 적용된다 / 사람들이 그들의 모든 수입을 사용하기 때문에 / 물품을 사기 위해.

단어 다시보기 문제를 풀기 전에 단어들을 30초 동안 다시 확인하세요.

01	hold	주장하다	a theory holds that	한 이론이 ~라고 주장하다
02	goods		sell goods	물품을 팔다
03	dismiss		dismiss workers	직원들을 해고하다
04	unemployment		Unemployment is impossible.	실업은 불가능하다.
05	picture		picture the level of spending	지출의 정도를 상상하다
06	apply		Say's Law applies.	세이의 법칙이 적용된다.
07	earning		use all their earnings	모든 수입을 사용하다
08	save		save some of it	그것의 일부를 저축하다
09	leakage		Savings are a leakage of spending.	저축은 지출의 누수이다.

⊕ 본문 문장 속에서 단어의 의미를 우리말로 해석해 보세요.

Say's Law applies / because people use all their earnings / to buy things.

➜ 세이의 법칙은 ____ / 사람들이 그들의 모든 ____을 사용하기 때문에 / 물품을 사기 위해.

2021 9월 학평 29번 문제

제한시간 80초

난이도 ★★★★★

STEP 2 • 수능 기출 제대로 풀기

C

다음 글의 밑줄 친 부분 중, 어법상 틀린 것은?

An economic theory of Say's Law holds that everything that's made will get sold. The money from anything that's produced is used to ① buy something else. There can never be a situation ② which a firm finds that it can't sell its goods and so has to dismiss workers and close its factories. Therefore, recessions and unemployment are impossible. Picture the level of spending like the level of water in a bath. Say's Law applies ③ because people use all their earnings to buy things. But what happens if people don't spend all their money, saving some of ④ it instead? Savings are a 'leakage' of spending from the economy. You're probably imagining the water level now falling, so there's less spending in the economy. That would mean firms producing less and ⑤ dismissing some of their workers.

*recession: 경기 후퇴

정답과 해설 p.31

STEP 3 • 수능 지문 제대로 복습하기

01 An economic theory of Say's Law holds / [that everything that's made will get sold]. // The money from anything that's produced / is used to buy something else.

(명사절(holds의 목적어) / 주격 관계대명사절 / 주어 / 주격 관계대명사절 / be used to+동사원형: ~하기 위해 사용되다)

02 There can never be a situation / [in which a firm finds / that it can't sell its goods / and so has to dismiss workers and close its factories].

(전치사+관계대명사 / 명사절 접속사 / 병렬구조)

03 Therefore, / recessions and unemployment are impossible. // Picture the level of spending / like the level of water in a bath.

(명령문(~하라) / 전치사(~처럼))

04 Say's Law applies / because people use all their earnings / to buy things. // But what happens / if people don't spend all their money, / saving some of it instead?

(to부정사의 부사적 용법(목적) / 분사구문)

05 Savings are a 'leakage' of spending / from the economy. // You're probably imagining the water level now falling, / so there's less spending in the economy.

(동사(현재진행))

06 That would mean / firms producing less / and dismissing some of their workers.

(병렬구조: 동명사(would mean의 목적어) 연결 / 의미상 주어)

01 경제 이론인 세이의 법칙은 주장한다**hold** / 만들어진 모든 물품이 팔리기 마련이라고. // 생산된 물품으로부터 나오는 돈은 / 다른 물품을 사는 데 사용된다.

02 상황은 절대 있을 수 없다 / 한 회사가 알게 되는 (상황) / 물품**goods**을 팔 수 없고 / 그래서 직원들을 해고해야**dismiss** 하고 공장의 문을 닫아야 함을.

03 따라서, / 경기 후퇴와 실업**unemployment**은 불가능하다. // 지출의 정도를 상상해보라**picture** / 욕조 안의 물 높이로.

04 세이의 법칙은 적용된다**apply** / 사람들이 그들의 모든 수입**earnings**을 사용하기 때문에 / 물품을 사기 위해. // 하지만 무슨 일이 일어날까 / 만약 사람들이 그들의 돈을 전부 사용하지 않고, / 대신 돈의 일부를 저축한다**save**면?

05 저축은 지출의 '누수**leakage**'이다 / 경제에서. // 당신은 아마 물의 높이가 지금 낮아지고 있는 것을 상상하고 있을 것이다 / 그래서 경제에서 지출이 적어지는 것을.

06 그것은 의미할 것이다 / 회사들이 더 적게 생산하고 / 일부 직원들을 해고하는 것을.

구문 Check up

① A firm finds that it can't sell its goods and so have / has to dismiss workers and close its factories.

can't sell과 병렬 연결되는 동사 자리인데, 문맥상 해고를 해야 한다는 의미이므로 has를 쓴다. have를 쓰면 sell과 마찬가지로 can't의 영향을 받아 '해고할 수 없어야 한다'는 어색한 의미가 된다.

② But what happens if people don't spend all their money, save / saving some of it instead?

if절의 동사는 don't spend로, 만약 save를 동사로 쓰고 싶다면 접속사가 있어야 하지만 접속사가 없기 때문에 분사구문인 saving을 쓴다.

정답 ① has ② saving

D

어법의 이해 +

STEP 1 • 수능에 진짜 나오는 단어

✔ 문제에 나오는 단어들을 확인하세요.

시간이 없다면 색으로 표시된 단어만이라도 꼭 외우고 넘어가세요!

01	phrase	n. 구절	the (✔ phrase) often used	종종 사용되는 구절
02	physical	a. 신체의	( ) health	신체 건강
03	processed food	가공식품	buy ( ) ( )s	가공식품을 사다
04	canned food	통조림 식품	buy ( ) ( )s	통조림 식품을 사다
05	packaged	a. 포장된	( ) goods	포장된 제품
06	contain	v. 담고 있다, 함유하다	( ) so many chemicals	너무 많은 화학물질을 함유하다
07	artificial	a. 인공적인	( ) ingredients	인공적인 재료
08	ingredient	n. 재료[성분]	contain so many ( )s	너무 많은 재료를 함유하다
09	label	n. 라벨 v. 라벨을 붙이다	food ( )s	식품 라벨
10	purpose	n. 목적	the main ( ) of food labels	식품 라벨의 주된 목적

+ 본문 문장 속에서 단어들을 확인해 보세요.

But do you really know what you are eating / when you buy processed foods, canned foods, and packaged goods?

하지만 여러분은 자신이 무엇을 먹고 있는 것인지 정말 아는가 / 여러분이 가공식품, 통조림 식품, 그리고 포장 제품을 살 때?

단어 다시보기 문제를 풀기 전에 단어들을 30초 동안 다시 확인하세요.

01	phrase	구절	the phrase often used	종종 사용되는 구절
02	physical		physical health	신체 건강
03	processed food		buy processed foods	가공식품을 사다
04	canned food		buy canned foods	통조림 식품을 사다
05	packaged		packaged goods	포장된 제품
06	contain		contain so many chemicals	너무 많은 화학물질을 함유하다
07	artificial		artificial ingredients	인공적인 재료
08	ingredient		contain so many ingredients	너무 많은 재료를 함유하다
09	label		food labels	식품 라벨
10	purpose		the main purpose of food labels	식품 라벨의 주된 목적

⊕ 본문 문장 속에서 단어의 의미를 우리말로 해석해 보세요.

But do you really know what you are eating / when you buy processed foods, canned foods, and packaged goods?

→ 하지만 여러분은 자신이 무엇을 먹고 있는 것인지 정말 아는가 / 여러분이 __________, __________, 그리고 __________을 살 때?

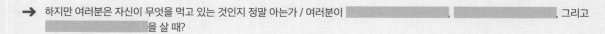

2020 3월 학평 29번 문제

제한시간 70초

난이도 ★★★☆☆

STEP 2 • 수능 기출 제대로 풀기

D

다음 글의 밑줄 친 부분 중, 어법상 틀린 것은?

"You are what you eat." That phrase is often used to ① show the relationship between the foods you eat and your physical health. But do you really know what you are eating when you buy processed foods, canned foods, and packaged goods? Many of the manufactured products made today contain so many chemicals and artificial ingredients ② which it is sometimes difficult to know exactly what is inside them. Fortunately, now there are food labels. Food labels are a good way ③ to find the information about the foods you eat. Labels on food are ④ like the table of contents found in books. The main purpose of food labels ⑤ is to inform you what is inside the food you are purchasing.

*manufactured: (공장에서) 제조된

**table of contents: (책 등의) 목차

정답과 해설 p.31

STEP 3 • 수능 지문 제대로 복습하기

01 "You are what you eat." // That phrase is often used / to show the relationship / between the foods you eat and your physical health.
be used to+동사원형: ~하는 데 사용되다
목적격 관계대명사 생략

02 But do you really know what you are eating / when you buy processed foods, canned foods, and packaged goods?
의문사절

03 Many of the manufactured products made today / contain so many chemicals and artificial ingredients / that it is sometimes difficult / to know exactly what is inside them.
주어(many of+복수명사) 과거분사(명사 수식) 동사(복수) so ~ that …: 너무 ~해서 …하다 가주어 진주어 의문사절

04 Fortunately, / now there are food labels. // Food labels are a good way / [to find the information about the foods you eat].
형용사적 용법
목적격 관계대명사 생략

05 Labels on food are like the table of contents / found in books.
전치사(~처럼) 과거분사(명사 수식)

06 The main purpose of food labels is / to inform you / [what is inside the food / you are purchasing].
주격보어 관계대명사 what절

01 '먹는 것이 여러분을 만든다.' // 그 구절**phrase**은 흔히 사용된다 / 관계를 보여주기 위해 / 여러분이 먹는 음식과 여러분의 신체 건강**physical health** 사이의.

02 하지만 여러분은 자신이 무엇을 먹고 있는 것인지 정말 아는가 / 가공식품**processed food**, 통조림 식품**canned food**, 그리고 포장 식품**packaged goods**을 살 때?

03 오늘날 만들어진 제조 식품 중 다수가 / 너무 많은 화학물질과 인공적인 재료를 함유하고**contain artificial ingredients** 있어서 / 때로는 어렵다 / 정확히 그 안에 무엇이 들어 있는지를 알기가.

04 다행히도, / 이제는 식품 라벨**food label**이 있다. // 식품 라벨은 좋은 방법이다 / 여러분이 먹는 식품에 관한 정보를 알아내는.

05 식품 라벨은 목차와 같다 / 책에서 볼 수 있는.

06 식품 라벨의 주된 목적**the main purpose**은 / 여러분에게 알려주는 것이다 / 식품 안에 무엇이 들어 있는지 / 여러분이 구입하고 있는.

구문 Check up

① Many of the manufactured products made today contain / contains so many chemicals and artificial ingredients.

주어가 <부분 of 전체> 형태의 <many of+복수명사>이므로, 동사는 전체에 수 일치하여 contain을 쓴다.

② Labels on food are like the table of contents finding / found in books.

the table of contents는 '발견되는' 대상이므로 수동의 의미를 갖는 과거분사 found를 쓴다.

정답 ① contain ② found

DAY 10

E

어법의 이해 +

STEP 1 • 수능에 진짜 나오는 단어

✔ 문제에 나오는 단어들을 확인하세요.

시간이 없다면 색으로 표시된 단어만이라도 꼭 외우고 넘어가세요!

01	comfort	n. 편안함	provide (✓ comfort)	편안함을 제공하다
02	appropriate	a. 적절한, 적당한	( ) for exercise	운동에 적절한
03	temperature	n. 기온	appropriate for the ( )	기온에 적절한
04	condition	n. 조건	environmental ( )s	환경적인 조건
05	environment	n. 환경	in warm ( )s	따뜻한 환경에서
06	capacity	n. 능력, 기능	have a ( )	기능이 있다
07	in contrast	그에 반해서	( ) ( ) = on the contrary	그에 반해서
08	layer	n. 층, 껴입기	face cold environments with ( )s	겹겹이 입어서 추운 환경에 대처하다
09	adjust	v. 조절하다	( ) body temperature	체온을 조절하다
10	sweat	v. 땀을 흘리다	avoid ( )ing	땀을 흘리는 것을 피하다

⊕ 본문 문장 속에서 단어들을 확인해 보세요.

Select clothing / appropriate for the temperature and environmental conditions / in which you will be doing exercise.

의류를 선택하라 / 기온과 환경 조건에 적절한 / 당신이 운동하고 있을.

단어 다시보기 문제를 풀기 전에 단어들을 30초 동안 다시 확인하세요.

01	comfort	편안함	provide comfort	편안함을 제공하다
02	appropriate		appropriate for exercise	운동에 적절한
03	temperature		appropriate for the temperature	기온에 적절한
04	condition		environmental conditions	환경적인 조건
05	environment		in warm environments	따뜻한 환경에서
06	capacity		have a capacity	기능이 있다
07	in contrast		in contrast = on the contrary	그에 반해서
08	layer		face cold environments with layers	겹겹이 입어서 추운 환경에 대처하다
09	adjust		adjust body temperature	체온을 조절하다
10	sweat		avoid sweating	땀을 흘리는 것을 피하다

⊕ 본문 문장 속에서 단어의 의미를 우리말로 해석해 보세요.

Select clothing / appropriate for the temperature and environmental conditions / in which you will be doing exercise.

→ 의류를 선택하라 / ________과 환경 ________에 ________ / 당신이 운동하고 있을.

2019 3월 학평 28번 문제

제한시간 80초

난이도 ★★★★★

STEP 2 • 수능 기출 제대로 풀기

E

(A), (B), (C)의 각 네모 안에서 어법에 맞는 표현으로 가장 적절한 것은?

Clothing doesn't have to be expensive to provide comfort during exercise. Select clothing appropriate for the temperature and environmental conditions (A) [which / in which] you will be doing exercise. Clothing that is appropriate for exercise and the season can improve your exercise experience. In warm environments, clothes that have a wicking capacity (B) [is / are] helpful in dissipating heat from the body. In contrast, it is best to face cold environments with layers so you can adjust your body temperature to avoid sweating and remain (C) [comfortable / comfortably].

*wick: (모세관 작용으로) 수분을 흡수하거나 배출하다

**dissipate: (열을) 발산하다

	(A)		(B)		(C)
①	which	……	is	……	comfortable
②	which	……	are	……	comfortable
③	in which	……	are	……	comfortable
④	in which	……	is	……	comfortably
⑤	in which	……	are	……	comfortably

정답과 해설 p.31

STEP 3 • 수능 지문 제대로 복습하기

01 Clothing doesn't have to be expensive / to provide comfort during exercise.
목적(~하기 위해)

주격 관계대명사+be동사(which is) 생략
02 Select clothing / appropriate for the temperature and environmental conditions / in which you will be doing exercise.
명령문(~하라)
전치사+관계대명사절

주어(불가산) 수 일치(단수)
03 Clothing that is appropriate for exercise and the season / can improve your exercise experience.
주격 관계대명사절

주어(복수) 수 일치
04 In warm environments, / clothes that have a wicking capacity / are helpful in dissipating heat from the body.
주격 관계대명사절 동사

that 생략
05 In contrast, / it is best to face cold environments with layers / so you can adjust your body temperature / to avoid sweating and remain comfortable.
가주어 진주어 ~하기 위해(목적)
동명사 (to) remain의 보어(형용사)

01 의류가 비쌀 필요는 없다 / 운동하는 동안 편안함을 제공하기**provide comfort** 위해.

02 의류를 선택하라 / 기온과 환경 조건에 적절한**appropriate for the temperature and environmental conditions** / 당신이 운동하고 있을.

03 운동과 계절에 적절한 의류는 / 운동 경험을 향상시킬 수 있다.

04 따뜻한 환경에서는**in warm environment** / 수분을 흡수하거나 배출할 수 있는 기능**capacity**을 가진 옷이 / 몸에서 열을 발산하는 데 도움이 된다.

05 반면**in contrast,** / 겹겹이 입어서**with layers** 추운 환경에 대처하는 것이 최선이다 / 체온을 조절하려면**adjust body temperature** / 땀을 흘리는 것을 피하고**avoid sweating** 쾌적한 상태를 유지하기 위해.

구문 Check up

① Clothing [don't / doesn't] have to be expensive to provide comfort during exercise.

주어가 Clothing으로 불가산명사이기 때문에 단수 취급하여 doesn't를 쓴다.

② Clothing [that / what] is appropriate for exercise and the season can improve your exercise experience.

앞에 선행사가 있고, 관계사절에 주어가 없기 때문에 주어를 대신할 관계대명사가 필요하다. 따라서 that이 적절하다.

정답 ① doesn't ② that

DAY 10

F

어법의 이해 ⊕

STEP 1 • 수능에 진짜 나오는 단어

✔ 문제에 나오는 단어들을 확인하세요.

시간이 없다면 색으로 표시된 단어만이라도 꼭 외우고 넘어가세요!

01	extremely	ad. 매우, 극도로	(✔ extremely) slow	매우 느린
02	float	v. 떠다니다	tend to ( ) on water	물에 떠다니는 경향이 있다
03	current	n. 흐름, 해류	ocean ( )s	해류
04	measure	v. 측정하다	difficult to ( )	측정하기 어려운
05	typically	ad. 전형적으로, 일반적으로	( ) used	일반적으로 사용되는
06	collect	v. 수집하다, 수거하다	( ) microplastics	미세 플라스틱을 수거하다
07	impact	n. 영향, 충격	( )s on marine environment	해양 환경에 미치는 영향
08	particle	n. 입자, 조각	tiny ( )s	작은 조각들
09	various	a. 다양한	( ) animals	다양한 동물
10	ocean	n. 바다, 대양	in the ( )	바다 속에
11	practical	a. 실질적인, 실천적인	a ( ) way	실질적인 방법
12	enormous	a. 거대한, 엄청난	( ) amounts of water	엄청난 양의 물
13	relatively	ad. 상대적으로, 비교적	( ) small	비교적 적은

⊕ 본문 문장 속에서 단어들을 확인해 보세요.

These tiny particles are known / to be eaten by various animals / and to get into the food chain.

이 작은 조각들은 알려져 있다 / 다양한 동물에게 먹혀 / 먹이 사슬 속으로 들어간다고.

단어 다시보기 문제를 풀기 전에 단어들을 30초 동안 다시 확인하세요.

01	extremely	매우, 극도로	extremely slow	매우 느린
02	float		tend to float on water	물에 떠다니는 경향이 있다
03	current		ocean currents	해류
04	measure		difficult to measure	측정하기 어려운
05	typically		typically used	일반적으로 사용되는
06	collect		collect microplastics	미세 플라스틱을 수거하다
07	impact		impacts on marine environment	해양 환경에 미치는 영향
08	particle		tiny particles	작은 조각들
09	various		various animals	다양한 동물
10	ocean		in the ocean	바다 속에
11	practical		a practical way	실질적인 방법
12	enormous		enormous amounts of water	엄청난 양의 물
13	relatively		relatively small	비교적 적은

⊕ 본문 문장 속에서 단어의 의미를 우리말로 해석해 보세요.

These tiny particles are known / to be eaten by various animals / and to get into the food chain.

→ 이 ____은 알려져 있다 / ____에게 먹혀 / 먹이 사슬 속으로 들어간다고.

2018 6월 학평 28번 문제

제한시간 80초

난이도 ★★★★★

STEP 2 • 수능 기출 제대로 풀기

F

다음 글의 밑줄 친 부분 중, 어법상 틀린 것은?

Plastic is extremely slow to degrade and tends to float, ① which allows it to travel in ocean currents for thousands of miles. Most plastics break down into smaller and smaller pieces when exposed to ultraviolet (UV) light, ② forming microplastics. These microplastics are very difficult to measure once they are small enough to pass through the nets typically used to collect ③ themselves. Their impacts on the marine environment and food webs are still poorly understood. These tiny particles are known to be eaten by various animals and to get into the food chain. Because most of the plastic particles in the ocean ④ are so small, there is no practical way to clean up the ocean. One would have to filter enormous amounts of water to collect a ⑤ relatively small amount of plastic.

*degrade: 분해되다

정답과 해설 p.32

STEP 3 • 수능 지문 제대로 복습하기

01 Plastic is extremely slow to degrade / and tends to float, / which allows it to travel in ocean currents / for thousands of miles.

관계대명사(계속적 용법) / allow+목적어+목적격 보어(to부정사)

02 Most plastics break down into smaller and smaller pieces / when exposed to ultraviolet (UV) light, / forming microplastics.

접속사가 남아있는 분사구문 (=when they are exposed~) / 분사구문(=and they form~)

03 These microplastics are very difficult to measure / once they are small enough to pass through the nets / typically used to collect them.

부사적 용법(형용사 수식) / 접속사(일단 ~하면) / ~하기에 충분히 / 과거분사(the nets 수식) / (=these microplastics)

04 Their impacts on the marine environment and food webs / are still poorly understood. // These tiny particles are known / to be eaten by various animals / and to get into the food chain.

수동태(be+p.p.) / 병렬연결(be known+to부정사: ~하다고 알려지다)

05 Because most of the plastic particles in the ocean are so small, / there is no practical way / to clean up the ocean.

주어(most of+복수명사) / 동사(복수) / 형용사적 용법

06 One would have to filter enormous amounts of water / to collect a relatively small amount of plastic.

부사적 용법(목적)

01 플라스틱은 매우extremely 느리게 분해되고 / 물에 떠다니는float 경향이 있다 / 이는 플라스틱으로 하여금 해류ocean current를 따라 돌아다니게 한다 / 수천 마일을.

02 대부분의 플라스틱은 점점 더 작은 조각으로 분해된다 / 자외선에 노출될 때 / 그리고 미세 플라스틱을 형성한다.

03 이러한 미세 플라스틱은 측정하기가measure 매우 어렵다 / 일단 그물망을 통과할 만큼 충분히 작아지면 / 그것들을 수거하는데collect 일반적으로typically 사용되는.

04 미세 플라스틱이 해양 환경과 먹이 그물에 미치는 영향impact은 / 아직도 제대로 이해되지 않고 있다. // 이 작은 조각particle들은 알려져 있다 / 다양한various 동물에게 먹혀 / 먹이 사슬 속으로 들어간다고.

05 바다ocean 속에 있는 대부분의 플라스틱 조각들은 매우 작기 때문에 / 실질적인practical 방법은 없다 / 바다를 청소할.

06 엄청난enormous 양의 물을 여과해야 할 수도 있다 / 비교적relatively 적은 양의 플라스틱을 수거하기 위해.

구문 Check up

① Plastic is extremely slow to degrade and tends to float, which allows it [travel / to travel] in ocean currents for thousands of miles.

5형식 동사 allow의 목적격보어는 to부정사가 되어야 하므로 to travel이 적절하다.

② Most plastics break down into smaller and smaller pieces when [exposing / exposed] to ultraviolet (UV) light, forming microplastics.

내용상 주어(Most plastics)와 분사의 관계가 수동이므로 과거분사 exposed가 되어야 한다.

정답 ① to travel ② exposed

STEP 1 • 수능에 진짜 나오는 단어

✔ 문제에 나오는 단어들을 확인하세요.

시간이 없다면 색으로 표시된 단어만이라도 꼭 외우고 넘어가세요!

01	strength	n. 강점	know one's (✔ strength)	강점을 알다
02	weakness	n. 약점	strengths and ( )es	강점과 약점
03	accept	v. 받아들이다	( ) one's weakness	약점을 받아들이다
04	role	n. 역할	accept one's ( )	역할을 받아들이다
05	improve	v. 개선하다, 향상시키다	( ) one's social image	사회적 이미지를 개선하다
06	step	n. 조치	( )s to improve	개선하기 위한 조치들
07	respond	v. 대응하다, 답하다	how to ( ) to life	삶에 대응하는 방법
08	excuse	n. 변명 v. 변명하다, 용서하다	end all the ( )s	모든 변명을 끝내다
09	personally	ad. 몸소, 개인적으로	( ) accept	스스로 받아들이다
10	responsibility	n. 책임	( ) for one's choices	자신의 선택에 대한 책임

⊕ 본문 문장 속에서 단어들을 확인해 보세요.

The beginning of growth comes / when you begin to personally accept responsibility for your choices.

성장의 시작은 일어난다 / 당신이 자신의 선택에 대한 책임을 스스로 받아들이기 시작할 때.

단어 다시보기 문제를 풀기 전에 단어들을 30초 동안 다시 확인하세요.

01	strength	강점	know one's strength	강점을 알다
02	weakness		strengths and weaknesses	강점과 약점
03	accept		accept one's weakness	약점을 받아들이다
04	role		accept one's role	역할을 받아들이다
05	improve		improve one's social image	사회적 이미지를 개선하다
06	step		steps to improve	개선하기 위한 조치들
07	respond		how to respond to life	삶에 대응하는 방법
08	excuse		end all the excuses	모든 변명을 끝내다
09	personally		personally accept	스스로 받아들이다
10	responsibility		responsibility for one's choices	자신의 선택에 대한 책임

⊕ 본문 문장 속에서 단어의 의미를 우리말로 해석해 보세요.

The beginning of growth comes / when you begin to personally accept responsibility for your choices.

→ 성장의 시작은 일어난다 / 당신이 자신의 선택에 대한 ______ 시작할 때.

2017 6월 학평 28번 문제

제한시간 70초

난이도 ★★★☆☆

STEP 2 • 수능 기출 제대로 풀기

G

다음 글의 밑줄 친 부분 중, 어법상 틀린 것은?

Are you honest with yourself about your strengths and weaknesses? Get to really know ① yourself and learn what your weaknesses are. Accepting your role in your problems ② mean that you understand the solution lies within you. If you have a weakness in a certain area, get educated and do ③ what you have to do to improve things for yourself. If your social image is terrible, look within yourself and take the necessary steps to improve ④ it, TODAY. You have the ability to choose how to respond to life. Decide today to end all the excuses, and stop ⑤ lying to yourself about what is going on. The beginning of growth comes when you begin to personally accept responsibility for your choices.

정답과 해설 p.32

STEP 3 • 수능 지문 제대로 복습하기

01 Are you honest with yourself / about your strengths and weaknesses? // Get to really know yourself / and learn what your weaknesses are.
병렬 연결(명령문)
의문사절(learn의 목적어)

02 Accepting your role in your problems means / [that you understand / the solution lies within you].
주어(동명사) 주어와 동사의 수 일치 목적절 접속사 that 생략

03 If you have a weakness in a certain area, / get educated / and do [what you have to do / to improve things for yourself].
명령문 관계대명사 what절(do의 목적어)
부사적 용법(목적)

04 If your social image is terrible, / look within yourself / and take the necessary steps / to improve it, / TODAY.
명령문의 목적어가 you이면 항상 yourself로 씀
재귀대명사
(=your social image)

05 You have the ability / to choose how to respond to life. // Decide today to end all the excuses, / and stop lying to yourself / about what is going on.
how+to부정사: ~하는 법
형용사적 용법
decide to-V: ~하기로 결심하다
stop+-ing: ~하는 것을 멈추다

06 The beginning of growth comes / when you begin to personally accept responsibility for your choices.

01 당신은 스스로에게 정직한가 / 당신의 강점과 약점**strengths and weaknesses**에 대하여? // 스스로에 대해 확실히 알고 / 당신의 약점이 무엇인지를 파악하라.

02 당신의 문제에 있어 자신의 역할을 받아들이는**accept your role** 것은 의미한다 / 당신이 이해함을 / 해결책도 당신 안에 있다는 것을.

03 만약 당신이 특정 분야에 약점이 있다면, / 배워서 / 해야만 할 것들을 행하라 / 스스로 상황을 개선하기**improve** 위해.

04 만약 당신의 사회적 이미지가 형편없다면, / 스스로를 들여다보고 / 필요한 조치를 취하라**take the necessary steps** / 그것을 개선하기 위해 / '오늘 당장'.

05 당신은 능력이 있다 / 삶에 대응하는 방법**how to respond to life**을 선택할. // 오늘 당장 모든 변명을 끝내기**end all the excuses**로 결심하고, / 스스로에게 거짓말하는 것을 멈춰라 / 일어나는 일에 대해.

06 성장의 시작은 일어난다 / 당신이 자신의 선택에 대한 책임**responsibility**을 스스로 받아들이기**personally accept** 시작할 때.

구문 Check up

① Accept / Accepting your role in your problems means that you understand the solution lies within you.

이 문장의 주어가 없고, 동사는 means이기 때문에 주어 역할을 하는 동명사 Accepting이 와야 한다.

② The beginning of growth comes when you begin to personal / personally accept responsibility for your choices.

begin의 목적어인 to부정사를 수식하기 위해 부사 personally를 쓴다. 준동사(to부정사, 동명사, 분사)는 부사의 꾸밈을 받는다.

정답 ① Accepting ② personally

A

글의 순서 배열

STEP 1 • 수능에 진짜 나오는 단어

문제에 나오는 단어들을 확인하세요.

시간이 없다면 색으로 표시된 단어만이라도 꼭 외우고 넘어가세요!

01	melt	v. 녹다, 녹이다	The ice (melt)ed.	얼음이 녹았다.
02	surface	n. 표면	the Earth's ( )	지구의 표면
03	trap	v. 가두다, 옥죄다	be ( )ped in a situation	어떤 상황에 갇히다
04	atom	n. 원자	( )s of hydrogen	수소 원자
05	combine into	~로 결합하다	( ) ( ) compounds	화합물로 결합하다
06	generally	ad. 대체로, 일반적으로	( ) true	일반적으로 맞는
07	unaided eye	육안	see with the ( ) ( )	육안으로 보다
08	arrange	v. 배치하다, 정리하다	( ) students into groups of five	학생들을 5명씩 그룹으로 배치하다
09	orderly	a. 질서 있는	an ( ), repeating pattern	질서 있고 반복적인 패턴

본문 문장 속에서 단어들을 확인해 보세요.

During this process, / atoms of the different compounds / arrange themselves into orderly, repeating patterns.

이 과정 동안, / 서로 다른 화합물의 원자가 / 질서 있고 반복적인 패턴으로 배열된다.

단어 다시보기 문제를 풀기 전에 단어들을 30초 동안 다시 확인하세요.

01	melt	녹다, 녹이다	The ice melted.	얼음이 녹았다.
02	surface		the Earth's surface	지구의 표면
03	trap		be trapped in a situation	어떤 상황에 갇히다
04	atom		atoms of hydrogen	수소 원자
05	combine into		combine into compounds	화합물로 결합하다
06	generally		generally true	일반적으로 맞는
07	unaided eye		see with the unaided eye	육안으로 보다
08	arrange		arrange students into groups of five	학생들을 5명씩 그룹으로 배치하다
09	orderly		an orderly, repeating pattern	질서 있고 반복적인 패턴

⊕ 본문 문장 속에서 단어의 의미를 우리말로 해석해 보세요.

During this process, / atoms of the different compounds / arrange themselves into orderly, repeating patterns.

➔ 이 과정 동안, / 서로 다른 화합물의 ________가 / ________________.

2023 3월 학평 37번 문제

제한시간 80초

난이도 ★★★★★

STEP 2 • 수능 기출 제대로 풀기

A

주어진 글 다음에 이어질 글의 순서로 가장 적절한 것은?

Natural processes form minerals in many ways. For example, hot melted rock material, called magma, cools when it reaches the Earth's surface, or even if it's trapped below the surface. As magma cools, its atoms lose heat energy, move closer together, and begin to combine into compounds.

(A) Also, the size of the crystals that form depends partly on how rapidly the magma cools. When magma cools slowly, the crystals that form are generally large enough to see with the unaided eye.

(B) During this process, atoms of the different compounds arrange themselves into orderly, repeating patterns. The type and amount of elements present in a magma partly determine which minerals will form.

(C) This is because the atoms have enough time to move together and form into larger crystals. When magma cools rapidly, the crystals that form will be small. In such cases, you can't easily see individual mineral crystals.

*compound: 화합물

① (A) — (C) — (B)
② (B) — (A) — (C)
③ (B) — (C) — (A)
④ (C) — (A) — (B)
⑤ (C) — (B) — (A)

정답과 해설 p.34

01 Natural processes form minerals in many ways.

02 For example, / hot melted rock material, called magma, / cools when it reaches the
 주어 수식 동사 부사절 접속사1
 Earth's surface, / or even if it's trapped below the surface. // As magma cools, / its atoms
 부사절 접속사2
 lose heat energy, / move closer together, / and begin to combine into compounds.
 동사1 동사2 동사3

03 During this process, / atoms of the different compounds / arrange themselves into
 주어(복수) 동사 목적어(=atoms)
 orderly, repeating patterns. // The type and amount of elements present in a magma /
 주어(A and B) 형용사구
 partly determine / which minerals will form.
 동사 목적어(의문사절: 어떤 ~할지)

 주격 관계대명사절(the crystals 수식)
04 Also, / the size of the crystals that form / depends partly on how rapidly the magma
 주어(단수) 동사
 cools. // When magma cools slowly, / the crystals that form / are generally large enough
 주어(복수) 동사 형/부+enough+to부정사:
 / to see with the unaided eye. ~할 만큼 충분히 …한/하게

05 This is because the atoms have enough time / to move together and form into larger
 이것은 ~하기 때문이다 enough+명+to부정사: ~할 만큼 충분한 …
 crystals. // When magma cools rapidly, / the crystals that form will be small. // In such
 주격 관계대명사절
 cases, / you can't easily see individual mineral crystals.

01 자연 과정은 많은 방법으로 광물을 형성한다.

02 예를 들어, / 마그마라고 불리는 뜨거운 용암 물질hot melted rock material은 / 지구의 표면surface에 도달할 때 식는다
 / 또는 심지어 표면 아래에 갇혔을trap 때도. // 마그마가 식으면서, / 마그마의 원자atom는 열에너지를 잃고, / 서로 더
 가까이 이동해 / 화합물로 결합하기combine into 시작한다.

03 이 과정 동안, / 서로 다른 화합물의 원자가 / 질서 있고orderly 반복적인 패턴으로 배열된다arrange. // 마그마에
 존재하는 원소의 종류와 양이 / 부분적으로 결정한다 / 어떤 광물이 형성될지를.

04 또한, / 형성되는 결정의 크기는 / 부분적으로는 마그마가 얼마나 빨리 식느냐에 좌우된다. // 마그마가 천천히 식으면, /
 형성되는 결정은 / 일반적으로generally 충분히 크다 / 육안unaided eye으로 볼 수 있을 만큼.

05 이것은 원자가 충분한 시간을 가지기 때문이다 / 함께 이동해 더 큰 결정을 형성할. // 마그마가 빠르게 식으면, / 형성되는
 결정은 작을 것이다. // 그런 경우에는 / 여러분은 개별 광물 결정을 쉽게 볼 수 없다.

구문 Check up

① The crystals that form are generally enough large /
large enough to see with the unaided eye.

〈형/부+enough+to부정사〉 어순에 맞춰 large enough를 써야 한다.

② The type and amount of elements present in a magma
partly determine / determining which minerals will
form.

주어인 The type and amount of elements 뒤로 동사가 필요하므로
determine이 적절하다. 'present ~ magma'는 주어를 꾸민다.

정답 ① large enough ② determine

B

글의 순서 배열

STEP 1 • 수능에 진짜 나오는 단어

✔ 문제에 나오는 단어들을 확인하세요.

시간이 없다면 색으로 표시된 단어만이라도 꼭 외우고 넘어가세요!

01	moral	n. 도덕(~s)	the laws of (✔ moral)s	도덕의 법칙들
02	performance	n. 연주, 수행	a bad ( )	나쁜 연주
03	not necessarily	반드시 ~인 것은 아닌	It is ( ) ( ) true.	그게 반드시 참인 것은 아니다.
04	accomplished	a. 숙달된	no matter how ( )	아무리 숙달되었더라도
05	tragic	a. 비극적인	a ( ) death	비극적인 죽음
06	in nature	사실상	tragic ( ) ( )	사실상 비극적인
07	somehow	ad. 어떻게든지	We must stop him ( ).	우리는 어떻게든지 그를 막아야만 해.
08	uplift	v. 고양시키다	( ) people	사람들을 고양시키다
09	doubtful	a. 미덥지 못한, 의심스러운	( ) quality	미덥지 못한 품질
10	character	n. 인격, 인물	a doubtful ( )	미덥지 못한 인물
11	composer	n. 작곡가	a world-famous ( )	세계적으로 유명한 작곡가
12	show off	뽐내다	They are just ( )ing ( ).	그들은 그저 뽐내고 있다.
13	task	n. 임무, 과업	a basic ( )	기본 임무
14	communicate	v. 전달하다	( ) the meaning	의미를 전달하다

⊕ 본문 문장 속에서 단어들을 확인해 보세요.

These doubtful characters aren't really listening / to what the composer is saying / — they're just showing off, / hoping / that they'll have a great 'success' with the public.

이 미덥지 못한 사람들은 정말로 듣고 있는 것이 아니다 / 작곡가가 말하는 것을 / 그들은 그저 뽐내고 있을 뿐이다, / 바라면서 / 대중적으로 큰 '성공'을 거두기를.

단어 다시보기 문제를 풀기 전에 단어들을 30초 동안 다시 확인하세요.

01	moral	도덕	the laws of morals	도덕의 법칙들
02	performance		a bad performance	나쁜 연주
03	not necessarily		It is not necessarily true.	그게 반드시 참인 것은 아니다.
04	accomplished		no matter how accomplished	아무리 숙달되었더라도
05	tragic		a tragic death	비극적인 죽음
06	in nature		tragic in nature	사실상 비극적인
07	somehow		We must stop him somehow.	우리는 어떻게든지 그를 막아야만 해.
08	uplift		uplift people	사람들을 고양시키다
09	doubtful		doubtful quality	미덥지 못한 품질
10	character		a doubtful character	미덥지 못한 인물
11	composer		a world-famous composer	세계적으로 유명한 작곡가
12	show off		They are just showing off.	그들은 그저 뽐내고 있다.
13	task		a basic task	기본 임무
14	communicate		communicate the meaning	의미를 전달하다

⊕ 본문 문장 속에서 단어의 의미를 우리말로 해석해 보세요.

These doubtful characters aren't really listening / to what the composer is saying / — they're just showing off, / hoping / that they'll have a great 'success' with the public.

→ 이 ________은 정말로 듣고 있는 것이 아니다 / ________가 말하는 것을 / 그들은 그저 ________ 뿐이다, / 바라면서 / 대중적으로 큰 '성공'을 거두기를.

2022 3월 학평 37번 문제

제한시간 80초

난이도 ★★★★☆

STEP 2 • 수능 기출 제대로 풀기

B

주어진 글 다음에 이어질 글의 순서로 가장 적절한 것은?

Robert Schumann once said, "The laws of morals are those of art." What the great man is saying here is that there is good music and bad music.

(A) It's the same with performances: a bad performance isn't necessarily the result of incompetence. Some of the worst performances occur when the performers, no matter how accomplished, are thinking more of themselves than of the music they're playing.

(B) The greatest music, even if it's tragic in nature, takes us to a world higher than ours; somehow the beauty uplifts us. Bad music, on the other hand, degrades us.

(C) These doubtful characters aren't really listening to what the composer is saying — they're just showing off, hoping that they'll have a great 'success' with the public. The performer's basic task is to try to understand the meaning of the music, and then to communicate it honestly to others.

*incompetence: 무능
**degrade: 격하시키다

① (A) — (C) — (B)
② (B) — (A) — (C)
③ (B) — (C) — (A)
④ (C) — (A) — (B)
⑤ (C) — (B) — (A)

정답과 해설 p.34

01 Robert Schumann once said, / "The laws of morals are those of art." // What the great
 동사(단수) =the laws 관계대명사 what절(주어)
man is saying here / is that there is good music and bad music.
 명사절 접속사(보어)

02 The greatest music, / (even if it's tragic in nature), / takes us to a world / higher than
 (): 삽입절(설령 ~일지라도) 형용사구
ours; / somehow the beauty uplifts us. // Bad music, on the other hand, degrades us.

03 It's the same with performances: / a bad performance isn't necessarily the result of
 반드시 ~는 아닌
incompetence.

04 Some of the worst performances occur / when the performers, / no matter how
 주어(some of+복수명사) 동사(복수) 아무리 ~하더라도(=however)
accomplished, / are thinking more of themselves / than of the music they're playing.
 they are 생략 목적격 관계대명사절

05 These doubtful characters aren't really listening / to what the composer is saying / —
 관계대명사 what절(전치사 to의 목적어)
they're just showing off, / hoping / that they'll have a great 'success' with the public.
 분사구문 명사절 접속사(hoping의 목적어)

06 The performer's basic task is / to try to understand the meaning of the music, / and
then to communicate it honestly to others.
 병렬연결(주격보어: ~것)

01 Robert Schumann은 말한 적이 있다 / "도덕morals의 법칙은 예술의 법칙이다"라고. // 여기서 이 위인이 말하고 있는
 것은 / 좋은 음악과 나쁜 음악이 있다는 것이다.

02 가장 위대한 음악은, / 설령 그것이 사실상 비극적tragic in nature일지라도, / 세상으로 우리를 데려간다 / 우리의
 세상보다 더 높은; / (즉) 어떻게든지somehow 아름다움은 우리를 고양시킨다uplift. // 반면에 나쁜 음악은 우리를
 격하시킨다.

03 연주performance도 마찬가지다: / 나쁜 연주가 반드시 무능의 결과는 아니다not necessarily.

04 최악의 연주 중 일부는 발생한다 / 연주자들이, / 아무리 숙달되었더라도accomplished, / 자기 자신을 더 생각하고 있을
 때 / 연주하고 있는 곡보다.

05 이 미덥지 못한 사람doubtful character들은 정말로 듣고 있는 것이 아니다 / 작곡가composer가 말하는 것을 / 그들은
 그저 뽐내고 있을show off 뿐이다, / 바라면서 / 대중적으로 큰 '성공'을 거두기를.

06 연주자의 기본 임무task는 / 음악의 의미를 이해하려고 노력하고서 / 그것을 다른 사람들에게 정직하게
 전달하는communicate 것이다.

구문 Check up	① That / What the great man is saying here is that there is good music and bad music.	② They're just showing off, hoping that / what they'll have a great 'success' with the public.
	앞에 선행사가 없고 뒤따르는 절이 불완전하므로 관계대명사 What이 적절하다.	동사 hope의 목적어로 명사절이 와야 하고 뒤따르는 절이 완전하므로 접속사 that을 쓴다.

정답 ① What ② that

C

글의 순서 배열

STEP 1 • 수능에 진짜 나오는 단어

문제에 나오는 단어들을 확인하세요.

시간이 없다면 색으로 표시된 단어만이라도 꼭 외우고 넘어가세요!

01	critical	a. 중요한	have the (✓ critical) skills	중요한 기술을 가지다
02	analyze	v. 분석하다	( ) the data	데이터를 분석하다
03	demonstrate	v. 보여주다, 입증하다	( ) the fact	사실을 입증하다
04	youth	n. 젊음, 젊은이(들)	a promising ( )	전도유망한 젊은이
05	fool	v. 속이다	be easily ( )ed	쉽게 속다
06	misinformation	n. 잘못된 정보	share ( )	잘못된 정보를 공유하다
07	especially	ad. 특히	( ) through social media	특히 소셜 미디어를 통해서
08	block	v. 막다	( ) misinformation	잘못된 정보를 막다
09	individual	n. 개인	every ( )	모든 개인
10	responsibility	n. 책임	take ( )	책임을 지다
11	threat	n. 위협	combat a ( )	위협에 맞서 싸우다
12	literate	a. 잘 분별하는	become information ( )	정보를 잘 분별하게 되다

⊕ 본문 문장 속에서 단어들을 확인해 보세요.

However, / every individual needs to take responsibility / for combating this threat / by becoming more information literate.

그러나 / 모든 개인은 책임을 질 필요가 있다 / 이러한 위협에 맞서 싸울 (책임) / 정보를 더 잘 분별하게 됨으로써.

단어 다시보기 문제를 풀기 전에 단어들을 30초 동안 다시 확인하세요.

01	critical	중요한	have the critical skills	중요한 기술을 가지다
02	analyze		analyze the data	데이터를 분석하다
03	demonstrate		demonstrate the fact	사실을 입증하다
04	youth		a promising youth	전도유망한 젊은이
05	fool		be easily fooled	쉽게 속다
06	misinformation		share misinformation	잘못된 정보를 공유하다
07	especially		especially through social media	특히 소셜 미디어를 통해서
08	block		block misinformation	잘못된 정보를 막다
09	individual		every individual	모든 개인
10	responsibility		take responsibility	책임을 지다
11	threat		combat a threat	위협에 맞서 싸우다
12	literate		become information literate	정보를 잘 분별하게 되다

⊕ **본문 문장 속에서 단어의 의미를 우리말로 해석해 보세요.**

However, / every individual needs to take responsibility / for combating this threat / by becoming more information literate.

→ 그러나 / 모든 ______은 ______을 질 필요가 있다 / 이러한 ______에 맞서 싸울 (책임) / 정보를 더 ______ 됨으로써.

2021 6월 학평 37번 문제

제한시간 70초

난이도 ★★★☆☆

STEP 2 • 수능 기출 제대로 풀기

C

주어진 글 다음에 이어질 글의 순서로 가장 적절한 것은?

People spend much of their time interacting with media, but that does not mean that people have the critical skills to analyze and understand it.

(A) Research from New York University found that people over 65 shared seven times as much misinformation as their younger counterparts. All of this raises a question: What's the solution to the misinformation problem?

(B) One well-known study from Stanford University in 2016 demonstrated that youth are easily fooled by misinformation, especially when it comes through social media channels. This weakness is not found only in youth, however.

(C) Governments and tech platforms certainly have a role to play in blocking misinformation. However, every individual needs to take responsibility for combating this threat by becoming more information literate.

*counterpart: 상대방

① (A) — (C) — (B)
② (B) — (A) — (C)
③ (B) — (C) — (A)
④ (C) — (A) — (B)
⑤ (C) — (B) — (A)

정답과 해설 p.35

STEP 3 • 수능 지문 제대로 복습하기

01 People spend much of their time / interacting with media, / but that does not mean / that people have the critical skills / to analyze and understand it.

spend+시간/돈+-ing: ~하는 데 시간/돈을 쓰다 / 지시대명사(=but 앞 내용) / 명사절 접속사 / to부정사의 형용사적 용법

02 One well-known study from Stanford University in 2016 / demonstrated / that youth are easily fooled by misinformation, / especially when it comes through social media channels.

명사절 접속사

03 This weakness is not found only in youth, however. // Research from New York University found / that people over 65 shared / seven times as much misinformation as their younger counterparts.

명사절 접속사 / 배수 표현(~ times)+원급 비교(as+형용사+명사+as): 몇 배 더 ~한

04 All of this raises a question: / What's the solution / to the misinformation problem?

05 Governments and tech platforms / certainly have a role to play / in blocking misinformation.

in+-ing: ~하는 데 있어 / to부정사의 형용사적 용법

06 However, / every individual needs to take responsibility / for combating this threat / by becoming more information literate.

every+단수 명사 / 수 일치 / by+-ing: ~함으로써(수단)

01 사람들은 많은 시간을 소비하지만 / 미디어와 상호작용하는 데, / 그렇다고 해서 그것이 의미하는 것은 아니다 / 사람들이 중요한**critical** 기술을 가지고 있다는 것을 / 미디어를 분석하고**analyze** 이해하는.

02 2016년 Stanford 대학의 한 잘 알려진 연구는 / 보여주었다**demonstrate** / 젊은이들**youth**이 잘못된 정보**misinformation**에 쉽게 속는다**be easily fooled**는 것을 / 특히**especially** 소셜 미디어 채널을 통하는 경우에.

03 그러나, 이러한 약점은 젊은이에게서만 발견되는 것은 아니다. // New York 대학의 조사에 따르면 / 65세 이상의 사람들이 공유한다고 한다 / 젊은이들보다 7배나 더 많은 잘못된 정보를.

04 이 모든 것이 의문을 제기한다. / 해결책은 무엇인가 / 잘못된 정보 문제에 대한?

05 정부와 기술 플랫폼은 / 분명 해야 할 역할을 가지고 있다 / 잘못된 정보를 막아내는**block** 데 있어서.

06 그러나 / 모든 개인**individual**은 책임**responsibility**을 질 필요가 있다 / 이러한 위협에 맞서 싸울**combat this threat** (책임) / 정보를 더 잘 분별하게**information literate** 됨으로써.

구문 Check up

① People over 65 shared seven times as many / much misinformation as their younger counterparts.

수식을 받는 명사 misinformation은 셀 수 없는 명사이므로 much로 수식한다.

② However, every individual need / needs to take responsibility for combating this threat.

<every+명사>는 단수 취급하므로 단수 동사 needs를 쓴다.

정답 ① much ② needs

D

글의 순서 배열

STEP 1 • 수능에 진짜 나오는 단어

✔ 문제에 나오는 단어들을 확인하세요.

시간이 없다면 색으로 표시된 단어만이라도 꼭 외우고 넘어가세요!

01	based on	~에 근거하여	(✔ based) (on) what we think	우리가 생각하는 바에 근거하여
02	majority	n. 대다수	the ( ) of people	대다수의 사람들
03	flat	a. 납작한, 편평한	believed the world was ( )	세상이 편평하다고 믿었다
04	reveal	v. 드러내다	the minor detail was ( )ed	사소한 상황이 드러났다
05	on a massive scale	대규모로, 대대적으로	change ( ) ( ) ( ) ( )	대대적으로 변화하다
06	trade	n. 무역 v. 거래하다	Spices were ( )d.	향신료가 거래되었다.
07	route	n. 도로	trade ( )s	무역로
08	perceive	v. 인지하다	( ) truth	진실을 인지하다
09	exploration	n. 탐험	There was very little ( ).	탐험이 거의 없었다.
10	edge	n. 가장자리	the ( ) of the earth	지구의 가장자리
11	allow for	가능하게 하다	( ) ( ) all kinds of things	온갖 종류의 것을 가능하게 하다
12	innovation	n. 혁신	all kinds of ( )s	모든 종류의 혁신
13	advancement	n. 진보	allow for all kinds of ( )s	모든 종류의 진보를 고려하다
14	assumption	n. 가정	a simple false ( )	단순한 잘못된 가정

⊕ 본문 문장 속에서 단어들을 확인해 보세요.

It wasn't until that minor detail was revealed / — the world is round — / that behaviors changed on a massive scale.

그런 사소한 사항이 드러나고 나서였다 / 세상은 둥글다는 / 대대적으로 행동이 변화한 것은.

단어 다시보기 문제를 풀기 전에 단어들을 30초 동안 다시 확인하세요.

01	based on	~에 근거하여	based on what we think	우리가 생각하는 바에 근거하여
02	majority		the majority of people	대다수의 사람들
03	flat		believed the world was flat	세상이 편평하다고 믿었다
04	reveal		the minor detail was revealed	사소한 상황이 드러났다
05	on a massive scale		change on a massive scale	대대적으로 변화하다
06	trade		Spices were traded.	향신료가 거래되었다.
07	route		trade routes	무역로
08	perceive		perceive truth	진실을 인지하다
09	exploration		There was very little exploration.	탐험이 거의 없었다.
10	edge		the edge of the earth	지구의 가장자리
11	allow for		allow for all kinds of things	온갖 종류의 것을 가능하게 하다
12	innovation		all kinds of innovations	모든 종류의 혁신
13	advancement		allow for all kinds of advancements	모든 종류의 진보를 고려하다
14	assumption		a simple false assumption	단순한 잘못된 가정

⊕ 본문 문장 속에서 단어의 의미를 우리말로 해석해 보세요.

It wasn't until that minor detail was revealed / — the world is round — / that behaviors changed on a massive scale.

→ 그런 사소한 사항이 ________ 나서였다 / 세상은 둥글다는 / ________ 행동이 변화한 것은.

2020 9월 학평 36번 문제

제한시간 70초

난이도 ★★★☆☆

STEP 2 • 수능 기출 제대로 풀기

D

주어진 글 다음에 이어질 글의 순서로 가장 적절한 것은?

> We make decisions based on what we *think* we know. It wasn't too long ago that the majority of people believed the world was flat.

(A) It wasn't until that minor detail was revealed — the world is round — that behaviors changed on a massive scale. Upon this discovery, societies began to travel across the planet. Trade routes were established; spices were traded.

(B) This perceived truth impacted behavior. During this period, there was very little exploration. People feared that if they traveled too far they might fall off the edge of the earth. So for the most part they didn't dare to travel.

(C) New ideas, like mathematics, were shared between societies which allowed for all kinds of innovations and advancements. The correction of a simple false assumption moved the human race forward.

① (A) — (C) — (B)
② (B) — (A) — (C)
③ (B) — (C) — (A)
④ (C) — (A) — (B)
⑤ (C) — (B) — (A)

정답과 해설 p.35

STEP 3 • 수능 지문 제대로 복습하기

01 We make decisions / based on [what we *think* we know]. // It wasn't too long ago / [that the majority of people believed the world was flat].
(관계대명사 what절 / 삽입구문 / 가주어 / 진주어(that절) / 더 이상 과학적 진리에 해당하지 않으므로 과거시제로 표현)

02 This perceived truth impacted behavior. // During this period, / there was very little exploration.
(과거분사(명사 앞에서 수식))

03 People feared / [that if they traveled too far / they might fall off the edge of the earth].
(접속사 that절 / 접속사(조건))

04 So for the most part they didn't dare to travel. // It wasn't until that minor detail was revealed / — (the world is round) — / that behaviors changed on a massive scale.
(대체로 / 감히 ~하다 / It isn't until ~ that…: ~하고 나서야 비로소 …하다 / ( ): 동격(=that minor detail))

05 Upon this discovery, / societies began to travel across the planet. // Trade routes were established; / spices were traded.

06 New ideas, like mathematics, / were shared between societies / which allowed for all kinds of innovations and advancements.
(관계대명사절)

07 The correction of a simple false assumption / moved the human race forward.
(주어 / 동사)

01 우리는 결정을 한다 / 우리가 안다고 '생각하는' 것에 기초하여**based on**. // 그다지 오래되지 않았다 / 대다수의 사람들**the majority of people**이 세상이 편평하다**flat**고 믿었던 것은.

02 이렇게 인지된**perceive** 사실은 행동에 영향을 미쳤다. // 이 기간 동안에는, / 탐험**exploration**이 거의 없었다.

03 사람들은 두려워했다 / 만약 그들이 너무 멀리 가면, / 지구의 가장자리**the edge of the earth**에서 떨어질까 봐.

04 그래서 대체로 그들은 감히 이동하지 않았다. // 그런 사소한 사항이 드러나고**reveal** 나서였다 / 세상은 둥글다는 (사항) / 대대적으로**on a massive scale** 행동이 변화한 것은.

05 이것이 발견된 후 곧, / 사람들은 세상을 돌아다니기 시작했다. // 무역 경로**trade route**가 만들어졌으며, / 향신료가 거래되었다**be traded**.

06 수학과 같은 새로운 개념이 / 사회들 사이에 공유되었다 / 모든 종류의 혁신과 진보**all kinds of innovations and advancements**를 가능하게 했던**allow for**.

07 단순한 잘못된 가정**false assumption**의 수정이 / 인류를 앞으로 나아가게 했다.

구문 Check up

① It wasn't too long ago that the majority of people believed the world is / was flat.

문장이 과거의 믿음을 나타내므로 시제를 일치하여 was로 쓴다.

② New ideas, like mathematics, were shared between societies where / which allowed for all kinds of innovations and advancements.

뒤에 주어 없는 불완전한 절이 나오므로 관계대명사 which를 써야 한다.

정답 ① was ② which

E

글의 순서 배열

STEP 1 • 수능에 진짜 나오는 단어

✔ 문제에 나오는 단어들을 확인하세요.

시간이 없다면 색으로 표시된 단어만이라도 꼭 외우고 넘어가세요!

01	vital	*a.* 중요한, 필수적인	the (✔ vital) difference	중요한 차이
02	unrealistic	*a.* 비현실적인	( ) ↔ realistic	비현실적인 ↔ 현실적인
03	optimist	*n.* 낙관론자	an unrealistic ( )	비현실적인 낙관론자
04	on the other hand	이와 달리	( ) ( ) ( ) ( ) = whereas	이와 달리
05	reward	*v.* 보상하다 *n.* 보상	( ) us for helping him	그를 도와준 것에 대해 우리에게 보상하다
06	positive	*a.* 긍정적인	( ) thinking	긍정적인 사고
07	transform	*v.* 변모시키다	be ( )ed overnight	하룻밤 사이에 변모되다
08	obstacle	*n.* 장애물, 방해물	( )s don't exist.	방해물은 존재하지 않는다.
09	strategy	*n.* 전략	the right ( )ies	적절한 전략들
10	need	*n.* 필요, 요구	a ( ) for food	음식의 필요
11	deal with	~을 다루다	( ) ( ) obstacles	장애물들을 다루다
12	preparation	*n.* 준비	( ) for the party	파티 준비

⊕ 본문 문장 속에서 단어들을 확인해 보세요.

They recognize the need / for giving serious thought / to how they will deal with obstacles.

그들은 필요를 인식한다 / 심각하게 고려할 / 어떻게 그들이 장애물을 다룰지에 대해.

단어 다시보기 문제를 풀기 전에 단어들을 30초 동안 다시 확인하세요.

01	vital	중요한, 필수적인	the vital difference	중요한 차이
02	unrealistic		unrealistic ↔ realistic	비현실적인 ↔ 현실적인
03	optimist		an unrealistic optimist	비현실적인 낙관론자
04	on the other hand		on the other hand = whereas	이와 달리
05	reward		reward us for helping him	그를 도와준 것에 대해 우리에게 보상하다
06	positive		positive thinking	긍정적인 사고
07	transform		be transformed overnight	하룻밤 사이에 변모되다
08	obstacle		Obstacles don't exist.	방해물은 존재하지 않는다.
09	strategy		the right strategies	적절한 전략들
10	need		a need for food	음식의 필요
11	deal with		deal with obstacles	장애물들을 다루다
12	preparation		preparation for the party	파티 준비

⊕ 본문 문장 속에서 단어의 의미를 우리말로 해석해 보세요.

They recognize the need / for giving serious thought / to how they will deal with obstacles.

➜ 그들은 ______를 인식한다 / 심각하게 고려할 / 어떻게 그들이 ______지에 대해.

2019 9월 학평 37번 문제

제한시간 80초

난이도 ★★★★★

STEP 2 • 수능 기출 제대로 풀기

E

주어진 글 다음에 이어질 글의 순서로 가장 적절한 것은?

To be successful, you need to understand the vital difference between believing you will succeed, and believing you will succeed easily.

(A) Unrealistic optimists, on the other hand, believe that success will happen to them — that the universe will reward them for all their positive thinking, or that somehow they will be transformed overnight into the kind of person for whom obstacles don't exist anymore.

(B) Put another way, it's the difference between being a realistic optimist, and an unrealistic optimist. Realistic optimists believe they will succeed, but also believe they have to make success happen — through things like careful planning and choosing the right strategies.

(C) They recognize the need for giving serious thought to how they will deal with obstacles. This preparation only increases their confidence in their own ability to get things done.

① (A) — (C) — (B)
② (B) — (A) — (C)
③ (B) — (C) — (A)
④ (C) — (A) — (B)
⑤ (C) — (B) — (A)

정답과 해설 p.36

STEP 3 • 수능 지문 제대로 복습하기

01 To be successful, / you need to understand the vital difference / between believing you will succeed, and believing you will succeed easily.

목적(~하려면) / 접속사 that 생략 / 접속사 that 생략 / between A and B: A와 B 사이(A, B 자리에 동명사)

02 Put another way, / it's the difference / between being a realistic optimist, / and an unrealistic optimist.

바꾸어 말하면, 다시 말해서

03 Realistic optimists believe they will succeed, / but also believe they have to make success happen / — through things like careful planning and choosing the right strategies.

접속사 that 생략 / 접속사 that 생략 / make+목적어+목적격 보어(원형부정사)

04 They recognize the need / for giving serious thought / to how they will deal with obstacles. // This preparation only increases their confidence / in their own ability to get things done.

전치사 to의 목적어(의문사절) / 형용사적 용법

05 Unrealistic optimists, on the other hand, / believe that success will happen to them / — that the universe will reward them / for all their positive thinking, / or that somehow they will be transformed overnight / into the kind of person for whom obstacles don't exist anymore.

여기서 that절은 모두 동사 believe의 목적어 역할을 하는 명사절 / 전치사+관계대명사절

01 성공하기 위해, / 당신은 중요한 차이**the vital difference**를 이해할 필요가 있다 / 당신이 성공할 것이라고 믿는 것과 당신이 쉽게 성공할 것이라고 믿는 것 사이의.

02 다시 말해서, / 그것은 차이이다 / 현실적인 낙관주의자가 되는 것과 / 비현실적인 낙관주의자**unrealistic optimist**가 되는 것 사이의.

03 현실적인 낙관주의자들은 그들이 성공할 것이라고 믿는다 / 뿐만 아니라, 그들은 그들이 성공이 일어날 수 있도록 만들어야 한다고 믿는다 / 신중한 계획과 적절한 전략**strategy**을 선택하는 것과 같은 것들을 통해.

04 그들은 필요**need**를 인식한다 / 심각하게 고려할 / 어떻게 그들이 장애물을 다룰지**deal with obstacles**에 대해. // 이런 준비**preparation**가 바로 자신감을 높여 준다 / 일이 수행되게 하는 그들 자신의 능력에 대한 (자신감).

05 반면에**on the other hand**, 비현실적인 낙관론자들은 / 성공이 그들에게 일어날 수 있다고 믿는다 / 즉 우주가 그들에게 보상할**reward** 것이라고 (믿는다) / 자신의 모든 긍정적인**positive** 사고에 대해, / 혹은 어떤 식으로든 그들이 하룻밤 사이에 변할**be transformed** 것이라고 (믿는다) / 장애물이 더 이상 존재하지 않는 그런 종류의 사람으로.

구문 Check up

① Unrealistic optimists, on the other hand, believe that success will happen to them / themselves.

will happen의 주어는 success인데, 목적어는 unrealistic optimists이다. 둘은 서로 다른 대상이므로, 재귀대명사가 아닌 인칭대명사 them이 어법상 맞다.

② They recognize the need for giving serious thought to what / how they will deal with obstacles.

뒤에 완전한 절이 나오므로 의문부사 how가 적절하다.

정답 ① them ② how

DAY 11

F

글의 순서 배열

STEP 1 • 수능에 진짜 나오는 단어

✔ 문제에 나오는 단어들을 확인하세요.

시간이 없다면 색으로 표시된 단어만이라도 꼭 외우고 넘어가세요!

01	interpersonal	a. 대인 관계의	(✔ interpersonal) messages	대인 관계에서의 메시지
02	combine	v. 결합하다	( )d with contents	내용과 결합된
03	content	n. 내용	a ( ) message	내용 메시지
04	refer to	언급하다, 지칭하다	( ) ( ) the real world	실제 세계를 지칭하다
05	external	a. 외부의	something ( )	외부적인 어떤 것
06	visualize	v. 시각화하다, 상상하다	( ) the same command	같은 명령을 상상하다
07	command	n. 명령, 요구 v. 명령하다	the simple ( )	간단한 명령
08	trainee	n. 수습 직원	say to a ( )	수습 직원에게 말하다
09	supervisor	n. 관리자, 감독관	see the ( )	관리자를 만나다
10	awkward	a. 어색한	( ) and out of place	어색하고 상황에 맞지 않는
11	violate	v. 위반하다	( ) the normal relationship	일반적인 관계를 위반하다
12	status	n. 사회적 지위, 상황	a ( ) difference	지위의 차이

⊕ 본문 문장 속에서 단어들을 확인해 보세요.

Even the use of the simple command shows / there is a status difference / that allows the supervisor to command the trainee.

이 간단한 명령의 사용도 보여준다 / 지위의 차이가 존재한다는 것을 / 관리자가 그 수습 직원에게 명령할 수 있게 하는.

단어 다시보기 문제를 풀기 전에 단어들을 30초 동안 다시 확인하세요.

01	interpersonal	대인 관계의	interpersonal messages	대인 관계에서의 메시지
02	combine		combined with contents	내용과 결합된
03	content		a content message	내용 메시지
04	refer to		refer to the real world	실제 세계를 지칭하다
05	external		something external	외부적인 어떤 것
06	visualize		visualize the same command	같은 명령을 상상하다
07	command		the simple command	간단한 명령
08	trainee		say to a trainee	수습 직원에게 말하다
09	supervisor		see the supervisor	관리자를 만나다
10	awkward		awkward and out of place	어색하고 상황에 맞지 않는
11	violate		violate the normal relationship	일반적인 관계를 위반하다
12	status		a status difference	지위의 차이

⊕ **본문 문장 속에서 단어의 의미를 우리말로 해석해 보세요.**

Even the use of the simple command shows / there is a status difference / that allows the supervisor to command the trainee.

→ 이 간단한 ______의 사용도 보여준다 / ______가 존재한다는 것을 / ______ ______ 수 있게 하는.

2018 6월 학평 35번 문제

제한시간 80초

난이도 ★★★★★

STEP 2 • 수능 기출 제대로 풀기

F

주어진 글 다음에 이어질 글의 순서로 가장 적절한 것은?

Interpersonal messages combine content and relationship dimensions. That is, they refer to the real world, to something external to both speaker and listener; at the same time they also refer to the relationship between parties.

(A) You can appreciate this most clearly if you visualize the same command being made by the trainee to the supervisor. It appears awkward and out of place, because it violates the normal relationship between supervisor and trainee.

(B) It also contains a relationship message that says something about the connection between the supervisor and the trainee. Even the use of the simple command shows there is a status difference that allows the supervisor to command the trainee.

(C) For example, a supervisor may say to a trainee, "See me after the meeting." This simple message has a content message that tells the trainee to see the supervisor after the meeting.

① (A) — (C) — (B)
② (B) — (A) — (C)
③ (B) — (C) — (A)
④ (C) — (A) — (B)
⑤ (C) — (B) — (A)

정답과 해설 p.36

STEP 3 • 수능 지문 제대로 복습하기

01 Interpersonal messages combine content and relationship dimensions. // That is, / they refer to the real world, / to something external to both speaker and listener; / at the same time / they also refer to the relationship between parties.

즉(=That is to say) / -thing으로 끝나는 명사는 형용사가 뒤에서 수식 / both A and B: A, B 둘 다

02 For example, / a supervisor may say to a trainee, / "See me after the meeting." // This simple message has a content message / that tells the trainee / to see the supervisor after the meeting.

주격 관계대명사 / 선행사 / 선행사에 수 일치

03 It also contains a relationship message / that says something / about the connection between the supervisor and the trainee.

=This simple message / 주격 관계대명사 / between A and B: A와 B 사이의

04 Even the use of the simple command shows / there is a status difference / that allows the supervisor to command the trainee.

접속사 that 생략 / 주격 관계대명사 / 5형식 동사(allow)+목적어+목적격 보어(to부정사)

05 You can appreciate this most clearly / if you visualize the same command being made / by the trainee to the supervisor.

지시대명사(=there is a status difference ~)

06 It appears awkward and out of place, / because it violates the normal relationship / between supervisor and trainee.

병렬연결 / 주격 보어(형용사) / 주격 보어(전치사구)

01 대인 관계에서의interpersonal 메시지는 내용 차원과 관계 차원을 결합한다combine. // 즉, / 그것들은 실제 세계를 지칭한다refer to / 즉 화자와 청자 모두에게 외부적인external 어떤 것을. / 동시에 / 당사자들 사이의 관계를 지칭하기도 한다.

02 예를 들어, / 한 관리자가 한 수습 직원trainee에게 말할 수 있다 / "회의 후에 저 좀 봅시다."라고. // 이 간단한 메시지는 내용content 메시지를 담고 있다 / 수습 직원에게 전달하는 / 회의 후에 관리자supervisor를 만나야 한다고.

03 그것은 또한 관계 메시지를 포함하고 있다 / 무언가를 말해 주는 / 관리자와 수습 직원 사이의 관계에 대해.

04 이 간단한 명령command의 사용도 보여준다 / 지위status의 차이가 존재한다는 것을 / 관리자가 그 수습 직원에게 명령할 수 있게 하는.

05 당신은 이것을 가장 명확하게 이해할 수 있을 것이다 / 만약 같은 명령이 내려진다고 상상해 본다면visualize / 수습 직원에 의해 관리자에게.

06 그것은 어색하고awkward 상황에 맞지 않아 보인다 / 그것이 일반적인 관계를 위반하기violate 때문에 / 관리자와 수습 직원 사이의.

구문 Check up

① This simple message has a content message that [tell / tells] the trainee to see the supervisor after the meeting.

관계대명사의 선행사(a content message)가 단수명사이므로 관계대명사절의 동사도 이에 수 일치해야 한다. 따라서 단수동사 tells를 써야 한다.

② It appears [awkward / awkwardly] and out of place, because it violates the normal relationship between supervisor and trainee.

2형식 동사(appear) 뒤에는 보어를 써야 하므로 형용사 awkward가 적절하다. 부사는 보어로 쓰이지 않는다.

정답 ① tells ② awkward

글의 순서 배열 +

STEP 1 • 수능에 진짜 나오는 단어

✔ 문제에 나오는 단어들을 확인하세요.

시간이 없다면 색으로 표시된 단어만이라도 꼭 외우고 넘어가세요!

01	implicit	a. 내재적인, 암묵적인	(✔ implicit) memory	내재적 기억
02	explicit	a. 외재적인, 명백한	( ) memory	외재적 기억
03	specific	a. 특정한	a ( ) topic	특정한 주제
04	consciously	ad. 의식적으로	( ) try to remember	의식적으로 기억하려고 하다
05	recall	v. 기억하다, 회상하다	( ) childhood memories	어린 시절의 기억을 회상하다
06	imprint	v. 각인하다	memories ( )ed in our minds	우리 마음속에 각인된 기억
07	autonomic	a. 자율적인	the brain's ( ) portion	뇌의 자율적인 부분
08	portion	n. 부분, 구역	a significant ( ) of the population	인구의 상당 부분
09	be supposed to	~할 예정이다	The event ( ) ( ) ( ) take place next week.	그 행사는 다음 주에 열릴 예정이다.

⊕ 본문 문장 속에서 단어들을 확인해 보세요.

Explicit memories, / on the other hand, / are the memories or the specific things / that you consciously try to recall.

외재적 기억들은 / 반면에 / 기억 혹은 특정한 것들이다 / 여러분이 의식적으로 기억하려고 노력하는.

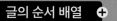

단어 다시보기 문제를 풀기 전에 단어들을 30초 동안 다시 확인하세요.

01	implicit	내재적인, 암묵적인	implicit memory	내재적 기억
02	explicit		explicit memory	외재적 기억
03	specific		a specific topic	특정한 주제
04	consciously		consciously try to remember	의식적으로 기억하려고 하다
05	recall		recall childhood memories	어린 시절의 기억을 회상하다
06	imprint		memories imprinted in our minds	우리 마음속에 각인된 기억
07	autonomic		the brain's autonomic portion	뇌의 자율적인 부분
08	portion		a significant portion of the population	인구의 상당 부분
09	be supposed to		The event is supposed to take place next week.	그 행사는 다음 주에 열릴 예정이다.

⊕ **본문 문장 속에서 단어의 의미를 우리말로 해석해 보세요.**

Explicit memories, / on the other hand, / are the memories or the specific things / that you consciously try to recall.

→ 외재적 기억들은 / 반면에 / 기억 혹은 ______ 것들이다 / 여러분이 ______.

2017 11월 학평 36번 문제

제한시간 80초

난이도 ★★★★★

STEP 2 • 수능 기출 제대로 풀기

G

주어진 글 다음에 이어질 글의 순서로 가장 적절한 것은?

Memory has two types — implicit and explicit memory. When you learn things without really thinking about it, it's implicit memory or body memory. Knowing how to breathe when you were born is an implicit memory.

(A) Explicit memories, on the other hand, are the memories or the specific things that you consciously try to recall. You use explicit memory every day on a conscious level.

(B) No one taught this to you. Some of the things you've learned since childhood also become implicit memories. Implicit memories are imprinted in the brain's autonomic portion; that is why even after years of not riding a bike you still know how to ride.

(C) Trying to find the keys, trying to remember when an event is supposed to take place, where it's going to be held, and with whom you are going. Explicit memories are the tasks you have written down on your calendar or planner.

① (A) — (C) — (B)
② (B) — (A) — (C)
③ (B) — (C) — (A)
④ (C) — (A) — (B)
⑤ (C) — (B) — (A)

정답과 해설 p.37

STEP 3 • 수능 지문 제대로 복습하기

01 Memory has two types / — implicit and explicit memory.
동격

02 When you learn things / without really thinking about it, / it's implicit memory or body memory.
without+동명사: ~하지 않고서

03 Knowing how to breathe when you were born / is an implicit memory. // No one taught this to you.
주어(동명사구) / 동사(단수) / 지시대명사(=how to breathe)

04 Some of the things / you've learned since childhood / also become implicit memories.
주어(부분+of+전체) / 목적격 관계대명사절 / 동사(the things에 수 일치)

05 Implicit memories are imprinted in the brain's autonomic portion; / that is why even after years of not riding a bike / you still know how to ride.
the reason 생략 / 이것이 ~한 이유다

06 Explicit memories, / on the other hand, / are the memories or the specific things / that you consciously try to recall.
선행사 / 목적격 관계대명사절

07 You use explicit memory every day / on a conscious level.

08 Trying to find the keys, / trying to remember / when an event is supposed to take place, / where it's going to be held, / and with whom you are going.
의문사절1 / 의문사절2 / 의문사절3(to remember의 목적어 병렬)

09 Explicit memories are the tasks / you have written down on your calendar or planner.
목적격 관계대명사절

01 기억은 두 가지 종류가 있는데, / 내재적 기억과 외재적 기억**implicit and explicit memory**이다.
02 여러분이 무언가를 배울 때 / 그것에 대해서 진정으로 생각하지 않고서 / 그것은 내재적 기억 혹은 신체 기억이다.
03 여러분이 태어났을 때 호흡하는 법을 아는 것은 / 내재적 기억이다. // 아무도 여러분에게 이것을 가르쳐 주지 않았다.
04 대상들 중 일부는 / 어릴 적부터 여러분이 배운 / 또한 내재적 기억들이 된다.
05 내재적 기억들은 뇌의 자율적 부분**autonomic portion**에 각인된다**imprint** / 이것은 자전거를 수년 동안 타지 않고서도 ~한 이유이다 / 여러분이 여전히 자전거 타는 법을 아는.
06 외재적 기억들은 / 반면에 / 기억 혹은 특정한**specific** 것들이다 / 여러분이 의식적으로 기억하려고 노력하는**consciously try to recall.**
07 여러분은 매일 외재적 기억을 사용한다 / 의식적 차원에서.
08 열쇠를 찾으려 노력하는 것, / 기억하려 하는 것 / 행사가 언제 개최될 예정이고**be supposed to take place**, / 그것이 어디서 개최될 것이며, / 그리고 여러분이 누구와 함께 거기 갈지를.
09 외재적 기억들은 과업들이다 / 여러분이 달력이나 일정표에 적어놓은.

구문 Check up

① Some of the things you've learned since childhood also become / becomes implicit memories.

Some of the things가 〈부분+of+전체〉 주어이므로, 전체 명사 the things에 수 일치시켜 become을 쓴다.

② Implicit memories are imprinted in the brain's autonomic portion; that is because / why even after years of not riding a bike you still know how to ride.

〈원인+that is why+결과〉 구조이다. 〈결과+that is because+원인〉를 구별해서 기억해 둔다.

정답 ① become ② why

DAY 12

A

주어진 문장 넣기 +

STEP 1 • 수능에 진짜 나오는 단어

✔ 문제에 나오는 단어들을 확인하세요.

시간이 없다면 색으로 표시된 단어만이라도 꼭 외우고 넘어가세요!

01	absorb	v. (정보를) 받아들이다	too much information to (✔ absorb)	받아들이기에 너무 많은 정보
02	evidence	n. 증거	( ) from the world	세상에서 얻은 증거
03	disinterested	a. 흥미를 잃은, 무관심한, 공평무사한	( ) curiosity	흥미를 잃은 호기심
04	decline	n. 감소 v. 줄어들다	the ( ) in curiosity	호기심의 감소
05	trace	v. (원인을) 찾다, 추적하다	be ( )d to childhood trauma	어린 시절 트라우마에서 원인을 찾다
06	neural	a. 신경의	( ) connections	신경 연결
07	mess	n. 엉망(인 상태)	a big ( )	엄청나게 엉망인 상태
08	intensely	ad. 매우, 강렬히	( ) rich	매우 풍부한
09	disordered	a. 무질서한	wildly ( )	대단히 무질서한
10	automatic	a. 자동적인	become ( )	자동적이 되다

+ 본문 문장 속에서 단어들을 확인해 보세요.

The baby's perception of the world / is consequently both intensely rich and wildly disordered.

세상에 대한 아기의 인식은 / 결과적으로 매우 풍부하면서도 상당히 무질서하다.

단어 다시보기 문제를 풀기 전에 단어들을 30초 동안 다시 확인하세요.

01	absorb	(정보를) 받아들이다	too much information to absorb	받아들이기에 너무 많은 정보
02	evidence		evidence from the world	세상에서 얻은 증거
03	disinterested		disinterested curiosity	흥미를 잃은 호기심
04	decline		the decline in curiosity	호기심의 감소
05	trace		be traced to childhood trauma	어린 시절 트라우마에서 원인을 찾다
06	neural		neural connections	신경 연결
07	mess		a big mess	엄청나게 엉망인 상태
08	intensely		intensely rich	매우 풍부한
09	disordered		wildly disordered	대단히 무질서한
10	automatic		become automatic	자동적이 되다

⊕ 본문 문장 속에서 단어의 의미를 우리말로 해석해 보세요.

The baby's perception of the world / is consequently both intensely rich and wildly disordered.

→ 세상에 대한 아기의 인식은 / 결과적으로 ____________________.

2023 6월 학평 39번 문제

제한시간 80초

난이도 ★★★★★

STEP 2 • 수능 기출 제대로 풀기

A

글의 흐름으로 보아, 주어진 문장이 들어가기에 가장 적절한 곳은?

> As children absorb more evidence from the world around them, certain possibilities become much more likely and more useful and harden into knowledge or beliefs.

According to educational psychologist Susan Engel, curiosity begins to decrease as young as four years old. By the time we are adults, we have fewer questions and more default settings. As Henry James put it, "Disinterested curiosity is past, the mental grooves and channels set." (①) The decline in curiosity can be traced in the development of the brain through childhood. (②) Though smaller than the adult brain, the infant brain contains millions more neural connections. (③) The wiring, however, is a mess; the lines of communication between infant neurons are far less efficient than between those in the adult brain. (④) The baby's perception of the world is consequently both intensely rich and wildly disordered. (⑤) The neural pathways that enable those beliefs become faster and more automatic, while the ones that the child doesn't use regularly are pruned away.

*default setting: 기본값
**groove: 고랑 ***prune: 가지치기하다

정답과 해설 p.38

STEP 3 • 수능 지문 제대로 복습하기

01 According to educational psychologist Susan Engel, / curiosity begins to decrease as young as four years old. // By the time we are adults, / we have fewer questions and more default settings. // As Henry James put it, / "Disinterested curiosity is past, / the mental grooves and channels set."

According to: ~에 따르면 / as young as: as+원급+as: ~만큼 …한 / By the time: ~할 무렵 / As: ~듯이

02 The decline in curiosity can be traced / in the development of the brain through childhood. // Though (it is) smaller than the adult brain, / the infant brain contains millions more neural connections.

can be traced: 조동사 수동태(조동사+be p.p.) / Though: 접속사(양보) / smaller than the adult brain: 보어(형용사구)

03 The wiring, however, is a mess; / the lines of communication between infant neurons / are far less efficient / than between those in the adult brain. // The baby's perception of the world / is consequently both intensely rich and wildly disordered.

far: 비교급 강조(훨씬) / both A and B: A, B 둘 다(형용사구 병렬)

04 As children absorb more evidence from the world around them, / certain possibilities become much more likely and more useful / and harden into knowledge or beliefs. // The neural pathways that enable those beliefs / become faster and more automatic, / while the ones that the child doesn't use regularly are pruned away.

As: ~함에 따라 / become: 동사1 / much more likely and more useful: 주격보어 / harden into knowledge or beliefs: 동사구2 / The neural pathways: 선행사(복수) / that enable those beliefs: 주격 관계대명사절 / while: ~반면에 / the ones: = the pathways / that the child doesn't use regularly: 목적격 관계대명사절 / are pruned away: 동사구(수동태)

01 교육 심리학자 Susan Engel에 따르면, / 호기심은 네 살 정도의 어린 나이에 줄어들기 시작한다. // 우리가 어른이 될 무렵, / 질문은 더 적어지고 기본값은 더 많아진다. // Henry James가 말했듯이, / "무관심한**disinterested** 호기심은 없어지고, / 정신의 고랑과 경로가 자리잡는다."

02 호기심의 감소**decline**는 원인을 찾을 수 있다**be traced** / 유년 시절을 통한 뇌의 발달에서. // 비록 성인의 뇌보다 작지만, / 유아의 뇌는 수백만 개 더 많은 신경**neural** 연결을 가지고 있다.

03 그러나 연결 상태는 엉망**mess**이라, / 유아의 뉴런 간의 전달은 / 훨씬 덜 효율적이다 / 성인 뇌의 그것들간의 전달보다. // 세상에 대한 아기의 인식은 / 결과적으로 매우**intensely** 풍부하면서도 대단히 무질서하다**disordered**.

04 아이들이 그들 주변의 세상으로부터 더 많은 증거**evidence**를 받아들임**absorb**에 따라, / 특정한 가능성들이 훨씬 더 커지고 더 유용해지며 / 지식이나 믿음으로 굳어진다. // 그러한 믿음을 가능하게 하는 신경 경로는 / 더 빠르고 자동적으로**automatic** 이루어지게 된다 / 아이가 주기적으로 사용하지 않는 경로는 제거되는 반면에.

구문 Check up

① [Despite / Though] smaller than the adult brain, the infant brain contains millions more neural connections.

뒤에 보어인 형용사구가 나오는 것으로 보아 접속사 Though가 적절하다. 접속사 뒤의 <주어(it = the infant brain)+동사(is)>는 생략되어 있다.

② The neural pathways that [enable / enables] those beliefs become faster and more automatic.

선행사가 복수명사이므로, 주격 관계대명사 뒤의 동사 또한 복수형인 enable로 써야 한다.

정답 ① Though ② enable

주어진 문장 넣기 ⊕

STEP 1 • 수능에 진짜 나오는 단어

✔ 문제에 나오는 단어들을 확인하세요.

시간이 없다면 색으로 표시된 단어만이라도 꼭 외우고 넘어가세요!

01	dawn	n. 새벽, 시작	at (✔ dawn)	새벽녘에
02	civilization	n. 문명	since the dawn of ( )	문명의 시작부터
03	ancestor	n. 선조	Our ( )s created myths.	우리 선조들은 신화를 만들었다.
04	inspire	v. 영감을 주다	( ) people to imagine	사람들로 하여금 상상하도록 영감을 주다
05	element	n. 요소	an important ( )	중요한 요소
06	narrative	n. 이야기, 서술	the popular ( )	유명한 이야기
07	identity	n. 정체성	cultural ( )ies	문화적 정체성
08	generation	n. 세대	past ( )s	과거 세대들
09	practical	a. 실용적인	on a ( ) level	실용적인 수준에서
10	keep track of	~을 기록하다, ~의 자국을 뒤밟다	( ) ( ) ( ) time	시간을 기록하다
11	essential	a. 필수적인	( ) to developing societies	사회를 발전시키는 데 필수적인
12	aid	n. 보조 도구	as ( )s to farming	농업의 보조 도구로서
13	navigation	n. 항해	a useful ( ) tool	유용한 항해 도구
14	vital	a. 필수적인	( ) for exploring new worlds	새로운 세계를 탐험하는 데 필수적인
15	remote	a. 외딴	in ( ) areas	외딴 지역에서

⊕ 본문 문장 속에서 단어들을 확인해 보세요.

Since the dawn of civilization, / our ancestors created myths and told legendary stories / about the night sky.

문명의 시작부터, / 우리 선조들은 신화를 만들었고 전설적 이야기를 했다 / 밤하늘에 대해.

단어 다시보기 문제를 풀기 전에 단어들을 30초 동안 다시 확인하세요.

01	dawn	새벽, 시작	at dawn	새벽녘에
02	civilization		since the dawn of civilization	문명의 시작부터
03	ancestor		Our ancestors created myths.	우리 선조들은 신화를 만들었다.
04	inspire		inspire people to imagine	사람들로 하여금 상상하도록 영감을 주다
05	element		an important element	중요한 요소
06	narrative		the popular narrative	유명한 이야기
07	identity		cultural identities	문화적 정체성
08	generation		past generations	과거 세대들
09	practical		on a practical level	실용적인 수준에서
10	keep track of		keep track of time	시간을 기록하다
11	essential		essential to developing societies	사회를 발전시키는 데 필수적인
12	aid		as aids to farming	농업의 보조 도구로서
13	navigation		a useful navigation tool	유용한 항해 도구
14	vital		vital for exploring new worlds	새로운 세계를 탐험하는 데 필수적인
15	remote		in remote areas	외딴 지역에서

⊕ 본문 문장 속에서 단어의 의미를 우리말로 해석해 보세요.

Since the dawn of civilization, / our ancestors created myths and told legendary stories / about the night sky.

→ ______의 ______부터, / 우리 ______은 신화를 만들었고 전설적 이야기를 했다 / 밤하늘에 대해.

2022 3월 학평 39번 문제

제한시간 80초

난이도 ★★★★★

STEP 2 • 수능 기출 제대로 풀기

B

글의 흐름으로 보아, 주어진 문장이 들어가기에 가장 적절한 곳은?

> Since the dawn of civilization, our ancestors created myths and told legendary stories about the night sky.

We are connected to the night sky in many ways. (①) It has always inspired people to wonder and to imagine. (②) Elements of those narratives became embedded in the social and cultural identities of many generations. (③) On a practical level, the night sky helped past generations to keep track of time and create calendars — essential to developing societies as aids to farming and seasonal gathering. (④) For many centuries, it also provided a useful navigation tool, vital for commerce and for exploring new worlds. (⑤) Even in modern times, many people in remote areas of the planet observe the night sky for such practical purposes.

*embed: 깊이 새겨 두다

**commerce: 무역

정답과 해설 p.38

STEP 3 • 수능 지문 제대로 복습하기

01 We are connected to the night sky in many ways. // It has always inspired(5형식 동사) people(목적어) / to wonder and to imagine.(목적격 보어(to부정사))

02 Since(전치사(~ 이래로)) the dawn of civilization, / our ancestors created myths and told legendary stories / about the night sky.

03 Elements of those narratives became embedded(become+수동태) / in the social and cultural identities of many generations.

04 On a practical level, / the night sky helped(5형식 동사) past generations(목적어) / to keep track of time and create calendars(목적격 보어(to부정사)) (선행사(복수)) / (which were 생략) essential to developing(전치사+동명사) societies / as(전치사(~로서)) aids to farming and seasonal gathering.

05 For many centuries, / it also provided a useful navigation tool, / (which was 생략) vital for commerce and for exploring new worlds.

06 Even in modern times, / many people(주어) in remote areas of the planet / observe(동사(복수)) the night sky / for such practical purposes.

01 우리는 많은 방식으로 밤하늘과 연결되어 있다. // 그것은 항상 사람들에게 영감을 주었다**inspire** / 궁금해하고 상상하도록.

02 문명**civilization**의 시작**dawn**부터, / 우리 선조**ancestor**들은 신화를 만들었고 전설적 이야기를 했다 / 밤하늘에 대해.

03 그러한 이야기**narrative**들의 요소**element**들은 깊이 새겨졌다 / 여러 세대**generation**의 사회적 그리고 문화적 정체성**identity**에.

04 실용적인**practical** 수준에서, / 밤하늘은 과거 세대들을 도왔다 / 시간을 기록하고**keep track of** 달력을 만들도록 / 이것은 사회를 발전시키는 데 필수적**essential**이었다 / 농업과 계절에 따른 수확의 보조 도구**aid**로서.

05 수 세기 동안, / 그것은 또한 유용한 항해**navigation** 도구를 제공하였다 / 무역과 새로운 세계를 탐험하는 데 필수적인**vital**.

06 심지어 현대에도 / 지구의 외딴**remote** 지역에 있는 많은 사람들이 / 밤하늘을 관찰한다 / 그러한 실용적인 목적을 위해.

구문 Check up

① It has always inspired people [wonder / to wonder].

동사 inspire의 목적격 보어 자리는 to부정사를 쓴다. 따라서 to wonder가 적절하다.

② Even in modern times, many people in remote areas of the planet [observe / observes] the night sky for such practical purposes.

문장의 주어는 many people이므로 복수에 수 일치한다. 따라서 observe가 적절하다.

정답 ① to wonder ② observe

DAY 12

C

주어진 문장 넣기

STEP 1 • 수능에 진짜 나오는 단어

✔ 문제에 나오는 단어들을 확인하세요.

시간이 없다면 색으로 표시된 단어만이라도 꼭 외우고 넘어가세요!

01	transfer	n. 이동, 전달 v. 전달하다, 이동시키다	the (✓ transfer) of food energy	식품 에너지의 이동
02	proportion	n. 부분, 비율	a large ( )	상당한 부분
03	potential	a. 잠재적인	the ( ) energy	잠재적 에너지
04	chain	n. 사슬, 띠	food ( )	먹이 사슬
05	organism	n. 유기체	through a series of ( )s	일련의 유기체들을 통해
06	in turn	이번에는, 차례차례	Rabbits ( ) ( ) are eaten.	이번에는 토끼가 먹힌다.
07	imply	v. 의미하다	( ) the sequence	연쇄를 의미하다
08	sequence	n. 연쇄, 연속	in the ( )	연쇄 과정에서
09	consumer	n. 소비자	from producer to ( )	생산자에서 소비자까지
10	restrict	v. 제한하다	The number is ( )ed.	수가 제한된다.
11	intake	n. 섭취량	the energy ( )	에너지 섭취량

⊕ 본문 문장 속에서 단어들을 확인해 보세요.

It has been observed / that at each level of transfer, / a large proportion, 80 – 90 percent, of the potential energy / is lost as heat.

관찰되어 왔다 / 각 이동 단계에서 / 잠재적 에너지의 상당한 부분인 80-90%가 / 열로 손실되는 것이.

단어 다시보기 문제를 풀기 전에 단어들을 30초 동안 다시 확인하세요.

01	transfer	이동, 전달 전달하다, 이동시키다	the transfer of food energy	식품 에너지의 이동
02	proportion		a large proportion	상당한 부분
03	potential		the potential energy	잠재적 에너지
04	chain		food chain	먹이 사슬
05	organism		through a series of organisms	일련의 유기체들을 통해
06	in turn		Rabbits in turn are eaten.	이번에는 토끼가 먹힌다.
07	imply		imply the sequence	연쇄를 의미하다
08	sequence		in the sequence	연쇄 과정에서
09	consumer		from producer to consumer	생산자에서 소비자까지
10	restrict		The number is restricted.	수가 제한된다.
11	intake		the energy intake	에너지 섭취량

⊕ 본문 문장 속에서 단어의 의미를 우리말로 해석해 보세요.

It has been observed / that at each level of transfer, / a large proportion, 80 – 90 percent, of the potential energy / is lost as heat.

➜ 관찰되어 왔다 / 각 ____ 단계에서 / ____ 에너지의 상당한 ____인 80-90%가 / 열로 손실되는 것이.

2021 6월 학평 39번 문제

제한시간 80초
난이도 ★★★★☆

STEP 2 • 수능 기출 제대로 풀기

C

글의 흐름으로 보아, 주어진 문장이 들어가기에 가장 적절한 곳은?

It has been observed that at each level of transfer, a large proportion, 80 – 90 percent, of the potential energy is lost as heat.

Food chain means the transfer of food energy from the source in plants through a series of organisms with the repeated process of eating and being eaten. (①) In a grassland, grass is eaten by rabbits while rabbits in turn are eaten by foxes. (②) This is an example of a simple food chain. (③) This food chain implies the sequence in which food energy is transferred from producer to consumer or higher trophic level. (④) Hence the number of steps or links in a sequence is restricted, usually to four or five. (⑤) The shorter the food chain or the nearer the organism is to the beginning of the chain, the greater the available energy intake is.

*trophic: 영양의

정답과 해설 p.39

STEP 3 · 수능 지문 제대로 복습하기

01 Food chain means the transfer of food energy / from the source in plants / through a series of organisms / with the repeated process of eating and being eaten.
과거분사 수식 / 병렬 구조(전치사 of의 목적어)

02 In a grassland, / grass is eaten by rabbits / while rabbits in turn are eaten by foxes. // This is an example of a simple food chain.
~한편

03 This food chain implies the sequence / [in which food energy is transferred / from producer / to consumer or higher trophic level].
전치사+관계대명사

04 It has been observed / [that at each level of transfer, / a large proportion, 80 – 90 percent, of the potential energy / is lost as heat].
가주어 / 진주어(that절) / 주어(부분+of+전체) / 동사(단수)

05 Hence / the number of steps or links in a sequence / is restricted, / usually to four or five.
the number of: ~의 수(단수 취급) / 수 일치

06 [The shorter the food chain / or the nearer the organism is / to the beginning of the chain], / the greater the available energy intake is.
병렬구조 / the 비교급 ~, the 비교급 …: ~하면 할수록 더 …하다

01 먹이 사슬food chain은 식품 에너지의 이동transfer을 의미한다 / 식물 안에 있는 에너지원으로부터 / 일련의 유기체organism들을 통해 / 먹고 먹히는 반복되는 과정 속에서 (이동하는 것).

02 초원에서 / 풀은 토끼에게 먹히지만 / 이번에는in turn 토끼는 여우에게 먹힌다. // 이것은 단순한 먹이 사슬의 예이다.

03 이 먹이 사슬은 연쇄sequence를 의미한다imply / 식품 에너지가 전달되는 (연쇄) / 생산자로부터 / 소비자consumer 또는 더 높은 영양 수준까지.

04 관찰되어 왔다 / 각 이동 단계에서 / 잠재적potential 에너지의 상당한 부분proportion인 80-90%가 / 열로 손실되는 것이.

05 그래서 / 하나의 연쇄(사슬) 안에 있는 단계나 연결의 수는 / 제한된다be restricted / 보통 4~5개로.

06 먹이 사슬이 짧을수록 / 또는 유기체가 가까울수록 / 하위 영양 단계에, / 이용 가능한 에너지 섭취량available energy intake이 더 커진다.

구문 Check up

① This food chain implies the sequence which / in which food energy is transferred from producer to consumer or higher trophic level.

the sequence를 수식하는 절이 완전한 문장이므로 <전치사+관계대명사>인 in which가 알맞다.

② Hence the number of steps or links in a sequence is / are restricted, usually to four or five.

'~의 수'를 의미하는 the number of는 단수 취급하므로 is를 쓴다.

정답 ① in which ② is

D

주어진 문장 넣기 ⊕

STEP 1 • 수능에 진짜 나오는 단어

✔ 문제에 나오는 단어들을 확인하세요.

시간이 없다면 색으로 표시된 단어만이라도 꼭 외우고 넘어가세요!

01	gender	n. 성별	(✔ gender) roles	성 역할
02	boundary	n. 경계	gender roles and ( )ies	성 역할과 경계
03	prior	a. 이전의	in ( ) generations	이전의 세대에
04	conflict	n. 갈등	between gender and ( ) styles	성별과 갈등 유형 사이
05	socialization	n. 사회화	( ) processes	사회화 과정
06	competitive	a. 경쟁적인	( ) work environments	경쟁적인 직업 환경
07	variability	n. 가변성	significant ( )	상당한 가변성
08	assertiveness	n. 단호함	( ) among women	여성들 사이의 단호함
09	resolution	n. 해결, 결정	conflict ( ) experts	갈등 해결 전문가
10	variation	n. 변화의 정도(차이)	within-group ( )s	그룹 내의 차이
11	stereotype	n. 고정관념 v. 고정관념을 가지다	the risks of ( )ing	고정관념을 갖는 것의 위험성
12	overgeneralization	n. 과잉 일반화	avoid ( )s	과잉 일반화를 피하다

⊕ 본문 문장 속에서 단어들을 확인해 보세요.

However, we live in a society / where gender roles and boundaries are not as strict / as in prior generations.

그러나, 우리는 사회에 살고 있다 / 성 역할과 경계가 엄격하지 않은 (사회) / 이전 세대만큼.

단어 다시보기 문제를 풀기 전에 단어들을 30초 동안 다시 확인하세요.

01	gender	성별	gender roles	성 역할
02	boundary		gender roles and boundaries	성 역할과 경계
03	prior		in prior generations	이전의 세대에
04	conflict		between gender and conflict styles	성별과 갈등 유형 사이
05	socialization		socialization processes	사회화 과정
06	competitive		competitive work environments	경쟁적인 직업 환경
07	variability		significant variability	상당한 가변성
08	assertiveness		assertiveness among women	여성들 사이의 단호함
09	resolution		conflict resolution experts	갈등 해결 전문가
10	variation		within-group variations	그룹 내의 차이
11	stereotype		the risks of stereotyping	고정관념을 갖는 것의 위험성
12	overgeneralization		avoid overgeneralizations	과잉 일반화를 피하다

⊕ 본문 문장 속에서 단어의 의미를 우리말로 해석해 보세요.

However, we live in a society / where gender roles and boundaries are not as strict / as in prior generations.

→ 그러나, 우리는 사회에 살고 있다 / ______ 과 ______ 가 엄격하지 않은 (사회) / ______ 세대만큼.

2020 9월 학평 39번 문제

제한시간 80초

난이도 ★★★★★

STEP 2 • 수능 기출 제대로 풀기

D

글의 흐름으로 보아, 주어진 문장이 들어가기에 가장 적절한 곳은?

However, we live in a society where gender roles and boundaries are not as strict as in prior generations.

Gender research shows a complex relationship between gender and conflict styles. (①) Some research suggests that women from Western cultures tend to be more caring than men. (②) This tendency may result from socialization processes in which women are encouraged to care for their families and men are encouraged to be successful in competitive work environments. (③) There is significant variability in assertiveness and cooperation among women, as well as among men. (④) Although conflict resolution experts should be able to recognize cultural and gender differences, they should also be aware of within-group variations and the risks of stereotyping. (⑤) Culture and gender may affect the way people perceive, interpret, and respond to conflict; however, we must be careful to avoid overgeneralizations and to consider individual differences.

정답과 해설 p.39

STEP 3 • 수능 지문 제대로 복습하기

01 Gender research shows a complex relationship / between gender and conflict styles. // Some research suggests / that women from Western cultures tend to be more caring than men.
(that: 명사절 접속사 / tend to: ~하는 경향이 있다)

02 This tendency may result from socialization processes / [in which women are encouraged to care for their families / and men are encouraged to be successful / in competitive work environments].
(in which: 전치사+관계대명사절 / are encouraged to care, are encouraged to be successful: 5형식의 수동태: be p.p+목적격보어(to부정사))

03 However, we live in a society / where gender roles and boundaries are not as strict / as in prior generations.
(where: 관계부사절 / not as ... as: 원급비교(~만큼 …하지 않은))

04 There is significant variability / in assertiveness and cooperation among women, / as well as among men.
(as well as: ~뿐만 아니라)

05 Although conflict resolution experts / should be able to recognize cultural and gender differences, / they should also be aware of / within-group variations and the risks of stereotyping.
(be aware of: ~을 알다 / within-group variations: 목적어1 / the risks of stereotyping: 목적어2)

06 Culture and gender may affect the way / people perceive, interpret, and respond to conflict; / however, we must be careful to avoid overgeneralizations / and to consider individual differences.
(관계부사 how 생략(the way와 how는 함께 쓸 수 없음) / be careful+to부정사: ~하도록 주의하다)

01 성별에 관한 연구는 복잡한 관계를 보여준다 / 성별과 갈등 유형**gender and conflict style** 사이의. // 몇몇 연구는 시사한다 / 서양 문화권에서 여성이 남성보다 더 주변을 돌보는 경향이 있다는 것을.

02 이런 경향은 사회화**socialization** 과정의 결과물일지 모른다 / 여성은 가족을 돌보도록 권장 받고, / 남성은 성공하도록 권장 받는 (사회화 과정) / 경쟁적인 직업 환경**competitive work environment**에서.

03 그러나, 우리는 사회에 살고 있다 / 성 역할과 경계**gender roles and boundary**가 엄격하지 않은 (사회) / 이전**prior** 세대만큼.

04 상당한 차이**significant variability**가 있다 / 여성들 사이에서도 단호함**assertiveness**과 협조성에 / 남성들 사이에서뿐만 아니라.

05 비록 갈등 해결**conflict resolution** 전문가는 / 문화적 차이와 성별의 차이를 인지할 수 있어야 하지만 / 그들은 또한 알고 있어야 한다 / 그룹 내의 차이**within-group variation**와 고정관념을 갖는 것의 위험성**the risks of stereotyping**도.

06 문화와 성별은 방식에 영향을 미칠 수도 있다 / 사람들이 인식하고, 해석하고, 갈등에 반응하는 (방식에). / 하지만 우리는 과잉 일반화**overgeneralization**를 피하도록 주의해야 한다 / 그리고 개인적인 차이를 고려하도록.

구문 Check up

① Some research suggests [which / that] women from Western cultures tend to be more caring than men.

동사 suggest의 목적어 자리에 명사절이 와야 하고, 뒤에 완전한 절이 나오고 있으므로 명사절 접속사 that을 쓴다.

② Culture and gender may affect [the way / the way how] people perceive, interpret, and respond to conflict.

관계부사 how는 the way와 함께 쓸 수 없으므로 the way만 써야 한다. 혹은 how만 써도 알맞다.

정답 ① that ② the way

DAY 12

E

주어진 문장 넣기 ⊕

STEP 1 • 수능에 진짜 나오는 단어

✔ 문제에 나오는 단어들을 확인하세요.

시간이 없다면 색으로 표시된 단어만이라도 꼭 외우고 넘어가세요!

01	in addition to	~ 이외에, ~에 더하여	(✓ in) (addition) (to) English	영어 이외에
02	undoubtedly	ad. 의심할 여지 없이, 분명히	( ) = certainly	의심할 여지 없이 (분명히)
03	comment	n. 언급, 의견	a positive ( )	긍정적인 의견
04	technical	a. 기술적인	the ( ) rehearsal	기술적인 예행연습
05	review	v. 재검토하다 n. 검토	( ) the rehearsal	예행연습을 재검토하다
06	contribution	n. 기여	a personal ( )	개인적인 기여
07	entire	a. 전체의	the ( ) company	일행 전체
08	nervousness	n. 긴장감	reduce ( )	긴장감을 줄이다
09	overwhelming	a. 견디기 어려운, 압도적인	seem ( )	견디기 어려워 보이다
10	pressure	n. 압박	a time ( )	시간적 압박
11	enthusiasm	n. 열정	good humor and ( )	기분 좋은 유머와 열정
12	tackle	v. 씨름하다, 해결하려 하다	( ) each task one by one	각 과제를 하나씩 해결하려 하다

⊕ 본문 문장 속에서 단어들을 확인해 보세요.

In addition to positive comments, / the director and manager will undoubtedly have comments / about what still needs work.

긍정적인 의견 이외에, / 총감독과 감독은 분명히 의견도 가지고 있을 것이다 / 아직 작업이 필요한 부분에 대한.

단어 다시보기 문제를 풀기 전에 단어들을 30초 동안 다시 확인하세요.

01	in addition to	~이외에, ~에 더하여	in addition to English	영어 이외에
02	undoubtedly		undoubtedly = certainly	의심할 여지 없이(분명히)
03	comment		a positive comment	긍정적인 의견
04	technical		the technical rehearsal	기술적인 예행연습
05	review		review the rehearsal	예행연습을 재검토하다
06	contribution		a personal contribution	개인적인 기여
07	entire		the entire company	일행 전체
08	nervousness		reduce nervousness	긴장감을 줄이다
09	overwhelming		seem overwhelming	견디기 어려워 보이다
10	pressure		a time pressure	시간적 압박
11	enthusiasm		good humor and enthusiasm	기분 좋은 유머와 열정
12	tackle		tackle each task one by one	각 과제를 하나씩 해결하려 하다

⊕ 본문 문장 속에서 단어의 의미를 우리말로 해석해 보세요.

In addition to positive comments, / the director and manager will undoubtedly have comments / about what still needs work.

→ 긍정적인 의견 ______, / 총감독과 감독은 ______ ______도 가지고 있을 것이다 / 아직 작업이 필요한 부분에 대한.

2019 9월 학평 39번 문제

제한시간 80초

난이도 ★★★★★

STEP 2 • 수능 기출 제대로 풀기

E

글의 흐름으로 보아, 주어진 문장이 들어가기에 가장 적절한 곳은?

> In addition to positive comments, the director and manager will undoubtedly have comments about what still needs work.

After the technical rehearsal, the theater company will meet with the director, technical managers, and stage manager to review the rehearsal. Usually there will be comments about all the good things about the performance. (①) Individuals should make mental and written notes on the positive comments about their own personal contributions as well as those directed toward the crew and the entire company. (②) Building on positive accomplishments can reduce nervousness. (③) Sometimes, these negative comments can seem overwhelming and stressful. (④) Time pressures to make these last-minute changes can be a source of stress. (⑤) Take each suggestion with good humor and enthusiasm and tackle each task one by one.

정답과 해설 p.39

STEP 3 • 수능 지문 제대로 복습하기

01 After the technical rehearsal, / the theater company will meet with the director, technical managers, and stage manager / to review the rehearsal.
부사적 용법(목적)

02 Usually there will be comments / about all the good things about the performance.
there be+주어(~가 있다)

03 Individuals should make mental and written notes / on the positive comments about their own personal contributions / as well as those directed toward the crew and the entire company.
대명사(=the positive comments) 과거분사(명사 수식)

04 Building on positive accomplishments / can reduce nervousness. // In addition to positive comments, / the director and manager will undoubtedly have comments / about what still needs work.
주어(동명사) 전치사 about의 목적어(관계대명사절)

05 Sometimes, these negative comments / can seem overwhelming and stressful. // Time pressures to make these last-minute changes / can be a source of stress.
2형식 동사 주격보어(형용사구) 형용사적 용법(명사 수식)

06 Take each suggestion with good humor and enthusiasm / and tackle each task one by one.
명령문1 명령문2

01 테크니컬 리허설(기술 예행연습)**technical rehearsal** 후에, / 극단은 총감독, 기술 감독들, 그리고 무대 감독을 만나서 / 리허설을 검토할**review** 것이다.

02 보통은 의견**comment**이 있을 것이다 / 공연에 대한 온갖 좋은 것들에 관한.

03 단원 개인들은 마음에 새기고 글로 적어놓아야 한다 / 그들의 개인적인 기여**personal contribution**에 대한 긍정적인 의견을 / 단원들과 극단 전체**entire company**에 대해 주어지는 (긍정적인) 의견뿐만 아니라.

04 긍정적인 성과를 바탕으로 하면 / 긴장감**nervousness**을 줄일 수 있다. // 긍정적인 의견 이외에**in addition to**, / 총감독과 감독은 분명히**undoubtedly** 의견도 가지고 있을 것이다 / 아직 작업이 필요한 부분에 대한.

05 때로, 이러한 부정적인 의견은 / 견디기 어렵고**overwhelming** 스트레스를 주는 것처럼 보일 수 있다. // 이렇게 마지막 순간의 변경을 해야 하는 시간적 압박**time pressure**은 / 스트레스의 원인이 될 수 있다.

06 각 제안을 좋은 기분으로 그리고 열정**enthusiasm**을 가지고 받아들이고 / 각 과제를 하나씩 해결해 나가라**tackle each task one by one**.

구문 Check up

① The director and manager will undoubtedly have comments about that / what still needs work.

전치사 about의 목적어 역할과 still needs work의 주어 역할을 동시에 할 수 있는 관계대명사는 what이다. 접속사 that 또는 관계대명사 that은 모두 전치사 뒤에 나올 수 없다.

② Sometimes, these negative comments can seem overwhelming / overwhelmingly and stressful.

동사 seem의 보어로는 형용사가 와야 한다. 따라서 overwhelming이 적절하다.

정답 ① what ② overwhelming

F

주어진 문장 넣기 ⊕

STEP 1 • 수능에 진짜 나오는 단어

✔ 문제에 나오는 단어들을 확인하세요.

시간이 없다면 색으로 표시된 단어만이라도 꼭 외우고 넘어가세요!

01	overlook	v. 간과하다, 무시하다	(✔ overlook) debt	빚을 간과하다
02	bracket	n. 계층	low-income ( )s	저소득층
03	acquire	v. 얻다, 획득하다	( ) basic necessities	생활필수품을 획득하다
04	necessity	n. 필수품, 필요성	basic ( )ies of life	기초적 생활 필수품
05	blame	v. 비난하다, 탓하다	( ) oneself	자신을 탓하다
06	individual	a. 개인의, 개인적인 n. 개인, 사람	( ) behavior	개인의 행동
07	beyond	prep. ~을 넘어서는	( ) our own control	우리의 통제 범위를 벗어난
08	sink	v. 가라앉다, 빠지다	( ) into the mud	진창 속에 빠지다
09	debt	n. 빚, 채무	sink into ( )	빚을 지다
10	abuse	n. 남용, 오용	credit card ( )	신용 카드의 남용
11	essential	a. 필수적인	( ) parts	필수적인 부분들
12	affect	v. 영향을 미치다	( ) the person's ability	개인의 능력에 영향을 미치다

⊕ 본문 문장 속에서 단어들을 확인해 보세요.

If a person sinks into debt / because of overspending or credit card abuse, / other people often consider the problem / to be the result of the individual's personal failings.

만약 한 사람이 빚을 진다면 / 과도한 지출이나 신용 카드의 남용 때문에 / 다른 이들은 종종 그 문제를 간주한다 / 그 사람의 개인적 실패의 결과라고.

단어 다시보기 문제를 풀기 전에 단어들을 30초 동안 다시 확인하세요.

01	overlook	간과하다, 무시하다	overlook debt	빚을 간과하다
02	bracket		low-income brackets	저소득층
03	acquire		acquire basic necessities	생활필수품을 획득하다
04	necessity		basic necessities of life	기초적 생활 필수품
05	blame		blame oneself	자신을 탓하다
06	individual		individual behavior	개인의 행동
07	beyond		beyond our own control	우리의 통제 범위를 벗어난
08	sink		sink into the mud	진창 속에 빠지다
09	debt		sink into debt	빚을 지다
10	abuse		credit card abuse	신용 카드의 남용
11	essential		essential parts	필수적인 부분들
12	affect		affect the person's ability	개인의 능력에 영향을 미치다

⊕ 본문 문장 속에서 단어의 의미를 우리말로 해석해 보세요.

If a person sinks into debt / because of overspending or credit card abuse, / other people often consider the problem / to be the result of the individual's personal failings.

→ 만약 한 사람이 ______ / 과도한 지출이나 ______ 때문에 / 다른 이들은 종종 그 문제를 간주한다 / ______의 개인적 실패의 결과라고.

2018 9월 학평 38번 문제

제한시간 80초

난이도 ★★★★★

STEP 2 • 수능 기출 제대로 풀기

F 글의 흐름으로 보아, 주어진 문장이 들어가기에 가장 적절한 곳은?

> However, thinking about it this way overlooks debt among people in low-income brackets who have no other way than debt to acquire basic necessities of life.

Have you heard someone say, "He has no one to blame but himself" for some problem? In everyday life we often blame people for "creating" their own problems. (①) Although individual behavior can contribute to social problems, our individual experiences are often largely beyond our own control. (②) They are determined by society as a whole — by its historical development and its organization. (③) If a person sinks into debt because of overspending or credit card abuse, other people often consider the problem to be the result of the individual's personal failings. (④) By contrast, at middle- and upper-income levels, overspending takes on a variety of meanings typically influenced by what people think of as essential for their well-being and associated with the so-called "good life" that is so heavily marketed. (⑤) But across income and wealth levels, larger-scale economic and social problems may affect the person's ability to pay for consumer goods and services.

정답과 해설 p.40

STEP 3 • 수능 지문 제대로 복습하기

01 Have you heard someone say, / "He has no one to blame but himself" / for some problem? // In everyday life / we often blame people / for "creating" their own problems.

(heard someone say: hear(지각동사)+목적어+목적격 보어(동사원형) / to blame: 형용사적 용법 / no one+but: ~외에 아무도 없다 / often: 빈도부사(일반동사 앞))

02 Although individual behavior can contribute to social problems, / our individual experiences / are often largely beyond our own control. // They are determined / by society as a whole — / by its historical development and its organization.

(Although: 비록 ~에도 불구하고 / are determined: 수동태(be+p.p.))

03 If a person sinks into debt / because of overspending or credit card abuse, / other people often consider the problem / to be the result of the individual's personal failings.

(consider the problem / to be ...: consider+목적어+목적격 보어(to부정사))

04 However, / thinking about it this way / overlooks debt among people in low-income brackets / [who have no other way than debt / to acquire basic necessities of life].

(thinking about it this way: 주어(동명사, 단수 취급) / overlooks: 동사 / people in low-income brackets: 선행사(사람) / who: 주격 관계대명사 / to acquire ...: 형용사적 용법)

05 By contrast, / at middle- and upper-income levels, / overspending takes on a variety of meanings / typically influenced by what people think of as essential / for their well-being / and associated with the so-called "good life" / that is so heavily marketed.

(influenced: 과거분사 수식 / influenced ~ and associated: 병렬연결 / what people think of as essential: 관계대명사 what절 / that is so heavily marketed: 주격 관계대명사절)

06 But across income and wealth levels, / larger-scale economic and social problems may affect the person's ability / to pay for consumer goods and services.

(to pay for ...: 형용사적 용법)

01 당신은 누군가 말하는 것을 들어본 적이 있는가 / "그는 자신 외에 다른 누구도 탓할**blame** 수 없다"고 / 어떤 문제에 대해? // 매일의 삶에서 / 우리는 종종 사람들을 비난한다 / 자신의 문제를 '만들어'낸다고.

02 비록 개인의**individual** 행동이 사회적 문제의 원인이 되기도 하지만 / 우리의 개인적 경험은 / 종종 우리의 통제 범위를 넘어선다**beyond our own control**. // 그것은 결정된다 / 사회 전반에 의해, / 즉 사회의 역사적 발달과 구조에 의해.

03 만약 한 사람이 빚을 진다면**sink into debt** / 과도한 지출이나 신용 카드의 남용**abuse** 때문에, / 다른 이들은 종종 그 문제를 간주한다 / 그 사람의 개인적 실패의 결과라고.

04 하지만 / 그것에 대해 이런 방식으로 생각하는 것은 / 저소득 계층**low-income bracket** 사람들이 진 빚을 간과한다**overlook** / 빚 외에 다른 방법이 없는 (사람들) / 기초적 생활 필수품을 얻을**acquire basic necessities of life** (방법).

05 대조적으로 / 중간 또는 상위 소득 계층에서 / 과도한 지출은 여러 다양한 의미를 가지는데, / 그 의미는 주로 사람들이 필수적**essential**이라고 생각하는 것에 영향을 받고 / 자신의 복지를 위해 (필수적이라고), / (그 의미는) 이른바 '좋은 삶'과 관련된다 / 집중적으로 마케팅의 대상이 된 ('좋은 삶').

06 하지만 소득과 부의 수준을 넘어, / 큰 규모의 경제적, 사회적 문제들은 개인들의 능력에 영향을 미칠지도**affect** 모른다 / 소비자 재화와 서비스에 대해 지불하는 (능력).

구문 Check up

① Have you heard someone say / to say, "He has no one to blame but himself" for some problem?

지각동사(hear)의 목적격 보어는 동사원형 또는 분사만 가능하므로 say 가 적절하다.

② However, thinking about it this way overlooks / overlook debt among people in low-income brackets who have no other way than debt to acquire basic necessities of life.

동명사(thinking)가 주어로 쓰이면 단수 취급하므로 단수동사 overlooks 가 적절하다.

정답 ① say ② overlooks

G

주어진 문장 넣기

STEP 1 • 수능에 진짜 나오는 단어

문제에 나오는 단어들을 확인하세요.

시간이 없다면 색으로 표시된 단어만이라도 꼭 외우고 넘어가세요!

01	expert	n. 전문가	done by an (✓ expert)	전문가에 의해서 행해진
02	graceful	a. 우아한	a ( ) dancer	우아한 무용수
03	harmonious	a. 조화로운	( ) activities	조화로운 활동들
04	awkward	a. 어색한	feel ( )	어색하게 느끼다
05	frustrating	a. 좌절감을 느끼게 하는	the most ( ) fact	가장 좌절감을 주는 사실
06	embarrassing	a. 당혹스럽게 하는	( ) experiences	당혹스러운 경험들
07	undergo	v. 겪다	( ) embarrassing experiences	당혹스러운 경험들을 겪다
08	slip	v. 발을 헛디디다, 미끄러지다	( ) and slide	발을 헛디뎌 미끄러지다
09	humiliating	a. 창피하게 하는	( ) experiences	창피한 경험들

본문 문장 속에서 단어들을 확인해 보세요.

Learning to ski / is one of the most embarrassing experiences / an adult can undergo.

스키 타는 것을 배우는 것은 / 가장 당혹스러운 경험들 중의 하나이다 / 성인이 겪을 수 있는.

단어 다시보기 문제를 풀기 전에 단어들을 30초 동안 다시 확인하세요.

01	expert	전문가	done by an expert	전문가에 의해서 행해진
02	graceful		a graceful dancer	우아한 무용수
03	harmonious		harmonious activities	조화로운 활동들
04	awkward		feel awkward	어색하게 느끼다
05	frustrating		the most frustrating fact	가장 좌절감을 주는 사실
06	embarrassing		embarrassing experiences	당혹스러운 경험들
07	undergo		undergo embarrassing experiences	당혹스러운 경험들을 겪다
08	slip		slip and slide	발을 헛디뎌 미끄러지다
09	humiliating		humiliating experiences	창피한 경험들

⊕ 본문 문장 속에서 단어의 의미를 우리말로 해석해 보세요.

Learning to ski / is one of the most embarrassing experiences / an adult can undergo.

→ 스키 타는 것을 배우는 것은 / 가장 ________ 경험들 중의 하나이다 / 성인이 ________ 수 있는.

2017 9월 학평 38번 문제

제한시간 80초
난이도 ★★★★★

STEP 2 • 수능 기출 제대로 풀기

G

글의 흐름으로 보아, 주어진 문장이 들어가기에 가장 적절한 곳은?

> But as soon as he puts skis on his feet, it is as though he had to learn to walk all over again.

Reading is like skiing. When done well, when done by an expert, both reading and skiing are graceful, harmonious activities. When done by a beginner, both are awkward, frustrating, and slow. (①) Learning to ski is one of the most embarrassing experiences an adult can undergo. (②) After all, an adult has been walking for a long time; he knows where his feet are; he knows how to put one foot in front of the other in order to get somewhere. (③) He slips and slides, falls down, has trouble getting up, and generally looks — and feels — like a fool. (④) It is the same with reading. (⑤) Probably you have been reading for a long time, too, and starting to learn all over again would be humiliating.

정답과 해설 p.40

STEP 3 • 수능 지문 제대로 복습하기

01 Reading is like skiing. // When done well, / when done by an expert, / both reading and skiing are graceful, harmonious activities.
(When done well, / when done: 접속사가 있는 분사구문)

02 When done by a beginner, / both are awkward, frustrating, and slow. // Learning to ski / is one of the most embarrassing experiences / an adult can undergo.
(When done by a beginner: 접속사가 있는 분사구문(=When both (reading and skiing) are done ~) / Learning to ski: 주어(동명사) / is: 동사(단수) / an adult can undergo: 관계대명사 that 생략)

03 After all, an adult has been walking for a long time; / he knows where his feet are; / he knows how to put one foot in front of the other / in order to get somewhere.
(; 세미 콜론(;): 접속사 역할 / where his feet are: 의문사절(목적어) / how to put one foot in front of the other: 의문사+to부정사구(~할 방법) / in order to get somewhere: to부정사의 부사적 용법(목적))

04 But as soon as he puts skis on his feet, / it is as though he had to learn to walk all over again.
(as soon as: ~하자마자 / as though: =as if(마치 ~처럼))

05 He slips and slides, / falls down, / has trouble getting up, / and generally looks — and feels — like a fool.
(has trouble getting up: have trouble+동명사: ~하는 데 어려움이 있다)

06 It is the same with reading. // Probably you have been reading for a long time, too, / and starting to learn all over again / would be humiliating.
(have been reading: 현재완료 진행형: have been+-ing / starting to learn all over again: 주어(동명사) / would be: 동사 / humiliating: 주격보어(현재분사: 능동))

01 읽는 것은 스키 타는 것과 같다. // 잘 되었을 때, / 전문가에 의해서 행해졌을**done by an expert** 때에는 / 읽는 것과 스키 타는 것은 모두 우아하고 조화로운 활동들**graceful, harmonious activities**이다.

02 초보자에 의해서 행해졌을 때에는, / 둘 다 어색하고**awkward** 좌절감을 느끼게 하며**frustrating** 느리다. // 스키 타는 것을 배우는 것은 / 가장 당혹스러운 경험들**embarrassing experiences** 중의 하나이다 / 성인이 겪을**undergo** 수 있는.

03 어쨌든, 성인은 오랫동안 걸어왔고 / 그는 자신의 발이 어디에 있는지 알며 / 그는 어떤 식으로 다른 발 앞에 한 발을 놓아야 하는지 안다 / 어딘가로 가기 위해.

04 하지만 그가 스키를 발에 신자마자, / 그것은 마치 그가 처음부터 다시 걷는 것을 배워야만 하는 것과 같다.

05 그는 발을 헛디뎌**slip** 미끄러지고, / 넘어지고, / 일어나는 데 어려움이 있고, / 대체로 바보같이 보이고 느껴지기도 한다.

06 읽는 것도 마찬가지이다. // 아마 여러분도 역시 오랫동안 읽기를 해왔으므로, / 처음부터 다시 배우기를 시작하는 것은 / 창피할**humiliating** 수 있다.

구문 Check up

① When doing / done by an expert, both reading and skiing are graceful, harmonious activities.

분사구문의 의미상 주어인 both reading and skiing이 '행해지는' 대상이므로 과거분사 done을 쓴다.

② Probably you have been reading for a long time, too, and starting to learn all over again would be humiliated / humiliating.

humiliate의 현재분사는 '창피함을 주는'의 의미이고 과거분사는 '창피함을 느끼는' 것이므로 여기서는 동명사 주어와 어울리는 의미가 되도록 현재분사로 쓴다. 따라서 humiliating이 적절하다.

정답 ① done ② humiliating

Review

DAY 10~12

☑ 종합 성적표

구분	공부한 날 ❶	결과 분석			틀린 이유 ❸
		출처	풀이 시간 ❷	채점 결과 (O, X)	
Day 10	월 일	학력평가 기출 2023년	분 초		
		학력평가 기출 2022년	분 초		
		학력평가 기출 2021년	분 초		
		학력평가 기출 2020년	분 초		
		학력평가 기출 2019년	분 초		
		학력평가 기출 2018년	분 초		
		학력평가 기출 2017년	분 초		
Day 11	월 일	학력평가 기출 2023년	분 초		
		학력평가 기출 2022년	분 초		
		학력평가 기출 2021년	분 초		
		학력평가 기출 2020년	분 초		
		학력평가 기출 2019년	분 초		
		학력평가 기출 2018년	분 초		
		학력평가 기출 2017년	분 초		
Day 12	월 일	학력평가 기출 2023년	분 초		
		학력평가 기출 2022년	분 초		
		학력평가 기출 2021년	분 초		
		학력평가 기출 2020년	분 초		
		학력평가 기출 2019년	분 초		
		학력평가 기출 2018년	분 초		
		학력평가 기출 2017년	분 초		

3일간 공부한 내용을 다시 보니, ……

❶ **매일 지문을 하루 계획에 맞춰 풀었다. vs. 내가 한 약속을 못 지켰다.**

<매3영 고1 기출>은 단순 문제풀이를 위한 책이 아니라, 매일 규칙적으로 영어를 공부하는 습관을 잡는 책입니다. 따라서 푸는 문제 개수는 상황에 따라 다르더라도 '매일' 학습하는 것이 중요합니다.

❷ **주어진 시간을 자꾸 넘긴다?**

풀이 시간이 계속해서 권장 시간을 넘긴다면 실전 훈련이 부족하다는 신호입니다. 아직 조급함을 가질 필요는 없지만, 매일의 문제 풀이에 더 긴장감 있게 임해보세요.

❸ **틀린 이유 맞춤 솔루션**: 오답 이유에 따라 다음 해결책을 참고하세요.

(1) 단어를 많이 몰라서
▶ <STEP 1 단어>에 제시된 필수 어휘를 매일 챙겨보고, SELF-TEST까지 꼼꼼히 진행합니다.

(2) 문장 해석이 잘 안 돼서
▶ <STEP 3 지문 복습>의 구문 첨삭과 끊어읽기 해설을 정독하며 문장구조를 보는 눈을 길러보세요.

(3) 해석은 되지만 내용이 이해가 안 되거나, 선택지로 연결을 못 해서
▶ <정답과 해설>의 해설과 오답풀이를 참고해 틀린 이유를 깊이 고민하고 정리해 보세요.

!

결론적으로, 내가 **취약한 부분**은 ____________ 이다. **취약점을 보완하기 위해서** 나는 ____________ 을/를 해야겠다.

3일 뒤 다시 봐야 할 문항과, 꼭 다시 외워야 할 사항·구문 등이 있는 페이지는 지금 바로 접어 두세요.

<매3영>이 제시하는 3단계로

유형 2일 훈련

DAY

13~14

공부한 날			출처	페이지
DAY 13	월	일	학력평가 기출 2023년 학력평가 기출 2022년 학력평가 기출 2021년 학력평가 기출 2020년 학력평가 기출 2019년 학력평가 기출 2018년 학력평가 기출 2017년	353
DAY 14	월	일	학력평가 기출 2023년 학력평가 기출 2022년 학력평가 기출 2021년 학력평가 기출 2020년 학력평가 기출 2019년 학력평가 기출 2018년 학력평가 기출 2017년	381

A

요약문 완성 ⊕

STEP 1 • 수능에 진짜 나오는 단어

✔ 문제에 나오는 단어들을 확인하세요.

시간이 없다면 색으로 표시된 단어만이라도 꼭 외우고 넘어가세요!

01	unless	conj. ~하지 않는 한	(✔ Unless) it harms you, just stay away from it.	그것이 네게 해를 끼치지 않는 한, 그냥 멀어져 있어라.
02	spoiled	a. 상한	( ) milk	상한 우유
03	label A as B	A를 B라고 분류하다	( ) foods ( ) good or bad	식품들을 좋거나 나쁘다고 분류하다
04	combination	n. 조합	( )s of foods	음식의 조합
05	add up to	결국 ~이 되다	( ) ( ) ( ) a healthful diet	결국 건강에 좋은 식단이 되다
06	raw	a. (익히지 않고) 생으로 먹는, 날것의	( ) broccoli	생으로 먹는 브로콜리
07	nutrient-dense	a. 영양이 풍부한	( ) foods	영양이 풍부한 식품들
08	occasionally	ad. 가끔, 때때로	( ) eat fried chicken	가끔 튀긴 치킨을 먹다
09	off track	궤도에서 벗어난	knock their diet ( ) ( )	그들의 식단을 궤도에서 벗어나게 하다
10	load up on	~을 실컷 먹다, ~로 배를 가득 채우다	( ) ( ) ( ) candy and chips	사탕과 감자 칩을 실컷 먹다

⊕ 본문 문장 속에서 단어들을 확인해 보세요.

But the person / who eats fried foods every day, / with few vegetables or fruits, / and loads up on supersized soft drinks, candy, and chips for snacks / has a bad diet.

하지만 사람은 / 매일 튀긴 음식을 먹고, / 채소나 과일을 거의 먹지 않으면서 / 간식으로 초대형 탄산음료, 사탕, 그리고 감자 칩을 실컷 먹는 / 나쁜 식단을 가진 것이다.

단어 다시보기 문제를 풀기 전에 단어들을 30초 동안 다시 확인하세요.

01	unless	~하지 않는 한	Unless it harms you, just stay away from it.	그것이 네게 해를 끼치지 않는 한, 그냥 멀어져 있어라.
02	spoiled		spoiled milk	상한 우유
03	label A as B		label foods as good or bad	식품들을 좋거나 나쁘다고 분류하다
04	combination		combinations of foods	음식의 조합
05	add up to		add up to a healthful diet	결국 건강에 좋은 식단이 되다
06	raw		raw broccoli	생으로 먹는 브로콜리
07	nutrient-dense		nutrient-dense foods	영양이 풍부한 식품들
08	occasionally		occasionally eat fried chicken	가끔 튀긴 치킨을 먹다
09	off track		knock their diet off track	그들의 식단을 궤도에서 벗어나게 하다
10	load up on		load up on candy and chips	사탕과 감자 칩을 실컷 먹다

⊕ 본문 문장 속에서 단어의 의미를 우리말로 해석해 보세요.

But the person / who eats fried foods every day, / with few vegetables or fruits, / and loads up on supersized soft drinks, candy, and chips for snacks / has a bad diet.

➔ 하지만 사람은 / 매일 튀긴 음식을 먹고, / 채소나 과일을 거의 먹지 않으면서 / 간식으로 초대형 탄산음료, 사탕, 그리고 감자 칩을 ________ / 나쁜 식단을 가진 것이다.

2023 6월 학평 40번 문제

제한시간 80초

난이도 ★★★★★

STEP 2 • 수능 기출 제대로 풀기

A

다음 글의 내용을 한 문장으로 요약하고자 한다. 빈칸 (A), (B)에 들어갈 말로 가장 적절한 것은?

Nearly eight of ten U.S. adults believe there are "good foods" and "bad foods." Unless we're talking about spoiled stew, poison mushrooms, or something similar, however, no foods can be labeled as either good or bad. There are, however, combinations of foods that add up to a healthful or unhealthful diet. Consider the case of an adult who eats only foods thought of as "good" — for example, raw broccoli, apples, orange juice, boiled tofu, and carrots. Although all these foods are nutrient-dense, they do not add up to a healthy diet because they don't supply a wide enough variety of the nutrients we need. Or take the case of the teenager who occasionally eats fried chicken, but otherwise stays away from fried foods. The occasional fried chicken isn't going to knock his or her diet off track. But the person who eats fried foods every day, with few vegetables or fruits, and loads up on supersized soft drinks, candy, and chips for snacks has a bad diet.

↓

> Unlike the common belief, defining foods as good or bad is not ___(A)___; in fact, a healthy diet is determined largely by what the diet is ___(B)___.

(A)		(B)	(A)		(B)
① incorrect	……	limited to	② appropriate	……	composed of
③ wrong	……	aimed at	④ appropriate	……	tested on
⑤ incorrect	……	adjusted to			

정답과 해설 p.42

STEP 3 • 수능 지문 제대로 복습하기

01 Nearly eight of ten U.S. adults believe / (that) there are "good foods" and "bad foods." // Unless we're talking about spoiled stew, poison mushrooms, or something similar, / however, / no foods can be labeled as either good or bad.

목적절(접속사 생략) / ~하지 않는 한(= if ~ not) / A be labeled as B: A가 B라고 분류되다

02 There are, however, combinations of foods / that add up to a healthful or unhealthful diet.

주어(선행사) / 주격 관계대명사절

03 Consider the case of an adult / who eats only foods thought of as "good" / — for example, raw broccoli, apples, orange juice, boiled tofu, and carrots. // Although all these foods are nutrient-dense, / they do not add up to a healthy diet / because they don't supply a wide enough variety of the nutrients we need.

명령문(~하라) / 주격 관계대명사 / 과거분사구 / 목적격 관계대명사절

04 Or take the case of the teenager / who occasionally eats fried chicken, / but otherwise stays away from fried foods. // The occasional fried chicken / isn't going to knock his or her diet off track. // But the person / who eats fried foods every day, / with few vegetables or fruits, / and loads up on supersized soft drinks, candy, and chips for snacks / has a bad diet.

명령문(~하라) / 주격 관계대명사절 / 동사1 / 동사2 / 주어(단수) / 주격 관계대명사절 / 동사1 / 동사2 / 동사

01 미국 성인 10명 중 거의 8명이 믿는다 / '좋은 음식'과 '나쁜 음식'이 있다고. // 우리가 상한**spoiled** 스튜, 독버섯, 또는 이와 유사한 것에 대해 이야기하고 있지 않는 한**unless**, / 하지만 / 어떤 음식도 좋고 나쁨으로 분류될**be labeled as either good or bad** 수 없다.

02 그렇지만 음식들의 조합**combination**이 있다 / 결국**add up to** 건강에 좋은 식단이나 건강에 좋지 않은 식단이 되는.

03 성인의 경우를 생각해보라 / '좋은' 음식이라고 생각되는 음식만 먹는 / 예컨대 생으로 먹는**raw** 브로콜리, 사과, 오렌지 주스, 삶은 두부와 당근 말이다. // 이 모든 음식들은 영양이 풍부하지만**nutrient-dense**, / 그것들은 결국 건강한 식단이 되지 않는다 / 그것들이 우리가 필요로 하는 충분히 다양한 영양소를 공급하지 않기 때문에.

04 또는 십 대의 경우를 예로 들어보자 / 튀긴 치킨을 가끔**occasionally** 먹지만 / 그렇지 않으면 튀긴 음식을 멀리하는. // 가끔 먹는 튀긴 치킨은 / 그 십 대의 식단을 궤도에서 벗어나게**off track** 하지 않을 것이다. // 하지만 사람은 / 매일 튀긴 음식을 먹고, / 채소나 과일을 거의 먹지 않으면서 / 간식으로 초대형 탄산음료, 사탕, 그리고 감자 칩을 실컷 먹는**load up on** / 나쁜 식단을 가진 것이다.

구문 Check up

① If / Unless we're talking about spoiled stew, poison mushrooms, or something similar, however, no foods can be labeled as either good or bad.

문맥상 '~하지 않는 한'의 의미이므로 Unless가 적절하다.

② Consider the case of an adult who eats only foods thought of / thought of as "good".

<think of A as B>의 수동태는 <A be thought of as B>이다. 따라서 전치사 as까지 다 써준 thought of as가 적절하다.

정답 ① Unless ② thought of as

B STEP 1 • 수능에 진짜 나오는 단어

요약문 완성 +

✔ 문제에 나오는 단어들을 확인하세요.

시간이 없다면 색으로 표시된 단어만이라도 꼭 외우고 넘어가세요!

01	layer	n. 층	another (✔ layer)	또 다른 층
02	soil	n. 흙, 토양	one layer of ( )	토양의 한 층
03	talent	n. 재능	a funny ( )	기이한 재능
04	concentration	n. 농도	at high ( )s	높은 농도에서
05	to one's advantage	~에게 유리한(하게)	use it ( ) ( ) ( )	그것을 나에게 유리하게 사용하다
06	redistribute	v. 재분배하다	( ) the wealth	부를 재분배하다
07	absorb	v. 흡수하다	( ) the metal	금속 원소를 흡수하다
08	concentrate	v. 농축하다	( ) the metal in the leaves	잎에 금속 원소를 농축하다
09	decay	v. 부패하다	( )ing leaves	부패해가는 잎
10	poison	v. (독성으로) 오염시키다, 중독시키다	( ) the soil	흙을 (독성으로) 오염시키다
11	immune to	~에 면역이 있는	not ( ) ( ) malaria	말라리아에 면역이 없는
12	toxic	a. 유독한	( ) effects	유독한 영향
13	eliminate	v. 제거하다	( ) toxins	유독 물질을 제거하다
14	competition	n. 경쟁(자)	eliminate ( )	경쟁(자)을 제거하다
15	neighbor	n. 이웃	He is my ( ).	그는 내 이웃이다.

+ 본문 문장 속에서 단어들을 확인해 보세요.

Second, / it absorbs manganese / as it grows, / concentrating the metal in its leaves.

둘째로, / 그것은 망가니즈를 흡수하여 / 성장하면서, / 그 금속 원소를 잎에 농축한다.

단어 다시보기 문제를 풀기 전에 단어들을 30초 동안 다시 확인하세요.

01	layer	층	another layer	또 다른 층
02	soil		one layer of soil	토양의 한 층
03	talent		a funny talent	기이한 재능
04	concentration		at high concentrations	높은 농도에서
05	to one's advantage		use it to my advantage	그것을 나에게 유리하게 사용하다
06	redistribute		redistribute the wealth	부를 재분배하다
07	absorb		absorb the metal	금속 원소를 흡수하다
08	concentrate		concentrate the metal in the leaves	잎에 금속 원소를 농축하다
09	decay		decaying leaves	부패해가는 잎
10	poison		poison the soil	흙을 (독성으로) 오염시키다
11	immune to		not immune to malaria	말라리아에 면역이 없는
12	toxic		toxic effects	유독한 영향
13	eliminate		eliminate toxins	유독 물질을 제거하다
14	competition		eliminate competition	경쟁(자)을 제거하다
15	neighbor		He is my neighbor.	그는 내 이웃이다.

⊕ 본문 문장 속에서 단어의 의미를 우리말로 해석해 보세요.

Second, / it absorbs manganese / as it grows, / concentrating the metal in its leaves.

➜ 둘째로, / 그것은 망가니즈를 ______ / 성장하면서, / 그 금속 원소를 잎에 ______.

2022 3월 학평 40번 문제

제한시간 80초

난이도 ★★★★★

STEP 2 • 수능 기출 제대로 풀기

B

다음 글의 내용을 한 문장으로 요약하고자 한다. 빈칸 (A), (B)에 들어갈 말로 가장 적절한 것은?

The common blackberry (Rubus allegheniensis) has an amazing ability to move manganese from one layer of soil to another using its roots. This may seem like a funny talent for a plant to have, but it all becomes clear when you realize the effect it has on nearby plants. Manganese can be very harmful to plants, especially at high concentrations. Common blackberry is unaffected by damaging effects of this metal and has evolved two different ways of using manganese to its advantage. First, it redistributes manganese from deeper soil layers to shallow soil layers using its roots as a small pipe. Second, it absorbs manganese as it grows, concentrating the metal in its leaves. When the leaves drop and decay, their concentrated manganese deposits further poison the soil around the plant. For plants that are not immune to the toxic effects of manganese, this is very bad news. Essentially, the common blackberry eliminates competition by poisoning its neighbors with heavy metals.

*manganese: 망가니즈(금속 원소) **deposit: 축적물

⬇

The common blackberry has an ability to ____(A)____ the amount of manganese in the surrounding upper soil, which makes the nearby soil quite ____(B)____ for other plants.

	(A)		(B)
①	increase	……	deadly
②	increase	……	advantageous
③	indicate	……	nutritious
④	reduce	……	dry
⑤	reduce	……	warm

정답과 해설 p.42

STEP 3 ● 수능 지문 제대로 복습하기

01 The common blackberry (Rubus allegheniensis) has an amazing ability / [to move manganese from one layer of soil to another / using its roots].
(to부정사의 형용사적 용법 / 분사구문)

02 This may seem like a funny talent / for a plant to have, / but it all becomes clear / when you realize the effect / it has on nearby plants. // Manganese can be very harmful to plants, / especially at high concentrations.
(의미상 주어+to부정사의 형용사적 용법 / 목적격 관계대명사 생략)

03 Common blackberry is unaffected / by damaging effects of this metal / and has evolved two different ways / of using manganese to its advantage. // First, / it redistributes manganese / from deeper soil layers to shallow soil layers / using its roots as a small pipe.
(from A to B / 분사구문)

04 Second, / it absorbs manganese / as it grows, / concentrating the metal in its leaves. // When the leaves drop and decay, / their concentrated manganese deposits / further poison the soil around the plant.
(as: ~함에 따라 / 분사구문(=and it concentrates ~) / 주어 / 부사 / 동사)

05 For plants / that are not immune to the toxic effects of manganese, / this is very bad news. // Essentially, / the common blackberry eliminates competition / by poisoning its neighbors with heavy metals.
(주격 관계대명사절 / by poisoning: ~함으로써)

06 → The common blackberry has an ability / [to increase the amount of manganese / in the surrounding upper soil], / which makes the nearby soil quite deadly for other plants.
(to부정사의 형용사적 용법 / which: = and it / makes: 5형식 동사 / the nearby soil: 목적어 / quite deadly for other plants: 목적격 보어(형용사구))

01 common blackberry(Rubus allegheniensis)는 놀라운 능력이 있다 / 토양**soil**의 한 층**layer**에서 다른 층으로 망가니즈를 옮기는 / 뿌리를 이용하여.

02 이것은 기이한 재능**talent**처럼 보일 수도 있다 / 식물이 가지기에는, / 그러나 전부 명확해진다 / 영향을 깨닫고 나면 / 그것이 근처의 식물에 미치는. // 망가니즈는 식물에 매우 해로울 수 있으며, / 특히 높은 농도**concentration**일 때 그렇다.

03 common blackberry는 영향을 받지 않는다 / 이 금속 원소의 해로운 효과에 / 그리고 두 가지 다른 방법을 발달시켰다 / 망가니즈를 자신에게 유리하게**to its advantage** 사용하는 (방법). // 첫째로, / 그것은 망가니즈를 재분배**redistribute**한다 / 깊은 토양층으로부터 얕은 토양층으로 / 뿌리를 작은 관으로 사용하여.

04 둘째로, / 그것은 망가니즈를 흡수하여**absorb** / 성장하면서, / 그 금속 원소를 잎에 농축한다**concentrate**. // 잎이 떨어지고 부패할**decay** 때, / 그것의 농축된 망가니즈 축적물은 / 그 식물 주변의 토양을 독성 물질로 더욱 오염시킨다**poison**.

05 식물에게 / 망가니즈의 유독한 영향에 면역이 없는**not immune to the toxic effects**, / 이것은 매우 나쁜 소식이다. // 본질적으로, / common blackberry는 경쟁자를 제거한다**eliminate competition** / 중금속으로 그것의 이웃**neighbor**을 중독시켜.

06 → common blackberry는 능력이 있는데 / 망가니즈의 양을 증가시키는 / 주변의 위쪽 토양의, / 그것은 근처의 토양이 다른 식물에게 꽤 치명적이게 되도록 만든다.

구문 Check up

① This may seem like a funny talent [of / for] a plant to have, but it all becomes clear when you realize the effect it has on nearby plants.

to부정사의 의미상 주어는 일반적으로 <for+목적격>으로 표시한다. of는 성격을 나타내는 형용사 뒤에만 쓴다.

② First, it redistributes manganese from deeper soil layers to shallow soil layers [uses / using] its roots as a small pipe.

이 문장의 동사는 redistributes이고, 이와 동사 use를 병렬연결시켜 줄 접속사가 없으므로 use는 분사구문인 using으로 쓴다.

정답 ① for ② using

C

요약문 완성 +

STEP 1 • 수능에 진짜 나오는 단어

✔ 문제에 나오는 단어들을 확인하세요.

시간이 없다면 색으로 표시된 단어만이라도 꼭 외우고 넘어가세요!

01	attend	v. 다니다, 출석하다	(✔ attend) the University of California	캘리포니아 대학을 다니다
02	toilet paper	화장지	rolls of ( ) ( )	몇 개의 두루마리 화장지
03	classic	a. 전형적인, 고전의	a ( ) situation	전형적인 상황
04	tragedy	n. 비극	the ( ) of the commons	공유지의 비극
05	common	a. 공통의, 흔한 n. 공유지(~s)	the ( )s	공유지
06	share	n. 몫 v. 공유하다	a fair ( )	정당한 몫
07	resource	n. 자원	the public ( )	공공재
08	behavior	n. 행동	( ) change	행동 변화
09	note	n. 쪽지	put a ( )	쪽지를 두다
10	remove	v. 치우다, 제거하다	( ) the toilet paper	화장지를 치우다
11	satisfaction	n. 만족	to her great ( )	그녀에게 아주 만족스럽게도
12	reappear	v. 다시 나타나다	( ) in a few hours	몇 시간 후에 다시 나타나다
13	note-free	a. 쪽지가 없는	a ( ) bathroom	쪽지가 없는 화장실

⊕ 본문 문장 속에서 단어들을 확인해 보세요.

To her great satisfaction, / one roll reappeared in a few hours, / and another the next day.

그녀에게 아주 만족스럽게도, / 몇 시간 후에 화장지 한 개가 다시 나타났다 / 그리고 그 다음 날에는 또 하나가 (다시 나타났다).

단어 다시보기 문제를 풀기 전에 단어들을 30초 동안 다시 확인하세요.

01	attend	다니다, 출석하다	attend the University of California	캘리포니아 대학을 다니다
02	toilet paper		rolls of toilet paper	몇 개의 두루마리 화장지
03	classic		a classic situation	전형적인 상황
04	tragedy		the tragedy of the commons	공유지의 비극
05	common		the commons	공유지
06	share		a fair share	정당한 몫
07	resource		the public resource	공공재
08	behavior		behavior change	행동 변화
09	note		put a note	쪽지를 두다
10	remove		remove the toilet paper	화장지를 치우다
11	satisfaction		to her great satisfaction	그녀에게 아주 만족스럽게도
12	reappear		reappear in a few hours	몇 시간 후에 다시 나타나다
13	note-free		a note-free bathroom	쪽지가 없는 화장실

⊕ **본문 문장 속에서 단어의 의미를 우리말로 해석해 보세요.**

To her great satisfaction, / one roll reappeared in a few hours, / and another the next day.

➔ 그녀에게 아주 ______스럽게도, / 몇 시간 후에 화장지 한 개가 ______ / 그리고 그 다음 날에는 또 하나가 (다시 나타났다).

2021 6월 학평 40번 문제

제한시간 80초
난이도 ★★★★☆

STEP 2 • 수능 기출 제대로 풀기

C

다음 글의 내용을 한 문장으로 요약하고자 한다. 빈칸 (A), (B)에 들어갈 말로 가장 적절한 것은?

A woman named Rhonda who attended the University of California at Berkeley had a problem. She was living near campus with several other people — none of whom knew one another. When the cleaning people came each weekend, they left several rolls of toilet paper in each of the two bathrooms. However, by Monday all the toilet paper would be gone. It was a classic tragedy-of-the-commons situation: because some people took more toilet paper than their fair share, the public resource was destroyed for everyone else. After reading a research paper about behavior change, Rhonda put a note in one of the bathrooms asking people not to remove the toilet paper, as it was a shared item. To her great satisfaction, one roll reappeared in a few hours, and another the next day. In the other note-free bathroom, however, there was no toilet paper until the following weekend, when the cleaning people returned.

⬇

A small ______(A)______ brought about a change in the behavior of the people who had taken more of the ______(B)______ goods than they needed.

(A)		(B)	(A)		(B)
① reminder	……	shared	② reminder	……	recycled
③ mistake	……	stored	④ mistake	……	borrowed
⑤ fortune	……	limited			

정답과 해설 p.43

STEP 3 • 수능 지문 제대로 복습하기

01 A woman named Rhonda / who attended the University of California at Berkeley / had a problem. // She was living near campus / with several other people / — none of whom knew one another.

과거분사 / 주격 관계대명사절 / whom의 선행사 / 부분표현+of+목적격 관계대명사 (계속적 용법)

02 When the cleaning people came each weekend, / they left several rolls of toilet paper / in each of the two bathrooms. // However, / by Monday / all the toilet paper would be gone.

by: ~ 무렵, 즈음

03 It was a classic tragedy-of-the-commons situation: // because some people took more toilet paper / than their fair share, / the public resource was destroyed for everyone else.

콜론: 부연 설명 / 비교급 표현

04 After reading a research paper about behavior change, / Rhonda put a note / in one of the bathrooms / asking people not to remove the toilet paper, / as it was a shared item.

접속사가 남아있는 분사구문(=After she read ~) / 수식어(ask+목적어+목적격보어)

05 To her great satisfaction, / one roll reappeared in a few hours, / and another the next day. // In the other note-free bathroom, / however, / there was no toilet paper / until the following weekend, / when the cleaning people returned.

등위접속사 / 반복되는 동사 reappeared 생략 / 관계부사절

06 → A small reminder brought about a change / in the behavior of the people / [who had taken more of the shared goods / than they needed].

주격 관계대명사절 / 과거완료(had p.p.)

01 Rhonda라는 여자는 / Berkeley에 있는 California 대학에 다니는**attend** / 한 가지 문제 상황이 있었다. // 그녀는 캠퍼스 근처에 살고 있었는데 / 여러 사람들과 함께 / 그들 중 누구도 서로를 알지는 못했다.

02 청소부가 주말마다 왔을 때, / 몇 개의 두루마리 화장지**toilet paper**를 두고 갔다 / 화장실 두 칸 각각에. // 그러나 / 월요일 즈음 / 모든 화장지가 없어지곤 했다.

03 그것은 전형적인 공유지의 비극 상황**a classic tragedy-of-the-commons situation**이었다. // 일부 사람들이 더 많은 휴지를 가져갔기 때문에 / 자신들의 정당한 몫**their fair share**보다 / 다른 모든 사람들을 위한 공공재**public resource**가 파괴됐다.

04 행동 변화**behavior change**에 대한 한 연구 논문을 읽고 나서, / Rhonda는 쪽지를 두었다**put a note** / 화장실 한 곳에 / 사람들에게 화장실 화장지를 가져가지**remove** 말라고 요청하는 / 화장실 화장지는 공유재이므로.

05 그녀에게 아주 만족**satisfaction**스럽게도, / 몇 시간 후에 화장지 한 개가 다시 나타났다**reappear** / 그리고 다음 날에는 또 하나가 (다시 나타났다). // 쪽지가 없는**note-free** 화장실에서는 / 하지만 / 화장지가 없었다 / 그 다음 주말까지 / 청소부가 돌아오는.

06 → 자그마한 상기물은 변화를 가져왔다 / 사람들의 행동에 / 더 많은 공유재를 가져갔던 / 그들이 필요한 것보다.

구문 Check up

① Because some people took more toilet paper than their fair share, the public resource destroyed / was destroyed for everyone else.

'공공재가 파괴되다'라는 수동의 의미이고 전체 문장의 동사가 필요하므로 was destroyed로 쓴다.

② After reading a research paper about behavior change, Rhonda put a note in one of the bathrooms asking people not removing / to remove the toilet paper.

5형식 동사 ask는 목적격 보어로 to부정사를 쓴다. 따라서 to remove가 적절하다.

정답 ① was destroyed ② to remove

D STEP 1 • 수능에 진짜 나오는 단어

요약문 완성

✔ 문제에 나오는 단어들을 확인하세요.

시간이 없다면 색으로 표시된 단어만이라도 꼭 외우고 넘어가세요!

01	evolutionary	a. 진화적인	many (✓ evolutionary) reasons	많은 진화적인 이유
02	cooperation	n. 협동, 협력	reasons for ( )	협력에 대한 이유
03	contact	n. 마주침, 접촉	eye ( )	눈 마주침
04	force	n. 힘	the most powerful human ( )	가장 강력한 인간의 힘
05	arguably	ad. 거의 틀림없이	She is ( ) the best singer.	그녀는 거의 틀림없이 가장 뛰어난 가수이다.
06	cooperative	a. 협조적인	quite ( )	꽤 협조적인
07	species	n. 종	a quite cooperative ( )	꽤 협조적인 종
08	noncooperative	a. 비협조적인	( ) on the road	도로에서 비협조적인
09	block	v. 차단하다	Our view is ( )ed.	우리 시야가 차단된다.
10	rearview	n. 후방	the ( ) mirror	백미러
11	confident	a. 자신감 넘치는	become ( )	자신 있어지다

⊕ 본문 문장 속에서 단어들을 확인해 보세요.

It is, arguably, the reason / why humans, normally a quite cooperative species, / can become so noncooperative / on the road.

그것은 거의 틀림없이 이유다 / 보통은 꽤 협조적인 종인 인간이 / 그렇게 비협조적이게 될 수 있는 (이유) / 도로에서.

단어 다시보기 문제를 풀기 전에 단어들을 30초 동안 다시 확인하세요.

01	evolutionary	진화적인	many evolutionary reasons	많은 진화적인 이유
02	cooperation		reasons for cooperation	협력에 대한 이유
03	contact		eye contact	눈 마주침
04	force		the most powerful human force	가장 강력한 인간의 힘
05	arguably		She is arguably the best singer.	그녀는 거의 틀림없이 가장 뛰어난 가수이다.
06	cooperative		quite cooperative	꽤 협조적인
07	species		a quite cooperative species	꽤 협조적인 종
08	noncooperative		noncooperative on the road	도로에서 비협조적인
09	block		Our view is blocked.	우리 시야가 차단된다.
10	rearview		the rearview mirror	백미러
11	confident		become confident	자신 있어지다

⊕ **본문 문장 속에서 단어의 의미를 우리말로 해석해 보세요.**

It is, arguably, the reason / why humans, normally a quite cooperative species, / can become so noncooperative / on the road.

➔ 그것은 ______ 이유다 / 보통은 꽤 ______인 인간이 / 그렇게 ______이게 될 수 있는 (이유) / 도로에서.

2020 3월 학평 40번 문제

제한시간 70초

난이도 ★★★☆☆

STEP 2 • 수능 기출 제대로 풀기

D 다음 글의 내용을 한 문장으로 요약하고자 한다. 빈칸 (A)와 (B)에 들어갈 말로 가장 적절한 것은?

While there are many evolutionary or cultural reasons for cooperation, the eyes are one of the most important means of cooperation, and eye contact may be the most powerful human force we lose in traffic. It is, arguably, the reason why humans, normally a quite cooperative species, can become so noncooperative on the road. Most of the time we are moving too fast — we begin to lose the ability to keep eye contact around 20 miles per hour — or it is not safe to look. Maybe our view is blocked. Often other drivers are wearing sunglasses, or their car may have tinted windows. (And do you really want to make eye contact with those drivers?) Sometimes we make eye contact through the rearview mirror, but it feels weak, not quite believable at first, as it is not "face-to-face."

*tinted: 색이 옅게 들어간

⬇

While driving, people become ____(A)____, because they make ____(B)____ eye contact.

	(A)		(B)
①	uncooperative	……	little
②	careful	……	direct
③	confident	……	regular
④	uncooperative	……	direct
⑤	careful	……	little

정답과 해설 p.43

STEP 3 ● 수능 지문 제대로 복습하기

01 While there are many evolutionary or cultural reasons for cooperation, / the eyes are one of the most important means of cooperation, / and eye contact may be the most powerful human force / we lose in traffic.

~하는 반면에 / one of the+최상급+복수명사 ~: 가장 ~한 것들 중 하나 / 목적격 관계대명사 생략

02 It is, arguably, the reason / [why humans, (normally a quite cooperative species), / can become so noncooperative / on the road].

관계부사절 / (=that) / 삽입구: humans 설명

03 Most of the time we are moving too fast / — we begin to lose the ability / to keep eye contact / around 20 miles per hour / — or it is not safe to look.

형용사적 용법 / 약, 대략 / ~마다 / 가주어 / 진주어

04 Maybe our view is blocked. // Often other drivers are wearing sunglasses, / or their car may have tinted windows. // (And do you really want to make eye contact / with those drivers?)

과거분사

05 Sometimes we make eye contact / through the rearview mirror, / but it feels weak, / not quite believable at first, / as it is not "face-to-face."

feel+형용사: ~하게 느껴지다 / =because

06 → While driving, / people become noncooperative, / because they make little eye contact.

접속사가 남아있는 분사구문 / 준부정어(거의 ~않다)

01 협동cooperation을 하는 진화적evolutionary이거나 문화적인 많은 이유가 있지만, / 눈은 가장 중요한 협동 수단 중 하나이고, / 시선의 마주침eye contact은 가장 강력한 인간의 힘force일지도 모른다 / 우리가 차량 운행 중에 잃는.

02 그것은 거의 틀림없이arguably 이유다 / 보통은 꽤 협조적인 종a quite cooperative species인 인간이 / 그렇게 비협조적noncooperative이게 될 수 있는 (이유) / 도로에서.

03 대부분의 시간에 우리가 너무 빨리 움직이고 있어서, / 우리는 능력을 잃기 시작한다 / 시선을 마주치는 (능력) / 시속 20마일 정도에서 / 혹은 (서로를) 보는 것이 안전하지 않다.

04 어쩌면 우리의 시야가 차단되어block 있을 수도 있다. // 흔히 다른 운전자들이 선글라스를 끼고 있거나 / 그들의 차는 색이 옅게 들어간 창문이 있을 수 있다. // (그리고 당신은 정말로 시선을 마주치고 싶은가 / 그러한 운전자들과?)

05 때로는 우리는 시선을 마주치지만 / 후방거울the rearview mirror을 통해, / 그것은 약하게 느껴지고 / 처음에는 전혀 믿을 수 없다 / '얼굴을 마주하고 있는 것'이 아니기 때문에.

06 → 운전하는 동안, / 사람들은 비협조적이 되는데, / 왜냐하면 그들이 거의 시선을 마주치지 않기 때문이다.

구문 Check up

① It is, arguably, the reason why / that humans, normally a quite cooperative species, can become so noncooperative on the road.

이유의 선행사 reason 뒤에는 관계부사 why가 오는데, 이는 that으로 대체되기도 한다. 따라서 why, that을 둘 다 써도 된다.

② Sometimes we make eye contact through the rearview mirror, but it feels not quite believable / believably at first, as it is not "face-to-face."

2형식 감각동사인 feels 뒤에 주격보어가 필요하므로 형용사 believable을 써야 한다. 부사는 주격보어가 될 수 없다.

정답 ① why, that ② believable

E

요약문 완성 +

STEP 1 • 수능에 진짜 나오는 단어

✔ 문제에 나오는 단어들을 확인하세요.

시간이 없다면 색으로 표시된 단어만이라도 꼭 외우고 넘어가세요!

01	goal	n. 목표	achieve a (✔ goal)	목표를 이루다
02	challenge	n. 도전, 어려움	a life ( )	인생의 어려움
03	undergo	v. 겪다, 받다	( ) surgery	수술을 받다
04	fantasize	v. 공상하다	( ) about winning	승리에 대해 공상하다
05	outcome	n. 결과	a positive ( )	긍정적인 결과
06	expectation	n. 기대	fantasy and ( )	공상과 기대
07	idealized	a. 이상화된	an ( ) future	이상화된 미래
08	based on	~에 기반하여	( ) ( ) past experiences	과거 경험에 기반하여
09	reveal	v. 드러내다, 보여주다	the results ( )	결과가 보여주다
10	engage in	~에 참여하다	( ) ( ) conversation	대화에 참여하다
11	desired	a. 바라던	the ( ) future	바라던 미래
12	recover	v. 회복하다	( ) from surgery	수술에서 회복하다
13	frustration	n. 좌절, 혼란	increase ( )	좌절을 증가시키다
14	discouraging	a. 의기소침해지게 하는	( ) experiences	의기소침하게 만드는 경험들

⊕ 본문 문장 속에서 단어들을 확인해 보세요.

While fantasy involves imagining an idealized future, / expectation is actually based on a person's past experiences.

공상은 이상화된 미래를 상상하는 것을 포함하는 반면 / 기대는 실제로 사람의 과거 경험에 근거한다.

단어 다시보기 문제를 풀기 전에 단어들을 30초 동안 다시 확인하세요.

01	goal	목표	achieve a goal	목표를 이루다
02	challenge		a life challenge	인생의 어려움
03	undergo		undergo surgery	수술을 받다
04	fantasize		fantasize about winning	승리에 대해 공상하다
05	outcome		a positive outcome	긍정적인 결과
06	expectation		fantasy and expectation	공상과 기대
07	idealized		an idealized future	이상화된 미래
08	based on		based on past experiences	과거 경험에 기반하여
09	reveal		the results reveal	결과가 보여주다
10	engage in		engage in conversation	대화에 참여하다
11	desired		the desired future	바라던 미래
12	recover		recover from surgery	수술에서 회복하다
13	frustration		increase frustration	좌절을 증가시키다
14	discouraging		discouraging experiences	의기소침하게 만드는 경험들

⊕ 본문 문장 속에서 단어의 의미를 우리말로 해석해 보세요.

While fantasy involves imagining an idealized future, / expectation is actually based on a person's past experiences.

→ 공상은 ______ 미래를 상상하는 것을 포함하는 반면 / ______는 실제로 사람의 과거 경험 ______.

2019 6월 학평 40번 문제

제한시간 70초

난이도 ★★★☆☆

STEP 2 • 수능 기출 제대로 풀기

E

다음 글의 내용을 한 문장으로 요약하고자 한다. 빈칸 (A)와 (B)에 들어갈 말로 가장 적절한 것은?

What really works to motivate people to achieve their goals? In one study, researchers looked at how people respond to life challenges including getting a job, taking an exam, or undergoing surgery. For each of these conditions, the researchers also measured how much these participants fantasized about positive outcomes and how much they actually expected a positive outcome. What's the difference really between fantasy and expectation? While fantasy involves imagining an idealized future, expectation is actually based on a person's past experiences. So what did the researchers find? The results revealed that those who had engaged in fantasizing about the desired future did worse in all three conditions. Those who had more positive expectations for success did better in the following weeks, months, and years. These individuals were more likely to have found jobs, passed their exams, or successfully recovered from their surgery.

↓

Positive expectations are more ____(A)____ than fantasizing about a desired future, and they are likely to increase your chances of ____(B)____ in achieving goals.

	(A)		(B)
①	effective	……	frustration
②	effective	……	success
③	discouraging	……	cooperation
④	discouraging	……	failure
⑤	common	……	difficulty

정답과 해설 p.43

STEP 3 • 수능 지문 제대로 복습하기

01 What really works / to motivate people to achieve their goals? // In one study, / researchers looked at / [how people respond to life challenges / including getting a job, taking an exam, or undergoing surgery].

motivate+목적어+목적격 보어(to부정사) / 의문사절 / 전치사(~을 포함해) / 동명사구1 / 동명사구2 / 동명사구3

02 For each of these conditions, / the researchers also measured / how much these participants fantasized about positive outcomes / and how much they actually expected a positive outcome.

measured의 목적어(의문사절) 병렬연결

03 What's the difference really between fantasy and expectation? // While fantasy involves imagining an idealized future, / expectation is actually based on a person's past experiences.

~인 반면에 / 과거분사

04 So what did the researchers find? // The results revealed / that those who had engaged in fantasizing about the desired future / did worse in all three conditions.

명사절 접속사 / 주격 관계대명사절

05 Those who had more positive expectations for success / did better in the following weeks, months, and years. // These individuals were more likely / to have found jobs, / passed their exams, or / successfully recovered from their surgery.

주격 관계대명사절 / 동사구(과거) / to have p.p.의 병렬구조(본동사 were보다 먼저 일어난 일)

06 → Positive expectations are more effective than fantasizing about a desired future, / and they are likely to increase your chances of success in achieving goals.

과거분사

01 무엇이 정말 효과가 있는가 / 사람들로 하여금 자신의 목표를 성취하도록**achieve a goal** 동기를 부여하기 위해서는? // 한 연구에서 / 연구자들은 살펴보았다 / 사람들이 인생의 과제**life challenge**에 대해 어떻게 대응하는가를 / 직장을 얻거나, 시험을 치거나, 수술을 받는**undergo surgery** 것과 같은.

02 이러한 각각의 상황에 대해, / 연구자들은 또한 측정했다 / 실험 참가자들이 긍정적인 결과**positive outcome**에 대해 얼마나 많이 공상했는지**fantasize**, / 그리고 그들이 실제로 긍정적인 결과를 얼마나 많이 기대했는지를.

03 공상과 기대**fantasy and expectation**의 차이는 진정 무엇인가? // 공상은 이상화된 미래**an idealized future**를 상상하는 것을 포함하는 반면 / 기대는 실제로 사람의 과거 경험에 근거한다**based on past experiences**.

04 그래서 연구자들은 무엇을 알아냈는가? // 그 결과는 보여주었다**reveal** / 바라던 미래에 대해 공상을 했던**engage in fantasizing about the desired future** 사람들은 / 세 가지 상황 모두에서 좋지 않았다는 것을.

05 성공에 대한 긍정적인 기대를 더 많이 했던 사람들은 / 다음 주, 다음 달, 다음 해에도 좋은 성과를 거두었다. // 이 사람들은 가능성이 더 높았다 / 직업을 구하고, / 시험에 합격하거나, / 수술에서 성공적으로 회복했을**recover from surgery**.

06 → 긍정적인 기대는 바라던 미래에 대해 공상하는 것보다 더 효과적이고 / 그것은 목표를 성취하는 데 있어 성공의 가능성을 높여주는 경향이 있다.

구문 Check up

① What really works to motivate people achieve / to achieve their goals?

동사 motivate의 목적격 보어로는 to부정사가 온다. 따라서 to achieve가 적절하다.

② These individuals were more likely to have found jobs, passed their exams, or successfully recover / recovered from their surgery.

<be likely+to부정사> 구문에서 완료형 to부정사(to have p.p.)가 쓰였고, 접속사 or가 이를 연결하고 있으므로 과거분사인 recovered를 쓴다.

정답 ① to achieve ② recovered

F

요약문 완성 +

STEP 1 • 수능에 진짜 나오는 단어

✔ 문제에 나오는 단어들을 확인하세요.

시간이 없다면 색으로 표시된 단어만이라도 꼭 외우고 넘어가세요!

01	predict	v. 예측하다	(✔ predict) the weather	날씨를 예측하다
02	outcome	n. 결과	the ( )s of sporting contests	스포츠 경기의 결과
03	vary	v. 달라지다, 다르다	( ) from week to week	매주 달라지다
04	feature	n. 특징 v. 특징으로 삼다	a ( ) of sport	스포츠의 한 특징
05	uncertainty	n. 불확실성	the ( ) of the result	결과의 불확실성
06	problematic	a. 문제가 많은	a ( ) case	문제가 많은 사례
07	guarantee	v. 보장하다	The quality of the contest cannot be ( )d.	경기 수준은 보장될 수 없다.
08	in respect of	~에 관해서	( ) ( ) ( ) the performance of star players	스타 선수의 경기력에 관해서
09	consistency	n. 일관성	display ( )	일관성을 보이다
10	solely	ad. 순전히, 오로지	based ( ) on winning	순전히 승리에만 기반한
11	facility	n. 시설	restore the ( )	시설을 복구하다
12	merchandise	n. 상품	a wide selection of ( )	다양하게 엄선한 상품
13	souvenir	n. 기념품	a ( ) shop	기념품 상점
14	core	a. 핵심적인	the ( ) product	핵심 제품

⊕ 본문 문장 속에서 단어들을 확인해 보세요.

It is the uncertainty of the result and the quality of the contest / that consumers find attractive.

바로 결과의 불확실성과 경기 질이다 / 소비자들이 매력적이라고 여기는 것은.

단어 다시보기 문제를 풀기 전에 단어들을 30초 동안 다시 확인하세요.

01	predict	예측하다	predict the weather	날씨를 예측하다
02	outcome		the outcomes of sporting contests	스포츠 경기의 결과
03	vary		vary from week to week	매주 달라지다
04	feature		a feature of sport	스포츠의 한 특징
05	uncertainty		the uncertainty of the result	결과의 불확실성
06	problematic		a problematic case	문제가 많은 사례
07	guarantee		The quality of the contest cannot be guaranteed.	경기 수준은 보장될 수 없다.
08	in respect of		in respect of the performance of star players	스타 선수의 경기력에 관해서
09	consistency		display consistency	일관성을 보이다
10	solely		based solely on winning	순전히 승리에만 기반한
11	facility		restore the facility	시설을 복구하다
12	merchandise		a wide selection of merchandise	다양하게 엄선한 상품
13	souvenir		a souvenir shop	기념품 상점
14	core		the core product	핵심 제품

⊕ 본문 문장 속에서 단어의 의미를 우리말로 해석해 보세요.

It is the uncertainty of the result and the quality of the contest / that consumers find attractive.

→ 바로 ____과 경기 질이다 / 소비자들이 매력적이라고 여기는 것은.

2018 11월 학평 40번 문제

제한시간 80초

난이도 ★★★★★

STEP 2 • 수능 기출 제대로 풀기

F

다음 글의 내용을 한 문장으로 요약하고자 한다. 빈칸 (A), (B)에 들어갈 말로 가장 적절한 것은?

We cannot predict the outcomes of sporting contests, which vary from week to week. This heterogeneity is a feature of sport. It is the uncertainty of the result and the quality of the contest that consumers find attractive. For the sport marketer, this is problematic, as the quality of the contest cannot be guaranteed, no promises can be made in relations to the result and no assurances can be given in respect of the performance of star players. Unlike consumer products, sport cannot and does not display consistency as a key feature of marketing strategies. The sport marketer therefore must avoid marketing strategies based solely on winning, and must instead focus on developing product extensions such as the facility, parking, merchandise, souvenirs, food and beverages rather than on the core product (that is, the game itself).

↓

Sport has the essential nature of being ____(A)____, which requires that its marketing strategies ____(B)____ products and services more than just the sports match.

(A)		(B)
① unreliable	……	feature
② unreliable	……	exclude
③ risky	……	ignore
④ consistent	……	involve
⑤ consistent	……	promote

정답과 해설 p.44

STEP 3 • 수능 지문 제대로 복습하기

01 We cannot predict the outcomes of sporting contests, / which vary from week to week.
선행사(복수) 계속적 용법

02 This heterogeneity is a feature of sport. // It is the uncertainty of the result and the quality of the contest / that consumers find attractive.
it is ~ that … 강조 구문: …한 것은 바로 ~이다

03 For the sport marketer, / this is problematic, / as the quality of the contest cannot be guaranteed, / no promises can be made in relations to the result / and no assurances can be given in respect of the performance of star players.
접속사(이유) 주어1 조동사 수동태1 주어2 조동사 수동태2 주어3 조동사 수동태3

04 Unlike consumer products, / sport cannot and does not display consistency / as a key feature of marketing strategies.
전치사(~와 달리) 전치사(~로서)

05 The sport marketer therefore must avoid marketing strategies / based solely on winning, / and must instead focus on developing product extensions / such as the facility, parking, merchandise, souvenirs, food and beverages / rather than on the core product (that is, the game itself).
동사1 동사2 A rather than B: B라기보다 A인

06 → Sport has the essential nature of being unreliable, / which requires that its marketing strategies (should) feature products and services / more than just the sports match.
요구 동사 명사절 접속사(목적절) 동사원형(~해야 한다)

01 우리는 스포츠 경기의 결과**outcome**를 예측할**predict** 수 없는데, / 이것은 매주 달라진다**vary**.

02 이러한 이질성이 스포츠의 특징**feature**이다. // 바로 결과의 불확실성**uncertainty**과 경기 질이다 / 소비자들이 매력적이라고 여기는 것은.

03 스포츠 마케팅 담당자에게 / 이것은 문제가 되는데**problematic**, / 왜냐하면 경기의 수준이 보장될**guarantee** 수 없고, / 경기 결과에 관해 어떤 약속도 할 수 없으며, / 스타 선수의 경기력에 관해**in respect of** 어떤 확신도 줄 수 없기 때문이다.

04 소비재와 다르게, / 스포츠는 일관성**consistency**을 보여줄 수도 없고 보여주지도 않는다 / 마케팅 전략의 중요한 특징인.

05 따라서 스포츠 마케팅 담당자는 마케팅 전략을 피해야 하고 / 순전히**solely** 승리에만 기반한 / 대신에 제품 확장 개발에 집중해야만 한다 / 시설**facility**, 주차, 상품**merchandise**, 기념품**souvenir**, 식음료 같은 / 핵심**core** 제품(즉, 시합 그 자체)보다는.

06 → 스포츠는 불확실하다는 본질적 속성을 갖고 있으며, / 이것은 스포츠 마케팅 전략이 상품과 서비스를 특징으로 삼기를 요구한다 / 단지 스포츠 경기보다는.

구문 Check up

① We cannot predict the outcomes of sporting contests, which vary / varies from week to week.

선행사 the outcomes가 복수명사이므로, 관계절의 동사 또한 복수형인 vary가 적절하다.

② It is the uncertainty of the result and the quality of the contest what / that consumers find attractive.

'it is ~ that …(…한 것은 ~하다)' 강조구문의 that이다. 뒤에 목적어가 없는 불완전한 문장이 나왔다.

정답 ① vary ② that

G

요약문 완성 +

STEP 1 • 수능에 진짜 나오는 단어

✔ 문제에 나오는 단어들을 확인하세요.

시간이 없다면 색으로 표시된 단어만이라도 꼭 외우고 넘어가세요!

01	psychologist	n. 심리학자	social (✔ psychologist)s	사회 심리학자들
02	weight	v. ~을 무겁게 하다	a ( )ed backpack	무거운 배낭
03	estimate	v. 추정하다, 어림잡다 n. 어림, 견적	( ) the cost	비용을 추정하다
04	steepness	n. 경사도	estimate the ( )	경사도를 추정하다
05	participant	n. 참가자	( )s in the marathon	마라톤 참가자
06	significantly	ad. 크게, 현저하게	( ) lower estimates	상당히 더 낮은 추정 (현저히 낮은 추정)
07	form	v. 형성하다, 만들다	newly ( )ed friends	새롭게 형성된(사귄) 친구
08	furthermore	ad. 게다가	( ) = moreover	게다가
09	involve	v. 포함하다	( )d in the study	연구에 포함된(참여한)
10	steep	a. 가파른	the ( ) hill	가파른 언덕
11	perceive	v. 인지하다	( ) a sound	소리를 인지하다

⊕ 본문 문장 속에서 단어들을 확인해 보세요.

Furthermore, / the longer the close friends had known each other, / the less steep the hill appeared / to the participants involved in the study.

게다가, / 그 친한 친구들이 서로 알았던 기간이 길면 길수록, / 언덕은 덜 가파르게 보였다 / 연구에 참여한 참가자들에게.

단어 다시보기 문제를 풀기 전에 단어들을 30초 동안 다시 확인하세요.

01	psychologist	심리학자	social psychologists	사회 심리학자들
02	weight		a weighted backpack	무거운 배낭
03	estimate		estimate the cost	비용을 추정하다
04	steepness		estimate the steepness	경사도를 추정하다
05	participant		participants in the marathon	마라톤 참가자
06	significantly		significantly lower estimates	상당히 더 낮은 추정
07	form		newly formed friends	새롭게 형성된(사귄) 친구
08	furthermore		furthermore = moreover	게다가
09	involve		involved in the study	연구에 포함된(참여한)
10	steep		the steep hill	가파른 언덕
11	perceive		perceive a sound	소리를 인지하다

본문 문장 속에서 단어의 의미를 우리말로 해석해 보세요.

Furthermore, / the longer the close friends had known each other, / the less steep the hill appeared / to the participants involved in the study.

→ ______, / 그 친한 친구들이 서로 알았던 기간이 길면 길수록, / 언덕은 덜 ______ 보였다 / 연구에 ______ ______에게.

2017 9월 학평 40번 문제

제한시간 70초

난이도 ★★★☆☆

STEP 2 • 수능 기출 제대로 풀기

G 다음 글의 내용을 한 문장으로 요약하고자 한다. 빈칸 (A)와 (B)에 들어갈 말로 가장 적절한 것은?

Social psychologists at the University of Virginia asked college students to stand at the base of a hill while carrying a weighted backpack and estimate the steepness of the hill. Some participants stood next to close friends whom they had known a long time, some stood next to friends they had not known for long, some stood next to strangers, and the others stood alone during the exercise. The participants who stood with close friends gave significantly lower estimates of the steepness of the hill than those who stood alone, next to strangers, or next to newly formed friends. Furthermore, the longer the close friends had known each other, the less steep the hill appeared to the participants involved in the study.

↓

According to the study, a task is perceived as less ____(A)____ when standing next to a ____(B)____ friend.

(A)		(B)
① difficult	……	close
② valuable	……	new
③ difficult	……	smart
④ valuable	……	patient
⑤ exciting	……	strong

정답과 해설 p.44

STEP 3 • 수능 지문 제대로 복습하기

01 Social psychologists at the University of Virginia / asked college students / to stand at the base of a hill / while carrying a weighted backpack / and estimate the steepness of the hill.

5형식 동사 / 목적어 / 병렬구조(목적격 보어)

02 Some participants stood next to close friends / whom they had known a long time, / some stood next to friends / they had not known for long, / some stood next to strangers, / and the others stood alone / during the exercise.

목적격 관계대명사절 / 관계대명사 whom 생략 / some ~ the others …: 어떤 사람들은 ~하고, 나머지 사람들은 …하다

03 The participants who stood with close friends / gave significantly lower estimates of the steepness of the hill / than those who stood alone, / next to strangers, / or next to newly formed friends.

주격 관계대명사절 / 비교급 수식 / 주격 관계대명사절

04 Furthermore, / the longer the close friends had known each other, / the less steep the hill appeared / to the participants involved in the study.

the 비교급 ~, the 비교급 …: ~하면 할수록 더 …하다 / 과거분사

05 → According to the study, / a task is perceived as less difficult / when standing next to a close friend.

접속사가 남아 있는 분사구문(=when people stand ~)

01 Virginia 대학의 사회 심리학자들**social psychologist**이 / 대학생들에게 요청했다 / 언덕 아래에 서 있도록 / 무거운 배낭**a weighted backpack**을 멘 채로 / 그리고 언덕의 경사도를 추정하도록**estimate the steepness**.

02 일부 참가자들**participant**은 친한 친구들 옆에 서 있었다 / 오랫동안 알아 왔던, / 몇몇은 친구들 옆에 서 있었고 / 안 지 오래되지 않은, / 몇몇은 낯선 사람 옆에 서 있었으며, / 다른 사람들은 혼자 서 있었다 / 그 활동을 하는 동안.

03 친한 친구들과 함께 서 있었던 참가자들은 / 그 언덕의 경사도를 상당히**significantly** 더 낮게 추정했다 / 혼자 서 있었던 사람들보다 / 혹은 낯선 사람 옆에 (서 있었던 사람들보다) / 혹은 새로 사귄 친구**newly formed friends** 옆에 (서 있었던 사람들보다).

04 게다가**furthermore**, / 그 친한 친구들이 서로 알았던 기간이 길면 길수록 / 언덕은 덜 가파르게**steep** 보였다 / 연구에 참여한**involved in the study** 참가자들에게.

05 → 연구에 따르면, / 과제가 덜 어렵게 지각된다**be perceived** / 친한 친구 옆에 서 있을 때.

구문 Check up

① Social psychologists at the University of Virginia asked college students to stand at the base of a hill and [estimated / estimate] the steepness of the hill.

문맥상 본동사 asked가 아닌 목적격보어 to stand와 병렬 연결되는 자리이므로 (to) estimate가 적절하다.

② According to the study, a task is perceived as less difficult when [stand / standing] next to a close friend.

접속사 when을 남긴 분사구문이 주어 없이 이어지므로 분사 standing이 적절하다.

정답 ① estimate ② standing

DAY 14

장문의 이해 +

A STEP 1 • 수능에 진짜 나오는 단어

✔ 문제에 나오는 단어들을 확인하세요.

시간이 없다면 색으로 표시된 단어만이라도 꼭 외우고 넘어가세요!

01	in the middle of	~ 도중에, 중간에	(✔ in) (the) (middle) (of) a game	게임 중간에
02	reproduce	v. 재현하다, 복제하다	( ) the glories	영광을 재현하다
03	from memory	기억해서, 외워서	speak ( ) ( )	외워서 말하다
04	randomly	ad. 무작위로	place the pieces on the board ( )	판에 말을 무작위로 배치하다
05	familiar	a. 친숙한, 익숙한	( ) patterns	익숙한 패턴
06	previously	ad. 이전에, 사전에	( ) held views	이전에 지녔던 견해들
07	beneficial	a. 유리한, 이로운	the ( ) effects of familiar structure on memory	익숙한 구조가 기억에 미치는 유익한 영향
08	expertise	n. 전문 지식	( ) in music	음악에 대한 전문 지식
09	accurately	ad. 정확하게	remember ( )	정확하게 기억하다
10	improve	v. 향상시키다, 높이다	( ) memory	기억력을 향상시키다
11	experienced	a. 숙련된, 경험이 많은	an ( ) dancer	숙련된 무용수
12	make up	~을 구성하다, 이루다	( ) ( ) a team	팀을 구성하다
13	routine	n. (안무 등의) 정해진 동작, 루틴	a dance ( )	춤의 정해진 동작

⊕ 본문 문장 속에서 단어들을 확인해 보세요.

Chess masters / shown a chess board in the middle of a game for 5 seconds / with 20 to 30 pieces still in play / can immediately reproduce the position of the pieces from memory.

체스의 달인들은 / 체스판을 게임 중간에 5초 동안 본 / 20~30개의 말들이 아직 놓여 있는 상태로 / 그 말들의 위치를 기억해서 즉시 재현할 수 있다.

단어 다시보기 문제를 풀기 전에 단어들을 30초 동안 다시 확인하세요.

01	in the middle of	~도중에, 중간에	in the middle of a game	게임 중간에
02	reproduce		reproduce the glories	영광을 재현하다
03	from memory		speak from memory	외워서 말하다
04	randomly		place the pieces on the board ramdomly	판에 말을 무작위로 배치하다
05	familiar		familiar patterns	익숙한 패턴
06	previously		previously held views	이전에 지녔던 견해들
07	beneficial		the beneficial effects of familiar structure on memory	익숙한 구조가 기억에 미치는 유익한 영향
08	expertise		expertise in music	음악에 대한 전문 지식
09	accurately		remember accurately	정확하게 기억하다
10	improve		improve memory	기억력을 향상시키다
11	experienced		an experienced dancer	숙련된 무용수
12	make up		make up a team	팀을 구성하다
13	routine		a dance routine	춤의 정해진 동작

⊕ **본문 문장 속에서 단어의 의미를 우리말로 해석해 보세요.**

Chess masters / shown a chess board in the middle of a game for 5 seconds / with 20 to 30 pieces still in play / can immediately reproduce the position of the pieces from memory.

→ 체스의 달인들은 / 체스판을 ______ 5초 동안 본 / 20~30개의 말들이 아직 놓여 있는 상태로 / 그 말들의 위치를 ______ 즉시 ______ 수 있다.

2023 3월 학평 41, 42번 문제

제한시간 120초
난이도 A-1 ★★★☆☆
A-2 ★★★★★

STEP 2 • 수능 기출 제대로 풀기

A 다음 글을 읽고, 물음에 답하시오.

Chess masters shown a chess board in the middle of a game for 5 seconds with 20 to 30 pieces still in play can immediately reproduce the position of the pieces from memory. Beginners, of course, are able to place only a few. Now take the same pieces and place them on the board randomly and the (a) difference is much reduced. The expert's advantage is only for familiar patterns — those previously stored in memory. Faced with unfamiliar patterns, even when it involves the same familiar domain, the expert's advantage (b) disappears.

The beneficial effects of familiar structure on memory have been observed for many types of expertise, including music. People with musical training can reproduce short sequences of musical notation more accurately than those with no musical training when notes follow (c) unusual sequences, but the advantage is much reduced when the notes are ordered randomly. Expertise also improves memory for sequences of (d) movements. Experienced ballet dancers are able to repeat longer sequences of steps than less experienced dancers, and they can repeat a sequence of steps making up a routine better than steps ordered randomly. In each case, memory range is (e) increased by the ability to recognize familiar sequences and patterns.

*expertise: 전문 지식 **sequence: 연속, 순서 ***musical notation: 악보

[A-1] 윗글의 제목으로 가장 적절한 것은?

① How Can We Build Good Routines?
② Familiar Structures Help Us Remember
③ Intelligence Does Not Guarantee Expertise
④ Does Playing Chess Improve Your Memory?
⑤ Creative Art Performance Starts from Practice

[A-2] 밑줄 친 (a)~(e) 중에서 문맥상 낱말의 쓰임이 적절하지 않은 것은?

① (a)
② (b)
③ (c)
④ (d)
⑤ (e)

정답과 해설 p.46

STEP 3 ● 수능 지문 제대로 복습하기

01 Chess masters / shown a chess board in the middle of a game for 5 seconds / with 20 to 30 pieces still in play / can immediately reproduce the position of the pieces from memory. // Beginners, of course, / are able to place only a few.
주어 / 과거분사구 / 동사구

02 Now take the same pieces / and place them on the board randomly / and the difference is much reduced. // The expert's advantage is only for familiar patterns / — those previously stored in memory. // Faced with unfamiliar patterns, / even when it involves the same familiar domain, / the expert's advantage disappears.
명령문1(~하라) / 명령문2(~하라) / 접속사(그러면 …) / =patterns / 분사구문

03 The beneficial effects of familiar structure on memory / have been observed for many types of expertise, / including music. // People with musical training / can reproduce short sequences of musical notation more accurately / than those with no musical training / when notes follow unusual sequences, / but the advantage is much reduced / when the notes are ordered randomly.
주어(복수) / 현재완료 수동태 / 비교급+than: ~보다 더 …하게

04 Expertise also improves memory for sequences of movements. // Experienced ballet dancers are able to repeat longer sequences of steps / than less experienced dancers, / and they can repeat a sequence of steps making up a routine better / than steps ordered randomly.
비교급+than: ~보다 더 …한 / 현재분사구

05 In each case, / memory range is increased by the ability / to recognize familiar sequences and patterns.
형용사적 용법

01 체스의 달인들은 / 체스판을 게임 중간에**in the middle of a game** 5초 동안 본 / 20~30개의 말들이 아직 놓여 있는 상태로 / 그 말들의 위치를 기억해서**from memory** 즉시 재현할**reproduce** 수 있다. // 물론 초보자들은 / 겨우 몇 개만 기억해 낼 수 있다.

02 이제 같은 말들을 가져다가 / 체스판에 무작위로**randomly** 놓아 보라 / 그러면 그 차이는 크게 줄어든다. // 전문가의 유리함은 익숙한**familiar** 패턴에 대해서만 있다 / 즉 전에**previously** 기억에 저장된 패턴. // 익숙하지 않은 패턴을 맞닥뜨리면, / 같은 익숙한 분야와 관련 있는 경우라도 / 전문가의 유리함은 사라진다.

03 익숙한 구조가 기억에 미치는 유익한**beneficial** 효과는 / 많은 유형의 전문 지식**expertise**에서 관찰되었다 / 음악을 포함해. // 음악 교육을 받은 사람이 / 짧은 연속된 악보를 더 정확하게**accurately** 재현할 수 있지만 / 음악 교육을 받지 않은 사람보다 / 음표가 특이한(→ 전형적인) 순서를 따를 때는 / 그 유리함이 훨씬 줄어든다 / 음표가 무작위로 배열되면.

04 전문 지식은 또한 연속 동작에 대한 기억을 향상시킨다**improve**. // 숙련된**experienced** 발레 무용수가 더 긴 연속 스텝을 반복할 수 있다 / 경험이 적은 무용수보다 / 그리고 그들은 정해진 춤 동작을 이루는**make up a routine** 연속 스텝을 더 잘 반복할 수 있다 / 무작위로 배열된 스텝보다.

05 각각의 경우, / 기억의 범위는 능력에 의해 늘어난다 / 익숙한 순서와 패턴을 인식하는.

B

장문의 이해

STEP 1 • 수능에 진짜 나오는 단어

✔ 문제에 나오는 단어들을 확인하세요.

시간이 없다면 색으로 표시된 단어만이라도 꼭 외우고 넘어가세요!

01	precious	a. 귀중한	a (✔ precious) watch	귀중한 시계
02	ordinary	a. 평범한	an ( ) watch	평범한 시계
03	search	v. 찾다, 수색하다 n. 찾기, 수색	( ) for his watch	그의 시계를 찾아 나서다
04	exhausted	a. 지친	become ( )	지치다
05	give up	포기하다	( ) ( ) all hope	모든 희망을 포기하다
06	call off	중지하다, 취소하다	( ) ( ) everything	모든 걸 취소하다
07	silence	n. 침묵	in ( )	침묵 속에서
08	delighted	a. 기쁜	( ) to get the watch back	시계를 되찾아 기쁜
09	reward	v. ~에게 보상을 주다 n. 보상	( ) the boy	소년에게 보상을 주다
10	attractive	a. 매력적인	an ( ) reward	매력적인 보상
11	entire	a. 전체의	the ( ) class	학급 전체
12	pile	n. 더미	a ( ) of books	책 더미
13	hay	n. 건초	the entire pile of ( )	전체 건초 더미

⊕ 본문 문장 속에서 단어들을 확인해 보세요.

The farmer gave up all hope of finding it / and called off the search.

그 농부는 시계를 찾을 거라는 모든 희망을 포기하고 / 찾는 것을 멈추었다.

단어 다시보기 문제를 풀기 전에 단어들을 30초 동안 다시 확인하세요.

01	precious	귀중한	a precious watch	귀중한 시계
02	ordinary		an ordinary watch	평범한 시계
03	search		search for his watch	그의 시계를 찾아 나서다
04	exhausted		become exhausted	지치다
05	give up		give up all hope	모든 희망을 포기하다
06	call off		call off everything	모든 걸 취소하다
07	silence		in silence	침묵 속에서
08	delighted		delighted to get the watch back	시계를 되찾아 기쁜
09	reward		reward the boy	소년에게 보상을 주다
10	attractive		an attractive reward	매력적인 보상
11	entire		the entire class	학급 전체
12	pile		a pile of books	책 더미
13	hay		the entire pile of hay	전체 건초 더미

⊕ 본문 문장 속에서 단어의 의미를 우리말로 해석해 보세요.

The farmer gave up all hope of finding it / and called off the search.

➜ 그 농부는 시계를 찾을 거라는 모든 희망을 ________ / ________을 ________.

2022 6월 학평 43, 45번 문제

제한시간 110초
난이도 B-1 ★★☆☆☆
B-2 ★★★☆☆

STEP 2 • 수능 기출 제대로 풀기

B

다음 글을 읽고, 물음에 답하시오.

(A) Once, a farmer lost his precious watch while working in his barn. It may have appeared to be an ordinary watch to others, but it brought a lot of happy childhood memories to him. It was one of the most important things to him. After searching for it for a long time, the old farmer became exhausted.

*barn: 헛간(곡물·건초 따위를 두는 곳)

(B) The number of children looking for the watch slowly decreased and only a few tired children were left. The farmer gave up all hope of finding it and called off the search. Just when the farmer was closing the barn door, a little boy came up to him and asked the farmer to give him another chance. The farmer did not want to lose out on any chance of finding the watch so let him in the barn.

(C) After a little while the boy came out with the farmer's watch in his hand. He was happily surprised and asked how he had succeeded to find the watch while everyone else had failed. He replied "I just sat there and tried listening for the sound of the watch. In silence, it was much easier to hear it and follow the direction of the sound." He was delighted to get his watch back and rewarded the little boy as promised.

(D) However, the tired farmer did not want to give up on the search for his watch and asked a group of children playing outside to help him. He promised an attractive reward for the person who could find it. After hearing about the reward, the children hurried inside the barn and went through and round the entire pile of hay looking for the watch. After a long time searching for it, some of the children got tired and gave up.

[B-1] 주어진 글 (A)에 이어질 내용을 순서에 맞게 배열한 것으로 가장 적절한 것은?

① (B) — (D) — (C)
② (C) — (B) — (D)
③ (C) — (D) — (B)
④ (D) — (B) — (C)
⑤ (D) — (C) — (B)

[B-2] 윗글에 관한 내용으로 적절하지 않은 것은?

① 농부의 시계는 어린 시절의 행복한 기억을 불러일으켰다.
② 한 어린 소년이 농부에게 또 한 번의 기회를 달라고 요청했다.
③ 소년이 한 손에 농부의 시계를 들고 나왔다.
④ 아이들은 시계를 찾기 위해 헛간을 뒤쳐나왔다.
⑤ 아이들 중 일부는 지쳐서 시계 찾기를 포기했다.

정답과 해설 p.46

STEP 3 • 수능 지문 제대로 복습하기

01 Once, a farmer lost his precious watch / while working in his barn. // It may have appeared to be an ordinary watch to others, / but it brought a lot of happy childhood memories to him. // It was one of the most important things to him. // After searching for it for a long time, / the old farmer became exhausted.

접속사가 남아있는 분사구문 / may have p.p. (~했을 수도 있다) / 접속사가 남아있는 분사구문 (=After he searched~)

02 However, / the tired farmer did not want to give up on the search for his watch / and [asked a group of children playing outside to help him]. // He promised an attractive reward / for the person who could find it.

ask+목적어+목적격 보어(to부정사) / 현재분사 / 주격 관계대명사절

03 After hearing about the reward, / the children hurried inside the barn / and went through and round the entire pile of hay / looking for the watch. // After a long time searching for it, / some of the children got tired and gave up.

접속사가 남아있는 분사구문(=After they heard~) / 동사1 / 동사2 / 분사구문

04 The number of children looking for the watch / slowly decreased / and only a few tired children were left. // The farmer gave up all hope of finding it / and called off the search.

주어(the number of+복수명사) / 현재분사(children 수식) / 동사 / =the watch

05 Just when the farmer was closing the barn door, / a little boy came up to him / and asked the farmer to give him another chance. // The farmer did not want to lose out / on any chance of finding the watch / so let him in the barn.

5형식 동사 / 목적어 / 목적격 보어(to부정사) / 동사1 / 동사2

06 After a little while / the boy came out with the farmer's watch in his hand. // He was happily surprised / and asked / how he had succeeded to find the watch / while everyone else had failed. // He replied / "I just sat there / and tried listening for the sound of the watch. // In silence, / it was much easier / to hear it and follow the direction of the sound." // He was delighted to get his watch back / and rewarded the little boy / as promised.

의문사절(asked의 목적어) / ~하기를 시도하다 / 가주어 / 진주어 / 감정 형용사+to부정사(원인)

01 어느 날, 한 농부가 그의 귀중한**precious** 시계를 잃어버렸다 / 헛간에서 일하는 동안. // 그것은 다른 이들에게는 평범한**ordinary** 시계로 보일 수도 있었지만 / 그것은 그에게 어린 시절의 많은 행복한 기억을 불러왔다. // 그것은 그에게 가장 중요한 것들 중 하나였다. // 오랜 시간 동안 그것을 찾아본**search for** 뒤에 / 그 나이 든 농부는 지쳐버렸다**exhausted.**

02 그러나, / 그 지친 농부는 그의 시계를 찾는 것을 포기하고**give up** 싶지 않았기에 / 밖에서 놀던 한 무리의 아이들에게 도와 달라고 요청했다. // 그는 매력적인 보상**attractive reward**을 약속했다 / 그의 시계를 찾을 수 있는 사람에게.

03 보상에 대해 듣고난 뒤, / 그 아이들은 헛간 안으로 서둘러 들어갔고 / 전체 건초 더미**entire pile of hay** 사이와 주변으로 걸어갔다 / 시계를 찾으러. // 시계를 찾느라 오랜 시간을 보낸 후, / 아이들 중 일부는 지쳐서 포기했다.

04 시계를 찾는 아이들의 숫자가 / 천천히 줄어들었고 / 지친 아이들 몇 명만이 남았다. // 그 농부는 시계를 찾을 거라는 모든 희망을 포기하고 / 찾는 것을 멈추었다**call off the search.**

05 농부가 막 헛간 문을 닫고 있었을 때 / 한 어린 소년이 그에게 다가와서 / 자신에게 또 한 번의 기회를 달라고 요청했다. // 농부는 놓치고 싶지 않아서 / 시계를 찾을 어떤 가능성도 / 그를 헛간 안으로 들어오게 해주었다.

06 잠시 후 / 그 소년이 한 손에 농부의 시계를 들고 나왔다. // 그는 행복에 겨워 놀랐고 / 물었다 / 소년이 어떻게 시계를 찾는 데 성공했는지를 / 다른 모두가 실패했던 반면. // 그는 답했다 / "저는 거기에 앉아서 / 시계의 소리를 들으려고 했어요. // 침묵**silence** 속에서, / 훨씬 쉬웠어요 / 그것을 듣고 소리의 방향을 따라가는 것이."라고. // 그는 시계를 되찾아 기뻤고**delighted** / 그 어린 소년에게 보상해 주었다 / 약속한 대로.

C

장문의 이해 +

STEP 1 • 수능에 진짜 나오는 단어

✔ 문제에 나오는 단어들을 확인하세요.

시간이 없다면 색으로 표시된 단어만이라도 꼭 외우고 넘어가세요!

01	passion	n. 열정	have a (✔ passion)	열정을 가지다
02	foot	n. 기슭	at the ( ) of the Himalayas	히말라야 산맥의 기슭에
03	preparation	n. 준비	all the necessary ( )s	모든 필요한 준비
04	set out	떠나다, 출발하다	( ) ( ) for a hunting trip	사냥 여행을 떠나다
05	previous	a. 이전의	the ( ) year	작년
06	fearlessly	ad. 두려움 없이	start ( ) licking the drum	두려움 없이 북을 핥기 시작하다
07	lick	v. 핥다	( ) the deerskin drum	사슴 가죽으로 만든 북을 핥다
08	palace	n. 궁궐	in the ( )	궁궐에서
09	spot	v. 발견하다	( ) a deer	사슴을 발견하다
10	aim	n. 겨냥, 목표	His ( ) was perfect.	그의 겨냥은 완벽했다.
11	arrow	n. 화살	one shot of an ( )	한 발의 화살
12	servant	n. 신하	an old ( )	한 나이 든 신하
13	belong to	~의 것이다	( ) ( ) her mate	그녀의 짝의 것이다

⊕ 본문 문장 속에서 단어들을 확인해 보세요.

Suddenly, / she started / fearlessly licking the deerskin drum.

갑자기, / 암사슴은 시작했다 / 사슴 가죽으로 만든 북을 두려움 없이 핥기 (시작했다).

단어 다시보기 문제를 풀기 전에 단어들을 30초 동안 다시 확인하세요.

01	passion	열정	have a passion	열정을 가지다
02	foot		at the foot of the Himalayas	히말라야 산맥의 기슭에
03	preparation		all the necessary preparations	모든 필요한 준비
04	set out		set out for a hunting trip	사냥 여행을 떠나다
05	previous		the previous year	작년
06	fearlessly		start fearlessly licking the drum	두려움 없이 북을 핥기 시작하다
07	lick		lick the deerskin drum	사슴 가죽으로 만든 북을 핥다
08	palace		in the palace	궁궐에서
09	spot		spot a deer	사슴을 발견하다
10	aim		His aim was perfect.	그의 겨냥은 완벽했다.
11	arrow		one shot of an arrow	한 발의 화살
12	servant		an old servant	한 나이 든 신하
13	belong to		belong to her mate	그녀의 짝의 것이다

⊕ 본문 문장 속에서 단어의 의미를 우리말로 해석해 보세요.

Suddenly, / she started / fearlessly licking the deerskin drum.

➔ 갑자기, / 암사슴은 시작했다 / 사슴 가죽으로 만든 북을 ______________ (시작했다).

2021 3월 학평 43, 45번 문제

제한시간 100초
난이도 C-1 ★★☆☆☆
C-2 ★★☆☆☆

STEP 2 • 수능 기출 제대로 풀기

C

다음 글을 읽고, 물음에 답하시오.

(A) Once upon a time, there lived a young king who had a great passion for hunting. His kingdom was located at the foot of the Himalayas. Once every year, he would go hunting in the nearby forests. He would make all the necessary preparations, and then set out for his hunting trip.

(B) Seasons changed. A year passed by. And it was time to go hunting once again. The king went to the same forest as the previous year. He used his beautiful deerskin drum to round up animals. But none came. All the animals ran for safety, except one doe. She came closer and closer to the drummer. Suddenly, she started fearlessly licking the deerskin drum.

*round up: ~을 몰다 **doe: 암사슴

(C) Like all other years, the hunting season had arrived. Preparations began in the palace and the king got ready for his hunting trip. Deep in the forest, he spotted a beautiful wild deer. It was a large stag. His aim was perfect. When he killed the deer with just one shot of his arrow, the king was filled with pride. The proud hunter ordered a hunting drum to be made out of the skin of the deer.

*stag: 수사슴

(D) The king was surprised by this sight. An old servant had an answer to this strange behavior. “The deerskin used to make this drum belonged to her mate, the deer who we hunted last year. This doe is mourning the death of her mate,” the man said. Upon hearing this, the king had a change of heart. He had never realized that an animal, too, felt the pain of loss. He made a promise, from that day on, to never again hunt wild animals.

*mourn: 애도하다

[C-1] 주어진 글 (A)에 이어질 내용을 순서에 맞게 배열한 것으로 가장 적절한 것은?

① (B) — (D) — (C)　② (C) — (B) — (D)
③ (C) — (D) — (B)　④ (D) — (B) — (C)
⑤ (D) — (C) — (B)

[C-2] 윗글에 관한 내용으로 적절하지 않은 것은?

① 왕은 매년 근처의 숲으로 사냥 여행을 갔다.
② 암사슴은 북 치는 사람으로부터 도망갔다.
③ 왕은 화살로 단번에 수사슴을 맞혔다.
④ 한 나이 든 신하가 암사슴의 행동의 이유를 알고 있었다.
⑤ 왕은 다시는 야생 동물을 사냥하지 않겠다고 약속했다.

정답과 해설 p.47

STEP 3 • 수능 지문 제대로 복습하기

01 Once upon a time, / there lived a young king / who had a great passion for hunting. //
도치(동사+주어) 주격 관계대명사절
His kingdom was located / at the foot of the Himalayas. // Once every year, / he would
~하곤 했다
go hunting / in the nearby forests. // He would make all the necessary preparations, / and then set out for his hunting trip.

02 Like all other years, / the hunting season had arrived. // Preparations began in the palace / and the king got ready for his hunting trip. // Deep in the forest, / he spotted a beautiful wild deer. // It was a large stag. // His aim was perfect. // When he killed the deer / with just one shot of his arrow, / the king was filled with pride. // The proud
~로 가득하다
hunter ordered / a hunting drum to be made out of the skin of the deer.
5형식 동사(order)+목적어+목적격 보어(to부정사)

03 Seasons changed. // A year passed by. // And it was time to go hunting once again.
비인칭주어 to부정사의 형용사적 용법
// The king went to the same forest / as the previous year. // He used his beautiful deerskin drum / to round up animals. // But none came. // All the animals ran for safety, / except one doe. // She came closer and closer / to the drummer. // Suddenly, /
전치사(~을 제외하고) 비교급+and+비교급: 점점 더 ~한
she started / fearlessly licking the deerskin drum.

04 The king was surprised by this sight. // An old servant had an answer / to this strange behavior. // "The deerskin used to make this drum / belonged to her mate, / the deer who
동격 과거분사(be used to+동사원형: ~하기 위해 쓰이다)
we hunted last year. // This doe is mourning the death of her mate," / the man said. //
목적격 관계대명사절
Upon hearing this, / the king had a change of heart. // He had never realized / that an
(up)on -ing: ~하자마자
animal, too, felt the pain of loss. // He made a promise, / from that day on, / to never again hunt wild animals.
to부정사의 형용사적 용법
to부정사를 꾸미는 부사구가 to와 동사원형 사이에 삽입됨

01 옛날 옛적에 / 젊은 왕이 살았다 / 사냥에 대해 엄청난 열정passion을 가진. // 그의 왕국은 위치해 있었다 / 히말라야 산맥의 기슭foot에. // 매년 한 번씩, / 그는 사냥하러 가고는 했다 / 근처의 숲으로. // 그는 모든 필요한 준비all the necessary preparations를 하곤 했다 / 그리고 자신의 사냥 여행을 떠나곤set out 했다.

02 다른 모든 해처럼, / 사냥철이 왔다. // 궁궐palace에서 준비가 시작되었고 / 왕은 자신의 사냥 여행을 갈 준비를 했다. // 숲 속 깊은 곳에서 / 그는 아름다운 야생 사슴을 발견했다spot. // 그것은 큰 수사슴이었다. // 그의 겨냥aim은 완벽했다. // 그 사슴을 잡고서 / 단 한 발의 화살arrow로 / 왕은 의기 양양했다. // 그 의기양양한 사냥꾼은 명령했다 / 그 사슴의 가죽으로 사냥용 북을 만들도록.

03 계절이 바뀌었다. // 1년이 지나갔다. // 그리고 또 다시 사냥하러 갈 때가 되었다. // 왕은 같은 숲으로 갔다 / 작년previous year과. // 그는 아름다운 사슴 가죽으로 만든 북을 사용하여 / 동물들을 몰았다. // 그러나 아무도 오지 않았다. // 모든 동물이 안전한 곳으로 도망쳤는데, / 암사슴 한 마리는 예외였다. // 암사슴은 점점 더 가까이 다가왔다 / 북 치는 사람에게. // 갑자기, / 암사슴은 시작했다 / 사슴 가죽으로 만든 북을 두려움 없이fearlessly 핥기lick (시작했다).

04 이 광경을 보고 왕은 놀랐다. // 한 나이 든 신하servant가 이유를 알고 있었다 / 이 이상한 행동의. // "이 북을 만드는 데 사용된 사슴 가죽은 / 암사슴의 짝의 것인데belong to her mate, / 우리가 작년에 사냥한 그 사슴입니다. // 이 암사슴은 짝의 죽음을 애도하고 있는 것입니다."/ 이라고 그 남자는 말했다. // 이 말을 듣자마자, / 왕의 마음이 바뀌었다. // 그는 전혀 몰랐었다 / 동물도 역시 상실의 고통을 느낀다는 것을. // 그는 약속했다 / 그날 이후 / 결코 다시는 야생 동물을 사냥하지 않겠다고.

D

장문의 이해 +

STEP 1 • 수능에 진짜 나오는 단어

✔ 문제에 나오는 단어들을 확인하세요.

시간이 없다면 색으로 표시된 단어만이라도 꼭 외우고 넘어가세요!

01	Fahrenheit	n. (온도) 화씨	65 degrees (✔ Fahrenheit)	화씨 65도
02	ideal	a. 이상적인	( ) for the sleep	수면에 이상적인
03	assume	v. 가정하다	( ) she wins the game	그녀가 그 게임을 이긴다고 가정하다
04	specific	a. 특정의, 구체적인	the ( ) temperature	특정 온도
05	recommendation	n. 권장, 추천	calorie ( )s	권장 칼로리
06	quantity	n. 양	( ) and quality of sleep	잠의 양과 질
07	clinician	n. 임상의사	sleep ( )s treating patients	환자를 치료하는 수면 임상의사
08	disbelieve	v. 불신하다	( ) the influence of temperature	온도의 영향을 불신하다
09	core	n. 중심(부)	( ) body temperature	심부체온
10	explore	v. 살펴보다	( ) related experiments	관련 실험들을 살펴보다

+ 본문 문장 속에서 단어들을 확인해 보세요.

A bedroom temperature of around 65 degrees Fahrenheit (18.3°C) / is ideal for the sleep of most people, / assuming standard bedding and clothing.

대략 화씨 65도(섭씨 18.3도)의 침실 온도가 / 대부분의 사람들의 수면에 이상적이다 / 표준적인 침구와 복장을 가정할 때.

단어 다시보기 문제를 풀기 전에 단어들을 30초 동안 다시 확인하세요.

01	Fahrenheit	화씨	65 degrees Fahrenheit	화씨 65도
02	ideal		ideal for the sleep	수면에 이상적인
03	assume		assume she wins the game	그녀가 그 게임을 이긴다고 가정하다
04	specific		the specific temperature	특정 온도
05	recommendation		calorie recommendations	권장 칼로리
06	quantity		quantity and quality of sleep	잠의 양과 질
07	clinician		sleep clinicians treating patients	환자를 치료하는 수면 임상의사
08	disbelieve		disbelieve the influence of temperature	온도의 영향을 불신하다
09	core		core body temperature	심부체온
10	explore		explore related experiments	관련 실험들을 살펴보다

⊕ 본문 문장 속에서 단어의 의미를 우리말로 해석해 보세요.

A bedroom temperature of around 65 degrees Fahrenheit (18.3°C) / is ideal for the sleep of most people, / assuming standard bedding and clothing.

→ 대략 ______ 65도(섭씨 18.3도)의 침실 온도가 / 대부분의 사람들의 수면에 ______이다 / 표준적인 침구와 복장을 ______ 때.

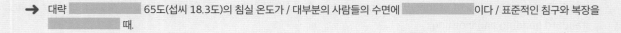

2020 9월 학평 41, 42번 문제

제한시간 120초
난이도 D-1 ★★★☆☆
D-2 ★★★★☆

STEP 2 • 수능 기출 제대로 풀기

D

다음 글을 읽고, 물음에 답하시오.

A bedroom temperature of around 65 degrees Fahrenheit (18.3°C) is ideal for the sleep of most people, assuming standard bedding and clothing. This (a) surprises many, as it sounds just a little too cold for comfort. Of course, that specific temperature will vary depending on the individual in question and their gender and age. But like calorie recommendations, it's a good target for the average human being. Most of us set bedroom temperatures higher than are ideal for good sleep and this likely contributes to (b) lower quantity and quality of sleep than you are otherwise capable of getting. Lower than 55 degrees Fahrenheit can be harmful rather than helpful to sleep, unless warm bedding or nightclothes are used. However, most of us fall into the (c) opposite category of setting a controlled bedroom temperature that is too high: 70 or 72 degrees. Sleep clinicians treating patients who can't sleep at night will often ask about room temperature, and will advise patients to (d) raise their current thermostat setpoint by 3 to 5 degrees from that which they currently use. Anyone disbelieving of the influence of temperature on sleep can explore some related experiments on this topic. Scientists have, for example, gently warmed the feet or the body of rats to encourage blood to rise to the surface of the skin and release heat, thereby decreasing core body temperature. The rats fell asleep far (e) faster than was otherwise normal.

*thermostat: 온도 조절 장치

[D-1] 윗글의 제목으로 가장 적절한 것은?

① Signs of Sleep Problems
② Stay Cool for Better Sleep
③ Turn Up the Heat in Your Room
④ How to Correct Bad Sleeping Posture
⑤ A Key to Quality Sleep: Clean Bedding

[D-2] 밑줄 친 (a)~(e) 중에서 문맥상 낱말의 쓰임이 적절하지 않은 것은?

① (a)
② (b)
③ (c)
④ (d)
⑤ (e)

정답과 해설 p.47

STEP 3 • 수능 지문 제대로 복습하기

01 A bedroom temperature of around 65 degrees Fahrenheit (18.3°C) / is ideal for the sleep of most people, / assuming standard bedding and clothing.
분사구문: 의미상 주어(막연한 일반인) 생략

02 This surprises many, / as it sounds just a little too cold for comfort. // Of course, / that specific temperature will vary / depending on the individual in question / and their gender and age.

03 But / like calorie recommendations, / it's a good target for the average human being.
전치사(~처럼)

04 Most of us set bedroom temperatures higher / than are ideal for good sleep / and this likely contributes to lower quantity and quality of sleep / than you are otherwise capable of getting.

05 Lower than 55 degrees Fahrenheit can be harmful / rather than helpful to sleep, / unless warm bedding or nightclothes are used.
~라기 보다는
~하지 않은 한(if ~ not)

06 However, / most of us fall into the opposite category / of setting a controlled bedroom temperature that is too high: / 70 or 72 degrees.
주격 관계대명사절

07 Sleep clinicians / treating patients who can't sleep at night / will often ask about room temperature, / and will advise patients / to raise their current thermostat set-point by 3 to 5 degrees / from that which they currently use.
현재분사구
advise+목적어+목적격보어(to부정사)
목적격 관계대명사절

08 Anyone disbelieving of the influence of temperature on sleep / can explore some related experiments / on this topic.
현재분사구

09 Scientists have, for example, gently warmed the feet or the body of rats / [to encourage blood to rise to the surface of the skin and release heat], / thereby decreasing core body temperature. // The rats fell asleep far faster / than was otherwise normal.
부사적 용법(목적)
분사구문(연속동작: 그리고 ~하다)
비교급 강조

01 대략 화씨**Fahrenheit** 65도(섭씨 18.3도)의 침실 온도가 / 대부분의 사람들의 수면에 이상적**ideal for the sleep**이다/ 표준적인 침구와 복장을 가정할**assume** 때.

02 이것은 많은 사람을 놀라게 한다 / 안락함을 위해서는 다소 너무 추운 것처럼 들리기 때문에. // 물론, / 그 특정**specific** 온도는 다를 것이다 / 해당되는 사람에 따라 / 그리고 그들의 성별 그리고 나이(에 따라).

03 하지만, / 권장**recommendation** 칼로리처럼, / 그것은 평균적인 사람에게 좋은 목표이다.

04 우리 대부분은 침실 온도를 더 높게 설정하는데 / 좋은 수면을 위해 이상적인 것보다, / 이는 수면의 양과 질**quantity and quality of sleep**을 낮추는 데 기여할 것이다 / 그렇게 하지 않는다면 당신이 얻을 수 있는 것보다.

05 화씨 55도보다 더 낮은 온도는 오히려 해로울 수 있다 / 잠을 자는 데 도움이 되기보다 / 따뜻한 침구와 잠옷이 사용되지 않는 이상.

06 하지만, / 우리 대부분은 정반대의 범주에 속한다 / 너무 높은 침실 온도를 설정하는 / 70도 또는 72도라는.

07 수면 임상의사**clinician**는 / 밤에 잠을 못 자는 환자를 치료하는 / 종종 침실 온도를 묻고, / 환자들에게 조언할 것이다 / 온도 조절 장치의 현재 설정 값을 3도에서 5도 가량 올리라고(→ 낮추라고) / 그들이 지금 사용하는 설정 값보다.

08 온도가 수면에 미치는 영향에 대해 불신하는**disbelieve** 사람은 누구든지 / 몇몇 관련 실험들을 살펴볼**explore** 수 있다 / 이 주제에 관한.

09 예를 들어, 과학자들은 쥐의 발이나 몸을 서서히 따뜻하게 했다 / 혈액을 피부의 표면으로 올라가게 하고 열을 방출시키기 위해 / 그리고 그럼으로써 심부체온**core body temperature**을 낮추었다. // 그 쥐들은 훨씬 더 빨리 잠들었다 / 그렇지 않았다면(체온을 낮추지 않았더라면) 평균적이었을 것(속도)보다.

E

장문의 이해 +

STEP 1 • 수능에 진짜 나오는 단어

문제에 나오는 단어들을 확인하세요.

시간이 없다면 색으로 표시된 단어만이라도 꼭 외우고 넘어가세요!

01	instruction	n. 지시	give (✓ instruction)s	지시하다
02	path	n. 길	follow the ( )	길을 따라가다
03	preparation	n. 대비, 준비	in ( ) for a test	시험을 대비해
04	log	n. 통나무	a fallen ( )	쓰러진 통나무
05	request	v. 요청하다	( ) a song	노래를 요청하다
06	location	n. 위치	a specific ( )	구체적인 위치
07	sink	v. 가라앉다, 내려앉다	a heart ( )s	심장이 내려앉다
08	leap	n. 도약	the ( ) to greatness	위대함으로의 도약
09	adequately	ad. 적절하게	prepare ( )	적절하게 준비하다
10	launch	v. 내던지다, 시작하다	( ) oneself into the air	자기 자신을 공중에 내던지다
11	regret	v. 후회하다	bitterly ( )	쓰라리게 후회하다

본문 문장 속에서 단어들을 확인해 보세요.

He gave them instructions / to follow the path to its end, / in preparation for a test later in the week.

스승은 그들에게 지시했다 / 그 길을 끝까지 따라가라고 / 그 주의 후반에 있을 테스트를 대비해.

단어 다시보기 문제를 풀기 전에 단어들을 30초 동안 다시 확인하세요.

01	instruction	지시	give instructions	지시하다
02	path		follow the path	길을 따라가다
03	preparation		in preparation for a test	시험을 대비해
04	log		a fallen log	쓰러진 통나무
05	request		request a song	노래를 요청하다
06	location		a specific location	구체적인 위치
07	sink		a heart sinks	심장이 내려앉다
08	leap		the leap to greatness	위대함으로의 도약
09	adequately		prepare adequately	적절하게 준비하다
10	launch		launch oneself into the air	자기 자신을 공중에 내던지다
11	regret		bitterly regret	쓰라리게 후회하다

⊕ 본문 문장 속에서 단어의 의미를 우리말로 해석해 보세요.

He gave them instructions / to follow the path to its end, / in preparation for a test later in the week.

→ 스승은 그들에게 ________했다 / 그 ________을 끝까지 따라가라고 / 그 주의 후반에 있을 테스트를 ______해.

2019 9월 학평 43, 45번 문제

제한시간 120초

난이도 E-1 ★★★★☆

E-2 ★★★☆☆

STEP 2 • 수능 기출 제대로 풀기

E 다음 글을 읽고, 물음에 답하시오.

(A) Two students met their teacher at the start of a track through a forest. He gave them instructions to follow the path to its end, in preparation for a test later in the week. The path split into two: one was clear and smooth, the other had fallen logs and other obstacles in the way. One student chose to avoid the obstacles, taking the easier path to the end. He felt clever as he ran without stopping.

(B) He requested that they join him at a specific location in three days. When they arrived, they could see a ravine that was a few meters wide. The students looked at their teacher and he said just one word. "Jump!" The first student looked at the distance and his heart sank. The teacher looked at him. "What's wrong? This is the leap to greatness. Everything that you've done until now should have prepared you for this moment."

*ravine: 계곡, 협곡

(C) The student shrugged his shoulders and walked away, knowing he hadn't prepared adequately for greatness. The second student looked at the teacher and smiled. He knew now that the obstacles that had been placed in his path were part of his preparation. By choosing to overcome challenges, not avoid them, he was ready to make the leap. He ran as fast as he could and launched himself into the air. He made it across!

(D) The second student chose to tackle the obstacles, battling through every challenge in his path. The student who chose the easy path finished first and felt proud of himself. "I'm glad I chose to avoid the rocks and logs. They were only there to slow me down," he thought to himself. The second student arrived at the finish feeling tired and regretting the path he had chosen. The teacher smiled at them both.

[E-1] 주어진 글 (A)에 이어질 내용을 순서에 맞게 배열한 것으로 가장 적절한 것은?

① (B) — (D) — (C)
② (C) — (B) — (D)
③ (C) — (D) — (B)
④ (D) — (B) — (C)
⑤ (D) — (C) — (B)

[E-2] 윗글에 관한 내용으로 적절하지 <u>않은</u> 것은?

① 스승이 두 제자에게 길을 끝까지 따라가라고 지시했다.
② 길이 두 갈래로 갈라져 있었다.
③ 첫 번째 제자는 계곡의 너비를 보고 자신감을 보였다.
④ 두 번째 제자는 스승을 보고 미소를 지었다.
⑤ 두 번째 제자는 자신의 선택을 후회하며 길의 끝에 도착했다.

정답과 해설 p.48

STEP 3 • 수능 지문 제대로 복습하기

01 Two students met their teacher / at the start of a track through a forest. // He gave them instructions / to follow the path to its end, / in preparation for a test later in the week. // The path split into two: / one was clear and smooth, / the other had fallen logs and other obstacles in the way.

형용사적 용법

02 One student chose to avoid the obstacles, / taking the easier path to the end. // He felt clever / as he ran without stopping. // The second student chose to tackle the obstacles, / battling through every challenge in his path. // The student who chose the easy path / finished first and felt proud of himself. // "I'm glad / I chose to avoid the rocks and logs.

분사구문 / 분사구문 / 주격 관계대명사절

03 They were only there / to slow me down," / he thought to himself. // The second student arrived at the finish / [feeling tired] / and [regretting the path he had chosen]. // The teacher smiled at them both. // He requested / that they join him / at a specific location in three days. // When they arrived, / they could see a ravine / that was a few meters wide. // The students looked at their teacher / and he said just one word. // "Jump!"

분사구문 병렬연결 / should 생략 / 요구 동사 / 접속사(목적절 연결) / 주격 관계대명사절

04 The first student looked at the distance / and his heart sank. // The teacher looked at him.// "What's wrong? // This is the leap to greatness. // Everything that you've done until now / should have prepared you for this moment." // The student shrugged his shoulders / and walked away, / knowing he hadn't prepared adequately for greatness. // The second student looked at the teacher / and smiled.

목적격 관계대명사절 / 분사구문

05 He knew now / that the obstacles that had been placed in his path / were part of his preparation. // By choosing to overcome challenges, / not avoid them, / he was ready to make the leap. // He ran as fast as he could / and launched himself into the air. // He made it across!

주어(복수) / 주격 관계대명사절 / 수 일치 / to 생략 / as+원급+as+주어+can[could]: 가급적 ~한

01 두 제자는 그들의 스승과 만났다 / 숲을 가로지르는 길의 출발선에서. // 스승은 그들에게 지시**instruction**했다 / 그 길을 끝까지 따라가라고**follow the path** / 그 주의 후반에 있을 테스트를 위한 준비**in preparation for a test**로. // 길은 두 갈래로 갈라졌는데, / 하나는 막힌 것이 없고 평탄했지만, / 다른 하나는 쓰러진 통나무들**fallen log**과 다른 장애물들이 길에 있었다.

02 한 제자는 그 장애물들을 피하기로 결정하고, / 끝까지 더 쉬운 길을 갔다. // 그는 자신이 똑똑하다고 느꼈다 / 한달음에 달려가면서. // 두 번째 제자는 장애물들에 덤벼들기로 결정했다 / 그의 길에 있는 모든 어려움을 통과해 싸우며. // 쉬운 길을 선택했던 제자가 / 먼저 마쳤고 자신을 자랑스럽게 느꼈다. // "난 기쁘다 / 내가 바위와 통나무들을 피하기로 선택해서."

03 그것들은 그곳에 있었을 뿐이야 / 내 속도를 늦추기 위해."/ 라고 그는 마음속으로 생각했다. // 두 번째 제자는 그 길의 끝에 도착했다 / 피곤함을 느끼고 / 그가 선택했던 길을 후회하며**regret**. // 스승은 그들 모두를 보며 미소를 지었다. // 그는 요청했다**request** / 그들에게 그와 만나자고 / 사흘 뒤에 특정 장소**a specific location**에서. // 그들이 도착했을 때, / 그들은 계곡을 볼 수 있었다 / 몇 미터 너비의. // 제자들은 그들의 스승을 보았고, / 스승은 딱 한 마디의 말을 했다. // "뛰어라!"

04 첫 번째 제자는 그 거리를 보고는 / 가슴이 내려앉았다**sink**. // 스승이 그를 쳐다보았다. // "뭐가 문제인가? // 이건 위대함을 위한 도약**leap to greatness**이다. // 네가 지금까지 해 온 모든 것이 / 이 순간을 위해 널 준비시켰어야 했다." // 그 제자는 그의 어깨를 으쓱하고는 / 떠나 버렸다 / 자신이 위대함을 위해 적절하게 준비하지**prepare adequately** 못했다는 것을 알고. // 두 번째 제자는 스승을 보고 / 미소를 지었다.

05 그는 이제 알았다 / 그의 길 위에 놓여 있던 장애물들이 / 그의 준비의 일부였다는 것을. // 어려움을 극복하는 것을 선택함으로써 / 어려움들을 피하는 것이 아니라, / 그는 도약할 준비가 되어 있었다. // 그는 가능한 한 빨리 달렸고 / 자신을 공중으로 내던졌다**launch oneself**. // 그는 건넜다!

F

장문의 이해 +

STEP 1 • 수능에 진짜 나오는 단어

✔ 문제에 나오는 단어들을 확인하세요.

시간이 없다면 색으로 표시된 단어만이라도 꼭 외우고 넘어가세요!

01	alive	a. 살아있는, 살아가는	every adult (✔ alive) today	현재를 살아가는 모든 어른
02	surface	n. 겉, 표면	on the ( )	겉보기에는
03	sentiment	n. 감정, 정서	the ( ) behind the phrase	그 표현 뒤의 감정
04	phrase	n. 구절, 표현	behind these ( )s	이러한 표현 뒤에
05	perception	n. 인지	our ( ) of it	그것에 대한 우리의 인지
06	influence	v. 영향을 주다	be heavily ( )d	매우 영향을 받다
07	absorb	v. 흡수하다	( ) information	정보를 흡수하다
08	task	n. 일, 임무	the enormous ( )	엄청난 임무
09	sensory	a. 감각의	( ) information	감각적 정보
10	alert	a. 기민한	an ( ) scientist	기민한 과학자
11	attentive	a. 집중하는, 주의하는	( ) in class	수업에 집중하는
12	ignore	v. 무시하다	( ) little events	사소한 사건들을 무시하다
13	predictable	a. 예측 가능한	The world becomes ( ).	세상이 예측 가능한 것이 된다.

+ 본문 문장 속에서 단어들을 확인해 보세요.

While different on the surface, / the sentiment behind these phrases is the same: / time feels like it moves faster / as we get older.

겉보기에는 다르지만 / 이러한 표현 뒤에 숨어있는 감정은 매한가지다 / 시간이 더욱 빨리 흐르는 것처럼 느껴진다 / 우리가 나이가 듦에 따라.

단어 다시보기 문제를 풀기 전에 단어들을 30초 동안 다시 확인하세요.

01	alive	살아있는, 살아가는	every adult alive today	현재를 살아가는 모든 어른
02	surface		on the surface	겉보기에는
03	sentiment		the sentiment behind the phrase	그 표현 뒤의 감정
04	phrase		behind these phrases	이러한 표현 뒤에
05	perception		our perception of it	그것에 대한 우리의 인지
06	influence		be heavily influenced	매우 영향을 받다
07	absorb		absorb information	정보를 흡수하다
08	task		the enormous task	엄청난 임무
09	sensory		sensory information	감각적 정보
10	alert		an alert scientist	기민한 과학자
11	attentive		attentive in class	수업에 집중하는
12	ignore		ignore little events	사소한 사건들을 무시하다
13	predictable		The world becomes predictable.	세상이 예측 가능한 것이 된다.

⊕ 본문 문장 속에서 단어의 의미를 우리말로 해석해 보세요.

While different on the surface, / the sentiment behind these phrases is the same: / time feels like it moves faster / as we get older.

→ ______________ 다르지만 / ______________________은 매한가지다 / 시간이 더욱 빨리 흐르는 것처럼 느껴진다 / 우리가 나이가 듦에 따라.

2018 9월 학평 41, 42번 문제

제한시간 120초
난이도 F-1 ★★★☆☆
F-2 ★★★★☆

STEP 2 • 수능 기출 제대로 풀기

F

다음 글을 읽고, 물음에 답하시오.

It's reasonable to assume that every adult alive today has, at some point in their life, expressed or heard from someone else a variation of the following: "Where did all the time go?" "I can't believe it's the New Year. Time flies!" "Enjoy it. One day you'll wake up and you'll be 50." While different on the surface, the sentiment behind these phrases is the same: time feels like it moves faster as we get older. But why does this happen? According to psychologist Robert Ornstein, the speed of time and our perception of it is heavily influenced by how much new information is available for our minds to absorb and process. In essence, the more new information we take in, the slower time feels. This theory could explain in part why time feels slower for children. Assigned the enormous task of absorbing and processing all this new perceptual and sensory information around them, their brains are continuously alert and attentive. Why? Because everything is ________. Consider the mind of a child: having experienced so little, the world is a mysterious and fascinating place. Adults and children may live in the same world, but reality for a child is vastly different — full of wonders and curiosities and miraculous little events that most adults ignore. Perhaps this is why we think so fondly about the joy of childhood, that freedom of mind and body before the world becomes familiar and predictable.

[F-1] 위 글의 제목으로 가장 적절한 것은?

① New Approach for Anti-aging
② Time Can Solve Every Concern
③ Time Management with Smart Devices
④ Reasonable Science behind Time Travel
⑤ Why Time Moves Faster as We Get Older

[F-2] 위 글의 빈칸에 들어갈 말로 가장 적절한 것은?

① unfamiliar
② organized
③ forgotten
④ meaningless
⑤ predetermined

정답과 해설 p.49

STEP 3 • 수능 지문 제대로 복습하기

01 It's reasonable / to assume / that every adult alive today has, / at some point in their life, / expressed or heard from someone else / a variation of the following: / "Where did all the time go?" / "I can't believe it's the New Year. / Time flies!" / "Enjoy it. / One day you'll wake up and you'll be 50."

(It's: 가주어 / to assume: 진주어 / that: 명사절 접속사(to assume의 목적어) / at some point in their life: 현재완료(have와 p.p. 사이에 삽입구))

02 While different on the surface, / the sentiment behind these phrases is the same: / time feels like it moves faster / as we get older. // But why does this happen? // According to psychologist Robert Ornstein, / the speed of time and our perception of it / is heavily influenced / by [how much new information is available / for our minds to absorb and process].

(While: ~하는 반면에, they are 생략 / as: ~함에 따라 / how ~: 의문사절 / for our minds: to부정사의 의미상의 주어 / to absorb and process: to부정사의 형용사적 용법)

03 In essence, / the more new information we take in, / the slower time feels. // This theory could explain / in part / why time feels slower for children. // [Assigned the enormous task of absorbing and processing / all this new perceptual and sensory information around them], / their brains are continuously alert and attentive.

(the 비교급 ~, the 비교급 …: ~할수록 …하다 / why ~: 의문사절(could explain의 목적절) / Assigned ~: 분사구문)

04 Why? // Because everything is unfamiliar. // Consider the mind of a child: / having experienced so little, / the world is a mysterious and fascinating place.

(having experienced so little: 완료분사구문(=As they experienced so little))

05 Adults and children may live in the same world, / but reality for a child is vastly different / —full of wonders and curiosities and miraculous little events / that most adults ignore. // Perhaps this is why we think so fondly / about the joy of childhood, / that freedom of mind and body / before the world becomes familiar and predictable.

(which is 생략 / that: 목적격 관계대명사절 / 선행사(the reason) 생략)

01 온당하다 / 생각하는 것은 / 현재를 살아가는**alive** 모든 어른들이 / 삶의 어느 순간에 / 표현하거나 다른 사람으로부터 들어보았을 것이라고 / 다음의 다양한 표현을: / "그 모든 시간이 어디로 간 거지?" / "벌써 새해라니 믿을 수 없어. / 시간은 빠르게 흘러가!" / "즐겨라! / 어느 날 깨어보면 너는 50살이 되어 있을 거야."

02 겉보기**surface**에는 다르지만 / 이러한 표현**phrase** 뒤에 숨어있는 감정**sentiment**은 매한가지다: / 시간이 더욱 빨리 흐르는 것처럼 느껴진다 / 우리가 나이가 듦에 따라. // 하지만 왜 이런 일이 일어나는 걸까? // 심리학자 Robert Ornstein에 따르면 / 시간의 속도와 그것에 대한 우리의 인지**perception**는 / 매우 영향을 받는다**be influenced** / 새로운 정보가 얼마나 많이 있는가에 / 우리의 마음이 흡수하고**absorb** 처리할 (정보).

03 핵심은, / 우리가 더 많은 새로운 정보를 받아들일수록 / 시간은 더 천천히 흐르는 것으로 느껴진다는 것이다. // 이 이론은 설명할 수 있다 / 부분적으로 / 왜 시간이 아이들에게는 천천히 가는 것으로 느껴지는지를. // 받아들이고 처리하는 엄청난 임무**task**가 주어져서 / 그들 주변에 있는 지각할 수 있고 느낄 수 있는**sensory** 이 모든 새로운 정보를, / 아이들의 뇌는 끊임없이 기민하고**alert** 주의하는**attentive** 상태가 된다.

04 왜 그런가? // 모든 것이 낯설기 때문이다. // 아이의 마음을 생각해보라: / 경험한 것이 거의 없어서 / 세상은 신비하고 흥미로운 장소이다.

05 어른들과 아이들은 똑같은 세상에 살지 모르지만 / 아이에게 현실은 매우 다른데, / 경이로움과 신기함, 그리고 기적 같은 작은 일들로 가득 차 있다 / 대부분의 어른들은 무시하는**ignore**. // 아마도 이것이 왜 우리가 그토록 애정 어리게 생각하는지에 대한 이유이다 / 어린 시절의 즐거움에 대해, / 즉 몸과 마음의 그러한 자유에 대해 / 세상이 친숙하고 예측 가능한**predictable** 것이 되기 이전의.

G

장문의 이해 +

STEP 1 • 수능에 진짜 나오는 단어

✔ 문제에 나오는 단어들을 확인하세요.

시간이 없다면 색으로 표시된 단어만이라도 꼭 외우고 넘어가세요!

01	popular	a. 인기 있는	a (popular) topic	인기 있는 주제
02	planet	n. 지구, 행성	across the ( )	세계 전역에서
03	extinct	a. 멸종된	( ) animals	멸종된 동물들
04	creature	n. 생명체	extinct ( )s	멸종된 생명체
05	fascinating	a. 매혹적인	( ) to children of all ages	모든 연령의 아이들에게 매혹적인
06	imagination	n. 상상	creative ( )	창의적인 상상
07	foster	v. 기르다	( ) creative thinking	창의적 사고력을 기르다
08	primary	a. 초등학교의, 초기의	( ) school teachers	초등학교 교사
09	inspire	v. 영감을 주다	( ) students	학생들에게 영감을 주다
10	footprint	n. 발자국	dinosaurs' ( )s	공룡 발자국
11	extinction	n. 멸종	the mass ( )	대량 멸종
12	fossil	n. 화석	dinosaur ( )s	공룡 화석

⊕ 본문 문장 속에서 단어들을 확인해 보세요.

Something about these extinct creatures from long ago / seems to hold almost everyone's attention, / young or old, boy or girl.

오래전 이 멸종된 생명체에 관한 무언가가 / 거의 모든 사람의 관심을 사로잡는 것처럼 보인다 / 남녀노소를 불문하고.

단어 다시보기 문제를 풀기 전에 단어들을 30초 동안 다시 확인하세요.

01	popular	인기 있는	a popular topic	인기 있는 주제
02	planet		across the planet	세계 전역에서
03	extinct		extinct animals	멸종된 동물들
04	creature		extinct creatures	멸종된 생명체
05	fascinating		fascinating to children of all ages	모든 연령의 아이들에게 매혹적인
06	imagination		creative imagination	창의적인 상상
07	foster		foster creative thinking	창의적 사고력을 기르다
08	primary		primary school teachers	초등학교 교사
09	inspire		inspire students	학생들에게 영감을 주다
10	footprint		dinosaurs' footprints	공룡 발자국
11	extinction		the mass extinction	대량 멸종
12	fossil		dinosaur fossils	공룡 화석

⊕ 본문 문장 속에서 단어의 의미를 우리말로 해석해 보세요.

Something about these extinct creatures from long ago / seems to hold almost everyone's attention, / young or old, boy or girl.

→ 오래전 이 __________에 관한 무언가가 / 거의 모든 사람의 관심을 사로잡는 것처럼 보인다 / 남녀노소를 불문하고.

2017 9월 학평 41, 42번 문제

제한시간 110초
난이도 G-1 ★★★☆☆
G-2 ★★★☆☆

STEP 2 • 수능 기출 제대로 풀기

G 다음 글을 읽고, 물음에 답하시오.

Without a doubt, dinosaurs are a popular topic for kids across the planet. Something about these extinct creatures from long ago seems to hold almost everyone's attention, young or old, boy or girl. Though we don't know a lot about dinosaurs, what we do know is fascinating to children of all ages. But why? "I think the reason kids like dinosaurs so much is that dinosaurs were big, were different from anything alive today, and are extinct. So they are imagination engines," explains Jack Horner, a technical advisor for the Jurassic Park films.

Teachers all over the country would agree. Dinosaurs are studied in classrooms each year, not only for the science behind the topic, but also because of the ______________ thinking it seems to foster in students. "The best part about this is what happens with their writing," Jennifer Zimmerman, a primary school teacher in Washington, D.C., says. "I think it's the mystery of dinosaurs — the fact that there are still so many things we don't know — that inspires them to use that topic in their journals." Children also feel powerful when asked to draw a dinosaur. Since no one knows what colors dinosaurs actually were, a child can use what information he has — and his imagination — to draw a dinosaur as he sees it.

[G-1] 위 글의 제목으로 가장 적절한 것은?

① Why Do Dinosaurs Fascinate Kids?
② A Mystery of Dinosaurs' Footprints
③ How Movies about Dinosaurs Are Made
④ The Next Mass Extinction Is Coming Up!
⑤ The Scientific Meaning Behind Dinosaur Fossils

[G-2] 위 글의 빈칸에 들어갈 말로 가장 적절한 것은?

① ethical
② spatial
③ creative
④ positive
⑤ realistic

정답과 해설 p.49

STEP 3 • 수능 지문 제대로 복습하기

01 Without a doubt, / dinosaurs are a popular topic for kids / across the planet. // Something about these extinct creatures from long ago / seems to hold almost everyone's attention, / young or old, boy or girl.
주어 / seem+to부정사: ~처럼 보인다

02 Though we don't know a lot about dinosaurs, / what we do know / is fascinating to children of all ages.
양보의 접속사: ~에도 불구하고 / 주어(관계대명사절) / 동사(단수)

03 But why? // "I think / the reason kids like dinosaurs so much is / that dinosaurs were big, / were different from anything alive today, / and are extinct. // So they are imagination engines," / explains Jack Horner, / a technical advisor for the Jurassic Park films.
관계부사 why 생략 / 명사절 접속사(보어) / alive는 늘 명사를 뒤에서 수식

04 Teachers all over the country / would agree. // Dinosaurs are studied in classrooms each year, / not only for the science behind the topic, / but also because of the creative thinking / it seems to foster in students.
A뿐만 아니라 B도 / 목적격 관계대명사 생략

05 "The best part about this / is what happens with their writing," / Jennifer Zimmerman, a primary school teacher in Washington, D.C., says. // "I think it's the mystery of dinosaurs / — the fact [that there are still so many things we don't know] / — that inspires them to use that topic in their journals."
관계대명사절 / 동격 / it that 강조 구문 / 동격의 that절 / 목적격 관계대명사 생략

06 Children also feel powerful / when asked to draw a dinosaur. // Since no one knows / what colors dinosaurs actually were, / a child can use what information he has / — and his imagination / — to draw a dinosaur as he sees it.
분사구문: 접속사를 남겨 의미를 명확하게 함 / 이유의 접속사: ~때문에 / 의문형용사절(어떤 ~인지) / 관계형용사절(모든 ~) / 부사적 용법(목적)

01 의심의 여지없이, / 공룡은 아이들에게 인기가 있는 주제**a popular topic**이다 / 세계 전역에서**across the planet**. // 오래전 멸종된 이 생명체**extinct creature**에 관한 무언가가 / 거의 모든 사람의 관심을 사로잡는 것처럼 보인다 / 남녀노소를 불문하고.

02 비록 우리가 공룡에 대해서 많이 알고 있지는 않지만, / 우리가 확실히 아는 것은 / 모든 연령의 아이들에게 매력적**fascinating**이다.

03 하지만 왜일까? // "나는 생각한다 / 아이들이 공룡을 그렇게 많이 좋아하는 이유는 / 공룡이 크고, / 오늘날 살아 있는 그 어떤 것과도 다르고 / 멸종되었기 때문이라고. // 따라서 그들은 상상력**imagination** 엔진이다" / 라고 Jack Horner는 설명한다 / Jurassic Park 영화의 기술 자문관인.

04 전국의 교사들은 / 동의할 것이다. // 공룡은 매년 교실에서 학습된다 / 그 주제 뒤에 숨겨진 과학을 위해서뿐만 아니라 / 창의적 사고력 때문이다 / 그것이 학생들에게 길러주는**foster** 것처럼 보이는.

05 "이에 대한 가장 좋은 점은 / 아이들의 글쓰기에서 나타나는 것이다," / 라고 Washington, D.C.의 초등학교**primary school** 교사인 Jennifer Zimmerman은 말한다. // 내가 생각하기엔 바로 공룡의 미스터리다 / 즉 여전히 우리가 알지 못하는 너무 많은 것이 있다는 그 사실이다 / 아이들로 하여금 자신들의 글에서 그 주제를 사용하도록 영감을 주는**inspire** 것은."

06 아이들은 또한 힘이 있다고 느낀다 / 공룡을 그리도록 요청받았을 때. // 아무도 모르기 때문에 / 공룡이 실제로 어떤 색이었는지 / 아이는 자신이 가진 모든 정보를 사용할 수 있다 / 그리고 상상력을 (사용할 수 있다) / 자신이 상상하는 대로 공룡을 그리기 위해서.

Review

DAY 13~14

☑ 종합 성적표

구분	공부한 날 ❶	결과 분석			틀린 이유 ❸
		출처	풀이 시간 ❷	채점 결과 (O, ×)	
Day 13	월 일	학력평가 기출 2023년	분 초		
		학력평가 기출 2022년	분 초		
		학력평가 기출 2021년	분 초		
		학력평가 기출 2020년	분 초		
		학력평가 기출 2019년	분 초		
		학력평가 기출 2018년	분 초		
		학력평가 기출 2017년	분 초		
Day 14	월 일	학력평가 기출 2023년	분 초		
		학력평가 기출 2022년	분 초		
		학력평가 기출 2021년	분 초		
		학력평가 기출 2020년	분 초		
		학력평가 기출 2019년	분 초		
		학력평가 기출 2018년	분 초		
		학력평가 기출 2017년	분 초		

2일간 공부한 내용을 다시 보니, ……

❶ **매일 지문을 하루 계획에 맞춰 풀었다. vs. 내가 한 약속을 못 지켰다.**

<매3영 고1 기출>은 단순 문제풀이를 위한 책이 아니라, 매일 규칙적으로 영어를 공부하는 습관을 잡는 책입니다. 따라서 푸는 문제 개수는 상황에 따라 다르더라도 '매일' 학습하는 것이 중요합니다.

❷ **주어진 시간을 자꾸 넘긴다?**

풀이 시간이 계속해서 권장 시간을 넘긴다면 실전 훈련이 부족하다는 신호입니다. 아직 조급함을 가질 필요는 없지만, 매일의 문제 풀이에 더 긴장감 있게 임해보세요.

❸ **틀린 이유 맞춤 솔루션**: 오답 이유에 따라 다음 해결책을 참고하세요.

(1) 단어를 많이 몰라서
 ▶ <STEP 1 단어>에 제시된 필수 어휘를 매일 챙겨보고, SELF-TEST까지 꼼꼼히 진행합니다.

(2) 문장 해석이 잘 안 돼서
 ▶ <STEP 3 지문 복습>의 구문 첨삭과 끊어읽기 해설을 정독하며 문장구조를 보는 눈을 길러보세요.

(3) 해석은 되지만 내용이 이해가 안 되거나, 선택지로 연결을 못 해서
 ▶ <정답과 해설>의 해설과 오답풀이를 참고해 틀린 이유를 깊이 고민하고 정리해 보세요.

!

결론적으로, 내가 **취약한 부분**은 ______ 이다. **취약점을 보완하기 위해서** 나는 ______ 을/를 해야겠다.

3일 뒤 다시 봐야 할 문항과, 꼭 다시 외워야 할 사항·구문 등이 있는 페이지는 지금 바로 접어 두세요.

Memo

Memo

Memo

고1

매일 3단계로 푸는 영어독해

전국연합 학력평가 기출

정답 및 해설

고1

매일 3단계로 푸는 영어독해

전국연합 학력평가 기출

정답 및 해설

DAY 01 글의 요지 / 주제 추론

A③ B① C⑤ D② E① F⑤ G②

A 정답 ③ 49% 2023 6월 학평

해석 우리가 듣기로, 컴퓨터화된 사회의 약속은 그것이 모든 반복적인 고된 일을 기계에 넘겨, 우리 인간들이 더 높은 목적을 추구하고 더 많은 여가 시간을 가질 수 있게 해준다는 것이었다. 일은 이렇게 풀리지는 않았다. 더 많은 시간 대신에, 우리 대부분은 더 적은 시간을 가진다. 크고 작은 회사들은 일을 소비자들의 등에 떠넘겼다. 회사에 맡겨 해결하던 부가가치 서비스의 일환으로, 우리를 위해 행해지던 것들을 이제 우리는 직접 하도록 기대받는다. 항공 여행의 경우, 항공사 직원이나 여행사 직원들에 의해 행해지던 일인 예약과 체크인을 이제는 우리가 직접 완수하도록 기대된다. 식료품점에서는 우리가 우리 식료품을 직접 봉지에 넣도록 기대되며, 일부 슈퍼에서는 우리가 구매한 물건을 직접 스캔하도록 기대된다.

해설 컴퓨터화된 사회는 우리에게 더 많은 여가 시간을 가져다줄 것으로 기대됐지만, 실상은 정반대의 일이 일어났다는 내용이다. 즉 고객이 직접 하는 일이 더 많아지게 됐다는 것이다. 따라서 요지로 가장 적절한 것은 ③ '컴퓨터화된 사회에서 소비자는 더 많은 일을 하게 된다.'이다.

오답 풀이

선택률	보기 해석
① 16%	여가가 오히려 '줄어든다'는 내용이 주제다.
② 5%	능률 향상에 관해서는 언급되지 않았다.
④ 5%	만족도에 관해서는 언급되지 않았다.
⑤ 25%	기계가 일자리를 대신할 줄 알았지만 오히려 인간이 직접 할 일이 더 '늘어났다'는 내용이 주제다.

구문 풀이 6행

Things that used to be done for us, as part of the value-added service of working with a company, **we are now expected to do** ourselves.

→ to do의 목적어가 문장 앞으로 나간 후 <주어+동사구>가 이어졌다. to do는 엄밀히 말하면 5형식 수동태 be expected의 보어이지만, 대략 'are ~ to do'까지를 하나의 동사구로 보고 목적어가 앞으로 나갔다고 이해하면 쉽다.

구문 플러스⁺ 목적어 도치

목적어를 강조하고자 문장 앞으로 빼면, 뒤에 <주어+동사>는 순서대로 나온다. 단, 목적어에 부정어구가 포함돼 있으면 의문문 어순 도치가 일어난다.

Something we'll never forget. → 목적어+주어+동사
cf. **Not a word** could I say. → 의문문 어순(조동사+주어+동사원형)

B 정답 ① 92% 2022 3월 학평

해석 많은 사람이 수면을 그저 뇌가 멈추고 신체가 쉬는 '가동되지 않는 시간'으로 본다. 일, 학교, 가족, 또는 가정의 책임을 다하기 위해 서두르는 와중에 사람들은 수면 시간을 줄이고, 그것이 문제가 되지 않을 것으로 생각하는데, 왜냐하면 이러한 모든 다른 활동들이 훨씬 더 중요해 보이기 때문이다. 하지만 연구는 수면 중에 수행되는 많은 매우 중요한 과업이 건강을 유지하는 데 도움이 되고 사람들이 최상의 수준으로 기능할 수 있게 해 준다는 것을 밝히고 있다. 잠을 자는 동안, 여러분의 뇌는 학습, 그리고 기억과 새로운 통찰을 만드는 것에 필수적인 경로를 형성하느라 열심히 일하고 있다. 충분한 수면이 없다면, 여러분은 정신을 집중하고 주의를 기울이거나 빠르게 반응할 수 없다. 수면 부족은 심지어 감정 (조절) 문제를 일으킬 수도 있다. 게다가, 계속된 수면 부족이 심각한 질병을 발생시킬 위험을 증가시킨다는 것을 점점 더 많은 증거가 보여준다.

해설 많은 사람들이 수면을 중요하게 생각하지 않지만, 실은 충분한 수면이 우리에게 중요하다는 내용이므로 정답은 ① '수면은 건강 유지와 최상의 기능 발휘에 도움이 된다.'이다.

오답 풀이

선택률	오답 풀이
② 3%	업무량과 수면 시간 사이의 관련성에 대해 언급하지 않았다.
③ 1%	균형 잡힌 식단에 대해 언급하지 않았다.
④ 2%	주위 사람들에 대한 영향에 대해 언급하지 않았다.
⑤ 1%	꿈의 내용에 대해 언급하지 않았다.

구문 풀이 2행

In a rush to meet work, school, family, or household responsibilities, people cut back on their sleep, **thinking it won't be a problem**, because all of these other activities seem much more important.

→ 문장의 동사는 cut back on이고, thinking ~ problem은 주어 people의 행위를 보충 설명하는 분사구문이다.

구문 플러스⁺ 분사구문

분사구문은 <접속사 + 주어 + 동사>의 부사절을 분사를 이용해서 간단한 부사구로 나타낸 것이다. 시간, 이유, 조건, 양보, 부대상황 등의 의미를 나타낸다.

As she came up the steps, Jane found her ring.
= **Coming up the steps**, Jane found her ring.

C 정답 ⑤ 54% 2021 9월 학평

해석 독자적으로 생각하고 자신이 믿는 것을 위해 싸우는 것도 중요하지만, 자신의 생각을 위해 싸우는 것을 중단하고 신뢰할 수 있는 집단이 가장 좋다고 생각하는 것을 받아들이는 쪽으로 나아가는 것이 현명한 때가 온다. 이것은 매우 어려울 수 있다. 하지만 여러분이 마음을 열고 신뢰할 수 있는 집단의 결론이 여러분이 생각하는 그 무엇보다 낫다는 믿

음을 갖는 것이 더 영리하고 궁극적으로 더 좋다. 만약 여러분이 그들의 생각을 이해할 수 없다면, 여러분은 아마도 단지 그들이 생각하는 방식을 보지 못하는 것이다. 모든 증거가 불리하고 신뢰할 수 있는 사람들이 당신에게 반대할 때 당신이 최선이라고 생각하는 것을 계속한다면, 당신은 위험할 정도로 자신감에 차 있는 것이다. 사실 대부분의 사람들은 믿을 수 없을 정도로 마음을 열 수 있는 반면에, 어떤 사람들은 자신이 옳지 않았을 때 옳았다고 확신하는 것으로부터 많은 고통을 반복적으로 겪고 난 후에도 그럴 수 없다는 것이다.

해설 자신의 생각을 고수하기보다 신뢰할 수 있는 집단의 의견을 들어야 한다는 내용이므로 정답은 ⑤ '자신의 의견이 최선이 아닐 수 있다는 것을 인정하는 것이 필요하다.'이다.

오답 풀이

선택률	오답 풀이
① 5%	진리에 도달하지 못하는 고통에 대한 언급이 없다.
② 7%	다른 사람의 의견을 받아들이는 것의 위험성에 대한 언급이 없다.
③ 4%	남을 설득하는 방법에 대한 언급이 없다.
④ 29%	믿을 만한 사람을 판단하는 방법에 대한 언급이 없다.

구문 풀이 2행

there comes a time when it's wiser to stop fighting for your view and move on to accepting what **a trustworthy group of people think** is best.

→ 관계사절에 <주어+동사>의 삽입 구문이 끼어든 형태이다. 이 때 삽입 구문의 동사는 believe, think, guess, know, suppose 등 생각이나 추측의 의미를 가진 동사가 쓰인다.

구문 플러스+ 관계대명사 삽입절

관계절이 <주격 관·대+(S'+V')+V~>의 구조이면 관계대명사 삽입절을 떠올리도록 한다.

I saw a man at the store **who I think is** my neighbor.
→ '내가 생각하기로 내 이웃인 남자'

The person **who we all believe is** the best candidate got the job.
→ '우리 모두가 믿기로 최적의 후보'

D 정답 ② 64% 2020 9월 학평

해석 인간뿐만 아니라 동물도 놀이 활동에 참여한다. 동물에게 있어 놀이는 오랫동안 미래 생존에 필요한 기술과 행동을 학습하고 연마하는 방식으로 여겨져 왔다. 아이들에게 있어서도 놀이는 발달하는 동안 중요한 기능을 한다. 유아기의 가장 초기부터, 놀이는 아이들이 세상과 그 안에서의 그들의 위치에 대해 배우는 방식이다. 아이들의 놀이는 신체능력, 즉 매일의 삶에 필요한 걷기, 달리기, 그리고 점프하기와 같은 기술을 발달시키기 위한 훈련의 토대로서 역할을 한다. 놀이는 또한 아이들이 사회적 행동을 시도하고 배우며, 성인기에 중요할 가치와 성격적 특성을 습득하도록 한다. 예를 들어, 그들은 다른 사람들과 경쟁하고 협력하는 방식, 이끌고 따르는 방식과 결정하는 방식 등을 배운다.

해설 놀이를 통해 아이의 신체 능력뿐만 아니라 사회화를 배울 수 있다고 했으므로 ② '아이의 발달에 놀이의 역할'이 주제로 적절하다.

오답 풀이

선택률	보기 해석
① 2%	창의적인 생각을 시도해보는 필요성
③ 5%	인간과 동물의 놀이의 차이
④ 21%	놀이에 있어 아이의 신체적인 능력의 영향
⑤ 6%	다양한 발달단계에서 아이의 욕구

구문 풀이 8행

Play also **allows** children **to try out and learn** social behaviors and **to acquire** values and personality traits ~

→ 동사 allow의 목적격 보어로 to부정사가 오며, to try out and learn, to acquire가 연결되어 있다.

구문 플러스+ 병렬 구조 (1)

형태가 같은 것끼리 접속사 and로 연결하여 글의 구조를 쉽게 파악하게 해준다.

They saw him **jump**, **snatch up slippers** and **run into the fence**.
목적격 보어

E 정답 ① 46% 2019 11월 학평

해석 여러분은 정보가 다른 뇌로 전달될 때까지 한 뇌에 머물러 있으며 대화 속에서 변하지 않는다고 말할 수 있다. 이는 여러분의 전화번호나 여러분이 열쇠를 놓아둔 장소처럼 '단순' 정보에 대해서는 사실이다. 하지만 이것은 지식에 대해서는 사실이 아니다. 지식은 판단에 의존하는데, 여러분은 다른 사람들 혹은 자신과의 대화 속에서 그 판단을 발견하고 다듬는다. 그러므로 여러분은 상세하게 이야기하거나 쓰고 그 결과를 비판적으로 되돌아볼 때까지 여러분 사고의 세부 내용을 알지 못한다. "내가 방금 이야기한 것이 바보 같은가, 혹은 내가 방금 쓴 것이 깊은 진실인가?" 말하거나 쓸 때, 여러분은 형편없는 생각들, 흔히 당황스러운 생각들을 발견하게 되고, 좋은 생각도 발견하게 되며, 때로는 유명하게 만들어 주는 생각도 발견하게 된다. 사고는 그 표현이 필요하다.

해설 사고 내용을 정확하게 알고 다듬어 나가려면 상세하게 이야기하거나 써보는 등 '표현'의 과정을 거치라는 내용이다. 따라서 주제로 가장 적절한 것은 ① '생각을 다듬는 데 있어 말하기나 글쓰기의 중요한 역할'이다.

오답 풀이

선택률	보기 해석
② 17%	당신의 생각을 사람들에게 전달할 설득력 있는 방법
③ 19%	글쓰기에 적합한 정보를 선택하는 데 중요한 조언
④ 9%	논리적 사고가 독해에 미치는 긍정적 영향
⑤ 8%	구어와 문어 사이의 거대한 격차

구문 풀이 8행

~ you uncover your bad **ideas**, often embarrassing **ones**, and good **ideas** too, sometimes fame-making **ones**. Thinking requires its expression.

→ 복수명사 ideas를 받는 부정대명사 ones를 썼다.

구문 플러스⁺ it vs. one

it: 앞에 나온 명사를 그대로 받을 때

one: 앞에 나온 명사와 같은 종류이면서 동일하지 않은 대상을 받을 때

→ 수식어구 동반 가능

A: Where did you put **the key**? / B: I think I've lost **it**.

I don't like this yellow **car**. I'd like a blue **one**.

관사+형용사

F 정답 ⑤ 70% 2018 9월 학평

해석 당신의 아이의 지능과 재능을 칭찬하는 것은 그의 자존감을 높이고 그에게 동기를 부여하는 것처럼 보일지도 모른다. 그러나 이런 종류의 칭찬은 역효과를 일으키는 것으로 밝혀진다. Carol Dweck과 그녀의 동료들은 일련의 실험적 연구들에서 그 효과를 보여주었다: "우리가 그들의 능력에 대해 아이들을 칭찬할 때, 아이들은 더 조심하게 된다. 그들은 도전을 피한다." 그것은 마치 그들이 자신들을 실패하게 만들고 당신의 높은 평가를 잃게 할지도 모를 어떤 것을 하길 두려워하는 것과 같다. 아이들은 또한 지능이나 재능이 사람들이 가지거나 가지지 못하는 어떤 것이라는 메시지를 받을지도 모른다. 이것은 아이들이 실수했을 때 무기력하게 느끼도록 만든다. 만약 당신의 실수가 당신이 지능이 부족하다는 것을 나타낸다면 향상하도록 노력하는 것이 무슨 소용이겠는가?

해설 아이들을 칭찬하는 것이 역효과를 일으킬 수도 있다는 내용이다. 따라서 정답은 ⑤ '아이의 지능과 재능에 대한 칭찬은 아이에게 부정적 영향을 끼친다.'이다.

오답 풀이

선택률	보기 해석
① 4%	놀이 시간의 부족에 대한 언급이 없다.
② 6%	구체적인 칭찬의 영향력에 대한 언급이 없다.
③ 12%	아이의 능력에 맞는 도전 과제는 언급되어 있지 않다.
④ 5%	자신의 잘못을 인정하는 태도는 칭찬의 역효과와 관계가 없다.

구문 풀이 7행

Kids might also get the message that intelligence or talent is something that people **either** have **or** don't have.

→ <either A or B>는 'A 또는 B 둘 중 하나'의 의미로, A와 B의 문법적 형태는 동일해야 한다.

구문 플러스⁺ either A or B

<either A or B>는 'A 또는 B 둘 중 하나'의 의미로 <either A or B>가 주어로 쓰이면 동사는 B에 일치시킨다.

Either he **or** I **am** going to enter the contest.

G 정답 ② 74% 2017 9월 학평

해석 새로운 기기, 옷, 혹은 무작위 잡동사니들을 사는 것은 그 자체로도 취미가 될 수 있다. 여러분이 다소 돈을 절약하고 싶다면, 물건을 사기보다는 무언가를 만드는 데서 즐거움을 찾도록 노력해라. 우리는 물건을 사는 것으로부터 얻는 (것과 똑같은) 만족감을 무언가를 만드는 것으로부터 얻는다. 만약에 여러분이 자랑스러워하는 무언가를 그리거나, 즐기는 무언가를 글로 쓴다면, 이제 여러분을 행복하게 만들어 주는 새로운 것을 삶에서 얻은 것이다. 새로운 기기를 사는 것이 여러분에게 비슷한 흥분감을 줄 수 있지만 그것은 아마도 더 일시적일 것이다. 물론, 우리가 추천하는 것도 돈이 들 수 있다. 그러나, 여러분이 돈을 쓸 수 없다면, 여러분은 언제나 온라인에서 공예기술에 관해서 더 배우거나 여러분이 이미 가지고 있는 것을 연습할 수 있다. 비록 여러분이 직접 무언가를 만드는 데 결국 돈을 쓰게 될지라도, 가치가 급격히 떨어지게 될 물건을 수집하기보다는 여러분은 적어도 기술을 키워 나가고 있는 것이다.

해설 단순히 소비하는 것이 아니라 무언가를 만드는 창의적인 일들에서 더 큰 만족을 느낄 수 있다고 말하고 있다. 따라서 정답은 ② '무언가를 만드는 것이 쇼핑보다 더 좋은 이유'이다.

오답 풀이

선택률	보기 해석
① 7%	취미로서의 기계 수집에 대한 오해들
③ 7%	값비싼 취미의 부정적인 효과
④ 6%	지혜롭게 옷을 구입하는 방법
⑤ 3%	취미로 옷 쇼핑하기

구문 풀이 2행

If you'd rather save your money, try finding pleasure in creating things **rather than** buying things.

→ <rather than~>은 '~하기 보다'라는 의미로 앞에 비교급이 없어도 쓸 수 있다.

구문 플러스⁺ rather than 구문

<prefer A to B>는 <prefer A rather than B>의 의미이다.

I **prefer** ramen **to** Gimbop.

→ I **prefer** ramen **rather than** Gimbop.

유형 플러스⁺ 글의 요지 / 주제 추론

글의 요지와 주제 추론은 글의 전체적인 내용을 파악하고 말하고자 하는 바를 압축한 답을 찾는 유형이다.

유형 해결 방법: 첫 문장 확인하기

① 첫 문장에서 사실적 정보, 글쓴이의 주장이나 의견을 직접 표현한다면 주제일 확률이 높다.

② 첫 문장이 두 가지 요소를 비교, 대조하여 강조하거나, 질문이나 문제점을 언급하는 경우 이에 대한 해결책이 요지나 주제일 수 있다.

③ 첫 문장이 잘못된 상식이나 정보를 제시하는 경우, 중반부에 역접 연결어가 등장하며 주제를 제시한다. 첫 문장과 대비되는 반전 내용이 답이 되기도 한다.

DAY 02 제목 추론

A② B② C① D⑤ E② F① G②

A 정답 ② 71%

2023 3월 학평

해석 성공은 여러분을 의도한 길에서 벗어나 틀에 박힌 편안한 생활로 이끌 수 있다. 여러분이 어떤 일을 잘하고 그것을 하는 데 대한 보상을 잘 받는다면, 그것을 즐기지 않게 되더라도 계속 그것을 하고 싶을 수도 있다. 위험한 점은, 어느 날 여러분이 주위를 둘러보며 여러분이 이 틀에 박힌 편안한 생활에 너무나 깊이 빠져 더는 태양을 보거나 신선한 공기를 마시지 못함을 알게 된다는 것이다. 그 틀에 박힌 생활의 양쪽 면이 너무나 미끄러워져서, 기어올라 나오려면 초인적인 노력이 필요할 것이고, 사실상 자신이 꼼짝할 수 없다는 것을 깨닫는다는 것이다. 그리고 그것은 많은 근로자가 현재 자신이 처해 있다고 걱정하는 상황이다. 열악한 고용 시장이 그들을 안정적이거나 심지어 보수가 좋을 수도 있지만, 궁극적으로는 만족스럽지 못한 일자리에 갇혀 있다고 느끼게 하였다.

해설 직업적 성공이 오히려 틀에 박힌 생활로 향하는 원인이 된다는 글로, 첫 문장에 주제가 잘 제시된다. 따라서 제목으로는 ② '성공적인 일자리의 덫'이 가장 적절하다.

오답 풀이

선택률	보기 해석
① 10%	자기 자신과 경쟁하지 말라
③ 5%	젊은이들을 위한 일자리를 더 창출하라
④ 8%	힘든 일자리의 공통점
⑤ 5%	영향력 있는 고용주가 되기 위한 로드맵

구문 풀이 7행

~ **it**'s a situation **that** many working people worry they're in now.

→ it(그것)은 앞 문장을 받는 대명사이고, that은 목적격 관계대명사이다. 'it ~ that …' 강조구문(…한 것은 바로 ~이다)과 혼동하지 않도록 한다.

구문 플러스⁺ 주의할 it ~ that 구문

- it(대명사=그것): that절은 다른 명사를 보충하는 수식어일 수 있음
- it(가주어) - that(진주어): it은 해석하지 않고, that절을 주어에 넣어 해석
- it is[was] ~ that …(강조구문): …한 것은 바로 ~이다

It's a lie **that** no one believes.
대명사 수식

It's a fact **that** earth is getting warmer.
가주어 진주어

It's the weather **that** bothers me the most.
강조구문

B 정답 ② 66%

2022 3월 학평

해석 감정을 정확하게 인식하고 그것에 이름을 붙일 수 있는 우리의 능력은 흔히 '감정 입자도'라고 불린다. Harvard 대학의 심리학자인 Susan David의 말에 의하면, "더 미묘한 차이가 있는 어휘로 감정에 이름을 붙이는 법을 배우는 것은 절대적으로 (사람을) 변화시킬 수 있다." David는 우리가 풍부한 감정 어휘를 갖고 있지 않으면 우리의 욕구를 전달하고 우리가 필요로 하는 지지를 다른 사람들로부터 얻는 것이 어렵다고 설명한다. 그러나 광범위한 다양한 감정을 구별할 수 있는 사람들은 "모든 것을 흑백 논리로 보는 사람들보다 평범한 존재로 사는 중에 겪는 좋은 일들과 궂은 일들을 관리하는 것을 훨씬 훨씬 더 잘한다." 사실, 감정 경험에 이름을 붙이는 과정은 더 탁월한 감정 조절 및 심리 사회적 행복과 관련되어 있다는 것을 연구 결과가 보여 준다.

해설 감정을 정확하게 인식, 구별하고 그것에 더 정교한 이름을 붙일수록 좋다는 내용이므로 가장 적절한 제목은 ② '감정에 세세한 이름을 붙이는 것은 유익하다'이다.

오답 풀이

선택률	오답 풀이
① 3%	진짜 우정은 감정적 논쟁을 견딘다
③ 22%	감정에 이름 붙이기: 행동보다 말이 쉽다
④ 4%	효율성을 위해 과업을 구별하고 이름 붙이라
⑤ 3%	용감해져서 당신의 욕구를 전달하라

구문 풀이 1행

Our ability to accurately recognize and label emotions **is often referred to as** *emotional granularity*.

→ 숙어 'refer to A as B (A를 B라고 부르다)'의 수동태 문장이다.

구문 플러스⁺ 수동태

'refer to A as B'의 수동태는 'A is referred to as B'가 된다.

People **refer to** him **as** 'the good man.'
→ He **is referred to as** 'the good man' (by people).

C 정답 ① 76%

2021 6월 학평

해석 사람들은 도시 발전에 대해 생각할 때, 수직 운송 수단의 중요한 역할을 거의 고려하지 않는다. 실제로 매일 70억회 이상의 엘리베이터 이동이 전세계 높은 빌딩에서 이루어진다. 효율적인 수직 운송 수단은 점점 더 높은 고층 건물을 만들 수 있는 우리의 능력을 확장시킬 수 있다. Illinois 공과대학의 건축학과 교수인 Antony Wood는 지난 20년 간의 엘리베이터의 발전은 아마도 우리가 높은 건물에서 봐왔던 가장 큰 발전이라고 설명한다. 예를 들어, 건설 중인 사우디 아라비아 Jeddah의 Jeddah Tower에 있는 엘리베이터는 660미터라는 기록적인 높이에 이를 것이다.

해설 수직 운송 수단이 고층 건물 건축에 중요한 역할을 한다는 내용이므로 가장 적절한 제목은 ① '엘리베이터들이 건물들을 하늘에 더 가깝게 만든다'이다.

오답 풀이

선택률	보기 해석
② 5%	더 높이 올라갈수록 더 경치가 좋다
③ 5%	엘리베이터를 싸고 빠르게 건설하는 방법
④ 6%	고대 도시와 현대 도시의 기능
⑤ 6%	건축의 진화: 인구과밀에 대한 해결책

구문 풀이 1행

When people think about the development of cities, **rarely do they** consider the critical role of vertical transportation.

→ Rarely 등의 부정어구로 시작되는 절의 '주어-동사' 부분은 의문문 어순으로 도치된다.

구문 플러스+ 부정어구 도치

Never, Rarely, Little 등의 부정어구로 절이 시작하면 '주어-동사' 순서에 도치가 발생한다.

Never has he done his homework.
Rarely does it melt under the Sun.
Little did I know that you would come so early.

D 정답 ⑤ 65% 2020 6월 학평

해석 여러분을 미소 짓게 만드는 온갖 사건들은 여러분이 행복감을 느끼게 하고, 여러분의 뇌에서 기분을 좋게 만들어주는 화학물질을 생산해내도록 한다. 심지어 스트레스를 받거나 불행하다고 느낄 때조차 미소를 지어보자. 미소에 의해 만들어지는 안면 근육의 형태는 뇌의 모든 "행복 연결망"과 연결되어 있고, 따라서 자연스럽게 여러분을 안정시키고 기분을 좋게 만들어주는 동일한 화학물질들을 배출함으로써 뇌의 화학 작용을 변화시킬 것이다. 연구자들은 스트레스가 상당한 상황에서 진정한 미소와 억지 미소가 개개인들에게 미치는 영향을 연구하였다. 연구자들은 참가자들이 미소 짓지 않거나, 미소 짓거나, (억지 미소를 짓게 하기 위해) 입에 젓가락을 옆으로 물고서 스트레스를 수반한 과업을 수행하도록 했다. 연구의 결과는 미소가 억지이든 진정한 것이든 스트레스가 상당한 상황에서 인체의 스트레스 반응의 강도를 줄였고, 스트레스로부터 회복한 후의 심박수도 낮추었다는 것을 보여주었다.

해설 연구에 따르면 미소는 그것이 진정한 것이든 억지이든 스트레스 상황을 극복하는 데 도움을 준다는 내용이므로, 가장 적절한 제목은 ⑤ '억지 미소도 스트레스를 줄이는 데 도움이 될까요?'이다.

오답 풀이

선택률	보기 해석
① 8%	스트레스 상황의 원인과 결과
② 4%	스트레스의 개인적인 징후와 양상
③ 12%	신체와 정신이 스트레스에 반응하는 방식
④ 8%	스트레스: 행복의 필요악

구문 풀이 1행

Every event that causes you to smile makes you feel happy and produces feel-good chemicals in your brain.

→ 이 문장의 주어는 Every event이고 동사는 makes와 produces가 and로 연결되고 있다.

구문 플러스+ every+단수명사의 수 일치

every는 의미상 복수이지만 단수 취급하므로 수 일치할 때 주의한다.

Every breath **takes** me closer to my baby.
수 일치

E 정답 ② 75% 2019 9월 학평

해석 Benjamin Franklin은 예전에 '너에게 친절을 행한 적이 있는 사람은 네가 친절을 베풀었던 사람보다도 너에게 또 다른 친절을 행할 준비가 더 되어 있을 것이다.'라는 옛 격언을 인용하며 동네에 새로 온 사람은 새 이웃에게 도움을 요청해야 한다고 제안했다. Franklin의 의견으로는, 누군가에게 무언가를 요구하는 것은 사회적 상호작용으로의 가장 유용하고 즉각적인 초대였다. 새로 온 사람 쪽에서의 그러한 요청은 자신을 좋은 사람으로 보여줄 수 있는 기회를 이웃에게 첫 만남에 제공했던 것이다. 또한 그것은 이제 후자(이웃)가 전자(새로 온 사람)에게 부탁할 수 있으며 그 보답으로 친밀함과 신뢰를 증진시킨다는 것을 의미했다. 그러한 방식으로, 양쪽은 당연한 머뭇거림과 낯선 사람에 대한 상호 두려움을 극복할 수 있을 것이다.

해설 도움을 요청하는 일이 친밀감과 신뢰의 관계를 키울 수 있는 일이라고 했기 때문에 ② '관계를 여는 도구: 부탁하기'가 정답이다.

오답 풀이

선택률	오답 풀이
① 4%	자신의 강점을 남들에게 보여주는 방법
③ 7%	우리는 왜 이방인을 돕는 데 주저하는가?
④ 6%	요구하는 바가 자신이 누구인가를 보여준다
⑤ 5%	이웃을 초대하는 정중한 방법들

구문 풀이 1행

Benjamin Franklin once **suggested** that a newcomer to a neighborhood **ask** a new neighbor to do him or her a favor, ~

→ 주장, 요구, 명령, 제안, 충고 등의 동사 뒤에 that절이 목적어로 나올 때, that절이 당위의 의미(~해야 한다)로 해석된다면 that절의 동사 자리에는 (should) 동사원형을 쓴다. 여기서도 a newcomer가 단수 주어이지만 ask가 원형으로 쓰였다.

구문 플러스⁺ that 목적절의 should 생략

주장 - insist
요구 - request, ask, demand
명령 - command, order + that S **(should)** V
제안 - suggest, propose ~해야 하다
충고 - recommend, advise

He **insisted** that she **leave** immediately.
She **suggested** that her son **practice** more.

F 정답 ① 73% 2018 6월 학평

해석 포유류는 다른 동물군에 비해 색이 덜 화려한 경향이 있지만 얼룩말은 두드러지게 흑백의 모습을 하고 있다. 이러한 높은 대비의 무늬가 무슨 목적을 수행할까? 색의 역할이 항상 명확한 것은 아니다. 줄무늬를 지님으로써 얼룩말이 얻을 수 있는 것이 무엇인지에 대한 이 질문은 과학자들을 1세기가 넘도록 곤혹스럽게 했다. 이 수수께끼를 풀기 위해, 야생 생물학자 Tim Caro는 탄자니아에서 얼룩말을 연구하면서 10년 이상을 보냈다. 그는 답을 찾기 전에 이론을 하나씩 하나씩 배제해 나갔다. 줄무늬는 얼룩말들을 시원하게 유지시켜 주지도 않았고, 포식자들을 혼란스럽게 하지도 않았다. 2013년에 그는 얼룩말의 가죽으로 덮인 파리 덫을 설치했고, 이와 대비하여 영양의 가죽으로 덮인 다른 덫들도 준비했다. 그는 파리가 줄무늬 위에 앉는 것을 피하는 것처럼 보인다는 것을 알게 되었다. 더 많은 연구 후에, 그는 줄무늬가 질병을 옮기는 곤충으로부터 얼룩말을 말 그대로 구할 수 있다는 결론을 내렸다.

해설 얼룩말의 줄무늬가 파리를 쫓는 역할을 할 수 있음을 밝히는 글이므로 ① '얼룩말의 줄무늬: 파리에 대한 자연 방어'가 정답이다.

오답 풀이

선택률	보기 해석
② 6%	어떤 포유류가 가장 색이 화려한 피부를 갖고 있는가?
③ 6%	어떤 동물이 얼룩말의 포식자인가?
④ 8%	무늬: 숨기 위한 것이 아니라 과시하기 위한 것
⑤ 5%	각각의 얼룩말은 고유의 독특한 줄무늬를 가지고 태어난다

구문 풀이 11행

After more research, he concluded that stripes can literally save zebras from **disease-carrying insects**.

→ '명사+분사' 형태의 복합형용사가 insects를 꾸민다. 수식받는 insects가 '병을 옮겨 다니는' 주체이므로 carrying을 현재분사로 썼다.

구문 플러스⁺ 복합형용사

'명사+분사'가 하이픈(-)으로 결합되어 하나의 형용사로 쓰일 때, 현재분사와 과거분사 중 무엇을 쓸지는 수식받는 명사를 기준으로 판단한다.

a **time-consuming** process
→ process가 '시간이 들게 하는' 주체
a **brightly-lit** corridor
→ corridor가 '불이 밝혀진' 대상

G 정답 ② 80% 2017 9월 학평

해석 과잉보호하는 부모들은 아이들이 모든 자연적 결과를 경험하지 못하게 막는다. 불행히도, 그들의 자녀는 종종 부모가 정한 규칙 이면의 이유를 명확하게 이해하지 못한다. 부모들이 아이들이 잘못된 선택을 하지 않도록 막았기 때문에 아이들은 결코 실패로부터 다시 일어나거나 실수로부터 회복하는 법을 배우지 못한다. 아이는 "밖에 날씨가 춥기 때문에 외투를 입어야지"라고 배우기보다는, "엄마가 시키니까 외투를 입어야지"라고 결론을 낼지도 모른다. 실제 세상이 주는 결과를 경험할 기회가 없으면, 아이들은 그들의 부모가 왜 특정한 규칙들을 만드는지 항상 이해하는 것은 아니다. 자연적 결과는 아이들의 선택이 가져오는 잠재적인 결과에 대해 생각하게 도와 그들이 성인기를 대비할 수 있도록 해준다.

해설 부모의 과잉보호가 아이의 성장을 가로막는 방해가 된다는 글이므로 ② '자연스러운 결과가 아이들을 가르치게 하라'가 정답이다.

오답 풀이

선택률	보기 해석
① 3%	가상현실의 어두운 면
③ 7%	많은 선택이 있을수록 더 많은 실수를 한다
④ 5%	관계를 개선할 수 있도록 아이의 말에 귀 기울이라
⑤ 4%	과잉보호 양육의 이점들

구문 풀이 1행

Overprotective parents **spare** kids **from** all natural consequences.

→ spare가 전치사 from을 만나면 '~하지 못하게 하다'라는 뜻으로도 쓰인다.

구문 플러스⁺ spare A from~ 구문

<spare A from~>는 <prevent A from~>과 같은 의미이다.

Medication **spared** him **from** feeling the pain.
→ Medication **prevented** him **from** feeling the pain.

유형 플러스⁺ 제목 추론

중심 내용을 상징적이고 함축적으로 나타내는 표현을 찾아낼 수 있는지를 묻는 유형이다.

제목 찾는 방법

① 글 초반부나 결론을 통해 주제를 파악한다.
② 글의 흐름을 바꿀 수 있는 연결사가 중간에 있는지 확인하고, 만일 있다면 역접어 뒤를 중점적으로 읽는다.
③ 영어로 제시된 선택지를 살펴보고, 주제에 관한 포괄적이고 일반적인 내용, 상징적이고 함축적인 내용을 고른다.

DAY 03 글의 목적 / 필자의 주장

A② B⑤ C④ D② E① F③ G①

A 정답 ② 95% 2023 9월 학평

해석 우리는 항상 우리 자녀에게 말과 행동으로 무언가를 가르치고 있다. 그들은 보면서 배운다. 그들은 듣고 또 '우연히 듣는 것'에서 배운다. 아이들은 인생에서 가장 중요한 것에 관한 부모의 가치관을 공유한다. 우리의 우선순위와 원칙, 그리고 훌륭한 행동에 대한 본보기는 우리 자녀가 다른 길이 유혹적으로 보일 때 올바른 길로 가도록 가르칠 수 있다. 아이들은 확고한 인격을 구성하는 가치를 단순히 그것에 대해 '들어서' 배우지 않는다는 것을 기억하라. 그들은 주변 사람들이 일상생활에서 그러한 가치에 따라 '행동'하고 '유지'하는 것을 보면서 배운다. 그러므로 여러분의 자녀에게 행동으로 삶의 모범을 보이라. 우리 일상생활에서, 우리는 자녀에게 우리가 타인을 존중하는 것을 보여줄 수 있다. 우리는 타인이 괴로워할 때 우리의 연민과 걱정을 그들에게 보여줄 수 있으며, 우리가 어려운 결정을 내릴 때에는 자제력과 용기와 정직을 보여줄 수 있다.

해설 아이들에게 행동으로 본보기를 보여서 올바른 길로 가도록 이끌 수 있다고 하므로, 필자의 주장으로 가장 적절한 것은 ② '자녀에게 행동으로 삶의 모범을 보여야 한다.'이다.

오답 풀이

선택률	보기 해석
① 1%	비교와 관련된 내용은 언급되지 않았다.
③ 1%	칭찬을 통해 강화하라는 내용은 언급되지 않았다.
④ 1%	자녀에게 생각할 시간을 주라는 내용은 언급되지 않았다.
⑤ 0%	부모의 인내심에 관해서는 언급되지 않았다.

구문 풀이 6행

Remember that children do not learn the values that make up strong character simply by **being *told*** about them.

→ 동명사의 의미상 주어인 children이 '듣는' 대상이다. 따라서 동명사의 수동태에 해당하는 <being p.p.> 형태를 썼다.

구문 플러스 동명사와 to부정사의 능동형과 수동형

동명사: V-ing(능동) / being p.p.(수동)
to부정사: to-V(능동) / to be p.p.(수동)

Loving your family is important.
능동(생략된 의미상 주어인 you가 '사랑하는' 주체)

She treasures the feeling of **being loved**.
수동(She가 '사랑받는' 대상)

I want you **to listen**.
능동(you가 '경청하는' 주체)

Everyone loves **to be listened to**.
수동(Everyone이 '경청되는' 대상)

B 정답 ⑤ 94% 2022 9월 학평

해석 부모님들/보호자들께,
학급 파티가 2022년 12월 16일 금요일 오후에 열릴 것입니다. 아이들은 사탕류, 감자칩, 비스킷, 케이크, 그리고 음료를 가지고 올 수 있습니다. 우리는 아이들이 집에서 만들거나 준비한 음식을 가져오지 않기를 요청합니다. 모든 음식은 성분을 명확하게 목록으로 작성하여 밀봉된 꾸러미로 가져와야 합니다. 과일과 채소는 가게에서 밀봉된 꾸러미로 사전 포장된 것이라면 환영합니다. 심각한 견과류 알레르기를 가진 아이들이 많이 있으니 견과류가 포함된 그 어떤 음식도 학교에 보내지 마십시오. 아이들이 가져오는 모든 음식의 성분을 주의 깊게 확인해 주십시오. 여러분의 지속적인 지원과 협조에 감사드립니다.
교장 Lisa Brown 드림

해설 학급 파티에 허용되는 음식과 그렇지 않은 음식을 안내하는 글이다. 따라서 정답은 ⑤ '학급 파티에 가져올 음식에 대한 유의 사항을 안내하려고'이다.

오답 풀이

선택률	보기 해석
① 0%	'일정 변경'에 대해 언급하지 않았다.
② 1%	'학교 식당'에 대해 언급하지 않았다.
③ 3%	알레르기 여부를 '조사'하려는 것은 아니다.
④ 0%	'학부모의 참여'를 독려하는 것은 아니다.

구문 풀이 4행

All food should arrive in a sealed packet **with the ingredients clearly listed**.

→ <with+명사+과거분사> 구조가 쓰였다. 의미는 '…가 ~된 채로'라고 해석한다.

구문 플러스 with+명사+분사

'with+명사+현재분사'는 '~가 …한 채로'라는 의미로, 명사와 분사와의 관계가 능동이고, 'with+명사+과거분사'는 '~가 …된 채로'라는 의미로, 명사와 분사와의 관계가 수동이다.

- She spoke **with tears falling down her cheeks**.
  → tears와 fall down her cheeks의 관계가 능동이므로 현재분사 falling이 쓰임
- Jack stood **with his arms folded**.
  → his arms와 fold의 관계가 수동이므로 과거분사 folded가 쓰임

C 정답 ④ 90% 2021 3월 학평

해석 Eastwood 도서관 회원들께,
Friends of Literature 모임 덕분에, 우리는 도서관 건물을 리모델링하기 위한 충분한 돈을 성공적으로 모았습니다. 우리 지역의 건축

업자인 John Baker씨가 우리의 리모델링을 돕기로 자원했지만, 그는 도움이 필요합니다. 망치나 페인트 붓을 쥐고 시간을 기부함으로써, 여러분은 공사를 도울 수 있습니다. Baker씨의 자원봉사 팀에 동참하여 Eastwood 도서관을 더 좋은 곳으로 만드는 데 참여하십시오! 더 많은 정보를 원하시면 541-567-1234로 전화해 주십시오.
Mark Anderson 드림

해설 도서관 리모델링 공사에 자원하기를 독려하는 글이다. 따라서 정답은 ④ '도서관 공사에 참여할 자원봉사자를 모집하려고'이다.

오답 풀이

선택률	보기 해석
① 2%	도서관 휴관에 대한 언급은 없다.
② 1%	아직 자원봉사자 모집 단계이다.
③ 4%	모금 행사는 이미 종료되었다.
⑤ 0%	글쓰기 대회에 대한 언급은 없다.

구문 풀이 5행

By grabbing a hammer or a paint brush and **donating** your time, you can help with the construction.

→ 수단을 나타내는 <by+동명사(~함으로써)> 구문이다.

구문 플러스 자주 쓰이는 전치사+동명사

by+동명사: ~함으로써
in+동명사: ~함에 있어, ~할 때
on+동명사: ~하자마자

By using a sunscreen, you can protect your skin from direct sunlight.
Eating healthy food plays a crucial role **in staying** in shape.
On arriving home, I took a shower.

D 정답 ② 84% 2020 3월 학평

해석 좋은 생각을 머릿속에 떠돌게 하는 것은 그것이 이루어지지 않게 하는 확실한 방법이다. 생명력을 얻는 유일한 좋은 생각은 적어둔 것이라는 점을 아는 작가들로부터 조언을 얻어라. 종이 한 장을 꺼내 언젠가 하고 싶은 모든 것을 기록하는데, 이 때 꿈이 100개가 되는 것을 목표로 해라. 여러분을 부르고 있는 그것들을 시작하도록 상기시키는 것과 동기 부여 요소를 갖게 될 것이고 또한 그 모든 것을 기억하는 부담을 갖지 않을 것이다. 꿈을 글로 적을 때 여러분은 그것을 실행하기 시작하는 것이다.

해설 생각을 구체화하고 생명력을 지니게 하는 것은 그것을 메모하고 목표로 할 때 이루어진다는 내용이므로 ② '하고 싶은 일을 적으라.'가 정답이다.

오답 풀이

선택률	보기 해석
① 4%	본인의 꿈에 관한 내용이다.
③ 4%	행동이 아니라 생각을 정리하는 것이다.
④ 3%	꿈, 목표를 적는 것이다.
⑤ 3%	실현 가능성과 상관 없이 적으라고 하고 있다.

구문 풀이 1행

Keeping good ideas floating around in your head is a great way **to ensure** that they won't happen.

→ to부정사가 앞의 명사를 수식하는 형용사 역할을 한다.

구문 플러스 to부정사의 형용사적 용법

to부정사가 앞에 있는 명사를 수식하는 형용사 역할을 하는 것을 말한다.

We need some food **to have for breakfast**.

E 정답 ① 73% 2019 3월 학평

해석 집중을 방해하는 것들이 너무 많이 있을 때, 공부에 전념하는 것은 힘들 수 있다. 많은 젊은이들이 숙제를 찔끔하는 것과 즉각적으로 메시지 주고받기, 전화로 잡담하기, SNS에 신상 정보 업데이트하기, 그리고 이메일 확인하기를 잔뜩 하는 것을 동시에 하고 싶어 한다. 여러분이 동시에 여러 가지 일을 처리할 수 있고 이러한 모든 일들에 집중할 수 있다는 것이 사실일지도 모르지만, 자신에게 솔직해지려고 노력해라. 여러분이 공부에 집중하되 (앞서 못했던) 그런 다른 소일거리를 하기 위해 규칙적인 휴식을 30분 정도마다 허락한다면 여러분은 아마도 가장 잘 공부할 수 있을 것이다.

해설 여러 일을 한꺼번에 하면 너무 산만해지기 때문에 ① '공부할 때는 공부에만 집중하라.'는 내용이다.

오답 풀이

선택률	보기 해석
② 1%	관계에 대한 글이 아니라 공부에 대한 글이다.
③ 18%	휴식할 때 휴식하더라도 공부할 때에는 공부에만 집중하라는 내용이다.
④ 4%	자투리 시간 활용에 대한 언급은 없다.
⑤ 2%	공부와 취미 활동을 동시에 하지 말라는 내용이다.

구문 풀이 1행

It can be tough **to settle down to study** when there are so many distractions.

→ 가주어 it은 의미가 없는 주어로 진주어는 뒤에 나오는 to부정사이다.

구문 플러스⁺ 가주어 it 문장

to부정사나 that절이 주어일 때 대신 it을 쓰고 to부정사, that절(진주어)는 뒤에 위치시키는 것을 말한다.

To have breakfast is good for health.
= **It** is good for health **to** have breakfast.

F 정답 ③ 88% 2018 9월 학평

해석 Stevens 씨께,
이것은 당신이 9월 26일 우리 가게에서 구매한 책상의 배송 상황 문의에 대한 회신입니다. 불행히도, 당신의 책상 배송이 가구 제조업체에서 우리 창고로 배송되는 동안 발생한 파손 때문에 예상된 것보다 더 오래 걸릴 것입니다. 우리는 제조업체로부터 똑같은 대체품을 주문했고, 그 배송이 2주 안에 이뤄질 것으로 예상합니다. 우리는 그 책상이 도착하자마자 당신에게 바로 전화해서 편리한 배송 시간을 정할 것입니다. 우리는 이 지연이 당신에게 일으킨 불편에 대해 유감으로 생각합니다.
진심을 담아,
Justin Upton 드림

해설 책상의 배송 지연 이유를 설명하고 있는 글이다. 따라서 정답은 ③ '상품의 배송 지연에 대해 설명하려고'이다.

오답 풀이

선택률	보기 해석
① 3%	영업시간 변경에 대한 언급이 없다.
② 2%	고객 서비스 조사와 관련이 없다.
④ 2%	환불 절차에 대한 언급이 없다.
⑤ 2%	항의가 아니라 사과를 하고 있다.

구문 풀이 3행

Unfortunately, the delivery of your desk will take longer than expected due to the damage that occurred **during** the shipment from the furniture manufacturer to our warehouse.
→ 시간 전치사 during이 기간을 나타낸다.

구문 플러스⁺ during vs. for

during과 for는 둘 다 '동안'의 의미이지만 during은 기간을 나타내는 명사, for는 숫자 표현과 함께 쓰인다.

- He was wounded **during** the war.
- She has been studying **for** three hours.

G 정답 ① 84% 2017 9월 학평

해석 행동을 기반으로 사람들을 판단하는 것은 쉽다. 우리는 종종 말보다 행동에 더 많은 가치를 두도록 배우고, 그럴 만한 충분한 이유가 있다. 다른 사람의 행동은 종종 그들이 하는 말보다 더 큰 목소리를 낸다. 하지만, 누군가가 난해한 행동을 보일 때, 여러분은 판단을 나중으로 유보하기를 원할 수도 있다. 사람들은 항상 그들의 행동으로 정의되는 것은 아니다. 누군가의 별로 바람직하지 않은 행동을 관찰한 후에 "그는 너무 거들먹거려," 또는 "그녀는 너무 심술궂어,"라고 보통 생각한다. 그러나 여러분은 그러한 추측을 즉시 내려서는 안 된다. 여러분은 그들을 낙인찍고 영원히 차단해 버리기 전에 다시 한번 기회를 줘야 한다. 여러분은 누군가가 훌륭한 동료 또는 절친한 친구라는 것을 알게 될 수도 있으니, 단시간의 관찰을 근거로 사람을 여러분의 삶에서 제거하지 말라.

해설 마지막 세 문장에서 겉으로 드러나는 행동으로 사람을 판단하기 쉽지만 그런 판단으로 낙인찍고 차단해 버리는 일이 없도록 하라는 필자의 주장을 알 수 있다. 따라서 정답은 ① '단시간의 관찰로 타인을 성급하게 판단하지 마라.'이다.

오답 풀이

선택률	보기 해석
② 2%	적성에 대한 언급이 없다.
③ 3%	타인에 대한 판단을 유보하라는 내용으로, 습관을 고치기 위한 노력은 언급되지 않았다.
④ 3%	칭찬에 대한 언급이 없다.
⑤ 6%	타인의 행동을 성급히 판단하지 말라는 글이지, 행동으로 모범을 보이라는 내용은 아니다.

구문 풀이 1행

We **are** often **taught to put** more value in actions than words, and for good reason.
→ <teach+목적어+to부정사>의 수동태이다.

구문 플러스⁺ 5형식 동사의 수동태

to부정사를 목적격보어로 취하는 5형식 동사가 수동태로 쓰이면 <be p.p.+to+동사원형> 형태가 된다.

My brother **taught** me **to swim**.
→ I **was taught to swim** by my brother.

유형 플러스⁺ 글의 목적 / 필자의 주장

주로 글 중후반부에서 답을 찾을 수 있는 쉬운 대의파악 유형이다.

① 목적을 나타내는 결정적 단서
: I'm writing to ~. Please ~. Would you like to ~?, I'd like to ask you to ~ 등

② 주장을 나타내는 결정적 단서
: 명령문, You[We] should/must/have to/need to ~, It's important/necessary ~ 등

A 정답 ④ 83% 2023 6월 학평

해석 위 도표는 1990년과 2019년의 지역별 총 토지 면적에서 산림 면적의 점유율을 보여준다. 아프리카의 전체 토지 면적에서 산림 면적의 점유율이 1990년과 2019년 둘 다 20%를 넘었다. 1990년 아메리카의 산림 면적 점유율은 42.6%였고, 이는 2019년보다 더 컸다. 아시아의 산림 면적 점유율은 1990년부터 2019년까지 10퍼센트포인트 넘게 감소했다. 2019년 유럽의 산림 면적 점유율은 다섯 개 지역 중 가장 컸고, 같은 해 아시아의 세 배(→두 배)가 넘었다. 오세아니아는 1990년과 2019년 사이에 총 토지 면적 중 산림 면적의 점유율 면에서 가장 작은 차이를 보였다.

해설 2019년 유럽의 산림 면적 점유율(46%)은 아시아의 점유율(20%)에 비해 두 배를 웃도는 수준이므로, 도표와 일치하지 않는 것은 이를 '세 배'로 잘못 기술한 ④이다.

오답 풀이

선택률	보기 해석
① 3%	아프리카의 산림 면적 점유율은 1990년에 25.3%, 2019년에 21.4%였다.
② 3%	2019년 아메리카의 산림 면적 점유율은 41.4%로, 1990년의 42.6%보다 줄어든 수치가 맞다.
③ 6%	아시아의 산림 면적 점유율은 1990년 32.4%에서 2019년 20%로 12.4퍼센트포인트 감소했다.
⑤ 3%	오세아니아의 산림 면적 점유율은 1990년에 22.6%, 2019년에 23.4%로, 둘 사이 격차는 다른 지역에 비해 가장 적다. 실제로 계산하지 않고 그림으로만 비교해도 충분하다.

구문 풀이 6행

In 2019, the share of forest area in Europe was **the largest among the five regions,** more than three times that in Asia in the same year.

→ <the+최상급(가장 ~한)> 구문이다.

구문 플러스⁺ the+최상급

최상급은 여러 대상 중 하나로 특정되는 것이 보통이므로 정관사 the와 함께 쓴다. 뒤에는 in/among/of 등 범위를 가리키는 표현이 나온다.

the tallest of the three
the fastest in our class

B 정답 ⑤ 72% 2022 3월 학평

해석 위 도표는 2020년도에 온라인 강의와 온라인 학습 자료를 이용한 영국 사람들의 비율을 연령 집단별로 보여 준다. 각 연령 집단에서 온라인 학습 자료를 이용한 사람들의 비율이 온라인 강의를 이용한 사람들의 비율보다 더 높았다. 모든 연령 집단 중, 25세에서 34세 연령 집단에서 온라인 강의를 이용한 사람들의 비율이 가장 높았다. 여섯 개의 연령 집단 가운데서, 65세 이상인 사람들이 온라인 강의를 이용할 가능성이 가장 낮았다. 여섯 개의 연령 집단 가운데서, 온라인 강의를 이용한 사람들의 비율과 온라인 학습 자료를 이용한 사람들의 비율 차이는 16세에서 24세 연령 집단에서 가장 컸다. 35세에서 44세, 45세에서 54세, 55세에서 64세(→삭제)의 각 연령 집단에서 다섯 명 중 한 명 이상의 사람들이 온라인 학습 자료를 이용했다.

해설 55세에서 64세 연령 집단에서는 20% 미만인 17%의 사람들이 온라인 학습 자료를 이용했으므로, 일치하지 않는 진술은 ⑤이다.

오답 풀이

선택률	보기 해석
① 2%	모든 연령 집단에서 온라인 학습 자료를 이용한 사람들의 비율이 온라인 강의를 이용한 사람들의 비율보다 더 높았다.
② 11%	25세에서 34세 연령 집단에서 온라인 강의를 이용한 사람들의 비율이 22%로 가장 높았다.
③ 7%	65세 이상 연령 집단에서 온라인 강의를 이용한 사람들의 비율이 2%로 가장 낮았다.
④ 6%	온라인 강의를 이용한 사람들의 비율과 온라인 학습 자료를 이용한 사람들의 비율 차이는 16세에서 24세 연령 집단에서 46% - 15% = 31%p로 가장 컸다.

구문 풀이 7행

Among the six age groups, **the gap** between the percentage of people who used online courses and that of people who used online learning materials **was** the greatest in the 16-24 age group.

→ 문장의 주어는 the gap으로, 전치사구(between ~)가 붙어 길어졌다. 이렇게 주어와 동사가 먼 경우, 동사의 수 일치에 주의한다.

구문 플러스⁺ 동사의 수 일치

동사의 수 일치는 그 동사가 속한 절의 진짜 주어(명사)를 찾아 그것에 일치시켜야 한다.

We all know that **people** with a nice attitude **are** always welcomed.
* 바로 앞의 a nice attitude에 수 일치 하지 않도록 주의

C 정답 ④ 80% 2021 9월 학평

해석 위 그래프는 2020년 미국 성인들을 대상으로 한 설문조사에 기반하여 네 가지 다른 종류의 정보 출처들에 대한 소비자의 신뢰 정도를 보여준다. 미국 성인의 절반 정도가 다른 사용자들이나 고객들로부터의 상품평에서 얻은 정보를 믿는다고 말했다. 이것은 다른 사용자들이나 고객들로부터의 상품평에 대해 불신을 갖는다고 말한 미국 성인들의 두 배 이상이다. 네 가지 다른 종류의 정보 출처들 중에서 신뢰와 불신 정도 사이의 가장 적은 차이는 회사나 상표의 그래프에서 보인다. 미국 성인의 1/5 보다 적은(→많은) 수치가 텔레비전 광고로부터의 정보를 신뢰한다고 말했는데, 그러한 정보를 불신하는 쪽의 수치가 이를 능가했다. 미국 성인의 15%만 인플루언서에게 제공받은 정보를 신뢰한다고 말했는데,

반면에 이보다 세 배 이상 많은 수치의 미국 성인들이 바로 그 정보 출처를 불신한다고 말했다.

해설 도표에 의하면 미국 성인의 23%가 텔레비전 광고로부터의 정보를 신뢰한다고 하는데, ④는 이 수치가 5분의 1(20%)보다 '적다(Fewer)'라고 하므로 도표의 내용과 일치하지 않는다.

오답 풀이

선택률	보기 해석
① 4%	49%가 다른 사용자들이나 고객들로부터의 상품평에서 얻은 정보를 믿는다.
② 6%	21%가 다른 사용자들이나 고객들로부터의 상품평에서 얻은 정보를 불신하고, 신뢰하는 49%는 21%의 두 배 이상이다.
③ 4%	신뢰와 불신 정도 사이의 가장 적은 차이는 7%p의 차이를 보이는 회사나 상표이다.
⑤ 3%	15%가 인플루언서의 정보를 신뢰하고, 48%가 불신하는데, 48%는 15%의 세 배 이상이다.

구문 풀이 10행

Only 15% of adults say they trust the information provided by influencers, while **more than three times as many adults** say they distrust the same source of information.

→ '배수사 as ~ as'는 '…의 몇 배만큼 ~한 (것)'을 의미한다. 위의 비교대상이 Only 15%라는 것을 맥락상 알 수 있기 때문에 <두 번째 as+비교대상>은 생략되어 있다.

구문 플러스+ 배수 표현

'몇 배만큼'이라는 의미일 때 <배수사+as ~ as> 또는 <배수사+비교급 than>으로 쓴다. 배수사는 <숫자+times>로 쓰는 것이 일반적이지만, 2배의 경우 twice로 쓴다.

The percentage this year is **three times as high as** last year.

D 정답 ⑤ 68% 2020 6월 학평

해석 위 도표는 2014년과 2016년에 영국인들이 인터넷 접속을 할 때 어떤 장치들이 가장 중요하다고 생각했는지를 보여 준다. 2016년도에 3분의 1이 넘는 영국 인터넷 사용자들은 스마트폰을 가장 중요한 인터넷 접속 장치로 생각했다. 같은 해에, 스마트폰이 인터넷 접속을 위해 가장 중요한 장치로서 노트북을 추월하였다. 2014년에, 영국 인터넷 사용자들은 인터넷 접속을 위한 가장 중요한 장치로 태블릿을 가장 적게 선택하는 경향이 있었다. 대조적으로, 2016년에는 인터넷 접속을 위한 가장 중요한 장치로 데스크톱을 가장 적게 선택하는 경향이 있었다. 인터넷 접속을 위한 가장 중요한 장치로 데스크톱을 선택한 영국 인터넷 사용자들의 비율은 2016년도에 2014년도 비율의 절반만큼 증가하였다(→ 감소하였다).

해설 2014년도에 데스크톱을 인터넷 접속을 위한 가장 중요한 장치로 고려한 영국 인터넷 사용자의 비율은 20%이고 2016년도에는 12%로, 절반만큼 증가한 것이 아니라 반대로 감소하였으므로, 일치하지 않는 진술은 ⑤이다.

오답 풀이

선택률	보기 해석
① 4%	36% 이상이므로 3분의 1 이상이라고 할 수 있다.
② 7%	2016년에 스마트폰이 노트북을 추월했다.
③ 9%	2014년에는 인터넷 접속 기기로 태블릿을 가장 적게 선택했다.
④ 10%	2016년에는 인터넷 접속 기기로 데스크톱을 가장 적게 선택했다.

구문 풀이 1행

The above graph shows what devices British people considered the most important **when connecting** to the Internet ~

→ 의미를 명확하게 하기 위해 접속사를 생략하지 않고 <접속사+-ing>의 분사구문이 쓰였다.

구문 플러스+ 분사구문

분사구문은 <접속사+주어+동사>의 부사절을 분사를 이용해서 간단한 부사구로 나타낸 것이다. 접속사는 흔히 생략되지만, 의미를 분명히 하기 위해 생략되지 않고 남는 경우도 있다.

분사구문 앞에 남을 수 있는 접속사(=부사절 접속사)

시간	when, while, since, before, after 등
이유	because, as, since 등
조건	if, unless
양보	although, (even) though, (even) if 등

E 정답 ④ 82% 2019 9월 학평

해석 위 그래프는 2011년에 실시한 16세부터 25세까지의 청년들의 발명 흥미 분야에 관한 조사의 결과를 보여 준다. 다섯 개 범주의 발명 분야 중에서 가장 높은 비율의 남성 응답자가 소비재를 발명하는 것에 대해 흥미를 나타냈다. 건강 과학 발명 분야에서, 여성 응답자의 비율은 남성 응답자의 비율보다 2배만큼 높았다. 환경 관련 발명 분야에서 남성과 여성 간 비율 점수의 차이가 가장 작았다. 웹 기반 발명 분야에서, 여성 응답자의 비율은 남성 응답자의 비율의 절반보다 적었다(→많았다). 기타 발명 분야의 범주에서 각 성별 집단의 응답자 비율은 10퍼센트보다 적었다.

해설 여성 응답자(14%)는 남성 응답자(26%)의 절반(13%)보다 많기 때문에 도표와 일치하지 않는 것은 ④이다.

오답 풀이

선택률	보기 해석
① 2%	남성 응답자는 소비재 발명에 대한 응답이 가장 높았다.
② 3%	건강 과학 발명은 여성 응답자가 2배 높았다.
③ 4%	남성, 여성 응답자 비율 차가 가장 작은 분야는 환경 발명 분야이다.
⑤ 6%	남성, 여성 응답 비율이 기타 발명에서는 10%보다 적었다.

구문 풀이 4행

For health science invention, the percentage of female respondents was **twice as high as that of male respondents.**

→ 지시대명사 that이 앞에 나온 the percentage를 받는다.

구문 플러스⁺ 비교대상의 병렬구조

<as ~ as> 또는 <비교급 than>의 비교대상은 서로 동일해야 한다. 중복을 피하기 위해 지시대명사 that/those를 흔히 활용한다.

Jen's smile was as pure as **that** of a kid.
(=smile)

Your prices are higher than **those** of your competitors.
(=prices)

F 정답 ④ 75% 2018 6월 학평

해석 위 그래프는 국제올림픽위원회의 메달 집계를 바탕으로 2016년 하계 올림픽 동안 상위 5개 국가들이 획득한 메달의 수를 보여주고 있다. 5개 국가들 중, 미국이 전부 약 120개로 가장 많은 메달을 획득하였다. 금메달의 경우, 영국이 중국보다 더 많이 획득하였다. 중국, 러시아, 독일은 각각 20개 미만의 은메달을 획득하였다. 미국이 획득한 동메달 수는 독일이 획득한 동메달 수의 두 배보다 적었다(→많았다). 상위 5개 국가는 총 40개 이상의 메달을 각각 획득하였다.

해설 미국이 획득한 동메달의 수(38개)는 독일이 획득한 동메달의 수(15개)의 두 배보다 많으므로 도표와 일치하지 않는 것은 ④이다.

오답 풀이

선택률	보기 해석
① 7%	미국은 5개 국가 중 전부 120개 이상으로 가장 많은 메달을 획득했다.
② 4%	영국(27개)은 중국(26개)보다 많은 금메달을 획득했다.
③ 8%	중국(18개), 러시아(17개), 독일(10개)은 모두 20개 미만의 은메달을 획득했다.
⑤ 3%	5개 국가 모두 총 40개 이상의 메달을 획득했다.

구문 풀이 7행

The number of bronze medals won by the United States was less than twice the number of bronze medals won by Germany.

→ <the number of ~>는 '~의 숫자'라는 의미이므로 단수 취급한다.

구문 플러스⁺ the number of vs. a number of

<the number of+명사>는 '~의 수'의 의미로 단수 취급하지만, <a number of+명사>는 '많은 ~'의 의미로 복수 취급한다.

- **The number of** students **is** increasing.
- **A number of** students **are** staying up late at night.

G 정답 ④ 90% 2016 9월 학평

해석 위 그래프는 여가 여행자들과 출장 여행자들이 호텔 선택 시 결정적인 요인으로 고른 상위 네 개의 호텔 편의 서비스를 보여준다. 두 유형의 여행자 모두에게 무료 Wi-Fi가 가장 인기 있는 선택이었다. 무료 조식은 두 유형의 여행자 모두에게서 2위에 올랐는데, 여가 여행자들 중 22퍼센트와 출장 여행자들 중 21퍼센트가 무료 조식을 선택했다. 출장 여행자들에게 대중교통에의 접근성은 무료 조식만큼 인기 있지 않았다. 여가 여행자의 15퍼센트(→10퍼센트)가 수영장을 가장 중요한 편의 서비스로 선택했고 반면 10퍼센트(→15퍼센트)가 무료 주차를 선택했다. 편안한 업무용 의자와 책상을 가지는 것이 출장 체류를 위한 상위 네 개의 편의 서비스 목록 중 가장 덜 인기 있는 선택이었다.

해설 도표에 따르면 여가 여행자의 10퍼센트가 수영장을, 15퍼센트가 무료 주차를 선택했다. 따라서 일치하지 않는 것은 ④이다.

오답 풀이

선택률	보기 해석
① 2%	두 유형 모두 무료 Wi-Fi를 주요하게 생각했다.
② 1%	두 유형 모두 무료 조식이 두 번째로 주요한 요소였다.
③ 3%	출장 여행자에게 무료 조식 다음으로 대중교통 접근성이 중요했다.
⑤ 1%	출장 여행자에게 마지막으로 중요한 항목이 바로 편안한 사무용 가구이다.

구문 풀이 6행

Accessibility to mass transportation is **not as popular as** free breakfast for business travelers.

→ 원급 비교의 부정문으로 '~만큼은 아닌'이라는 뜻이다.

구문 플러스⁺ 원급 비교

<as ~ as>는 비슷한 두 대상을 비교할 때 쓰는 표현으로, 부정문인 <not as[so] ~ as>는 <less+원급+than>으로 바꿔 쓸 수 있다.

- She is as tall as her father. (그녀는 아빠만큼 크다.)
- She is not as talkative as her brother.
(그녀는 오빠만큼 수다스럽지 않다.)
→ She is less talkative than her brother.
(그녀는 오빠보다 덜 수다스럽다.)

유형 플러스⁺ 도표의 이해

도표 유형은 그래프의 정보를 파악하는 문제로 내용의 일치와 불일치를 찾는 유형이기 때문에 각 문장과 도표를 비교하여 읽어야 한다. 비교급, 최상급, 배수 표현 등을 익혀두어야 한다.

도표에 자주 쓰이는 단어

증가	increase, rise, raise, grow, multiply
감소	decrease, fall, drop, reduce, decline, diminish
정도	sharply, rapidly, drastically, slightly, slowly, gradually, steadily, continuously
배수	a half, half of, double, twice, three times

A 정답 ④ 49% 2023 6월 학평

해석 자기 직업에서 높은 수준으로 수행하는 사람들은 흔히 다른 사람들에게 즉각적인 신뢰를 얻는다. 사람들은 그들을 존경하고, 그들처럼 되고 싶어 하고, 그들과 연결되어 있다고 느낀다. 그들이 말할 때, 다른 사람들은 비록 그들의 기술 분야가 그들이 주는 조언과 전혀 관련이 없을지라도 경청한다. 세계적으로 유명한 농구 선수를 생각해 보라. 그는 농구를 하면서 그간 벌었던 것보다 광고로 더 많은 돈을 벌었다. 그것이 그가 광고하는 제품에 대한 지식 때문일까? 아니다. 그것은 그가 농구로 할 수 있는 것 때문이다. 올림픽 메달리스트 수영 선수도 마찬가지이다. 사람들은 그가 수영장에서 할 수 있는 것 때문에 그의 말을 경청한다. 그리고 어떤 배우가 우리에게 특정 자동차를 운전해야 한다고 말할 때, 우리는 엔진에 대한 그의 전문 지식 때문에 경청하는 것은 아니다. 우리는 그의 재능을 존경하기 때문에 경청한다. 탁월함이 연결된다. 만약 당신이 어떤 분야에서 높은 수준의 능력을 갖고 있다면, 다른 사람들은 그것 때문에 당신과 연결되기를 원할 수도 있다.

해설 전문 분야에서 두각을 나타내거나 전문성을 인정받은 사람은 바로 그 점 때문에 다른 분야에서도 타인의 신뢰를 더 얻기 쉽다는 내용이다. 즉 그 사람의 ④ '탁월함' 때문에 사람들이 그와 연결되고자 한다는 것이다.

오답 풀이

선택률	보기 해석
① 10%	Patience(인내)
② 13%	Sacrifice(희생)
③ 18%	Honesty(정직)
⑤ 11%	Creativity(창의성)

구문 풀이 10행

People listen to him because of **what he can do in the pool**.

→ what이 이끄는 명사절이 전치사 because of의 목적어 역할을 한다.

구문 플러스⁺ 전치사 뒤의 what절

what은 전치사 뒤에 나오는 목적절을 이끌 수 있는 반면, that은 이끌 수 없다.

He couldn't say a word because of **what**(→ that X) **he had done**.

B 정답 ② 42% 2022 9월 학평

해석 우리는 로봇이 우리의 직업을 빼앗고 있다고 걱정하지만, 그만큼 흔한 문제는 로봇이 우리의 판단력을 빼앗고 있다는 것이다. 오늘날의 경제 배후에서 아주 흔한 거대한 창고에서, 인간 '집게들'은 서둘러서 선반에서 상품을 집어내고 그것들이 포장되고 발송될 수 있는 곳으로 이동시킨다. 그들의 귀에는 헤드폰이 있는데, 한 소프트웨어 프로그램인 'Jennifer'의 목소리가 그들 움직임의 가장 작은 세부 사항들을 조종하면서, 그들에게 어디로 갈지와 무엇을 할지를 말한다. Jennifer는 실수를 줄이고 생산성을 최대화하기 위해 지시 사항을 아주 작은 덩어리로 쪼갠다. 예를 들어, 인간 작업자는 선반에서 책 18권을 집어내기보다는, 5권을 집어내라고 정중하게 지시받을 것이다. 그러고 나서 또 다른 5권을. 그러고 나서 다시 또 다른 5권을. 그러고 나서 또 다른 3권을 (집어내라고 지시받을 것이다). 그러한 조건에서 일하는 것은 사람을 살로 만들어진 기계로 격하시킨다. Jennifer라는 장치는 우리에게 생각하거나 적응하라고 요구하기보다는 사고 과정을 가져가고, 작업자들을 약간의 시각적인 처리 과정과 한 쌍의 마주 보는 엄지손가락을 가진 값싼 자원으로 취급한다.

해설 창고에서 로봇 Jennifer가 세부 사항들까지 사람들에게 조종·지시하여 인간 작업자들이 단순한 기계 취급을 받고 있다는 내용이다. 즉, 로봇이 우리의 ② '판단력'까지 앗아가는 상황이다.

오답 풀이

선택률	보기 해석
① 15%	reliability(신뢰도)
③ 11%	endurance(인내력)
④ 19%	sociability(사교성)
⑤ 12%	cooperation(협동성)

구문 풀이 1행

We worry that the robots are taking our jobs, but **just as common a problem** is that the robots are taking our judgment.

→ <as+형용사+관사+명사A+as+명사B>는 '(명사B)만큼 (형용사)한 (명사A)'라고 해석하며, 두 번째 as부터의 부분은 맥락에 따라 생략되기도 한다. 관사의 위치에 주의한다.

구문 플러스⁺ 관사의 어순

관사는 본디 형용사 앞에 위치하는데(관사+형용사+명사), so/too/as 뒤에서는 '형용사+관사+명사' 어순이 된다.

It was **so beautiful a day**. (매우 ~한 …)
It is **too small a car** to take you all. (너무 ~한 …)
He is **as great a statesman** as ever lived. (~만큼 …한 ~)

C 정답 ⑤ 46% 2021 3월 학평

해석 좋은 보살핌을 제공하는 것의 가장 중요한 측면 중 한 가지는 반드시 동물의 욕구가 일관되게 그리고 예측 가능하게 충족되도록 하는 것이다. 사람과 마찬가지로, 동물은 통제감이 필요하다. 그러므로 충분한 음식을 제공받고 있을지라도 음식이 언제 (눈에) 보일지 모르고 일관된 일정을 알 수 없는 동물은 괴로움을 겪을지도 모른다. 우리 동물의 환경이 예측 가능하도록 보장함으로써 우리는 통제가 있다는 느낌을 줄 수 있다. 즉, 마실 수 있는 물이 늘 있고, 물이 늘 같은 곳에 있다. 아침에 일어날 때 그리고 저녁 산책을 한 후에 늘 음식이 있다. 불편할 정도로 참을 필요 없이 (변을) 배설할 수 있는 시간과 장소가 늘 있을 것이다. 사람 친구는 한순간에는 애정을 주다가 그 다음에는 애정을 주지 않기보다는 일관된 정서적 지지를 보여주면 좋다. 기대할 수 있는 것이 무엇인지 알고 있을 때, 동물은 자신감과 차분함을 더 많이 느낄 수 있다.

해설 글에 따르면, 동물에게 좋은 보살핌이란 욕구를 충족할 수 있는 일관된 환경을 제공하여 통제감을 제공하는 것이다. 즉, 우리 동물의 환경이 ⑤ '예측 가능하도록' 보장하여 통제가 있다는 느낌을 주는 것이다.

오답 풀이

선택률	보기 해석
① 6%	silent(고요한)
② 32%	natural(자연스러운)
③ 8%	isolated(고립된)
④ 6%	dynamic(역동적인)

구문 풀이 3행

So an animal who may get enough food **but** doesn't know when the food will appear **and** can see no consistent schedule may experience distress.

→ 관계대명사절의 동사구가 등위접속사 but과 and의 병렬구조로 길어졌다.

구문 플러스⁺ 등위접속사

등위접속사란, 단어와 단어, 또는 구와 구, 문장과 문장을 대등하게 잇는 접속사이다. 대표적인 등위접속사로 and, but, or 등이 있다.

I like James **and** Jenny.
He began **but** couldn't finish the project.

D 정답 ② 41% 2020 6월 학평

해석 다른 과학자의 실험 결과물을 읽을 때, 그 실험에 대해 비판적으로 생각하라. 당신 자신에게 물어라. 관찰들이 실험 도중에 혹은 후에 기록되었나? 결론이 합리적인가? 그 결과들은 반복될 수 있는가? 정보의 출처는 신뢰할 만한가? 당신은 실험을 수행한 그 과학자나 그룹이 한쪽으로 치우치지 않았는지 역시 물어야 한다. 한쪽으로 치우치지 않음은 당신이 실험의 결과로 특별한 이익을 얻지 않는다는 것을 의미한다. 예를 들면, 만약 한 제약 회사가 그 회사의 새로운 제품 중 하나가 얼마나 잘 작용하는지 시험해보기 위한 실험 비용을 지불한다면, 특별한 이익이 관련된 것이다. 만약 실험이 그 제품이 효과 있음을 보여준다면, 그 제약 회사는 이익을 본다. 따라서, 그 실험자들은 객관적이지 않다. 그들은 결론이 제약 회사에 우호적이고 이익을 주도록 보장할지도 모른다. 결과들을 평가할 때, 있을 수 있는 어떤 치우침에 대해 생각하라!

해설 실험과정이 기록되고 결론이 합리적이어야 하며 한쪽으로 치우치지 않아야 한다. 따라서 어느 한 쪽의 이익이 된다면 이는 ② '객관적이지' 않다.

오답 풀이

선택률	보기 해석
① 14%	inventive(창의적인)
③ 21%	untrustworthy(신뢰할 수 없는)
④ 15%	unreliable(믿을 수 없는)
⑤ 6%	decisive(결단력 있는)

구문 풀이 4행

You should also ask **if** the scientist or group conducting the experiment was unbiased.

→ 접속사 if가 명사절을 이끌면 '~인지 아닌지'의 뜻으로 해석한다.

구문 플러스⁺ if의 역할과 의미

If 접속사가 부사절에 쓰일 때는 조건을 나타내고 명사처럼 동사의 목적어 역할을 하면 '~인지 아닌지'의 의미이다.

She asked **if** he left school. (명사절: 목적어 역할)

E 정답 ① 32% 2019 6월 학평

해석 창의력은 우리가 일반적으로 인간만이 특별히 가지고 있다고 간주하는 능력이다. 인류 역사를 통틀어, 우리는 지구상에서 가장 창의적인 존재였다. 새는 둥지를 틀 수 있고, 개미는 개미탑을 쌓을 수 있지만, 지구상의 그 어떤 다른 종도 우리 인간이 보여주는 창의력 수준에 가까이 도달하지 못한다. 하지만, 불과 지난 10년 만에 우리는 로봇 개발처럼, 컴퓨터로 놀라운 것을 할 수 있는 능력을 습득하였다. 2010년대의 인공 지능의 급속한 발전으로 컴퓨터는 몇 가지를 언급하자면, 이제 얼굴을 인식하고, 언어를 번역하고, 여러분을 대신해 전화를 받고, 시를 쓸 수 있으며 세계에서 가장 복잡한 보드게임에서 선수들을 이길 수 있다. 갑작스럽게, 우리는 우리의 창의력이 경쟁할 상대가 없지 않게 되는 가능성에 직면해야 할 것이다.

해설 인공지능의 엄청난 발전으로 창의력이 더 이상 인간만의 고유한 능력이 아니며 로봇이 인간을 능가할 수도 있기 때문에, 인간의 창의력은 ① '경쟁할 상대가 없는' 것이 아니게 될 가능성에 직면하게 된다는 내용이다.

오답 풀이

선택률	보기 해석
② 14%	learned(습득된)
③ 16%	universal(보편적인)
④ 22%	ignored(무시된)
⑤ 13%	challenged(이의가 제기된)

구문 풀이 1행

For all of human history, we **have been** the most creative beings on Earth.

→ For가 기간을 나타내므로, 주절의 동사 have been이 현재완료 시제로 쓰였다.

구문 플러스⁺ 현재완료

계속, 경험, 완료, 결과의 의미를 나타내는 시제로, 주로 기간의 부사구와 함께 쓰인다.

We **have been** married **for** ten years. (계속)
They **have been** to Jeju five times before. (경험)

F 정답 ② 62% 2018 6월 학평

해석 동기 부여의 한 가지 결과는 상당한 노력을 필요로 하는 행동이다. 예를 들면, 만약 좋은 차를 사고자 하는 동기가 있다면, 당신은 온라인으로 차들을 검색하고, 광고를 자세히 보며, 자동차 대리점들을 방문하는 것 등을 할 것이다. 마찬가지로, 몸무게를 줄이고자 하는 동기가 있다면, 당신은 저지방 식품을 사고, 더 적은 1인분의 양을 먹으며, 운동을 할 것이다. 동기 부여는 목표를 더 가까이 가져오는 최종 행동을 이끌 뿐만 아니라, 준비 행동에 시간과 에너지를 쓸 의지를 만들기도 한다. 따라서 새 스마트폰을 사고자 하는 동기가 있는 사람은 그것을 위해 추가적인 돈을 벌고, 가게에 가기 위해 폭풍 속을 운전하며, 그것을 사려고 줄을 서서 기다릴지도 모른다.

해설 동기 부여는 어려운 일을 하게끔 만든다는 내용이므로 상당한 ② '노력'을 필요로 하는 일이라고 하는 것이 적절하다.

오답 풀이

선택률	보기 해석
① 14%	risk(위험)
③ 5%	memory(기억)
④ 6%	fortune(돈, 행운)
⑤ 10%	experience(경험)

구문 풀이 5행

Motivation **not only** drives the final behaviors that bring a goal closer **but also** creates willingness to expend time and energy on preparatory behaviors.

→ <not only A but also B>는 같은 형태끼리 연결한다.

구문 플러스⁺ not only A but also B

<not only A but also B>는 'A뿐만 아니라 B도'의 의미로 <B as well as A>와 같다.

He **not only** cleaned the house **but also** washed the dishes.
→ He washed the dishes **as well as** cleaned the house.

G 정답 ① 54% 2017 11월 학평

해석 여러분의 상사가 여러분 자녀의 이름과 나이를 모두 기억해주고, 주기적으로 여러분 자리에 들러서 그들에 관해 물어봐주고, 그런 뒤 여러분이 그들에 관해 이야기할 때 들어준다고 잠시 상상해 보자. 바로 그 상사가 여러분에게 여러분이 개발해야 할 능력을 이야기해주고 그 특정 능력을 여러분이 교육받을 기회를 열어준다고 상상해 보자. 가족상이 있고, 여러분의 상사가 도와주려는 표시로 장례식 후에 회사에서 여러분의 가족들에게 식사를 제공하게 해준다고 상상해 보자. 이 모든 것들은 실제 시나리오인데, 어떻게 생각하는가? 이런 배려와 관심의 행동을 했던 모든 상사는 열렬히 충성스러운 부하 직원을 두고 있다. 이들은 자기 상사를 위해 한층 더 노력하기를 전혀 사리지 않는 부하 직원을 두고 있다. 이들은 출근하는 것을 즐기며, 회사 돈을 아끼고 매출을 증대시킬 창의적인 아이디어를 자진해서 제안한다. 이런 상사들은 자기 팀원들에게 무엇을 달리 할지 말해줘서가 아니라, 배려를 통해서 팀원들의 행동에 영향을 끼친다.

해설 첫 세 문장에서 상사가 직원의 역량 계발 뿐 아니라 자녀나 가족사까지 살뜰히 챙겨주는 상황을 언급하고 있다. 이는 모두 ① '배려'의 예시에 해당한다.

오답 풀이

선택률	보기 해석
② 9%	warning(경고)
③ 14%	training(훈련)
④ 10%	pretending(겉치레)
⑤ 10%	evaluating(평가)

구문 풀이 3행

Imagine that same boss tells you about a skill you need to develop and opens up an opportunity **for you to be trained** on that particular skill.

→ opportunity를 꾸미는 형용사적 용법의 to부정사이다. 바로 앞의 <for+목적격>은 의미상 주어이다.

구문 플러스⁺ to부정사의 의미상 주어

부정사의 의미상 주어는 보통 <for+목적격>으로 표시하지만, 성격을 나타내는 형용사가 앞에 있으면 예외적으로 <of+목적격>으로 표시한다.

It's natural **for her** to say so. → 일반 형용사
It's nice **of you** to see him off. → 사람 성격 형용사

A 정답 ① 43% 2023 3월 학평

해석 Lewis Carroll의 <Through the Looking-Glass>에서 붉은 여왕은 Alice를 시골을 통과하는 경주에 데리고 간다. 그들은 달리고 또 달리지만, 그러다가 Alice는 자신들이 출발했던 나무 아래에 여전히 있음을 발견한다. 붉은 여왕은 Alice에게 "'여기서는' 보다시피 같은 장소에 머물러 있으려면 네가 할 수 있는 모든 뜀박질을 해야 한단다."라고 설명한다. 생물학자들은 때때로 이 '붉은 여왕 효과'를 이용해 진화 원리를 설명한다. 만약 여우가 더 많은 토끼를 잡기 위해 더 빨리 달리게 진화한다면, 그러면 오직 가장 빠른 토끼만이 충분히 오래 살아 훨씬 더 빨리 달리는 새로운 세대의 토끼를 낳을 텐데, 이 경우 당연하게도 가장 빠른 여우만이 충분한 토끼를 잡아 번성하여 자기 유전자를 물려줄 것이다. 그 두 종은 달린다고 해도 제자리에 머무를 뿐이다.

해설 '붉은 여왕 효과'를 적용해 생물계의 유전을 설명하는 글이다. 아무리 전속력으로 뛰고 있어도 모두가 그렇게 뛰는 한 차이가 생기지 않고 '같은 장소에 머물게 된다'는 내용으로 보아, 여우와 토끼 둘 다 더 빨리 뛰게 진화한다면 결국 둘 다 ① '제자리에 머무를 뿐이다'라는 결론이 적합하다.

오답 풀이

선택률	보기 해석
② 11%	결국 더 천천히 걷게 된다
③ 20%	서로 결코 마주치지 않는다
④ 13%	변화에 적응하지 못할 것이다
⑤ 13%	자기 부모보다 더 빨리 뛸 수 없다

구문 풀이 6행

If foxes evolve to run faster **so (that)** they can catch more rabbits, **then** only the fastest rabbits will live long enough to make a new generation of bunnies that run even faster ~

→ 문장은 전체적으로 <if ~ then …(만약 ~한다면, 그렇다면 …하다)> 구조이며, so (that)은 목적의 부사절을 이끈다.

구문 플러스⁺ **목적 부사절 so that**

접속사 so that은 '~하기 위해, ~하도록'이라는 목적의 의미로 주절을 보충한다.

We'll give you these free samples **so that** you **can** try out our products. → 조동사 can과 흔히 함께 쓰임

B 정답 ③ 41% 2022 6월 학평

해석 1992년 프린스턴 대학의 한 연구에서, 연구 과학자들은 두 개의 다른 쥐 집단을 관찰했다. 한 집단은 글루타민산염 수용체에 대한 유전자를 변형함으로써 지적으로 우월하게 만들어졌다. 글루타민산염은 학습에 필수적인 뇌 화학 물질이다. 다른 집단도 지적으로 열등하도록 유전적으로 조작되었는데, 이 역시 글루타민산염 수용체에 대한 유전자를 변형함으로써 이루어졌다. 그 후 똑똑한 쥐들은 표준 우리에서 길러졌고, 반면에 열등한 쥐들은 장난감과 운동용 쳇바퀴가 있고 사회적 상호작용이 많은 큰 우리에서 길러졌다. 연구가 끝날 무렵, 비록 지적으로 열등한 쥐들이 유전적으로 불리했지만, 그들은 그들보다 유전적으로 우월한 쥐들만큼 잘 수행할 수 있었다. 이것은 천성(선천적 성질)에 대한 양육(후천적 환경)의 진정한 승리였다. 유전자는 여러분 주변에 있는 것에 따라 켜지거나 꺼진다.

해설 유전적으로 지능이 낮은 쥐들이 '좋은 환경 덕분에' 유전적으로 지능이 높은 쥐들만큼 잘 수행하게 되었다는 내용이다. 즉, 환경에 따라 유전적 불리함을 극복할 수 있다는 것이므로 정답은 ③ '여러분 주변에 있는 것에 따라'가 적절하다.

오답 풀이

선택률	보기 해석
① 14%	생존을 위해 자력으로
② 10%	사회적 상호작용에서 벗어나서
④ 29%	유전적 우월함에 따라
⑤ 7%	스스로를 즐겁게 하기 위하여

구문 풀이 4행

The other group was genetically manipulated to be intellectually inferior, **(which was)** also done by modifying the gene for the glutamate receptor.

→ 콤마 뒤에 이어지는 부분은 which was가 생략된 계속적 용법의 관계대명사절이다. 선행사는 콤마 이전의 내용 전체이다.

구문 플러스⁺ **계속적 용법의 which**

선행사가 단어뿐 아니라 구, 절로 확장될 수 있다는 것이 특징이다.

I bought some new shoes, **which** are very comfortable.
You need to finish this task by the end of the day, **which** means you'll have to work efficiently.

C 정답 ⑤ 67% 2021 9월 학평

해석 많은 진화 생물학자들은 인간이 경제적인 이유로 언어를 발달시켰다고 주장한다. 우리는 거래해야 했고, 거래하기 위해서는 신뢰를 확립해야 했다. 언어는 당신이 누군가와 거래할 때 매우 편리하다. 초창기의 두 인간은 3개의 나무로 만든 그릇을 6다발의 바나나와 거래하기로 동의할 수 있었을 뿐만 아니라 규칙을 정할 수도 있었다. 그 그릇들을 만드는 데 무슨 나무가 사용되었나? 어디서 그 바나나를 얻게 되었나? 단지 제스처와 혼란스런 소음만을 사용해서는 그 상업 거래는 거의 불가능했을 것이고, 합의된 조항에 따라서 그것을 실행하는 것이 신뢰라는 결속을 만든다. 언어는 우리가 구체적이도록 해주고, 이것이 대화가 중요한 역할

을 하는 지점이다.

해설 언어를 통하여 상업 거래를 할 수 있었다는 내용이므로 인간이 ⑤ '경제적인 이유로 언어를 발달시켰다'가 빈칸에 들어가야 한다.

오답 풀이

선택률	보기 해석
① 14%	의사소통하기 위해 몸짓 언어를 사용했다
② 4%	누구에게 의존해야 하는지 본능적으로 알았다
③ 7%	스스로의 필요를 위해 규칙들을 종종 바꾸었다
④ 5%	그들 스스로의 생존을 위해 독립적으로 살았다

구문 풀이 6행

That business deal **would have been** nearly impossible using only gestures and confusing noises, ~

→ would have p.p.가 가정법 과거완료의 의미(만일 ~했더라면 …했었을 것이다)를 나타낸다.

구문 플러스+ would have p.p.

과거에 대한 추측 표현으로, 가정법 과거완료의 의미를 내포하기도 한다. 즉 '실제로 ~하지 않았지만 했더라면 …했을 것이다'의 의미인 것이다.

I **wouldn't have made** it without your help.
→ 실제로는 도움이 있었지만, '없었더라면 못 했을 것이다'라는 의미

D 정답 ① 27% 2020 9월 학평

해석 신생아와 유아는 흔들림에 의해 편안해지는데, 이것은 이런 움직임이 자궁 안에서 그들이 경험했던 것과 유사하기 때문이고, 그들이 이런 친숙한 느낌에서 편안해지는 것이 틀림없다는 말을 자주 듣는다. 이것은 사실일 수 있지만, 현재까지 임신 기간 동안 엄마가 움직이는 시간의 양과 흔들림에 대한 신생아의 반응 사이에 상당한 관계가 있음을 입증하는 설득력 있는 데이터는 없다. 신생아가 부드러운 흔들림을 젖을 먹는 것과 연관시키게 된다는 생각도 그만큼 가능할 법하다. 부모는 흔들어 주는 것이 신생아를 달래 준다는 것을 알고 있어서, 그들은 젖을 주는 동안 부드럽고, 반복적인 움직임을 매우 자주 제공한다. 음식의 등장은 일차 강화물이기 때문에, 신생아는 아마도 움직임을 좋아하게 되고, 그 이유는 그들이 연관 학습의 과정을 통해 조건화되어 왔기 때문이다.

해설 신생아와 유아가 흔들림을 선호하는 이유로 수유와의 관련성을 제시하고 있으므로, ① '움직임을 좋아하게 되고'가 적절하다.

오답 풀이

선택률	보기 해석
② 21%	지속적인 수유를 원하고
③ 14%	심한 흔들림을 싫어하고
④ 18%	음식의 맛을 기억하고
⑤ 17%	엄마와 유대를 형성하고

구문 풀이 3행

This may be true; however, to date there are no **convincing** data

→ 현재분사 convincing이 명사 data를 꾸며주는 형용사 역할을 하고 있다.

구문 플러스+ 분사의 쓰임

분사는 기본적으로 문장에서 형용사 역할을 하지만 위치와 명사와의 관계에 따라 쓰임이 달라진다.

한정적 용법
- 명사를 앞에서 수식

Look at the **dancing** girl over there. (저 곳에서 춤추는 소녀를 봐라.)

The road was blocked by a **fallen** tree. (길은 넘어진 나무로 막혔다.)

서술적 용법
- 주격 보어로 쓰이는 분사

They came **running**. (그들은 뛰어서 왔다.)
They were **excited**. (그들은 흥분됐다.)
- 목적격 보어로 쓰이는 분사

She saw a big eagle **flying** above her.
(그녀는 그녀 위로 큰 독수리가 날아다니는 것을 보았다.)

E 정답 ④ 64% 2019 9월 학평

해석 비전은 움직이는 목표물을 쏘아 맞히는 것과 같다. 많은 것들이 미래에 잘못될 수 있고, 더 많은 것들이 예측할 수 없는 방식들로 변할 수 있다. 그러한 일들이 일어날 때, 당신은 새로운 현실에 당신의 비전을 맞출 수 있도록 준비되어야 한다. 예를 들어, 한 사업가의 낙관적인 예측은 그가 예견할 수 없었을 방식으로 잔혹한 경기 침체나 공격적인 경쟁에 의해 날아갈 수 있다. 혹은 또 다른 시나리오에서는 그의 판매가 급등하거나 그의 수익이 훨씬 더 나아질 수 있다. 어떤 상황에서도, 그가 새로운 데이터에 직면했을 때 그의 기존의 비전을 고수하는 것은 어리석은 일이 될 것이다. 필요할 때 당신의 비전을 수정하거나 심지어 그것을 버리는 것은 잘못된 것이 아니다.

해설 미래의 변화에 맞게 비전을 수정하거나 버리는 것이 중요하다는 내용이므로 ④ '새로운 현실에 비전을 맞출'이 답이다.

오답 풀이

선택률	보기 해석
① 9%	자신의 비전을 다른 사람들에게 논리적으로 설명할
② 11%	자신이 내린 잘못된 결정을 방어할
③ 7%	경험을 공유할 수 있는 공동체를 세울
⑤ 6%	앞으로의 경제를 예측할 수 있게 전문가들과 상담할

구문 풀이 7행

In any event, he will be foolish **to stick to his old vision in the face of new data.**

→ to부정사의 부사적 용법 중 판단(foolish)의 이유를 나타내는 것으로 '왜 멍청한가'를 설명하고 있다.

구문 플러스⁺ 판단의 근거를 제시하는 to부정사

to부정사가 판단을 나타내는 형용사와 쓰여 그 이유를 나타낸다.

• She was smart **to get the highest score in math**.
('똑똑하다'는 판단)

F 정답 ④ 45% 2018 9월 학평

해석 만약 당신이 10층 건물 꼭대기에서 구슬이 떨어지는 데 시간이 얼마나 걸리는지 물리학자에게 묻는다면, 그는 아마 진공상태에서 구슬이 떨어지는 것을 가정하고 그 질문에 답할 것이다. 실제로 건물은 공기로 둘러싸여 있는데, 이것은 떨어지는 구슬에 마찰을 가하며 속도를 떨어뜨린다. 그러나 그 물리학자는 구슬에 가해지는 마찰이 너무 작아서 그것의 효과는 무시할 수 있다는 점을 지적할 것이다. 구슬이 진공상태에서 떨어진다고 가정하는 것은 그 답에 큰 영향을 주지 않고 그 문제를 단순화한다. 경제학자들도 같은 이유로 가정을 한다. 가정은 복잡한 세상을 단순화하고 이해하기 더 쉽게 만들 수 있다. 예를 들어, 국제무역의 효과를 연구하기 위해 우리는 세상이 단 두 국가로만 구성되었고, 각각의 국가들이 두 상품만을 생산한다고 가정할 수 있다. 그렇게 함으로써, 우리는 문제의 본질에 우리의 사고를 집중할 수 있다. 따라서 우리는 복잡한 세상에서의 국제무역을 이해하는 더 나은 위치에 있게 된다.

해설 가정은 문제를 단순화하여 이해를 더 쉽게 만든다고 했으므로, 이를 통해 ④ '문제의 본질에 우리의 사고를 집중할' 수 있다고 하는 것이 가장 적절하다.

오답 풀이

선택률	보기 해석
① 7%	소비자 권리의 침해를 예방할
② 22%	문화적 다양성의 가치를 이해할
③ 7%	실험실에서 실험자들의 안전을 보장할
⑤ 17%	물리학과 경제학의 차이를 깨달을

구문 풀이 8행

Assumptions can simplify the complex world and make **it** easier **to understand**.

→ to부정사가 목적어이지만 대신 가목적어 it을 쓰고 to부정사를 목적격 보어 뒤에 위치시킨다.

구문 플러스⁺ 가목적어 it

5형식 문장에서 to부정사구가 목적어로 쓰이면, 목적어를 뒤로 보내고 가목적어를 쓴다. 따라서 <동사+가목적어(it)+목적격 보어+진목적어(to부정사)>의 어순을 갖는다.

5형식 가목적어 문장에 많이 쓰이는 동사

make, find, consider, think, call, keep, leave 등

G 정답 ② 60% 2017 9월 학평

해석 Houston 공항의 임원들은 수하물을 찾는 데 걸리는 시간에 대한 많은 불평에 직면했다. 그래서 그들은 수하물 담당자들의 수를 늘렸다. 비록 이것이 기다리는 평균 시간을 8분으로 줄였지만 불평은 멈추지 않았다. 도착 게이트에서 수하물을 찾는 곳까지 도달하는 데 약 1분의 시간이 걸리고 탑승객들은 그들의 가방을 기다리며 7분을 더 보냈다. 그 해결책은 도착 게이트를 수하물 찾는 곳으로부터 더 멀리 이동시키는 것이었고 그 결과 탑승객들이 수하물 찾는 곳으로 걸어가는 데 약 7분의 시간이 걸렸다. 이는 불평이 거의 0으로 줄어드는 결과를 가져왔다. 연구는 사용된 시간이 사용되지 않은 시간보다 더 짧게 느껴진다는 것을 보여준다. 사람들은 보통 그들이 기다렸던 시간에 대해 과장하며, 그들이 가장 성가신 것으로 여기는 것은 사용되지 않은 채로 보낸 시간이다. 그래서 탑승객들을 더 오래 걷게 함으로써 그들의 시간을 차지하는 것은 그들에게 그렇게 오래 기다릴 필요가 없다는 생각을 갖게 했다.

해설 같은 시간이어도 아무것도 안 하고 기다리는 것보다 본인이 뭔가를 하면 그 시간을 짧게 느끼기 때문에 정답은 ② '그들을 더 오래 걷게 함'이다.

오답 풀이

선택률	보기 해석
① 10%	그들을 줄 세워 기다리게 하는 것
③ 8%	더 많은 광고를 만드는 것
④ 10%	불평으로 그들을 성가시게 하는 것
⑤ 9%	수하물을 다룰 직원을 더 고용하는 것

구문 풀이 4행

It took about a minute to get from the arrival gate to baggage claim, so the passengers spent seven more minutes waiting for their bags.

→ <it takes+시간+to부정사>는 '~하는 데 (시간)이 걸리다'라는 의미의 구문이다.

구문 플러스⁺ it takes ~ / it costs ~

보통 '시간이 걸리다'는 <it takes + 시간 + to부정사>로, '비용이 들다'는 <it costs + 비용 + to부정사>로 나타낸다.

It costs a lot of money **to get** this dress.

유형 플러스⁺ 빈칸 추론

주어진 지문의 내용을 기반으로 빈칸에 들어갈 어구를 찾는 유형으로, 지문 속에서 단서를 찾아 추론하여야 한다.

① 빈칸에 들어갈 말과 동일한 맥락의 내용이 예시, 재진술 등의 형태로 제시될 수 있다. 이 경우 해당 내용과 같은 의미가 되도록 빈칸을 채운다.
② 빈칸에 들어갈 말과 반대되는 맥락의 내용이 대조, 대비, 비교 등의 형태로 함께 제시될 수 있다. 이 경우 해당 내용과 반대의 의미가 되도록 빈칸을 채운다.

DAY 07 함축적 의미 추론 / 무관한 문장 찾기 A① B③ C③ D③ E③ F③ G④

A 정답 ① 50% 2023 6월 학평

해석 왜 당신은 고객이 구매품에 어떻게 반응하는지 신경 쓰는가? 좋은 질문이다. 구매 후 행동을 이해함으로써, 당신은 그 영향력과 구매자가 제품을 재구매할지(그리고 그 사람이 제품을 가질지 또는 반품할지)의 가능성을 이해할 수 있다. 당신은 구매자가 다른 사람들에게 당신에게서 제품을 구매하도록 권장할지 아닐지도 또한 알아낼 것이다. 만족한 고객은 당신의 사업을 위한 무급 대사가 될 수 있으므로, 고객 만족은 할 일 목록의 최상단에 있어야 한다. 사람들은 자기가 아는 사람들의 의견을 믿는 경향이 있다. 사람들은 언제든 광고보다 친구를 더 신뢰한다. 그들은 광고는 '좋은 면'을 말하려고 돈을 받고, 제품과 서비스를 구매하도록 그들을 설득하는 데 이용된다는 것을 알고 있다. 판매 후 고객의 만족을 지속 관찰하여, 당신은 부정적인 입소문 광고를 피할 수 있는 능력을 얻는다.

해설 소비자의 구매 후 행동을 관찰하면 그 소비자가 다른 사람들에게 제품을 사도록 권하는지 아닌지 알 수 있다는 내용으로 보아, 밑줄 부분은 만족한 소비자가 '홍보를 자청해서 해준다'는 의미임을 알 수 있다. 따라서 함축된 의미로 가장 적절한 것은 ① '아무 대가 없이 남들에게 제품을 추천해주다'이다.

오답 풀이

선택률	보기 해석
② 12%	제조업자들에게 제품에 대한 피드백을 주다
③ 12%	남의 말을 믿지 못하는 사람이 되다
④ 12%	제품을 해외에 광고해준 데 대한 보상을 받다
⑤ 14%	가격 걱정 없이 제품을 사다

구문 풀이 4행

You'll also determine **whether** the buyer will encourage others to purchase the product from you.

→ 접속사 whether(~인지 아닌지)가 이끄는 명사절이 determine의 목적절이다.

구문 플러스⁺ 접속사 whether

명사절 접속사: ~인지 아닌지
부사절 접속사: ~이든 아니든 간에

Let's check **whether** it's true. → 명사절
Whether it's true or not, we don't trust him. → 부사절

B 정답 ③ 83% 2022 6월 학평

해석 한 심리학 교수가 학생들에게 스트레스 관리 원칙을 가르치던 중 물이 든 유리잔을 들어 올리고 "제가 들고 있는 이 물 잔은 얼마나 무거울까요?"라고 물었다. 학생들은 다양한 대답을 외쳤다. 그 교수가 답했다. "이 잔의 절대적 무게는 중요하지 않습니다. 이는 제가 이 잔을 얼마나 오래 들고 있느냐에 달려 있죠. 만약 제가 이것을 1분 동안 들고 있다면, 꽤 가볍죠. 하지만, 만약 제가 이것을 하루 종일 들고 있다면 이것은 제 팔에 심각한 고통을 야기하고 잔을 바닥에 떨어뜨리게 할 것입니다. 각 사례에서 잔의 무게는 같지만, 제가 오래 들고 있을수록 그것은 저에게 더 무겁게 느껴지죠." 학생들은 동의하며 고개를 끄덕였고, 교수는 말을 계속했다. "여러분이 인생에서 느끼는 스트레스들도 이 물잔과 같습니다. 만약 아직도 어제 받은 스트레스의 무게를 느낀다면, 그것은 잔을 내려놓아야 할 때라는 강력한 신호입니다."

해설 물잔을 오래 들고 있으면 그 무게를 견딜 수 없게 되는 것처럼, 스트레스 또한 오래 영향받으면 견디기 어렵다는 내용이다. 물잔을 스트레스에 비유하고 있으므로, '잔을 내려놓다'는 ③ '마음에서 스트레스를 떠나 보내다'의 의미이다.

오답 풀이

선택률	보기 해석
① 4%	잔에 더 많은 물을 붓다
② 1%	실수를 하지 않기 위한 계획을 세우다
④ 10%	스트레스의 원인에 대해 생각하다
⑤ 1%	다른 사람들의 의견을 받아들이는 법을 배우다

구문 풀이 10행

If you still feel the weight of yesterday's stress, it's a strong sign **that** it's time to put the glass down.

→ 동격의 that절이 앞의 a strong sign의 내용을 자세히 설명하고 있다.

구문 플러스⁺ 동격의 that절

that절이 앞의 명사를 추가 설명하고 그 절의 문장성분이 완전할 때, 이를 동격절이라고 한다.

There exists a possibility **that** he went there.

C 정답 ③ 46% 2021 6월 학평

해석 우리는 사건을 선택적으로 해석하는 경향이 있다. 만약 우리가 일이 "이렇게" 또는 "그렇게" 되기를 원한다면, 우리는 틀림없이 그러한 관점을 뒷받침하는 방식으로 증거를 선택하거나 쌓거나 배열할 수 있다. 선택적인 지각은 우리에게 두드러져 보이는 것에 기반을 둔다. 그러나 우리에게 두드러져 보이고 있는 것은 우리의 목표, 관심사, 기대, 과거의 경험 또는 상황에 대한 현재의 요구와 매우 관련 있을지도 모른다. — "망치를 손에 들고 있으면, 모든 것은 못처럼 보인다." 이 인용문은 선택적 지각의 현상을 강조한다. 만약 우리가 망치를 사용하기를 원하면, 우리 주변의 세상은 마치 못으로 가득 찬 것처럼 보이기 시작할지도 모른다!

해설 일이 "이렇게" 또는 "그렇게" 되기를 원할 때, 그런 방향을 뒷받

침해주는 근거만을 선택적으로 지각하게 된다는 내용이다. 일이 특정한 방식으로 이루어지기를 원하는 상황의 예시로서 '망치를 사용하기를 원한다'는 말이 나오고 있으므로, 이는 ③ '특정한 방식으로 무언가를 하려고 의도하다'를 의미한다.

오답 풀이

선택률	보기 해석
① 7%	두드러지기를 꺼리다
② 9%	우리의 노력을 무의미하게 만들다
④ 22%	다른 사람들이 우리의 관점과 비슷한 관점을 갖기를 소망하다
⑤ 13%	다른 사람들에게 수용되는 사고방식을 갖다

구문 풀이 3행

Selective perception is based on what **seems** to us **to stand out**.

→ 동사 seem은 to부정사와 함께 쓰이며, '-하는 것으로 보이다'라는 수동의 의미를 갖지만 능동태로 쓴다.

구문 플러스 seem/appear의 쓰임

seem/appear to-V: ~한 것 같다
seem/appear like+명: ~인 것 같다
It seems/appears that ~: ~한 것 같다

He **seems to be** nervous.
Winning the lottery **seems like** a dream.
It appears that there has been some misunderstanding.

D 정답 ③ 76% 2020 3월 학평

해석 일부 사람들에게 주의를 기울이고 다른 사람들에게 그렇게 하지 않는 것이 여러분이 남을 무시하고 있다거나 거만하게 굴고 있다는 것을 의미하지는 않는다. 그것은 단지 명백한 사실을 나타낼 뿐인데, 우리가 가능한 대로(최대한) 주의를 기울이거나 관계를 발전시킬 수 있는 사람의 수에 한계가 있다는 것이다. 일부 과학자는 우리가 안정된 사회적 관계를 지속할 수 있는 사람의 수가 우리의 뇌에 의해 자연스럽게 제한되는 것일지도 모른다고까지 믿는다. (여러분이 다른 배경의 사람들을 더 많이 알수록, 여러분의 삶은 더 다채로워진다.) Robin Dunbar 교수는 우리의 마음은 실제로 최대 약 150명의 사람과 의미 있는 관계를 형성할 수 있을 뿐이라고 설명했다. 그것이 사실이든 아니든, 우리가 모든 사람과 진정한 친구가 될 수 있는 것은 아니라고 가정하는 것이 안전하다.

해설 우리가 의미 있는 관계를 맺는 수가 한정되어 있다고 했으므로 다른 배경의 사람을 알수록 더 다채로워진다는 ③은 관련이 없다.

오답 풀이

선택률	보기 해석
① 4%	첫 문장이 주어인 It으로 연결된다. 즉 남들에게 주의를 다 기울이지 못하는 상황은 거만함 등 다른 이유 때문이 아니라 우리가 관심을 줄 수 있는 사람 수에 제한이 있기 때문임을 설명하는 것이다.
② 6%	돈독한 관계 맺기가 가능한 사람 수에 '제한'이 있다는 것이 과학자들에 의해서도 지지된다는 내용이다. 즉 ①을 뒷받침하는 문장이다.
④ 7%	①, ②에서 말하는 제한된 수가 '150명' 정도라는 구체적 숫자를 제시하고 있다.
⑤ 4%	앞 내용(that)이 사실이든 아니든, 우리가 모두와 친구가 될 수 없는 것은 분명하다는 내용이다.

구문 풀이 1행

Paying attention to some people and not others doesn't mean you're being dismissive or arrogant.

→ 동명사구 주어는 단수 취급한다.

구문 플러스 명사구 주어의 수 일치

동명사구, to부정사구 주어는 단수 취급한다.

Swimming in the pool is fun.
To stop learning is to stop growing.

E 정답 ③ 59% 2019 3월 학평

해석 기술은 의문의 여지가 있는 이점을 지니고 있다. 우리는 너무 많은 정보와 올바른 정보만을 사용하여 의사결정 과정을 간소하게 하는 것 사이에서 균형을 이루어야 한다. 인터넷은 어떤 문제에 대해서도 너무 많은 무료 정보를 이용 가능하게 만들어서 우리는 어떤 결정을 하기 위해서 그 모든 정보를 고려해야 한다고 생각한다. 그래서 우리는 계속 인터넷에서 답을 검색한다. 이것이 우리가 개인적, 사업적, 혹은 다른 결정을 하려고 애쓸 때, 전조등 불빛에 노출된 사슴처럼, 우리를 정보에 눈멀게 만든다. 오늘날 어떤 일에 있어서 성공하기 위해서는, 우리는 눈먼 사람들의 세계에서는 한 눈으로 보는 사람이 불가능해 보이는 일을 이룰 수 있다는 것을 명심해야 한다. 한 눈으로 보는 사람은 어떤 분석이든 단순하게 하는 것의 힘을 이해하고, 직관이라는 한 눈을 사용할 때 의사 결정자가 될 것이다.

해설 직관적이고 간결한 결정을 위해 인터넷에 있는 너무 많은 정보의 양을 적절하게 조절할 필요가 있다고 하고 있으므로, '정보에 눈먼다'는 ③ '너무나 많은 정보 때문에 의사 결정을 할 수 없는'의 의미로 볼 수 있다.

오답 풀이

선택률	보기 해석
① 9%	다른 사람들의 생각을 수용하지 않는
② 11%	무료 정보에 접근할 수 없는
④ 10%	이용 가능한 정보의 부족에 무관심한
⑤ 8%	의사 결정의 위험을 기꺼이 무릅쓰는

구문 풀이 6행

This makes us information blinded ~ **when trying** to make personal, business, or other decisions.

→ 분사구문은 접속사와 주어를 생략하고 -ing 구문으로 쓰지만 종종 접속사를 생략하지 않기도 한다.

구문 플러스 접속사가 있는 분사구문

분사구문은 접속사(as, because, when, if, although 등)와 주어를 생략하지만 의미를 명확하게 하기 위해 접속사를 그대로 두기도 한다.

While walking down the street, I ran into Jason.
(= While I was walking ~)

유형 플러스 함축적 의미 추론

글의 전체적인 맥락 속에서 밑줄 친 어구가 의미하는 바를 추론하는 유형이다. 글의 핵심에 관련된 비유적인 표현에 밑줄이 있고 그 의미를 재진술하는 선택지를 골라야 하는 경우가 대부분이다.

① 글의 핵심 소재와 주제를 잘 파악해야 한다.
② 지문의 밑줄 친 어구를 선택지의 표현으로 바꾸어 써도 기존의 맥락과 의미가 유지되어야 한다.

F 정답 ③ 49% 2018 9월 학평

해석 물은 궁극적인 공유 자원이다. 한때, 강들은 끝없는 것처럼 보였고 물을 보호한다는 발상은 어리석게 여겨졌다. 그러나 규칙은 변한다. 사회는 반복적으로 수계(水系)를 연구해 왔고 현명한 사용을 재정의해 왔다. 현재 에콰도르는 자연의 권리를 헌법에 포함시킨 지구상 첫 번째 국가가 되었다. 이러한 움직임은 강과 숲이 단순히 재산이 아니라 그들 스스로가 번영할 권리를 가진다고 주장한다. (수로 기반 교통체제를 발달시키는 것은 에콰도르의 교통 기반 시설을 현대화시킬 것이다.) 이 헌법에 따라 시민은 강의 건강은 공공의 선에 필수적임을 인식하며, 훼손된 (강) 유역을 대표해서 소송을 제기할 수도 있다. 더 많은 권리들이 자연의 권리를 인정하고 있으며 에콰도르의 주도를 따를 것으로 기대된다.

해설 사람들이 자연을 그들에게 속한 재산이 아닌, 번영할 권리를 가진 주체로 보기 시작했다는 내용이므로, 자연의 권리 인정이 글의 핵심 주제이다. 따라서 강을 훼손하고 수로를 발달시키는 것을 긍정적으로 이야기하는 ③은 글의 흐름에 어울리지 않는다.

오답 풀이

선택률	보기 해석
① 7%	사회에서 물의 현명한 사용을 계속 재정의해왔다는 내용에 이어, '현재 에콰도르'의 사례를 언급한다.
② 10%	①의 '자연권을 인정하려는' 노력이 This move로 이어진다. 또한 ①의 the rights of nature가 their own right to flourish라는 표현으로 구체화되었다.
④ 26%	the constitution이 ①에 언급된 에콰도르의 헌법(its constitution)을 다시 가리킨다. 강의 건강을 인정했으므로 여기에 근거해 소송까지 이뤄질 수 있다는 보충 설명이 연결되는 문맥이다.
⑤ 6%	에콰도르의 선례를 많은 국가들이 따를 것이라는 전망을 결론으로 제시하고 있다.

구문 풀이 1행

Once, watercourses seemed boundless and **the idea of protecting water was considered silly**.

→ and 뒤는 5형식 문장의 수동태 구문이다. 본래의 5형식 문장은 'people considered the idea of protecting water silly'였다.

구문 플러스 5형식의 수동태

<동사+목적어+목적격 보어>의 5형식 문장이 수동태(be p.p.)로 쓰일 때는 목적어가 주어 자리로 가며, 동사에 따라 목적격 보어의 형태가 바뀌기도 하고 바뀌지 않기도 한다.

- I considered her story **interesting**.
  → Her story was considered **interesting**. (대부분의 보어: 그대로)
- She made me **do** my homework.
  → I was made **to do** my homework. (원형부정사 보어 → to부정사로)

G 정답 ④ 70% 2017 9월 학평

해석 역사를 공부하는 것은 여러분을 함께 말하기에 더 유식하거나 재밌는 사람으로 만들어 줄 수 있거나 모든 종류의 멋진 직업, 탐구, 그리고 경력으로 이어질 수 있다. 하지만 훨씬 더 중요한 것은, 역사를 공부하는 것이 우리가 인류의 '중대 문제'를 묻고 답하는 데 도움을 준다는 점이다. 만약 여러분이 현재 무언가가 왜 발생하고 있는지 알기를 원한다면, 여러분은 사회학자나 경제학자에게 물어볼지도 모른다. 그러나 만약 여러분이 (그에 대한) 깊은 배경지식을 알고 싶다면, 여러분은 역사가에게 질문한다. (역사가와 같은 직업은 드문 직업이고, 이것이 아마 여러분이 역사가를 만나 본 적이 없는 이유일 수 있다.) 그것은 그들이 과거를 알고 이해하며 현재와의 복잡한 상관관계를 설명할 수 있는 사람이기 때문이다.

해설 역사를 공부하는 이유를 설명하는 글로, 역사가라는 직업의 희귀함에 대해 언급하고 있지는 않다. 따라서 정답은 ④이다.

오답 풀이

선택률	보기 해석
① 4%	앞에서 역사 공부가 중요한 이유를 언급한 데 이어, '그보다 더 중요한' 진짜 이유를 언급하고 있다.
② 13%	갑자기 경제학자나 사회학자가 등장해 흐름과 무관해 보이지만, ③과 함께 읽으면 자연스럽다. 현재 일어나는 상황을 알려면 사회학자나 경제학자에게 물으면 되지만, 그 배경을 알려면 역사학자에게 물어야 한다는 예시로 ①의 내용을 뒷받침하는 것이다.
③ 8%	②에 이어지는 보충 설명으로, 글의 핵심을 담고 있기도 하다. 어떤 일의 깊은 배경을 이해하는 데 도움을 주고, 인류의 '중대 질문'에 답하게 하는 존재들이 바로 역사학자들이라는 내용이다.
⑤ 3%	③과 연결되어 그 이유를 설명하는 문장이다. 즉 '왜 사건 배경을 알고 싶을 때 역사학자들에게 물어야 하는지'를 설명하는 부분이다.

구문 풀이 3행

But even more importantly, studying history **helps us ask and answer** humanity's Big Questions.

→ help는 <help +목적어+목적격 보어>의 5형식 동사로 목적격 보어로 동사원형이나 to부정사를 쓴다.

구문 플러스+ 5형식의 목적격 보어 형태

5형식 동사의 목적격 보어는 그 형태가 다양하다.

Don't call me **a liar**! (명사)
Studying history can make you **more knowledgeable**. (형용사)
I helped her **(to) laundry clothes**. (동사원형 혹은 to부정사)

유형 플러스+ 무관한 문장 찾기

흐름상 무관하거나 주제와 반대되는 문장을 찾아내는 유형이다.

① 번호(①~⑤)가 시작되기 전 문장에서 주제에 대한 힌트를 얻는다.
② 핵심어가 들어 있지 않는 문장이 없나 살핀다.
③ 모두 핵심어가 포함돼 있다면, 주제와 반대되는 문장을 찾아야 한다.

A 정답 ③ 89% 2023 6월 학평

해석 Gary Becker는 1930년 Pennsylvania 주 Pottsville에서 태어났고 New York City의 Brooklyn에서 자랐다. 교육을 제대로 받지 못한 그의 아버지는 금융과 정치 문제에 깊은 관심이 있었다. 고등학교를 졸업한 후, Becker는 Princeton University로 진학했고, 거기서 그는 경제학을 전공했다. Princeton University에서의 경제학 교육이 '현실적인 문제를 다루고 있는 것처럼 보이지 않았기' 때문에 그는 그곳에서 그가 받은 경제학 교육에 불만족했다. 그는 1955년에 University of Chicago에서 경제학 박사 학위를 취득했다. 차별의 경제학에 대한 그의 박사 논문은 노벨상 위원회에 의해 경제학에 대한 중요한 기여로 언급되었다. 1985년부터, Becker는 <Business Week>에 경제학적 분석과 아이디어를 일반 대중에게 설명하는 경제학 칼럼을 정기적으로 기고했다. 1992년에, 그는 노벨 경제학상을 수상했다.

해설 'He was dissatisfied with his economic education at Princeton University ~'에서 Gary Becker는 프린스턴에서의 경제학 교육이 실질적 문제를 다루지 않는다고 생각해 불만족했다고 한다. 따라서 일치하지 않는 것은 ③이다.

오답 풀이

선택률	보기 해석
① 1%	~ grew up in Brooklyn, New York City.
② 2%	His father ~ had a deep interest in financial and political issues.
④ 4%	He earned a doctor's degree in economics from the University of Chicago in 1955.
⑤ 2%	Since 1985, Becker had written a regular economics column in *Business Week*, ~

구문 풀이 12행

In 1992, he **was awarded the Nobel Prize** in economic science.

→ 4형식 동사 award가 수동태로 바뀌고, 원래 문장의 직접목적어가 <be p.p.> 뒤에 그대로 목적어로 쓰였다.

구문 플러스⁺ 4형식 문장의 수동태

4형식 문장은 본래 목적어를 2개 취하므로, 수동태로 바뀌어도 <be p.p.> 뒤에 목적어가 1개 남는다.

He **was given drugs** to relieve the pain.

B 정답 ③ 94% 2022 6월 학평

해석 피아니스트, 작곡가, 그리고 빅 밴드 리더인 Claude Bolling은 1930년 4월 10일 프랑스 칸에서 태어났지만, 그의 삶의 대부분을 파리에서 보냈다. 그는 젊었을 때 클래식 음악을 공부하기 시작했다. 그는 학교 친구에게 재즈의 세계를 소개받았다. 후에 Bolling은 최고의 재즈 음악가들 중 한 명인 Fats Waller의 음악에 관심을 가졌다. 그는 10대 때 프랑스의 아마추어 대회에서 Best Piano Player 상을 수상하며 유명해졌다. 그는 또한 성공적인 영화 음악 작곡가였고, 100편이 넘는 영화의 음악을 작곡했다. 1975년에, 그는 플루트 연주자 Rampal과 협업했고, <Suite for Flute and Jazz Piano Trio>를 발매했으며, 그것으로 가장 잘 알려지게 되었다. 그는 두 아들 David와 Alexandre를 남기고 2020년 사망했다.

해설 20대가 아니라 10대에 Best Piano Player 상을 받았다고 하므로 ③이 정답이다.

오답 풀이

선택률	보기 해석
① 1%	Pianist ~ was born on April 10, 1930, in Cannes, France
② 1%	He was introduced to the world of jazz by a schoolmate
④ 2%	He was also a successful film music composer
⑤ 1%	In 1975, he collaborated with flutist Rampal

구문 풀이 8행

In 1975, he collaborated with flutist Rampal and published *Suite for Flute and Jazz Piano Trio*, **which** he became most well-known for.

→ 콤마 뒤의 which는 계속적 용법으로, 해석은 앞 문장의 내용에 이어서 한다.

구문 플러스⁺ 관계대명사의 계속적 용법

콤마 뒤의 관계대명사는 앞말에 이어서 '~ 그리고/그런데 그 사람은/그것은 …'이라고 해석한다.

He has two daughters, **who** became teachers.
그는 딸이 둘 있다. 그리고 그들은 교사가 되었다.
She was stunning in the black dress, **which** she borrowed from her sister.
그녀는 검은 드레스를 입으니 정말 멋졌다. 그런데 그것을 그녀는 언니에게서 빌렸다.

C 정답 ③ 66% 2021 6월 학평

해석 Lithops는 독특한 바위 같은 겉모양 때문에 종종 '살아있는 돌'로 불리는 식물이다. 이것은 원산지가 남아프리카 사막이지만, 식물원과 종묘원에서 흔히 팔린다. Lithops는 수분이 거의 없는 빡빡한 모래 토양과 극히 높은 온도에서 잘 자란다. Lithops는 작은 식물로, 토양의 표면 위로 1인치 이상 거의 자라지 않고 보통 단 두 개의 잎을 가지고 있다. 두꺼운 잎은 동물 발의 갈라진 틈이나 함께 모여있는 한 쌍의 회갈색 빛을 띠는 돌과 닮았다. 이 식물은 실제 줄기는 없고 식물의 대부분이 땅속에 묻혀 있다. 겉모양은 수분을 보존하는 효과를 가지고 있다.

해설 Lithops는 토양의 표면 위로 1인치 이상 자라는 일이 거의 없다고 하므로 ③이 정답이다.

오답 풀이

선택률	보기 해석
① 1%	Lithops are plants that are often called 'living stones'
② 3%	They are native to the deserts of South Africa
④ 18%	The plants have no true stem and much of the plant is underground.
⑤ 11%	Their appearance has the effect of conserving moisture.

구문 풀이 8행

The plants have no true stem and **much of the plant is** underground.

→ <much of+단수명사>가 주어이므로, 뒤에 단수동사 is가 나왔다. 이 <much of+단수명사>는 <부분 of 전체> 표현의 일종이다.

구문 플러스⁺ 〈부분 of 전체〉의 수 일치

<부분 of 전체>가 주어이면 동사는 전체 명사에 수 일치한다.

Many of the students here **wear** glasses.
(전체=복수)

Much of the water was wasted along the way.
(전체=불가산)

D 정답 ③ 83% 2020 9월 학평

해석 Jessie Redmon Fauset은 1884년 New Jersey의 Snow Hill에서 태어났다. 그녀는 Cornell University를 졸업한 최초의 흑인 여성이었다. Fauset은 소설, 시, 단편 소설, 수필을 쓰는 것 외에도, Washington, D.C.의 공립학교에서 프랑스어를 가르쳤고, 저널 편집자로서 일했다. 편집자로 일하는 동안, 그녀는 Harlem Renaissance(흑인 예술 문화 부흥 운동)의 많은 유명한 작가들을 고무시켰다. 비록 그녀는 소설가보다 편집자로서 더 유명하지만, 많은 비평가들은 그녀의 소설 <Plum Bun>을 Fauset의 가장 뛰어난 작품으로 간주한다. 그 속에서, 그녀는 한 흑인 소녀의 이야기를 하는데, 그 소녀는 백인으로 여겨질 수 있었지만 결국에는 자신의 인종적 정체성과 자부심을 주장한다. Fauset은 1961년 4월 30일에 Philadelphia에서 심장병으로 사망했다.

해설 Jessie Redmon Fauset은 소설가보다 편집자로 더 유명했다고 하므로 ③이 정답이다.

오답 풀이

선택률	보기 해석
① 1%	the first black woman to graduate from Cornell University
② 5%	taught French in public schools in Washington, D.C.
④ 7%	she tells the story of a black girl
⑤ 1%	died of heart disease April 30, 1961, in Philadelphia

구문 풀이 8행

~ she tells the story of a black girl **who could pass for** white **but** ultimately **claims** her racial identity and pride.

→ 동사 claims가 문맥상 could pass와 병렬 연결되었다. 'a black girl'이 인종적 정체성과 자부심을 '주장한' 것이기 때문이다.

구문 플러스⁺ 병렬구조 (2)

등위접속사 앞뒤로 무엇이 병렬구조를 이루는지 파악하려면 형태뿐 아니라 문맥도 잘 살펴야 한다.

She **found out** who ate the last slice of cake but **didn't say** anything about it.
→ 과거시제 동사가 3개 등장하지만, ate는 문맥상 who절의 동사이며 found out과 didn't say만 병렬 연결됨

E 정답 ④ 87% 2019 9월 학평

해석 Mary Cassatt은 부유한 가정의 다섯 아이들 중 넷째로 Pennsylvania에서 태어났다. Mary Cassatt과 그녀의 가족은 유년 시절에 유럽 전역을 여행했다. 그녀가 화가가 되려고 결심했을 때 그녀의 가족은 찬성하지 않았지만, 그녀의 열망은 매우 강해서, 미술을 그녀의 진로 분야로 삼기 위한 과정을 용감하게 밟아나갔다. 그녀는 먼저 필라델피아에서 공부했고 그러고 나서 그림을 공부하기 위해 파리로 갔다. 그녀는 Edgar Degas의 작품에 감탄했고 파리에서 그를 만날 수 있었는데, 그것은 큰 영감이 되었다. 비록 그녀는 자기 자녀는 없었지만, 아이들을 사랑했고 그녀의 친구들과 가족의 자녀의 초상화를 그렸다. Cassatt은 70세에 시력을 잃었고, 슬프게도 노년에는 그림을 그릴 수 없었다.

해설 Mary Cassatt은 아이들을 좋아하고 아이들 그림을 많이 그렸지만 자신의 아이는 없었다고 하므로 ④가 정답이다.

오답 풀이

선택률	보기 해석
① 2%	Mary Cassatt and her family traveled throughout Europe in her childhood.
② 3%	Her family did not approve when she decided to become an artist
③ 3%	She admired the work of Edgar Degas and was able to meet him in Paris
⑤ 3%	Cassatt lost her sight at the age of seventy

구문 풀이 8행

Though she never had children of her own, she loved children and painted portraits of the children of her friends and family.

→ 양보의 의미인 부사절 접속사는 even though, although, even if 등이 있다.

구문 플러스⁺ 양보의 부사절

접속사 though, even though, even if, although 등은 '~에도 불구하고, ~라 하더라도'라는 양보의 의미를 나타낸다.

We should try to do our best **even if** we fail.

F 정답 ③ 82% *2018 9월 학평*

해석 Eddie Adams는 펜실베니아 주 New Kensington에서 태어났다. 그는 십대 시절에 자신의 고등학교 신문 사진 기자가 되어 사진에 대한 열정을 키웠다. 졸업 후, 그는 미국 해병대에 입대했고, 그곳에서 종군 사진 기자로 한국 전쟁 장면을 촬영했다. 1958년, 그는 필라델피아에서 발간된 석간 신문 <Philadelphia Evening Bulletin>의 직원이 되었다. 1962년에 그는 연합통신사(AP)에 입사했고, 10년 뒤 연합통신사를 떠나 <Time> 잡지사에서 프리랜서로 일했다. 그가 베트남에서 촬영한 <Saigon Execution> 사진은 그에게 1969년 특종기사 보도 사진 부문의 퓰리처상을 가져다 주었다. 그는 350개가 넘는 잡지 표지에 실린 Deng Xiaoping, Richard Nixon, George Bush와 같은 정치 지도자들의 사진을 촬영했다.

해설 Eddie Adams는 1962년 연합통신사(AP)에 입사했고 10년 후에 <Time> 잡지사에 입사했기 때문에 ③ '1962년부터 *Time* 잡지사에서 일했다.'가 내용과 다르다.

오답 풀이

선택률	보기 해석
① 3%	He developed his passion for photography in his teens
② 4%	where he captured scenes from the Korean War as a combat photographer
④ 3%	The ~ photo he took in Vietnam earned him the Pulitzer Prize
⑤ 5%	He shot more than 350 covers of magazines with portraits of political leaders

구문 풀이 3행

After graduating, he joined the United States Marine Corps, **where** he captured scenes from the Korean War as a combat photographer.

→ 장소 선행사를 수식하기 위해 부사 역할과 접속사 역할을 동시에 하는 관계부사 where를 쓴다.

구문 플러스⁺ 관계부사의 계속적 용법

관계부사 where, when은 관계대명사와 마찬가지로 계속적 용법으로 쓸 수 있다.

She went into the room, **where** her little daughter was asleep. (= and there ~)

They decided to postpone their wedding till next year, **when** they expect things to improve. (= and then ~)

G 정답 ④ 85% *2016 9월 학평*

해석 Edith Wharton은 1862년에 뉴욕시의 한 부유한 가정에서 태어났다. 가정에서 개인 교사들에 의해 교육을 받은 그녀는 일찍이 독서와 글쓰기를 즐겼다. 그녀의 첫 번째 소설인 <The Valley of Decision>이 1902년에 출판된 후, 그녀는 많은 소설을 집필했고 몇몇은 그녀에게 폭넓은 독자층을 가져다 주었다. Wharton은 또한 건축에 매우 큰 애정이 있었고 그녀는 자신의 첫 번째 실제 집을 설계하여 건축했다. 1차 세계대전 동안 그녀는 프랑스와 벨기에의 고아들을 돕는 데 많은 시간을 쏟았고 그들을 부양하기 위해 기금을 모으는 것을 도왔다. 전쟁 후 그녀는 프랑스의 Provence에 정착했으며 거기에서 <The Age of Innocence>의 집필을 끝마쳤다. 이 소설은 Wharton이 1921년 Pulitzer상을 받을 수 있게 했으며 그녀는 이 상을 받은 최초의 여성이 되었다.

해설 전쟁 후 Provence에 정착하며 <The Age of Innocence>의 집필을 끝마쳤다고 했기에 정답은 ④이다.

오답 풀이

선택률	보기 해석
① 4%	her first novel ~ was published in 1902
② 3%	had a great love of architecture, and she designed and built her first real home
③ 5%	assisting orphans from France and Belgium
⑤ 1%	~ Pulitzer Prize, making her the first woman to win the award

구문 풀이 9행

This novel won Wharton the 1921 Pulitzer Prize, making her the first woman **to win the award**.

→ to부정사가 형용사적 용법으로 앞의 명사를 수식한다.

구문 플러스⁺ to부정사의 형용사적 용법

to부정사가 형용사처럼 명사를 수식하는 것을 말한다.

I need some water **to drink**.

유형 플러스⁺ 내용 일치 / 불일치

글의 세부 정보가 일치 또는 불일치하는지 판단하는 유형이다.

유형 해결 방법

① 선택지를 먼저 읽고 어떤 정보를 확인해야 하는지 살펴본다.

② 지문 속 정보의 제시 순서와 선택지의 순서는 동일하므로, 위에서부터 차례대로 각 선택지의 정보가 있는 부분을 빠르게 찾아 대조한다.

DAY 09 어휘의 이해

A④ B⑤ C③ D③ E① F⑤ G③

A 정답 ④ 36% 2023 3월 학평

해석 산업 사회가 1940년대와 1950년대 동안 더 부유해지고, 더 경쟁적이 되고, 더 지리적으로 퍼지면서 판매 개념에 주요한 철학적 변화가 일어났다. 이로 인해 기업은 구매자 및 고객과 더 긴밀한 관계를 발전시켜야 했고, 이것은 결과적으로 기업이 적당한 가격에 양질의 제품을 생산하는 것으로는 충분하지 않다는 것을 깨닫게 했다. 사실, 고객이 실제로 원하는 제품을 내놓는 것이 마찬가지로 매우 중요했다. 1908년에 Henry Ford는 가장 많이 팔렸던 T모델 Ford를 딱 한 색상(검은색)으로만 생산했지만, 현대 사회에서는 이것이 더 이상 가능하지 않았다. 사회의 현대화는 생산이 그 자체의 수요를 창출할 것이라는 견해를 강화하는(→ 파괴하는) 마케팅 혁명으로 이어졌다. 고객과 그들의 다양하고 흔히 복잡한 욕구를 충족하고자 하는 욕망이 기업의 초점이 되었다.

해설 ④가 포함된 문장 앞뒤는 차가 한 가지 색상으로만 생산되어도 일단 만들어놓으면 팔리던 시대는 가고, 고객의 다양한 수요에 부응할 필요가 생겼다는 문맥이다. 따라서 ④에는 strengthened 대신 destroyed를 써야 한다.

오답 풀이

선택률	보기 해석
① 12%	closer(더 긴밀한)
② 16%	essential(매우 중요한)
③ 27%	possible(가능한)
⑤ 9%	meet(충족하다)

구문 풀이 9행

The modernization of society led to a marketing revolution that destroyed **the view that** production would create its own demand.

→ 동격의 that절이 앞의 the view의 내용을 자세히 설명하고 있다.

구문 플러스⁺ 동격절을 유도하는 추상명사

동격의 that절은 흔히 fact, idea, news, rumor, view, evidence, feeling 등의 추상명사와 어울려 쓰인다.

the evidence that he stole the necklace
the rumor that the boss will leave the company

B 정답 ⑤ 55% 2022 9월 학평

해석 어떤 허브는 다소 마법처럼 특정 장기의 기능을 향상시키고, 그 결과 특정한 질병을 "고친다"고 널리 알려져 있다. 그러한 진술은 비과학적이고 근거가 없다. 때때로 허브는 효과가 있는 것처럼 보이는데, 이는 당신의 신체로부터 그것들을 제거하려는 당신 몸의 적극적인 시도 속에서 그것들이 혈액 순환을 증가시키는 경향이 있기 때문이다. 그것은 일시적으로 좋은 기분을 만들어 줄 수 있는데, 이는 마치 당신의 건강 상태가 향상된 것처럼 보이게 만든다. 또한 허브는, 다른 아무 방법과 마찬가지로, 위약 효과를 가지고 있는데, 그래서 당신이 더 나아졌다고 느끼도록 도와준다. 어떠한 경우든, 건강을 되찾게 하는 지성을 가진 것은 허브가 아니라 바로 당신의 몸이다. 허브가 어떻게 당신의 몸을 더 건강해지는 방향으로 인도하는 데 요구되는 지성을 가질 수 있겠는가? 그것은 불가능하다. 어떻게 허브가 당신의 몸 안으로 들어가 영리하게 당신의 문제를 해결할 수 있는지를 상상해 보라. 만약 당신이 그렇게 해 본다면 당신은 그것이 얼마나 불가능하게 보이는지를 알게 될 것이다. 그렇지 않다면, 그것은 허브가 인간의 몸보다 덜(→더) 지적이라는 것을 의미하는 것이 되는데, 이는 정말로 믿기 어렵다.

해설 허브는 건강에 도움이 되지 않고, 허브가 아닌 우리 몸 자체가 우리의 건강을 되찾게 한다는 내용의 글이다. 마지막 문장은 '그렇지 않다면(만약 허브가 우리 몸의 문제를 해결할 수 있다면)'의 상황을 가정하는데, 이 상황은 허브가 인간의 몸보다 ⑤ '더(more)' 지적인 상황을 가정하는 것이다.

오답 풀이

선택률	보기 해석
① 8%	increase(증가시키다)
② 12%	temporary(일시적인)
③ 15%	regain(되찾다)
④ 10%	fix(고치다)

구문 풀이 11행

Try to imagine **how herbs might come into your body and intelligently fix your problems.** If you try to do that, you will see **how impossible it seems.**

→ 두 문장에서 모두, how는 목적어 기능의 의문사절을 이끈다. how herbs ~ problems에서의 how는 '어떻게'의 의미이고, how impossible ~ seems에서의 how는 '얼마나'의 의미이다.

구문 플러스⁺ 의문부사 how

how는 '어떻게, 얼마나'의 의미를 나타내며, '얼마나'라는 의미일 때는 보통 <how+형/부+주어+동사> 형태로 쓴다.

I don't know **how** he finds the time to read so many books. → 어떻게
Don't you see **how** pretty you are when you smile? → 얼마나

C 정답 ③ 56% 2021 3월 학평

해석 기본적인 어떤 것의 가격이 크게 하락할 때, 온 세상이 바뀔 수 있다. 조명을 생각해 보자. 아마 여러분은 어떤 유형의 인공조명 아래에서 이 문장을 읽고 있을 것이다. 또한, 여러분은 독서를 위해 인공조명을 이용하는 것이 그럴 만한 가치가 있는지에 대해 아마 한번도 생각하지 않았을 것이다. 조명 값이 너무 싸서 여러 분은 생각 없이 그것을 이용한다. 하지만 1800년대 초반에는, 같은 양의 조명에 대해 오늘날 지불하고 있는 것의 400배만큼의 비용이 들었을 것이다. 그 가격이면, 여러분은 비

용을 의식할 것이고 책을 읽기 위해 인공조명을 이용하기 전에 다시 한 번 생각할 것이다. 조명 가격의 증가(→ 하락)는 세상을 밝혔다. 그것은 밤을 낮으로 바꾸었을 뿐 아니라, 자연광이 들어올 수 없는 큰 건물에서 우리가 살고 일할 수 있게 해 주었다. 만약 인공조명의 비용이 거의 공짜 수준으로 하락하지 않았더라면 우리가 오늘날 누리는 것들은 거의 불가능할 것이다.

해설 어떤 것의 가격이 크게 하락하여 세상에 큰 변화가 생긴 것에 대한 예시로 조명 가격의 변화를 설명하는 내용의 글이다. 조명 가격은 과거에 매우 비쌌지만 현재는 너무 싸다고 하였으므로 ③ '증가'를 '감소(decrease)'로 바꾸어야 한다.

오답 풀이

선택률	보기 해석
① 11%	cheap(저렴한)
② 8%	notice(의식하다)
④ 10%	natural(자연의)
⑤ 13%	possible(가능한)

구문 풀이 9행

Not only did it turn night into day, **but** it allowed us to live and work in big buildings that natural light could not enter.

→ 'A뿐만 아니라 B도'라는 의미의 상관접속사인 <not only A but (also) B> 구문으로, A에 해당하는 절이 부정어구인 not only로 시작하기 때문에 주어-동사 어순이 도치되었다.

구문 플러스⁺ 상관접속사

상관접속사는 등위접속사(and, but, or 등)와 의미를 좀 더 보강해주는 단어들이 짝을 이룬 접속사로, 대개 같은 품사나 형태의 어구를 연결한다.

- not only A but also B: A뿐만 아니라 B도
  She wanted **not only** this one **but also** that one.
- either A or B: A와 B 둘 중 하나
  I will **either** play tennis **or** go hiking.

D 정답 ③ 70% 2020 6월 학평

해석 뇌는 몸무게의 2퍼센트만을 차지하지만 우리의 에너지의 20퍼센트를 사용한다. 갓 태어난 아기의 경우, 그 비율은 자그마치 65퍼센트에 달한다. 그것은 아기들이 항상 잠을 자는 부분적인 이유이자 — 아기들의 성장하는 뇌가 그들을 소진시킨다 — 많은 체지방을 보유하는 이유인데, 필요할 때 (체지방을) 에너지 저장고로 사용하기 위함이다. 근육은 전체(에너지)의 약 4분의 1 정도로 훨씬 더 많은 에너지를 사용하기도 하지만, 우리가 많은 근육을 가지고 있기도 하다. 실제로, 물질 단위당, 뇌는 다른 기관보다 훨씬 더 많은 에너지를 사용한다. 그것은 우리 장기 중 뇌가 단연 가장 에너지 소모가 많다는 것을 의미한다. 하지만 그것은 또한 놀랍도록 효율적이다. 뇌는 하루에 약 400칼로리의 에너지만 필요로 하는데, 블루베리 머핀에서 얻는 것과 거의 같다. 머핀으로 24시간 동안 노트북을 작동시켜서 얼마나 가는지 보라.

해설 뇌가 대부분의 에너지를 (A) 소진시키고(exhaust) 다른 기관보다 물질 단위당 (B) 더 많은(more) 에너지를 쓰지만, 필요로 하는 에너지와 비교해 보면 (C) 효율적(efficient)이라는 내용이다. 따라서 정답은 ③이다.

오답 풀이

선택률	보기 해석
① 3%	warn(경고하다), less(더 적은), efficient(효율적인)
② 7%	warn(경고하다), more(더 많은), efficient(효율적인)
④ 15%	exhaust(소진시키다), more(더 많은), creative(창의적인)
⑤ 2%	exhaust(소진시키다), less(더 적은), creative(창의적인)

구문 풀이 5행

Our muscles use **even** more of our energy, about a quarter of the total, but we have a lot of muscle.

→ even은 비교급을 강조하는 부사로 '훨씬, 매우'라는 의미이다.

구문 플러스⁺ 비교급 강조

비교급을 강조하는 부사는 '훨씬'이라는 뜻으로, very는 쓰지 않는다.

His house was **much more** expensive than yours.
※ 비교급 강조 부사: even, much, far, a lot, still 등

E 정답 ① 49% 2019 6월 학평

해석 학교 과제는 전형적으로 학생들이 혼자 하도록 요구해 왔다. 이러한 개별 생산성의 강조는 독립성이 성공의 필수 요인이라는 의견을 반영했던 것이다. 타인에게 의존하지 않고 자신을 관리하는 능력을 가지는 것이 모든 사람에게 요구되는 것으로 간주되었다. 따라서, 과거의 교사들은 모둠 활동을 덜 자주 마련했으며, 학생들에게 팀워크 기술을 배우도록 권장하는 것도 덜 했다. 그러나 뉴 밀레니엄 시대 이후 기업들은 향상된 생산성을 요구하는 더 많은 국제적 경쟁을 경험하고 있다. 이러한 상황은 고용주들로 하여금 노동 시장의 초입자들이 전통적인 독립성뿐만 아니라 팀워크 기술을 통해 보여지는 상호 의존성도 입증해야 한다고 요구하도록 만들었다. 교육자의 도전 과제는 학생들이 팀에서 잘 수행할 수 있도록 하는 학습 기회를 늘려주는 동시에 기본적인 기술에서의 개별 능력을 보장하는 것이다.

해설 글에 따르면, 과거의 학교 과제는 학생들이 혼자 하는 (A) 개별(individual) 생산성을 강조하였기 때문에 모둠 활동이나 팀워크 기술은 (B) 덜(less) 권장되었다. 그러나 상호 의존성이 요구되는 시대적 분위기 속에서, 개별 능력을 보장하는 동시에 팀에서 잘 수행할 수 있도록 하는 학습 기회를 (C) 늘려주는(adding) 것이 교육자의 과제이다. 따라서 정답은 ①이다.

오답 풀이

선택률	보기 해석
② 4%	collective(단체의), less(덜), decreasing(줄여주는)
③ 18%	individual(개별의), less(덜), decreasing(줄여주는)
④ 5%	collective(단체의), more(더), decreasing(줄여주는)
⑤ 24%	individual(개별의), more(더), adding(늘려주는)

구문 풀이 5행

Consequently, teachers in the past less often arranged group work or **encouraged students to acquire teamwork skills**.

→ want, allow, encourage 등의 5형식 동사는 목적어 다음에 목적격 보어로 to부정사가 온다.

구문 플러스⁺ 목적격 보어 - to부정사

want, allow, enable, encourage, ask 등의 동사는 목적어 다음에 목적격 보어로 to부정사가 오는 것에 유의한다.

I just **want** you **to focus on study**.
It can **enable** students **to perform well in teams**.

F 정답 ⑤ 47% 2018 9월 학평

해석 사람들은 선천적으로 사건의 원인을 찾는, 즉, 설명과 이야기를 구성하려는 경향이 있다. 그것이 스토리텔링이 그토록 설득력 있는 수단인 한 가지 이유이다. 이야기는 우리의 경험을 떠올리게 하고 새로운 경우의 사례를 제공한다. 우리의 경험과 다른 이들의 이야기로부터 우리는 사람들이 행동하고 상황이 작동하는 방식에 관해 일반화하는 경향이 있다. 우리는 사건에 원인을 귀착시키고 이러한 원인과 결과 쌍이 이치에 맞는 한, 그것을 미래의 사건을 이해하는 데 사용한다. 하지만 이러한 인과관계의 귀착은 종종 잘못되기도 한다. 때때로 그것은 잘못된 원인을 연관시키기도 하고, 발생하는 어떤 일에 있어서 원인이 하나만 있지 않기도 하다. 오히려 모두 그 결과의 원인이 되는 복잡한 일련의 사건들이 있다. 만일 사건들 중에 어느 하나라도 발생하지 않았었다면, (지금의) 결과는 유사할(→다를) 것이다. 하지만 원인이 되는 행동이 단 하나가 아닐 때조차도, 사람들이 하나(원인 행동 하나)를 선정하는 것을 막지는 못한다.

해설 사람들은 인과관계를 일반화하는 경향이 있는데, 이러한 일반화가 잘못되기도 한다고 말한 뒤, 어떤 결과의 원인으로 복잡한 일련의 사건들이 있다고 했다. 따라서 그 중 하나라도 발생하지 않았다면 결과가 ⑤ '다를(different)' 것이라는 표현이 문맥상 적절하다.

오답 풀이

선택률	보기 해석
① 8%	persuasive(설득력 있는)
② 12%	generalizations(일반화)
③ 16%	pairings(쌍)
④ 16%	wrong(잘못된)

구문 풀이 10행

~ if any one of the events **would not have occurred**, the result **would be** different.

→ 의미상 혼합가정법 문장으로, 과거에 상황이 달랐더라면 지금의 결과도 달랐을 것이라는 가정을 나타낸다.

구문 플러스⁺ 혼합가정법

<가정법 과거완료 종속절+가정법 과거 주절>이 합쳐진 형태로, 시제를 알 수 있는 부사구가 함께 쓰이곤 한다.

If he **had saved** more money when he was young, he **wouldn't be** in debt now.

G 정답 ③ 58% 2017 9월 학평

해석 인류 역사의 시작부터, 사람들은 세상과 그 세상 속에 있는 그들의 장소에 관하여 질문해 왔다. 초기 사회에 있어, 가장 기초적인 의문에 대한 대답은 종교에서 발견되었다. 그러나 몇몇 사람들은 그 전통적인 종교적 설명이 충분하지 않다는 것을 알게 되었고, 이성에 근거하여 답을 찾기 시작하였다. 이러한 변화는 철학의 탄생을 보여주었고, 우리가 아는 위대한 사상가들 중 첫 번째 사람은 Miletus의 Thales였다. 그는 우주의 본질을 탐구하기 위해 이성을 사용하였고, 다른 사람들도 이와 같이 하도록 권장하였다. 그는 자신의 추종자들에게 자신의 대답뿐만 아니라 어떤 종류의 설명이 만족스러운 것으로 여겨질 수 있는가에 대한 생각과 함께 이성적으로 생각하는 과정도 전했다.

해설 글에 따르면, 세상과 장소에 관한 의문에 대하여 초기 사회에서는 그 답을 (A) 종교(religion)에서 찾으려 했지만, 몇몇 사람들이 이성에 근거하여 답을 찾기 시작하는 (B) 변화(shift)가 일어났다. 그 중 첫 번째 사상가 Thales는 (C) 이성적으로(rationally) 생각하는 과정을 전했다. 따라서 정답은 ③이다.

오답 풀이

선택률	보기 해석
① 12%	religion(종교), consistency(일관성), rationally(이성적으로)
② 16%	religion(종교), shift(변화), irrationally(비이성적으로)
④ 4%	science(과학), shift(변화), irrationally(비이성적으로)
⑤ 7%	science(과학), consistency(일관성), rationally(이성적으로)

구문 풀이 7행

He used reason **to inquire** into the nature of the universe, and encouraged others **to do** likewise.

→ to inquire는 '~하기 위해서'는 목적을 나타내는 to부정사이고 to do는 동사 encouraged의 목적격보어에 해당한다.

구문 플러스⁺ to부정사의 역할

to부정사는 명사, 형용사, 부사 역할로 쓰인다.

It is easy **to judge people** based on their actions. (명사 역할-주어)
I need a pen **to write with**. (형용사 역할-명사 수식)
She goes to work **to earn money**. (부사 역할-목적)

유형 플러스⁺ 어휘의 이해

밑줄 친 어휘 다섯 개 중 전체적인 맥락과 맞지 않는 것을 찾는 유형으로, 대개 들어가야 할 단어의 '반의어'가 들어가 있어 문제가 된다.

① 글의 핵심 소재와 맥락을 잘 파악하고, 각 선지가 이와 어울리는지 확인한다.
② 정답 선지의 '반의어'를 넣었을 때 전체적인 맥락과 잘 어울려야 한다.

DAY 10 어법의 이해

A④ B③ C② D② E③ F③ G②

A 정답 ④ 28% 2023 9월 학평

해석 'Monday Morning Quarterback(월요일 아침 쿼터백: 일이 이미 벌어진 후 이러쿵저러쿵하는 사람)'이라는 이름이 존재하는 이유가 있다. 주말 경기에 대해 토론하는 팬들의 소셜 미디어의 댓글만 읽어봐도, 여러분은 얼마나 많은 사람들이 자기가 경기장에 있는 사람들보다 더 성공적으로 경기를 뛰고, 감독하고, 스포츠팀을 관리할 수 있다고 믿는지 금방 알 수 있다. 이것은 이사회실에서도 마찬가지이다. 스포츠 사업에서 수년간의 훈련을 받고 전문적인 학위를 가진 학생들과 전문가들 또한, 전문 지식이 전혀 없는 친구들, 가족, 혹은 심지어 완전한 타인으로부터 일하는 방법에 대한 충고를 듣고 있는 자신을 발견할지도 모른다. 스포츠 경영 임원진들은 각자 자기 분야에서 수십 년의 지식과 경험을 가지고 있다. 하지만, 그들 중 많은 사람들이 그들에게 사업 운영 방식을 알려주는 팬들과 지역 사회 구성원들의 비난에 직면한다. 의사에게 수술하는 방법을 알려주거나, 회계사에게 세금을 준비하는 방법을 알려주는 사람은 거의 없지만, 스포츠 조직이 어떻게 관리되어야 하는지에 대한 피드백은 많은 사람들이 제공한다.

해설 ④가 포함된 문장에서, '말하는' 주체는 fans and community members인 반면, 말을 듣는 대상은 executives이다. 즉 telling의 의미상 주어와 목적어가 서로 달라 재귀대명사를 쓰면 안 된다. 따라서 ④의 themselves를 them으로 바꾸는 것이 옳다.

오답 풀이

선택률	보기 해석
① 19%	동사 could play, coach, and manage를 꾸미고 있으므로 부사가 적절하게 쓰였다.
② 32%	<find+목적어+분사> 형태의 5형식 구조이다. 문맥상 목적어 themselves가 조언을 '받는' 것이어서 수동을 나타내는 <being+p.p.> 형태를 썼다. being이 진행의 의미를 강조한다.
③ 12%	주어는 have 바로 앞의 management가 아닌, 맨 앞의 복수명사 Executives이다. 따라서 주어와 동사의 수 일치가 적절하게 이루어졌다.
⑤ 9%	'~하는 방식'이라는 의미의 how절은 명사절 역할을 하므로 전치사 뒤에 쓸 수 있다.

구문 풀이 12행

Very few people tell their doctor **how to perform surgery** or their accountant **how to prepare their taxes** ~

→ or로 연결된 <how+to부정사>가 tell의 직접목적어이다.

구문 플러스 〈의문사+to부정사〉 형태의 목적어

what to-V: 무엇을 ~할지 / who(m) to-V: 누가/누구를 ~할지
where to-V: 어디서 ~할지 / when to-V: 언제 ~할지
how to-V: 어떻게 ~할지

I don't know **what to talk about on the first date**.
Let's decide on **where to go for our vacation**.

B 정답 ③ 70% 2022 9월 학평

해석 인간의 뇌는 15,000년에서 30,000년 전 크기가 정점에 도달한 이후 부피가 약 10퍼센트만큼 줄어든 것으로 밝혀졌다. 한 가지 가능한 이유는, 인간이 수천 년 전에, 죽임을 당하는 것을 피하기 위해 항상 포식자들에 대해 빈틈이 없어야 했던 위험한 포식자들의 세계에서 살았다는 것이다. 오늘날, 우리는 우리 자신을 효율적으로 길들여 왔고, 생존의 많은 과업이 ― 즉각적인 죽음을 피하는 것부터, 은신처를 짓는 일과 음식을 얻는 일까지 ― 더 넓은 사회로 위탁되어 왔다. 또한, 우리는 우리의 조상보다 더 작은데, 가축이 그들의 야생 사촌들보다 일반적으로 더 작은 것은 가축 동물들의 한 특징이다. 이것의 어떤 것도 우리가 더 어리석다는 것을 의미하지는 않지만 ― 뇌 크기가 반드시 인간 지능의 지표는 아니다 ― 그러나 그것은, 오늘날 우리의 뇌가 다르게, 그리고 우리 조상들보다 아마도 더 효율적으로 구성되어 있다는 것을 의미할지도 모른다.

해설 주어가 many of the tasks of survival이므로 복수로 수 일치하여, ③의 has를 have로 바꾸어 써야 한다.

오답 풀이

선택률	보기 해석
① 4%	뒤에 과거 부사구(ago)가 오므로 자동사 peak를 과거시제로 알맞게 썼다.
② 9%	a world of dangerous predators를 수식하는 관계부사절을 이끈다.
④ 7%	가주어 it에 대한 진주어 that절을 이끈다.
⑤ 7%	brains를 대신하는 대명사이다.

구문 풀이 2행

One possible reason is that many thousands of years ago humans lived in **a world of dangerous predators where they had to have their wits about them at all times to avoid being killed.**

→ 관계부사절 where ~ killed가 선행사 a world of dangerous predators를 수식한다. where절은 <주어+타동사+목적어+부사구> 구조로, 빠진 문장 성분 없이 완전하다.

구문 플러스 관계부사 vs. 관계대명사

관계부사(where, when, how, why)는 완전한 절을 이끌어 선행사를 수식하며, <전치사+관계대명사>로 바꾸어 쓸 수 있다. 이와 대조적으로, 관계대명사가 단독으로 쓰였을 때는 불완전한 절이 연결된다.

- I know the house **where(=in which)** a criminal lives.
  → 뒤따르는 절이 완전하다. (lives = 자동사)
- I know the house **which** the rich man owns.
  → 뒤따르는 절이 불완전하다. (owns = 타동사)

C 정답 ② 45% 2021 9월 학평

해석 경제이론인 Say의 법칙은 만들어진 모든 물품이 팔리기 마련이라고 주장한다. 모든 생산된 물품으로부터 나오는 돈은 다른 물품을 사는 데 사용된다. 한 회사가 물품을 팔 수 없게 되어서 직원들을 해고하고 공장의 문을 닫아야 하는 상황은 절대 있을 수 없다. 따라서, 경기 후퇴와 실업은 불가능하다. 지출의 정도를 욕조 안의 물높이로 상상해 보라. Say의 법칙은 사람들이 그들의 모든 수입을 물품을 사는 데 사용하기 때문에 적용된다. 하지만 만약 사람들이 그들의 돈을 전부 사용하는 대신, 돈의 일부를 모은다면 무슨 일이 일어날까? 경제에서 저축은 지출의 '누수'이다. 당신은 아마 물의 높이가 지금 낮아지고, 그래서 경제에서 지출이 적어지는 것을 상상하고 있을 것이다. 그것은 회사들이 더 적게 생산하고 일부 직원들을 해고하는 것을 의미할 것이다.

해설 밑줄 친 부분 뒤에 완전한 절이 뒤따르고 있으므로 관계대명사를 쓸 수 없다. 따라서 ② 자리에는 관계부사 where 혹은 <전치사+관계대명사> in which가 어법상 알맞다.

오답 풀이

선택률	보기 해석
① 8%	be used to가 '~에 익숙하다'의 의미일 때는 to 뒤에 명사 또는 동명사가 오지만, 여기서는 '~하기 위해 이용되다'라는 의미로 to부정사를 쓴다.
③ 9%	뒤에 완전한 절이 오므로 because of가 아닌 because를 쓴다.
④ 25%	all their money라는 불가산명사를 지칭하므로 단수로 쓴다.
⑤ 12%	앞의 동명사 producing과 병렬구조를 이룬다.

구문 풀이 11행

That would mean **firms producing** less and **dismissing** some of their workers.

→ <mean+동명사(~하는 것을 뜻하다)> 구문으로, firms는 동명사의 의미상 주어이다.

구문 플러스⁺ to부정사와 동명사를 모두 목적어로 취하는 동사

의미 차이가 있는지 없는지 나누어 기억한다.

- 의미 차이가 없는 동사
  : love, like, start, begin, continue, cease
- 의미 차이가 있는 동사

remember / forget	+ to-V: (앞으로) ~할 일을 기억하다/잊다 + V-ing: (이미) ~한 일을 기억하다/잊다
regret	+ to-V: ~하게 되어 유감이다 + V-ing: ~한 것을 후회하다
mean	+ to-V: ~할 작정이다 + V-ing: ~을 뜻하다

cf. 동명사를 목적어로 취하지만, 의미상 주의할 동사

try	+ V-ing: 한번 ~해보다 + to-V: ~하려고 노력하다 → 부사적 용법
stop	+ V-ing: ~하기를 관두다 + to-V: ~하려고 멈추다 → 부사적 용법

D 정답 ② 63% 2020 3월 학평

해석 '먹는 것이 여러분을 만든다.' 그 구절은 흔히 여러분이 먹는 음식과 여러분의 신체 건강 사이의 관계를 보여주기 위해 사용된다. 하지만 여러분은 가공식품, 통조림 식품, 포장 식품을 살 때 자신이 무엇을 먹고 있는 것인지 정말 아는가? 오늘날 만들어진 제조 식품 중 다수가 너무 많은 화학물질과 인공적인 재료를 함유하고 있어서 때로는 정확히 그 안에 무엇이 들어 있는지 알기가 어렵다. 다행히도, 이제는 식품 라벨이 있다. 식품 라벨은 여러분이 먹는 식품에 관한 정보를 알아내는 좋은 방법이다. 식품 라벨은 책에서 볼 수 있는 목차와 같다. 식품 라벨의 주된 목적은 여러분이 구입하고 있는 식품 안에 무엇이 들어 있는지 여러분에게 알려주는 것이다.

해설 '너무 ~해서 …하다'라는 의미의 <so ~ that ...> 구문의 that절을 이끌어야 하므로 ② which를 that으로 바꿔야 한다.

오답 풀이

선택률	보기 해석
① 7%	be used to가 '~에 익숙하다'일 때는 동명사가 오지만 여기서는 to부정사로 '~하기 위해 이용되다'라는 의미이다.
③ 3%	앞의 명사를 수식하는 to부정사이다.
④ 16%	전치사 like로, 뒤에 명사구가 나왔다.
⑤ 8%	핵심 주어가 단수인 purpose이므로 is가 알맞다.

구문 풀이 1행

That phrase **is often used to show** the relationship between the foods you eat and your physical health.

→ <be used to+동사>와 <be used to+(동)명사>의 의미 차이에 주의한다.

구문 플러스⁺ used to / be used to

used to 동사원형 → ~하곤 했다
be used to 동사원형 → ~하는 데 사용되다
be used to (동)명사 → ~에 익숙하다

E 정답 ③ 46% 2019 3월 학평

해석 운동하는 동안 편안함을 제공하기 위해 의류가 비쌀 필요는 없다. 기온과 당신이 운동하고 있을 환경 조건에 적절한 의류를 선택하라. 운동과 계절에 적절한 의류는 운동 경험을 향상시킬 수 있다. 따뜻한 환경에서는 수분을 흡수하거나 배출할 수 있는 기능을 가진 옷이 몸에서 열을 발산하는 데 도움이 된다. 반면, 땀을 흘리는 것을 피하고 쾌적한 상태를 유지하기 위해 체온을 조절하려면 겹겹이 입어서 추운 환경에 대처하는 것이 최선이다.

해설 (A) 뒤따르는 절이 완전하므로 <전치사+관계대명사>인 in which가 어법에 맞다.
(B) 주어가 clothes이므로 수 일치하여 are를 쓴다.
(C) 동사 remain의 보어로는 형용사 comfortable이 어법에 맞다. 따라서 정답은 ③이다.

오답 풀이

선택률	보기 해석
① 7%	(A) which, (B) is가 적절하지 않다.
② 13%	(A) which가 적절하지 않다.
④ 6%	(B) is, (C) comfortably가 적절하지 않다. 부사는 문장의 보어 역할을 할 수 없다.
⑤ 26%	(C) comfortably가 적절하지 않다.

구문 풀이 3행

Clothing that **is** appropriate for exercise and the season can improve your exercise experience. In warm environments, **clothes** that **have** a wicking capacity are helpful in dissipating heat from the body.

→ 주격 관계대명사절의 동사는 선행사에 수 일치하므로, Clothing을 꾸미는 that절의 동사는 단수(is)로, clothes를 꾸미는 that절의 동사는 복수(have)로 쓰였다.

구문 플러스 관계대명사절 속 동사의 수 일치

주격 관계대명사절 안의 동사는 선행사에 수 일치한다.

a girl who always **smiles** → 단수
girls who **have** confidence → 복수

F 정답 ③ 35% 2018 6월 학평

해석 플라스틱은 매우 느리게 분해되고 물에 떠다니는 경향이 있는데 이는 플라스틱으로 하여금 해류를 따라 수천 마일을 돌아다니게 한다. 대부분의 플라스틱은 자외선에 노출될 때 점점 더 작은 조각으로 분해되어 미세 플라스틱을 형성한다. 이러한 미세 플라스틱은 일단 그것들을 수거하는 데 일반적으로 사용되는 그물망을 통과할 만큼 충분히 작아지면 측정하기가 매우 어렵다. 미세 플라스틱이 해양 환경과 먹이 그물에 미치는 영향은 아직도 제대로 이해되지 않고 있다. 이 작은 조각들은 다양한 동물에게 먹혀 먹이 사슬 속으로 들어간다고 알려져 있다. 바다 속에 있는 대부분의 플라스틱 조각들은 매우 작기 때문에 바다를 청소할 실질적인 방법은 없다. 비교적 적은 양의 플라스틱을 수거하기 위해 엄청난 양의 물을 여과해야 할 수도 있다.

해설 to collect의 의미상 주어는 그물망(the nets)이고, 목적어는 미세 플라스틱(these microplastics)이므로 주어와 목적어가 지칭하는 대상이 다르다. 따라서 재귀대명사를 쓸 수 없으므로 ③ themselves를 them으로 고쳐야 한다.

오답 풀이

선택률	보기 해석
① 8%	앞 문장 전체를 선행사로 받는 계속적 용법의 관계대명사 which는 적절하다.
② 25%	연속동작의 의미를 나타내는 분사구문을 이끄는 현재분사 forming은 적절하다.
④ 12%	복수 주어(most of the plastic particles)를 받는 동사 are가 적절하다.
⑤ 17%	형용사(small)를 수식하는 부사 relatively는 적절하다.

구문 풀이 4행

These microplastics are very difficult to measure once they are **small enough to pass** through the nets typically used to collect them.

→ <enough to부정사>는 부사나 형용사 다음에 쓰여 '…할 만큼 충분히 ~하다'로 해석한다.

구문 플러스 형용사 enough to부정사

<형용사 enough to부정사>는 '…하기에 충분히 ~하다'의 의미로 <so 형용사 that ~ can …> 구문으로 바꿀 수 있다.

The man was **lucky enough to win** the lottery.
→ The man was **so lucky that he could win** the lottery.

G 정답 ② 60% 2017 6월 학평

해석 당신은 당신의 강점과 약점에 대하여 스스로에게 정직한가? 스스로에 대해 확실히 알고 당신의 약점이 무엇인지를 파악하라. 당신의 문제에 있어 자신의 역할을 받아들이는 것은 해결책도 당신 안에 있다는 것을 이해함을 의미한다. 만약 당신이 특정 분야에 약점이 있다면, 배워서 스스로 상황을 개선하기 위해 해야만 할 것들을 행하라. 만약 당신의 사회적 이미지가 형편없다면, 스스로를 들여다보고 그것을 개선하기 위해 필요한 조치를 오늘 당장 취하라. 당신은 삶에 대응하는 방법을 선택할 능력이 있다. 오늘 당장 모든 변명을 끝내기로 결심하고, 일어나는 일에 대해 스스로에게 거짓말하는 것을 멈춰라. 성장의 시작은 당신이 자신의 선택에 대한 책임을 스스로 받아들이기 시작할 때 일어난다.

해설 accepting으로 시작하는 동명사구가 주어이므로 ②에는 단수형 동사 means가 와야 한다.

오답 풀이

선택률	보기 해석
① 4%	명령문 주어(you)와 동일한 대상을 가리키는 목적어인 재귀대명사 yourself가 와야 한다.
③ 12%	동사 do의 목적어 역할을 할 명사가 필요하고 뒤따르는 절이 불완전하므로 선행사를 포함하는 관계대명사 what을 쓴다.
④ 7%	지칭하는 your social image가 단수이므로 it으로 대신한다.
⑤ 14%	stop의 목적어로 동명사 lying을 사용하는 것이 적절하다.

구문 풀이 8행

Decide today **to end** all the excuses, and **stop lying** to yourself about what is going on.

→ to end는 동사 decide의 목적어이고, lying은 동사 stop의 목적어 역할을 한다.

구문 플러스 동명사 또는 to부정사를 목적어로 취하는 동사

- 동명사를 목적어로 취하는 동사: mind, avoid, give up, finish, enjoy, recommend, suggest, stop 등
- to부정사를 목적어로 취하는 동사: decide, want, wish, desire, plan, refuse 등

We **enjoyed dancing** all night. (to dance X)
She **decided to go** to college. (going X)

유형 플러스 어법의 이해

① 다섯 개의 밑줄 친 표현 중 틀린 것을 고르는 유형
② 네모 안에 주어진 표현 중 알맞은 것을 고르는 유형

유형 해결 방법
① 주요 빈출 문법 정리
② 문장의 기본 구성 요소인 주어, 동사를 파악
③ 문맥의 흐름에 적합(수동태/능동태 등)한지 확인

A 정답 ② 37% 2023 3월 학평

해석 자연 과정은 많은 방법으로 광물을 형성한다. 예를 들어, 마그마라고 불리는 뜨거운 용암 물질은 지구의 표면에 도달할 때, 또는 심지어 표면 아래에 갇혔을 때도 식는다. 마그마가 식으면서, 마그마의 원자는 열에너지를 잃고, 서로 더 가까이 이동해 화합물로 결합하기 시작한다.
(B) 이 과정 동안, 서로 다른 화합물의 원자가 질서 있고 반복적인 패턴으로 배열된다. 마그마에 존재하는 원소의 종류와 양이 어떤 광물이 형성될지를 부분적으로 결정한다.
(A) 또한, 형성되는 결정의 크기는 부분적으로는 마그마가 얼마나 빨리 식느냐에 좌우된다. 마그마가 천천히 식으면, 형성되는 결정은 일반적으로 육안으로 볼 수 있을 만큼 충분히 크다.
(C) 이것은 원자가 함께 이동해 더 큰 결정을 형성할 충분한 시간을 가지기 때문이다. 마그마가 빠르게 식으면, 형성되는 결정은 작을 것이다. 그런 경우에는 개별 광물 결정을 쉽게 볼 수 없다.

해설 주어진 글은 광물 형성 과정을 화제로 언급하며, 마그마가 식는 것에 관해 언급한다. (B)에서는 '이 식어가는 과정'에서 광물의 종류가 결정된다고 설명하며, (A)는 광물의 크기가 마그마가 식는 속도에 좌우된다는 점을 추가로 언급한다. (C)는 왜 속도에 좌우되는 것인지 그 이유를 설명한다. 따라서 ② '(B)-(A)-(C)'가 글의 순서로 가장 자연스럽다.

오답 풀이

선택률	보기 해석
① 7%	주어진 글의 마지막 부분은 '결정 형성'을 본격적으로 언급하기 앞서 마그마가 식는다는 내용을 다룬다. 따라서 결정 형성을 전제로 크기에 관해 추가로(Also) 언급하는 (A)부터 연결하는 것은 부자연스럽다.
③ 32%	(B)는 결정의 '종류와 양'을, (C)는 결정의 '크기'를 언급하여 서로 소재가 겹치지 않는다. 따라서 (B)-(C)의 흐름은 부자연스럽다.
④ 17%	주어진 글에서 '결정의 크기'를 언급하지 않으므로, '더 큰 결정이 만들어지는 이유'를 설명하는 (C)부터 연결하는 것은 부적절하다.
⑤ 8%	④와 동일

구문 풀이 11행

The type and amount of elements present in a magma partly determine **which minerals will form**.

→ 동사 determine의 목적어로 which 의문사절이 나왔다. 이 which는 의문형용사로, 뒤에 나오는 minerals를 수식하면서 명사절을 이끈다.

구문 플러스⁺ 의문사절

의문사가 이끄는 명사절은 문장의 주어, 목적어, 보어 역할을 한다.

What she does for living is unknown. → 주어
We don't know **where the money goes**! → 목적어
The question is **what caused the car crash**. → 보어

B 정답 ② 55% 2022 3월 학평

해석 Robert Schumann은 "도덕의 법칙은 예술의 법칙이다"라고 말한 적이 있다. 여기서 이 위인이 말하고 있는 것은 좋은 음악과 나쁜 음악이 있다는 것이다.
(B) 가장 위대한 음악은, 설령 그것이 사실상 비극적일지라도, 우리의 세상보다 더 높은 세상으로 우리를 데려간다. 즉 어떻게든지 아름다움은 우리를 고양시킨다. 반면에 나쁜 음악은 우리를 격하시킨다.
(A) 연주도 마찬가지다. 나쁜 연주가 반드시 무능의 결과는 아니다. 최악의 연주 중 일부는 연주자들이 아무리 숙달되었더라도 연주하고 있는 곡보다 자기 자신을 더 생각하고 있을 때 발생한다.
(C) 이 미덥지 못한 사람들은 작곡가가 말하는 것을 정말로 듣고 있는 것이 아니다. 그들은 대중적으로 큰 '성공'을 거두기를 바라며 그저 뽐내고 있을 뿐이다. 연주자의 기본 임무는 음악의 의미를 이해하려고 노력하고서 그것을 다른 사람들에게 정직하게 전달하는 것이다.

해설 좋은 음악과 나쁜 음악이 있다고 이야기하는 주어진 글 뒤에 이를 구체적으로 비교하여 설명하는 (B)가 오고, 나쁜 음악과 연결지어 나쁜 연주 또한 마찬가지임을 설명하는 (A)가 오는 것이 자연스럽다. 마지막으로 나쁜 연주자들에 대한 이야기가 (C)의 '이 미덥지 못한 사람들'로 이어진다. 따라서 정답은 ② '(B)-(A)-(C)'이다.

오답 풀이

선택률	보기 해석
① 7%	(B)의 '나쁜 음악'에 대한 이야기가 먼저 나와야 (A)의 '나쁜 연주'에 대한 설명이 자연스러워진다.
③ 19%	(A)의 '나쁜 연주자들'에 대한 이야기가 먼저 나와야 (C)의 '이 미덥지 못한 사람들'에 대한 설명이 자연스러워진다.
④ 10%	주어진 글에서 '미덥지 못한 사람들'로 볼 만한 대상이 언급되지 않으므로 (C)가 처음에 연결되기는 부자연스럽다.
⑤ 7%	④와 동일

구문 풀이 5행

Some of the worst performances occur when the performers, **no matter how accomplished (they are)**, are thinking more of themselves than of the music they're playing.

→ no matter how는 양보 부사절(아무리 ~하더라도)을 이끌며, <no matter how+형/부+주어+동사> 어순으로 쓰인다. 여기서 <주어+동사>는 생략되었다.

구문 플러스⁺ 부사절 축약

시간, 조건, 양보의 부사절에서 <대명사 주어+be동사>는 생략되기도 한다.

He always works hard **while (he is) on duty**.
If (it is) necessary, I can come at once.

C 정답 ② 70% 2021 6월 학평

해석 사람들은 미디어와 상호작용하는 데 많은 시간을 소비하지만, 그렇다고 해서 사람들이 미디어를 분석하고 이해하는 데 중요한 기술을 가지고 있는 것은 아니다.
(B) 2016년 Stanford 대학의 한 잘 알려진 연구는 특히 소셜 미디어 채널을 통해 젊은이들이 잘못된 정보에 쉽게 속는다는 것을 보여주었다. 그러나 이러한 약점은 젊은이에게서만 발견되는 것은 아니다.
(A) New York 대학의 조사에 따르면 65세 이상의 사람들이 젊은이들 보다 7배나 더 많은 잘못된 정보를 공유한다고 한다. 이 모든 것이 의문을 제기한다: 잘못된 정보 문제에 대한 해결책은 무엇인가?
(C) 정부와 기술 플랫폼은 분명 잘못된 정보를 막아내는 데 있어 해야 할 역할을 가지고 있다. 그러나 모든 개인은 정보를 더 잘 분별함으로써 이러한 위협에 맞서 싸울 책임을 질 필요가 있다.

해설 사람들이 미디어를 제대로 분석하고 이해하지 못하고 있음을 설명하는 주제문 뒤에 이를 뒷받침하는 연구 결과에 대한 (B)가 오고, 그 뒤에 젊은이들뿐만 아니라 노인들도 그러하다는 추가적인 내용을 다루는 (A)가 와야 한다. 마지막으로, 앞서 서술한 문제에 대한 해결책을 다루는 (C)가 오는 것이 자연스럽다. 따라서 정답은 ② '(B)-(A)-(C)'이다.

오답 풀이

선택률	보기 해석
① 6%	주어진 글과 (A)는 얼핏 주제-예시로 자연스럽게 연결되지만, (B)를 보면 마지막 문장이 '젊은이들만 문제가 아니라'는 내용이다. 이 지적이 먼저 나오고, '노인들은 더 심각함'을 언급하는 (A)가 나와야 흐름이 더 자연스럽다.
③ 8%	(B)의 마지막 내용이 '젊은이들만이 문제가 아니라'는 것인데 이를 뒷받침하는 사례는 (C)가 아닌 (A)에 나온다. (C)는 정부와 개인이 둘 다 노력해야 한다는 해결책에 관해서만 언급한다.
④ 10%	주어진 글에서 모든 개인이 미디어를 잘 분석하고 이해하지는 못한다고 언급한 후, (B)-(A)가 사례를 제시하므로 (C)보다 먼저 나와야 한다. (C)는 (A) 마지막에서 언급한 '해결책'의 내용을 다룬다.
⑤ 4%	④와 동일

구문 풀이 13행

However, **every individual needs** to take responsibility for combating this threat by becoming more information literate.

→ every 뒤의 명사는 단수 명사로 쓰고, 단수 취급하여 수 일치한다.

구문 플러스⁺ 주의할 수 일치

every/each+단수명사+단수동사
each of the+복수명사+단수동사

Every student is required to attend the lecture.
Each student has the opportunity to ask questions.
Each of the students has a unique perspective on the issue.

D 정답 ② 60% 2020 9월 학평

해석 우리는 우리가 안다고 '생각하는' 것에 기초하여 결정을 한다. 대다수의 사람들이 세상이 편평하다고 믿었던 것은 그다지 오래되지 않았다.
(B) 이렇게 인지된 사실은 행동에 영향을 미쳤다. 이 기간 동안에는, 탐험이 거의 없었다. 사람들은 만약 그들이 너무 멀리 가면, 지구의 가장자리에서 떨어질까 봐 두려워했다. 그래서 대체로 그들은 감히 이동하지 않았다.
(A) 대대적으로 행동이 변화한 것은 그런 사소한 사항, 곧 세상은 둥글다는 것이 드러나고 나서였다. 이것이 발견된 후 곧, 사람들은 세상을 돌아다니기 시작했다. 무역 경로가 만들어졌으며, 향신료가 거래되었다.
(C) 사회들 사이에 모든 종류의 혁신과 진보를 가능하게 했던 수학과 같은 새로운 개념이 공유되었다. 단순한 잘못된 가정의 수정이 인류를 앞으로 나아가게 했다.

해설 우리가 생각하는 것에 따라 결정한다는 내용의 첫 문장 뒤에, 세상이 편평하다고 생각했던 과거의 인식을 예시로서 언급하고, (B)에서 그 생각으로 인해 사람들이 탐험을 거의 하지 않았음을 설명한다. 그 후, (A)에서 시간이 흘러 인식이 변하자 행동도 변했음을 이야기하고, (C)에서 '잘못된 가정의 수정이 인류를 앞으로 나아가게 했다'고 요약한다. 따라서 정답은 ② '(B)-(A)-(C)'이다.

오답 풀이

선택률	보기 해석
① 7%	주어진 글과 (A)는 자연스러워 보이지만, This perceived truth로 주어진 글의 마지막 문장을 받는 (B)를 맨 마지막에 연결할 수는 없다.
③ 18%	(B)에서 옛날 사람들은 지구가 편평하다는 믿음 때문에 여행도 잘 못했다고 하는데, 이 뒤에 새로운 개념이 진보를 낳는다는 내용의 (C)를 연결하면 소재가 달라져서 흐름이 부자연스럽다.
④ 7%	편평한 지구를 믿었던 과거 사람들에 대한 이야기가 마무리되지 않았는데 새로운 개념을 언급하는 (C)부터 연결할 수는 없다.
⑤ 5%	④와 동일

구문 풀이 3행

It wasn't until that minor detail was revealed — the world is round — **that** behaviors changed on a massive scale.

→ <not until A B(A하고 나서야 비로소 B하다)의 not until A를 <it is ~ that …(…한 것은 바로 ~이다)> 구문으로 강조한 것이다. <it is not until A that B>를 하나의 숙어처럼 기억해 두도록 한다.

구문 플러스⁺ not until A B

not until A B = it is not until A that B
= A하고 나서야 비로소 B하다

Not until the sun set did they realize they were lost.
→ 부정어구로 시작되므로 주절(B)이 도치됨
= **It was not until** the sun set **that** they realized they were lost.
→ 주절(B) 도치 X

E 정답 ③ 38% 2019 9월 학평

해석 성공하려면, 당신은 당신이 성공할 것이라고 믿는 것과 당신이 쉽게 성공할 것이라고 믿는 것 사이의 중요한 차이를 이해할 필요가 있다.
(B) 다시 말해서, 그것은 현실적인 낙관주의자가 되는 것과 비현실적인 낙관주의자가 되는 것 사이의 차이이다. 현실적인 낙관주의자들은 그들이 성공할 것이라고 믿을 뿐만 아니라, 그들이 신중한 계획과 적절한 전략을 선택하는 것과 같은 것들을 통해 성공이 일어날 수 있도록 만들어야 한다고 믿는다.
(C) 그들은 어떻게 그들이 장애물을 다룰지에 대해 심각하게 고려할 필요가 있다는 것을 인식한다. 이런 준비가 바로 일이 수행될 수 있게 만드는 그들 자신의 능력에 대한 자신감을 높여 준다.
(A) 반면에, 비현실적인 낙관론자들은 성공이 그들에게 일어날 수 있다는 것, 즉 우주가 그들에게 자신의 모든 긍정적인 사고에 대해 보상할 것이라고, 혹은 어떤 식으로든 그들이 하룻밤 사이에 장애물이 더 이상 존재하지 않는 그런 종류의 사람으로 변할 것이라고 믿는다.

해설 성공에 대한 두 가지 다른 태도를 말하는 주제문 뒤에 이를 다시 설명하는 (B)가 오고, 그 태도 중 하나인 현실적 낙관주의자에 대한 설명인 (C)가 와야 한다. 그 뒤에 이것과 반대 태도를 나타내는 비현실적인 낙관주의자에 대한 내용의 (A)가 오는 것이 자연스럽다. 따라서 정답은 ③ '(B)-(C)-(A)'이다.

오답 풀이

선택률	보기 해석
① 7%	(A)의 on the other hand로 보아, (A) 앞에는 '비현실적 낙관론자'와 반대되는 대상이 언급돼야 하는데, 주어진 글에는 그런 대상이 나오지 않는다.
② 25%	(B)-(A)가 역접어(on the other hand)로 자연스럽게 연결되는 것 같지만, (C)에서 현실적 낙관주의자에 대한 설명을 마무리한 뒤 (A)로 넘어가는 것이 적절하다.
④ 12%	주어진 글과 (C)를 바로 연결하면 (C)의 They가 누구를 가리키는지 불분명해진다. 주어진 글에 They가 받을 만한 '복수인 사람'이 언급되지 않기 때문이다.
⑤ 14%	④와 동일

구문 풀이 4행

Unrealistic optimists, on the other hand, believe **that** success will happen to them — **that** the universe will reward them for all their positive thinking, **or that** somehow they will be transformed overnight into the kind of person for whom obstacles don't exist anymore.

→ believe의 목적절이 <A or B> 형태로 병렬 연결되는데, A 뒤에 A와 동격인 that절이 삽입되었다. 즉, <A, A', or B>의 구조인 것이다.

구문 플러스⁺ 삽입구문

앞말의 내용을 자세히 풀어쓰거나 내용을 덧붙이고 싶을 때 콤마(,)나 줄표(—)를 이용해 내용을 추가할 수 있다.

They are, **as far as I know**, unreliable people.
→ 부사처럼 중간에 삽입('내가 아는 한')

F 정답 ⑤ 40% 2018 6월 학평

해석 대인 관계에서의 메시지는 내용 차원과 관계 차원을 결합한다. 즉, 그것들은 화자와 청자 모두에게 외부적인 어떤 것인, 실제 세계를 지칭한다. 동시에 당사자들 사이의 관계를 지칭하기도 한다.
(C) 예를 들어, 한 관리자가 한 수습 직원에게 "회의 후에 저 좀 봅시다."라고 말할 수 있다. 이 간단한 메시지는 수습 직원이 회의 후에 관리자를 만나야 한다는 것을 전달하는 내용 메시지를 담고 있다.
(B) 그것은 또한 관리자와 수습 직원 사이의 관계에 대해 무언가를 말해주는 관계 메시지를 포함하고 있다. 이 간단한 명령의 사용도 관리자가 그 수습 직원에게 명령할 수 있게 하는 지위의 차이가 존재한다는 것을 보여준다.
(A) 만약 수습 직원에 의해 관리자에게 같은 명령이 내려진다고 상상해 본다면 당신은 이것을 가장 명확하게 이해할 수 있을 것이다. 관리자와 수습 직원 사이의 일반적인 관계를 위반하기 때문에 그것은 어색하고 상황에 맞지 않아 보인다.

해설 메시지는 내용뿐 아니라 당사자간의 관계를 보여주기도 한다는 주제문 뒤에 관리자와 수습 직원의 구체적인 예를 언급하는 (C)가 오고, 그들의 대화가 관계 메시지를 포함하고 있다는 내용의 (B)가 와야 한다. 그 뒤에 이것을 반대 상황에 대입하면 더 잘 이해할 수 있다는 내용의 (A)가 오는 것이 자연스럽다. 따라서 정답은 ⑤ '(C)-(B)-(A)'이다.

오답 풀이

선택률	보기 해석
① 10%	(A)의 this에 주어진 글 내용을 넣어도 자연스럽게 읽히는 듯하지만, the same command에서 막힌다. 주어진 글에는 '명령'이 언급되지 않기 때문이다.
② 10%	(B)에 주어진 글과 마찬가지로 relationship이 언급되므로 얼핏 보면 바로 이어지는 것 같지만, 연결어와 내용을 잘 봐야 한다. also가 있는 (B)는 '관리자와 수습 직원' 사이의 메시지에 관해 '추가로' 설명하는 단락이다. 그런데 주어진 글에는 이 두 대상이 언급조차 되지 않는다.
③ 21%	주어진 글에 (B)를 연결한다 하더라도, (C)-(A)의 흐름 또한 부자연스럽다. (C)는 상사가 부하 직원에게 지시하는 상황만을 언급하는데, (A)에서는 직원이 상사에게 명령하는 반대 상황을 생각해보면 '이것'을 알 수 있다고 한다. 이 '이것'이 가리키는 바를 (C)-(A)만 읽어서는 알 수 없다.
④ 16%	(C) 다음 (A)-(B)를 연결하면, (A)의 this가 (B)의 It이 각각 무엇을 뜻하는지 애매해진다. (A)~(C)를 전체적으로 읽고 내용을 대강 아는 상태에서는 무의식적으로 대명사에 올바른 대상을 넣어가며 읽게 되므로 의미상의 공백에 둔감해질 수 있기 때문에 주의해야 한다.

구문 풀이 11행

Even the use of the simple command shows **(that)** there is a status difference **that** allows the supervisor to command the trainee.

→ 첫 번째 that은 shows의 목적절을 이끄는 접속사로, 문장에서 생략되었다. 두 번째 that은 a status difference를 꾸미는 주격 관계대명사이다.

구문 플러스 that vs. what

관계대명사 that과 명사절 접속사 that의 구분은 뒤따르는 절이 완전한지 여부로 나뉘고, 관계대명사 what과 that의 구분은 앞에 선행사가 있는지 여부로 나뉜다.

앞구조	종류	뒷구조
선행사 X	접속사 that	완전한 문장
선행사 O	관·대 that	불완전한 문장
선행사 X	관·대 what	불완전한 문장

I didn't know **that** he likes you. → 접속사 that
The car **that** she drives is brand new. → 관계대명사 that
I know **what** I need. → 관계대명사 what(선행사 포함)

G 정답 ② 49% 2017 11월 학평

해석 기억은 두 가지 종류가 있는데, 내재적 기억과 외재적 기억이다. 여러분이 무언가에 대해서 진정으로 생각하지 않고서 배울 때, 그것은 내재적 기억 혹은 신체 기억이다. 태어났을 때 호흡하는 법을 아는 것은 내재적 기억이다.
(B) 아무도 여러분에게 이것을 가르쳐 주지 않았다. 또한 어릴 적부터 여러분이 배운 것 중 일부는 내재적 기억들이 된다. 내재적 기억들은 뇌의 자율적 부분에 각인된다. 이 이유로 자전거를 수년 동안 타지 않고서도 여전히 자전거 타는 법을 알고 있다.
(A) 반면에 외재적 기억들은 여러분이 의식적으로 기억하려고 노력하는 기억 혹은 특정한 것들이다. 여러분은 매일 의식적 차원에서 외재적 기억을 사용한다.
(C) 열쇠를 찾으려 노력하는 것, 행사가 언제 개최될 예정이고, 어디서 개최될 것이며, 누구와 함께 거기 갈지 기억하려 하는 것(이 외재적 기억의 예시이다). 외재적 기억들은 여러분이 달력이나 일정표에 적어놓은 과업들이다.

해설 주어진 글에서는 기억의 두 종류를 언급한 후, 태어났을 때 호흡하는 법이 두 기억 중 내재적 기억과 관련 있다고 설명한다. (A)는 이 호흡법을 this로 받은 후, 내재적 기억의 예시를 보충 설명한다. 한편 (A)는 on the other hand로 흐름을 반전시키며, 외재적 기억을 언급한다. (C)는 외재적 기억의 사례를 든다. 따라서 순서로 가장 자연스러운 것은 ② '(B)-(A)-(C)'이다.

오답 풀이

선택률	보기 해석
① 8%	(B)가 아직 내재적 기억에 관해 언급하는데, (A)가 먼저 연결되어 흐름이 외재적 기억으로 넘어가면 (B)가 연결되기 어렵다.
③ 12%	(B)는 내재적 기억, (C)는 외재적 기억에 관한 내용이므로 둘 사이에는 (A)의 역접 연결어(on the other hand)가 반드시 필요하다.
④ 7%	주어진 글 마지막 부분이 내재적 기억의 예를 언급하므로, 외재적 기억의 예를 언급하는 (C)가 흐름 반전의 연결어 없이 바로 이어질 수는 없다.
⑤ 4%	④와 동일

구문 풀이 3행

Knowing how to breathe when you were born **is** an implicit memory.
→ 핵심 주어가 동명사이므로 단수 취급하여 is를 썼다.

유형 플러스 글의 순서 배열

주어진 글 뒤에 (A), (B), (C)의 글을 순서대로 배치하는 유형이다.

단서가 될 수 있는 표현들

인칭대명사	성(性)과 수가 일치하는 명사를 포함하는 문장 뒤에 이어져야 한다.
지시대명사	명사가 언급된 문장 뒤에 이어져야 하며 수 일치에 주의해야 한다.
one, the other, another	one이 먼저 나오고, 뒤에 추가의 another나 두 당사자 중 '상대방'을 가리키는 the other를 연결해준다.
(the) others	some과 연결된 경우 some이 포함된 단락 뒤에 위치해야 한다.
reason(s)	앞에 나온 원인에 관한 결론을 이끄는 문장으로 원인이 포함된 단락 뒤에 위치해야 한다.

DAY 12 주어진 문장 넣기

A⑤ B② C④ D③ E③ F④ G③

A 정답 ⑤ 28% (2023 6월 학평)

해석 교육 심리학자 Susan Engel에 따르면, 호기심은 네 살 정도의 어린 나이에 줄어들기 시작한다. 우리가 어른이 될 무렵, 질문은 더 적어지고 기본값은 더 많아진다. Henry James가 말했듯이, "흥미를 잃은 호기심은 없어지고, 정신의 고랑과 경로가 자리잡는다." 호기심의 감소는 유년 시절을 통한 뇌의 발달에서 원인을 찾을 수 있다. 비록 성인의 뇌보다 작지만, 유아의 뇌는 수백만 개 더 많은 신경 연결을 가지고 있다. 그러나 연결 상태는 엉망이라, 유아의 뉴런 간의 전달은 성인 뇌에서의 전달보다 훨씬 덜 효율적이다. 결과적으로 세상에 대한 아기의 인식은 매우 풍부하면서도 대단히 무질서하다. 아이들이 그들 주변의 세상으로부터 더 많은 증거를 받아들임에 따라, 특정한 가능성들이 훨씬 더 커지고 더 유용해지며 지식이나 믿음으로 굳어진다. 그러한 믿음을 가능하게 하는 신경 경로는 더 빠르고 자동적으로 이루어지게 되고, 반면에 아이가 주기적으로 사용하지 않는 경로는 제거된다.

해설 ⑤ 앞에서 유아 뇌의 신경 연결이 수는 대단히 많지만 그만큼 무질서하다고 하는데, ⑤ 뒤는 갑자기 '믿음'을 언급하므로 흐름이 어색하게 끊긴다. 따라서 '아이들이 세상에서 더 많은 것을 배워가며 믿음을 굳혀 간다'는 주어진 문장을 ⑤에 넣어 흐름을 자연스럽게 만들어 주어야 한다.

오답 풀이

선택률	보기 해석
① 8%	앞뒤로 모두 '호기심의 감소'에 관해 언급하므로 흐름이 끊기지 않는다.
② 22%	앞에서 유아 뇌의 발달을 언급한 뒤, 뒤에서 배경 설명으로 유아 뇌가 어떤 상태인지 부연하는 자연스러운 흐름이다.
③ 22%	앞에서 유아 뇌에는 연결이 많다고 하고, 뒤에서는 '그런데' 이 연결이 엉망임을 지적하고 있다. however가 있어 흐름 전환이 자연스럽게 일어난다.
④ 22%	앞에서 말한 아이들 뇌의 특성으로 인해 유추할 수 있는 결론(consequently)을 자연스럽게 정리한다.

구문 풀이 1행

As children absorb more evidence from the world around them, certain possibilities become much more likely and more useful ~

→ As는 여기서 '~함에 따라'라는 접속사이다.

구문 플러스 as의 다양한 의미

접속사: ~할 때, ~하므로, ~함에 따라, ~듯이 등
전치사: ~로서

He led a successful career **as** a politician.
→ 전치사(~로서)

As we grow old, our eyes undergo changes.
→ 접속사(~함에 따라)

B 정답 ② 30% (2022 3월 학평)

해석 우리는 많은 방식으로 밤하늘과 연결되어 있다. 그것은 항상 사람들이 궁금해하고 상상하도록 영감을 주었다. 문명의 시작부터, 우리 선조들은 밤하늘에 대해 신화를 만들었고 전설적 이야기를 했다. 그러한 이야기들의 요소들은 여러 세대의 사회적 그리고 문화적 정체성에 깊이 새겨졌다. 실용적인 수준에서, 밤하늘은 과거 세대들이 시간을 기록하고 달력을 만들도록 도왔고 이는 농업과 계절에 따른 수확의 보조 도구로서 사회를 발전시키는 데 필수적이었다. 수 세기 동안, 그것은 또한 무역과 새로운 세계를 탐험하는 데 필수적인, 유용한 항해 도구를 제공하였다. 심지어 현대에도 지구의 외딴 지역에 있는 많은 사람들이 그러한 실용적인 목적을 위해 밤하늘을 관찰한다.

해설 ② 다음 문장에 '그러한 이야기들'이 등장하는데, ② 앞에 '그러한 이야기들'이 뜻하는 바가 나오지 않아 흐름이 어색하다. 따라서 '밤하늘에 대한 신화와 전설적 이야기(=그러한 이야기들)'에 대해 설명하는 주어진 문장을 ②에 삽입하여 글의 흐름을 자연스럽게 만들어주어야 한다.

오답 풀이

선택률	보기 해석
① 14%	우리가 밤하늘에 연관되어 있다고 말한 뒤, 그 예시로 밤하늘이 우리의 호기심과 상상력을 자극한다고 설명한다.
③ 26%	밤하늘이 우리의 사회문화적 정체성과 연관된다고 이야기한 뒤, 이번에는 밤하늘이 우리에게 어떻게 실용적으로 활용되는지를 설명한다. 글의 초점이 자연스럽게 전환되었다.
④ 18%	밤하늘의 실용적 활용에 대해 연이어 설명한다.
⑤ 10%	밤하늘의 실용적 활용 방식이 지금까지도 이어지고 있음을 설명한다.

구문 풀이 6행

On a practical level, the night sky helped past generations to keep track of time and create calendars **— essential to developing societies as aids to farming and seasonal gathering.**

→ 대시(—) 뒷부분은 which was가 생략된 것으로, 앞의 'to keep track of time and create calenders'에 대해 부연 설명한다.

구문 플러스

문장부호로서의 대시(—)는 문장 내에서 흐름을 짧게 중단시키고 부연 설명을 덧붙일 때 쓴다.

- You may think she is a liar — **she isn't**. → 부연 설명
- When we try something — **for example, playing the piano** — for the first time, it is not easy. → 삽입구로 쓰임

C 정답 ④ 55% 2021 6월 학평

해석 먹이 사슬은 식물 안에 있는 에너지원으로부터 먹고 먹히는 반복되는 과정 속에서 일련의 유기체를 통해 일련의 식품 에너지가 이동하는 것을 의미한다. 초원에서 풀은 토끼에게 먹히지만 이번에는 토끼는 여우에게 먹힌다. 이것은 단순한 먹이사슬의 예이다. 이 먹이사슬은 식품 에너지가 생산자로부터 소비자 또는 더 높은 영양 수준으로 전달되는 연쇄를 의미한다. 각 이동 단계에서 잠재적 에너지의 상당한 부분인 80-90%가 열로 손실되는 것으로 관찰되어 왔다. 그래서 하나의 연쇄(사슬) 안에 있는 단계나 연결의 수는 보통 4~5개로 제한된다. 먹이 사슬이 짧을수록 또는 유기체가 하위 영양 단계에 가까울수록 이용 가능한 에너지 섭취량이 더 커진다.

해설 ④ 이전 문장에서 먹이사슬을 통해 음식의 에너지가 전달된다고 하였는데, Hence로 시작하는 ④ 이후 문장에서 이 때문에 먹이사슬 단계의 수가 제한된다는 갑작스러운 결론을 내린다. 즉, ④ 이전 문장이 ④ 이후 문장에 대한 적절한 원인이 아니므로, ④에 적절한 원인(에너지 전달과정에서 에너지 손실이 발생함)을 설명하는 주어진 문장을 넣어 원인-결과의 흐름을 자연스럽게 만들어주어야 한다.

오답 풀이

선택률	보기 해석
① 7%	먹이사슬의 정의가 구체적인 예시로 이어지고 있다.
② 10%	풀, 토끼, 여우의 이야기를 대명사 This로 받으며 앞의 내용이 단순한 먹이사슬의 예시라고 정리한다.
③ 16%	먹이사슬과 그 과정 중 발생하는 에너지 전달에 대한 설명이 이어지고 있다.
⑤ 11%	먹이사슬 단계 제한에 관한 추가 설명이 이어지고 있다.

구문 풀이 10행

The shorter the food chain **or the nearer** the organism is to the beginning of the chain, **the greater** the available energy intake is.

→ <the 비교급, the 비교급> 구문으로, '~할수록 ~하다'의 의미를 갖는다. 앞 절이 등위접속사 or이 붙은 병렬구조로 길어졌다.

구문 플러스 the 비교급 ~, the+비교급 …

'~할수록 더 …하다'의 의미로, 이 구문이 쓰이면 글의 주제문인 경우가 많다.

The faster you drive, **the more** dangerous it becomes.
부사(drive 수식) 형용사(becomes의 보어)

D 정답 ③ 47% 2020 9월 학평

해석 성별에 관한 연구는 성별과 갈등 유형 사이의 복잡한 관계를 보여준다. 몇몇 연구는 서양 문화권에서 여성이 남성보다 더 주변을 돌보는 경향이 있다는 것을 시사한다. 이런 경향은 여성은 가족을 돌보도록 권장 받고, 남성은 경쟁적인 직업 환경에서 성공하도록 권장 받는 사회화 과정의 결과물일지 모른다. 그러나 우리는 성 역할과 경계가 이전 세대만큼 엄격하지 않은 사회에 살고 있다. 남성들 사이에서뿐만 아니라 여성들 사이에서도 단호함과 협조성에는 상당한 정도의 차이가 있다. 갈등 해결 전문가는 문화적 차이와 성별의 차이를 인지할 수 있어야 하지만, 그들은 또한 그룹 내의 차이와 고정관념을 갖는 것의 위험성도 알고 있어야 한다. 문화와 성별은 사람들이 인식하고, 해석하고, 갈등에 반응하는 방식에 영향을 미칠 수도 있지만, 우리는 과잉 일반화를 피하고 개인적인 차이를 고려하도록 주의해야 한다.

해설 ③ 앞에는 사회화 과정에서 여성과 남성이 서로 다른 것을 권장 받는다는 내용이 나오지만 ③ 이후에는 같은 성별 안에서도 차이가 있다고 말하고 있으므로 내용이 달라진다. 따라서, However로 시작하는 주어진 문장을 넣어 흐름을 자연스럽게 만들어야 한다.

오답 풀이

선택률	보기 해석
① 4%	성별과 갈등 유형 사이의 관계를 구체적 예시로 설명한다.
② 6%	성별에 따른 경향이 다르게 나타나는 이유를 사회화 과정으로 설명한다.
④ 25%	하나의 성별 안에서도 다양한 차이가 있음을 말하며, 고정관념의 위험성을 지적한다.
⑤ 15%	문화와 성별에 대한 과잉 일반화를 피해야 한다는 내용으로 마무리한다.

구문 풀이 5행

This tendency may result from socialization processes in which women **are encouraged to care for** their families and men are encouraged to be successful in competitive work environments.

→ 5형식 동사 encourage의 수동태로, <be p.p.> 뒤에 to부정사가 따라왔다.

구문 플러스 수동태

수동태의 시제

현재	is/are+p.p. (~되다)
과거	was/were+p.p. (~되었다)
미래	will be+p.p. (~될 것이다)
현재완료	has/have been+p.p. (~되어 왔다)
과거완료	had been+p.p. (~되어 왔었다)
진행	be being+p.p. (~되는 중이다)

수동태로 쓰일 수 없는 동사

① 자동사는 목적어가 없으므로 수동태로 쓰일 수 없다.
(appear, disappear, become, come, exist, happen, consist of 등)
② 상태동사는 타동사더라도 수동태로 쓰일 수 없다.
(have, resemble 등)

E 정답 ③ 43% 2019 9월 학평

해석 테크니컬 리허설(기술 연습) 후에, 극단은 총감독, 기술 감독들, 그리고 무대 감독을 만나서 리허설을 검토할 것이다. 보통은 공연에 대한 온갖 좋은 것들에 관한 의견이 있을 것이다. 개인은 단원들과 극단 전체에 대해 주어지는 긍정적인 의견뿐만 아니라, 그들의 개인적인 기여에 대한 긍정적인 의견도 마음에 새기고 글로 적어놓아야 한다. 긍정적인 성과를 바탕으로 하면 긴장감을 줄일 수 있다. 긍정적인 의견 이외에, 총

감독과 감독은 분명 아직 작업이 필요한 부분에 대한 의견도 가지고 있을 것이다. 때로, 이러한 부정적인 의견은 견디기 어렵고 스트레스를 주는 것처럼 보일 수 있다. 이렇게 마지막 순간의 변경을 해야 하는 시간적 압박은 스트레스의 원인이 될 수 있다. 각 제안을 좋은 기분으로 그리고 열정을 가지고 받아들이고 각 과제를 하나씩 해결해 나가라.

해설 ③ 앞에서는 리허설에 대한 긍정적인 의견을, ③ 뒤에서는 부정적인 의견을 이야기한다. 즉 ③에서 흐름이 어색하게 끊기므로, In addition to로 시작하는 주어진 문장을 넣어 흐름을 자연스럽게 만들어 주어야 한다.

오답 풀이

선택률	보기 해석
① 11%	긍정적 의견에 개인들이 어떻게 반응해야 하는지 설명한다.
② 24%	긍정적 의견으로 코멘트를 시작하는 것의 이득을 설명한다.
④ 13%	부정적 의견이 스트레스가 될 수 있음을 설명한다.
⑤ 7%	부정적 의견이 주는 압박과 스트레스를 설명하고, 이에 대응하는 방법을 말한다.

구문 풀이 11행

Time pressures **to make these last-minute changes** can be a source of stress.

→ 이 문장의 주어는 Time pressures이고 동사는 can be이다. 다만 주어를 수식하는 to부정사 때문에 주어가 길어졌다.

구문 플러스 수식어가 들어가 길어진 주어와 동사 찾기

문장이 복잡해 보일 때는 기본적으로 동사를 중심으로 주어를 찾는다.

The climatic change the trees underwent **is getting** worse.
수식절(목적격 관·대 생략)

F 정답 ④ 42% 2018 9월 학평

해석 누군가 어떤 문제에 대해 "그는 자신 외에 다른 누구도 탓할 수 없다"고 말하는 것을 들어본 적이 있는가? 매일의 삶에서 우리는 사람들이 자신의 문제를 '만들어'내는 것을 종종 비난한다. 비록 개인의 행동이 사회적 문제의 원인이 되기도 하지만 우리의 개인적 경험은 종종 우리의 통제 범위를 넘어선다. 그것은 사회 전반, 즉 사회의 역사적 발달과 구조에 의해 결정된다. 만약 한 사람이 과도한 지출이나 신용 카드의 남용 때문에 빚을 진다면 다른 이들은 종종 그 문제가 그 사람의 개인적 실패의 결과라고 간주한다. 하지만 그것에 대해 이런 방식으로 생각하는 것은 빚을 지는 것 외에 기초적 생활 필수품을 얻을 다른 방법이 없는 저소득 계층 사람들이 진 빚을 간과한다. 대조적으로 중간 또는 상위 소득 계층에서 과도한 지출은 여러 다양한 의미를 가지는데, 그 의미는 주로 사람들이 자신의 복지를 위해 필수적이라고 생각하는 것에 영향을 받고, 집중적으로 마케팅의 대상이 된 이른바 '좋은 삶'과 관련된다. 하지만 소득과 부의 수준을 넘어, 큰 규모의 경제적, 사회적 문제들은 소비자 재화와 서비스에 대한 개인들이 지불하는 능력에 영향을 미칠지도 모른다.

해설 개인적 경험이 개인의 탓뿐 아니라 사회적 요인에 영향을 받을 수 있다는 내용이다. ④ 앞에서는 어떤 사람이 빚을 지면 흔히 '그 사람 탓'이라고 생각하는 경우를 예로 들고, 주어진 문장은 '이런 식의 생각'이 구조적으로 빚을 질 수밖에 없는 저소득 사람들을 고려하지 않은 생각임을 비판한다. 이어서 ④ 뒤는 '저소득 사람들'과는 반대되는(By contrast) 대상으로 중간 이상 계층을 언급하며, 이들의 과도한 지출은 또 의미가 다르다는 설명을 이어 간다. 따라서 주어진 문장은 ④에 들어가야 가장 자연스럽다.

오답 풀이

선택률	보기 해석
① 6%	개인의 행동은 개인의 '통제 범위를 넘어서는' 경우가 있다고 말하며, 앞에서 말한 통념을 반박한다.
② 14%	개인적 경험이 사회에 의해 결정됨을 강조한다.
③ 28%	앞서 언급한 내용에 대해 예시를 들어 설명한다.
⑤ 8%	중간 또는 상위 소득 계층의 과도한 지출은 마케팅의 대상이 된 것과 관련 있음을 설명하면서, 개인들은 경제적, 사회적 영향을 받음을 다시 강조한다.

구문 풀이 9행

If a person sinks into debt because of **overspending or credit card abuse**, other people often consider the problem to be the result of the individual's personal failings.

→ because of는 '~ 때문에'라는 의미로, of가 전치사이기 때문에 명사나 동명사 등이 온다.

구문 플러스 because of vs. because

because of와 because는 둘 다 이유를 나타내지만 전치사인 because of 뒤에는 명사(구)가, 접속사인 because 뒤에는 절이 온다. because of는 due to와 동일한 의미이다.

He couldn't go to the party **because of** his homework.
→ He couldn't go to the party **because** he had homework.

G 정답 ③ 48% 2017 9월 학평

해석 읽는 것은 스키 타는 것과 같다. 잘 되었을 때, 즉, 전문가에 의해서 행해졌을 때에는 읽는 것과 스키 타는 것은 모두 우아하고 조화로운 활동들이다. 초보자에 의해서 행해졌을 때에는, 둘 다 어색하고 좌절감을 느끼게 하며 느리다. 스키 타는 것을 배우는 것은 성인이 겪을 수 있는 가장 당혹스러운 경험들 중의 하나이다. 어쨌든, 성인은 오랫동안 걸어왔고 그는 자신의 발이 어디에 있는지 알며 그는 어딘가로 가기 위해 어떤 식으로 한 발을 다른 발 앞에 놓아야 하는지 안다. 하지만 그가 스키를 발에 신자마자, 그것은 마치 그가 처음부터 다시 걷는 것을 배워야만 하는 것과 같다. 그는 발을 헛디뎌 미끄러지고, 넘어지고, 일어나는 데 어려움이 있고, 대체로 바보같이 보이고 느껴지기도 한다. 읽는 것도 마찬가지이다. 아마 여러분도 역시 오랫동안 읽기를 해왔으므로, 처음부터 다시 배우기를 시작하는 것은 창피할 수 있다.

해설 ③ 이전 문장에서는 사람이 잘 걷는다고 이야기하다가, ③ 이후 문장에서는 갑자기 사람이 잘 걷지 못한다고 이야기한다. 이렇게 ③에서 흐름이 어색하게 끊기므로, ③에 But으로 시작하는 주어진 문장을 넣어 전환을 자연스럽게 만들어주어야 한다.

오답 풀이

선택률	보기 해석
① 4%	읽기와 스키의 공통점을 언급한 후, 스키에 대해 설명한다.
② 15%	스키를 배우는 것이 성인에게 당혹스러운 경험이라고 말한 후, 성인들은 걷는 방법을 잘 알고 있음을 언급한다.
④ 26%	스키를 배울 때 어려움이 있듯, 읽기도 마찬가지라 말한다.
⑤ 5%	읽기를 처음부터 다시 배우는 어려움을 이어 설명한다.

구문 풀이 9행

He slips and slides, falls down, has trouble getting up, and generally **looks** – and **feels** – **like a fool**.

→ 동사 look, feel 다음에는 형용사가 오지만 look like, feel like 다음에는 명사가 온다.

구문 플러스⁺ 감각동사와 지각동사

주어의 느낌을 전달하는 감각동사는 <주어+감각동사+주격보어>의 2형식 구조로 쓴다. 반면 주어가 대상을 어떻게 인지하였는지를 나타내는 지각동사는 <주어+지각동사+목적어+목적격보어>의 5형식 구조로 쓴다. 같은 동사라도 문장의 의미에 따라 구조가 다르므로 유의한다.

감각동사로 쓰인 경우

It **feels** soft. → 형용사 보어

He **looks** like a fool. → <like+명> 보어

지각동사로 쓰인 경우

I could **feel** him move. → 원형부정사 보어

유형 플러스⁺ 주어진 문장 넣기

다섯 군데의 빈칸 중에 주어진 문장이 들어갈 위치를 찾는 문제로 문장과 문장 사이의 연결이 자연스럽도록 해야 한다.

① 먼저 핵심 소재를 파악한다. 주어진 문장을 먼저 읽어 내용을 파악한다.
② 정관사, 대명사, 지시어 등을 살펴보아 문장 간의 관계를 유추한다.
흐름이 갑자기 어색해지는 부분이 있다면 주어진 문장을 대입해본다.

DAY 13 요약문 완성

A② B① C① D① E② F① G①

A 정답 ② 49% 2023 6월 학평

해석 미국 성인 10명 중 거의 8명이 '좋은 음식'과 '나쁜 음식'이 있다고 믿는다. 하지만, 우리가 상한 스튜, 독버섯, 또는 이와 유사한 것에 대해 이야기하고 있지 않는 한, 어떤 음식도 좋고 나쁨으로 분류될 수 없다. 그렇지만, 결국 건강에 좋은 식단이나 건강에 좋지 않은 식단이 되는 음식들의 조합이 있다. '좋은' 음식이라고 생각되는 음식만 먹는 성인의 경우를 생각해보라. 예컨대 생브로콜리, 사과, 오렌지 주스, 삶은 두부와 당근 말이다. 이 모든 음식들은 영양이 풍부하지만, 우리가 필요로 하는 충분히 다양한 영양소를 공급하지 않기 때문에 그것들은 결국 건강한 식단이 되지 않는다. 또는 튀긴 치킨을 가끔 먹지만, 그렇지 않으면 튀긴 음식을 멀리하는 십 대의 경우를 예로 들어보자. 가끔 먹는 튀긴 치킨은 그 십 대의 식단을 궤도에서 벗어나게 하지 않을 것이다. 하지만 채소나 과일을 거의 먹지 않으면서 매일 튀긴 음식을 먹고, 간식으로 초대형 탄산음료, 사탕, 그리고 감자 칩을 실컷 먹는 사람은 나쁜 식단을 가진 것이다.
→ 통념과 달리, 음식을 좋고 나쁨으로 정의하는 것은 (A) 적절하지 않으며, 사실 건강에 좋은 식단은 대체로 그 식단이 무엇으로 (B) 구성되는지에 의해 결정된다.

해설 절대적으로 좋은 식단과 나쁜 식단이 있다기보다 조합이 중요하다는 내용이다. 첫 세 문장에서 핵심 내용을 확인할 수 있다. 따라서 ② '적절한 - ~로 구성된'이 요약문의 빈칸에 적절하다.

오답 풀이

선택률	보기 해석
① 17%	incorrect(부정확한), limited to(~로 제한된)
③ 9%	wrong(틀린), aimed at(~을 목표로 한)
④ 13%	appropriate(적절한), tested on(~에 시험된)
⑤ 12%	incorrect(부정확한), adjusted to(~에 맞춰진)

구문 풀이 5행

Consider the case of an adult who eats only foods **(that are) thought of as** "good" ~
→ <think of A as B>의 수동태인 <A be thought of B>이다. <주격 관계대명사+be동사>는 생략되고 'thought of as ~'와 같이 과거분사구만 남았다.

구문 플러스+ 구동사의 수동태

구동사가 수동태(be p.p.)로 바뀌면 동사의 일부인 부사/전치사까지 p.p. 뒤에 모두 써주고, 이어서 <by+목적격>을 붙여준다. 이 경우 전치사가 연속적으로 나와 어색해 보이지만 문법적으로 이상이 없다.

a girl (who is) **looked after by** her big sister

B 정답 ① 48% 2022 3월 학평

해석 common blackberry(Rubus allegheniensis)는 뿌리를 이용하여 토양의 한 층에서 다른 층으로 망가니즈를 옮기는 놀라운 능력이 있다. 이것은 식물이 가지기에는 기이한 재능처럼 보일 수도 있지만, 그것이 근처의 식물에 미치는 영향을 깨닫고 나면 전부 명확해진다. 망가니즈는 식물에 매우 해로울 수 있으며, 특히 고농도일 때 그렇다. common blackberry는 이 금속 원소의 해로운 효과에 영향을 받지 않으며, 망가니즈를 자신에게 유리하게 사용하는 두 가지 다른 방법을 발달시켰다. 첫째로, 그것은 뿌리를 작은 관으로 사용하여 망가니즈를 깊은 토양층으로부터 얕은 토양층으로 재분배한다. 둘째로, 그것은 성장하면서 망가니즈를 흡수하여 그 금속 원소를 잎에 농축한다. 잎이 떨어지고 부패할 때, 그것의 농축된 망가니즈 축적물은 그 식물 주변의 토양을 독성 물질로 더욱 오염시킨다. 망가니즈의 유독한 영향에 면역이 없는 식물에게 이것은 매우 나쁜 소식이다. 본질적으로, common blackberry는 중금속으로 그것의 이웃을 중독시켜 경쟁자를 제거한다.
→ common blackberry는 주변의 위쪽 토양의 망가니즈의 양을 (A) 증가시키는 능력이 있는데, 그것은 근처의 토양이 다른 식물에게 꽤 (B) 치명적이게 되도록 만든다.

해설 글에 따르면, common blackberry는 깊은 토양층의 망가니즈를 자신의 뿌리를 이용하여 흡수한 뒤, 그것을 잎에 농축한다. 그리고 그 잎이 떨어져 부패하면서, 얕은 토양층의 망가니즈 농도가 높아진다. 즉, common blackberry 주변의 위쪽 토양의 망가니즈의 양이 증가하는 것이다. 이는 근처의 다른 식물에게 유독한 영향을 줄 수 있다. 따라서 요약문의 빈칸에는 ① '증가시키다 - 치명적인'이 적절하다.

오답 풀이

선택률	보기 해석
② 20%	increase(증가시키다), advantageous(유리한)
③ 9%	indicate(의미하다), nutritious(영양분이 있는)
④ 13%	reduce(감소시키다), dry(건조한)
⑤ 8%	reduce(감소시키다), warm(따뜻한)

구문 풀이 3행

~ it all becomes clear when you realize the effect **it has on nearby plants.**
→ 목적격 관계대명사가 생략된 형용사절이 the effect를 꾸민다.

구문 플러스+ 관계대명사의 생략

주격: be동사와 함께 생략하며, 단독 생략 불가
목적격: 자유롭게 생략

a rule **(that is)** accepted without proof → <주격 관·대+be동사> 생략
a rule **that** has few exceptions → 생략 X
a rule **(that)** everyone should follow → 목적격 관·대 생략

C 정답 ① 58% 2021 6월 학평

해석 Berkeley에 있는 California 대학에 다니는 Rhonda라는 여자는 한 가지 문제 상황이 있었다. 그녀는 여러 사람들과 함께 캠퍼스 근처에 살고 있었는데 그들 중 누구도 서로를 알지는 못했다. 청소부가 주말 마다 왔을 때 화장실 두 칸 각각 몇 개의 두루마리 화장지를 두고 갔다. 그러나 월요일 즈음 모든 화장지가 없어지곤 했다. 그것은 전형적인 공유지의 비극 상황이었다. 일부 사람들이 자신들이 사용할 수 있는 몫보다 더 많은 휴지를 가져갔기 때문에 그 외 모두를 위한 공공재가 파괴됐다. 행동변화에 대한 한 연구논문을 읽고 나서, Rhonda는 화장실 화장지는 공유재이므로 사람들에게 가져가지 말라고 요청하는 쪽지를 화장실 한 곳에 두었다. 아주 만족스럽게도, 몇 시간 후에 화장지 한 개가 다시 나타났고 그 다음 날에는 또 하나가 다시 나타났다. 하지만 쪽지가 없는 화장실에서는 청소부가 돌아오는 그 다음 주말까지 화장지가 없었다.
→ 자그마한 (A) 상기물은 그들이 필요한 것보다 더 많은 (B) 공유재를 가져갔던 사람의 행동에 변화를 가져왔다.

해설 Rhonda의 쪽지가 상기물로서 작용하여, 공유재였던 휴지를 필요 이상으로 가져갔던 사람들의 행동을 변화시켰다. 따라서 요약문의 빈칸에는 ① '상기물 - 공유된'이 들어가야 한다.

오답 풀이

선택률	보기 해석
② 11%	reminder(상기물), recycled(재활용의)
③ 15%	mistake(실수), stored(저장된)
④ 12%	mistake(실수), borrowed(빌려간)
⑤ 3%	fortune(부), limited(제한된)

구문 풀이 10행
~ one roll reappeared in a few hours, and another (**reappeared**) the next day.
→ 반복되는 동사 reappeared를 생략하였다.

구문 플러스 등위접속사 생략 구문

등위접속사 and, or, but, so 뒤에서 앞말과의 중복을 피하기 위해 뒷말 일부를 생략하기도 한다.

I went to the store, and she **(went)** to the bank.

D 정답 ① 73% 2020 3월 학평

해석 협동을 하는 진화적이거나 문화적인 많은 이유가 있지만, 눈은 가장 중요한 협동 수단 중 하나이고, 시선의 마주침은 우리가 차량 운행 중에 잃는 가장 강력한 인간의 힘일지도 모른다. 그것은 보통은 꽤 협조적인 종인 인간이 도로에서 그렇게 비협조적이 될 수 있는 이유라고 주장할 수 있다. 대부분의 시간에 우리가 너무 빨리 움직이고 있어서, 우리는 시속 20마일 정도에서 시선을 마주치는 능력을 잃기 시작하거나, 혹은 (서로를) 보는 것이 안전하지 않다. 어쩌면 우리의 시야가 차단되어 있을 수도 있다. 흔히 다른 운전자들이 선글라스를 끼고 있거나 그들의 차는 색이 옅게 들어간 창문이 있을 수 있다. (그리고 당신은 정말로 그러한 운전자들과 시선을 마주치고 싶은가?) 때로는 우리는 후방거울을 통해 시선을 마주치지만, '얼굴을 마주하고 있는 것'이 아니기 때문에 약하게, 처음에는 전혀 믿을 수 없게 느껴진다.
→ 운전하는 동안, 사람들은 (A) 비협조적이 되는데, 왜냐하면 그들이 (B) 거의 시선을 마주치지 않기 때문이다.

해설 협동은 눈빛을 교환하고 얼굴을 마주할 때 나타나기 때문에, 운전할 때 서로를 볼 수 없는 사람들은 비협조적일 수 밖에 없다고 말하고 있다. 따라서 정답은 ① '비협조적인 - 거의 없는'이다.

오답 풀이

선택률	보기 해석
② 8%	careful(주의하는), direct(직접적인)
③ 3%	confident(자신이 있는), regular(정기적인)
④ 7%	uncooperative(비협조적인), direct(직접적인)
⑤ 6%	careful(주의하는), little(거의 없는)

구문 풀이 1행
While there are many evolutionary or cultural reasons for cooperation, the eyes are **one of the most important means of cooperation** ~
→ <one of the+최상급+복수명사>는 '가장 ~한 것들 중 하나'라는 의미이다.

구문 플러스 one of the+복수명사

<one of the+(최상급)+복수명사>가 주어로 나오면 단수 취급한다.

One of the most beautiful cities in the world **is** Venice.
→ 핵심 주어: One(단수)

E 정답 ② 78% 2019 6월 학평

해석 무엇이 정말 사람들로 하여금 자신의 목표를 성취하도록 동기를 부여하기 위해 효과가 있는가? 한 연구에서, 연구자들은 사람들이 직장을 얻거나, 시험을 치거나, 수술을 받는 것과 같은 인생의 과제에 어떻게 대응하는가를 살펴보았다. 이러한 각각의 상황에 대해, 연구자들은 또한 실험 참가자들이 긍정적인 결과에 대해 얼마나 많이 공상했는지, 그리고 그들이 실제로 긍정적인 결과를 얼마나 많이 기대했는지를 측정했다. 공상과 기대의 차이는 진정 무엇인가? 공상은 이상화된 미래를 상상하는 것을 포함하는 반면, 기대는 실제로 사람의 과거 경험에 근거한다. 그래서 연구자들은 무엇을 알아냈는가? 그 결과는 바라던 미래에 대해 공상을 했던 사람들은 세 가지 상황 모두에서 성과가 좋지 않았다는 것을 보여주었다. 성공에 대한 긍정적인 기대를 더 많이 했던 사람들은 다음 주, 달, 해에도 좋은 성과를 거두었다. 이 사람들은 직업을 구하고, 시험에 합격하고, 수술에서 성공적으로 회복했을 가능성이 더 높았다.
→ 긍정적인 기대는 바라던 미래에 대해 공상하는 것보다 더 (A) 효과적이고, 그것은 목표를 성취하는 데 있어 (B) 성공의 가능성을 높여 주는 경향이 있다.

해설 긍정적인 기대와 공상의 차이를 말하며 긍정적 기대가 성공의 가능성을 높여준다고 말하고 있으므로 ② '효과적인 - 성공'이 적절하다.

오답 풀이

선택률	보기 해석
① 6%	effective(효과적인), frustration(좌절)
③ 6%	discouraging(실망스러운), cooperation(협조)
④ 5%	discouraging(실망스러운), failure(실패)
⑤ 2%	common(일반적인), difficulty(어려움)

구문 풀이 12행

These individuals were more likely to **have found** jobs, **passed** their exams, or successfully **recovered** from their surgery.

→ <to have p.p.>는 본동사의 시제보다 먼저 일어난 일을 나타낸다.

구문 플러스⁺ to부정사의 시제

일반적으로 to부정사는 <to+동사원형>의 형태지만 본동사보다 이전 시제를 나타낼 때는 <to+have+p.p.>로 쓴다.

to부정사의 두 가지 형태

단순형	to+동사원형	He seems **to be** rich. → 지금 부유해보임
완료형	to+have+p.p.	He seems **to have been** rich. → 과거에 부유했던 것으로 보임

F 정답 ① 32% *2018 11월 학평*

해석 우리는 스포츠 경기의 결과를 예측할 수 없는데, 이것은 매주 달라진다. 이러한 이질성이 스포츠의 특징이다. 소비자들이 매력적이라고 여기는 것은 바로 결과의 불확실성과 경기 질이다. 스포츠 마케팅 담당자에게 이것은 문제가 되는데, 왜냐하면 경기의 수준이 보장될 수 없고, 경기 결과에 관해 어떤 약속도 할 수 없으며, 스타 선수의 경기력에 관해 어떤 확신도 줄 수 없기 때문이다. 소비재와 다르게, 스포츠는 마케팅 전략의 중요한 특징인 일관성을 보여줄 수도 없고 보여주지도 않는다. 따라서 스포츠 마케팅 담당자는 순전히 승리에만 기반한 마케팅 전략을 피해야 하고, 대신에 핵심 제품(즉, 시합 그 자체)보다는 시설, 주차, 상품, 기념품, 식음료 같은 제품 확장 개발에 집중해야만 한다.

→ 스포츠는 (A) 불확실하다는 본질적 속성을 갖고 있으며, 이로 인해 스포츠 마케팅 전략은 단지 스포츠 경기보다는 상품과 서비스를 (B) 특징으로 삼아야 한다.

해설 처음과 마지막에 힌트가 있다. 스포츠는 그 결과를 예측하거나 장담할 수 없기에, 스포츠 마케팅을 할 때는 시합이라는 핵심 제품에만 집중하기보다는 제품 확장에도 관심을 기울여야 한다는 것이다. 따라서 답으로는 ① '불확실한 - 특징으로 삼다'가 적절하다.

오답 풀이

선택률	보기 해석
② 15%	unreliable(불확실한), exclude(제외하다)
③ 6%	risky(위험한), ignore(무시하다)
④ 19%	consistent(일관성 있는), involve(포함하다)
⑤ 19%	consistent(일관성 있는), promote(홍보하다)

구문 풀이 2행

It is the uncertainty of the result and the quality of the contest **that** consumers find attractive.

→ it is A that B 강조 구문이다. <find+목적어+형용사> 구조의 5형식 문장에서 목적어인 'the uncertainty ~ and the quality ~'를 강조하고, that 뒤에 <주어+동사+목적격 보어>만을 남겼다.

구문 플러스⁺ it is A that B 강조 구문

- A에는 명사구 또는 부사구가 나오는데, 사람/사물 명사면 that 대신 who/which를, 부사구면 의미에 따라 when/where 등을 쓸 수 있다.
- 동사나 형용사는 A 자리에 들어갈 수 없다.

It was Sam **that[who]** told me the news. → 명사 강조
It was yesterday **that[when]** he called me. → 부사 강조
It is natural **that** you feel sad after losing your best friend.
→ 가주어-진주어 구문

G 정답 ① 77% *2017 9월 학평*

해석 Virginia 대학의 사회 심리학자들이 대학생들에게 무거운 배낭을 멘 채로 언덕 아래에 서서 언덕의 경사도를 추정하도록 요청했다. 그 활동을 하는 동안 일부 참가자들은 오랫동안 알아 왔던 친한 친구들 옆에 서 있었고, 몇몇은 안 지 오래되지 않은 친구들 옆에 서 있었고, 몇몇은 낯선 사람 옆에 서 있었으며, 다른 사람들은 혼자 서 있었다. 친한 친구들과 함께 서 있었던 참가자들은 혼자이거나, 낯선 사람 옆이거나, 또는 새로 사귄 친구 옆에 서 있었던 사람들보다 그 언덕의 경사도를 상당히 더 낮게 추정했다. 게다가, 그 친한 친구들이 서로 알았던 기간이 길면 길수록, 연구에 참여한 참가자들에게 언덕은 덜 가파르게 보였다.

→ 연구에 따르면, (B) 친한 친구 옆에 서 있을 때 과제가 덜 (A) 어렵게 지각된다.

해설 옆에 선 사람과 친할수록 언덕이 덜 가파르다고 느낀다는 마지막 문장의 내용을 통해 '친한' 친구가 옆에 있을 때 과제를 '덜 어렵게' 느낀다는 것을 알 수 있다. 따라서 정답은 ① '어려운 - 친한'이다.

오답 풀이

선택률	보기 해석
② 10%	valuable(가치 있는), new(새로운)
③ 5%	difficult(어려운), smart(똑똑한)
④ 4%	valuable(가치 있는), patient(인내심 많은)
⑤ 1%	exciting(흥미로운), strong(강한)

구문 풀이 9행

Furthermore, **the longer** the close friends **had known** each other, **the less steep** the hill appeared to the participants involved in the study.

→ 문장은 전체적으로 <the 비교급 ~, the 비교급 …(~할수록 더 …하

다)> 구문이다. 실험 상황보다 더 이전에 있었던 일을 묘사하기 위해 과거완료 시제(had known)가 등장했다.

구문 플러스⁺ 과거완료

두 과거 사건의 선후 관계를 나타내는 시제로, 기준 시점보다 더 이전에 있었던 일을 묘사한다.

Your secretary said you **had already left**.
'말한' 것보다 먼저 떠남

유형 플러스⁺ 요약문 완성

주어진 글의 내용을 요약하고 그 요약문에 들어갈 적절한 표현을 고르는 문제 유형이다.

문제 해결 방법

① 요약문을 먼저 읽고 내용을 파악한다.
② 핵심어, 반복 어휘의 다른 표현에 주목한다.
③ 주제를 요약하는 표현에 유의한다.

DAY 14 장문의 이해

A1 ② A2 ③ B1 ④ B2 ④ C1 ② C2 ② D1 ② D2 ④ E1 ④ E2 ③ F1 ⑤ F2 ① G1 ① G2 ③

A 정답 1. ② 69% 2. ③ 45% 2023 3월 학평

해석 체스판을 게임 중간에 20~30개의 말들이 아직 놓여 있는 상태로 5초 동안 본 체스의 달인들은 그 말들의 위치를 기억해서 즉시 재현할 수 있다. 물론 초보자들은 겨우 몇 개만 기억해 낼 수 있다. 이제 같은 말들을 가져다가 체스판에 무작위로 놓으면 그 차이는 크게 줄어든다. 전문가의 유리함은 익숙한 패턴, 즉 전에 기억에 저장된 패턴에 대해서만 있다. 익숙하지 않은 패턴을 맞닥뜨리면, 같은 익숙한 분야와 관련 있는 경우라도 전문가의 유리함은 사라진다.

익숙한 구조가 기억에 미치는 유익한 효과는 음악을 포함해 많은 유형의 전문 지식에서 관찰되었다. 음표가 특이한(→ 전형적인) 순서를 따를 때는 음악 교육을 받은 사람이 음악 교육을 받지 않은 사람보다 짧은 연속된 악보를 더 정확하게 재현할 수 있지만, 음표가 무작위로 배열되면 그 유리함이 훨씬 줄어든다. 전문 지식은 또한 연속 동작에 대한 기억을 향상시킨다. 숙련된 발레 무용수가 경험이 적은 무용수보다 더 긴 연속 스텝을 반복할 수 있고, 무작위로 배열된 스텝보다 정해진 춤 동작을 이루는 연속 스텝을 더 잘 반복할 수 있다. 각각의 경우, 기억의 범위는 익숙한 순서와 패턴을 인식하는 능력에 의해 늘어난다.

A1

해설 두 번째 단락 첫 줄에서 요약하듯, '익숙한 구조가 기억에 미치는 유익한 효과'에 관해 설명하는 글이다. 따라서 제목으로 가장 적절한 것은 ② '익숙한 구조는 우리가 기억하는 것을 돕는다'이다.

오답 풀이

선택률	보기 해석
① 5%	어떻게 좋은 루틴을 만들어 나갈까?
③ 7%	지능은 전문 지식을 보장하지 못한다
④ 12%	체스를 하는 것은 기억력을 높여줄까?
⑤ 4%	창의적인 예술 공연은 연습에서 시작된다

A2

해설 무작위로 배열된 정보에서는 전문가의 유리함이 두드러지지 않고, '익숙한' 정보에서 유리함이 두드러진다는 내용으로 보아, (c)의 unusual을 conventional로 바꿔야 한다. 따라서 정답은 ③이다.

오답 풀이

선택률	보기 해석
① 11%	difference(차이)
② 24%	disappears(사라지다)
④ 9%	movements(동작)
⑤ 11%	increased(늘어난)

구문 풀이 5행

Now **take** the same pieces and **place** them on the board randomly **and** the difference is much reduced.

→ <명령문+and …(~하라, 그러면 …)>의 구조이다. take와 place가 병렬 연결되었다.

구문 플러스 명령문+등위접속사

명령문+and: ~하라, 그러면 …
명령문+or: ~하라, 그러지 않으면 …

Hurry, **and** you'll catch the bus. → 서둘렀을 때의 결과
Hurry, **or** you'll be late. → 서두르지 않았을 때의 결과

B 정답 1. ④ 80% 2. ④ 79% 2022 6월 학평

해석 (A) 어느 날, 한 농부가 헛간에서 일하는 동안 그의 귀중한 시계를 잃어버렸다. 그것은 다른 이들에게는 평범한 시계로 보일 수도 있었지만 그것은 그에게 어린 시절의 많은 행복한 기억을 불러왔다. 그것은 그에게 가장 중요한 것들 중 하나였다. 오랜 시간 동안 그것을 찾아본 뒤에 그 나이 든 농부는 지쳐버렸다.

(D) 그러나, 그 지친 농부는 그의 시계를 찾는 것을 포기하고 싶지 않았기에 밖에서 놀던 한 무리의 아이들에게 도와 달라고 요청했다. 그는 그의 시계를 찾는 사람에게 매력적인 보상을 약속했다. 보상에 대해 듣고난 뒤, 그 아이들은 헛간 안으로 서둘러 들어갔고 시계를 찾으러 전체 건초더미 사이와 주변으로 걸어갔다. 시계를 찾느라 오랜 시간을 보낸 후, 아이들 중 일부는 지쳐서 포기했다.

(B) 시계를 찾는 아이들의 숫자가 천천히 줄어들었고 지친 아이들 몇 명만이 남았다. 그 농부는 시계를 찾을 거라는 모든 희망을 포기하고 찾는 것을 멈추었다. 농부가 막 헛간 문을 닫고 있었을 때 한 어린 소년이 그에게 다가와서 자신에게 또 한 번의 기회를 달라고 요청했다. 농부는 시계를 찾을 어떤 가능성도 놓치고 싶지 않아서 그를 헛간 안으로 들어오게 해주었다.

(C) 잠시 후 그 소년이 한 손에 농부의 시계를 들고 나왔다. 그는 행복에 겨워 놀랐고 다른 모두가 실패했던 반면 소년이 어떻게 시계를 찾는 데 성공했는지를 물었다. 그는 "저는 거기에 앉아서 시계의 소리를 들으려고 했어요. 침묵 속에서, 그것을 듣고 소리의 방향을 따라가는 것이 훨씬 쉬웠어요."라고 답했다. 그는 시계를 되찾아 기뻤고 그 어린 소년에게 약속한 대로 보상해 주었다.

B1

해설 (D)에서 아이들이 시계를 찾기 시작하다 (B)에서 그만두고, 한 명의 아이만이 다시 시계를 찾으려 한 후, (C)에서 결국 시계를 찾는 흐름이 자연스럽다. 따라서 정답은 ④ '(D)-(B)-(C)'이다.

오답 풀이

선택률	보기 해석
① 6%	많은 아이들이 적극적으로 시계를 찾기 시작하는 (D)가 맨 처음에 나와야 한다.
② 3%	①과 동일
③ 5%	①과 동일
⑤ 3%	결국 시계를 찾는 내용의 (C)는 시계를 찾는 과정인 (B)보다 뒤에 나와야 한다.

B2

해설 (D)의 '~ the children hurried inside the barn ~'에 따르면, 아이들은 시계를 찾기 위해 헛간을 '나오지' 않고 '들어갔으므로', 정답은 ④이다.

오답 풀이

선택률	보기 해석
① 3%	(A) it brought a lot of happy childhood memories to him
② 6%	(B) a little boy ... asked the farmer to give him another chance
③ 4%	(C) the boy came out with the farmer's watch in his hand
⑤ 5%	(D) some of the children got tired and gave up

구문 풀이 8행

However, the tired farmer did not want to give up on the search for his watch and **asked a group of children playing outside to help him.**

→ 'ask+목적어+목적격 보어(to부정사)'의 5형식 구조가 쓰였다. 그리고 현재분사구 playing outside가 명사 children을 수식하고 있다.

구문 플러스⁺ ask의 다양한 문장구조

- ask+간접목적어+직접목적어 → 4형식
- ask+목적어+to부정사 → 5형식
- ask that+주어+(should)+동사원형 → 가정법 현재 명사절

She asked **me an embarrassing question**.
She asked me **to check out** some books.
She asked that we **be sure** to lock the door. → that절: '~해야 하다'

C 정답 1. ② 84% 2. ② 81% 2021 3월 학평

해석 (A) 옛날 옛적에 사냥에 대해 엄청난 열정을 가진 젊은 왕이 살았다. 그의 왕국은 히말라야 산맥의 기슭에 위치해 있었다. 매년 한 번씩, 그는 근처의 숲으로 사냥하러 가고는 했다. 그는 모든 필요한 준비를 하고 자신의 사냥 여행을 떠나고는 했다.
(C) 다른 모든 해처럼, 사냥철이 왔다. 궁궐에서 준비가 시작되었고 왕은 자신의 사냥 여행을 갈 준비를 했다. 숲 속 깊은 곳에서 그는 아름다운 야생 사슴을 발견했다. 그것은 큰 수사슴이었다. 그의 겨냥은 완벽했다. 단 한 발의 화살로 그 사슴을 잡고서 왕은 의기양양했다. 그 의기양양한 사냥꾼은 그 사슴의 가죽으로 사냥용 북을 만들도록 명령했다.
(B) 계절이 바뀌었다. 1년이 지나갔다. 그리고 또 다시 사냥하러 갈 때가 되었다. 왕은 작년과 같은 숲으로 갔다. 그는 아름다운 사슴 가죽으로 만든 북을 사용하여 동물을 몰았다. 그러나 아무도 오지 않았다. 모든 동물이 안전한 곳으로 도망쳤는데, 암사슴 한 마리는 예외였다. 암사슴은 북 치는 사람에게 점점 더 가까이 다가왔다. 갑자기, 암사슴은 두려움 없이 사슴 가죽으로 만든 북을 핥기 시작했다.
(D) 이 광경을 보고 왕은 놀랐다. 한 나이 든 신하가 이 이상한 행동의 이유를 알고 있었다. "이 북을 만드는 데 사용된 사슴 가죽은 암사슴의 짝의 것인데, 우리가 작년에 사냥한 그 사슴입니다. 이 암사슴은 짝의 죽음을 애도하고 있는 것입니다."라고 그 남자는 말했다. 이 말을 듣자마자, 왕의 마음이 바뀌었다. 그는 동물도 역시 상실의 고통을 느낀다는 것을 전혀 몰랐었다. 그는 그날 이후 다시는 결코 야생 동물을 사냥하지 않겠다고 약속했다.

C1

해설 (C)에서 수사슴을 사냥하고, (B)에서 그 수사슴의 가죽으로 만든 북을 친 후 벌어진 일에 대한 신하의 설명이 (D)에서 이어지는 것이 자연스럽다. 따라서 ② '(C)-(B)-(D)'가 정답이다.

오답 풀이

선택률	보기 해석
① 2%	수사슴을 잡은 이야기(C)가 수사슴 북을 친 이야기(B)보다 뒤에 나오는 것이 부자연스럽다.
③ 6%	왕이 사냥을 하지 않기로 했다는 다짐(D)이 제일 뒤에 와야 한다.
④ 3%	③과 동일
⑤ 2%	③과 동일

C2

해설 (B)의 마지막 문장에 따르면, 암사슴은 북 치는 사람에게 다가와 북을 핥았다. 따라서 일치하지 않는 것은 ②이다.

오답 풀이

선택률	보기 해석
① 2%	(A) Once every year, he would go hunting in the nearby forests.
③ 6%	(C) he killed the deer with just one shot of his arrow
④ 6%	(D) An old servant had an answer to this strange behavior.
⑤ 2%	(D) He made a promise, from that day on, to never again hunt wild animals.

구문 풀이 3행

He **would** make all the necessary preparations, and then set out for his hunting trip.

→ 조동사 would는 '~하곤 했다'로 해석되기도 한다.

구문 플러스⁺ 조동사 would

조동사 would는 여러가지 의미를 가지고 있다. 문맥에 맞게 적절히 해석하여야 한다.

He said he **would** come early. (will의 과거형)
Would you mind leaving us alone? (정중한 요청)
If you had seen it, you **would** have felt happy. (~했을 것이다)
My grandmother **would** bake cookies for us. (~하곤 했다)

D 정답 1. ② 68% 2. ④ 53% 2020 9월 학평

해석 표준적인 침구와 복장을 가정할 때, 대략 화씨 65도(섭씨 18.3도)의 침실 온도가 대부분의 사람들의 수면에 이상적이다. 이것은 안락함을 위해서는 다소 너무 추운 것처럼 들리기 때문에 많은 사람을 놀라게 한다. 물론, 그 특정 온도는 해당되는 사람과 그들의 성별 그리고 나이에 따

라 다를 것이다. 하지만, 권장 칼로리처럼, 그것은 평균적인 사람에게 좋은 목표이다. 우리 대부분은 침실 온도를 좋은 수면을 위해 이상적인 것보다 높게 설정하는데, 이는 그렇게 하지 않는다면 당신이 얻을 수 있는 것보다 수면의 양과 질을 낮추는 데 기여할 것이다. 따뜻한 침구와 잠옷이 사용되지 않는 이상 화씨 55도보다 더 낮은 온도는 잠을 자는데 도움이 되기보다 오히려 해로울 수 있다. 하지만, 우리 대부분은 70도 또는 72도라는 너무 높은 침실 온도를 설정하는 정반대의 범주에 속한다. 밤에 잠을 못 자는 환자를 치료하는 수면 임상의사는 종종 침실 온도를 묻고, 환자들에게 온도 조절 장치의 현재 설정값을 그들이 지금 사용하는 설정값보다 3도에서 5도 가량 올리라고(→낮추라고) 조언할 것이다. 온도가 수면에 미치는 영향에 대해 불신하는 사람은 누구든지 이 주제에 관한 몇몇 관련 실험들을 살펴볼 수 있다. 예를 들어, 과학자들은 혈액을 피부의 표면으로 올라가게 하고 열을 방출시키기 위해 쥐의 발이나 몸을 서서히 따뜻하게 했고, 그렇게 해서 심부체온을 낮추었다. 그 쥐들은 그렇지 않았다면(체온을 낮추지 않았더라면) 평균적이었을 것(속도)보다 훨씬 더 빨리 잠들었다.

D1

해설 이 글은 우리가 예상한 것보다 더 낮은 온도일 때 숙면을 할 수 있다고 말하고 있기 때문에 ② '더 나은 수면을 위해 서늘하게 유지하라'가 제목으로 적절하다.

오답 풀이

선택률	보기 해석
① 4%	수면 장애의 징후
③ 16%	방 온도를 높여라
④ 5%	나쁜 잠자리 자세를 고치는 방법
⑤ 3%	질 높은 수면의 핵심: 깨끗한 침구

D2

해설 계속해서 방의 온도를 낮추는 것이 수면에 도움이 된다고 했으므로 반대로 높이라고 말하는 ④ (d)가 어색하다.

오답 풀이

선택률	보기 해석
① 7%	surprises(놀라게 하다)
② 19%	lower(낮추다)
③ 11%	opposite(정반대의)
⑤ 8%	faster(더 빨리)

구문 풀이 18행

The rats fell asleep far faster than was **otherwise** normal.

→ 부사 otherwise는 '그렇지 않으면'의 의미다.

구문 플러스+ 부사 otherwise

otherwise(그렇지 않으면)는 가정법적 의미를 나타낼 때도 있다.

The newspaper disclosed crimes that **would otherwise have remained** unreported to the public.

→ '만일 그 신문에서 보도하지 않았더라면'과 같이, 실제 과거와 반대되는 내용을 가정

E 정답 1. ④ 59% 2. ③ 60% 2019 9월 학평

해석 (A) 두 제자는 숲을 가로지르는 길의 출발선에서 그들의 스승과 만났다. 스승은 그들에게 그 주의 후반에 있을 테스트를 대비해 그 길을 끝까지 따라가라고 지시했다. 길은 두 갈래로 갈라졌는데, 하나는 막힌 것이 없고 평탄했지만, 다른 하나는 쓰러진 통나무들과 다른 장애물들이 길을 막고 있었다. 한 제자는 그 장애물들을 피하기로 결정하고, 끝까지 더 쉬운 길을 갔다. 그는 한달음에 달려가면서 자신이 똑똑하다고 느꼈다.

(D) 두 번째 제자는 그의 길에 있는 모든 어려움을 통과해 싸우며, 장애물들에 덤벼들기로 결정했다. 쉬운 길을 선택했던 제자가 먼저 마쳤고 자신을 자랑스럽게 느꼈다. "난 내가 바위와 통나무들을 피하기로 선택해서 기쁘다. 그것들은 내 속도를 늦추기 위해 그곳에 있었을 뿐이야."라고 그는 마음속으로 생각했다. 두 번째 제자는 피곤함을 느끼고 그가 선택했던 길을 후회하며 그 길의 끝에 도착했다. 스승은 그들 모두를 보며 미소를 지었다.

(B) 그는 그들에게 사흘 후에 특정 장소에서 그와 만나자고 했다. 그들이 도착했을 때, 그들은 몇 미터 너비의 계곡을 볼 수 있었다. 제자들은 그들의 스승을 보았고, 스승은 딱 한 마디의 말을 했다. "뛰어라!" 첫 번째 제자는 그 거리를 보고는 가슴이 내려앉았다. 스승이 그를 쳐다보았다. "뭐가 문제인가? 이건 위대함을 위한 도약이다. 네가 지금까지 해 온 모든 것이 이 순간을 위해 널 준비시켰어야 했다."

(C) 그 제자는 그의 어깨를 으쓱하고는 자신이 위대함을 위해 적절하게 준비하지 못했다는 것을 알고 떠나 버렸다. 두 번째 제자는 스승을 보고 미소를 지었다. 그는 이제 그의 길 위에 놓여 있던 장애물들이 그의 준비의 일부였다는 것을 알았다. 그는 어려움들을 피하는 것이 아니라, 극복하는 것을 선택함으로써 도약할 준비가 되어 있었다. 그는 가능한 한 빨리 달렸고 자신을 공중으로 내던졌다. 그는 건넜다!

E1

해설 (A)에 등장한 한 제자 다음에 (D)의 두 번째 제자가 등장하는 것이 순서상 적합하고, 그 사흘 뒤 이야기인 (B)가 다음에 오며, 두 제자의 새로운 테스트에 대한 각기 다른 태도에 대한 (C)가 이어지는 것이 자연스럽다. 따라서 정답은 ④ '(D)-(B)-(C)'이다.

오답 풀이

선택률	보기 해석
① 6%	(D)에 이어 사흘 후의 이야기가 (B)에 나온다. 일화 구조의 지문에서는 시간 힌트를 잘 봐야 한다.
② 12%	①과 동일
③ 11%	계곡에서 뛰라는 스승의 지시가 (B)에 먼저 나온 후에, 이에 대한 제자들의 반응인 (C)가 나와야 한다.
⑤ 10%	③과 동일

E2

해설 (B)에 따르면 첫 번째 제자는 계곡을 보고 마음이 철렁했다(his heart sank)고 한다. (C)를 함께 참고하면, 계곡 너비를 보고도 자신감을 갖고 성공한 이는 두 번째 제자임을 알 수 있다. 따라서 일치하지 않는 것은 ③이다.

오답 풀이

선택률	보기 해석
① 3%	(A) He gave them instructions to follow the path to its end
② 2%	(A) The path split into two
④ 12%	(C) The second student looked at the teacher and smiled.
⑤ 20%	(D) The second student arrived at the finish feeling tired and regretting the path he had chosen.

구문 풀이 3행

The path split into two: **one** was clear and smooth, **the other** had fallen logs and other obstacles in the way.

→ 영어의 문장부호 중 콜론(:)은 인용문이나 보충 설명이 뒤에 나올 때 쓴다. 여기서는 앞의 two를 one과 the other로 나누어 보충 설명하기 위해 썼다.

구문 플러스⁺ 콜론(:) / 세미콜론(;)

콜론: 인용문이나 보충 설명
Don't forget the words: "Look before you leap."

세미콜론: and, but, so 등의 의미로 문장을 연결
I don't really care for Jim; however, I'd rather care for Jim than Jack.

F 정답 1. ⑤ 71% 2. ① 56% 2018 9월 학평

해석 현재를 살아가는 모든 어른들이 삶의 어느 순간에 다음의 다양한 표현을 사용하거나 다른 사람으로부터 들어보았을 것이라고 생각하는 것은 온당하다. "그 모든 시간이 어디로 간 거지?" "벌써 새해라니 믿을 수 없어. 시간은 빠르게 흘러가!" "즐겨라! 어느 날 깨어보면 너는 50살이 되어 있을 거야." 겉보기에는 다르지만 이러한 표현 뒤에 숨어있는 감정은 매한가지다: 우리가 나이가 듦에 따라 시간이 더욱 빨리 흐르는 것처럼 느껴진다. 하지만 왜 이런 일이 일어나는 걸까? 심리학자 Robert Ornstein에 따르면 시간의 속도와 그것에 대한 우리의 인지는 우리의 마음이 흡수하고 처리할 새로운 정보가 얼마나 많이 있는가에 매우 영향을 받는다. 핵심은, 우리가 더 많은 새로운 정보를 받아들일수록 시간은 더 천천히 흐르는 것으로 느껴진다는 것이다. 이 이론은 왜 시간이 아이들에게는 천천히 가는 것으로 느껴지는지를 부분적으로 설명할 수 있다. 그들 주변에 있는 지각할 수 있고 느낄 수 있는 이 모든 새로운 정보를 받아들이고 처리하는 엄청난 임무가 주어져서, 아이들의 뇌는 끊임없이 살피고 주의하는 상태가 된다. 왜 그런가? 모든 것이 낯설기 때문이다. 아이의 마음을 생각해보라: 경험한 것이 거의 없어서 세상은 신비하고 흥미로운 장소이다. 어른들과 아이들은 똑같은 세상에 살지 모르지만 아이에게 현실은 매우 다른데, 대부분의 어른들은 무시하는 경이로움과 신기함, 그리고 기적 같은 작은 일들로 가득 차 있다. 아마도 이것이 왜 우리가 어린 시절의 즐거움, 즉 세상이 친숙하고 예측 가능한 것이 되기 이전의 몸과 마음의 그러한 자유에 대해 그토록 애정 어리게 생각하는지에 대한 이유이다.

F1

해설 나이가 듦에 따라 시간이 빨리 흐르는 것처럼 느껴지는 이유에 대해 설명하는 글이므로 제목으로 가장 적절한 것은 ⑤ '왜 우리가 나이가 들수록 시간은 빠르게 움직이나'이다.

오답 풀이

선택률	보기 해석
① 6%	노화방지에 대한 새로운 접근
② 6%	시간이 모든 걱정을 해결할 수 있다
③ 6%	스마트 장치를 이용한 시간 관리
④ 8%	시간 여행에 숨은 합리적 과학

F2

해설 아이들은 어른들과는 달리 경험한 것이 거의 없어서 새로운 정보를 끊임없이 받아들인다는 내용이므로, 아이들에게는 모든 것이 ① '낯설다'고 하는 것이 가장 적절하다.

오답 풀이

선택률	보기 해석
② 10%	organized(정돈된)
③ 11%	forgotten(잊힌)
④ 11%	meaningless(의미 없는)
⑤ 9%	predetermined(미리 결정된)

구문 풀이 8행

In essence, **the more** new information we take in, **the slower** time feels.

→ <the 비교급 ~, the 비교급 …>의 문장으로 '~하면 할수록 더욱 …하다'라는 뜻이다.

구문 플러스⁺ the 비교급 ~, the 비교급 … (2)

<the+비교급> 뒤에는 주어와 동사가 차례로 온다. '점점 더 ~한'이라는 의미의 <비교급 and 비교급> 구문과 구분하도록 한다.

- **The higher** it gets, **the colder** the air becomes.
- The weather becomes **colder and colder**.

G 정답 1. ① 77% 2. ③ 76% 2017 9월 학평

해석 의심의 여지없이, 공룡은 세계 전역에서 아이들에게 인기가 있는 주제이다. 오래전 멸종된 이 생명체에 관한 무언가가 남녀노소를 불문하고 거의 모든 사람의 관심을 사로잡는 것처럼 보인다. 비록 우리가 공룡에 대해서 많이 알고 있지는 않지만, 우리가 확실히 아는 것은 모든 연령의 아이들에게 매력적이다. 하지만 왜일까? "아이들이 공룡을 그렇게 많이 좋아하는 이유는 공룡이 크고, 오늘날 살아 있는 그 어떤 것과도 다르고 멸종되었기 때문이라고 생각한다. 따라서 그들은 상상력 엔진이다."라고 Jurassic Park 영화의 기술 자문관인 Jack Horner는 설명한다. 전국의 교사들은 동의할 것이다. 공룡은 그 주제 뒤에 숨겨진 과학뿐만 아니라 그것이 학생들에게 길러주는 것처럼 보이는 창의적 사고력 때문에 매년 교실에서 학습된다. "이에 대한 가장 좋은 점은 아이들의 글쓰기에서 나타나는 것이다."라고 Washington, D.C.의 초등학교 교사인

Jennifer Zimmerman은 말한다. "내가 생각하기에 아이들로 하여금 자신들의 글에서 그 주제를 사용하도록 영감을 주는 것은 다름 아닌 공룡의 미스테리, 즉 여전히 우리가 알지 못하는 너무나 많은 것이 있다는 사실이다." 아이들은 또한 공룡을 그리도록 요청받았을 때 힘이 있다고 느낀다. 공룡이 실제로 어떤 색이었는지 아무도 모르기 때문에 아이는 자신이 상상하는 대로 공룡을 그리기 위해서 자신이 가진 모든 정보와 상상력을 사용할 수 있다.

G1

해설 첫 문장에 이 글의 주제로서 공룡이 아이에게 인기가 있다는 것이 나와 있다. 따라서 정답은 ① '왜 공룡이 아이들을 매혹시키는가'이다.

오답 풀이

선택률	보기 해석
② 4%	공룡 발자국의 미스터리
③ 5%	공룡 영화는 어떻게 만들어지는가
④ 2%	다음 대규모 멸종이 다가오고 있다!
⑤ 8%	공룡 화석 이면의 과학적 의미

G2

해설 공룡이 학습되는 이유는 과학적 내용뿐만 아니라 아이들에게 주는 영감, 곧 ③ '창의적인 사고'를 가능하게 하기 때문이다.

오답 풀이

선택률	보기 해석
① 4%	ethical(윤리적인)
② 4%	spatial(공간적인)
④ 5%	positive(긍정적인)
⑤ 8%	realistic(현실적인)

구문 풀이 15행

Since no one knows **what** colors dinosaurs actually were, a child can use **what** information he has - and his imagination - to draw a dinosaur as he sees it.

→ <what+명사>가 의문형용사(어떤 ~인지)와 관계형용사(모든 ~)의 의미로 각각 쓰였다.

구문 플러스 〈what+명사〉의 해석

<what+명사>는 보통 '어떤 ~인지'의 의미이지만, 간혹 '모든 ~'의 의미일 수도 있다.

I know **what method** he used.
'그가 어떤 방법을 썼는지' → 의문형용사 what
She gave me **what little money** she had.
'그녀가 가진 얼마 안 되는 모든 돈' → 관계형용사 what

유형 플러스 장문의 이해

장문의 지문을 읽고 해당 지문과 관련된 여러 유형의 문제를 동시에 풀어야 한다. 주로 다음과 같은 조합으로 하나씩 출제된다.

① 주제or제목 + 빈칸or어휘 → 최근에는 주로 어휘만 나옴
- 소재를 둘러싼 논리와 맥락을 올바르게 파악하여야 한다.

② 순서 + 지칭 + 내용불일치
- 스토리의 흐름과 구체적인 내용을 빠르게 파악하여야 한다.

Memo

Memo